JOHN SEARLE AND HIS CRITICS

ⅉB

PHILOSOPHERS AND THEIR CRITICS

General Editor: Ernest Lepore

Philosophy is an interactive enterprise. Much of it is carried out in dialogue as theories and ideas are presented and subsequently refined in the crucible of close scrutiny. The purpose of this series is to reconstruct this vital interplay among thinkers. Each book consists of a contemporary assessment of an important living philosopher's work. A collection of essays written by an interdisciplinary group of critics addressing the substantial theses of the philosopher's corpus opens each volume. In the last section the philosopher responds to his critics, clarifies crucial points of the discussion, or updates his or her doctrines.

JOHN SEARLE AND HIS CRITICS

Edited by

Ernest Lepore and Robert Van Gulick

BLACKWELL
Oxford UK & Cambridge USA

First published 1991
Reprinted in paperback 1993

Blackwell Publishers, Inc.
238 Main Street, Suite 501,
Cambridge, Massachusetts 02142, USA

108 Cowley Road, Oxford OX4 1JF, UK

Library of Congress Cataloging in Publication Data
John Searle and his critics/edited by Ernest Lepore and Robert Van Gulick.
p.   cm.
Includes bibliographical references.
ISBN 0–631–15636–4;   0–631–18702–2 (pbk.)
1. Searle, John R.   I. Lepore, Ernest, 1950–   .   II. Van Gulick.
Robert
B1649.S264J64   1991
128'.2'092—dc20   90–33297
                                                                                    CIP

British Library Cataloguing in Publication Data
A CIP catalogue record for this book is available from the British Library.

NWST
IADK 3129

Typeset in Linotron 202 on 9½pt Ehrhardt by Best-set Typesetter Ltd.
Printed in Great Britain by T.J. Press (Padstow) Ltd, Padstow, Cornwall

Contents

Notes on Contributors

WILLIAM P. ALSTON is Professor of Philosophy at Syracuse University. He is the author of *Philosophy of Language, Epistemic Justification: Essays in the Theory of Knowledge*, and *Divine Nature and Human Language: Essays in Philosophical Theology*.

KARL-OTTO APEL is Professor of Philosophy at the Johann Wolfgang Göethe University. Among his publications are *Toward a Transformation of Philosophy*, *Charles S. Pierce: From Pragmatism to Pragmaticism*, and *Understanding and Explanation: A Transcendental Pragmatic Perspective*.

DAVID M. ARMSTRONG is the Challis Professor of Philosophy at the University of Sydney. His publications include *A Materialist Theory of Mind, Universals and Scientific Realism*, and *What is a Law of Nature?*

TYLER BURGE is Professor of Philosophy at the University of California at Los Angeles. He has published widely on topics in the philosophy of language, philosophy of mind, philosophy of logic, and history of philosophy.

MARVIN BELZER is Professor of Philosophy at Duke University. He has published on topics in the philosophy of law, deontic logic and defeasible reasoning systems.

JONATHAN BENNETT is Professor of Philosophy at Syracuse University. Among his publications are *Linguistic Behavior, A Study of Spinoza's Ethics*, and *Events and their Names*.

ALAN CODE is Associate Professor of Philosophy at the University of California at Berkeley. He has published on a variety of topics in metaphysics and ancient philosophy.

HUBERT DREYFUS is Professor of Philosophy at the University of California at Berkeley. He is the author of *What Computers Can't Do: A Critique of Artificial Reason*, co-author with Paul Rabinow of *Michael Foucault: Beyond Structuralism and Hermeneutics*, and of *Mind over Machine: The Power of Human Intution and Expertise in the Era of the Computer* co-authored with Stuart Dreyfus.

WALTER J. FREEMAN is Professor of Physiology and Anatomy at the University of California at Berkeley. In addition to his many research publications he is the author of *Mass Action in the Nervous System: Examination of the Neurophsiological Basis of Adaptive Behavior through EEG*.

CAROL FELDMAN is Professor of Psychology at New York University. She has published widely in psychology and is the author of *The Development of Adaptive Intelligence: A Cross-Cultural Study.*

ALASTAIR HANNAY is Professor of Philosophy at the University of Trondheim. He is the Editor of the journal *Inquiry*, and the author of *Kierkegaard* in the Arguments of the Philosophers Series.

JÜRGEN HABERMAS is Professor of Philosophy at the Johann Wolfgang Göethe University. His published works include *A Theory of Communicative Action*, *Knowledge and Human Interests*, and *On the Logic of the Social Sciences.*

ERNEST LEPORE is Professor of Philosophy at Rutgers University. He has published on a variety of topics in the philosophy of mind and the philosophy of language.

BARRY LOEWER is Professor of Philosophy at Rutgers University. He has published widely on topics in the philosophy of science, the philosophy of mind and logic.

JOHN MCDOWELL is University Professor at the University of Pittsburgh. He has published on a wide variety of topics in philosophy and has co-edited several collections of philosophical essays including *The Varieties of Reference*, and *Truth and Meaning.*

NORMAN MALCOLM is Susan Lynn Sage Professor Emeritus of Philosophy at Cornell University. His publications include *Knowledge and Certainty, Problems of Mind: Descartes to Wittgenstein*, and *Nothing is Hidden: Wittgenstein's Criticism of His Early Thought.*

BRIAN O'SHAUGHNESY is Lecturer on Philosophy at University of London. He has published widely in philosophy and is the author of *The Will: A Dual Aspect Theory.*

CHRISTINE SKARDA is a theoretical neuroscientist associated with the laboratory of Walter J. Freeman at the University of California at Berkeley. She has published on the neurophysiology of brain dynamics, issues in cognitive science and the structure of scientific explanation.

IRVIN ROCK is Visiting Professor of Psychology at the University of California at Berkeley. In addition to his many research publications he is the author of *An Introduction to Perception, Orientation and Form*, and *The Logic of Perception.*

BARRY STROUD is Professor of Philosophy at University of California at Berkeley. Among his publications are *The Significance of Philosophical Skepticism*, and *Hume* in the Arguments of the Philosophers Series.

RAIMO TUOMELA is Professor of Philosophy at the University of Helsinki. His published works include *Theoretical Concepts, Human Action and Its Explanation*, and *A Theory of Social Action.*

PETER VAN INWAGEN is Professor of Philosophy at Syracuse University. Among his publications are *An Essay on Free Will* and *Material Beings.*

ROBERT VAN GULICK is Associate Professor of Philosophy and Director of the Cognitive Science Program at Syracuse University. He has published on a variety of topics in the philosophy of psychology and philosophy of mind.

JEROME WAKEFIELD is Assistant Professor at the Columbia University School of Social Work. He has published on topics in the philosophical foundations of psychotherapy and psychoanalysis.

EDDY ZEMACH is Professor of Philosophy at the Hebrew University of Jerusalem. He has published on a wide variety of philosophical topics.

Editors' Introduction

For more than three decades John Searle has been developing and elaborating a unified theory of language and mind. What has emerged is an impressive and detailed account of intentionality embracing both mental states and linguistic behavior. Though the developing theory has been presented in the steady stream of books and published articles over the past 30 years (listed in the bibliography of this volume), two works stand out as major landmarks in the ongoing process: the publication of *Speech Acts, An Essay in the Philosophy of Language* in 1969 and *Intentionality, An Essay in the Philosophy of Mind* in 1983. Both these seminal works offer structural theories; i.e. they analyze the items within their domains (speech acts and mental states respectively) as having a structure which allows for variation along a number of parameters (e.g. propositional content and direct of fit). It is by appeal to these structural categorizations that the theories explain the distinctive features of the items in their domains and their interrelations.

The first of these two key books analyzes speech acts in terms of a specific structure distinguishing illocutionary force from propositional content and provides a detailed scheme for classifying and explaining the major categories of speech acts in terms of a limited stock of conditions including input–output conditions, preparatory conditions, propositional content conditions, and sincerity conditions. However, the primary role in Professor Searle's taxonomy is played by what he calls essential conditions, those that concern the illocutionary point of a given type of speech act; the illocutionary point of an assertion is to represent how things are, and the point of a directive is to get someone to do something in response to the directive. The theory is wide-ranging and ambitious; it provides accounts of reference, meaning, the dependence of speech acts on social institutions, and even of how to derive an ought from an is. Over the past 20 years *Speech Acts* has stimulated a great quantity of important research and had a worldwide impact on the study of language and linguistic behavior.

In writing *Intentionality* Professor Searle undertook a yet more ambitious project: to provide a general theory of the structure of intentional mental states, including those states of mind from whose intrinsic intentionality linguistic phenomena derive their intentionality. Intentional states, like speech acts, are analyzed in terms of a definite structure of the form $F(p)$, with F representing the psychological mode of a state and p its propositional content. Certain key notions, such as conditions of satisfaction and direction of fit, are carried over from speech act theory and applied in novel ways to intentional mental states. And a wide variety of new and important concepts, such as those of the network and the background, are introduced specifically to account for the intentionality of mental states. Both of the latter concepts concern the larger context within which a given state must occur in order to be of the intentional type it is. While the sort of intentional holism connected with the network is a generally accepted feature in recent theorizing about intentional states, Professor Searle's theory is quite innovative in arguing that intentional states can exist only against a background of nonintentional mental phenemona such as basic skills and abilities.

Going against the mainstream current in recent philosophy of mind, Professor Searle identifies the primary forms of intentionality not as belief and desire but as perception and action and offers subtle and exciting analyses of each. With respect to the intentionality of perception he identifies an essentially self-reflexive element in the conditions of satisfaction for perceptual states. For example, the satisfaction conditions for the state that Sally is in when she sees a car include not only there being a car before her but that car's being the cause of that very state. A similarly self-referential element appears in his account of action; the satisfaction conditions for an intention require that the intended act come about as a result of the very intention. His theory also introduces the key notion of intentional causation and an important theoretical distinction between prior intentions and intentions in action.

Professor Searle's theory of intentionality has a great many consequences for major philosophical issues and questions in other disciplines such as the mind/body problem, the problem of linguistic meaning, and questions about the nature of psychological and social explanation.

Professor Searle's approach throughout *Intentionality* is naturalistic and nonreductionistic. His goal is to offer a detailed theory of the structure of intentionality and not to explain intentional phenomena in terms of nonintentional features of the world. He nonetheless regards intentionality as a biological phenomenon which is to be ultimately explained in terms of the physical and biological structure of the brain. He argues that the mind–body problem can be resolved by understanding mental phenomena as being caused by and realized in the physical structure of the brain. At a metaphysical level, the relation between mind and body, he holds, need be no more troublesome than that between liquidity and molecular structure.

Professor Searle has strongly criticized much of the recent philosophical literature on the nature of mentality for approaching mental phenomena from a primarily third-person point of view; in contrast he has stressed the need to understand them from a first-person subjective point of view. Indeed, he has argued that our very idea of a mental state is essentially bound up with the subjective experiential nature of conscious mental states. While he acknowledges the existence of unconscious mental states, he holds that our idea of an unconscious mental state is simply that of a state which though not conscious could become conscious and as such have a subjective experiential aspect.

The issue of linguistic meaning is analyzed within his general theory as involving a double level of intentionality. The intentionality of language, he argues, is derived from the intrinsic intentionality of mental states. Speech acts as actions are to be understood within his general theory of action. The making of an assertion by uttering "It is snowing", involves two levels of intentionality. The speaker has an intention in action to produce that particular string of words, but he also has an intention that that utterance should have certain conditions of satisfaction and should have the illocutionary point of representing how the world is. Thus meaning involves the intentional imposition of conditions of satisfaction onto conditions of satisfaction; the speaker intentionally imposes conditions of satisfaction on the utterance which is itself the condition of satisfaction of his intention in action.

Again going very much against the mainstream current, Searle has argued against the existence or need for any intermediate level theories between the many levels of intentional explanation and the many levels of neurophysiological explanation. In particular, Searle has argued against the need for any computational theory to mediate between the intentional and the neurophysiological. Searle has also taken his account of intentionality to entail a limited skepticism about the prospects of the social sciences by arguing that they will never achieve laws of the sort found in such natural sciences as chemistry and physics.

Given their scope and boldness, Searle's views have, not surprisingly, provoked a great deal of criticism and dissent. Major philosophical theories invariably meet such disagreement within the philosophical community, since the search for philosophic truth must of necessity proceed through a collective process of conjecture and refutation, a process of argument and counterargument of analysis and counterexample. However, it is not the norm for such criticism to come from outside the philosophical community. Contemporary academic philosophers seldom engage the spirited interest of those working in other disciplines, and it is rare indeed for a philosophical thesis to provoke an extended and sometimes heated exchange in a general intellectual forum such as *the New York Review of Books*, but such indeed has been the response to some of John Searle's work, especially his anti-computationalist arguments. The breadth and intensity of the response to his views has been due in part to his willingness to speak out plainly and candidly, exposing without reluctance what he regards as intellectual pretension, misguided theorizing, or simple nonsense. The debates occasioned by these negative evaluations have been lively indeed, but his critics in these exchanges have rarely addressed or been well informed about the details of his positive theories regarding the structure of intentionality

The interdisciplinary group of critics – philosophers, psychologists, and neuro-scientists – referred to in the title of this volume are of quite a different sort. Their contributions are specifically addressed to the substantial theses of Professor Searle's theory of intentionality. Their essays raise detailed and often subtle critical questions about such issues as his account of linguistic meaning, the notion of satisfaction, the status of the background, the intentionality of perception, and the implications of his theory for questions about realism, the mind/body problem, and the nature of the social sciences.

The essays are collected in seven parts on the basis of their topics:

1. Meaning and Speech Acts
2. The Mind–Body Problem
3. Perception and the Satisfaction of Intentionality
4. Reference and Intentionality
5. The Background of Intentionality and Action
6. Social Explanation
7. Applications: Ontology and Obligation

Each part concludes with a critical essay in which Professor Searle gives a statement of his current thinking on the relevant issues and responds in turn to each of the papers in the section.

The resulting exchange of views clarifies Professor Searle's theory on many key points, such as the status of the background as mental though nonintentional and the exact role of self-relexivity in the intentionality of perception. It also serves to contrast Professor Searle's views with others in the current literature and to locate them within the logical geography of theories on the key issues. For example, the papers in part I together with Professor Searle's reply make clear that his view of speaker meaning occupies an intermediate position between those of Griceans who wish to account for linguistic meaning in terms of individual communicative intentions and those of more socially oriented theories that analyze linguistic meaning in terms of conditions that are essentially social, normative and require reciprocity between speaker and audience.

The combination of 21 critical essays and seven substantial responses has produced a lengthy volume. However, we believe the reader will find that the quality of the exchange and the importance of the issues discussed justify so large a work. To prevent it from being even longer, we have not used this introduction to provide a survey or precis of Professor Searle's views; the discussions in this volume are largely self-contained and the reader interested in further details of Professor Searle's views should consult the publications listed in the bibliography of this book. Nor have we exercised the usual editorial perogative to include essays of our own as contributions to the volume; to include more than 21 essays would threaten to cross the border into excess. We have been glad simply to bring together Professor Searle and 21 incisive critics for the serious and comprehensive dialogue that his rich and original theories merit.

Ernest Lepore
Robert Van Gulick

For Dagmar, Francesca and Virginia

Part   I
Meaning and Speech Acts

1

How do Gestures Succeed?

JONATHAN BENNETT

1 Meaning and Intention: Why it Matters

If we human beings are to command a whole, clear view of ourselves, we need to understand those aspects of our nature that we share with many other kinds of animal and the aspects that are, so far as we know, unique to ourselves; and we need to be able to hold the two sets of aspects together in a single, coherently integrated picture. Perhaps the biggest single obstacle to our doing this is *language*. It is so conspicuously unique to our species that it tends to impede our view of anything else that is special about us, and yet it is so pervasive and familiar that in a certain way it tends to drop out of sight. If we are to be able to see it as a separable but pervasive part of the human condition, we need to get it in focus – to stand back from it, and from ourselves, just far enough to see how our language relates to the rest of us. Paul Grice's paper "Meaning," with help from two subsequent papers in which he developed the central idea there presented, helps us to do this and thus to see ourselves whole and clear.[1]

In these papers Grice explains the concept of *meaning* in psychological terms: an analysis of "By making that gesture, Joe means that he is hungry" in terms of what Joe intends to achieve by making the gesture. Once we are straight about how *meaning* fits into the human condition, there is no insuperable obstacle to bringing *language* into the picture; for language is basically and essentially and almost exclusively a systematic vehicle of meaning, and the concept of *system* is one that we understand. All that remains, if Grice is right, is to ground intention in our deeper natures. All sorts of people, functionalists and others, are working on the project of explaining intentional psychology in terms of biology, and there are good grounds for optimism. In short: we have a link from biology to psychology, another from that to meaning, and a third from that to language. When these are all worked out properly, that will be a great achievement – one of the greatest achievements that could be expected of philosophers. Grice's contribution is the forging of the middle link, which elucidates the concept of meaning in terms of more general psychological terms.

2   Grice's Theory

It is plausible to think that meaning is essentially tied to communication, so that what someone means by a noise or gesture may be explained or analyzed or defined in terms of what he intends to communicate to his audience. This general idea breaks down into two main cases. The person intends (1) to get his audience to believe that P, or (2) to get his audience to do A, where A is some kind of action. In (1) a *statement* is made, in (2) an *injunction* is uttered – using "injunction" to cover commands, requests, bits of advice, and any other utterances whose immediate purpose is to influence the audience's behavior.

I give pride of place to the split between statements and injunctions because it is deep and central. Kinds of speech act that belong to neither of these categories, though they contribute greatly to the richness of our scene, are not necessary to language as such, are explicable in terms of statements and injunctions, and should be introduced at a later stage. For now I shall confine myself to statements; but everything I shall say can *easily* be adapted for injunctions as well.

The suggestion is that "By doing x, S means that P" means about the same as "By doing x, S intends to get someone to believe that P." It has long been known that our ordinary notion of *meaning that P* is not captured by this analysis, because we often do things intending to get others to believe that P without meaning that P by what we do. For example, I might show you a photograph of McStiggins streaking at a football game, intending thereby to get you to think that he has be-haved in that way; but in showing you the photograph I don't *mean that* McStiggins has streaked at a football game. Showing you that photograph isn't remotely like the making of a statement.

On the other hand, if I show you a *drawing* of McStiggins streaking at a football game, intending to make you think that he has behaved like that, that is a more plausible candidate for meaning. What is the difference? It is that the photograph's status as evidence that P has nothing to do with why I showed it to you, whereas the drawing can serve for you as evidence about McStiggins's behavior only if you think I showed it to you for that purpose. If in the second case I sanely show you the drawing as a way of getting you to think that (P) McStiggins streaked at a football game, I must be intending that you take it as evidence that P; but that could only be *intention-dependent* evidence; and that, according to Grice, is what marks off meaning from other kinds of belief-production.

That is how I express Grice's theory. He puts it like this: In doing x, S means that P if and only if:

> In doing x (1) S intends to get an audience to believe that P, and (2) S expects this to come about through the audience's realizing that (1) is the case.

A similar story holds for injunctions. Compare these two cases in which I do something intending to get you to close the window. (a) I act the part of someone suffering from a draft on the back of his neck (or I show that I *am* suffering from a draft); I want you to take this as evidence that the draft is bothering me, and to close the window. (b) I go through a mock-performance of someone suffering from a draft, and then make a big to-do of looking at the window. Nobody could possibly take my shivers and neck-rubs as natural, uncontrived expressions of suffering from a draft, and I don't expect you to do so. Rather, I want you to take them as evidence that I want you to close the window, and to be led by that to close the window. How can I expect you to take such a transparent charade as evidence that I want you to close the window? By taking it that I am offering the charade for that purpose. So the core of this injunction, as of the statement, is the attempt to give *intention-dependent* evidence for something.

3 Meaning-Nominalism and Other Complaints

A great feature of this account of the concept of meaning is that it helps us to see that meaning doesn't necessarily involve rules or conventions. Uttering x and thereby meaning that P can be a one-shot deal, though of course there *can* be conventions for meaning (and a language is a system of such conventions). Analogously, we could have a convention for driving on the right, but the notion of driving on the right can be fully understood without bringing in the concept of convention. One of the things I did in my book *Linguistic Behaviour* was to show how to take the concept of convention (as analyzed by David Lewis] and the concept of meaning (as analyzed by Grice), to hold them apart and then bring them together in a fruitful combination.

Some of the earliest attacks on Grice's work on meaning focused on its "meaning-norminalist" aspect, that is, its treating meaning as something that can occur in an isolated case that owes nothing to rules or regularities or conventions. None of these attacks was convincing, because they were all backing a loser. An early paper of Searle's, a modified version of which is in his book *Speech Acts*, purported to show that Grice's analysis was wrong because, as Searle put it, "Meaning is more than a matter of intention, it is also a matter of convention."[2] But Searle's attempt to show this relies on a discussion that becomes vague at crucial points, and on a supposed counterexample to Grice which I have argued (to my own satisfaction) doesn't work.[3]

Those who hold that meaning requires convention must conclude that Grice's analysans is too weak to be sufficient for meaning. Strawson has given another reason for the same conclusion; but he did not offer it as fatal, because he rightly through that the trouble could be repaired without detriment to the main thrust of the analysis.[4]

That's enough about the charge that Grice's analysans is too weak for meaning. My main topic comes from the correct accusation that the analysans is too strong.

My purpose in saying to you that P need not be to convince you that P; it may instead be to show you that *I* know that P, or to *remind* you that P. We can easily weaken the account of what the "speaker" intends enough to take in these two possibilities: replace "intend to get the audience to believe that P" by "intend to get the audience to believe that the speaker believes that P" or "intends to get the audience to bring actively to mind the belief that P" or the like.

Something along these lines might be made to yield the view – which some have found plausible – that in statement-making the primary aim of the speaker is to produce *understanding* in the hearer. Of course that would be no help in an analysis of meaning if "y understands x" has to be explained as "y knows what x means"; but it *may* be possible to bring understanding into the picture while avoiding that circularity.

4   Absent audience

Amendments of the kind I have described so far leave the spirit of the analysis untouched. But other troubles are more recalcitrant. According to a recent paper of Searle's, one may speak to someone in a statement-making kind of way without caring what effect one has on the person. He writes:

> Why can there not be cases where one says something, means it, and does not intend to produce understanding in the hearer? In a case, for example, where I know that my hearer is not paying attention to me I might feel it my duty to make a statement even though I know he will not understand me. In such cases the speech act is indeed defective, because the speaker fails to secure illocutionary up-take; but even in such cases it seems clear that the speaker means *something* by what he says even though he knows his speech act is defective.[5]

That seems right, and there are other kinds of example as well. Someone who speaks to himself does not even *have* an audience, yet his use of language is presumably meaningful. It isn't a mere accident that he mutters "I wish I were dead!" rather than "Oh, let it last for ever!"

The morning after I discussed this subject in public for the first time, the morning newspaper carried a comic strip in which the eggregious Andy Capp looks carefully to left and to right, sees that the bar is empty except for the barman who is dozing, and shouts "Drinks all round!" He then turns to the reader and confides: "I've always wanted to say that." That final frame forces the point home: when Andy Capp says "Drinks all round!", it's not just that his words mean something – *he* means something by them. So Grice's analysans is too strong.

In *Linguistic Behaviour*, which amends and develops and builds on Grice's theory of meaning, I proposed that we to stop trying to formulate conditions that are not only sufficient for meaning but also *necessary* for it:

> If a community's verbal behaviour was indistinguishable from that of the characters in Chekhov's *The Three Sisters*, say, that might suffice to qualify it as linguistic; but such a specialized example does not illuminate the concept of meaning or of language. What we need, at a minimum, is a statement of conditions which are strong enough to be sufficient for meaning and yet *weak enough to be instructive* . . . .[That] restores the problem to the form: how can we get something strong enough but not too strong?[6]

My point was that the search for a biconditional analysis is a search for conditions that are strong enough to be sufficient for the analysandum yet *weak enough to be necessary* for it; and I was proposing that we give up looking for this much weakness, and settle for something that is present throughout a subclass of instances of meaning that is large and central enough to serve as a good basis upon which to understand all the cases of meaning that lie outside it. I think of it as a secure base-camp from which one can make brief forays into the surrounding territory.

5 Explaining the Absent Audience Cases

Virtually all the cases of meaning that stubbornly resist Gricean analysis – such as Andy Capp's offer of drinks – have in common that they involve *language*, that is, systematic conventional meaning. I contend that if we start with meaning as an isolated phenomenon, we shall encounter hardly any such cases. So we can use Grice's analysis for the notion of meaning as an isolated phenomenon, then bring in *convention*, move from that to *language*, and then be in a position to open the flood-gates to all the fancy meaningful things we can do because we have language. (I cannot prove this; I'm offering it as a plausible conjecture.)

What, then, should we say about Andy Capp's offer? It is obviously true and unproblematic for Gricean theory to say that he utters a sentence whose conventional meaning is an offer of drinks to all the members of a present audience. But what makes it the case that Andy himself means something by the sentence (or by uttering it)? I suggest that it is this fact:

> A full explanation of why he utters that sentence rather than some other will involve some fact about what he takes the conventional meaning of the sentence to be.

And what makes it true that Andy means the sentence as an offer of drinks is this:

> A full explanation of why he utters that sentence rather than some other will involve the fact that he takes that sentence to mean conventionally an offer of drinks.

Something along those lines will probably serve for all the other cases that are not enclosed within the base camp, not captured by the initial Gricean story.[7] Some of them will have flavors of their own, coming from special links between the speaker's mind and the conventional meaning of what he utters; it is not to be expected that all this could be expressed in a unitary account. But the above treatment is the part of the story that is common to all the cases, and will be *most* of the story in each individual case.

6 A Pocket of Resistance

John Bricke has suggested to me that some cases of "no-intended-audience" meaning don't involve meaning conventions. I sit in my study replaying in my mind a recent conversation with a colleague; it suddenly dawns on me that I have said something stupid or harmful, and that the damage cannot be undone; and I make a slashing movement across my left wrist with my right forefinger, meaning by this something like "I'm so angry with myself that I could kill myself." The case is not offered as one in which that is literally *true*, just as one in which it is *meant*; similarly, one might utter those words meaning something by them yet not speaking truly.

For this example to embarrass my Gricean program, it must involve "non-natural meaning," as Grice calls it. That is, my gesture must be something by which *I* mean that I am angry etc.; it mustn't be the case merely that my gesture "means that" I am angry etc. in the way that my sniffling "means that" I have a cold. But I find it intuitively plausible to suppose that the gesture is meaningful in the former way, which makes this a problem for my program.

I allowed for this by saying that "virtually all," rather than "all" *simpliciter*, the no-intended-audience cases involve language. What can I say about the ones that don't? If there are any, i.e. if cases like Bricke's really do involve non-natural meaning, then the sorties from the Gricean base-camp will not all use the tactic of explaining what the speaker means in terms of how his mind relates to what his utterance conventionally means. I could live with that loss of unitariness in the procedure, but I don't know what other procedure(s) to use for the recalcitrant cases. I find it reasonable to suppose that the person who makes the finger-across-wrist gesture may *mean that P* by it, for a certain P; but I don't yet know how to justify or explain that intuition on the basis of any general truths about meaning.

7   Representation to the Rescue?

Despite this unsolved problem, I think that my base-camp strategy is reasonable and principled, not a mere *ad hoc* retreat in the face of the no-intended-audience problem. It may be the best that can be done. Given the great variety and complexity of things we can do with language, it would be surprising if we could capture the phenomenon of *meaning* that lies at their core in a single unitary analysis.

Still, it would be nice if we could: the old idea of *necessary and sufficient conditions* is still attractive, if only we could implement it for the concept of meaning.

Searle suggests that we can. This is in the recent paper of his, in the Grandy and Warner volume mentioned above, in which he denies that someone who means must intend to affect an audience. Searle argues there that Grice has given us a theory not of meaning but of communication; that the characteristically Gricean flourish – the piece about intending to affect someone through his realizing what you are up to – is true of communication; and that meaning can be analyzed in terms that don't involve any thought of an audience.

According to Searle, for someone to mean that P by uttering x is for him to utter x *intending that it represent the state of affairs that P* ("Meaning, Communication, and Representation," p. 216). This looks promising: it leaves the audience out of the picture, while making it easy for it to be brought into it: when I do something intending it to represent the state of affairs that P, I may intend further that my audience recognize this first intention and be led by it to believe that P, or to bring it about that P. Searle shows that if you handle meaning in his way, and then take the most natural further step to communication, you will end up with an account of the latter that really is Gricean; so Grice is allowed his success, not at the ground floor where he thought it was taking place, but one level up, as a natural consequence of Searle's account of the ground floor.

This bypasses the worst obstacles to a Gricean biconditional about meaning by offering only a Gricean biconditional about communication, with this resting on a non-Gricean, Searlean biconditional about meaning. This is neat and pleasing and plausible. It would be hard to resist *if* one were satisfied that the notion of *representation* could be adequately explained without help from any such notions as those of meaning and communication. For example, it might be that "x represents the state of affairs that P" means something like "Somebody produces x as part of an attempt to get someone else to have the thought that P" or, worse still, "somebody produces x thereby meaning that P." If we can't explain *representation* except in such terms as those, Searle's account is vitiated by circularity.

8 What is Representation?

The first step in Searle's account of representation says that for x to represent that P, someone must produce or use x with the intention that it represent that P. This implies that Searle's basic analysandum is not *x represents that P* but *S produces or uses x intending it to represent that P*; and the circularity problem then arises in connection with the latter.

Searle knows it, and expresses himself cautiously about his chances of success:

> What exactly do I intend . . . when I intend that [x] represent [that P]? The answer to that question, if it is to have any real explanatory power, should be given in terms that employ no such semantic notions as reference, truth, meaning, propositions, etc. Perhaps, in the end, it will prove impossible to give an answer that does not employ such notions. However, at least a start on such an answer can be made by showing how representing relates to intentional behaviour generally. ("Meaning, Communication, and Representation," pp. 214f)

He confidently offers a conditional of the form "If (representation) then (such and such)", apparently having doubts only about whether its converse is true. He seems to think that it may be, for he more than once says that representation consists "at least in part" in his necessary condition, hinting that the latter *may* be sufficient too. Shortly after that Searle speaks of "my account of representation," suggesting that he thinks the account is complete, or probably or nearly so.

If none of these is true, then why should we think his account can be completed without vicious circularity or regress? And if we don't think that, why should we regard this as a significant rival to the Gricean base-camp strategy?

The question of whether Searle's account is complete or at least completable without circularity would be crucial if the account were correct as far as it goes. But it is not. What Searle offers is not even necessary for representation. For the remainder of this dicsussion, the topic will not be partialness but untruth. Here is Searle's supposed necessary condition for represenation:

> Whenever S produces x with the intention that it represent a state of affairs A then it must be the case that S produces x with the intention that a criterion of success of his action should be that A obtains, independently of the utterance.[8]

In discussing this, I shall assume that "He intends that a criterion of success of his action should be that P" means something of the form "He intends it to be the case that: he performs an action for which a criterion of success is P," rather than of the form "He intends it to be the case, with respect to the action that he performs, that a criterion of success for it be P." What is being said is not that he intends to confer upon a certain action a certain relational property; rather, something is said about what kind of action he intends to perform. If this is wrong, I am lost right at the outset.

Throughout the next three sections, I shall further assume that "A criterion of success for what x intends to do is P" entails "If not-P then x fails in what he intends to do." Searle would reject that entailment, I think, but it matters to see that he *must* reject it; in section 12 I shall consider what notion of "condition of success" he might use that would not have that consequence.

9   Representation and Truth

Now, to understand Searle's conditional, we must understand its phrase "success of his action." I think Searle means by it "his success in using x to represent that P," so that the conditional entails that *S hasn't succeeded in using x to represent that P unless P*. That reading seems to be implied by this:

> My intention to represent can at least in part be analysed as the intention that certain conditions of success of the utterance be satisfied. How exactly can we specify these? The most obvious way would be to ask what counts as a failure. When would we say the speaker had made a "mistake"? In the case of the broken crankshaft an obvious mistake would be made if S's crankshaft were not broken. If S's crankshaft is not broken then he has made a mistake in representing it as broken.[9]

Something similar happens here:

> The difference between saying it is raining and meaning it, and saying it without meaning it can be got at by examining the question, what counts as a mistake? What counts as a relevant objection? If I say "It's raining" and mean it, then if I look out of the window and see that the sun is shining and the sky is blue, I am committed to recognizing these states of affairs as relevant to my utterance ... ("Meaning, Communication, and Representation," p. 217)

Well, "relevant" is safely weak; but my concern is with Searle's use of the stronger words "mistake" and "objection." Judging by these two passages, and by his "criterion of success" conditional, Searle is evidently taking representation to be *true* representation.

This is too narrow a base upon which to erect a theory of meaning. In Searle's "crankshaft" example, the protagonist does think his crankshaft is broken, and has intentions which cannot be realized if the crankshaft is sound. But there are plenty of cases of communication (and thus of meaning (and thus of representation)) where S intends to produce a false belief in the mind of the audience, by using x to represent that P when in fact not-P. In such a case, S has succeeded in representing that P, in every ordinary sense of "represent", and he may well mean that P as well; yet this lies outside the purview of Searle's account.

Incidentally, Searle would not be helped by a weaker reading of his conditional according to which its consequent merely says that S intends to be doing *something* such that: if not-P then he fails in it. If S is lying, he may represent (and mean) that

P when really not-P, and may succeed gloriously all down the line, failing in nothing that he intends to do.

10   A Base-Camp Strategy for Searle?

Searle might reply that non-liars are central and basic to his analysis of meaning, and that he plans to build his account on them and then move out to capture the liars. This resembles my base-camp way of relating no-intended-audience cases to Grice's account, but is worse than it in two ways. (1) With few exceptions, one can see how to operate from the Gricean base-camp, whereas the corresponding task for Searle looks hopeless: how can his partial treatment of representation help us to understand the ordinary notion according to which one can represent that P as part of a deliberate attempt to deceive? (2) With my strategy, the basic central class of cases is marked off by the Gricean account, with no threat of circularity or regress. Searle's basic, central class of cases, on the other hand, contains . . . what? All Searle tells us is that in each member of the class: "There is some P such that: S intends to be doing something that he cannot succeed in unless P is true independently of what he is doing." Because Searle does not say that this fits only items that fall within the class in question, his is admittedly an incomplete account of the latter. If it is even that, however, it must have some power to guide one's mind towards the class of cases that Searle has in mind; and I don't see how anyone could be thus guided by it except *through* the thought: "Ah yes, in each of these cases the 'something' that S intends to be doing is truthfully representing that P." So I think that Searle's account, as well as being incomplete, is covertly circular.

A completely different line that Searle may want to take to deal with lying will be discussed in section 12.

11   Trouble with Injunctions

Searle's account, as so far reported, does not fit injunctions. Indeed, the "criterion of success" conditional is false of *every* injunction. When I say to you "Please close the door," I presumably intend to represent your closing the door; and my success does not require that that should obtain independently of my utterance – quite the contrary. (The "independently of S's utterance" clause is needed for statements. Without it Searle's conditonal would apply whenever someone tries to *make it the case* that P, that is, intends something in which he must fail unless P; and that would cover so much ground other than representation as to be an intolerably feeble "start" on an account of representation.)

Searle knows this. When he re-runs his partial account of representation in the context of language, he leads off with the words: "For simple indicative sentences of the sort used to make statements . . ." (pp. 217f), and a page later he writes: "So far we have considered only the nature of meaning and representation as they apply to utterances of the statement class." He proceeds to discuss four other kinds of illocutionary act; but I shall bypass three of them and concentrate on injunctions, which Searle calls "directives."

He offers a necessary condition for an utterance to be meant as a directive. If S uttered x meaning it as a directive to H to do A, Searle says, then

> In the uttering of x S intended that a criterion of success of the uttering of x will be that
> H does A, at least partly because of the recognition by H that S intends the uttering of
> x as a reason for doing A.

This, like Grice's similar account, doesn't fit the case where S shouts "Close the door!" without caring whether H obeys, or even (relying on H's counter-suggestability) as a way of keeping the door open.

There are two ways in which Searle might try to deal with this.

The first way is through a base-camp strategy such as I suggested he might adopt to cover lying statements. (The present difficulty is the injunctive analogue of the liar difficulty.) Searle might say that he is offering a partial analysis of a large central class of injunctions, on the basis of which he can then explain the marginal kinds of case that do not satisfy his necessary condition – namely the ones in which the commander is not trying to be obeyed.

This is less open to criticism than the base-camp treatment of the liar, if only because where injunctions are concerned the base-camp can be established without circularity. But that very advantage also disqualifies this approach as an alternative to Grice, for it is Grice's own analysis that has established the base camp. Searle's own partial account of directives is nakedly Gricean, as indeed it has to be; I shall return to that point in section 13 below.

12   A Special Notion of Success?

The second way of dealing with the problem is by using "failure" and "mistake" in explaining "conditions of success," Searle suggests that he means by "success" what it ordinarily means. (See the passages quoted in section 9 above.) But perhaps he can cancel that suggestion and claim to be using "success" as a technical term with a special meaning. If so, then he might say that the indifferent or wily enjoiner is not a counterexample to his conditional, and that in thinking otherwise I have been construing "success" in a naively narrow (or shallow) way. He could point out that whatever S wants H to do, if S intends to be uttering a command then he intends something such that if H doesn't close the door it "fails" in the sense that it is *not obeyed*; and that, he could say, is a kind of failure in a command, whatever the further purposes of the commander may have been.

The problem of lying statements might also be approached in that way. When someone makes a statement (Searle might say), no matter what his ultimate purpose, the statement's being false is a kind of failure.

Hints of this line of thought can be found in what Searle writes. A little before his discussion of injunctions, he says:

> The different illocutionary points can be defined at least partly in terms of the different
> conditions of success that the speaker intends in making the utterance. In each case the
> essential condition on the speech act will be specified as a necessary condition of the
> success of the utterance as intended, when the utterance is intended as a member of
> the relevant class. The basic idea here is the old one that the meaning of a statement is
> somehow given by its truth conditions, the meaning of a command by its obedience
> conditions, and so on.[10]

This pretty clearly implies that if I intend my utterance as stating that P, there is *some* success that I cannot have unless P; and if I intend it as an injunction to do A, there is some success that I cannot have unless A is done.

On this understanding of what Searle is saying, the notion of "success" is being divorced from that of what S is, in the ordinary sense, trying or intending to do; we have to regard his utterance as falling even if *he* is perfectly satisfied with every aspect of the situation, and not because of any relevant ignorance or error.

A newcomer to this scene could be forgiven for protesting that nothing properly called "success" could be thus divorced from the notion of what an informed agent would count as success. We old hands know better: we have the idea of statements as fixed by truth-conditions, and of injunctions as fixed by obedience conditions, and we can think of the satisfaction of those as a kind of "success" of the utterance, whatever the utterer may be up to. We are accustomed to thoughts like this: "Whichever direction of fit we are interested in, a lack of fit in a particular situation is a lack of fit, and so something which is in itself unsatisfactory."[11] But when we understand what Searle is saying in this way, we are going *through* our grasp of what statements and injunctions are, and so once again the procedure is circular.

Searle's book *Intentionality*, though published long before the paper I am discussing, was written long after. I have gone to the book for help with this matter, but have been disappointed. "Conditions of success" are there usually called "conditions of satisfaction," and "satisfaction" must be the most frequently used technical term in the book. Searle doesn't define it, however, nor does it occur in his index. As applied to mental states, it boils down to the two theses that a belief is satisfied only if it is true, and a desire is satisfied only if what is desired is obtained, and Searle makes no attempt to justify his evident assumption that those two theses involve a single sense of the term "satisfaction." In defence and explanation of the peculiar notion of "psychological state that can be satisfied" Searle offers a putative technical sense of "satisfy" according to which "x satisfied y" is true if y is a desire and x "satisfies" it in the ordinary sense *or if y is a belief and x makes it true.* This seems to be incurably disjunctive; I can find no unitary sense of "satisfy" that produces this result.

(Searle wants "satisfaction" so as to have a solid account of the genus Intentionality, an account which neatly bifurcates down the road to yield the species belief and desire. The split, according to Searle, comes from a difference in "direction of fit" between the state and what "satisfies" it: with beliefs the direction runs from world to mental state, with desires it runs the other way. Having criticized the part of this story that lies upstream from the fork, I should add that the fork itself is suspect. Explaining "direction of fit" in terms of statements and injunctions rather than beliefs and desires, Searle says that statements are "supposed in some way to match an independently existing world" whereas imperatives are "supposed to bring about changes in the world" (*Intentionality*, p. 7), and speaks of where the "fault" or the "responsibility" lies if fit is not achieved. One sees what he is getting at, of course, but these merely suggestive remarks do not locate any clean, worthwhile concept of direction of fit. From the functionalist standpoint that Searle rejects, the whole idea of a unified story that forks down the road is mistaken. Functionalists are in a position to see (and if they bothered with details they *would* see) that the concepts of belief and desire are deeply different in structure, having almost nothing in common except the formal feature of being a psychological propositional attitude.)

13   The Disunity in Searle's Account

Searle's partial account of meaning tells one story for statements and a different one for injunctions, with no significant overlap between the two. The word "represent" occurs with statements and not with injunctions, and although it probably could be dragged into the latter as well, it wouldn't then answer to the only partial account Searle has given of it because that includes the "independently of the utterance" clause.

A Gricean account respects the difference between statements and injunctions, linking one with trying to produce belief and the other with trying to produce action. But it also has an underlying unity, in the idea that each kind of attempt involves a reliance on the Gricean mechanism of intention-dependent evidence for what the speaker believes or wants. Searle could have that unity too, but he would say that it exists not on the ground floor of meaning but up at the level where communication is to be found.

It looks as though Searle *cannot*, down at what he takes to be the ground floor, say anything substantive about statements and injunctions at once. What I am not sure of is whether he would mind this. There is in fact a discomfort, an awkwardness, about trying to get a picture of Searle's picture of the situation. On the face of it, we are to be offered an account of illocutionary acts from which everything perlocutionary is excluded, Grice's fault being that he let the latter in on his ground floor. But the account that Searle offers as a rival to Grice's is confined to statements, and the demarcation line around statements itself involves some reference to what the utterer intends to result from what he is doing. Here is why.

The concept of an injunction cannot be explained without reference to an intended effect on an audience, that is, without reference to intended effects of the kind Searle calls "perlocutionary"; so the concept of a statement must at least involve enough about perlocutionary intentions to ensure that statements are not injunctions. And so it is in Searle's account, where representation as it occurs in statements is partly explained in terms of a person's intending something in which he will fail unless P is the case *independently of his action*, which implies that he intends that it *not* be the case that his action or utterance make it the case that P. That intention is very abstract or general, or as we sometimes say it is "negative"; but it is perlocutionary for all that. And of course when Searle moves over to injunctions the perlocutionary content gets even greater, because now the speaker has a "positive" intention to achieve a certain perlocutionary effect.

14   Summary

Searle's use of "representation" to explain meaning seems not to be a strong rival to Grice's because it is not and apparently cannot be accompanied by a non-circular account of what representation is. Searle does not claim to tell more than a part of the story – a necessary condition for representation – but even that is false on its most natural interpretation, and seems to be true only when understood in a manner that makes the account circular. Furthermore, the account is not even *prima facie* plausible when applied to injunctions; for them a quite different story must be told, in which "represent" has no urgent work to do. Finally, the concept of an intended audience is involved in the very distinction between statements and injunctions, and thus in the foundations of Searle's own account of meaning.[12]

NOTES

1 H. P. Grice, "Meaning", *Philosophical Review* 66 (1957), pp. 377–88; "Utterer's Meaning, Sentence-Meaning, and Word-Meaning," *Foundations of Language* 4 (1968), pp. 225–42; "Utterer's Meaning and Intentions," *Philosophical Review* 78 (1969), pp. 147–77.

2 John R. Searle, "What is a Speech Act?" in M. Black (ed.), *Philosophy in America* (Cornell University Press: Ithaca, NY, 1965), pp. 221–39, p. 230.

3 John R. Searle, "What is a Speech Act?" and *Speech Acts* (Cambridge University Press: Cambridge, 1969), pp. 47–50; Jonathan Bennett, "The Meaning-Nominalist Strategy," *Foundations of Language* 10 (1973), pp. 141–68, pp. 164f.

4 P. F. Strawson, "Intention and Convention in Speech Acts," reprinted in his *Logico-Linguistic Papers* (Methuen: London, 1971), pp. 149–69. The best way to meet Strawson's point, I believe, is that presented in Jonathan Bennett, *Linguistic Behaviour* (Cambridge University Press: Cambridge, 1976; Hackett: Indianapolis, 1989), pp. 126f.

5 John Searle, "Meaning, Communication, and Representation," in R. Grandy and R. Warner (eds), *Philosophical Grounds of Rationality: Intentions, Categories, Ends* (Oxford University Press: Oxford, 1986), pp. 209–26, p. 211.

6 Bennett, *Linguistic Behaviour*, pp. 22f. The same device deals also with some difficulties that *could* be handled within the Gricean framework. They are so handled by Stephen R. Schiffer, *Meaning* (Oxford University Press: Oxford, 1972), but the result of thus soldiering on with biconditionals is that one ends up with an analysis that is not useful because it is too heavy to lift.

7 It also fits all the Gricean cases, where real audiences are genuinely offered drinks. The two classes come apart in their further details: they need different accounts of *how* the conventional meaning of the sentence figures in the explanation of why the speaker utters what he utters.

8 Searle, "Meaning, Communication, and Representation," p. 215. How does this "show how representing relates to intentional behaviour generally?" Only by implying that when we intend to represent, as when we intend to do anything else, we may succeed or fail. This isn't much of "a start" towards analyzing the concept of representation in a way that would fit it to support a theory of meaning. Furthermore, there is reason to think that Searle would not claim even that thin connection; for his notion of "conditions of success" seems in the event to have nothing to do with succeeding or failing.

9 Searle, "Meaning, Communication, and Representation," p. 215, lightly edited for brevity.

10 "Meaning, Communication, and Representation,' p. 230, quoted with harmless omissions.

11 Ross Harrison, "Ethical Consistency," in R. Harrison (ed.), *Rational Action: Studies in Philosophy and Social Science* (Cambridge University Press: Cambridge, 1979), pp. 29–45, p. 35.

12 I have been helped by the comments of William P. Alston on a draft of this paper, and by correspondence with John Searle.

2

Comments on John Searle: "Meaning, Communication, and Representation"

JÜRGEN HABERMAS

I

Every analysis of the processes of linguistic communication is guided by intuitions. We think we know what it takes to perform a successful speech act. My comments indirectly serve to compare two intuitions of this kind.

The intentionalist view assumes that a speaker S successfully performs a given speech act if he makes the addressee, A, recognize the (intended) meaning or intention (intention$_1$) conveyed by an expression x. S achieves this goal by getting the addressee to recognize also this communicative intention (intention$_2$) in uttering x. In this view, the communication process consists in conveying speaker's ideas to an addressee. The addressee acquires these ideas by means of the expression x, which S uses with a certain communicative intention: S makes A understand something by means of x.

The intersubjectivist view assumes that S successfully performs a given speech act if he reaches an understanding with the addressee about something in the world. Thus, the intentionalist description is replaced not only by a more complex (and vaguer) one, but by a *different* conceptualization. In producing the utterance x the speaker S allows the addressee the option of responding with "yes" or "no". It is the achievement of a mutual consensus with respect to a (potentially questionable) matter, and not the transfer of ideas, that serves here as a model of communication. Language is not regarded as a means for the transfer of the subjective contents; but as a medium in which the participants can intersubjectively share their understanding of a given subject matter. The expression x is not a device used by an individual to communicate something by making the addressee recognize his belief or intention; rather, the expression x is an element from a commonly used repertoire which enables the participants to understand the same matter in the same way.

The intentionalist can provide a more elegant explanation on the basis of fewer assumptions because he grounds the phenomenon of communication in the general conditions for the successful performance of intentional actions. If this model of communication is correct, the intentionalist might also hope to explain the rule system of a natural language that determines the meaning of conventionally produced expressions. That is, he might hope to explain what the intersubjectivist presupposes in his description of the communication process. Within the limits of this paper, I cannot go into the details of the criticism of this method of explanation.[1] I am only interested in the fact that John Searle, despite his earlier criticism of Grice, does not want to dismiss totally the explanatory power of the intentionalist approach. In fact, he gave his speech act theory an intentionalist turn.[2] In 1969, Searle showed that the understanding of a speech act cannot be described as a perlocutionary effect.[3] A speech act cannot be adequately analyzed on the teleological model of purposive action because the propositional content the speaker wants to communicate is not exhausted by the subjective content of a speaker's intention. In accordance with Austin, Searle described the understanding of a speech act as the illocutionary goal that primarily arises out of what is said and not out of what the speaker intends. The goal intended by the speaker is that the addressee recognize that the conditions for a correctly performed speech act are satisfied. The understanding of a speech act requires the knowledge of these conditions.

Searle originally analyzed such conditions on the basis of sentences which typically occur in standard speech acts and in doing so he *presupposed* that both speaker and hearer speak the same language, that is, they share an understanding of the same language. However, more recently he believes that he can renounce such a strong presupposition, and that he can treat the common language itself as a phenomenon which needs to be explained. On these grounds he revives the intentionalist approach; at the same time he maintains the semantically motivated separation of the meaning of a given language expression from speaker's intention. According to his own understanding Searle appears to be even more radical in his criticism of Grice by deriving the semantic notion of meaning from the cognitive intentions which are supposedly not only more basic than language but are also independent of the interaction situation. Like Husserl, he understands "meaning" as the content of a representation (*Vorstellung*). Of course, Searle differs from Husserl in that he analyzes meanings in terms of the so-called satisfaction conditions, because the representations in which meanings are grounded have a direction of fit and do represent states of affairs; that is, representations have a propositional structure. Such a mentalistic notion of meaning allows Searle to retain Grice's model in a modified form.

By using an expression x the speaker has the intention$_2$ of getting the addressee to recognize his intention$_1$. However, according to Searle's revision, the intention$_1$ has the structure of a representation "p" which is true if "p" obtains. Therefore, the speaker can impose on the expression x the conditions for the existence of an *a fortiori* conceived state of affairs. Furthermore, he can measure the success of communicating this representation according to whether the addressee, on the basis of the truth conditions on x, is able to recognize the state of affairs represented by the speaker.

From my point of view, a speech act, which the speaker uses in order to come to an agreement with the addressee about something, expresses simultaneously (a) a certain speaker intention, (b) a certain state of affairs, and (c) an interpersonal relationship. According to the original intentionalist view, the whole communication process can be explained from the perspective of the speaker and his intentions in such a way that (c) and (b) are derived from (a). Searle expands this model because he sees that with the representation of states of affairs, a relation to the world of events and objects and a dimension of validity come into play which essentially provide the criteria for a successful performance of a communicative intention. While retaining the intentionalist approach, Searle modifies his explanation strategy to the effect that successful communication now depends on the successful representation of states of affairs, namely that both (c) and (a) are derived from (b). Such a strategy requires that at least the following two important theses be justified:

1   Mental representation of states of affairs in terms of an analysis in terms of satisfaction conditions is more basic than linguistic representation.
2   Illocutionary types can be distinguished like representation of states of affairs and corresponding propositional attitudes of the speaker.

I am going to use one of Searle's own examples for discussing the first thesis: that linguistic notions can be analyzed in terms of intentional notions. With this reduction thesis Searle wants to ground the theory of language in the philosophy of mind. The question is, whether representational content is prior to language or whether it in turn borrows its own propositional structure from the grammatical from of assertive sentences (in section II). I will then proceed with a discussion of the second thesis: that the theory of intentionality provides a conceptual frame for the classification of speech acts. The question is, whether the meaning of a speech act is determined by the satisfaction conditions of a representational content imposed on the linguistic expression or whether it has to be explained in terms of validity conditions that only gain their determination by an interpretational process terminating in the intersubjective recognition of corresponding validity claims (in section III). This will be followed by a brief exposition of an alternative approach (in section IV). In the end I will elucidate this intersubjectivist view on communication with reference to Searle's recent analysis of performatives (section V).

II

The sentence "The crankshaft of this engine is broken" denotes the state of affairs in which the crankshaft of this engine is broken.[4] This linguistically represented state of affairs can be distinguished from the communication of the represented state of affairs in a similar way as the above mentioned sentence from a constative speech act in which a speaker uses this sentence with communicative intention. Searle now suggests replacing the assertive sentence by a drawing, and thereby replacing the linguistic by a graphic representation of the same state of affairs. He imagines that a driver who does not know the language of the country, could in this manner convey to a mechanic which part of his car needs to be repaired. The drawing representing a broken carnkshaft can also be made without any intention to use it for such a communicative purpose. The graphic representation of an object can be complete quite independently of any communicative intention and use, provided it is so accurate that the represented state of affairs is recognizable. The same holds true when S replaces his drawing with other expressions, for example, with gestures or word symbols:

> We may say that whenever S produces x with the intention that it represents a state of affairs A then it must be the case that S produces x with the intention that a criterion of success of his action should be that A obtains, independently of the uttering. (P. 215).

Of course, Searle would not have chosen the example of a graphic representation had he intended to make only the trivial claim that we can bring before our eyes a linguistically representable state of affairs independently of actual communicative intentions. Clearly, the example should serve to support the less trivial claim that we can visualize a certain state of affairs *in mente* without using *any* language whether for the purposes of representation or communication. Thesis (1) can then be interpreted in such a way as to state that we are capable of this not only when we do not use a language but also when we have no command of a language at all. However, the cited derivation example does not provide any argument in support of this thesis. In the quoted remark Searle already presupposes that S makes (or chooses) his drawing (or some other x) with the intention that it should allow recognition of a certain state of affairs A. An observer who can speak a language can also interpret the drawing of the broken crankshaft the same way. However, pictures themselves do not represent any states of affairs. As Searle himself observes, the relation between the depicted object and the object itself is of a different nature. The drawing somehow copies a broken crankshaft, and its useful-ness depends on whether it sufficiently *resembles* the pictured object. However, the similarity constitutes a necessary but not a sufficient condition for the interpretation, that the represented crankshaft expresses the fact that the crankshaft is broken.

The similarity relation between the picture and the original may as such support the role of a deictic gesture or of an index. It points to a certain object and serves to lift up this one object from the multitude of all the possible objects and thereby to identify it. However, the drawing itself does not represent a certain state of affairs. It is not equivalent to an assertion which could be true or false. The cartographic representation of a mountain range may be more or less accurate – truth or falsity can only hold of the interpretations which we base on the look of the map, which we, in a way, derive from it: for example, we may infer that the mountain ranges are separated by wide valleys or that the highest peak lies 3,000 meters above sea level. And in the same way we can *infer* from the drawing of a broken crankshaft the proposition that the represented crankshaft is broken. However, only an interpreter who *in advance* knows what it means to represent certain states of affairs is able to understand that the drawing of a broken crankshaft is meant as a sign with the propositional content that the crankshaft is broken. The interpreter could not *see* at all that the drawing, by imitating a certain object, in fact represents a certain state of affairs if he did not already know a language and from his language use knew how states of affairs are linguistically represented.[5]

This consideration casts shadows of a doubt on the reduction thesis. In view of the method of analysis, that Searle uses since his intentionalist turn, we might become even more skeptical.[6] It is still the theory of speech acts, as presented in 1969, which provides the conceptual machinery for the subsequent analysis of intentionality; the contents of intentional states and the psychological modes with directions of fit are mirror-images of what has been presented before in terms of grammatical features and conditions of successful performance of speech acts. So, the suspicion arises that linguistic features, which first get transferred back to the mental states, then show up again, on the level of an intentionalist analysis of language, as a kind of re-import of language's own products. I will not face this issue straight on but take an indirect route.

The priority of meaning over intention can be reversed in any case only under the premise that communication within a community of speakers is secondary to the capacity for representation possessed by the individual mind or brain. Searle's underlying picture is the operation of an isolated brain in the vat. This premise again is only compatible with the ontology of a single subject confronting the world, whereas the world is conceived as the sum total of states of affairs which can either be perceived as existing or brought into existence by intervention. This empiricist ontology allows for just two directions in which the subject can relate a predetermined representational or propositional content to the world. In the following section I will focus on the problem, whether this frame provides sufficient conceptual space for an adequate classification of speech acts.

III

Even if it were possible to defend the first thesis mentioned above, it would still be necessary to justify the second one, which Searle states as following: the different types of speech acts must be analyzed in terms of the different ways in which they can be related to the satisfaction conditions for the originally mentally represented states of affairs:

> Different kinds of illocutionary acts, insofar as they have propositional contents, can be regarded as different modes in which utterances represent reality . . . If we see the basic form of the illocutionary act as F(p) . . . then the illocutionary points will determine the different ways in which ps are related to the world. (P. 219)

Given that utterances owe their meanings to the representation of states of affairs, we can understand the uttered sentence if we know the conditions which make it true. This holds for assertive sentences that are used in constative speech acts. However, most speech acts are not about the existence of states of affairs. Yet, if the relation of representing something also determines the meaning of non-constative speech acts, the illocutionary types must be distinguishable by the attitude of a single speaker toward the represented states of affairs and according to the mode *in which* his utterance represents a certain state of affairs:

> The basic idea here is the old one, that the meaning of a statement is somehow given by its truth conditions; the meaning of a command is given by its obedience conditions; the meaning of a promise is given by its fulfilment conditions, a.s.o. (P. 220)

Thus, the mode of speech act changes with the propositional attitude of the speaker and with the kind of satisfaction conditions that he imposes on the propositional content.

Since the representation relation allows only two directions of fit truth conditions are fulfilled when the words fit the asserted states of affairs (or the world) $\downarrow$, and success-conditions are fulfilled when the desired states of affairs (or the world) are made to fit the words $\uparrow$. Therefore, Searle explains the first three of his five basic types of speech acts in the following way: an utterance x belongs to the class of "constatives," "directives," or "commissives," if its success can be judged according to the following criteria:

> the state of affairs "p" expressed by "x" exists independently of the speaker and his utterance;
> the state of affairs "p" expressed by "x" comes to exist on the basis of the fact that the speaker or his addressee regard "x" at least partially to be the cause for bringing about "p."

I would like to show by a couple of counterexamples that the propositional attitude and the direction of fit (together with the relation of the speaker and hearer) do not suffice to determine the illocutionary type. Let us first consider an order which according to context can be interpreted as a request, complaint, command, etc. (but, as we shall see, also as a threat):

(1) I order you to give Y the required amount of money.

Who understands (1) can paraphrase the illocutionary sense of this speech act roughly as follows: S gives the addressee A to understand that he should bring about that "p." However, it is not sufficient for A to know under what conditions the desired state of affairs would be brought about. The hearer can understand the speech act only if, in addition to these success conditions, he knows the conditions which authorize the speaker to give the order and which allow the speaker to expect that he can expect that the addressee will perform the required action. Apart from the *success conditions* for "p," the hearer must also know the *normative conditions* which authorize the speaker to direct a certain speech act to the hearer. This requirement clearly follows from the fact that a speaker who utters (1) and who cannot rely on his role as a supplicant, friend, neighbor or superior, on *any* normative context, has to draw upon a sanctioning potential instead, in order to replace the missing normative validity claim by a claim based on power. In the case of negative sanctioning, for example, the bare imperative turns into a threat:

(2) I order you to give Y the required amount of money – otherwise, I'll notify the police that . . .

In place of the missing authorizing conditions which, as distinct from (1), cannot be inferred from the preceding clause which lacks illocutionary force, sanctioning conditions step in which are expressed in the subsequent clause. (2) has to be understood as an indirect speech act. Its literal meaning expresses an illocutionary point different from the speaker's intention. The threat which the speaker actually intends to convey would have to be literally expressed roughly in the following way:

(2a) If you don't give Y the required amount of money, I'll notify the police that . . .

In this context it is important to realize that examples (1) and (2), where (2) is interpreted as (2a), obviously are not speech acts of the same type, even though they both meet the same conditions which determine the illocutionary type of directives in Searle's theory. They fulfill the same success conditions for "p" (with the same direction of fit) and require the same propositional attitude of the speaker, nevertheless, they do not have the same illocutionary meaning. As we will see, threats do not have proper illocutionary force at all.[6] Searle might object that orders as well as imperaties deprived of their normative backing and threats *do* belong to the same class of directives and that they are distinguished only by having different modes of achieving the same illocutionary point.[7] While orders appeal to a position of authority or to some (intersubjectively recognized) normative context, bare imperatives and explicit threats invoke sanctions. This much admitted, it should be clear, however, that there still is a difference in illocutionary meaning. The illocutionary point of an order "p" is, that the hearer, recognizing the corresponding conditions of success, realizes that he is supposed to bring about "p" in a specific way, namely by way of obeying, which means by meeting a normative expectation of the speaker. For him the expected behavior falls under the description of "following a previously established and intersubjectively recognized norm." In the case of bare imperatives or threats the expected behavior does not fit this description, at least not from the actor's view. It has quite a different meaning, that of avoiding negative consequences which the hearer had to suffer otherwise. With Searle we may say that the hearer is intentionally caused to perform the required action by orders as well as by imperatives and threats; but then we mean in each case something different by "intentional causation." It is true that in both cases speech acts constitute for the hearer at least partially a reason to bring about a certain state of affairs; but the types of reason they constitute are distinct in an interesting way. Reasons for redeeming the validity claim raised with an order are reasons for everybody, at least for all the parties who recognize the authorizing norms or institutions. On the other hand, reasons for submitting to a power claim linked to bare imperatives or threats do not belong to this set of general reasons; they are specific in the sense that they count as reasons only for the more or less rational choice of a particular person with particular preferences in a particular situation. This difference becomes obvious when the hearer rejects respective speech acts. In the case of an order the hearer denies that the speaker is duly authorized to expect the requested behavior of him:

(1′) No, you can't command me to do anything.

In the second case, however, he challenges only certain existential presuppositions of the claimed sanction potentials:

(2′) No, you don't possess any compromising material against me.

While general reasons can facilitate an uncoerced agreement between speaker and hearer, specific reasons, in the sense illustrated by the latter case, mediate an influence that one partly exerts on the attitudes of the other.

To this objection Searle could respond by drawing attention to his distinction between successful and successful but defective speech acts. Everything then hinges on which kind of deficiency we mean. If we describe the lack of authorizing conditions as a failure in preparatory conditions, as Searle has suggested, we would miss the point. Illocutionary acts owe their motivating force to the validity claims they carry, since these claims – like truth-claims – are capable of intersubjective recognition to the extent that they are based on reasons which count as reasons for all parties involved. Bare imperatives and threats are deprived of this illocutionary force; there is no claim to validity associated with them, but a power claim instead; they are not oriented toward the possibility of common agreement, but to the causal effects of speaker's influence on the hearer.[8]

IV

Before I draw some conclusions let us return to the issue of classification. The same analysis which I have proposed for normatively authorized directives also applies to commissives.

(3) I promise you to give Y the required sum of money.

An addressee can understand the utterance as a promise only if he knows the conditions under which a responsible actor can make a commitment and thereby bind his own will, i.e. can obligate himself to do something. The negation in the following example refers to these autonomy conditions which in (1) complement the success conditions for "p":

(3') No, you are much too unreliable a person to take such promises seriously.

In order to understand a directive or commissive speech act, the hearer must know not only the satisfaction conditions for the state of affairs expressed in it but also the conditions under which it can be regarded as legitimate or as binding.

This view is grounded in the formal-pragmatic generalization of a basic insight of truth-conditional semantics. Therefore, it is to be expected that constative speech acts would easily fit into this pattern of analysis. In this respect, however, there is a striking asymmetry. The validity of constative speech acts seems to depend only on the satisfaction of the truth conditions for the assertoric sentence (p). But, in accordance with our analysis so far, for the validity of orders or promises the satisfaction of the corresponding success conditions for the state of affairs "-that p" expressed in the propositional component is not sufficient. Now, this asymmetry dissolves as soon as one realizes that the speaker, also with his constative speech acts must intend something more and different than what is expected from him on the basis of the intentionalistic interpretation – namely, to get the hearer to recognize that he considers "p" to be true (intention$_1$) and that he would like to let him know this (intention$_2$). The speaker wants to communicate to the hearer not only intention$_1$ that *he* has (that he believes that "p"), but he also wants to communicate to him the fact "p" (so that the addressee *himself* should believe that "p"). The illocutionary purpose does not consist simply in letting the addressee know what the speaker believes, rather it consists in getting the addressee to have the *same* view of which the speaker is convinced. In short, the addressee is asked to accept the speaker's assertion as valid. This is what communication of facts is all about. The intentionalist description that the speaker intends to produce in the hearer the belief that the speaker is committed to the existence of a certain state of affairs comes close to a distortion. In order to achieve the illocutionary purpose, it is not sufficient that the speaker imposes truth conditions for the mental representation of a state of affairs on the expression x, and that he lets the addressee know them by uttering x (the assertoric sentence) likewise impregnated with the truth conditions. Rather, it is also necessary that the speaker confronts the addressee with his *claim* that the conditions which make the statement true are indeed satisfied.

As with orders or promises, in a constative speech act the speaker makes a challengeable claim which the hearer should accept. In contrast to nonconstative speech acts, this claim refers to the fact that the conditions, which make the employed assertoric sentence true, are satisfied. On the other hand, the validity claims which are associated with orders and promises relate *directly* to the normative conditions which entitle one party to expect that the other party will make the represented state of affairs true. The claim to propositional truth relates to the existence of a state of affairs, in other words to the fact "p." The claim to normative validity relates to the legitimacy of the expectation that one or the other participant should bring about a represented state of affairs "-that p."

The main point I should like to make here is the inadequacy of the intentionalist model. It condems the hearer to a peculiar passivity. It deprives him of the option of taking the speaker's utterance seriously, i.e. to accept it as valid or to reject it as invalid. However, the communication process is incomplete without the *option* of taking a stand with "yes" or "no."

With a speech act, the speaker gives the addressee not only the chance to learn of his intentions. He claims further that he has reasons that can move the hearer to accept a statement as true, an order as legitimate, a promise as binding or – as I should like to add at this point – an avowal as sincere. The speaker cannot achieve his illocutionary purpose of conveying a fact, giving an order, making a promise or revealing an experience, if he does not at the same time make known the *conditions* under which his utterance *could* be accepted as valid: that is, in *claiming* that these conditions are satisfied he implicitly offers to provide the reasons for their validity, if necessary. The hearer must be able to have the opportunity to anticipate the reasons for accepting a statement as true, an order as legitimate, a promise as binding, an avowal as authentic or sincere (or alternatively for questioning such a claim). The hearer cannot understand the speech act if he does not know the conditions for taking a yes/no position. The illocutionary meaning of a statement, an order, an avowel or a confession would remain hidden from the addressee if he could know only that the speaker has a certain intentional state: that he believes that "p"; that he wants the hearer to bring about "p"; or that he himself has the intention of bringing about "p"; or that he wants to reveal the content of a belief, a feeling, a desire, an intention, etc.

Obviously, to understand the meaning of a grammatical expression, on the one hand, and to reach a mutual understanding about something by means of an utterance which is accepted as valid, on the other, is not the same. One must also distinguish between an utterance which is believed to be valid and a valid one. Nevertheless, it is not possible to separate fully questions of meaning from questions of validity. The basic question, namely what it means to understand the meaning of a linguistic expression, cannot be isolated from the question, in which context the expression could be accepted as valid. We would not know what it takes to understand the meaning of a linguistic expression if we did not know how we *could* use it to reach an agreement with somebody about something. It already follows from the conditions for understanding of linguistic expressions that the speech acts which can be formed with their help are based on the possibility of a rationally motivated consensus on what is being said. The orientation toward the possible validity of utterances does not only belong to the pragmatic conditions of communication but to the conditions of understanding the language itself. Within the language the dimensions of meaning and validity are intertwined.

On the basis of this intersubjectivist concept of language, illocutionary types can be identified according to the validity claims associated with them.[9] In order to discover the validity claims themselves, we can start with the heuristic question: in what sense can speech acts as a whole be negated? If we, for example, consider under which aspects an illocutionarily ambiguous sentence such as

    (4)   I will give Y the required amount of money.

can be negated, we arrive at exactly three validity claims.

    (4')   No, you are much too unreliable in such things.
    (4'')   No, you don't really mean what you say.
    (4''')   No, this is not going to happen.

In the first case the hearer understands the utterance as a promise and he denies that the speaker is sufficiently autonomous to fulfill such as obligation. In the second case, the speaker understands the utterance as a declaration of an intention and he doubts the seriousness or sincerity of the uttered intention.[10] In the third case, the hearer understands the utterance as a prediction and he denies the truth of the future assertion about the future. Any illocutionary act can be challenged on the basis of legitimacy or veracity as well as truth. For example, an order such as (1) can be negated not only with respect to the authorization of the speaker but also with respect to the sincerity of the expressed speech intention or with respect to the truth of the existential presuppositions of the expressed propositional content.

V

If we consider Searle's analysis of the conditions for speech acts as a whole, then the three above-mentioned validity claims can be found in his scheme of analysis under a different description.

In a discussion, Searle proposed to analyze the legitimacy claim in terms of his preparatory conditions, the veracity claim in terms of his sincerity conditions, and the truth claim in terms of his essential conditions. The fact that such a translation is possible shows the sharpness and complexity of Searle's analyses. John Searle was the first to understand clearly the structure of speech acts. Moreover, his pioneering insights transcend the conceptual framework that is based on the intentionalist model. But the proposed concept of validity claim would have to lose its point if it were transposed into that model. Certainly, validity conditions or satisfaction conditions are semantic concepts which also have correlates in the domain of mental states. However, a private access to validity conditions, which is either prior to language or only a monologue, can be defended only at the cost of what I take to be an untenable correspondence theory of truth. Therefore, I suggest that the validity conditions should not be considered in isolation but in pragmatic connection with validity claims and with potential grounds for the redemption of such claims. Validity claims open to criticism and designed for intersubjective recognition constitute the rails without which the speaker could not reach his illocutionary purpose.

In a recent paper on Performatives[11] Searle comes fairly close to a recognition of the intersubjective nature of meaning and validity. The analysis of performatives leads into the very center of a theory which takes off from Austin's observation of the peculiar character of speech acts which allow us to do something in saying it. In the standard form of a speech act F(p) the performative sentence makes explicit the illocutionary force "F" of an utterance containing "p." On the issue of how performatives work, there prevail two competing intepretations, one of which treats performatives as simple statements while the other maintains that performatives do not admit of truth and falsity and therefore lack meaning in any proper sense. Both interpretations are strongly counterintuitive.

Performative sentences like "I state that...", "I promise you...", "I confess that..." etc. constitute in fact performances which cannot be confirmed or falsified like full-fledged assertions. They do not operate under a claim to truth. This is revealed by the fact that they first have to undergo a transformation from the second person (performative) perspective of the speaker into the third-person perspective of an observer before they themselves can be true or false. This same transformation shows, however, that performative sentences have a meaning, too. Obviously, the following sentences:

(5)   I order you to come.
(5′) He orders him to come.

have the same meaning, if references are preserved. But at the same time the illocutionary force switches over into the propositional content and thereby loses, if not its meaning, at least its force: it is included in the topic of another – constative – speech act. Uttered in the second-person attitude performative sentences have a meaning (a) only in connection with some other proposition or propositional content, and (b) only as a kind of escort in the back, which is articulated in an unthematic and implicit way. These and other features can be explained as soon as we realize that performative sentences (like other illocutionary indicators) are self-referential and self-executive expressions for the very act of raising a validity claim for a sentence of propositional content. Searle states the problem clearly. The difficulties into which his own proposal runs are instructive; they disclose an underlying intuition close to our own.

Searle explains the meaning of sentences, the performance of which constitute the act they say they are, by taking recourse to declarations – a last class of speech acts we have not discussed so far. Uttering a sentence such as "I hereby order you to come" functions, according to Searle, "as a performative, and hence as a declaration because (a) the verb 'order' is an intentional verb, (b) ordering is something you can do by manifesting the intention to do it, and (c) the utterance is both self-referential and executive, as indicated by the word 'hereby.'"[12]

Without going into the details I will explain – and question – the declarative character of performatives. Searle has introduced declaratives as speech acts that both express a propositional content and make it true. In concluding a contract or closing a meeting I let what I say be the case by saying it. Within the limits of this model Searle somewhat paradoxically postulates for declarations that they simultaneously satisfy both directions of fit: they state a fact and produce it. The paradox disappears with the observation of how the authorizing or legitimizing conditions of contract law or business procedures back those speech acts. It is because of this legal or institutional, in any case normative, background that declarations can produce a change in the arena of legitimate interpersonal relationships and thereby create new social facts. Compared with directives and commissives declaratives display features of both types; like orders they rely on a normative context and like promises they draw from the normative resource of a speaker's responsibility.

Searle, however, makes a further move; he now interprets the performative character of all classes of illocutionary acts in the light of the illocutionary force of declarations. This proposal faces two major difficulties. It first explodes the architecture of the classification of speech acts because declartions would lose their distinctive place in it if they were to explain the performative character of *all* speech acts. Of greater interest is the second one. Since many performatives do not appeal to or rely on a normative backing, the illocutionary point of declaratives would lose its specificity. Consequently Searle is pushed forward to redifferentiate the illocutionary meaning of declaratives. Besides "extralinguistic declaratives" – such as pronouncing a couple man and wife or declaring war – Searle introduces another category of "linguistic declarations," which are neither attached to particular institutions like marriage or warfare, nor supported by some informal value consensus on the background. However, once *all* illocutionary acts gain a declarative force so that this force extends to requests, promises and avowals as well as statements which then is the meaning preserved for the force of such "linguistic declarations?" Properly speaking there cannot be any declaration without a dependence on authorizing or legitimizing conditions of the sort that have the power to create new social facts. If his analysis leads Searle nevertheless to refer to some declarative force inherent in speech itself, the intuition behind this peculiar force might well match what I prefer to call the rationally motivating force of validity claims that are in need of intersubjective recognition. Searle elucidates the intrinsically linguistic force of the very act of raising a claim to validity with the force of an institution that enables a speaker, via his social roles, literally to call something into existence. In order to turn the elucidation into an explanation, Searle has to assimilate language to institutions. Language, however, is an institution only in a metaphorical sense. Thus Searle's explanation of how performatives work reaches no further than this metaphor.

NOTES

1 J. Habermas, "Intentionalistische Semantik," in J. Habermas (ed.), *Vorstudien und Ergänzungen zur Theorie des kommunikativen Handelns*, Sohrkamp: Frankfurt am Main, 1984, pp. 441ff.
2 Cf. K. O. Apel, "Is Intentionality more Basic than Linguistic Meaning?" chapter 3 below.
3 J. Searle, *Speech Acts*, Cambridge University Press: Cambridge, 1969, pp. 49ff.
4 In the following quotations I refer to J. Searle, "Meaning, Communication, and Representation," in R. E. Grandy and R. Warner (eds), *Philosophical Grounds of Rationality: Intentions,*

Categories, Ends, Oxford University Press: Oxford, 1986. The page numbers in the text refer to this paper. Searle describes his theory in *Intentionality, An Essay in the Philosophy of Mind*, Cambridge University Press: Cambridge, 1983.

5 The history of the philosophy of consciousness from Descartes to Husserl shows that it is not a coincidence that the basic terms of mentalism are determined by the concept of objects, i.e. by the subject–object relation. It was only the linguistic turn introduced by Frege which led to the insight that in analogy to sentences concepts also manifest a propositional structure. Cf. E. Tugendhat, *Vorlesungen zur Einführung in die sprachanalytische Philosophie*, Frankfurt am Main, 1976.

6 J. Searle, "Intentionality and Method," *Journal of Philosophy*, 1981, pp. 720ff.

7 I am grateful to Chris Latiolais for this indication.

8 Bare imperatives and threats are examples of perlocutionary acts which play an instrumental role in the context of success-oriented acts. They have lost their illocutionary *force* and borrow their illocutionary *meaning* from other contexts of use in which the utterance of the same sentences is mainly determined by communication goals. Such speech acts which have become perlocutionarily *independent* are not oriented toward the rationally motivated attitude of an addressee and in so far as they are not they do not rely on a potential of general reasons which are unspecific with respect to the addressee.

9 Cf. my classification proposal in J. Habermas, *Theorie des kommunikative Handelns*, Sohrkamp: Frankfurt am Main, 1981, Bd. 1, pp. 427ff.

10 Given that the class of expressive speech acts can be defined under the aspect of the veracity claim posited by the speaker for the utterance of a subjective experience to which he has a privileged access, avowels may serve as prototypes of such expressive speech acts. Differing from Searle, I would not classify congratulations, excuses, saying "thank you," etc. as expressive speech acts; they can succeed even though the speaker does not mean what he says. As in the case of bets and christening the illocutionary sense of these regulatory speech acts is determined by an institutionalized background. Given that the normative conditions are not violated, saying "thank you" can also be valid even if it is not seriously meant that way.

11 J. Searle, "How Performatives Work," *Linguistics and Philosophy* 12, 1989, pp. 535–58.

12 Ibid., p. 23.

3

Is Intentionality more Basic than Linguistic Meaning?

KARL OTTO APEL

1 The Problem

In what follows, I should like to tackle a general and fundamental controversy which has concerned philosophers of this century, the question of whether intentional consciousness or language has methodological priority in the determination of meaning. The question can be stated as follows: What is more basic for the grounding of a theory of meaning? The meanings of signs fixed by linguistic convention, or the meaning which we give to these signs on the basis of our pre-linguistic intentionality, as we impose physical signs to convey them?

If we pose the question in this way, then the historical situation in the early twentieth century looked more or less like this. First, Husserl's phenomenology developed an intentionalist theory of meaning which was prelinguistically oriented in the sense alluded to above. In that theory, the "intentional acts" of the "ego-consciousness" (which could in principle be understood as the acts of a solipsistic-autarkic and thus transcendental consciousness) were held to be responsible for the original constitution of all linguistically expressible meaning. This theory of meaning, which was in the transcendental-phenomenological sense intentionalist, was, however, supplanted, in the wake of the "linguistic turn" of analytic philosophy, by a linguistically oriented theory of meaning. In this process, we can distinguish between two phases which are usually differentiated as the *philosophy of ideal language* and the *philosophy of ordinary language*. In the present context, I should like to emphasize that the first phase, as a phase of formal semantics of propositional sentences, abstracted more or less coherently from the so-called pragmatic dimension of the use of language by speakers and hearers, whilst the second phase re-introduced this pragmatic dimension as an integrative function of natural language, as for example in Wittgenstein's language-game theory and, particularly, in speech act theory. The results of the speech act approach, in particular, now clearly show that in the second phase, alongside Austin's theory, which was primarily oriented toward language conventions, theories of meaning also appeared which once again sought to reduce linguistic meaning to pre-linguistic mental intentions (in the broadest sense). Among these (in the broader sense) *intentionalist* meaning theories, we can distinguish, so far as I can see, two differently inflected approaches.

First, there is the approach of Paul Grice.[1] Apart from what is generally a mental-ist reductionism, this approach has few similarities with the Husserlian theory of meaning, since it distinguishes as the basis of its reduction not the total spectrum of the intentionality of mind, but only so-called action-intentions in the narrower sense and thus reduces the concept of meaning-intention to that of the purposively rational production of language-action effects in the consciousness of hearers. If one conceives these intended effects with Austin as "perlocutionary effects," then this approach can best be compared with Max Weber's conception of social actions as reciprocal purposively rational actions; this means that it should here be possible to reduce linguistic communication to strategic interaction, more or less in the way that it is analyzed in economic game-theory. I have criticized this version of intentionalist meaning theory elsewhere.[2]

Very different from this end, to all appearances more related to Husserl's theory of meaning, is the intentionalist-meaning theory elaborated by John Searle in his recent book *Intentionality*. Here, or so it seems, the original act of meaning con-stitution on the part of the intentionality of mind is rather, as in Husserl's theory, uncoupled from that communicative purposive rationality which is directed towards the production of effects in the consciousness of hearers. And it is not only un-coupled from the purposive intentionality that is directed toward "perlocutionary effects," but also, surprisingly, from that intentionality which is directed toward "illocutionary effects," i.e. toward the communication of meaning in general. Searle himself formulates this point in the following way:

> Communicating is a matter of producing certain effects on one's hearers, but one can intend to represent something without caring at all about the effects on one's hearers. One can make a statement without intending to produce conviction or belief in one's hearers or without intending to get them to believe that the speaker believes what he says or indeed without even intending to get them to understand it at all. There are therefore two aspects to meaning intentions, the intention to represent and the inten-tion to communicate. The traditional discussion of these problems, my own work included, suffers from a failure to distinguish between them and from the assumption that the whole account of meaning can be given in terms of communication intentions. On the present account, representation is prior to communication and representing intentions are prior to communication intentions. Part of what one communicates is the content of one's representations, but one can intend to represent something with-out intending to communicate. (*Intentionality*, pp. 165–6)

The significance of this uncoupling of meaning intention from communication intention lies, in my view, in the following assumption: it is supposed to be possible to understand the structure of a statement as the structure of a speech acts – and this at the same time means the structure of a sentence which not only has a pro-positional content which *represents a fact*, but also a *performative* component, which indicates the illocutionary force of the statement – without in principle presup-posing a communication intention, i.e. without presupposing also that a statement which *actualiter* is not to be *imparted* must nonetheless in principle – apart from the representation function of the propositional sentence content – always imply the structure of a potential act of communication.

It seems to me that the retrogression to a point before the "linguistic turn" in *Intentionality* is bound up with this uncoupling of meaning-intention from communication-intention. In a way that is very similar to Husserl, Searle here goes back to the *Intentionality of the Mind* in the broadest sense – i.e. intentional states like convictions, wishes and, among other things, action-intentions – in order to clarify the various meanings of speech acts, and particularly also the possibility of various classes of speech acts on this basis. Searle's definitive programmatic formulations on this read as follows:

> A natural consequence of the biological approach advocated in this book is to regard meaning, in the sense in which speakers mean something by their utterances, as a special development of more primitive forms of Intentionality. So construed, speakers' meaning should be entirely definable in terms of more primitive forms of Intentionality. (Ibid., p. 160)

On the basis of the "forms of Intentionality" referred to here (which can ultimately be analyzed into "psychological notions such as belief, desire and intention", ibid., p. 161), it ought also be possible to explain the possible forms of meaning, and thus the possible classes of speech acts:

> The Intentionality of the mind not only creates the possibility of meaning, but it limits its forms. . . . Another aim, then, of the analysis of meaning is to show how the possibilities and limitations of meaning derive from the Intentionality of the mind. (Ibid., pp. 166–7)

From these considerations, the following *basic question* regarding the explanation of the possibility of linguistic meaning arises for Searle – and once again this is similar to Husserl (and the whole of pre-"linguistic turn" philosophy): "The problem of meaning is how does the mind impose Intentionality on entities that are not intrinsically Intentional? How is it possible that mere things can represent?" (Ibid., p. 167).

It is very characteristic that Searle elucidates this basic question using the example of a signal gesture, the meaning of which is specifically agreed upon beforehand.

> Suppose that you and I have arranged in advance that if I raise my arm that act is to count as a signal that such and such is the case. Suppose, in a military context, I signal to you on a hill while I am standing on another hill that the enemy has retreated, and by pre-arrangement I signal this by raising my arm. (Ibid., p. 167)

Is not the real basic question of the constitution of linguistic meaning through the intentionality of mind simply displaced here, since agreement as to the meaning of the signal already presupposes the existence of linguistic meaning conventions?

This same objection also forces itself upon us when Searle explains the problem of the constitution of meaning in the following way:

> The problem of meaning would arise even for people who were communicating with each other without using a common language. It sometimes happens to me in a foreign country, for example, that I attempt to communicate with people who share no common language with me. In such a situation the problem of meaning arises in an acute form, and my question is: What is it about my intentions in such a situation take makes them specifically meaning intentions? In such a situation I mean something by my

gestures, whereas in another situation, by making the very same gestures, I might not
mean anything. (Ibid., p. 164)

This situation also seems to me poorly fitted to illustrate the problem of the *constitution* of meaning; for it has to be admitted that the meaning of the gestures which are
here used in non-linguistic communication are for their part already dependent
upon a language, and that this is the case both for Searle, who ascribes meaning to
his gestures, and for those to whom the message is addressed who understand the
meaning of the gestures in the light of their language. To this extent the example is
far from giving us an idea of the kind of meaning-intentions, which one might assume people to have, who – wholly without the presupposition of a shared language
– could communicate with anybody. (Even animals such as bees or dolphins seem
in their communication to presuppose a linguistic code – though this may be more
determined by instinct than by convention.)

Only at the following point does Searle seem to pose the question of the constitution of meaning in a radical form.

Suppose there was a class of beings who were capable of having intentional states like
belief, desire, and intention, but who did not have a language, what more would they
require in order to be able to perform linguistic acts? (Ibid., p. 176)

And yet in this case one might be tempted to reply that it is difficult to conceive of
there being any kind of being to whom one could ascribe *differentiated intentional
states* – such as those we call "belief," "desire" or "intention" – without having to
presuppose at the same time that they possess a form of speech, whether it be a
conventional or an instinct-related sign-code. At most – surely – one can assume
that, in the case of human evolution, on the one hand the differentiation of intentional states and of possible meaning-intentions and, on the other, the differentiation of the conventional meanings of language, have conditioned one another
reciprocally. However, such as assumption would by no means justify a unilateral
reduction of the possible linguistic meanings to nonlinguistic intentions of mind.

The foregoing remarks on the peculiarity of the Searlian theory of meaning
may, for the time being, suffice to explain why I would like once again, in relation
to this approach, to raise the question set out in the title of my paper. From the
perspective of the "linguistic turn" of contemporary philosophy I should also like to
question both the independence of human meaning-intentions from communication-
intentions and their independence from language.

In seeking to do this, I am particularly motivated by the following circumstance.
In his *Speech Acts*, Searle was able to appear as a representative of the "linguistic
turn." At least this is how Jürgen Habermas and I saw him. In more precise terms,
he seemed to us to represent a *linguistic pragmatics* in which the semantics of linguistic sentences in Austin's sense was integrated with the pragmatics of speech
acts which were normally produced by the uttering of sentences and thus linguistic meaning could be understood for the first time from the standpoint of the
performative-propositional dual structure of all explicit linguistic sentences.[5] Through
this approach, it seemed to me that the *propositional representation-function* of meaning was both distinguished from the performatively indexed *communication*-function
and also made to depend upon it. In the dependence also of the actual isolated
representation-performance on the potential *communication*-performance – for

example of the representation-performance of a statement on the information-performance of the statement which normally belongs to it – there seemed to me also to be implied, that both the representation function of meaning and also the performatively indexed communication function were in principle always already co-determined by a (differentiated) language used and developed in communication. Against the background of this reading, which may perhaps have been based on a misunderstanding, *Intentionality*, in which the "philosophy of language" was to be traced back to a "philosophy of mind," seemed to me evidence of an astonishing turn, both in respect of the development of "analytic philosophy" and of the development of Searle's philosophy, the consistency and coherence of which seemed to me to be put in question.

In what follows I should like to try more precisely to explicate this impression of an astonishing turn and the underlying understanding of the development of "linguistic-analytic philosophy" and in particular the philosophy of Searle. In doing so, I should at all events like to defend my original understanding of the speech act theory of Searle I (i.e. the Searle Speech Acts as I have described him just above) – whether or not this is based on a misunderstanding – as the basis for a defence of the "linguistic turn" in the sense of its possible integration with the "pragmatic turn" and therefore also a theory of self-reflexive meaning intentions.

2   On the Prehistory of Intentional Semantics in Analytic Philosophy: The Supplementing of the "Linguistic Turn" with the "Pragmatic Turn" and Question as to Whether the Two can be Unified

In this context the next question which arises is the following: What are we to understand by the term "linguistic turn" in the philosophy of this century, and to what extent has linguistic philosophy been elevated, through it, to the status of a rival of the philosophy of mind so far as methodological priority is concerned?

The "linguistic turn" in analytic philosophy, phase 1

A short and very clear answer to this question has, in my view, been given by Wittgenstein, the real inaugurator of the "linguistic turn". And it was provided in a dictum which retrospectively summarizes the central import of the *Tractatus Logico-Philosophicus*. It reads:

> The limit of language shows itself in the impossibility of describing the fact which corresponds to a sentence . . . without simply repeating the sentence. (We are here dealing with the Kantian solution to the problem of philosophy.)[6]

This, in my view, is where the *transcendental-philosophical nub of the linguistic turn* becomes clear and precisely in the fact that Kant's "highest principle of synthetic judgments" – "The conditions of possiblity of experience are at the same time the conditions of possibility of the objects of experience" is reinterpreted in terms of linguistic philosophy. It then reads more or less as follows: *The conditions of possibility of the description of experienceable facts* – propositional sentences as representations of facts – *are at the same time the conditions of possibility of the describable facts.*

The nub of this transcendental-philosophical interpretation of the *Tractatus* (which has been fully elaborated by Erik Stenius)[7] also reveals itself in my view in

Tarski's famous definition schema for the *semantic* – and this means referring *a priori* to a (formalized) language – explication of the concept of truth, which reads: "'For all p, "p" is a true sentence if and only if p'. For example, 'the proposition "the cat is on the mat" is true if and only if the cat is on the mat.'"[8] One might here be tempted to enquire further: "When is it the case that the cat is on the mat?" In other words, on what demonstrable conditions can we say that this is the case? Wittgenstein and Tarski would, however, have to reply that we simply cannot *describe* this without repeating the *propositional sentence*, in which the fact as such is *described*. The representation of the world through language – or, more exactly here, through the structure of the propositional sentence – simply cannot be circumvented. In this stands revealed the methodological primacy of the *a priori of language*.

A phenomenologist who, with Husserl, subscribed to the *primacy of consciousness of given phenomena* could here make the following objection: I can, however, become convinced through *perception* that my simple opinion that the cat is on the mat (and not, for example, on the window seat) corresponds to a phenomenally given fact. This perceived state of affairs can even be photographed and then all those who viewed the photograph could be convinced that a fact corresponds or corresponded to my opinion. By this means then, to the phenomenally given perceived state of affairs is ascribed the status of an *objective truth criterion*, which *transcends* the mere verbal description of the fact in a propositional sentence.

Is the thesis of the methodological impossibility of circumventing the linguistic representation of the world refuted by this objection?

The answer is yes and no, depending on what aspect of this impossibility we are speaking of.

In fact, in my view, we can see from the phenomenological argument that it is possible to go beyond the descriptive representation of a fact by means of a propositional sentence in one particular respect, namely in regard to the *perceptual identification of the given phenomenon*, which provides my consciousness with the *evidence of the correspondence* between the merely asserted fact and the phenomenally given fact. In this way it can in fact be proved that the *evidence* of consciousness cannot be reduced to a mere psychologically relevant *evidence feeling*, as the representatives of the "linguistic turn" have occasionally asserted. For example, the possibility of taking a photograph shows the distinction between an objective evidence criterion and a purely subjective evidence feeling. And to this extent *the evidence of consciousness* is at least a necessary – i.e. indispensable – criterion of the confirmation and disconfirmation of scientific hypotheses through perceptual judgments; it is not, as Popper thinks, a merely psychologically relevant *cause* (*Ursache*) of the subjective acceptance of basic propositions of science, but an epistemologically relevant ground (*Grund*) of their inter-subjective acceptance.[9]

In so far as the evidence of consciousness attests a correspondence for self-reflexion between the intentionally meant (*gemeint*) and the phenomenally given fact, to that extent also a phenomenological way out of the well-known *circulus vitiosus* of the metaphysical and purely logical-semantic *correspondence theory* of truth opens up here. This circle consists in the fact that the correspondence between a true proposition and an abstract fact can only be explicated in the following way: A true proposition is one which corresponds to a fact, and a fact is something which corresponds to a *true proposition*. This vicious circle – which is also the cause of the *criteriological irrelevance* of the Tarskian definition of truth – is now clearly broken by the *criterion of evidence for correspondence between the meant and the phenomenally given.* In short, the propositional representation of the world of experience can in fact be transcended *in respect of the perceptual identification of phenomenal evidence;* and in *this* respect, it is not *language* which is the essential (nichthintergehbar) *a priori* of experience, but the *consciousness of the perceptual evidence.*

And yet the nub of the Wittgensteinian explication of the "linguistic turn" is not refuted by the phenomenological evidence theory of truth in the respect in which it was really meant: as a reference to the *linguistic a priori of the describabiliy* of experienceable facts. One can easily satisfy onself of this from the following example. Let us assume that an explorer presents us with a photograph depicting something of which no one can *say what it is;* nonetheless what is depicted may be characterized in terms of particular qualities of color and form. In this case, we can certainly see a *perceptual confrontation with a qualitatively given phenomenon,* but there is no *interpretative determination* of the given phenomenon *as something,* because the corresponding possibility of a *linguistic-propositional* description is not available. Here we can see that the *perceptual evidence of consciousness* of a given phenomenon is perfectly compatible with a dependence on the linguistic *a priori* of the *knowledge* (*Erkenntnis*) *of something as something.* This can be seen even more precisely in terms of a semiotic epistemology.

The founder of pragmatic semiotics and phenomenology (or Phaneroscopy), Charles Peirce, speaks in this case (concurring with the phenomenology of Husserl), of *phenomenal evidence* – and he speaks, in fact, in terms of the categories of *Firstness* (that is, qualitative so-being) and *Secondness* (that is, an encounter between the ego and the non-ego) and he explains that objectivization and intentional memorability of the phenomenal evidence through the iconic sign-function of the photograph; yet, unlike Husserl, he does not in this case speak of *truth* in the sense of knowledge. For this, in Pierce's view, an *intersubjectively valid interpretation* of the meaning of the given phenomenon in terms of the category of *Thirdness* would be needed, i.e. the *mediation* of the immediate givenness of the phenomenon through the conceptual universal of linguistic symbols.[10] With this, in my view, the nub of the Wittgensteinian discovery of the *propositional linguistic a priori* is for the first time brought into its proper relation to the phenomenological insight into the possibility and epistemological indispensability of *perceptual evidence* in the sense of the *a priori of consciousness.* So much for the first (semiotic) connection between the *a priori* of language and the *a priori* of consciousness where knowledge is concerned.

Yet with the consideration of the *perceptual identification* of an object or objects by propositions, not only is an epistemologically relevant connection between phenomenology and linguistic philosophy instituted, but in the process, the very *abstractness* of the linguistic philosophy of the early Wittgenstein and the logical semantics of Carnap and Tarski depending upon it are brought into question. To what extent is this so?

The supplementing of the "Linguistic Turn" with the "Pragmatic Turn" and the Question of Whether the Two can be Unified

Analytic philosophy was, in its early – logical-semantic – phase, oriented toward *propositions* and not, for example, toward *speech acts.* This means that it abstracted from what Charles Morris would later call the *pragmatic dimension* of intentional and interpretative use of sentences by speakers and hearers in particular situations. It nonetheless sought to take into account in the *semantic* dimension of the meaning of propositions not only their *intensional meaning* but also their *extensional reference* to real facts (*Sachverhalte*) and this meant chiefly the reference of the various subjects of the propositions to real objects, for instance of "cat" and "mat" in the sentence "the cat is on the mat." The sentence indeed expresses that in respect of the cat and the mat as its logical and ontological subjects, the relation or fact pertains that the cat is on the mat.

At this point, we do however see a *pragmatic deficit* in the abstract theory of *logical semantics* since, in order to confirm the *real reference* of the subjects of the proposition, the analysis of the language-immanent *semantic reference* of subjects of the proposition is not sufficient. If it were, then the subject of the proposition, "The present king of France is bald" or the subject of the sentence "Witches ride on broomsticks" would also have to possess a real reference. But these subjects have at best fictive reference; for their real reference cannot be revealed by a corresponding *identification of objects existing in space and time.*

Thus the location of the *real reference* of subjects of propositions comes down to the *identification of the intended (gemeint) objects.* In order for this even to be considered possible however, it must first be presupposed that a proposition *is intended or interpreted by a speaker or a hearer as a perceptual judgment and can correspondingly be verified by the identification of the object meant.* This can also be expressed in the following way: the *two-term* basis of logical semantics, which is oriented toward abstract propositions, must be extended in the direction of the *three-term* basis of the pragmatically integrated semiotics of Charles Peirce. For the identification in the real world of an object intended in language is a matter of the *intentional and interpretative use of language by a speaker or hearer.*

At this point, the question once again arises whether the *pragmatic* extentions of the analysis of the sign function in the sense indicated here can be unified with the "linguistic turn" in philosophy inaugurated by Wittgenstein. Does it not rather lead to a restoration of the methodological primacy of the *philosophy of mind* – since undoubtedly the *reflexively self-certain intention* of the speaker establishes the possible referential "fulfillment" of the meaning of a proposition? To this extent does the establishment of meaning not seem to be a matter of the *intentional consciousness* concerned?

In fact this consideration leads us directly to one of the central theses of Professor Searle's book *Intentionality.*

3 The Intentionalistic Meaning Theory of John Searle as Interpretation of the "Pragmatic Turn" from the Point of View of the Philosophy of Mind

Essentially, Searle grounds the priority of the philosophy of mind or intentionalist meaning theory by means of the following argument. It is the *intentional states* of consciousness – such as, for example, convictions, wishes, fears, hopes and (action-)intentions in the narrower sense – which ultimately determine the *conditions of satisfaction*, with the help of which the *meaning* of *speech acts* can be understood (*Intentionality*, p. 11).

According to Searle, the determination of the "conditions of satisfaction" of speech acts by intentional states of mind occurs in the following way. The intentional states can express themselves in "physical entitites" – such as noises or marks on paper – and impose on the "expressions" which arise in this way the "conditions of satisfaction of special speech acts." Thus, for example, upon a *statement* they can impose the condition of corresponding with a fact of which the speaker is *convinced*; or, upon a *command* the condition of bringing about a state of affairs *desired* by the speaker by the person to whom the command is addressed; or upon a *promise* the condition of bringing about a state of affairs that is desirable for the hearer by the speaker, who *intends* this. According to Searle, in the case of a *statement*, the "direction of fit" of the conditions of satisfaction is laid down by the speaker's underlying conviction; and this in fact occurs in the direction of "word-to-world direction of fit." In the case of an *order* and of *promises*, by contrast, the direction of fit of the conditions of satisfaction is established in terms of an actively produced adaptation of the world to the expression ("world-to-word direction of fit"). Searle summarizes the main semantic import of his argument as follows:

> the key to the problem of meaning is to see that in the performance of the speech act the mind intentionally imposes the same conditions of satisfaction on the physical expression of the expressed mental state, as the mental state has itself. (Ibid., p. 164)

On the basis of this argument regarding the determination of the conditions of satisfaction of speech acts by the underlying *intentional states of mind*, Searle arrives at the following theses in regard to the relationship between *intentionality* and *linguistic meaning*.

> So construed, speakers' meaning should be entirely definable in terms of more primitive forms of Intentionality. And the definition is nontrivial in this sense: we define speakers' meaning in terms of forms of Intentionality that are not intrinsically linguistic. If, for example, we can define meaning in terms of intentions we will have defined a linguistic notion in terms of a nonlinguistic notion even though many, perhaps most, human intentions are in fact linguistically realized.
>   On this approach the philosophy of language is a branch of the philosophy of mind. In its most general form it amounts to the view that certain fundamental semantic notions such as meaning are analyzable in terms of even more fundamental psychological notions such as belief, desire and intention. (Ibid., pp. 160–1)

The challenge of the latest attempt at an intentionalistic theory of meaning is here formulated with sufficient clarity. The question now arises what argument a defender of the "linguistic turn," and therefore of the methodolgical priority of the linguistic *a priori*, can summon against it.

4   Critique of the Intentionalistic Meaning Theory of Searle II (i.e. the Searle of *Intentionality*) by Recourse to the Pragmatic Extension of the "Linguistic Turn" Suggested by Austin and Searle I

The Integration of the "Linguistic Turn" and the "Pragmatic Turn" in Contemporary Philosophy in the Work of Austin and Searle I

I should first like to recap the results of our earlier confrontation between the key Wittgensteinian argument of the *propositional linguistic a priori* and the phenomenological defence of the *a priori of consciousness*. We established the following point: in respect of the perceptual evidence of the phenomenal givenness of the factual content asserted in a proposition, the *a priori of consciousness* does in fact have *priority*; for in this regard, it is up to me, the subject of consciousness, to establish whether the intentionality of my conviction of the existence of a fact is fulfilled by the given phenomenon. This is clearly quite in line with Searle's thesis that the intentional state of mind – here the conviction of the existence of a fact – ultimately determines the conditions of satisfaction for the speech act that consists in asserting a fact.

We have, however, also established that Wittgenstein's argument in respect of the propositional *linguistic a priori of describability* of facts of experience is not refuted by the dependency of the *perceptual fulfillment-evidence* on the *intentionality of consciousness*. In relation to Searle's thesis, we can now formulate this as follows: in respect of the *pure phenomenal-evidence* the *intentional state of consciousness* does indeed impose conditions of satisfaction on the speech act of assertion. In other words, my *conviction decides* which *phenomenon* I can recognize as fulfilling the condition of satisfaction of my assertive; in respect of the *intersubjectively valid interpretability* of the phenomenal evidence, however, the imposition of conditions of satisfaction – and, before this, the intentional content of consciousness of the conviction of an existing fact – is dependent on the *linguistic proposition* through which the intended fact can be *described*. That is to say that the linguistically established meaning decides *as what* I can mean a fact of whose existence I am convinced, and in the case of its existence, *as what* I can point to it.

If one wished to abstract from this *mediation* of the establishment of conditions of satisfaction, and indeed prior to this of the intentional content of consciousness, *through the linguistic a priori*, then there would remain merely a *direct interpretation-free relation* between the *intentionality of consciousness* and the *given phenomenon*. I could, for example, mean that there was behind me precisely *something like what was depicted on the explorer's previously uninterpretable photo*. Through this quasi-language-independent intentionality a condition of satisfaction would in fact also be laid down. I could confirm that it had been fulfilled by turning round and stating "Yes, that was exactly what I meant." But *what*, in this case, would I have meant as an existing fact? In this case, I could not state this in a *publicly or intersubjectively comprehensible form*. My language-independent laying-down and testing of the conditions of satisfaction of my fact-intention would in a certain sense be carried out in terms of the *methodical solipsism* of the pre-linguistically oriented *evidence-phenomenology* of Edmund Husserl. And such a case would not indeed be a case of recognition or verification, as I have sought to indicate in opposition to Husserl; but it could be thought of as a *deficient mode* of verification. For example, all the members of an expedition to whom a photograph was shown could corroborate that they had seen *something of this sort*, without being able to *say what* it was. Intentional *meaning or thinking (Meinen)* and the conditions of satisfaction of conviction of the existence of a fact established by it could in this case only be explicated, to use Peirce's terms, in terms of "Firstness" (so-being of perceptual qualities) and "Secondness" (encounter of the ego with the non-ego), but not however in terms of "Thirdness" (interpretability *as something*). But Searle was certainly not referring to such a case in his argument on the determination of the conditions of satisfaction of an assertive by a conviction. And yet, I might assert that only the case described above fulfills in an exact sense the condition which Searle gives for his meaning theory, which is that of a *unilateral* dependence of linguistic meaning on the allegedly more fundamental intentionality of consciousness. In keeping with our analysis so far, I would like by contrast to propose in the normal cases of assertives and underlying convictions the thesis of a *reciprocal dependence of a priori of consciousness and linguistic a priori*:

1. In my view, in regard to the establishment of *interpretation-free evidence of fulfillment*, the propositional meaning of my assertive is in fact methodological dependent on the intentional content of consciousness of my conviction (and this dependence corresponds in fact to an empirical-genetic priority of intentionality of consciousness over the linguistic *a priori*, for I must first have a conviction before I can – legitimately – assert anything).

2. But, conversely, in regard to the possible *intersubjectively valid meaning* of the intentional content of my conviction, and therefore in regard to the possible *interpretability* of the evidence of fulfillment established by it, there exists a dependence of the intentionality of consciousness on the linguistic *a priori*.

However, in our analysis of the intentionalist semantics of Searle we have only made use of the version of the "linguistic turn" that goes back to the Wittgenstein of the *Tractatus*. That is to say, we have indeed introduced the concept of the *speech act* – of assertion, for example – but, in the sense of the linguistic *a priori* of intersubjectively valid assertion, we have only brought out the *propositional content* of the speech act. This is, in fact, relevant as *a priori of description and interpretation*, when we are concerned with the possible public meaning of a conviction as *representation* of an existing fact. But *speech act theory* – in its foundation by J. L. Austin and, more particularly its elaboration by Searle in his earlier book *Speech Acts* – has in my view also demonstrated the following:

It is not only in respect of the *representation of facts* in the *propositional content* of speech acts but also in respect of the so-called "illocutionary force" of our speech acts that all publicly valid meaning of our meaning-intentions is pre-determined by *linguistic conventions*. This *pragmatic-communicative* meaning of speech acts too can be pre-shaped through the corresponding sentences or phrases in terms of the *semantics* of a particular language ("langue.") This is precisely what Austin showed by his discovery of linguistic *performatives*.[11] The point of this discovery is much less to be seen in such socially institutionalized performative formulas as "I hereby baptize you ..." or "I hereby name you ...," or "I hereby announce my resignation" and such like, than it is in the later proof, that *all* linguistic *sentences* can be made explicit in the sense of the *illocutionary acts* expressed through them. Thus I can express an assertion through the sentence: "I hereby assert, that 'p,'" a command through the sentence, "I command you to bring about 'p'" and a promise through the sentence "I hereby promise you that I shall bring about 'p.'" It can be seen here that the so to speak *possible public meaning of communicative intentions* in the sense of the *illocutionary force of speech acts* is already *conventionally institutionalized*, before the special social institutionalization of perfomative formulas, at the level of language.

It was precisely this point which Searle seemed to me to be making in *Speech Acts*, with the "principle of expressibility" (*Speech Acts*, pp. 19–21) and the attendant comments on that principle, as, for example, in the following passage:

There are, therefore, not two irreducibly distinct semantic studies, one a study of the meanings of sentences and one a study of the performance of speech acts. For just as it is part of our notion of the meaning of a sentence that a literal utterance of that sentence with that meaning in a certain context would be the performance of a particular speech act, so it is part of our notion of a speech act that there is a possible sentence (or sentences) the utterance of which in a certain context would in virtue of its (or their) meaning constitute a performance of that speech act. (*Speech Acts*, pp. 17–18)

It seemed to me that in this passage there was formulated the program for an integration of *propositional semantics* with the *pragmatics of contextualized speech acts* and, therefore also with the *theory of intentionality*. This interpretation also appears to me to be corroborated by the following passage in *Foundations of Illocutionary Logic*,[12] in which "illocutionary force" is expressly explicated as a "component of the meaning" of sentences:

Part of the meaning of an elementary sentence is that its literal utterance in a given context constitutes a performance or attempted performance of an illocutionary act of a particular illocutionary force. Thus, for example, it is part of the meaning of the English sentence, (22) "Is it raining?", that its successful literal and serious utterance constitutes the asking of a question as to whether it is raining. Every complete sentence, even a one-word sentence, has some indicator of illocutionary force; therefore, no semantical theory of language is complete without an illocutionary component." (Ibid., p. 7)

What is happening here is, therefore, a pragmatic extension of the concept of linguistic meaning in the sense of the semantically pre-structured illocutionary force of speech acts. From this I drew the conclusion that the "principle of expressibility" is to be understood in a dual sense:

First, in the sense that one *can* in principle say what one means (irrespective of an actually always existing *pragmatic difference* between *linguistic competence* and general *communicative competence* which is such that the latter is obliged, and able, to compensate for deficiencies in one's own linguistic competence or of the conventional resources of language through non-verbal language use and the paralinguistic use of signs).

Second, in the sense that one is also in principle obliged to express all one's meaning-intentions *explicitly in language* if the validity claim of *intersubjective intelligibility* attaching to one's meaning intention is to be publicly redeemed. The *intersubjective validity of meaning* is thus constituted initially at the level of linguistic expression.

In order to say what one means, one is thus, in the sense of this second interpretation of the "principle of expressibility," also forced – so to speak – to *mean* what one can *say*. This means that the realization of the possibility asserted in the "principle of expressibility" includes a process of mutual adaptation and correction of meaning-experiences and meaning-intentions of individuals on the one hand and of the conventional meaning-fixations of the language community on the other (in which, in processes of inter-lingual translation, the conventional meanings of individual languages are also open for correction in the sense of progressive realization of *universal* validity of meaning, somewhat in the sense of the progressive realization of what Peirce called the "ultimate logical interpretant" of linguistic signs).

At least this second interpretation now stands, it seems to me, in contradiction to the extraordinary turn taken by Searle II, who in *Intentionality* asserts a unilateral dependence of linguistically expressed meaning on the more fundamental intentionality of mind. For in respect of *intersubjective intelligibility and validity* there still exists, as has been demonstrated above, a priority of *linguistic meaning convention* over *meaning intention*, insofar as this latter is dependent on linguistic expression. This is so for Austin and Searle I even in the sense that not only the meaning of *propositional sentence contents* but also the *illocutionary force* of speech acts can be pre-determined by linguistic conventions. In the sense of the implicit doctrine of the speech act theory of Austin and Searle I, one could thus, in my opinion, arrive at the following conclusion: not only in regard to the *representation of facts in linguistic propositions*, but also in regard to the *illocutionary force of speech acts*, which can be expressed in performative phrases, our meaning intentions are dependent on linguistic *conventions* as a condition of possibility of *valid* intersubjective *meaning*. In short, one might arrive at the conclusion that the concept of *intersubjectively valid meaning* is to be defined in terms of what Habermas called the *performative-propositional "dual structure"* of linguistically expressible meaning.[13]

If we take this *pragmatically* enhanced explication of a concept of meaning oriented toward the "linguistic turn," then we arrive at consequences which seriously diverge from the *intentionistically* oriented meaning theory of Searle II.

Let us now attempt to clarify this by a critical reconstruction of the Searlian explication of meaning in the light of "conditions of satisfaction."

The Inadequacy of the Explication of Illocutionary Meaning in Concepts of "Conditions of Satisfaction of Intentional States"

It seems clear, first of all, that this theorem of Searle's represents an extrapolative generalization of the explication of sentence meaning in the light of truth-conditions, which goes back to Frege and Wittgenstein.[14] The Searlian extrapolation and generalization of verificationism in the direction of "conditions of satisfaction" is clearly, in essence, a product of the fact that he is concerned not merely with the meaning of statements, but with the meaning of sentences through which possible *speech acts of all types* can be expressed, such as, for instance, commands, requests and promises etc. as well as assertions.

The extrapolative generalization of the verificationist explication of meaning then takes the following form:

> In Wittgenstein's *Tractatus*, it was stated that "To understand a proposition means to know what is the case, if it is true." (4.024)

In Searle II, the relation runs more or less as follows: to understand the meaning of a linguistically explicitly expressed speech act means to know what conditions of satisfaction are laid down for it through the underlying intentional content of consciousness. In the case of an assertive, this means to know what correspondence to a fact exists in accordance with the "word to world direction of fit;" in the case of a command, by contrast, it means to know what active changing of the world (or, alternatively, what failure of the world to change) exists in accordance with the "world-to-word direction of fit." Even in the case of a *promise*, in Searle's view the understanding of its meaning depends on one's knowing what satisfaction or fulfillment is to be expected in terms of "world-to-word direction of fit."

In this way, it appears, an elegant and plausible extension of the previously accepted explication of meaning in concepts of truth-conditions can be arrived at; and this extension of "verificationism" does, moreover, represent, in Searle's opinion, an argument for the possibility of an intentionalist reduction of the concept of meaning; for the conditions of satisfaction are ultimately determined by intentional states of mind. Yet, against this basic conception of Searle's we can now raise objections on two counts:

1   Firstly, the same is true of the "conditions of satisfaction" of speech acts of all types as we have already demonstrated in relation to the "truth conditions" of statements: the propositional contents of speech acts are dependent on intentional states of mind only to the same extent as these latter are at the same time also already dependent on linguistic meaning conventions in their intersubjectively intelligible meaning. (A unilateral language-independent determination of the conditions of fulfillment of convictions by the corresponding intentional states of mind is indeed – as we have shown – only conceivable in cases of non-interpretable, but nonetheless perceptible and memorable pure "so-being phenomena" – in the sense of Peirce's category of "Firstness.")

2   Secondly, however, we can in fact also demonstrate the following. The apparently very elegant extrapolation and generalization of the *verificationist* explication of meaning in concepts of *conditions of satisfaction* or *conditions of fulfillment* cannot in principle do justice to the linguistic differentiation of illocutionary meaning.

Thus, for example, the conditions of satisfaction or fulfillment in the case of *commands*, *requests*, *demands*, and even of *compulsions* – like "Hands up!" – refer in like fashion to the speaker's *wishes* (more precisely: not to the actual wishes but to the intentions of will that can be supposed on the basis of the particular speech acts) as the determining intentional states of mind: but the *linguistic differentiation* of the various *illocutionary* meanings of the speech acts cited is clearly not explicated in that relationship. All that is explicated is the specific *propositional* meaning which may be the same in the various illocutionary acts – for example, the meaning *that the door is to be opened* – and, in addition to that, the fact that the hearer is to *bring about* the propositionally represented state of affairs. But with this, for example, the following is not explicated:

> in the case of a *command*, the expectation of a compliance which depends on the understanding of the illocutionary meaning implies that the door is opened because the command is respected as proper and issued by an authorized person;
> in the case of a *request*, the expectation of a compliance which depends on the understanding of the illocutionary meaning implies that the door is opened because the addressee considers the request worthy of fulfillment;
> in the case of a *demand*, the expectation of a compliance which depends on the understanding of the illocutionary meaning implies that the door is opened because the addressee considers the request legitimate;
> in the case of a *compulsion*, the expectation of compliance, because the addressee fears negative consequences for himself in the case of non-compliance.

It is clear here that in all four cases *of directive* speech acts, not only the signalization of the *conditions of satisfaction* of a *wish*, but also – above and beyond this – the *signalization of the reasons for compliance with it* belong to the illocutionary force and thus to the explicatable meaning of the speech act.

Normally – i.e. in the case of a serious and sincere directive speech act – the communication of the reasons for compliance will also belong to the intentionality of the speaker's wish, which is part of the speech act, yet this component of illocutionary meaning can precisely not be made intelligible *solely* from the intentionality of the pre-communicative wish: it does, rather, presuppose in principle the linguistic differentiation of illocutionary meaning, just as the propositional content of the wish presupposes the corresponding content of a linguistic sentence. The only aspect (*Moment*) of illocutionary force in every speech act which does in fact depend on the intentional state of mind of the speaker *alone*, is *sincerity* or *seriousness of intention*. However this aspect is usually taken for granted in normal cases and thus cannot contribute anything to the *constitution* of illocutionary meaning. (Matters are the same here as with the uninterpreted perceptual evidence, which we have shown above to be determined as intentional state through conviction alone.)

The irrelevance of the intentional state of mind that is not dependent on the illocutionary force of the speech act – for example, of a *secret* wish – can be clearly seen from the following case, which, even in Searle's view, can certainly not be accounted a normal case of understanding of and compliance to commands: in Richard Wagner's *Ring of the Nibelungen* the god Wotan orders the Valkyrie Brünhilde to aid Hunding to victory over Siegmund. The Valkyrie however aids Siegmund, because she knows Wotan's real wish and would like to fulfill it. With this *realization of the conditions of satisfaction of the intentional state of mind* of the god, she has not, however, obeyed his *command* and is punished accordingly. (Naturally, she has also not fulfilled the will intentions that may be supposed from the command; but *these* intentions are precisely *a priori* dependent in their meaning on the establishment of that meaning in language!)

In fact Searle himself, in *Foundations of Illocutionary Logic* – i.e. in a book which draws, so to speak, on the speech act theory of Searle I – distinguished, apart from the five "illocutionary points or purposes" which determined the "four possible "directions of fit" (Ibid., pp. 51ff), six further components of illocutionary force, which are not concerned – at least in part – with the intentional states which determine the "conditions of satisfaction" of speech acts:

For example – as component 3 – he specifies "the mode of achievement:" "A special way or special set of conditions under which their illocutionary point has to be achieved in the performance of the speech act" (Ibid., p. 15). This component seems to me to be best suited to come into consideration in the explication of illocutionary force in the examples of *directive* speech acts cited by me above; for Searle explains the function of the "mode of achievement" as follows:

> For example, a speaker who issues a command from a position of authority does more than someone who makes a request. Both utterances have the same illocutionary point, but the command achieves that illocutionary point by way of *invoking the position of authority of the speaker*. (Ibid., p. 15; my emphasis)

As a further component which comes into consideration in the explication of illocutionary force in the case of a command Searle's fifth component – that of "pre-

paratory conditions" – can be cited. Here we should have to enlist the following
exemplary determination of functions by Searle: For example, a speaker must
satisfy the preparatory condition of being in a position of authority before he can
non-defectively issue an utterance with the mode of achievement of a command"
(ibid., p. 18). Having regard simply to these "components of illocutionary force," it
becomes possible to say that if one takes them seriously as components of meaning,
then it is not clear how the following programmatic thesis of the book *Intentionality*,
which I cited at the beginning can be validated:

> speakers' meaning should be entirely definable in terms of more primitive forms of
> Intentionality. And the definition is nontrivial in this sense: we define speakers' mean-
> ing in terms of Intentionality that are not intrinsically linguistic. (Ibid., p. 160)

Yet this reference to the conditions cited by Searle himself as constitutive of the illocutionary meaning of speech acts still does not seem to me to express in adequate
form the *necessity of extending* the explication of illocutionary meaning in terms of
conditions of satisfaction. It is admittedly interesting in fact that the illocutionary force of *directive* speech acts, precisely insofar as it is determined by the *pre-
illocutionary intentionality of the speaker*, can be explicated in terms of "conditions
of satisfaction" and their "direction of fit." One has understood precisely the pre-
illocutionary intentionality of these acts if one knows when their *conditions of
satisfaction* are fulfilled; and precisely to that extent the explication of the meaning
of *directive* speech acts, exactly like that of *assertive* speech acts, can be made explicit
in terms of the *conditions of fulfillment of propositional contents*; and this clearly means
that, to this same extent, what in the broadest sense must be called the *verificationist*
method of explication of meaning can be extrapolatively generalized.

Here, in my view, the following question arises: Why in fact is it the case that one
has not sufficiently understood, for example, an *improper* or *unauthorized* command
or an *illegitimate request* or a *compulsion* if one only knows its conditions of satisfaction, whereas on the basis of that knowledge one can very well have sufficiently
understood a false statement? To this question which in my opinion arises in a way
that cannot be ignored in respect of the illocutionary force of *directive speech acts*,
even the reference to components (3) and (5) of illocutionary force introduced
by Searle does not seem to represent a satisfactory answer – even though these
meaning-components already extend, as has been said, well beyond the program
of an intentionalist semantics.

At this point, it seems to me that an extension – or, if the reader prefers, a deep-
ening – of the philosophical presuppositions of the possible *explication of meaning*
is required – an extension which understands the *truth conditions* in the light of
which the propositional content of speech acts or sentences can be explicated not
as a special case of the *conditions of satisfaction* of *intentional states*, but as a special
case of the *validity conditions* of *illocutionary acts*. In other words, we must take seriously the idea of the integration of semantics and pragmatics – as suggested by
Austin and Searle I – in the sense of an extension of the "linguistic turn." And
insofar as the extension of the "linguistic turn" has to take into account all functions of language and all relations of language to the world, it ought to be possible
to understand the *meaning* of speech acts – beyond the *intended proposition-related
conditions of satisfaction* in terms of *validity conditions*.

5   The Explication of the Illocutionary Force of Speech Acts in Terms of Validity Conditions. Speech Act Theory in the Light of a Universal or Transcendental Pragmatics of Language

The possibility, and indeed the necessity of explicating the meaning of speech acts in terms of *validity conditions* is, in my view, overlooked because it is normally easy to refer back the validity conditions of assertives – i.e. the truth conditions of propositions asserted – to the conditions of satisfaction or fulfillment of the asserted propositions. Thus here the conditions of satisfaction or fulfillment can *grosso modo* be equated with the *validity conditions* of the *act of assertion*. A statement seems *true* and, at the same time, *intersubjectively valid* to the extent that the conditions of satisfaction can be fulfilled. In the case of commands, demands, suggestions etc., the *conditions of satisfaction* or *conditions of fulfillment* quite obviously cannot be equated with *validity conditions*. For compliance with an order, demand or suggestion in no way shows that the command was *legal* or *legitimate*, that the demand was *justified* or the suggestion *appropriate*, just as non-compliance in no way proves that it was not valid.

It can, however, now be argued that the understanding of the *illocutionary force* of a command very much implies the understanding of the *validity* of the command, a validity that is to be respected, and thus, in normal cases of compliance with the command, implies the supposition of its *legitimacy* or *legality* in the sense of positive law. In the case of a demand, it is not a supposition of its institutional legitimacy, but an understanding of its *moral justification* or *non-justification* which in this sense is part of the understanding of the illocutionary force. Even in the case of a demand that can only be made if backed up by a threat of violence – a *compulsion* such as, e.g. "Hand over your head!" – understanding of the *illegality* and the moral *illegitimacy* of the demand actually forms part of the understanding of its illocutionary meaning. However, in this case non-compliance is determined by *reasons* deriving from the deficient *validity* of the demand, but compliance, on the other hand, is determined by reasons which have nothing to do with the validity of the speech act, but which derive for the addressee solely from the speaker's *position of power*. Should we here suppose the existence of a further possible basis of illocutionary force besides *validity*? This is a point I shall return to.

We must, however, now ask why it is that, in the case of *directive* speech acts – such as commanding, requesting, demanding etc. – the conditions of fulfillment of the propositional content "p" diverge from the *validity conditions* of the speech act, whereas this is not the case for *assertive* speech acts. From the formulation of this question, it clearly follows that the answer cannot lie in the fact that in the case of *assertive* speech acts no difference whatever exists between their proposition-related *truth* and their speech act-related *validity*. Such a difference does, rather, exist, insofar as the proposition-related truth is related to the *world of objects and facts*, but the speech act-related validity, by contrast, is related to the *intersubjective recognition of validity claims*. However, in the case of *assertive* speech acts, there precisely exists no possible *divergence* but rather a necessary *convergence* between the proposition-related conditions of fulfillment *qua* truth conditions and conditions of intersubjective validity. Why is this not the case with *directive* speech acts?

The answer to this question is, in my view, to be found in the fact that the redemption or legitimation of the validity claim of *assertive* speech acts – i.e. the fulfillment of the truth conditions of their propositional contents which it is asserted are fulfilled – is dependent on the existence of facts which exist independently of the speech act in the external world, whereas this cannot be the case with *non-assertive* – e.g. *directive* – speech acts. With *directive* speech acts, the validity claim which contributes to the constitution of the illocutionary force does not reside in the fact that, for its propositional content, a representation of already existing facts in the external world is being asserted, but, first, in the fact that a demand is made upon the addressees to bring about the existence of a state of affairs in the external world (or cause this to be brought about) and, secondly, in the fact that for the *appropriateness* or *correctness* of this demand *grounds* are claimed which may also be binding for the addressees or have the power to motivate them. To put it a different way: the difference between the validity claim of *assertive* and *directive* speech acts corresponds to the hiatus between *is* and *ought* and the redemption or legitimation of the ought-related validity claim cannot be based upon existing facts or states of affairs in the external world, but must be based upon *socially valid* or – in the case where all conventions are being challenged – on *universally valid norms*.

With this answer to the question as to the difference between the validity conditions – and therefore also of the illocutionary force – of *assertive* and *directive* speech acts a *relationship of language to the world* is clearly being claimed, which cannot be referred back to a relationship of *representation of facts in propositions*. One might call this the relationship to the *world of the intersubjective validity of social norms*; and it is clear that it is also already claimed in the *performative-illocutionary* semantic aspect of *assertive* speech acts, yet in such a way that the redemption of this validity claim – i.e. the *truth-claim* as an assertive's claim to *intersubjective validity* – cannot come into conflict with the fulfillment of the proposition-related truth-conditions. In contrast to this, there always exists a potential conflict between the redemption of the proposition-related *conditions of fulfillment* or *conditions of satisfaction* of *directive* speech acts and the redemption of their *validity claim*, for example in the case of the acceptance or non-acceptance of a command or demand whose validity claim is problematic.

Employing Searle's terminology, one might say that in the understanding of the illocutionary force of directive speech acts, it is not simply a question of understanding the "world-to-word direction of fit" in the sense of proposition-related conditions of *satisfaction* and determining whether one *can* fulfill these conditions, but it is at the same time also a question of understanding the "relation of fit" assumed (or not assumed) by the speaker between the directive claim of his speech act and the *world of social norms* and determining whether one *ought* to respect and therefore accept the directive claim *as right and proper, i.e. as consonant with intersubjectively valid norms*.

Does this distinction between the validity claims of *assertive* and *directive* speech acts exhaust the field of the possible *validity claims* of speech acts and the field of their possible *relations to the world*?

It seems to me possible in principle to regard so-called *commissive* speech acts as a complementary counterpart to *directive* speech acts: their *illocutionary force* similarly presupposes the *intersubjective recognition of the validity of social norms*, but it does so in such a way that the validity of the self-obligation of speakers, not the claim of an obligation on the part of the addressee, is deduced. This is the case, for example, with all contracts – and even with the social contract, through which many philosophers wish to ground the validity of norms in general. It is clearly apparent here that the norm which dictates that promises – and also contracts – are to be *kept* cannot be founded through actual promises or contracts, but represents a condition of possibility of the validity of promises and contracts. We can here see emerge with great intensity the difference between the *social validity of norms* which can be grounded by means of contracts and the *universal validity of norms*, as it has to be taken into consideration *a priori* for the *pacta sunt servanda*. I shall return to this point later. Lastly, so-called *declarative* speech acts could be understood as a social institutionalization and autonomization of that function which all speech acts fulfill in their *performative* dimension: the function of *constituting social facts*. Thus the illocutionary force of *declarative* speech acts also depends primarily on the *inter-subjective validity of social norms*, whilst their *conditions of satisfaction* – which are dependent on the normative validity of the constitution of social facts – must lie in the reciprocal correspondence of the "word-to-world" and "world-to-word" directions of fit.

However, even if these classifications are justified, the distinction between the *normative socially oriented validity claim and relation to the world* and the *truth claim and relation to the world that are oriented to facts in the external world* does not seem to me to exhaust the sphere of the possible validity claims of speech acts or of their relations to be world, for in the case of *expressive* speech acts there is a further specific validity claim which is part of the illocutionary force and has a specific relation to the world, which as such can neither be referred back to the *proposition-related truth claim* of *assertive* speech acts nor to the *performative-communicative validity claim* of *directive* speech acts. In the case, for example, of congratulations, condolences and apologies, and a fortiori of avowals, confessions, vows, and pro-testations, it is neither the *existence* of propositionally represented facts (*Sachverhalte*) – or, alternatively, the *truth* of the propositions representing them – nor the inter-subjective *validity of norms* of what ought to be in the social world, that provides the speech act with its legitimacy. It is here, rather, the *sincere* – or possibly *authentic* – *expression* of the *psychical inner world* of the speaker.

The fact that a *validity claim* is present here can be seen, in my view, in the fact that the *sincerity* of, for example, *condolences*, *apologies*, or *declaration of love* can be put into question and that in this case it can be made the theme of assurance in expressive speech acts of another type, for example in *protestations* or *vows*. In the latter case, one could, following Searle's terminology, say that *assurance* is con-cerned with the question that the "relation of fit" between what has been expressed linguistically and the inner world of the speaker on which doubt has been cast does in fact exist. (It is indeed interesting here that, in the case of the *sincerity claim*, this is only *affirmed* or *declared*, and is not, by contrast – as in the case of the *truth claim* and the *normative legitimacy claim* – *grounded* and *redeemable* by argument. One can, at most, point out that one may *redeem* the sincerity claim of the expressive speech act *through behavioral practice*. This criterion also shows, in my view, that it is wrong to regard *confessions, protestations* and *vows* as special *intensive* forms of *assertive* speech acts. What is particularly intensive here is not able – by contrast with a *proof* – to reinforce the *truth*-claim of an assertive. When strictly understood, i.e. *rationa-liter*, it merely reinforces the sincerity claim of the what has been linguistically expressed in the sense that it provides an assurance that the expressive speech act corresponds with the psychical inner world of the speaker, i.e. with his/her *feelings* and also with his/her *will-intentions* and *convictions*. If the validity of the principle of *fallibility* is assumed, one cannot, in the strict sense, avow that a fact is the case or a statement is true. One can only avow that one is convinced of the truth of one's statement or that one believes, "to the best of one's knowledge," that one's statement is justified.)

Against the introduction of the *sincerity claim* as a separate validity claim for a special class of speech acts, one could perhaps argue that the *condition of sincerity* represents a precondition for the success of all speech acts. This seems to me, however, to be in no way incompatible with the assumption of the special *sincerity claim* of *expressive* speech acts. It seems to me merely to make clear that all the *validity claims* and *relations to the world* that have so far been introduced are presupposed in all speech acts – and this means in speech in general – as transcendental-pragmatic conditions of their possibility, whereas they also form the dominant validity claim of a particular class of speech act (or – in the case of *directive* and *commissive* speech acts – form the dominant validity claim of two complementary classes of speech acts). This fact that *assertive* speech acts, for example, in the context of *argumentation*, as assertions of truth *qua* intersubjective validity always also presuppose the *intersubjective validity of moral norms of an ideal community of argument* is of crucial importance for the ultimate grounding of ethics, as can only be briefly indicated here (see below, p. 53f.).

In this, I have sketched out a philosophical "architectonics" (Kant) of speech act theory or of the meaning explication inherent in it in the sense of *three different validity claims* and the *relations to the world* and *redemption dimensions* inherent in them in the sense of possible *relations of correspondence*. This was first developed in this triadic form by Habermas, following Searle I,[15] and it is significantly corroborated in Karl Bühler's "language theory," i.e. in his well-known theory of the three essential "language functions:" "representation," "expression," and "appeal."[16]

Bühler's theory – which has also been adopted by Karl Popper – does however require one essential correction: the non-representative functions – "expression" and "appeal" – are, from a semiotic point of view, in no way mere "symptom-" or "signal-functions," which we might be said, in contradistinction to the "representation-function" of propositions, to share with animals. The *non-representative* functions of *subjective-self-reflexive expression of intentions* and of *communicative appeal* in the sense of the positing of validity claims can rather be expressed wholly "symbolically" – namely through performatives – and likewise performed responsibly. This is precisely what has been shown by Austin's discovery of "performatives" and the possible knowledge, which can be drawn from his work and that of Searle I, of the *performative-propositional dual structure* of all sentences, which are explicitly semantically prestructured by the *illocutionary force* and the *propositional meaning* of speech acts. The fact that we are *not* here dealing with language functions which we share with the animals is particularly shown in the "three-beam nature" (Bühler) not only of the *meaning* of sentences and speech acts, but of the *validity claims* inherent in their *illocutionary force*. Recent experiments with chimpanzees have suggested that we should acknowledge that these animals are very probably capable of *propositional representation of the world* in non-verbal sign language; however, we ourselves are not for the time being willing to believe in the capacity of Washoe and Sarah to effect the *illocutionary expression of validity claims in dual-structure-sentences*.[17]

From these considerations on the three-dimensional philosophical architectonics of the theory of meaning-explication outlined here and its correspondence to Bühler's three "language-functions", I should like to return to the question of the reducibility – or non-reducibility – of linguistic meaning to pre-linguistic mental intentionality. I do not wish to contest that there are three different directions of possible intentionality of meaning corresponding to the three language functions and validity claims. If this were not the case, then one would have to be able to conceive the *expression* function – and in fact the *appeal* function, with Bühler, as *pre-symbolic* functions. One may, however, assert that only *language* or *linguistic communication* can elucidate the "three-beam nature" of meaning and the three-dimensionality of validity claims and relations to the world. For, with mental intentionality, every meaning intention – whether it be directed toward factual representation, toward an appeal to interlocutors or toward self-expression – must ultimately assume the structure of the *subject–object relation*.

This is precisely attested by this history of philosophy, particularly the history of the moderns since Descartes – with its aporetic tendency to conceive the *reflexion* problem as a problem of *self-objectivization* (or, alternatively, of the *infinite hierarchy of metalevels*) and – correspondingly – simply to overlook the always already complementarily presupposed dimension of *communicative understanding* and the *intersubjective validity of deontic norms*. (This oversight seems to me to form the cause of the characteristic blindness of *scientistically* oriented philosophy for the dimension of intersubjectively recognized *ethical norms* that is always already presupposed in objective knowledge.)

On the other hand, the orientation to *language-functions* can help toward an extended – or more profound – philosophical "architectonics" – an architectonics which overcomes the *one-dimensionality of the modern subject-object relation* (and with it also the one-dimensionality of the explication of linguistic meaning in terms of *truth*-conditions of propositions or the fulfillment conditions or conditions of satisfaction of intentional states of mind) in favor of the *three-dimensionality of linguistic meaning, validity claims, and relations to the world* as the possible conditions of redemption of validity claims. We might, therefore, in summary, say that in language an architectonics of meaning of validity dimensions is laid down which is a fitting basis for *theoretical* and also *practical* philosophy (in the dimension of sincere or authentic self-expression, it also seems that we see a *necessary* condition of *aesthetics* emerge).

I have in this regard argued, with Habermas, for the philosophical architectonics of a "universal pragmatics of language," which I myself interpret as a *transcendental pragmatics of language*. I should like to clarify the degree to which this is justified by examining the as yet unelucidated and unresolved problem of this study. I have, in the foregoing, (see above, p. 47) referred to a circumstance which might be regarded as putting into question the whole conception of the *explication of illocutionary force in terms of validity conditions* which has been argued up to now. I am referring to the case or type of case – only inadequately exemplified in the example of *compulsion* – in which the compliance with a directive speech act ensues not "on the basis of" a redeemable *validity claim*, but "on the basis" of a consideration of the *power position of the speaker* or of the *positive or negative consequences for the addressee of complying or not complying* which are dependent upon that position of power.

We are not only talking here about criminal extortion, as in the sentence

"Give me your money!" but about the broad spectrum of all those, perfectly civil "suggestions" which are obeyed on opportunistic grounds and thus out of thoroughly rational motivation. In this, in my opinion, we can distinguish two sub-classes of cases: on the one hand the broad spectrum of those cases in which the suggestion of compliance is not effected through *open threats or offers*, but through *concealed strategic use of language* – as for example, rhetorical persuasion, suggestion of conclusions, suggestion through advertizing, diplomatic hints etc; on the other hand, the relatively clearly circumscribable realm of openly strategic communication – for example, the mode of hard negotiations in the political or economic spheres.

Do these facts from practical life not expose the conception of the explication of illocutionary force in terms of validity conditions as being from the outset the product of an "idealistic fallacy?" And is this not an argument for completely leaving out of account the concept of *validity* – at least that of *moral validity* – in the analysis of the illocutionary force of speech acts, and confining ourselves to a, so to speak, "value-neutral" analysis of the mechanism through which "uptake" and *acceptance* – and therefore the *illocutionary* and *perlocutionary* effect – of speech acts can be achieved?

In his *Theory of Communicative Action*, Habermas has given roughly the following answer to this question:[19] *First*, he pointed out that one cannot adequately understand actual validity-*claims qua* components of the illocutionary force of speech acts if one does not understand them in the light of *intersubjectively valid norms*, i.e. of norms which actually constitute the *social world* and which virtually make a universal validity claim, which – in the case of its being questioned – can be tested at the level of "argumentative discourse" in the light of universally valid principles. *Second*, Habermas has shown – in my view, convincingly – that all cases of *concealed strategic language use* can be understood as "parasitic" upon language use that is oriented toward *validity claims* and their social binding force. This is alright so far as it goes, yet as an answer it is, in my view, still inadequate in both its parts.

In its *first part*, it is not adequate insofar as Habermas ultimately seeks to contrive the *founding* of the virtually universal validity claims of social norms at the level of argumentative discourse by ultimately referring to the *functional necessity* of the norms in the "lifeworld." In the lifeworld, however – or more precisely in actually existing socio-cultural "forms of life" – not only do quite distinct and mutually incompatible social norms function, but they do moreover always function in the form of compromises with the strategic form of "communicative action-coordination" (Habermas). These few comments are enough, in my view, to reveal the attempt to *found* the validity of social norms *by recourse to their function* in the "life world" as a *petitio principii*. And yet it is does in my view remain correct for Habermas to refer to the virtually universal validity-*claims* of lifeworld acts of communication. Yet one cannot found this *claim* by *reference to itself*; one would rather have to be able to refer to the *necessary acceptance* of certain universally valid norms. This leads us to the second part of Habermas's answer.

In this second part of the answer, Habermas has in fact shown in relation to the actual compromise between *language use oriented toward validity claims* and *concealed strategic language use* that people in these cases have always already implicitly *acknowledged the priority of language use oriented toward validity claims*. They *show* this precisely by the fact that they only allow strategic suggestions to be effective in *concealed* form, in that, for example, in cases of intentions to *persuade*, they simultaneously feign a desire to *convince* by argument. To this extent, the *parasitism* argument does in fact work here. Yet precisely this argument cannot be applied in relation to *openly strategic* language use, for example in relation to the field of hard – political or economic – negotiations mentioned above. For, in these cases, the speaker in no way *shows* by the form of his language use that he has already acknowledged the priority of the communication form oriented toward validity claims. Rather, he takes up his position *openly* upon the *standpoint of power* and can, for that very reason, use *language* in a way that is "oriented toward agreement" ("verständigungs-orientiert") in Habermas's sense.

Does this then reveal the definitive aporia in the universal pragmatic conception of the explication of illocutionary meaning in terms of *validity conditions?* (in favor, for instance, of the neo-Nietzscheanism flourishing in French post-structuralism – e.g. in Foucault and his disciples).

In my opinion this is in no way the case. One may no longer shy away from the – apparently so esoteric – *transcendental pragmatic* radicalization of *language pragmatics*. In relation to the second part of Habermas's answer, the two following supplementary considerations are necessary.

Whoever – in hard negotiations, for example – openly speaks from the *standpoint of power*, does not need to recognize the priority of the illocutionary force of speech acts that is oriented toward *validity claims* so long as he does not seek to *argue* for his standpoint. However, as soon as he becomes involved in doing that, i.e. as soon as he wants to know *who is right*, he is already implicitly recognizing the *equal right of his interlocuter* and thereby a *part of the moral basic norms of an ideal community of argument.* (A further part, which I do not need to go into here, lies, in my view in the *basic norm of shared responsibility* of those engaged in the argument for the solution of all problems facing them, which is implicitly acknowledged in *serious questioning*). Insofar as he does this, he also of course recognizes the *priority* of communication that is oriented toward *validity claims* and moreover also an *ethical principle* for the testing in argument of moral validity claims.

Since *argumentative discourse* is methodically *indispensable* for those who wish to know who is right (those who philosophize are always such people as wish to know who is right and wish to decide this by argument – not by force or negotiation!), it follows that we have also uncovered a principle of a possible ultimate grounding of the universal validity of validity-claims through the *reflexive recourse to the presuppositions of argumentative* discourse: *those norms can be regarded as ultimately grounded which on the level of argumentative discourse concerning validity claims cannot be contested without performative self-contradiction – and for that very reason cannot be grounded by logical derivation (whether deductive or inductive).*[20]

In saying this, we have supplied a *transcendental-pargmatic completion of the first part of Habermas's answer* to our question. We no longer need to suggest, in the form of a *petitio principii*, that the virtually universal validity claims of human discourse have their sufficient grounding *in themselves* or in their *lifeworld function*; and we can also contest their radical questioning by movements of enlightenment from the Greek Sophists to Nietzsche and Foucault. Where the skeptic and relativist is prepared to argue, we can confound him on the grounds that *as argumentative language being*, he has always already necessarily recognized the basis of the intersubjective validity of all three validity claims, which contribute to constituting the illocutionary force of speech acts – the basis of the *truth claim*, the *sincerity claim*, and the *claim to normative rightness*. (Addition for the extremely cautious: in the case where the skeptic refuses to argue, this does not of course reveal any aporia in the idea of grounding by argumentation. It merely follows that the skeptic can no longer join in the discussion and that now only those who will argue, can present their thoughts – theories or hypotheses – *about the skeptic*: which may, for example, run to the conjecture that the skeptic wished to avoid a possible refutation or – in the really serious case – that a case of existential despair or a collapse of communicative competence requiring therapy was involved.

So much for the transcendental-pragmatic grounding of the explication of il-locutionary meaning in terms of *validity*-conditions. The man in whose honor this *Festschrift* has been prepared has indeed warned in his *Speech Acts* against the "ivresse des grands profondeurs." He may forgive the writer of this article that he could only make the philosophical import of speech act theory clear to himself through re-transcendentalization (even Rorty may forgive me!). The transcendental-pragmatic interpretation of speech act theory certainly means no return to the phil-osophy of "transcendental consciousness" and its functions of world-constitution (from Kant to Husserl). There remains only Kant's question of the *conditions of possibility of validity*. The answer to this question is, however, supplied by reflec-tion on *language-functions*, as this can be carried out as a reflection on the *conditions of validity of current philosophical argumentation*.

NOTES

1   On this point, see the following: H. P. Grice, "Meaning," in *Philosophical Review* 66 (1957), pp. 377–88; "Utterer's Meaning, Sentence-Meaning and Word-Meaning," in *Foundations of Language* 4 (1968); "Utterer's Meaning and Intentions," in *Philosophical Review*, 78 (1969), pp. 147–77; S. Schiffer, *Meaning* (Oxford University Press: Oxford, 1972); J. Bennett, *Linguistic Behaviour* (Cambridge University Press: Cambridge, 1976); G. Meggle, *Grundbegriffe der Kom-munikation* (W. de Gruyter: Berlin/New York, 1981).

2   K. -O.Apel, "Intentions, Conventions, and Reference to Things, Dimensions of Understand-ing Meaning in Hermeneutics and in Analytic Philosophy of Language," in, H. Parret and J. Bouveresse (eds), *Meaning and Understanding*, (W. de Gruyter: Berlin/New York, 1981), pp. 79–111; "Läßt sich ethische Vernunft von strategischer Zweckrationalität unterscheiden? Zum Problem der Rationalität sozialer Kommunikation und Interaktion," in *Archivio di Filosofia* 51 (1983), pp. 375–434; "Linguistic Meaning and Intentionality. The Compatibility of the 'Linguistic Turn' and the 'Pragmatic Turn' of Meaning-Theory within the Framework of a Transcendental Semiotics," in H. Silverman and D. Welton (eds), *Critical and Dialectical Phenomenology* (State University of New York Press: Albany, 1987), pp. 2–53

3   J. R. Searle, *Intentionality: An Essay in the Philosophy of Mind* (Cambridge University Press: Cambridge, 1983).

4   J. R. Searle, *Speech Acts* (Cambridge University Press: Cambridge, 1969), pp. 43ff.

5   See the articles of J. Habermas and K.-O. Apel in Apel (ed.), *Sprachpragmatik und Philosophie* (Suhrkamp: Frankfurt am Main, 1976), and my article "Linguistic Meaning and Intentionality."

6   L. Wittgenstein, *Vermischte Bemerkungen* (Suhrkamp: Frankfurt am Main, 1977), p. 27.

7   See E. Stenius, *Wittgenstein's 'Tractatus'* (Basil Blackwell: Oxford, 1964).

8   See A. Tarski, "Die semantische Konzeption der Wahrheit und die Grundlagen der Semantik," in J. Sinnreich (ed.), *Zur Philosophie der idealen Sprache* (Deutscher Taschenbuch Verlag: Munich, 1972), pp. 53ff.

9   See K. R. Popper, *Logic of Scientific Discovery* (Hutchinson: London, 1959), pp. 95ff, and 105.

10   On Peirce, see K. -O.Apel, *Charles Peirce, From Pragmatism to Pragmaticism* (University of Massachusetts Press: Amherst, Mass., 1981), and "C. S. Peirce and the Post-Tarskian Problem of an Adequate Explication of the Meaning of Truth, Towards a Transcendental-Pragmatic Theory of Truth," in E. Freeman (ed.), *The Relevance of Charles Peirce* (The Hegeler Institute: Le Salle, Ill., 1983), pp. 189–223; Apel, "Linguistic Meaning and Intentionality"; "Das Problem der phänomenologischen Evidenz im Lichte einer transzendentalen Semiotik," in M. Benedikt and R. Burger (eds), *Die Krise der Phänomenologie und die Pragmatik des Wissenschaftsfortschritts* (Oesterreichische Staatsdruckerei: Vienna, 1986), pp. 78–99.

11   See J. L. Austin, *How To Do Things With Words* (Oxford University Press: Oxford, 1962); K.-O.Apel, "Austin und die Sprachphilosophie der Gegenwart," in H. Nagl-Docekal (ed.), *Überlieferung und Aufgabe, Festschrift für E. Heintel* (W. Braumüller: Vienna, 1982), vol. I, pp. 183–96; "Die Logos-Auszeichnung der menschlichen Sprache. Die Philosophische Relevanz der Sprechakttheorie", in H.-G. Bosshardt (ed.), *Sprache interdisziplinär* (W. de Gruyter: Berlin/New York, 1986), pp. 45–87.

12   See J. R. Searle and D. Vanderveken, *Foundations of Illocutionary Logic* (Cambridge University Press: Cambridge, 1985).

13   See J. Habermas, "Vorbereitende Bemerkungen zu einer Theorie der kommunikativen Kompetenz," in J. Habermas and N. Luhmann, *Theorie der Gesellschaft oder Sozialtechnologie?* (Suhrkamp: Frankfurtam Main, 1971, pp. 101–41; "Was heißt Universalpragmatik und Philosophie?" in K.-O.Apel (ed.), *Sprachpragmatik und Philosophie* (see note 5).

14   A similar extrapolation was already made by Peter Strawson in *Individuals*, pp. 313f, and in "Meaning and Truth" (see *Logico-Linguistic Papers* (Methuen: London, 1971), p. 178.

15   See the works cited at n. 13 and J. Habermas, *Theory of Communicative Action* (Beacon Press: Boston, Mass., 1985) vol. 1, chapters 1 and 3.

16   See K. Bühler, *Sprachtheorie* (G. Fischer: Jena, 1934).

17   On this, see K.-O.Apel, "Die Logoauszeichnung der menschlichen Sprache."

18   See K.-O.Apel, "Das Apriori der Kommunikationgemeinschaft und die Grunlagen der Ethik," in K.-O.Apel, *Towards a Transformation of Philosophy* (Routledge and Kegan Paul: London, 1980), and "The Common Presuppositions of Hermeneutics and Ethics. Types of Rationality beyond Science and Technology," in J. Sallis (ed.), *Research in Phenomenology*, 9 (1979), pp. 35–53.

19   On what follows, see Habermas, *Theory of Communicative Action*, vol. 1, chapter 3, and K. -O.Apel, "Sprachliche Bedeutung, Wahrheit und normative Gültigkeit. Die soziale Bindekraft der Rede im Lichte einer transzendentalen Sprachpragmatik," in *Archivio di filosofia* (1987). See particularly J. Habermas, *Moralbewußtsein und Kommunikatives Handeln* (Suhrkamp: Frankfurt am Main, 1983), pp. 88, 108, 110, 112.

20   See K.O-Apel, "The Problem of Philosophical Fundamental Grounding in Light of a Transcendental Pragmatic of Language," in *Man and World*, 8 (1975), pp. 239–79, reprinted in K. Baynes et al. (eds), *After Philosophy – End or Transformation?* (MIT Press: Cambridge, Mass., 1987), pp. 250–90. On this, see, W. Kunemann, *Reflexive Letztbegründung. Untersuchungen zur Transzendentalpragmatik* (Alber: Freiburg, 1985), and D. Böhler, *Rekonstruktive Pragmatik. Von der Bewußtseinsphilosophie zur Kommunikationreflexion* (Suhrkamp: Frankfurt am Main, 1985).

4

Searle on Illocutionary Acts

WILLIAM P. ALSTON

Preliminaries

Over the past few decades John Searle has produced the most influential and important discussion of illocutionary acts in print. He has been foremost among those who have taken the torch from J. L. Austin[1] and developed a theory of illocutionary acts that occupies a prominent position in the philosophy of language. The crucial contributions are to be found in his book *Speech Acts*[2] (hereinafter *SA*) and in his essays, "A Taxonomy of Illocutionary Acts" (hereinafter TIA) and "Indirect Speech Acts."[3] More recently in *Intentionality (hereinafter IN)*[4] he has used his account of illocutionary acts as the basis of a general theory of intentionality and in the process made some additions to the account.

This essay will be concerned with the fundamentals of Searle's theory. Space constraints prevent me from going into the uses Searle makes of this account in the philosophy of mind and elsewhere. I shall subject the theory to a detailed critical analysis, hoping thereby to extract some important morals for our thinking about the topic.

I should warn the reader at the outset that any opposition between Searle and myself is far from being of the most fundamental sort. On the contrary, my own work on illocutionary acts has been very much in the same ball park as Searle's, as will become clear in this essay. The reader may be tempted to regard our differences as another case of Tweedledum and Tweedledee and wonder whether this trip was necessary. Nevertheless, I submit that these differences, though minute compared with, say, the differences between Searle and Davidson, Quine, or Goodman are well worth airing. Precisely because they are relatively subtle, I shall have to examine the fine details of Searle's account, a treatment it has thus far lacked, since critics have focused on more sweeping oppositions between extensional and intensional theories, and between illocutionary and perlocutionary, accounts of meaning.

Quibbles aside, I share with Searle the same initial intuitive concept of an illocutionary act, not only with respect to the paradigmatic core, but even with respect to the fringe areas. My favorite way of introducing the concept is this. Illocutionary acts are what are typically reported by our *oratio obliqua* devices for reporting speech, the devices that tell us *what* the speaker says (in a sense of "what he says" that does not mean "what sentences he uttered"), devices that make explicit the "content" of the utterance. Such devices consist of (a) a principal verb that specifies the type of illocutionary act involved, or as Searle likes to say, specifies the "illocutionary force" of the act, and (b) a content specifying phrase, typically a "that..." clause or an infintive construction. Here is a small sample.

1   A told B that B had left his lights on.
2   A predicted that the strike would be over soon.
3   A suggested to B that they go to a movie.
4   A asked B for a match.
5   A advised B to sell his utilities stock.
6   A promised B to read his paper.
7   A expressed considerable enthusiasm for B's proposal.
8   A reminded B that it was almost 9:00.
9   A exhorted B to try to finish before the week was out.
10 A congratulated B on his performance.
11 A announced that the meeting had been cancelled.
12 A admitted that the gate was open.

The problem, stated most generally, is to specify what it is to perform an act of the sort exemplified by this list.

Preparatory Conditions for Promising

Searle has developed his theory from an analysis of one type of illocutionary act, promising. So far as I am aware, this is the only detailed analysis that he has provided; the broader theory consists of generalizations to other cases and informal comments about similarities and differences between illocutionary acts of various types. Therefore it will repay us to look carefully at the account of promising.

I   Given that a speaker S utters a sentence T in the presence of a hearer H, then, in the literal utterance of T, S sincerely and non-defectively promises that p to H if and only if the following conditions 1–9 obtain.

1   Normal input and output conditions obtain.
2   S expresses the proposition that p in the utterance of T.
3   In expressing that p, S predicates a future act A of S.
4   H would prefer S's doing A to his not doing A, and S believes H would prefer his doing A to his not doing A.
5   It is not obvious to both S and H that S will do A in the normal course of events.
6   S intends to do A.
7   S intends that the utterance of T will place him under an obligation to do A.
8   S intends (i-1) to produce in H the knowledge (K) that the utterance of T is to count as placing S under an obligation to do A. S intends to produce K by means of the recognition of i-1, and he intends i-1 to be recognized in virtue of (by means of) H's knowledge of the meaning of T.
9   The semantical rules of the dialect spoken by S and H are such that T is correctly and sincerely uttered if and only if conditions 1–8 obtain. (*SA*, pp. 57–61)

Each of these conditions is alleged to be necessary, and their conjunction sufficient, for "sincerely and non-defectively promising that p to H." Be that as it may, not all of the conditions are necessary for promising *tout court*. We can have a clear case of promising without (4). Thus I might say to you, "I promise to take you to the meeting tomorrow," where, unbeknownst to me, you would prefer not to be taken by me but for fear of offending me you do not make this explicit. Here I could still be making the promise; I could rightly be taken to have assumed an obligation to take you to the meeting and I could justly be blamed for not doing so. The second part of (4), also, could be violated without inhibiting the promise. I might realize, or believe incorrectly, that you would prefer not to go to the meeting with me, but utter the above sentence all the same. Perhaps I am motivated to make you uncomfortable. Then, so long as you do not make explicit that you had rather not go with me and so long as I do not make explicit that I believe that you had rather not, I could still rightly be taken to have made the promise, and justly reproached for not carrying through. Similar points could be made about conditions (5) and (6).

Condition (1) is not necessary for promising either. To develop this we will first have to look into how Searle understands this condition.

> I use the terms "input" and "output" to cover the large and indefinite range of conditions under which any kind of serious and literal linguistic communication is possible. "Output" covers the conditions for intelligible speaking and "input" covers the conditions of understanding. Together they include such things as that the speaker and hearer both know how to speak the language; both are conscious of what they are doing; they have no physical impediments to communication, such as deafness, aphasia, or laryngitis; and they are not acting in a play or telling jokes, etc. (*SA*, p. 57)

Searle also says: "I am construing condition 1. broadly enough so that together with the other conditions it guarantees that H understands the utterance . . ." (*SA*, p. 61)

Now clearly it is not necessary for my promising you to do A that you not be deaf or that I not have laryngitis. More seriously, it is not necessary that you understand what I said. To be sure, if you did not understand me, you didn't realize that I made the promise and hence would not be disposed to hold me to it. And, no doubt, if I realize that you didn't hear or understand me and take no steps to correct that situation, we don't have a clear case of promising. But none of that implies that your actually understanding me is required for my having made a promise. Suppose that I mistakenly think that you heard and understood me when I said "I promise to take you to the meeting tomorrow." When I come to pick you up you are surprised and ask me what I am doing. I then might well say, "Didn't you hear me when I promised to take you?" thereby presupposing that I did promise, even if you didn't hear me. Or suppose that I fail to show up, and a third party who heard my utterance upbraids me for not keeping the promise. I can hardly defend myself on the grounds that I had made no such promise.[5]

Searle will, quite justly, respond to all this by pointing out that his conditions were presented as necessary, not for promising *tout court*, but for "sincere and non-defective promising." And where I promise you to do A, and you don't understand what I said, or you would prefer that I not do A, the promise is surely defective.

But the trouble with taking "non-defective promising" as our analysandum is that there are indefinitely many ways in which promises can be defective, *vis-à-vis* their standard social function. Thus I might promise to do something it is impossible for me to do[6] or very foolish for me to do. The promisee might not take me seriously; he might even be the sort of person who never takes promises seriously, a person to whom it is useless to make promises. The consequences of my keeping the promise may be disastrous, as it would if I were the President and promised Senator Helms to drop the H-bomb on Teheran. The promiser might be an unreliable person, though sincere at the moment. And so on. Thus even if we leave out defects that are not distinctive of promises, such as conceptual confusions and bad pronunciation, there are very many ways in which promises can be defective. The absence of all these would have to be specified as conditions of "non-defective promising," and it is dubious that such a list could be completed. Even if it could it would be too unwieldy to be usable, and in any event would not provide a way of getting at what is essential to promising. Searle has a sense that some possible defects of promises are such that the absence of the defect is "intrinsic to the notion" of promising (*SA*, p. 54), and it is the absence of these defects that he includes in his analysis. But he has done nothing to support this supposition, nor do I see how he could.[7]

Suppose, then, we set out to say what it is to promise H to do A, whether "defectively" or not. The aim is to produce an account that will cover all clear cases of promising. The only qualification to be made on this is that I mean the account to cover only *intentional* promisings, if indeed there are unintentional promises and if some unintentional promises count as clear cases.[8] Now it does seem that conditions like (4) and (6) have something to do with promising; surely, for example, it is essential to promising that, as Searle says, it involves an expression of an intention to do what is promised. But how are we to incorporate this into a necessary condition for promising, given that an insincere promise still counts as a promise?

Searle himself has shown us the way:

> A promise involves an expression of intention, whether sincere or insincere. So to allow for insincere promises, we need only to revise our conditions to state that the speaker takes responsibility for having the intention rather than stating that he actually has it. A clue that the speaker does take such responsibility is the fact that he could not say without absurdity, e.g., "I promise to do A but I do not intend to do A". To say, "I promise to do A" is to take responsibility for intending to do A, and this condition holds whether the utterance was sincere or insincere. (*SA*, p. 62)

The notion of taking responsibility for the satisfaction of conditions is one that I used in the analysis of illocutionary acts in "Linguistic Acts"[9] and in *Philosophy of Language*,[10] as a way of bringing in conditions such as (4) and (6). We may save both, in an analysis of promising *tout court*, by prefacing each with "S takes responsibility for its being the case that ... "

We must be careful to understand "take responsibility" here in a rather special way. The idea is not that the speaker took responsibility for state of affairs C in the sense that he acknowledged having brought C into existence. It is more like the way in which, when I become the head of a department or agency, I take responsibility for the efficient and orderly conduct of its affairs. I am responsible for the work of my subordinates being done properly, not in the sense that I have done the work myself but in the sense that I am rightly held to blame if the work is not done properly. I am the one who must "respond" to complaints about that work. It is in this sense that S takes responsibility for conditions (4) and (6) being satisfied in promising H to do A. S, in uttering some appropriate sentence, knowingly lays himself open to complaints, objections, correction, blame, or some such response, in case (4) or (6) is not satisfied. We may take the following as explaining the phrase, "In uttering sentence, T, S took responsibility for its being the case that p":

> R1 In uttering T, S knowingly took on a liability to (laid himself open to) blame (censure, reproach, being taken to task, being called to account), in case of not-p.[11]

Where I say something that renders me liable to blame or correction in case of not-p, we may say that in saying what I said I "purport" or "implicitly claim" that p, or "represent" it as being the case that p. Thus we could alternatively explain "In uttering T, S took responsibility for its being the case that p" as follows:

> R2 In uttering T, S represents it as being the case that p.

In the sequel I shall abbreviate these formulations by "S R's that p."

Let's nail down the point that S's R'ing (4) and (6) are necessary conditions of promising to do A, even though (4) and (6) themselves are not. Suppose S said "I'll write those letters tomorrow" (in a context that clearly indicates that this would normally be taken as a promise). H replies, "You know you don't have any intention of writing those letters tomorrow," or "What makes you think I care whether you write them or not?" S then replies, "So what?" or "What does that have to do with it?" thereby indicating that he does not take the failure of condition (4) or (6) to be just grounds for complaint. Of course, S may just be pretending not to see the point, and he may, in spite of his disclaimer, be quite well aware that there is something wrong with what he said if H's allegations are correct. But let's suppose that he is sincere and that he really doesn't take the complaints to be relevant. In that case we must conclude that S did not promise H to do A, or at least did not mean to do so, did not intentionally make that promise. He may have been just expressing an intention or making a prediction (or even practicing pronunciation), but he certainly didn't intend to be making a promise.

It will be noted that Searle's condition (5) has not figured in this discussion. That is because I have my doubts as to whether it is necessary for promising, even with the "take responsibility" preface. So far as I can see, I could have promised you to do A even if it is obvious to both of us that I will do A, and even if I do not represent (5) as being the case. There might be "ritual" or institutional reasons for me to "nail the matter down" by explicitly making a promise, as would be the case where I am taking the oath of office and promise to faithfully discharge my duties. However I am inclined to include a condition not mentioned by Searle for which S is *ipso facto* taking responsibility in promising to do A, namely, that it is possible for S to do A. Having promised to do A I cannot avoid recognizing the allegation that it is not possible for me to do A as a relevant complaint. Thus I will replace Searle's (5) with:

> (5) (S takes responsibility for its being the case that) it is possible for S to do A.

Some readers may feel that, having rejected Searle's program of specifying conditions for "non-defectively promising" as being too undiscriminating, I am hoist with my own petard in that I am unable to prevent all the myriad forms of defects from reentering the back door as states of affairs for the non-obtaining of which S is taking responsibility. If it is necessary for promising to do A that S take responsibility for its being the case that she intends to do A, isn't it equally necessary that she take responsibility for A's being a sensible thing to do, or for there being some chance of the auditor's taking her seriously? Doesn't she have to recognize the non-obtaining of these conditions as a legitimate basis for blame, just as much as she does for the non-obtaining of Searle's (4) and (6)?

No. To be sure, these are or can be legitimate grounds for complaint or criticism, but they are not connected with the *concept* of promising in the same way. If one refuses to recognize the foolishness or imprudence of doing A as rendering one liable to blame or censure for promising to do A, that may show that one is lacking in practical sense, but it has no tendency to show that one was not really promising. One can respond by saying: "So what! I just feel like doing it, and I don't go for all that prudence stuff. I prefer to do what I feel like doing at the moment." In that case we may condemn the promiser for being frivolous or irresponsible, but we would have no solid grounds for denying that she had made the promise. On the other hand, if one seriously sloughs off as irrelevant a complaint that it is impossible for her to do A, that does show that she didn't really intend to be promising, either because she doesn't understand what it is to promise or because she was making some other use of her utterance. This gives us a way of separating out those "defects" that figure in the concept of promising.

Other Conditions for Promising

Now for Searle's (7), which, let's remember, runs as follows:

> (7) S intends that the utterance of T will place him under an obligation to do A.

Of this condition Searle writes:

> The essential feature of a promise is that it is the undertaking of an obligation to perform a certain act. I think that this condition distinguishes promises (and other members of the same family such as vows) from other kinds of illocutionary acts. (*SA*, p. 60)

And he goes on to call this the "essential condition." I agree, with qualifications to be noted. The basic point of promising to do A, as contrasted with predicting that one will do A or expressing an intention to do A, is that one places oneself under a *prima facie* obligation to do A. But this makes it all the more surprising that Searle formulated this "essential" condition as simply requiring that S *intend* his utterance to place him under the obligation rather than as:

S's utterance of T places him under an obligation to do A.

After all the actual engendering of the obligation is what Searle has said to be essential. It is true that after the passage just quoted from page 60, Searle writes: "Notice that in the statement of the condition, we only specify the speaker's intention; further conditions will make clear how that intention is realized (*SA*, p. 60)." However it is not at all clear to me that all of Searle's nine conditions taken together entail that S does have even a *prima facie* obligation to do A. Suppose that, in a deranged state but not so deranged that I cannot have the intentions and beliefs required by the conditions, I say to you "I promise to blow up the earth tomorrow," and all of Searle's conditions are satisfied. No one I think, would take me to have even a *prima facie* obligation to blow up the earth. In any event, so long as there is even a doubt that the other conditions, taken together, entail that the intention specified in (7) will be realized, we may as well explicitly require that it is. I therefore propose to alter Searle's (7) to:

(7) By his utterance of T S carries out an intention to place himself under an obligation to do A.

We could have moved further from Searle by dropping the requirement of the intention on S's part. But we will want to retain that so long as we are restricting ourselves to intentional promises.

It is clear that (7) is indeed essential: (4)–(6) alone, whether in Searle's version or ours, conditions that Searle felicitously calls "preparatory," cannot make the utterance a case of promising. In fact, if all that S is doing is representing it as being the case that (4)–(6) hold, he is *asserting* that these conditions hold, rather than promising anything. These conditions figure in a case of promising only by being presupposed as a background for doing what is the heart of promising, namely, laying an obligation on oneself by one's utterance.

But in coming to appreciate the essentiality of (7) we may wonder whether (4)–(6) are required. So long as I lay a *prima facie* obligation on myself to do A by saying what I say, haven't I promised to do A, whatever else is the case? No. There are two points to be made here. First, these preparatory conditions are doing some work in distinguishing promising from other "commissives," all of which involve laying an obligation on oneself. Thus I can contract to do A without taking responsibility for its being the case that the other party to the contract would prefer my doing A to my not doing A. But, second, a more fundamental point is that both promising and other commissives – contracting, vowing, betting, etc. – are distinguished from other cases of engendering obligations by utterances by the fact that they are what we might call cases of *explicitly* taking on an obligation by an utterance. In commissives the action one takes on an obligation to perform is explicitly involved in the propositional content of the act (the proposition expressed by one's utterance), and the commitment of the speaker is also carried by the utterance. These are cases of "coming right out and saying" that one is hereby bound to do so-and-so, not in the sense that one says *that* in so many words but in the sense that one's commitment and what one is committing onself to do are embodied in the rules governing one's linguistic devices.[12] In these respects all "commissives" are contrasted with other cases in which one takes on an obligation by an utterance, but where the commitment and/or what one is committed to is not made explicit by the utterance. For an example, consider my accepting an offer of a faculty position. In doing so I acquire an obligation to meet my classes on time, even though I didn't explicitly promise, or otherwise commit myself to do so. The other conditions in the analysis, (4)–(6) in particular, ensure that the act is of the explicit commitment sort. Thus, e.g., if I undertake an obligation to do A by an utterance and am also, in that utterance, taking responsibility for its being the case that you would prefer my doing A to my not doing A, and that it is possible for me to do A, I am doing something that carries an explicit commitment to my doing A in particular.

This brings us to (8), which requires that S intends to get H to realize that S is promising to do A. We can save ourselves the trouble of considering whether this is a necessary condition of promising, since in *IN* Searle explicitly abandons the view that any intention to communicate is necessary for illocutionary act performance (see pp. 165–9). Instead let's take a brief look at Searle's (9).

> (9) The semantical rules of the dialect spoken by S and H are such that T is correctly and sincerely uttered if and only if conditions 1–8 obtain.

The idea back of this condition is that the rules of a natural language render a given sentence standardly usable for performing illocutionary acts of a certain type by requiring, for correct utterance of the sentence, that the necessary conditions for performing illocutionary acts of that type are satisfied.[13] Thus "I promise to pay you back in a week" is standardly usable to promise to pay the hearer back within a week of the time of utterance, just because it is part of the semantics of English that S correctly utters that sentence only if H would prefer S's paying him/her back within a week to S's not doing so, only if S intends to pay H back within a week of the utterance, and so on.[14] If this is the way the semantics of sentences goes, we have what I call an "illocutionary-act-potential" theory of sentence meaning, according to which what it is for a sentence to have a certain meaning is whatever it takes for that sentence to be standardly usable to perform illocutionary acts of a certain type. Against this background, (9) has the effect of requiring that T be a sentence that, by virtue of its meaning, is standardly usable to promise to do A.

A serious difficulty for (9) is posed by the fact that promises are most frequently made without using sentences the meaning of which makes it explicit that it is a promise that is being made, or even makes it explicit just what sort of future action of S is in question. It is the exception rather than the rule that promises are made by using the full formula "I promise that . . ." More typically one just says "I'll do A" or the like, leaving it to the context to make clear that this has the force of a promise. And, with the right kind of contextual support – someone's just having asked "Do you solemnly swear . . . ?" – one can make a promise just by saying "I do," thereby uttering a sentence the meaning of which does not make explicit what he is promising to do, much less that it is a promise.

Searle will, no doubt, answer that he has already pointed out that "I confine my discussion to full blown explicit promises and ignore promises made by elliptical turns of phrase, hints, metaphors, etc." (*SA*, p. 55–6) However, since this leads to the analysis failing to cover most of the clear cases of promising, the restriction is surely ill advised. Stated most generally, the basic trouble with (9) is that it ignores the enormous importance of context in communication and approaches the matter as if, in normal cases, the full content of the illocutionary act is carried by the meaning of the sentential vehicle. However this point can be easily accommodated by adding to (9): "or a sentence that the context makes clear is being used as elliptical for a sentence that satisfies the first disjunct."

There is still the point that it is possible for S and H to be using a private code in which T is set aside for this use, even though neither it, nor anything for which it is elliptical, enjoys that status in any full blown natural language. But perhaps we can understand Searle's "dialect" in a wide enough sense to cover this eventuality. Even so, there is the case in which S mistakenly supposes that H is party to the convention that makes T so usable. Suppose I am speaking to a foreigner whom I mistakenly suppose to understand English. Could I be promising to help him get a taxi, even though there is no dialect we share in which my sentence is cut out for that job? Or if that is not possible, perhaps it is something special about promises, having to do with the serious practical commitment they involve. Consider a kind of illocutionary act that lacks that dimension, telling H that something is the case. Can't it be true that I told H something though, unbeknownst to me, H doesn't sufficiently understand the language I am speaking. ("I told him where the railway station is, but it turned out that the dummy couldn't understand a word I said.") On the other hand, if it is quite clear to me that my utterance, in context, will give H no sufficient clue as to my illocutionary act, it is, at least, not clear that I have told him anything. We can best handle these matters by simply attaching the "take responsibility" preface to (9) as well. That would rule out the case in which S simply ignores the chances for communication, while at the same time allowing that illocutionary act performance does not require a sentential vehicle that actually fits the hearer's condition.

Thus the version of (9) to which we have been led is the following.

(9) S takes responsibility for its being the case that either (a) T is such that the semantical rules of a dialect spoken by S and H are such that T is suited by virtue of its meaning to be used to promise that A, or (b) the context makes it clear that T is uttered as elliptical for a sentence that satisfies (a).

That leaves us with (2) and (3), which require that S express a proposition that predicates a future act A of S. This is, no doubt, necessary, but it does not require separate statement. If S takes responsibility for the satisfaction of (4)–(6), he has *ipso facto* expressed the proposition that S does A in the future. S could not take responsibility for, e.g., intending to do A (represent himself as intending to do A) without expressing the proposition that he will do A. In fact, that is one revealing way of bringing out what it is to express a proposition; the proposition gets "expressed" by virtue of the fact that it enters into the conception of what S is taking responsibility for. Each of the conditions (4)–(6) has to do, in one way or another, with S's doing A in the future.

Let's sum up the results of this examination of Searle's account of promising. Our revised version will look like this.

II S promised to H to do A in uttering T *iff*:

A In uttering T S took responsibility for its being the case that (represented it as being the case that):
1 H would prefer S's doing A to S's not doing A.[15]
2 It is possible for S to do A.
3 S intends to do A.
4 Either (a) T is such that the semantical rules of a dialect spoken

by S and H are such that T is suited by virtue of its meaning to be used to promise to do A, or (b) the context makes it clear that T is uttered as elliptical for a sentence that satisfies (a).

B   S's utterance of T carries out S's intention to place S under a *prima facie* obligation to do A.

Some morals can be drawn from the difference between I and II. The most fundamental and important difference is that, with respect to Searle's (4)–(6) and (9), we have shifted from a straightforward requirement of objective states of affairs to the "internalized" requirement that S take responsibility for these states of affairs' obtaining. Without rehashing the specific reasons for this shift in each case, let me say more generally that it reflects what I take to be the most basic truth about illocutionary acts and, indeed, about contentful or meaningful speech generally. This is the point that what makes the utterance of a sentence a case of promising to do A, asserting that p, or performing an illocutionary act of any other type, is not some set of "natural" facts, such as those required by Searle's (4)–(6), but rather a "normative fact." What most basically changes when one moves from just vocalizing or testing a microphone to saying something with a propositional content and an illocutionary force, is that one changes one's "normative status" in a certain way, one "sticks one's neck out," one renders oneself liable or responsible in a new way; one opens oneself up to pertinent censure, reprimand, or correction, in case certain conditions are not satisfied.[16] This basic difference has several important consequences.

First, it ensures the intentionality of the act without the need for any explicit requirement of this, at least as far as those aspects of the act embodied in the "take responsibility" condition are concerned. For I can't be taking responsibility for condition C holding in uttering T, without meaning to be doing whatever it is that this assumption of responsibility entails that I am doing. I may not have consciously put together the various "take responsibility" conditions into a single-act concept; and so I might not be explicitly thinking of myself as intending to perform that act. Nevertheless my intentions will be such as to amount, in effect, to a intention to perform the act that one performs if and only if one takes responsibility for those conditions in uttering a sentence. In so far as there are aspects of the act that fall outside the "take responsibility" conditions, as is the case even with II, intentionality will have to be specified separately for them. I myself am inclined to push the ideas of this revision all the way and make illocutionary-act performance solely a matter of taking responsibility for the holding of certain conditions, but I will not be able to develop that in this paper. (See the works cited in note 14.)

Second, it makes possible a much more integrated account. Disparate material becomes unified under the "take responsibility for" rubric. Again, if the whole analysis were so subsumed, the account would be even more highly integrated.

Third, II provides a natural, intuitive bridge between the analysis of an illocutionary-act type and the content of the rules subjection to which renders a sentence usable to perform illocutionary acts of that type. To see this, consider how one takes responsibility for certain conditions holding in uttering a sentence. What button does one push? Of course, one could say to oneself while uttering the sentence, or just before, "I hereby render myself liable to complaint in case of not-p." But if that were required for taking responsibility an infinite regress would loom. For whatever one is doing, illocution-wise, in uttering this last sentence would itself involve some taking of responsibility and so another public or private utterance, and . . . Moreover, whether or not I go through some verbal or non-verbal mental perform- ance of assuming responsibility, how is it to be communicated to my hearer what I am taking responsibility for? How can I genuinely render myself liable to blame if no one else knows about it? What kind of liability would that be? Searle will say, no doubt, that S intends to get it across to H that he is taking responsibility for C by picking the right kind of sentential vehicle, one governed by a rule that requires the necessary conditions of performing this illocutionary act, as conditions of correct utterance. Something like this is, no doubt, the case. Nevertheless, and this is the point I have been leading up to, II provides a much closer connection between the conditions of promising and their reflection in the rules governing an appropriate sentence than does I. For the standard way of taking responsibility for conditions holding in uttering a sentence, and perhaps the only way, is to recognize that, under appropriate conditions, the sentence is subject to a rule that requires those condi- tions for correct utterance, and to utter one's sentence *as* subject to such a rule (in other words, satisfy whatever speaker intention conditions there are for the sentence's being subject to that rule on a particular occasion). For all practical purposes, and ignoring *outré* cases, to take responsibility for C's obtaining in utter- ing T *is* to utter T as subject to a rule that requires C as a condition of correct utterance. Thus at the very heart of our analysis of promising to do A there is the notion of the content of a rule that will render a sentence usable for promising to do A. Indeed, this paragraph indicates that we could redo the analysis of a particular illocutionary-act concept as, at least in part, uttering a sentence as subject to a certain rule, thus bringing the illocutionary-act-potential conception of sentence meaning explicitly into the analysis of illocutionary act concepts.

A Taxomony of Illocutionary Acts

We have devoted a great deal of attention to promising, naturally enough since it is the one kind of illocutionary act that Searle treats in detail. It is now time to look at the general picture of illocutionary acts that emerges from this account of promis- ing. Here I will draw both on the brief suggestions in *SA* and the more extended treatments in TIA and chapter 6 of *IN*.

Searle's procedure in *Speech Acts* is to take the analysis of promising as a model for the construction of analyses of other illocutionary act concepts. Thus any such analysis will involve the following elements (omitting (1), (8), and (9) as containing nothing distinctive of one kind of act rather than another, except for variable filler that is taken from the other conditions).

1 Restrictions on the propositional content. With requests it has to do with a future act of H; with thanks it has to do with a past act of H; with assertions there is no restriction; and so on.
2 Preparatory conditions, analogous to (4) and (5) in the analysis of promising. For example, for requesting we have the condition that H is able to do A.
3 The essential condition, analogous to (7) in the analysis of promising. I will have much to say about this.

4   The sincerity condition, the psychological state expressed. For assertions this
     is a belief, for requests a desire, and so on.

Thus we get the following analysis of requesting (leaving out the analogues of
(1), (8), and (9) from the analysis of promising).

III   S requests H to do A in uttering T in the presence of H *iff*:

A   In uttering T S expresses a proposition that predicates a future act of H.
B   H is able to do A and S believes H is able to do A.
C   It is not obvious to both S and H that H will do A in the normal course
     of events of his own accord.
D   S wants H to do A.
E   T counts as an attempt to get H to do A.[17]

Of course, just as with promising, what figures here as B–D are not really necessary as they stand; it is only necessary that S take responsibility for their being the
case.

This generalization is least successful on the essential condition. For promising
and other commissives the production of what may felicitously be called a "conventional effect" is essentially tied up with the performance of the act. I haven't succeeded in promising you to do A unless I have laid on myself a *prima facie* obligation
to do A. This deserves to be regarded as the center of the act, by reference to which
the other conditions are to be understood. As Searle says, "In general, the essential
condition determines the others" (*SA*, p. 69). But there isn't really anything in
stating or requesting that is as analogous to the essential condition for promising
as Searle supposes. As we have just seen, Searle takes the essential condition of
a request to be that it "counts as an attempt to get H to do A." But this is, of course,
not anything brought about by the utterance; if it obtains at all it is, rather, a status
of the utterance. And even there it cannot be construed as a *conventional* status, one
the utterance enjoys by virtue of falling under some rule or convention. Whether
something was an attempt on my part to achieve a goal, G, is, rather, a matter of fact,
a matter of whether a certain intention, aim, or motive played a certain role in my
action; and no convention can determine whether that is the case. But suppose we
drop the aim at as much commonality with promising as would be achieved by
identifying a conventional effect or status that is essential to requesting, and change
the essential condition to "T is (rather than 'counts as') an attempt to get H to do
A." Now we no longer have a necessary condition. I could request you to do A
without attempting to get you to do A. I might hope that you do not accede to the
request, making it only because it is my duty to do so or in order to satisfy some
third party.[18] At most, it is a necessary condition of requesting H to do A that S take
responsibility for attempting to get H to do A.

As for asserting or stating that p, Searle says in *SA* (p. 66), that the essential
condition is that the utterance "counts as an undertaking to the effect that p represents an actual state of affairs." In TIA this becomes "a representation of how
something is" (p. 2). From the same article, "The point or purpose of the members
of the assertive class is to commit the speaker (in varying degrees) to something's
being the case, to the truth of the expressed proposition" (p. 12). This strikes me
as quite a mixed bag. "Undertaking" and "commitment" sound like normative

statuses engendered by the utterance, analogous to the obligation on the speaker engendered by the promise; while being a representation does not seem to carry that force, depending on how "representation" is to be understood here. Moreover, the undertaking or commitment in question is naturally understood as the same sort of thing I have been calling "taking responsibility" for a certain state of affairs obtaining. On that reading of the "essential condition" for asserting, it is something involved in all illocutionary acts; so that what is distinctive about asserting would be that it lacks features possessed by acts of other types, not that its "essential condition" is peculiar to it, as is the case with promising, or rather with commissives generally. But the chief difficulty about all these versions is that rather than providing one condition among others that make up the analysandum, as with the essential condition for promising, they simply present the total package in different words. To be sure, these locutions cry out for considerable explanation, but "commiting oneself to something being the case" or "representing how something is," is naturally understood as just *being* asserting that p, the whole ball of wax. And in that case we have merely provided a rather obscure synonym for the analysandum rather than digging into its structure.

Let's now turn to TIA, where Searle introduces some new categories. He identifies "twelve significant dimensions of variation in which illocutionary acts differ one from another" (p. 2) and differentiates some broad categories of illocutionary acts in terms of (some of) these dimensions. Neither here nor, so far as I know, in any other published work subsequent to *SA* does Searle put forward any analyses of particular illocutionary act concepts; rather he indicates in broad terms how various categories of illocutionary acts differ from each other. I shall take what he gives us and subject it to critical scrutiny without reminding the reader at each point of what he does not provide. However, at some point we must return to the question of whether, or to what extent, Searle means the ideas introduced in these later works to supersede the account of *SA* or whether, or to what extent, the new ideas are designed to be supplementary.[19]

In TIA Searle distinguishes the following categories of illocutionary acts: Assertives, Directives, Commissives, Expressives, and Declarations. The dimensions of difference that he chiefly relies on to differentiate and characterize these categories are the following: point (or purpose); direction of fit between words and the world; psychological state expressed. His explanation of these dimensions leaves much to be desired.

Point (or purpose) is not explained (except by saying that it corresponds to the essential condition in *SA*) but only illustrated. The need to go beyond a basic grasp of these English words is underlined by two considerations: (1) If the purpose is the speaker's purpose and the point is a standard, social, institutional, or conventional one, these may diverage. Perhaps the standard point of making a promise is to commit the speaker to do what is promised; but my purpose in making a particular promise may be to discomfit you. (2) In any event, a speaker will normally have more than one purpose in saying something, and an utterance may well have more than one point. I normally always have the purpose, in speaking, to get you to understand what I am saying, and I usually have further purposes as well, e.g., to inform the hearer of something or to get the hearer to do something. Searle does say: "The point or purpose of a type of illocution I shall call its *illocutionary point*" (p. 3), and he further says: "For many, perhaps most, of the most important illocutionary acts, there is no essential periocutionary intent [i.e., intent to produce a certain effect in one's audience] associated by definition with the corresponding verb" (p. 3).[20] But this helps us only if we already have the idea of what constitutes a distinctively *illocutionary* point, and that is exactly what needs explanation.

So far as I can see, Searle is simply relying on the supposition that every illocutionary-act concept carries with it a particular point or purpose that is obviously basic to that illocutionary-act type, in that it goes toward making particular utterances acts of that type. And perhaps we can handle the point-purpose alternative by simply taking these to be alternative terms for that end for the sake of which, most basically, illocutionary acts of that type are typically or standardly performed. That still leaves us with the contrast between the notion just adumbrated and the notion of a necessary condition of the performance of an act of that type. With respect to the alleged point or purpose of directives, I have already pointed out that such a purpose on the part of the speaker is not a necessary condition of, e.g., requesting H to do A. But it still could be maintained that the basic social or communicative point of directives is to get a hearer to perform a certain action. I will suppose that Searle is best interpreted here as dealing with basic social points of performing illocutionary acts of certain types.

Searle explains direction of fit as follows. "Some illocutions have as part of their illocutionary point to get the words (more strictly, their propositional content) to match the world, others to get the world to match the words" (TIA, p. 3). The former direction of fit is termed "word-to-world" and is illustrated by assertives. The latter direction is termed "world-to-word" and is illustrated by directives and commissives.

Note that the direction of fit is explained as an aspect of the illocutionary point. This reinforces my previous suggestion that the "purpose or point" is best thought of as attaching to the illocutionary act type standardly or typically, rather than being something that must be involved in a particular case if that case is to fall under that type. One can make an assertion without its being any part of one's purpose to make the words fit the world, as when one is deliberately lying. And so with directives and commissives, as we have seen.

But even with that understanding it is only with directives, of the categories already discussed here, that the direction of fit can be seen to be an aspect of the illocutionary point specified. Since the illocutionary point of a directive was specified as "attempting to get H to do A," that is obviously one way of trying to "get the world to fit the words." But if the illocutionary point of a commissive is to lay the speaker under an obligation to do A, that does not necessarily carry with it the purpose of getting the "world to match the worlds", i.e., bringing it about that what is promised is actually done. No doubt, sincere promises are made with the intention of doing what is promised. But even here it would be a distortion to think of the promise as typically made in order to get oneself to do A, as if one felt that one needed that goad to rouse one from one's lethargy. Ordinarily one just has the intention to do A and feels no need to institute the obligation as an extra motivating force. And where one is insincere in promising to do A one certainly doesn't do so in order to get A done. A similar story is to be told for asserting, whether the point is specified as *representing* how something is or *committing* the speaker to something's being the case. When lying I make such a commitment and represent it as being the case that p, without in any way having the purpose of making my words match the world, i.e., asserting what is true.[21] Hence, given Searle's specification of the illocutionary points of these categories, he cannot reasonably suppose that the direction of fit is an aspect thereof.

Searle does at least hint at an alternative way of thinking of direction of fit. In *IN* we find the following.

> The members of the assertive class of speech acts . . . are supposed in some way to match an independently existing world . . . But the members of the directive class of speech acts . . . and the members of the commissive class . . . are not supposed to match an independently existing reality but rather are supposed to bring about changes in the world so that the world matches the propositional content of the speech act . . . If the statement is not true, it is the statement which is at fault, not the world; if the order is disobeyed or the promise broken it is not the order or promise which is at fault, but the world in the person of the disobeyer of the order or the breaker of the promise. Intuitively we might say the idea of direction of fit is that of responsibility for fitting. (*IN* p. 7)

Whether this is an alternative suggestion depends on how we unpack this figurative idea of statements, orders, and promises being at fault, or their being *supposed* to do or be something. A natural way of reading it is in terms of what the point or purpose of the act is, and we have seen that this will not do. The notion of *conditions of satisfaction*, which Searle makes central in *IN*, might give us an alternative reading. We shall come back to that after looking further at the taxonomy in TIA.

The third dimension of variation featured by Searle in TIA is *expressed psychological states*. This is relatively unproblematic, except for the fact that Searle makes no attempt to explain what notion of "express" is involved here. He does make it explicit that one can be expressing a belief, e.g., even if one has no such belief; so it is clear that this is not the notion of a manifestation, evincing, or betrayal of the state in question. If I do not intend to do A nothing can be a manifestation of that intention. But Searle does not tell us what alternative concept of expressing will allow for the non-existence of what is expressed. He does note that "it is linguistically unacceptable (though not self-contradictory) to conjoin the explicit performative verb with the denial of the expressed psychological state. Thus one cannot say 'I state that p but do not believe that p,' 'I promise that p but I do not intend that p,' etc." (TIA, pp. 4–5) This strongly suggests our old friend, taking responsibility. For the unacceptability and pragmatic paradoxicality of "I loc that p, but not-q" (where "loc" stands for some illocutionary verb) is precisely an indication that in loc'ing that p I am thereby taking responsibility for its being the case that q. That explains the pragmatic paradox; I would be simultaneously taking responsibility for its being the case that q and taking responsibility for its not being the case that q (the latter in denying that q). But if that is the way the wind blows, we need a way of distinguishing expressing a psychological state from asserting that one has it; for both will equally involve taking responsibility for its being the case that one has the state. More work is neeeded here.[22]

To sum up this rather scattered discussion of TIA, Searle distinguishes three categories of illocutionary acts as follows.

Commissives: Point or purpose – to commit the speaker to some future course of action.

Direction of fit – world to words.
Psychological state expressed – intention.
Assertives: Point or purpose – to commit the speaker to something's being
                  the case.
                  Direction of fit – words to world.
                  Psychological state expressed – belief.
Directives: Point or purpose – an attempt by the speaker to get the hearer
                  to do something.
                  Direction of fit – world to words.
                  Psychological state expressed – desire.

Now let's look at the other two categories. So far we have heard nothing of those speech acts that got Austin launched onto his seminal investigation, those in which someone brings about some normative, institutional, or conventional state of affairs by (apparently) saying that it obtains: acts like hiring of firing someone, adjourning a meeting, or sentencing a convict. Searle uses the term "declarations" for this category. He quite properly takes the basic point of the act to be what has just been indicated, the engendering of the conventional state of affairs specified in the propositional content.[23] However, with respect to direction of fit, he makes the odd ruling that there is a two-way direction. His fullest explanation of this is found in *IN*:

> Since the illocutionary point of the declaration is to bring about some new state of affairs solely in virtue of the utterance, declarations have both directions of fit. One brings it about that p by way of representing it as being the case that p. Thus "I now pronounce you man and wife" makes it case that you are man and wife (world-to-word direction of fit) by way of representing it as being the case that you are man and wife (word-to-world direction of fit). (*IN*, p. 171)

Thus, in effect, Searle takes a declaration to be a combination of an assertive and something extra that is made possible by extra-linguistic convention that saying something of the right sort, in the satisfaction of certain further conditions, is sufficient to bring it about that p. This is further borne out by his saying "This analysis has the consequence that a declaration expresses both a belief and a desire. A man who sincerely declares the meeting adjourned must want to adjourn the meeting and must believe that the meeting is thereby adjourned" (*IN*, p. 172).[24] Thus a declaration contains all three basic features of an assertive: the illocutionary point, the direction of fit, and the psychological state expressed.

I see no reason to agree with this. It is true that the declarative act of adjourning a meeting involves the same propositional content as the assertive act of reporting that the meeting is adjourned. But then any non-assertive act will contain the same propositional content as some assertion. Asking you to close the door involves the same propositional content as asserting that the door is closed. In attributing an assertion of the propositional content to the declarer but not to the requester Searle is presumably moved by the fact that the declarer seems to be asserting that the state of affairs in question obtains, as when I adjourn the meeting by saying "The meeting is adjourned." However, this holds only for some ways of making declarations. I can also adjourn a meeting by pounding the gavel and saying "That's it." And in any event, Austin and others have given strong reasons for denying that what Searle calls declarations really are, even in part, assertions. Space constraints forbid my pursuing this issue.

Searle also distinguishes a category of *expressives*, the illocutionary point of which "is to express the psychological state specified in the sincerity condition about a state of affairs specified in the propositional content" (TIA, p. 15) Presumably this is supposed to be the same sense of "express" as that in which assertives, commissives, directives, and declarations express psychological states of various kinds. Thus expressives would seem to be distinguished by, *inter alia*, the fact that something which is a feature of all illocutionary acts is here the basic illocutionary point. As for direction of fit, Searle declares there to be none. There is, to be sure, a propositional content involved when, e.g., I thank you for writing a letter of recommendation for me or congratulate you on getting the fellowship, but, says Searle, since the truth of that proposition (that you wrote a letter for me, or that you won the fellowship) is presupposed rather than asserted, we are not trying to get the words to match the world in the expressive act. (TIA, pp. 15–16; *IN*, p. 173). It certainly seems right that these propositions are *presupposed* in these illocutionary acts, but it is not clear that this rules out a direction of fit. Surely my speech act of thanking just mentioned is criticizable in case you wrote no such letter, just as much as it would be if I had asserted that you wrote the letter. Presuppositions are "supposed" to be true, just as assertions are. In defending his position in TIA Searle says: "In performing an expressive, the speaker is neither trying to get the world to match the words nor the words to match the world; rather the truth of the expressed proposition is presupposed" (p. 15). This seems right. But likewise, as we saw earlier, no such attempt is being carried out in typical cases of assertives or commissives. I can't see that Searle has a strong case for his denial of direction of fit, even given his way of identifying the propositional content. And he will have an even weaker case if the propositional content of my thanking you for writing a letter of recommendation for me is: *my being grateful to you for writing a letter of recommendation for me.*[25] There is a simple and, I think, quite convincing reason for this choice. The attitude of the speaker is just as much a part of what must be understood by the hearer if she is to grasp the illocutionary act being performed as is the object of that attitude, while at the same time the attitude does not constitute the illocutionary force of the act; hence it must be part of the propositional content. We can see that the attitude doesn't constitute the illocutionary force by noting that other acts with other illocutionary forces could have the propositional content specified above, e.g., someone else's telling someone that I am grateful to you for writing that letter for me. Thus I find Searle's specification of the propositional content incomplete. And once we get the full story it becomes even more implausible, on Searle's grounds, to deny a words-to-world direction of fit. Surely, if I thank you for doing A without being grateful at all to you for doing A, my utterance is criticizeable for failing to match the facts in something very much like the way in which my asserting that I am so grateful would have been.[26]

Thus Searle's classification of illocutionary acts is deeply flawed. I believe that a simpler, more defensible, and more natural classification can be achieved by taking illocutionary acts to consist solely in R'ing conditions in the utterance of sentences (or surrogates for sentences). Major categories can then be distinguished by differenes in the patterns of conditions R'd. But I will not have time to develop that in this paper. (See the forthcoming book mentioned in note 14.)

74 *William P. Alston*

Intentions to Represent and Conditions of Satisfaction

Before drawing the multiple strands of this discussion together into a final assessment, we must look at some new resources deployed in Searle's 1983 book, *Intentionality* (*IN*), and foreshadowed, in part, in "Meaning, Communication, and Representation" (MCR). *IN* is mostly devoted to using material from his theory of illocutionary acts in developing a general account of intentional psychological states and activities, but in the process Searle alters and enriches the former. For one thing, as we noted earlier, he renounces any supposition that intention to communicate with, or be understood by, a hearer is necessary for illocutionary-act performance, and he had already in *SA* denied that any intention to produce other effects on hearers was required. In *IN* the intention required for an (intentional) illocutionary act is said to be an intention to *represent* (pp. 167–9). But what is it to intend to represent something or other by one's utterance? "... the representing intention is a matter of imposing the conditions of satisfaction of an Intentional [psychological] state on an overt act, and thereby expressing that Intentional state" (p. 169). And what is meant by "conditions of satisfaction"? To this, the key contribution of *IN* to the subject, we must now turn.

Since I am not convinced that Searle has given the kind of explanation of this term he needs to give, I had better exhibit his own words to the reader.

> The notion of conditions of satisfaction applies quite generally to both speech acts and Intentional states in cases where there is a direction of fit. We say, for example, that a statement is true or false, that an order is obeyed or disobeyed, that a promise is kept or broken. In each of these we ascribe success or failure of the illocutionary act to match reality in the particular direction of fit provided by the illocutionary point. To have an expression, we might label all these conditions "conditions of satisfaction" or "conditions of success." So we will say that a statement is satisfied if and only if it is true, an order is satisfied if and only if it is obeyed, a promise is satisfied if and only if it is kept, and so on. Now, this notion of satisfaction clearly applies to Intentional states as well. My belief will be satisfied if and only if things are as I believe them to be, my desires will be satisfied if and only if they are fulfilled, my intentions will be satisfied if and only if they are carried out. That is, the notion of satisfaction seems to be intuitively natural to both speech acts and Intentional states and to apply quite generally, wherever there is a direction of fit. (*IN*, p. 10)

This is Searle's best shot as explaining "conditions of satisfaction," and I'm afraid it doesn't take us very far. The suggestion, so far as illocutionary acts are concerned, is that conditions of satisfaction are necessary and sufficient conditions for the act's being successful, in the way in which, e.g., a statement is successful *iff* it is true, an order is successful *iff* it is obeyed, and so on. Now clearly this is only one dimension of success or failure. Just what counts as success for a particular statement or order depends on what the speaker was aiming to accomplish. If, in stating that the prospects of nuclear war have increased, my aim, or one of my aims, was to alarm the auditor, then my act is successful in that respect *iff* the auditor is alarmed. If my aim is issuing an order is to get you to realize what a big shot I am, then my act is successful in that respect *iff* you come to realize what a big shot I am. Clearly Searle means to identify conditions of satisfaction with conditions of certain sorts of success rather than others. But how does he explain which these are? For one thing, he lists the appropriate conditions for different sorts of illocutionary acts – truth for statements, etc. But this hardly throws light on the general concept of conditions of satisfaction. What he gives us in the way of a more general formula is this: "we ascribe success or failure of the illocutionary act to match reality in the particular direction of fit provided by the illocutionary point." So the particular kind of success involved is success in carrying out the "illocutionary point," including the particular direction of fit aimed at. In MCR this is spelled out a little more fully. It is because the defining point of an assertion is to commit the speaker to the truth of the propositional content that the crucial requirement of success is the truth of the proposition, independent of the utterance. It is because the defining point of directives is to get the hearer to do something and to do it because of the utterance, that the crucial condition of success here is obedience. And so on. Thus the notion of conditions of satisfaction for illocutionary acts is derived from the previous specification of illocutionary points and directions of fit, and so is heir to all the ills that plague the latter. Conditions of satisfaction do not, contrary to what one might at first suppose, give us a new and independent way of analyzing illocutionary-act concepts.

To be sure, if Searle had some independent account of conditions of satisfaction for intentional psychological states, he could then build his account of conditions of satisfaction for illocutionary acts on that. For the heart of the treatment of illocutionary acts in *IN* is the doctrine that one performs an illocutionary act by intending one's utterance to represent something, and to intend that is to intend that the utterance have the same conditions of satisfaction as a certain psychological state, the one expressed.

> How is it possible that mere things can represent? And the answer I am proposing is that the utterance act is performed with the intention that the utterance itself has conditions of satisfaction. The conditions of satisfaction of the belief that the enemy is retreating are transferred to the utterance by an Intentional act. (*IN*, p. 167)
>
> the representing intention is a matter of imposing the conditions of satisfaction of an Intentional state on an overt act, and thereby expressing that Intentional state. (*IN*, p. 169)

However the conceptual dependence seems to be in the opposite direction. The theory of speech acts is used to provide resources for the conceptualization of intentional psychological states. So no help is to be expected from that quarter.

Even though the account in *IN* fails to provide any really new tools for digging into the structure of illocutionary-act concepts, it does mark a definite advance on the earlier accounts in clearly recognizing that intentions to communicate are not necessary, in general, for illocutionary-act performance.[27] But Searle leaves us with an unresolved problem concerning the exact place of "intentions to represent" in the total illocutionary-act concept. Does he suppose that they are sufficient as well as necessary for illocutionary-act performance. He does not, so far as I am aware, explicitly address this question, but the discussion in *IN* strongly suggests a positive answer.

Intentions to represent are introduced in chapter 6 of *IN*, "Meaning," as an answer to the question "What does his intention add to that physical event [the utterance] that makes that physical event a case of the speaker's meaning something by it?"

(p. 161); and, indeed, these intentions are referred to as "meaning intentions" throughout the chapter. So the intention to represent is supposed to be constitutive of speaker meaning. Furthermore Searle supposes that the categories of illocutionary acts constitute the ways in which a speaker can mean something (pp. 166ff), and he regularly refers to particular meaning intentions as, e.g., intending the raising of the arm *as a directive* (more specifically, a particular directive) (p. 170).[28] Thus the "meaning intention" takes the place of condition (8) in the original pattern of analysis for promising, which was supposed to bring out what it is to *mean* the utterance as a certain promise.

But although in *SA* Searle regarded condition (8) as only part of the story, and indeed dependent on other parts, in *IN* he seems to suppose that the meaning intention does the whole job. He repeatedly says that the meaning intention determines that the illocutionary acts has the conditions of satisfaction that it has (e.g., pp. 164, 165, 167–8, 169). But presumably he thinks that when the conditions of satisfaction of an act have been fully determined it is thereby determined what illocutionary act that is.

Now I could enter into the question of whether the intention to perform an illocutionary act of a certain type is necessary or sufficient for doing so. But this would be a tortuous discussion, requiring us to go into special problems about special types of illocutionary acts, as well as into questions about the possibility of unintentional illocutionary acts; and we have no time for that. Instead I shall use my little remaining space to consider whether Searle's way of specifying "meaning intentions" in *IN* make them sufficient even for *intending* to perform an illocutionary act of a certain sort.

Their insufficiency is most obvious with respect to directives and commissives. Here is Searle's account of the content of the meaning intention for ordering you to retreat, by raising one's arm.

> My arm goes up as a result of this intention in action, and my arm going up has as conditions of satisfaction, with the world-to-mind (or utterance) direction of fit, that you retreat and that you retreat because my arm going up has those conditions of satisfaction. (*IN*, p. 170)

And here is his specification of the content of the meaning intention for promising to advance on the enemy by raising one's arm.

> My arm goes up as a result of this intention in action, and my arm going up has as conditions of satisfaction with the world-to-mind (or utterance) direction of fit that I advance on the enemy and that I do so, at least in part, because my arm going up has those conditions of satisfaction. (*IN*, p. 171)

Now the most obvious way in which these intentions are not sufficient for an intention to perform the illocutionary act in question is that they do not guarantee an intention to realize what Searle specifies as the essential condition in each case. For the order, that essential condition was said to be that the utterance is an attempt to get H to do A. But we have already seen that, putting it in these terms, an utterance can be endowed with these conditions of satisfaction without the speaker making any such attempt. This will be the case where I issue an order because it is my duty to do so, without having an interest in your carrying it out. As for the promise, one can issue an utterance with this world-to-words condition of satisfaction without thereby intending to lay on oneself an obligation to advance. This is most obvious where I *enjoin* or *urge* myself to advance. In doing that I produce the utterance with the intention specified here (at least I do so if this approach to specifying intentions to represent is at all sound), without intending to obligate myself to advance. Intentions like the second one just quoted do not distinguish promising to do A from urging oneself to do A.[29]

This will have to suffice for a brief indication of the inadequacy of these "meaning intentions" for the task. The basic trouble is this: there is more to illocutionary-act performance than the satisfaction of what Searle calls "conditions of satisfaction"; hence the intention to endow one's utterance with such conditions does not amount to an intention to perform an illocutionary act of a certain specific sort. The conditions of satisfaction mark out broader caregories and require supplementation before any particular order or promise has been uniquely picked out.

Envoi

I must apologize for subjecting the reader to so much detail, but without it I could not make clear what I take to be defective in Searle's account. I take Searle's approach to be sound in many of its most general features – the independence of the illocutionary from the perlocutionary, the tie between illocutionary-act potential and sentence meaning, and the crucial role of rules – as well as in many of its details. However, I have tried to show that he has not given proper appreciation to the normative, regulative element in illocutionary act concepts, how taking responsibility for the holding of certain conditions is at the heart of illocutionary-act performance.[30] Because of this he has been led into various implausible and inadequate views. The stated conditions for performing illocutionary acts of a certain type are, in many instances, not necessary. Notions like "point or purpose," "direction of fit," and "conditions of satisfaction" are either not sufficiently explained, or they fail to cover the specified territory, or they fail to provide the desired illumination. As a result we come away without either a model of analysis for particular illocutionary act concepts, or a taxonomy of such types, that is adequate to the subject matter. I suggest that by taking the notion of *taking responsibility for the satisfaction of conditions in uttering a sentence* as the heart of the matter we can provide an illuminating and extensionally adequate account of the matter that ties things together in a natural and intuitive manner. Searle is to be commended for his ingenuity in achieving as much as he has within his self-imposed limitations, but further advance in the subject requires that these limitations be transcended.[31]

NOTES

1   J. L. Austin, *How To do Things with Words* (Clarendon Press, Oxford: 1962).
2   Cambridge University Press, Cambridge: 1969. Hereinafter *SA*.
3   In *Expression and Meaning* (Cambridge University Press, Cambridge: 1979). Hereinafter TIA.
4   Cambridge University Press, Cambridge: 1983. Hereinafter *IN*. Some of the developments in

this book are foreshadowed in an earlier written, though later published, essay, "Meaning, Communication, and Representation," in *Philosophical Grounds of Rationality: Intentions, Categories, Ends*, ed. R. E. Grandy and R. Warner (Clarendon Press, Oxford: 1986).

5   As we shall see, in *IN* Searle recognizes that successful communication is not, in general, necessary for illocutionary-act performance.

6   Searle claims, correctly I believe, that his condition (6) implies ths S believes that it is possible for him to do what he had promised to do (*SA*, p. 60). But nothing in his analysis requires that this be in fact possible.

7   To be sure, as I will contend later, sincerity (intending to do what is promised) comes into the analysis of promising in a way that, e.g., advisedness or prudence does not. But my point here is that we cannot exhibit this differential centrality by thinking of them as defects. In defending his approach Searle argues that because of the looseness of many of our concepts we can best proceed by confining ourselves to "simple and idealized" cases (*SA*, pp. 55–6) I have no quarrel with this general methodological point. However I still contend that "non-defective promising" is too squishy a notion to be a useful idealization.

8   I'm afraid that in this paper I will not have time to go into the question of unintentional illocutionary acts. Since the intentional–unintentional distinction plays no role in my differences with Searle, I believe it is safe to ignore those issues.

9   *American Philosophical Quarterly* 13 (1963), pp. 1–9.

10 Prentice-Hall Englewood Cliffs, NJ: (1964).

11 Note that R1 makes it explicit that taking responsibility for p is a matter of S's *instituting* a certain normative state of affairs, rather than a matter of S's recognizing an antecedently existing state of affairs. Moreover, it is not just that the liabilities in question are inaugurated by S's saying what he says; a certain intention on his part is required as well, at least for normal cases. It is, to a certain extent, up to S whether, when he utters "I promise to do A," he has taken responsibility for, e.g., (4) and (6). If he intended to be practicing pronunciation or testing a microphone (and the context were not such as to carry the inevitable suggestion that he was seriously promising), he would not be liable to negative reactions in case (4) or (6) is not the case.

One might think that the end of R1 should read "in case S is not justified is supposing that p." For where p is not the case S will not be held blameworthy provided he had every reason to think that p is the case. But, without contesting the point, I will stick to R1 as given, for the sake of simplicity, and handle this point by recognizing that S's being justified in believing that p will serve as an excuse, and exculpate from blame, even if p is not the case.

12 This is true as stated only in those cases in which one chooses a sentence that is maximally explicit as to what one is doing. To make the formulation strictly accurate, we have to add the disjunct, "or one utters something as elliptical for such a device." See the discussions a few pages down the road for more details.

13 This is true, as stated, only for univocal sentences. Where a sentence has more than one meaning in the language, it is rather that some one of a disjunction of sets of such requirements is required for correct utterance.

14 Of course, in our account these are not themselves necessary conditions of making the promise. That means that on our account the conditions of correct utterance for a sentence standardly usable to promise to do A are somewhat differently related to the conditions for making the promise. See my "Sentence Meaning and Illocutionary Act Potential," *Philosophical Exchange* 2 (3) (Summer, 1977), and, for much more detail, my unpublished manuscript, *Illocutionary Acts and Sentence Meaning*.

15 In this version we don't need the second part of Searle's (4), which requires that S believe this to be the case. I can't represent it as being the case that p without representing myself as believing that p.

16 To be sure, Searle's (7), especially as we have beefed it up, embodies a normative element into the concept of promising. But, as we shall see, it is dubious that this kind of normativity is found in illocutionary acts generally, whereas I propose to analyze all illocutionary acts in

terms of the speaker's taking responsibility for various conditions' holding. Moreover, even for promising, my account represents promising as much more thoroughly a normative state of affairs.

17 This analysis is constructed on the basis of Searle's chart on pp. 66–7, rather than being Searle's *ipsissima verba*.

18 Searle acknowledges this kind of point in *IN*, p. 169, though his remarks there are confined to stating.

19 In none of these works does Searle systematically address himself to the question of how different act types within a broad category are to be differentiated. He does throw out some suggestions. For example, "'boast' and 'complain'. . . both denote assertives with the added feature that they have something to do with the interest of the speaker," while "'conclude' and 'deduce' are also assertives with the added feature that they mark certain relations between the assertive illocutionary act and the rest of the discourse or the context of utterance" (TIA, p. 13). But apart from the point that this is quite unspecific as to what it has to do with the interest of the speaker or as to what relations between the act and the rest of the discourse are in question, we are given no hint as to just how these matters come into the analysis. Is it that these relations to the rest of the discourse are themselves necessary conditions for the utterance's being an act of that type, or is it only necessary that the speaker take responsibility for these conditions holding? Or do they enter in some other fashion?

20 Presumably this is restricted to "many, or most" because, as we have already seen, Searle takes the illocutionary point of directives to be that they are attempts to get the hearer to do something; thus here the "illocutionary point" is a perlocutionary purpose. This further complicates the situation.

21 Note that the direction of fit must be interpreted somewhat differently for the two directions or else worse consequences ensue. For the world-to-word direction the purpose is quite straightforwardly to *bring it about* that the relevant portion of the world match some specification verbally expressed in the illocutionary act. One issues an order in order to bring it about that the addressee's behavior make true the proposition expressed. (Of course we have seen that this is not really true of, e.g., promises, but still this is clearly Searle's intended interpretation.) But if we were to understand the word-to-world direction in this way, we would be saddled with the preposterous notion that one makes a statement in order to bring it about that the proposition expressed matches the facts, rather than making the statement because one supposes that the match already obtains. A more charitable interpretation would be that one chooses one's words (the proposition expressed) in such a way as to exploit an already existing match; i.e., one avoids choosing words that do not reflect such a match. I am grateful to Jonathan Bennett for helping me to see this point.

22 For a development of an illocutionary concept of expressing, along the lines just (partially) adumbrated, see my "Expressing," in *Philosophy in America*, ed. Max Black (Cornell University Press, Ithaca, NY: 1965), pp. 15–34.

23 Again we have the question of whether the "point or purpose" must be realized in each individual case, i.e., whether that realization is a necessary condition for an utterance to count as an act of that sort. Am I still performing the *illocutionary act* of firing someone if the act misfires (e.g., I lack proper authority) so that the hearer's employment is not actually terminated? (Clearly I didn't fire him in a full-blooded sense of that term.) This is a long story into which I cannot go here. See my unpublished manuscript, *Illocutionary Acts and Sentence Meaning*.

24 In TIA Searle had denied that declarations express anything (p. 19).

25 Searle never evinces awareness of this or any other alternative to his way of picking out a propositional content.

26 To be sure, this raises questions as to how expressing gratitude is to be distinguished from asserting that one is grateful. Again, see my forthcoming book.

27 There are other contributions we will not have time to go into. Most importantly, there is stress on the way in which "meaning intentions" (the intentions that confer conditions of satisfaction on the utterance and thereby allow it to represent something) involve self-

reference, in that they are typically intentions to bring about something as a result of the intention.

28 On p. 163 he says that the short answer to the question as to what kind of intention makes an utterance meaningful is that it is an intention to perform an illocutionary act; while the longer answer involves explaining the structure of intentions to represent, i.e., "meaning intentions."

29 There is also the point that the intentions Searle specifies do nothing to distinguish different kinds of directives or commissives from each other. But in this paper we have been confining ourselves to issues concerning the main categories of illocutionary acts.

30 I certainly recognize that Searle has given proper recognition to this element in his account of linguistic meaning as consisting in the governance of linguistic elements by rules.

31 Thanks are due to Jonathan Bennett for many helpful comments on this paper.

5

Response: Meaning, Intentionality, and Speech Acts

JOHN R. SEARLE

Systematic study in the theory of speech acts has now gone on for over 30 years. During that time there has been genuine progress, and something like consensus has emerged on many issues. Speech act theory has two features which would have enormously pleased its founder, J. L. Austin, because he regarded them as essential to fruitful intellectual work: First, it is possible for different people to work on the theory. It is not the property of one person or even of one ideological group. And second, agreement is possible. People of widely differing ideologies and philosophical commitments can agree on the facts about promises, assertions, apologies, etc.

Among the items in the area of general agreement that I hope to take for granted in this discussion are the following: there is a distinction between illocutionary force and propositional content so that, in general, speech acts have the structure F(p), where "F" marks the illocutionary force and "p" marks the propositional content. This distinction supersedes Austin's original distinction between illocutionary acts and locutionary acts. In the performance of a speech act, it is essential to distinguish different sorts of conditions on successful and non-defective performance. Among these are input–output conditions, preparatory conditions, propositional content conditions, sincerity conditions, and essential conditions. Various of these conditions, especially the essential condition, form the basis of any fruitful taxonomy of speech acts. Not everyone agrees which taxonomy is best, but the one that I have developed divides illocutionary forces into assertives (statements, assertions, etc.), directives (orders, requests, etc.), commissives (promises, vows, etc.), expressives (thanks, apologies, etc.) and declarations (declaring war, adjourning a meeting, etc.).[1] This taxonomy is based on illocutionary point, and illocutionary point is itself explained in terms of the essential conditions on the speech act.

An understanding of illocutionary point or purpose is central to the understanding of speech acts because each genuine illocutionary act has an illocutionary point or purpose built into it in virtue of its being an act of that type. Any given speech act may, of course, be performed for a number of purposes. A man might make a promise for all sorts of reasons. But if he makes a promise, then in virtue of its being a promise, it is the undertaking of an obligation to do something for the hearer. This feature is the mark of the illocutionary point: it is the point or purpose which the act has in virtue of being an act of that type.

The notions introduced so far also relate to another notion which I have found useful, but which is not universally accepted, the notion of direction of fit. The illocutionary force with which a proposition is presented in the performance of a speech act will determine the way in which the proposition is supposed to fit reality. Statements are supposed to represent how things are, and thus they can be assessed as true or false. Orders and commands do not represent how things are, but roughly speaking, how the speaker is trying to get the hearer to make things be; and such speech acts cannot be assessed as true or false, but rather as obeyed or disobeyed. Similarly, promises cannot be assessed as true or false but only as kept or broken. To mark these distinctions, I say that statements have the word-to-world direction of fit; promises, orders, commands, etc. have the world-to-word direction of fit. No doubt these notions merit further clarification and elucidation; however, I really do not have any doubts about the validity and usefulness of these fundamental notions: the notions of illocutionary force, propositional content, direction of fit, sincerity conditions, etc.

In recent years, I have been trying to ground the theory of speech acts in the theory of the mind, specifically in the theory of Intentionality. The results of this investigation are much more controversial and many of the commentators have made objections to this part of my work on speech act theory. I think that most researchers would agree that the general project must be right, because we know in advance that speech acts are a subclass of human actions, and thus we should be able to state what speech acts have in common with human actions in general simply in virtue of being acts and how they are special, how they differ by way of being speech acts. We know, furthermore, that human actions are themselves expressions of human Intentionality: intentions, beliefs, desires, etc. So, in advance we have very good reasons for supposing that the attempt to ground speech act theory in the theory of the mind is well-motivated. The main issue is how to do it exactly.

There is one further notion I need to introduce because it provides the connecting link between the theory of mind, including the theory of action, on the one hand, and the theory of speech acts, as a special case, on the other. That is the notion of "conditions of satisfaction." The intuitive idea behind it is very simple: what stands to statements being true, is what stands to orders being obeyed, is what stands to promises being kept, etc. And where psychological states are concerned what stands to beliefs being true, is what stands to wishes being fulfilled, is what stands to intentions being carried out, etc. Every Intentional state and every speech act that has a direction of fit will be satisfied or unsatisfied depending on whether or not the actual fit comes about. Notice that there is nothing essentially semantic, in the linguistic sense, about the notion of conditions of satisfaction, since we need this notion to account for the Intentionality of psychological states quite independently of the expression of Intentional states in language.

It seems to me that the notion of conditions of satisfaction helps us to elucidate semantic notions precisely because it is a psychological notion applied to semantics. We know what it is for a belief to be true or false, or a wish to be fulfilled or unfulfilled, an intention to be carried out or not carried out, quite independently of our theory of speech acts. It seems to me that the notion of conditions of satisfaction is so general, so powerful, and so useful that the question of elucidating it further is one of achieving pedagogical success rather than philosophical justification. One item of clarification I shall mention immediately because it leads to some misunderstanding in Bennett's paper: "satisfaction" here is a technical term. It has no essential connection with feeling satisfied or feeling good. Thus, for example, a man who predicts disaster will have a prediction which is satisfied if and only if disaster ensues, even though the ensuing disaster does not leave the man himself satisfied. He may be quite miserable.

Once we have the notion of conditions of satisfaction as it applies across many forms of Intentionality, both psychological and linguistic, then the general structure of the modes of illocutionary meaning is so ludicrously simple that I am embarrassed that it did not occur to me many years earlier. The key to understanding meaning is to see that meaning is special among forms of Intentionality in that, in general, it involves the intentional imposition of conditions of satisfaction onto conditions of satisfaction. A hint of this double level of Intentionality is already contained in our ordinary locutions. Such sentences as "John believes that p" can stand on their own. But the sentence "John means that p" or "John meant that p" invite completion. They invite completion in the form "By saying such and such John meant that p" or "By doing such and such John meant that p." But since the doing and the saying are Intentional and since the propositional content marked by "p" is also Intentional, how do we account for the relationships between the Intentionality of the sheer act of uttering and the Intentionality marked by the propositional content of the total speech act? And how do we do that in a way that will give us a precise account of meaning in its various illocutionary modes? How, since it is essential to get absolutely clear about these points, and since it seems to me that neither Bennett nor Habermas, and possibly not even Apel nor Alston, has really understood me on this issue, I am going to go through a simple example, step by step, to try to make it clearer.

Imagine that a speaker utters the sentence "It is raining." The making of this utterance is an intentional action and as such it was performed with a certain intention in action. Like any intention in action that intention has conditions of satisfaction. In this case, part of the conditions of satisfaction are that the intention should result in the production of a certain utterance. If the intention is satisfied a certain set of sounds, amounting to a certain sentence token, will come out of the speaker's mouth. So far, as characterized, that intention does not involve any meaning at all. It is just a matter of making sounds that happen to be a part of a language. What is added when we say that the speaker not only intentionally *uttered* "It is raining" but he *meant* that it is raining? Well, normally he will have had the intention to perform a certain type of *speech act*, to make the *statement* that it is raining. He did not just intend to utter a sentence, but he intended to utter that sentence by way of making statement. "Yes, but what exactly is the intention to make the statement?" Well, actually that is a complicated matter, because the intention to make a statement is a very complex intention. But what I am trying to analyze here are the very bare bones of that component of the intention to make a statement which includes the essential aspect of our pretheoretical notion of saying something and *meaning* something. And the answer I am proposing is the common sense one: the very bare bones of the intention to state are the intention that one's utterance should be *meaningful* in the quite specific sense that it should be a *representation* of a state of affairs.

So far so good, however we are still left with this puzzling word "representation." But that is a notion we can elucidate, because it can be entirely cashed out in terms of such notions as Intentional content, direction of fit and conditions of satisfaction. Now, notice that though these notions have an application to semantics, none of them is a linguistic semantic notion as such. They are all Intentional notions and are part of the apparatus that we need to characterize Intentionality in general. In this case, to say that the speaker intended that the utterance represent how things are is simply to say that he intended that his utterance have certain conditions of satisfaction with a certain direction of fit. But since the making of the utterance itself was the condition of satisfaction of part of his intention, it follows that the meaning intention is the intention that those condition of satisfaction should themselves have conditions of satisfaction. *And that is the essence of speaker's meaning: the intentional imposition of conditions of satisfaction on conditions of satisfaction.* Meaning is thus a form of derived Intentionality. Strictly speaking, the notion of meaning applies to, e.g., utterances, but not to, e.g., beliefs. Utterances have *derived* Intentionality; beliefs have *intrinsic* Intentionality. Notice a crucial feature of this account: *the intention that the utterance has conditions of satisfaction is not the same as the intention that the conditions of satisfaction should be, in fact, satisfied.* This is why, as we shall see in more detail later, false statements and lies are perfectly meaningful speech acts.

Furthermore, part of the beauty of this analysis is that it is easily extendable to all of the various modes of meaning that have a direction of fit, because they all show the same formal structure of imposing conditions of satisfaction on conditions of satisfaction. In directives, we cannot just represent any state of affairs but rather we must represent the state of affairs of the hearer performing a certain course of action. And in commissives, to take another example, we must represent the state of affairs of the speaker performing a certain course of action. Furthermore, the conditions of satisfaction of most directives and commissives are self-referential because the meaning intention will be satisfied (and hence the speech act will be satisfied) only if – in the case of most directives – the hearer brings about the conditions of satisfaction because of the issuance of the directive in question; and – in the case of most commissives – only if the speaker brings about the conditions of satisfaction because of the making of the commissive in question. In ordinary English, we can put this point as follows: an order is obeyed in the strict sense only if the hearer does what he does by way of obeying the order, and a promise is kept only if the promissor does what he does by way of keeping the promise.

Furthermore, another attractive feature of this account is that Grice's analysis of the intention to communicate now falls into place automatically. Acts of communication are peculiar among examples of human behavior in that the intention to perform the act will succeed if the audience recognizes the intention to perform it. As soon as my audience recognizes that I intend to tell them something and what it is that I intend to tell them, I have succeeded in telling them. This feature is certainly not true of human behavior generally. If, for example, someone intends to become President of the United States and other people recognize his intention, he is still not President. So, what is so special about speech acts that they have this Gricean reflexive feature in this communicative success? At one level the answer to that question is fairly clear: the intention to communicate is the intention to produce understanding in the hearer. And the hearer will understand the speaker if he recognizes the speaker's intention; so the intention to produce understanding involves the intention that that very intention should be recognized, and the recognition of that intention constitutes understanding by the hearer, and hence communication from speaker to hearer. But at a much deeper level we can see why meaning intentions lend themselves to this feature of communicability in a way that other intentions do not. Characteristically, human intentions are designed to produce some further effects on the world. But meaning intentions are simply the intentions that some of those effects, such as utterances, should themselves have conditions of satisfaction. So meaning intentions are, so to speak, designed for communicability because the only further effect needed or intended for communication is that the hearer should recognize the utterance as the bearer of the meaning intention.

Of course, this analysis so far is designed only to give us the bare bones of the modes of meaning and not to convey all of the subtle distinctions involved in actual discourse. It is important to emphasize this because, in various ways, Bennett, Habermas, and Apel, all object that this analysis cannot account for all the richness and variety of actual speech acts in actual natural language. Of course not. It was not designed to address that issue.

I now want to consider what I take to be the most powerful and salient objections made to the foregoing account by my critics.

Jonathan Bennett

Since Bennett attempts to defend the Gricean account of meaning and attacks my views from that perspective, I will begin by repeating some of my objections to Grice.

Grice attempted to analyze meaning in terms of communication, but there are notorious counterexamples to his analysis. Many of these are cases where the speaker says something and means something by it but does not intend to communicate at all. It is revealing that Grice kept changing his views on what exactly the speaker's intended effects on the hearer were supposed to be – were they beliefs, beliefs that the speaker believed something or what? But the really radical problem is this: *a speaker can say something, mean something by it, and not intend to communicate anything to anybody.* Bennett acknowledges these cases but his description of them as "no intended audience" really misses the point. The point is not necessarily that there is no intended *audience*, but audience or no, there is no intended *communication*.

These cases have an enormous theoretical consequence we should ponder: if there are such cases, and there surely are, then there must be something which the speaker fails to intend to communicate in these cases which he does intend to communicate in the standard or, as Bennett calls them, the "base camp" cases. And that component, whatever it is, looks like it might be the core of meaning, because it is the meaning which was left over when we carved off the intention to communicate and found we still had meaning. The problem is not that there are a *few* counterexamples which are an embarrassment to the Gricean program, but rather that *meaningful utterances in general are counterexamples to Grice*, because in general with meaningful utterances we can carve off the intention to communicate to some hearer and still have a meaningful utterance left over.

The point is so crucial that I cannot help repeating it once more: In a *successful speech act* the speaker intentionally produces an effect on a hearer. And if he achieves that effect he will have successfully communicated. But the intention to achieve that effect cannot be the essence of *meaning*, because one can say something and mean something by it and not have that intention. And what this shows us is not that there are a few counterexamples to the project of analyzing meaning in terms of the intention of communicate but, roughly speaking, meaningful utterances in general are counterexamples; because, even in the normal case where the speaker does intend to communicate, there must be some meaning to be communicated. Thus, not surprisingly, we must separate the intention which is the essence of meaning from the intention to communicate.

So much for Bennett's "base camp" strategy. There is no camp there, it is just more wilderness.

Now, what about this "essence of meaning", this "content to be communicated," etc.? At this point I stop crticizing Bennett's attempt to defend Grice and present my own response to his objections in light of what I said above:

It is clear in general what the package to be communicated is: speech acts in general have the form F(p), and it is the intention to produce an object with that form that constitutes saying something and meaning something by it. In the normal speech act one will intend that one's hearer recognize the package for what it is; that is, one intends that the hearer know that one is performing a speech act and (*à la* Grice), one intends that he knows it by means of getting him to recognize one's intention that he should know it.

To illustrate this, let us remind ourselves of the naive example I mentioned earlier. I say "It is raining"; I mean what I say and intend to *communicte my meaning* (note the locution, which implies a distinction between meaning and communication) to you, the hearer. How does it work?

Well, at least this much has to happen: In making the utterance, I intend to represent assertively the state of affairs that it is raining, (that is the F(p) part) and I intend you to recognize that representation, by means of getting you to recognize my intention that you should recognize it (and that is the Gricean communication part). Frankly, this distinction between the representing intentions and communication intention seems to me obvious.

But now let us go to work on the F(p) part. Bennett doubts that we can analyze that structure without using semantic notions. But, notice that the structure of the speech act, F(p), and the structure of the corresponding Intentional state, S(p), are exactly parallel. Futhermore, they have exactly the same conditions of satisfaction: e.g. my statement that it is raining will be true iff my belief that it is raining is true. Also, the Intentional state is the sincerity condition on the assertion: when I say it is raining I express the belief that it is raining; and if I say it is raining but do not believe it is raining, I am lying.

These very tight connections are not accidental and they suggest the following explanation: To say something and mean it is to impose the conditions of satisfaction of the belief onto the utterance. Since the utterance is itself the condition of satisfaction of the intention to make it, the essence of meaning is the intentional imposition of conditions of satisfaction onto conditions of satisfaction.

And this double level of Intentionality is what makes lies possible: One can intend that one's utterance has, e.g., truth conditions without believing or intending that those conditions actually obtain. With that much in hand, let us turn to Bennett's specific objections. I will present them and my answers in the form of an imaginary dialogue between JB and JRS:

Objection 1, JB: If you take the normal notions of "success" or "satisfaction" where "A criterion of success for what x intends to do is P" entails "If not P then x fails in what he intends to do" then you get absurd results.

Answer, JRS: Of course. You would get the result, e.g. that the making of a false statement is not the making of a statement at all; and the account of lies would be self-contradictory. Since, I believe, most of your objections rest on a misunderstanding of the notion of conditions of satisfaction and its implications both for the analysis of Intentionality, in general, and the analysis of meaning, in particular, I will try to state these points as precisely as I can in such a short compass. In making a false statement the speaker nonetheless succeeds in making a statement. He succeeds in making the statement even though the statement fails in achieving its conditions of satisfaction, and he can do this precisely because of the double level of Intentionality involved in the notion of speaker-meaning. The speaker can *succeed* in making a statement even though the statement itself *fails* in achieving its truth conditions, its conditions of satisfaction, because *in making the statement the speaker both intends to produce an utterance and intends that the utterance should have conditions of satisfaction.* The speaker succeeds in both of these even though the utterance itself fails in achieving the conditions of satisfaction that the speaker has intentionally imposed upon it. From this point it is easy to see how lies are possible: the speaker can impose conditions of satisfaction, in this case truth conditions, on utterances, even when he knows or believes that those truth conditions are not, in fact, satisfied. Just as a speaker can succeed in making a statement, even though the statement is, unknown to him, false; so he can succeed in making a statement, even though he knows or believes that the statement is, in fact, false. And indeed he may make it with the intention that it not succeed in satisfying the conditions of satisfaction that he has intentionally imposed upon it.

Now, I said that most of your objections derive from a misunderstanding of the notion of conditions of satisfaction, and indeed, I believe that, up until section 12 of your paper, the objections you make are for the most part irrelevant to my actual views, since they are based on ignoring the way the Intentional phenomena relate to their conditions of satisfaction. When the speaker makes the statement that it is raining, the conditions of satisfaction are that the *utterance* should have the conditions of satisfaction (in this case, truth conditions) that it is raining, not that the *speaker* should have those conditions of satisfaction. And that is why a *speaker succeeds* in lying precisely because his *utterance fails* to be true. For a detailed account of all these relations see chapters 1 to 6 of *Intentionality*, especially chapter 6.[2]

Objection 2, JB: Well, all the same if "conditions of satisfaction" is supposed to be a technical notion it is incurably disjunctive. It is supposed to apply to both beliefs and desires, but they are really quite different.

Answer, JRS: Actually, once you grant that the same propositional content can be common to both a belief and a desire, it follows trivially that they both have the same conditions of satisfaction. I can both believe it to be the case and want it to be the case, e.g., that it is raining. These, therefore have the same conditions of satisfaction. So, *once you grant the possibility of sameness of content between both beliefs and desires, you have already granted a unitary notion of conditions of satisfaction applying to both beliefs and desires.*

Indeed the notion covers a whole lot more than just beliefs and desires. I like to use them as examples for pedagogical purposes, but the biologically primary forms of Intentionality are perception and action. Then further down the road come memory and prior intentions, and only very derivatively do we get beliefs and desires. They arise when the causal conditions are removed from the Intentional contents. Conditions of satisfaction do not "neatly bifurcate," as you say; they are all over the place. The basic idea, however, is one which, I believe, you would accept: Intentional contents, as expressed in propositional contents of Intentional states, speech acts, etc., relate Intentional entities to the world. Now, if you tell the story about those relations between content and reality, you get conditions of satisfaction. The notion applies quite generally, but it is not thereby ambiguous.

Objection 3, JB: But why is not that account circular? Are you not just using our understanding of meaning to explain meaning?

Answer, JRS: Well, that sort of circularity is always a danger, but I do not think I am guilty of it here. Clearly, Intentional representation, in general, does not pre-suppose linguistic representation, because there are lots of animals, small children, and even adults who have Intentional representations without language. We have a notion of Intentionality which is prior to meaning, so there is no circularity in explaining meaning using Intentionality.

Objection 4, JB: All the same, you do not have a unitary account of meaning; because you still have to define injunctions in terms of intended effects on hearers, rather than defining them in terms of pure representations as you do with statements.

Answer JRS: Actually, it is precisely because there is a unitary account of meaning in terms of conditions of satisfaction as determined by the propositional content that there is a special reference to the hearer in the case of directives (what you call "injunctions"). Once again, what you take as an objection, I regard as a substantiation of the thesis I am advancing, so it is, perhaps, important to try to state it with some precision: my general account of meaning is given in terms of representation. Representation is then further analyzed using the apparatus of the theory of Intentionality – conditions of satisfaction, direction of fit, etc. Now given such a general account of the content of different types of speech acts in terms of representation, we can see that a special feature of the content of many directives, e.g. orders, is that *they represent the state of affairs of the hearer doing the thing he is ordered to do because he is ordered to do it.* Thus, the conditions of satisfaction of such directives make an essential reference to an effect on a hearer. It is not a counterexample to the view that meaning can be analyzed in terms of representa-tion, that in the case of directives representations make special reference to the hearer; on the contrary, it is precisely a feature of the general account in terms of representations that it shows the different sorts of representational content involved in different sorts of speech acts. A *general* theory of representational contents includes and explains the *special* features of different types.

But notice that even for directives we need to distinguish meaning from communication, even though in directives the illocutionary point is defined in terms of potential perlocutionary effects. A speaker may, for example, feel it his duty to issue an order, even though he is convinced that there is no possibility that it will be obeyed or even understood. In such a case he means something by what he says but does not intend to communicate that meaning. A defective speech act, to be sure, but nonetheless a meaningful one.

Objection 5, JB: All the same your analysis gives only necessary but not sufficient conditions.

Answer, JRS: That's right. I am providing only necessary but not sufficient conditions for the performance of certain meaning bearing acts, i.e., illocutionary acts. There is a deep reason for this. To repeat a point I made earlier, I am only trying to capture the bare bones of the structure of the Intentionality in the speech act. But, of course, actual speech acts will have all sorts of social, institutional and interpersonal constraints. To understand all of these constraints requires much more than just an understanding of the bare bones of the Intentionality of meaning. It requires, for example, understanding the difference between making a statement and making a conjecture; or, in the case of directives it involves understanding the difference between giving an order, a command, and making a request. Now, all of these directives have a common bare bones underlying structure. But, on top of that structure is a whole lot of the flesh and tissue provided by organized, historically situated societies. The particular forms in which different types of illocutionary acts manifest themselves seem to me to be immensely socially contingent. They can be structured in all sorts of different ways in different societies. But the underlying biological basis by which the mind relates to reality is common to all societies; and on the vision of language that I am attempting to articulate, language is the public manifestation in communicative expression of a common underlying biology.

The basic message I want to get across in this discussion is this: the Gricean enterprise contains an absolutely fundamental mistake in confusing meaning with communication. Now, once that distinction is made clear, then you can see that Grice's mistake here is a sympton of a much deeper mistake. It is mistaken to attempt to give an analysis of meaning without a general account of Intentionality. Meaning is a special form of Intentionality, by which entites such as utterances acquire a further Intentionality.

Jürgen Habermas[3]

Habermas's article presents a strong statement of the differences that he sees between his approach to problems in the philosophy of language and my own. I think, in fact, that at one level the differences in the two approaches are not as great as he thinks, and part of my reply, but only part, will be designed to show that much of what he takes to be a difference in thesis is, in fact, a difference in emphasis. In some cases, we are not offering competing answers to the same question, but non-competing answers to quite different questions. However, at a much deeper level perhaps a great difference remains, and if so, I hope to uncover its true nature.

Habermas believes that there are two competing approaches to the philosophy of language which he calls "intentionalist" and "intersubjectivist." On the intentionalist approach the meaning of an utterance is essentially a matter of the speaker's intentions. The intersubjectivist or social view sees the successful performance of a speech act as a successful attempt to reach an understanding with a hearer about something in the world. And, one might add, the intersubjectivist view emphasizes the responsibilities and the validity claims made by the speaker and responded to by the hearer in the actual social dynamics of the speech situation.

Habermas presents these as rival approaches, but they are not necessarily in conflict. They could reasonably be interpreted as answers to two different questions. The intentionalist view, as I see it, tries to describe the bare skeletal structure of the basic speech acts. In the statement of the intentionalist view, I am, as I said in my reply to Bennett, trying to get behind the incredible social complexity of actual speech, to discover the underlying lineaments, the basic intentionalistic form that admits of such very diverse expressions in society. The intersubjectivist view is not really a rival view at all. It merely describes an extension of the phenomena that are described by the intentionalist view. The picture I have is this: The basic structure of meaning and communication is as I have described it in *Intentionality*. Now on top of that basic foundation, societies erect elaborate and complex structures of particular sorts of speech acts, involving constitutive rules and institutional facts of the sorts I described in *Speech Acts*. The "intentionalist" view of *Intentionality* is not in conflict with the "intersubjectivist" view of *Speech Acts*, rather the former is the condition of possibility of the latter. For example, the basic structure allows for commissive speech acts where the speaker simply "gives his word" that he will do something. Within that structure social institutions allow for such distinctions as those between promises, vows, pledges, threats, contracts, warranties, and bets.

On this construal, Habermas's counterexamples are not really counterexamples to the intentionalist thesis. In what he takes to be an objection to me, he points out correctly that the understanding of certain preparatory conditions is essential to understanding certain sorts of speech acts. For example, to understand an order issued from a position of authority the hearer "must know the conditions which authorize the speaker to give the order" (p. 22). But this is not an objection to my account; it simply repeats a point I made in *Speech Acts*. Furthermore, some of the features that Habermas mentions are simply features of *conversations* as opposed to features of *individual speech acts*. It is characteristic of a normal conversation that each participant takes turns of being now a speaker, now a hearer, and the overall aim of a conversation is to reach agreement, to reach what he calls a "mutual consensus with respect to a (potentially questionable) matter." But notice that there is no inconsistency between saying on one hand that each individual speech act is designed to communicate an Intentional content from speaker to hearer (the intentionalist view), and on the other saying that the overall aim of the conversation is to achieve consensus (the intersubjectivist view). On one interpretation then, Habermas's views are not inconsistent with mine, rather they are a repetition of some and a natural extension of others. Notice, furthermore, that the intersubjectivist view presupposes the intentionalist view, because in order for there to be intersubjective consensus in conversation there have to be Intentional contents that are communicated in the first place. Without speech acts there is no conversation.

All of this is also related to a misunderstanding which Habermas has of the evolution of my views, a misunderstanding which is probably my fault, because I have not made my exposition fully clear. My attempt to give an Intentionalistic account of meaning is not intended as a rejection of the project that I originally stated in *Speech Acts*. It is rather an attempt to go deeper, to provide the project with a more thorough grounding in the basic Intentionality of the mind. I am not rejecting the idea that actual institutional structures, such as the social structures of making promises, or making assertions, require systems of constitutive rules. Rather, what I am trying to do is to locate the most fundamental forms of Intentionality which are expressed in different institutional structures in different societies. To repeat the point I made in response to Bennett, I am trying to show the skeleton that underlies the skin and clothing of the illocutionary organism. I do not say that the skeleton is all there is, but, I do say that there is a skeleton.

Now here is my puzzle: why cannot Habermas agree with the picture I have just outlined? It seems intuitively obvious and would remove even the appearance of disagreement between us. But a clue that there is some deeper disagreement emerges when he makes the, to me, astounding claim that threats do not have illocutionary force at all. He objects to my treating both orders made within a recognized instution and orders backed by threats as being the same type of speech acts (namely, orders) because they have the same conditions of satisfaction in the same illocutionary mode.

To try to make clear the difference between us let us go through an example:

1 The captain says to the private, "Leave the room."
2 The gunman says to the victim, "Leave the room, or I will shoot you."

On my account the first is an order made from a recognized position of authority. The second is also an order, but it is made by way of a conditional threat. Both utterances clearly have the illocutionary force of orders and the second has the additional illocutionary force of a threat.

Taxonomically, there is no problem for me at all, so what is Habermas's objection? His answer is that in the second case there is no "intersubjectively recognized normative context" and hence "Threats do not have proper illocutionary force at all." But what difference does that make to illocutionary force? How are the premises supposed to imply the conclusion? It just seems mysterious that anybody would suppose that in every case the very existence of illocutionary force should depend on the possibility of accepting of some normative claim.

The solution to the mystery is this: Habermas thinks that the existence of validity claims is not a *consequence* of the analysis of certain sorts of speech acts, rather he thinks that the validity claims are *constitutive* of all speech acts. And for that reason he thinks that the very performance of the meaningful speech act in communication requires that the speaker is actually trying to get the hearer to *agree* with the speaker about, for example, the three validity claims of truth, sincerity and legitimacy. Thus, *successful* communication requires actual agreement about these validity claims. In this connection, about assertions, he says, "the illocutionary purpose does not consist simply in letting the addressee know what the speaker believes, rather it consists in *getting the addressee to have the same view of which the speaker is convinced. In short the addressee should accept the speaker's assertion as valid*" (my italics). He also makes the, to me, amazing claim that, "The speaker successfully performs a given speech act if he reaches an understanding with the addressee about something in the world." So on this view a threat or a "bare imperative" is not even a candidate for illocutionary force since there is no question of getting agreement between speaker and hearer on validity claims.

Thus it turns out his picture is really radically distinct from mine. On my view, a speaker can perform an illocutionary act in a meaningful utterance and produce perfect understanding in the hearer even though the hearer does not agree and the speaker may be totally indifferent as to whether or not he agrees. Indeed on my view unless the hearer understands at least something, there is nothing for him to agree or disagree about. On Habermas's view there is no communication, no understanding, and indeed no "proper" illocutionary force unless the speaker and the hearer could come to agreement, until they could both say "yes" to the same claims.

Well how is one to chose between these views? Could we treat them as different ways of describing the same phenomena without really being inconsistent with each other?

Actually I think Habermas's view is deeply flawed and cannot be rescued by saying that it is just an alternate use of technical terms such as "illocutionary force." I have already suggested the reason: we cannot analyze meaning, communication and speech acts in terms of the attempt to achieve consensus because unless there is actual understanding of a meaningful speech act in successful communication there is nothing for the consensus to be about, there is no way to specify the terms of the consensus. If for example I say, "Bush is doing a good job," before you can agree or disagree you have to *understand* me. I have to succeed in *communicating a meaning* in the performance of my speech act before the question of consensus can arise. The attempt to achieve consensus cannot *constitute* meaning, understanding, communication, etc., because it *presupposes* all these phenomena. Furthermore we cannot appeal to the validity claims in the explanation of the speech act, for the validity claims have to be explained in terms of the structure of specific sorts of speech acts which in turn have to be explained in terms of the underlying Intentionality, as we shall see.

Habermas thinks this view "condemns the hearer to a peculiar passivity." But this is not so. The hearer can be as active as he likes, but he needs to understand what is being said before he can jump into action with such validity claim challenges as "That's false"; "You are a liar" and "You don't have enough evidence to say that."

In short, Habermas has the role of consensus in the theory of speech acts back to front, and I think this is closely related to a similar problem with his notion of validity claims. Habermas takes the existence of the validity claims as a primitive given. I think they require explanation. I think my analysis enables me to explain them, whereas his analysis precludes their explanation.

The whole issue of validity claims requires more discussion than I can give it here, but the suggestion that I want to put forward, and illustrate with at least one example is that it is philosophically illegitimate to assume validity claims as something given to us. They are part of our problem not part of its solution. I think a theory of speech acts of the sort that I advance offers an explanation of validity claims, and without such a theory I do not believe there is an explanation. I will take a simple case and show why it is so.

Let us suppose that in the course of a discussion with my colleagues I make the following claim: "The University budget will not permit us to expand the library in the next year." And suppose that this is a conversation in which we are trying to achieve mutual consensus about various matters of university policy. So, we meet all of Habermas's claims to the effect that the purpose of the discussion is to arrive at some mutual consensus. Now, in my *statement* there are several validity claims which can be revealed by the following challenges:

1 What you say is false. There is a plenty of money in the University budget.
2 You do not actually believe what you are saying. You have some strategic motive for trying to deceive us.
3 You do not really have enough evidence to say that. The figures about next year's budget are not yet available.

Now, notice that all of these complaints are directed at internal features of my statement. That is, they are not like, for example:

4 You are talking too loudly; you are disturbing the people in the next room.

The relevance of such complaints is already determined by the internal features of the speech act in question. And the three validity claims in question are those of (1) truth, (2) sincerity, and (3) legitimacy, in this case having sufficient evidence for one's claims.

I believe Habermas and I both agree that these are validity claims on the speech act of asserting. But notice they are all strictly derivable from my account of the structure of assertions. The three sorts of conditions in question are specifically:

1 The essential condition on assertion. A statement is a commitment to the truth of a proposition.
2 The sincerity condition. In making a statement the speaker expresses a belief in the truth of the proposition expressed.
3 The preparatory condition. The speaker is required to have evidence or reasons for a statement.

That is, Habermas's validity claims derive exactly from my conditions on illocutionary acts as stated in *Speech Acts*. But now, what in turn is the basis for these conditions? Notice that the essential condition is primary. Since the speech act is a commitment to the truth of a proposition, it necessarily commits the speaker to believing the truth of the proposition. And where the speaker is making a *statement*, as opposed to, e.g. expressing a supposition, the speaker will also be committed to having grounds or reasons for the truth of the proposition. These features in turn derive from the most fundamental features of the Intentionality of the phenomena. The speaker is intentionally representing to us a certain state of affairs. That intention commits him to the existence of that state of affairs. But his commitment to the existence of that state of affairs is already an expression of a belief in the existence of that state of affairs. And the form of strong commitment involved in making an assertion (as opposed, for example, to making a mere conjecture) commits the speaker to being able to provide reasons or evidence for his claim. In short, I do not disagree that there are validity claims involved in the speech act. On the contrary, that there are validity claims seems to me a strict consequence of my analysis. However, what I do claim is that *it is philosophically back to front to suppose that the validity claims provide a basis for the understanding of the phenomena of speech acts, rather it is the theory of speech acts that has to explain the validity claims.*

To summarize: the basic difference between Habermas and me on this issue can be stated as follows. The existence of elaborate social institutions that enable us to perform such complex illocutionary acts as making assertions, promises, and commands, is a social development of more primitive underlying forms of Intentionality. Once these logical relations are made perfectly explicit you can see which speech acts involve which validity claims, and you can see why the validity claims are a strict logical consequence of the structure of the speech act in question. On Habermas's view, on the other hand, we are supposed to take the existence of the validity claims as a kind of primitive given, and construe a speech act as essentially an attempt to get consensus between the speaker and hearer. I hope in this brief discussion I have made it clear why I think the advantage lies with my theory rather than with Habermas's.

There is another area of genuine disagreement between me and Habermas, and it is really too large to settle in the confines of this discussion. But, I would like to put my finger on it. Habermas sees the basic structure of the Intentional state as essentially derived from the propositional structure of sentences of natural languages. But Habermas claims that the reason that we are inclined to ascribe that kind of a structure to Intentional states is precisely because we already find it in the structure of the expressed speech act. Similar objections are made by Bennett and Alston. I believe that their claim is mistaken, but it is very hard to know how to go about refuting it. The reason that it is so hard, of course, is that anything that I say has to be said in a language, and any articulation I give of more primitive prelinguistic forms of Intentionality will always be done in language. So, it looks like I am simply using linguistic forms to explicate Intentionality, and thus it looks like the Intentionality is intrinsically linguistic. But now ask yourself, "How did the speech acts get this extraordinary shape?" and "Why is it that psychological states have exactly the same shape?" Is it because mankind first learned how to talk and then learned how to experience, feel and think? I think the answer is that biological forms of Intentionality are primary; linguistic forms are derived. Of course, for any developed speaker of a language there is an inextricable intermingling of the linguistic and the intentional; and that is just another way of saying that most of our intentional states come to us linguistically and could not exist without linguistic forms of expression.

The picture that I have is this: a human child begins with prelinguistic forms of Intentionality. By a kind of bootstrapping effect the child acquires primitive linguistic expressions of that Intentionality. But a little bit of language goes a long way; and the child develops a richer Intentionality which it could not have developed without linguistic forms. This richer Intentionality enables a further richer linguistic development which in turn enables richer Intentionality. All the way up to the developed adult, there is a complex series of developmental and logical interactions between Intentionality and language. Most forms of adult Intentionality are essentially linguistic. But the whole edifice rests on biological primitive forms of prelinguistic Intentionality.

Finally, about performatives. The notion of a "performative" is one of the most confused and misused in recent philosophy of language. Originally, Austin opposed performatives to constatives, but that opposition failed for reasons that he made clear. Every utterance is a *performance* in the sense that every utterance is a speech act, but not every utterance is thereby a *performative*. Within utterances, i.e. speech acts, there is a sub-class of utterances that are performed by way of using a word that names the very type of act of being performed. These and only these are performative utterances. Thus, "I order you to leave the room" is a performative, and it is a performative used to make an order. "Leave the room," on the other hand, is a sentence used to make an order, but the making of an order with this sentence, is not a *performative*, though, of course, it is a *performance*.

I hope these distinctions are clear because they are essential to understanding my dispute with Habermas about the character of performatives: all speech acts are performances, but only a *very* restricted class of speech acts are performatives. The only speech acts that literally have a performative character are those which are performed by way of a performative verb or some other such performative expression. Such speech acts work by way of the speaker performing an act by declaring that he is performing it, thus all performatives are members of the class of declarations, in my taxonomy.[4]

Habermas makes two objections to this. First, he says this analysis "explodes the architecture of the classification of speech acts because declarations would lose their distinctive place in it, if they were to explain the performative character of all speech acts" (p. 28 above). And secondly, "since most performatives do not appeal to or rely on normative backing, the illocutionary point of declaratives will lose its specificity" (p. 28 above).

It seems to me that Habermas is mistaken on both these points. I believe that my account of performatives strengthens the taxonomy rather than weakens it. What it shows is that the power of declarations is more extensive than I had originally thought. For example, one can perform an assertive, either by uttering an indicative statement "It is raining," or by way of declaring that one is performing the assertive, "I hereby state that it is raining." In the latter case, one actually performs two speech acts in one utterance: One makes a declaration but one thereby makes a statement because one's declaration creates the statement that one is making. But such facts in no way detract from the validity of, for example, the categories of assertives and directives. Furthermore, we avoid the mistake of supposing that all utterances are performatives; rather performatives, strictly speaking, are included in the class of declarations. It is a mistake, I believe, for Habermas to speak of "the performative character of all speech acts." As I said above, if this notion is to have a clear use at all, only a very restricted class of speech acts are performatives.

Furthermore it is not sufficient to say that this merely reflects a different use of the term "performative" on Habermas's part and on my own. If one treats every utterance as a performative, then the mistake is not merely terminological but prevents us from giving a coherent account of the relationship between, for example, the utterance "It is raining," which is not a performative, and "I hereby state that it is raining," which is a performative. The attempts to treat the ordinary indicative sentences without a performative verb as "implicit performatives" have, in my view, invariably been unsuccessful, and have not resulted in a coherent account of the relationship between performative verbs and the rest of the language.[5]

His second objection is more puzzling: "Mot performatives do not appeal to or rely on normative backing." I think, in fact, that almost all performatives require a normative backing, and for the same reason that speech acts in general require normative backing. They are, with few exceptions, social acts performed within a social institution of language. When Habermas says that on my analysis "all illocutionary acts gain a declarative force," it seems to me he is confusing the performance with a performative. Again, it is only a restricted class of speech acts that have a declarative force, those that are explicitly performed by declarations. Most types of speech acts can be performed by declaration, simply by using the appropriate performative verb. But one seldom uses performative verbs in ordinary discourse (for example, how many performative verbs have I used in this reply to Habermas?).

Finally, when he says in objecting to my account of performatives, that language is not a human institution, I really cannot imagine why he or anyone else would say that. On just about any definition of "institution," language is a paradigm, perhaps *the* paradigm of a human institution. If he wants to deny this, surely the onus is on him to provide an argument.

Bennett and Habermas represent opposite ends of a spectrum within the theory of speech acts. Roughly speaking, one might say that Bennett thinks my views are not enough like Grice's, Habermas thinks they are altogether too much like Grice's. Apel's discussion is of a piece with Habermas's, and I now turn to it.

Karl-Otto Apel

I believe Apel's argument is best construed as a continuation of the basic disagreement between Habermas and me: On my view, speaker's meaning can be explained in terms of more fundamental Intentional notions such as belief, desire, and especially intention-in-action. Apel believes that any explanation of meaning essentially depends on social conventions of the sort that are embodied in the conventional meaning of linguistic expressions. the actual structure of his arguments against me is not all that easy to discern. Part of the difficulty is due to the fact that in various ways he misstates my views. Once these confusions are removed is there still a serious disagreement between us? Let us see.

First, Apel persistently confuses a *correspondence* approach to language with a *verificationist* approach. I hold what might be called a correspondence theory of language. I believe that, in general, a statement, if true, corresponds to the state of affairs that makes it true; an order, if obeyed, corresponds to the behavior by the hearer that constitutes its obedience; a promise, if kept, corresponds to the behavior by the speaker that constitutes its fulfillment; etc. But none of this has anything to do with vertificationism. Apel persistently describes my view as "verificationism"; but I reject verificationism and I think in the end, if verificationist assumptions are followed to their limit, they will inevitably lead to some kind of idealism. But whether I am right about that, I am not a verificationist by any standard definition of the term.

Second, again like Habermas, he persistently confuses the illucutionary component of the speech act with a performative component. The structure of the illocutionary act is $F(p)$, where the "F" marks the illocutionary force and the "p" marks the propositional content. A very small class of illocutionary acts are performed by way of uttering a performative expression. These and only these are properly described as performatives. Though every speech act is indeed a *performance*, only a very small class are *performatives*. Apel consistently describes the "illocutionary" component of an illocutionary act as a "performative" component, but I believe that is a mistake, for reasons I pointed out in my reply to Habermas.

Third, there is a kind of implied and sometimes explicit idealism in Apel's account. He says: "The conditions of possibility of the description of experienceable facts . . . are at the same time the conditions of possibility of the describable facts" (p. 35 above). But on a natural interpretation that seems to be false. When, for example, Kepler described the planetary orbits, the "conditions of possibility" of his *describing* involved a lot of linguistic expressions and mathematical symbols; but the actual *facts* concerning the planetary orbits did not depend on the existence of any linguistic expressions or mathematical symbols. Those facts were there before any human beings existed on earth and will be there long after we are all gone. Does anyone seriously deny this?

In a similar vein he quotes Wittgenstein to the effect that it is impossible to describe the fact that corresponds to a sentence without simply repeating the sentence. Wittgenstein is mistaken: there are lots of ways of describing the facts which correspond to sentences without simply repeating the sentences. Indeed, that is what we are all now trying to do. In this discussion all of the participants are trying to explain the structure of the facts which correspond to puzzling sentences about meaning and speech acts, such sentences as "S meant that p" or "S performed the speech act of asserting that p." But notice that not one of us has carried on the discussion by simply repeating sentences of the form "S meant that p" or "S performed the speech act of asserting that p."

Fourth, Apel objects to my analysis on the grounds that there are a lot of speech acts in which the various components of the F in the F(p) structure of the illocutionary act cannot be explained in non-linguistic terms, but rather require what he calls the "linguistic differentiation of illocutionary meanings". Thus, for example, the differences between commands, request, suggestions, orders, pleadings, etc. could not be intended by speakers who did not have a language, much less could they be understood by hearers who did not have a language.

But I agree completely with this point, and it is not an objection to my account. It is emphatically not part of my claim that there are no illocutionary acts which are so to speak essentially linguistic. It is *not* my view that all speech acts could be performed by beings who had no language at all, *nor* is it my view that all speech acts have conditions of satisfaction which can be specified in terms that make no reference to conventions of language.

The thesis I defend is *not* that every speech act could have been performed without language. In fact, I regard that thesis as most implausible. Rather I claim that the *form* of the meaning intention can be specified without any essential reference to linguistic elements. The form of the meaning intention involves the intentional imposition of conditions of satisfaction on conditions of satisfaction. It thus needs to be distinguished from the communication intention which involves the intent that the hearer should recognize the meaning intention and its content. But neither of these so far makes any reference to linguistic elements. Now, all of this is consistent with the fact that in real life many and indeed nearly all actual speech acts are performed in language and could not be performed by beings that lack a language. Since Apel shares this misunderstanding with Habermas and Bennett, it presumably reveals an unclarity in my original exposition.

Suppose we subtract these four features of his account. Is there an argument left against my view, is there a genuine disagreement between us? Yes, I think there is. I think if one takes his paper as a totality, one finds that he shares with Habermas a conception of the speech act which is radically different from mine.

I believe his basic agrument can be stated as a series of steps:

1   The basic unit of speaker's meaning is the illocutionary act.
2   Illocutionary acts are constituted by validity claims.
3   Validity claims are essentially intersubjective.
4   Intersubjective validity claims require social conventions as a condition of their possibility.
5   Therefore, it is wrong to try to explain meaning in terms of prelinguistic forms of Intentionality, because the Intentionality of meaning requires linguistic conventions as a condition of its possibility.

My reply to this argument can be stated very briefly. Apel shares with Habermas a misunderstanding of the role of the validity claims in the constitution of the speech act. The speech act, like any act, is constituted by the fact that it meets certain conditions. Speech acts, unlike most other acts, have a rather heavily articulated structure and one can, in general, distinguish input–output conditions, preparatory conditions, propositional content conditions, sincerity conditions, and essential conditions. Thus, for example, there is no way that I can give an order without attempting to get the hearer to do something (*essential condition*), the order must represent what it is that the hearer is supposed to do (*propositional content condition*), the order expresses the desire on my part that the hearer do the thing he is ordered to do (*sincerity condition*) and I must be in a position of authority or power over the hearer in order to issue the order, and the hearer must be able to do the thing ordered (*preparatory conditions*).

The validity claims discussed by Habermas and Apel are just these various conditions generalized. I am indeed committed to satisfying these conditions whenever I issue an order, because it is the satisfaction of these conditions that constitutes the speech act's being an order. But Habermas and Apel want to add something to what I have just said which is not implied by the theory of speech acts and is not true independently. They want to claim that whenever I issue a speech act, it is part of the structure of my speech act that I am attempting to get the hearer to *agree* to the validity (or rightness or justification or truth, etc.) of the various conditions on the speech act. Thus, for example, on their account, whenever I issue an order I am seeking not merely that the hearer should do the thing ordered, but that he should recognize my sincerity, my justification for issuing the order, etc.

As I suggested in my reply to Habermas, this extension of the theory of speech acts seems to me to be simply not true. A man may issue an order (or a statement or a promise or an apology, etc.) and not care at all whether the speaker accepts it, agrees with it, recognizes its truthfulness, sincerity, valldity, etc. It is not part of the constitution of the *meaning* of a speech act that the speaker must seek from the hearer a recognition of the validity of its performance under these various headings.

It is important to state this point precisely: in the constitution of the illocutionary act it is necessary to distinguish the meaning of the utterance from the intent to communicate that meaning to the hearer. Now, if the speech act is successful the speaker will not only mean something but the hearer will *understand* what he *means*. I was concerned to analyze *meaning*; but now, in addition to meaning and understanding, there are various *perlocutionary* effects that the speaker may wish to produce in the hearer, such as getting the hearer to *agree*. These are important in the context of utterances, *but they are not part of the constitution of the meaning of the utterance*. I believe this is obvious in the case of speech acts where there is no implied moral claim, such as in threats, or orders backed by brute force, that the constitution of the speech act contains no implied moral claim, and that is why cases like these are such as embarrassment to the Habermas–Apel account. But the same point holds in general. To repeat: one can issue a speech act, for example, simply because one feels it is one's duty to issue it. And one can issue a meaningful speech act even in cases in which one had no intention of having one's validity claims recognized by the hearer. To take a famous case, when Galileo said "Eppure si muove," he had no intention of getting his hearers to agree to his validity claims, because he knew there was no possibility of their doing so.

In short, both Habermas and Apel have confused the fact that the performance of the speech act commits the speaker to the conditions of its successful performance with the quite independent and, I believe, false claim that the performance of the speech act necessarily involves an attempt to get the hearer to agree with the speaker on a whole series of validity claims. Of course, communication works best when there is a spirit of cooperation between speaker and hearer. And in such cases, the speaker will attempt to elicit precisely the sorts of agreement that Apel is referring to. But it is a mistake to suppose that the features which are characteristic of *successful cooperation and communication are* part of the *definition of the meaning*. I think a careful analysis of the sort that I propose will show that one can say something, mean what one says, and not get agreement on the sorts of validity claims that Habermas and Apel discuss.

William Alston

Alston and I agree on so many fundamental points about the nature of speech acts that this is perhaps a good time for me to acknowledge my indebtedness to discussions which he and I had about speech acts in the early 1960s. He has influenced my views in ways that are greater than either he or I were aware of at the time. In this brief response I will simply list some points in which there are still areas of disagreement and possibly misunderstandings.

1   I think he fails to see the intuitively plausible sense in which we can distinguish between internal and external criticisms of a speech act such as, e.g., promising. A speech act, like any other act, is subject to a range of criticisms; and some of these criticisms have to do with the sort of speech act it is. Thus, if someone makes a promise and I say to him "But you do not really intend to keep it," that is an internal criticism because it is directed to his utterance *qua promise*. But if I simply say to him "Speak louder I cannot hear you" then I am indeed criticizing his speech act but it

is not *qua* promise but rather *qua* utterance. Intuitively, there is clearly a distinction, as exemplified by these two cases, between internal and external criticisms.

And it is this distinction between internal and external criticisms which justified me in analyzing *sincere* and *non-defective* promises, in a way that I believe can enable me to distinguish defects in the speech act, which have to do with the fact that it is a promise, from those defects which have nothing to do with its character as a promise.

2   He thinks that if I make a promise to do something awful, I don't even have a "*prima facie* obligation" to do it. I have never been able to find a coherent notion of *prima facie* obligations,[6] but it seems intuitively clear to me that a speaker who successfully and non-defectively promises, undertakes an obligation; and this point seems to me valid, even though the obligation may be ridiculous or too stupid to be worth considering, or overridden by other considerations. An argument for this is that there must be a difference between the speaker who has made a promise and the speaker who has done nothing whatever. The promisor has an obligation, even though it is overriden. But unless there were an obligation there would nothing to override.

3   Alston says that I have abandoned the view that the intention to communicate is necessary for the performance of illocutionary acts. But that is not quite right. In general, the successful performance of an illocutionary act requires successful communication. The point that I have been making, however, is that in the theory of meaning, we need to distinguish the intention to represent, in one illocutionary mode or another, from the intention to communicate that representation to a speaker. In nearly all cases, successful illocutionary acts include both. This is a point I discussed in response to Bennett.

4   I do not really think there is a substantive disagreement between me and Alston on the question of whether or not the analysis of speech acts is better pursued in terms of a discussion of actual states of affairs or in terms of the question of the speaker *taking responsibility* for those states of affairs. The whole point of the discussion in terms of responsibility is to mark the fact that there is a reference to states of affairs; and in the case in which the speaker succeeds in his responsibilities, the state of affairs he is taking responsibility for will actually obtain. Thus, it is possible to do the analysis either in terms of the commitment to the *states of affairs* or in terms of the correlative responsibility. The point is: taking responsibility is what counts from the point of view of Intentionality, but if the speaker succeeds, then the things he takes responsibility for must actually obtain. So, you can do the analysis either way.

5   On the question of whether or not directives count as attempts by the speaker to get the hearer to do something, I think Alston's intuitions and mine are simply in disagreement. It seems to me intuitively obvious that any directive counts as an attempt by the speaker to get the hearer to do something; and this point holds even in cases in which the speaker does not, in fact, want the hearer to do it. In such cases, the speaker still did, so to speak, officially try to get the hearer to do it. A clue to this fact is that if the hearer does the things he is told by the speaker to do, he can always give as a reason for his doing it, that he was ordered to do it by the speaker.

And the speaker cannot evade the charge that he tried to get the hearer to do it by pleading that he really did not want the hearer to do the thing he ordered him to do.

6 I think that Alston has not understood my notion of illocutionary point. Of course, a speaker may have any number of different points or purposes in performing a speech act. But the *illocutionary point* is the point that the act has in virtue of its being an act of that type. I think this leads Alston to make some mistakes about the notion of lying which are similar to those which Bennett makes. He says that one can make an assertion without its being any part of one's purpose to make the words fit the world, as when one is deliberately lying. But that is not a correct description of the situation. In the case of a lie the speaker is still *committed* to having his words fit the world. If he were not so committed there would be nothing wrong with lying. In this connection Alston also complains that I do not give an adequate explanation of the notion of direction of fit. Well, any philosophically difficult concept is always subject to further elucidation, but I have attempted to explain it in *Intentionality* to such an extent that I do not feel seriously concerned with this objection. In any case, I reject Alston's conclusion that I cannot reasonably suppose that direction of fit is determined by illocutionary point. I try to show that it is in every case.

7 Alston objects to my use of the notion of conditions of satisfaction in a way which is similar to the objections of both Bennett and Habermas. He seems to think that the analysis of Intentional states in terms of conditions of satisfaction essentially requires a reference to the conditions of satisfaction of speech acts. But in my view that is not correct. I do, in fact, pedagogically tap the speaker's intuitions about speech acts in order to get the right intuitions about Intentional states. Thus, the direction of pedagogy is to explain Intentionality by means of language. But the direction of logical analysis is precisely the reverse. The conditions of satisfaction of linguistic entities are derived from those of Intentional states and not conversely.

I am immensely grateful for the sheer intelligence and thoughtfulness of the contributions to this section. One of the best things that can happen to a philosopher is to have intelligent critics, such as those I have been attempting to answer.

NOTES

1 J. R. Searle, "A Taxonomy of Illocutionary Acts," in Language, Mind and Knowledge, ed. Keith Gunderson, Minnesota Studies in the Philosophy of Science (University of Minnesota Press: Minnesota, 1975).

2 Part of the difficulty in this discussion is that both Bennett and Habermas are working from a very early version of my views on meaning. The article "Meaning, Communication, and Representation" was written for publication in the Grice *Festschrift* in early 1974. Because of the incredible delays in the publication of that volume, the article did not appear until mid-1986. In the meantime I had developed my views to their present form in *Intentionality*, published in 1983.

3 For a better understanding of Habermas's views I am very much indebted to Thomas Judge "The Locus of Meaning: Habermas and Searle on Communication," unpublished undergraduate Honors Thesis, Department of Philosophy, University of California at Berkeley.

4 For a further discussion of performatives see J. R. Searle, "How Performatives Work," in

Linguistics and Philosophy, vol. 12 (Netherlands, Kluwer Academic Publishers, 1989), pp. 535–58.

5   J. R. Searle, "Speech Acts and Recent Linguistics," in *Developmental Psycholinguistics and Communication Disorders*, Annals of the New York Academy of Sciences, 1975.

6   J. R. Searle, "*Prima Facie* Obligations," in *Practical Reasoning*, J. Raz (ed.) (Oxford University Press: Oxford, 1978); also, Searle, reply to Loewer and Belzer, this volume.

Part   II
The Mind–Body Problem

6

Aristotle, Searle, and the Mind–Body Problem

ALAN CODE

(1) John Searle presents a solution to the mind–body problem that involves treating mental phenomena as physical properties caused by and realized in a system of physical micro-elements. The mental and the physical do not, on the proffered view, form mutually exclusive classes – rather, the mental is included within the physical. The mind–body problem was generated in the seventeenth century when, as a part of the radical rejection of Aristotelian physics, the psychological could no longer be treated as a part of the physical.[1] Aristotle considered the soul and its faculties to be causally primitive physical powers, and as such, not caused or explained by the behavior of the elements of which the body is composed. In one respect, Searle's view is like Aristotle's. Both treat the psychological as a part of the physical. However, they differ in a number of respects. Most importantly, Searle does not think that human mental capacities are causally primitive.

(2) Searle believes that the mind–body problem has long seemed to be intractable because philosophers have been unable to see how the following two theses could *both* be true:

  (a) Mental phenomena are caused by processes going on in the brain. (This thesis can be abbreviated as "Brains cause minds.")
  (b) Mental phenomena are features of the brain.[2]

If both are accepted as true, then the attempt to provide an account of the mental which is continuous with a post-Aristotelian physical science will be possible. However, there are four features of the mental that have been thought to pose serious problems for any such account: consciousness, intentionality, subjectivity, and mental causation. An adequate solution to the mind–body problem must not, Searle thinks, involve the repudiation of any of these four features of the mental, but rather must show how these four features are to be incorporated into a single model satisfying theses (a) and (b).

  To demonstrate that these two theses can both be true together, he sketches a model according to which mental phenomena are macro-features of that micro-system which constitues the brain, and as such, mental phenomena are both caused by and realized in that very micro-system. In these respects, though certainly not in all, mental phenomena are analogous to such macro-properties of molecular structures as liquidity and solidity. Solidity, for instance, is a physical property at the macro-level; it is caused by the behavior of entities at the level of micro-elements, and is a property that is realized in the physical system of micro-elements, the behavior of which causes the system to have that property. In much the same way, a mental phenomenon is a macro-property of a complex neurophysiological system of micro-elements such that the mental phenomenon in question is a property realized in that system of micro-elements, the behavior of which causes the mental phenomenon.

(3)   Thesis (a) is intended to be an empirical generalization drawn from contemporary neurophysiology. Searle does not wish to commit himself to any particular neurophysiological explanation of any particular kind of mental phenomenon, nor to the view that at the present time neurophysiology can provide even *prima facie* explanations for all types of mental phenomena. He does, however, wish to endorse the claim that *in principle* all mental phenomena *can* be explained using the type of explanations currently sought and offered by neurophysiologists. Our scientific conception of ourselves as ultimately composed of micro-elements, the behavior of which is the subject matter of physics, leads us to attempt causal explanations of mental phenomena in terms of a series of neurophysiological events,[3] and it is to this type of explanation that thesis (a) is committed.

Searle does not think that thesis (a) presupposes or entails thesis (b) – the thesis that mental phenomena are features of the brain. The fact that a series of events in the brain causes some mental phenomenon does not by itself entail that the mental phenomenon takes place in the brain, much less that it is a property inhering in the brain. A neurophysiological causal account of mental phenomena does not by itself entail that the mental phenomena occur in the brain. This view is part of a philosophical interpretation of the causal story provided by science. In so far as neurophysiology does no more than investigate and discover the physical causes of mental phenomena, it does not itself contain the view that mental phenomena occur in the body, or in some sub-system of the body.

Furthermore, the conjunction of (a) and (b) does not by itself entail that any causal explanation (much less a neurophysiological one) can be given of the mental phenomena *qua* mental. Suppose, for instance, that MP is Patrick's belief that it is raining, that MP is in fact a macro-neurophysiological state caused by something taking place in his brain, and that we have just given a causal explanation of the neurophysiological state which is, in fact, MP. What we have given is a causal explanation of MP *qua* macro-neurophysiological state. However, our ability to give, such an explanation should not simply be equated with the ability to give a causal explanation of MP *qua* mental phenomenon.

The neurophysiological explanation of MP might actually fail to explain why MP is a belief, just as it might fail to explain why MP has the particular content that it does (i.e., it might not explain why MP is a belief *that it is raining*). Imagine: we have Patrick sitting in Searle's laboratory; Searle's scientist has isolated a macro-feature of Patrick's brain and given a causal explanation of that macro-feature in neuro-physiological terms; and we even grant that the macro-feature he has isolated is in fact identical with Patrick's belief that it is raining. In this scenario, Patrick's belief is caused by something taking place in the brain and is also a feature realized in his brain. Searle's two theses are honored. However, Patrick's belief, which is itself a property of his brain, has properties of its own. It has, for instance, the property of being a belief, and the property of having as its content the proposition that it is raining. We have as yet not been told that a neurophysiological explanation can be given of these *mental* properties of his belief that it is raining. Searle's two theses, taken by themselves, are noncommittal on this point. Objections to the claim that physical causality is sufficient to account for mental properties are not properly addressed to these theses. By the same token, theses (a) and (b) do not by themselves support this claim.

(4)   Searle is not, however, noncommittal as to whether the mental properties of mental phenomena are caused by the brain. He holds that *both* mental phenomena *and* their properties are caused by and realized in the brain. It is important to see this because (a) and (b) are actually consistent with a functionalist account of the mind – an account that he explicitly rejects. Searle's position is not simply that (a) and (b) are both true. His position is that the mind–body problem can be solved only by showing how (a) and (b) are both acceptable, and this in turn requires coming up with a *viable* model of the mental that satisfies both. Some functionalist accounts may be compatible with both (a) and (b). However, Searle thinks that the problems involved in these accounts are so serious that functionalism cannot, in any convincing way, show how these two theses can both be true.

The model he does present, which compares mental phenomena with such macro-properties as solidity and liquidity, is a crucial and indispensable part of the exposition of his view. As a macro-level property, solidity itself has all sorts of properties such as *rigidity* and *resistance to pressure*.[4] These properties of solidity are themselves physical properties that are caused by and realized in exactly the same system of micro-elements, the behavior of which causes solidity.

The mental properties of mental phenomena are analogous to (for instance) rigidity. MP (that is, Patrick's belief that it is raining) corresponds to solidity, and the property of having as its content *that it is raining* corresponds to rigidity. Just as rigidity is caused by and realized in the system of micro-elements that causes solidity, so too the content of a mental phenomenon is caused by and realized in the brain. Searle's view, that the mental properties of mental phenomena are caused by the brain, is not supposed to follow merely from the acceptance of (a) and (b), but rather is supposed to be a consequence of the model that he suggests for showing how both can be true. Searle's view is not functionalist. Neither is Aristotle's.

(5)   We have seen that Searle views both mental phenomena and their mental properties as physical properties at the macro-level, and treats them as caused by the behavior of the micro-elements. Aristotelian physics, however, although it treats the psychological as a part of the physical, firmly rejects the idea that the psychological is caused by anything at the elemental level. The nature of the material elements is such that on their own they cannot lead to psychological activity. We now turn to a brief consideration of the Aristotelian conception of the psychological.

(6)   Aristotle resisted Platonic soul/body dualism and replaced it with a hylomorphic conception of soul. According to this conception, all living things are com-

posites of matter and form, where the matter is the body and the form is the soul. Psychological activity is the exercise of various faculties of the form (i.e., the soul), the form being the first, or primary, source of being for the material composite.[5]

Such a view embodies a commitment to a thesis, or set of theses, concerning the relations that obtain between the psychological and the physical, and hence also a commitment to a view about the relationship between psychology and physics. Recently there has been much discussion among students of Aristotle regarding the precise nature of that commitment, and much debate as to whether his hylo-morphism involves an endorsement of some version of materialism, physicalism or functionalism, and if so, to which version.

There is an unstated assumption made in these recent discussions. It is the very assumption that Searle rejects in his solution to the mind–body problem: the idea that psychological properties or entities on the one hand, and physical properties or entities on the other, form mutually exclusive classes. The various recent debates about Aristotle's conception of the soul concern the correct characterization of the relationships that obtain between members of the two classes. For Aristotle, however, psychological properties *are* also physical.

(7) A number of contemporary scholars have argued that Aristotle's conception of the psychological bears significant affinities to functionalist accounts of the mental. What these scholars have in mind can, I think, be explained as follows.[6] For any actual occurrence of some type or kind of psychological phenomenon, one may draw a distinction between the material in which the phenomenon is realized, and the role which that phenomenon plays in the overall functioning of a system which contains the phenomenon as a member. Let us call the properties that the particular occurrence has in virtue of its material composition its "M-properties," and those it has in virtue of its functional role its "F-properties." Functional role may put some restrictions on the material composition (you can't make a saw out of water), and hence the F-properties of a psychological phenomenon might well put restrictions upon the M-properties of the material in which the F-property is realized. Nonetheless, the F-properties of a mental phenomenon are neither reducible to, nor derivable from, its M-properties.

The psychological properties, or "P-properties," according to a functionalist account, are without exception F-properties. So, a particular psychological phenomenon may be seen as a kind of composite of matter and form, an F-property realized in matter suitable for that form or F-property. Since the F-properties of a psychological phenomenon are not had by that phenomenon by virtue of its material composition, the relation between the F-properties and the M-properties is purely contingent. In this sense psychological entities are *compositionally plastic*. Beliefs, desires, and the like can be given different kinds of material realizations, including the possibility of realization in some kind of spiritual, non-physical matter. The compositional plasticity of the psychological allows for the possibility that two creatures that differ greatly in physical constitution might nonetheless be in exactly the same psychological state.

(8) It is impossible that Aristotle should have had anything resembling a functionalist account of the psychological. By this I do not mean that for Aristotle the various faculties of soul are not defined in terms of their functions. Of course they are. However, the exercise of a faculty of soul just is its function. For instance,

seeing is the function in terms of which sight is defined. In denying that Aristotle could have been a functionalist I am denying that seeing (the psychological activity itself) is characterized in functional terms; or that thinking (the psychological activity itself) is characterized in functional terms. Seeing is receiving the form of the "see-able" without the matter; thinking (*noesis*) an intelligible, and immaterial, essence is (correctly called) a "thinking" of that essence in virtue of the fact that the actuality of the intellect (*nous*) is the same as the actuality of the immaterial essence which is being thought. Aristotle is not characterizing these activities in terms of their functional role, and a functionalist should recoil in horror at his accounts as to what makes seeing seeing, or what makes thinking thinking. However, Aristotle does not deny, but rather accepts, the idea that the faculties of soul are defined by reference to their function (that is, by reference to their exercise, or "second actuality").

Furthermore, I do not mean to deny that the faculties of soul are in *some* sense "plastic." Sight, for example, must be realized in a transparent body, and since both water and air are transparent, it could be realized in either. However, if our eyes were made of air, they would leak too easily, and for that reason our eyes have water.[7] Thus sight could inform a body made of air or a body made of water, and it is a contingent fact that it is realized in water. This does not show compositional plasticity in the sense required by a functionalist. All that this shows is that sight is a power that, in principle, could be present in different kinds of materials. The same could be said of heat. For Aristotle, heat is a power defined in terms of what it does (its function); it separates things by drawing like to like. Furthermore, heat can be present in different kinds of material, and in that sense is "plastic." But despite the fact that heat is defined in terms of its function, and can be present in different kinds of matter, Aristotle obviously does not have a "functionalist" account of heat. Aristotle's soul, like Searle's mind, is a physical property.

(9)   Aristotle's conception of soul is an integral part of his physics, and presupposes some of the basic principles constitutive of that physics. Once the physics is rejected, the psychology goes with it. To think that Aristotle had anything like a functionalist account of the soul is completely to misunderstand the relationship between Aristotelian psychology and the fundamental principles constitutive of his physics. His account of the soul is not compatible with Cartesian physics, since for Aristotle the soul is the nature of a certain kind of physical body, and as such is responsible for its natural motions. However, Descartes totally rejects the idea that there are specifically different kinds of bodies endowed with specifically different essences or natures serving as internal causal principles of natural changes. Functionalism, on the other hand, in virtue of the compositional plasticity of functional states is logically consistent with Cartesian physics (though it is not consistent with Cartesian psychology). A functionalist need not accept Cartesian physics, but could. So, since Aristotle's conception of the soul is not compatible with Cartesian physics, but the functionalist account of the mind is, it follows that Aristotle's conception of soul is not, and does not involve, a functionalist account of the mind.

The characteristic problems and projects of modern philosophy begin with the seventeenth-century scientific revolution and its rejection of Aristotle's irreducibly teleological physics. Functionalism is a post-Cartesian philosophical position in the philosophy of mind, and as such is not wedded to the ideas of Aristotelian physics that were rejected in the seventeenth century. For the Aristotelians, the mind had a secure place in nature. They viewed the mind as a faculty of human soul, and thought that the relation between soul and body was that of form to matter. For them, human mind is a faculty that a human has in virtue of its formal nature. With the sole exception of *nous* (intellect), the exercise of any faculty of soul is the operation of a bodily organ.[8] Thinking is not the function of a bodily organ – after all, God thinks, but being perfect can have no matter, and hence no body. The objects of thought for an Aristotelian are immaterial, and so thought itself must be immaterial.

(10)   As long as we stick to a physics that allocates to each kind of natural body a unique formal nature, our mental activity can be assigned to our form, essence or nature. However, once we reject that kind of physics we can no longer treat a mental phenomenon as the operation of the essential nature of a certain kind of physical body. Hence with the new physics the relation between the mental and the physical immediately becomes problematic in a way that it could not have been for a scholastic Aristotelian.

It is particularly informative to invoke Descartes at this point. For him, the body is a machine, and the various bodily organs are parts of the machine. The functioning of those organs is not due to "animal soul," but can be explained solely in terms of whatever mechanical principles govern *inanimate* matter. Descartes defines the nature of body as extension, and mechanical principles are those governing body and its modes (figure, magnitude, and motion). For Descartes, there are not specifically different kinds of body having specifically different kinds of natures or essences, and *man* is most emphatically not a kind of physical body possessed of a unique internal nature, human soul. The only nature that a body has *qua* body is extension, and that is not an internal causal principle governing its natural motions or changes.

Since mental activity is not the operation of a bodily organ (as any good scholastic knows), the Cartesian mechanical principles that govern body cannot account for thought. The old Aristotelian view about mind's place in nature is no longer acceptable, and the new approach to physics does not seem to be hospitable to the mental as a part of the physical. So, what is the relation between thinking and the physical? The Cartesian dualist addresses the new problem by invoking two distinct types of substance: soul and body. The soul and the body are distinct substances that causally interact (in both directions), though each can exist without the other. Furthermore, the mind is a substance the nature of which is to think, whereas the body is a substance the nature of which is extension. The body can no more be the subject of mental properties than the mind can have a spatial location. After all, if thought cannot be derived from extension (the nature of body) and its modes, and yet thought must be a natural activity of that which thinks, it follows not only that thought cannot be an attibute of a body, but also that it must be an attribute of something the nature of which is to think. Thus the *res cogitans* – a substance the nature of which is to think.

(11)   In the seventeenth century various philosophers proposed other views about the relation of the mental to the corporeal, most notably Leibniz's monadology and Spinoza's monism, both of which are more Aristotelian than Descartes. Skipping

over a tremendous amount of history to the latter part of the twentieth century, we find a number of philosophers proposing functionalism as the correct account of the relation between the mental and the physical. Aha! Mental phenomena are compositionally plastic functional states. Although functionalism does not (logically) require physicalism, nonetheless functional states can (in principle) be realized in neurophysiological configurations, regardless of whether they could also be realized in other ways. Hence, functionalism provides a way of treating physical systems as the bearers of mental predicates. For a functionalist, there is no need to introduce a separate substance, the Cartesian *res cogitans*, to be the subject of such mental predicates, because a human being is a physical object that is the subject of such mental predicates as those expressing belief, desire, and so on. My beliefs, for example, are neurophysiological states that play a certain functional role. In general, mental predicates are characterized by input/output relations (and relations to other mental predicates).

(12)   So, why can't Aristotle be a functionalist? According to Aristotle, there are just four basic elements: earth, water, air and fire. Each element has its own natural place. Down is the place of earth, up for fire, with water just above down and air just below up. The natural motion of an element is a rectilinear path towards its natural place, and any element not in its proper place will move in a straight line towards that place unless either (1) it is already there, or (2) something prevents it. Furthermore, an element will stay at rest in its natural place unless something forces it to move somewhere else. Each of these elements is a natural body in the sense that each has a nature (or *phusis*) that is an internal principle of such natural change and resistance to change.[9]

According to Aristotelian physics, *all* sub-lunary bodies are ultimately composed of these four elements.[10] Furthermore, a great deal of their behavior is due to the natures of these basic elemental constituents. Nonetheless, the characteristic behavior of a composite natural body cannot be accounted for in terms of these elemental natures. This is true for the extremely simple reason that the natural motions of the four elements are towards four different regions. Were its only natural principles those of its material elements, the elements contained in any composite body would, if nothing prevented, naturally separate from each other as they moved towards their respective places.[11] Hence, the natural body would disintegrate, decompose and decay unless it had something in it to counteract the natural motions of its material elements.

Each non-elemental natural body has a nature unique to bodies of that kind, and its natural behavior (including its resistance to disintegration and decay) is due to that nature, and not to the natures of the elements of which it is composed. For Aristotle the nature of a living thing is its form, which in turn is to be identified with its soul. The soul is the causal principle that counteracts the natural migrations of the elements to their natural places. In *Metaphysics*, Book VII Aristotle identifies the soul of a living thing with its form and essence, and says that this is a primary, or primitive, substance. It is a basic causal principle, and its causal efficacy cannot be derivative from the causal powers of elemental matter, for part of its causal job is to counteract the natural motions of the elements. It is a primitive causal power that exists in matter together with such causal powers as the hot and the cold, the fluid and the dry.

(13)   Although the ancient Greeks were concerned with the relationship between thinking and the body, they were not confronted with the problem as to how thought is related to a serious post-Aristotelian physics. Hence they were not concerned with our mind–body problem. Searle is. Our mind–body problem results from accepting a physics that refuses to utilize souls as basic, irreducible causal principles. Searle proposes to solve that mind–body problem by showing how the mind can be a physical property and nonetheless not be causally primitive. His work is not a return to Aristotle, but rather is best seen as showing us why the rejection of Aristotle's physics need not involve a rejection of the idea that the mental is a part of the physical. For an Aristotelian, however, despite the fact that the capacity for thought is a part of the internal nature of a certain kind of physical body, thinking as such is, due to the immaterial nature of its objects, itself immaterial. Human thinking is both *physical* and *immaterial*. Descartes rejected the Aristotelian physics, but still endorsed the immateriality of thought. The psychological was no longer regarded as a part of the physical, and given the new approach to physics, would not again be so-regarded until the legacy of Aristotle's *nous* could be laid to rest.[12]

NOTES

1   Consideration of neo-Platonism is necessary for a full story, but falls outside the scope of this paper.
2   See chapter 1 of *Minds, Brains and Science* (Harvard University Press: Cambridge, Mass., 1984); also chapter 10 of *Intentionality* (Cambridge University Press: Cambridge, 1983). As Searle makes clear, he does not mean to commit himself to the claim that mental phenomena are features solely of the brain, as opposed to being features of the entire central nervous system. For brevity he talks as though his view is that they are features of the brain alone.
3   Just so long as psychological capacities are not viewed as causally primitive.
4   Solidity, of course, is not itself rigid. Solidity is, on the common sense level, defined in terms of such properties as rigidity. This is analogous to saying that beliefs are defined, on the common-sense level, in terms of their mental properties such as content.
5   For Aristotle, "psychological activity" includes growth, nutrition, sexual generation, as well as perception, self-initiated locomotion, remembering, dreaming, imagination, and thinking. (The list is not exhaustive.) Thus much that we currently consider to be physical (e.g., growth) is for Aristotle psychological. In a limited way, Searle can be seen as returning to a conception of the mental as continuous with life processes and enlivening capacities. Searle does not, of course, treat growth, digestion, and the like as mental, but rather treats the mental capacities of living things as themselves physical properties (at the macro-level).
6   M. Nussbaum and H. Putnam defend a functionalist reading of Aristotle in "Changing Aristotle's Mind", written in response to criticism of their position lodged by M. F. Burnyeat in "Is an Aristotelian Philosophy of Mind Still Credible?" (both in *Essays on Aristotle's De Anima*, ed. M. Nussbaum and A. Rorty (Oxford University Press: Oxford, 1990)). (See also S. Marc Cohen, "The Credibility of Aristotle's Philosophy of Mind," in *Aristotle Today*, M. Matthen (ed.); (Academic Printing and Publishing: Edmonton, Alta., 1987), who questions whether Burnyeat has succeeded in refuting the functionalist interpreters of Aristotle.) Burnyeat argues that Aristotle's theory of perception cannot be freed from certain Aristotelian physical assumptions that (1) have been rejected since the seventeenth century, and (2) given compositional plasticity, are not required by a functionalist account of the mental. In section 9 I elaborate upon this type of argument by contrasting Aristotle and Descartes on the nature of a body. Since on my account perception is physiological, and Burnyeat argues that

physiological conditions are not sufficient for perception, he may not agree with my elaboration.

7   *Sense and Sensibilia*, Book 2.
8   It is the only faculty of soul that is not the form of a bodily organ, thus leaving open the possibility that perhaps this part of the form of our body could exist without that body.
9   See *Physics*, Book II, 1.
10 *Generation and Corruption*, II.8.
11 *De Anima*, II.4.
12 I would like to thank H. P. Grice for helpful discussion about Searle's philosophy of mind.

7

Mind/Brain Science: Neuroscience on Philosophy of Mind

WALTER J. FREEMAN
CHRISTINE A. SKARDA

1 Introduction

With the advent of behaviorism it became fashionable to claim that neuroscience is irrelevant to cognitive science, and since the introduction of the computer, philosophers of a functionalist persuasion have pointed to the symbolic processing model to support this view. Fortunately, this line of thinking did not stop most of the minds/brains in neuroscience from pursuing research that ran directly counter to the functionalist doctrine. Neuroscientists never believed that knowing how the brain functions is irrelevant to cognitive theory: functionalism looked nice on paper to those who knew nothing about how brains work, but it was based on profoundly anti-biological assumptions which, far from encouraging interdisciplinary exchange, prompted most neuroscientists to ignore what was going on in cognitive science. Today, as functionalism gives way to "neurophilosophy" (Churchland, 1986) and "neural network" models replace some forms of symbol-based processing in artificial intelligence, cognitive and neuroscientists should look at what is being said by their colleagues in both disciplines.

John Searle's work in philosophy of mind has distinguished itself for many reasons, chief among these being that he never accepted functionalism and, unlike many philosophers, always enthusiastically embraced neuroscience. We suggest that his contributions deserve serious consideration, in turn, by neuroscientists. Of special interest in this respect are Searle's views on the mind/brain. Our comments focus on four of these: (1) the relation between brains and computers; (2) the issue of levels of description; (3) Searle's model for interpreting how the mind/brain functions; and (4) his characterization of perceptual states. Recent findings in neuroscience corroborate many of Searle's claims and support his view that there is no mind/body problem except in the minds of some philosophers. But our research also suggests that some traditional, time-worn and no longer valid physiological concepts persist in Searle's characterization of how the mind/brain works which lead to problems that neuroscience may help to solve. We address these issues in an attempt to contribute to a future mind/brain science that is being envisaged by many researchers today, including Searle.

2 Brains and Computers

Searle has presented a forceful and convincing argument against the view that intelligence is formal symbol manipulation (Searle, 1980). This view, which we also believe to be false, says that the brain produces intelligent behavior because at the functional level of description the brain is a device formally manipulating symbols according to rules. This view characterizes classical cognitivism; it is still not uncommon to read that a model that does without symbols and rules at the functional level is "noncognitive" (Earle, 1987).

Evidence from our laboratory indicates that brain functioning does not resemble the rule-driven symbol-manipulating processes characteristic of digital computers (Skarda and Freeman, 1987). Electroencephalogram (EEG) research on pre-attentive sensory processing taking place in the olfactory bulb suggests that brains use the functional architecture of distributed, self-organizing networks similar in many ways to some types of present-day connectionist models. The essential feature of connectionist or so-called "neural net" models is that a distributed system of interacting simple elements can produce intelligent behavior without the rules and programs that were previously thought to be required. Learning takes place by strengthening and weakening connection strengths between units in the network in parallel. When the network is activated each unit computes its own level of activity in terms of input from other units and a predetermined threshold value. The global pattern of activity resulting from these simultaneous, independent, parallel computations constitutes the state of the system at each moment.

To support Searle's claim with an appeal to connectionist systems, however, we believe it is important to distinguish two camps of connectionist models, one typified by so-called PDP models (Hinton, 1985; Rumelhart et al., 1986), the other characterized by self-organizing dynamical systems (Amari, 1983; Anderson et al., 1977; Freeman, 1987; Grossberg, 1981; Hopfield, 1982; Kohonen, 1984). Not every connectionist network can be said to operate in the absence of symbols or symbol-like elements. Systems that fall within the PDP class of connectionist models use globally distributed dynamics, but there is a sense in which this class of systems still uses internal "representations" in the production of behavior. Systems like these, which rely on feed-forward connectivity and back propogation for error correction, have their "goals" externally imposed: they require a "teacher" or set of correct answers to be instilled by the system's operator. These answers are paradigmatic patterns with reference to which the output of the system is corrected via back propagation and error correction. The teacher used by such systems may not be contained in a program, but it nonetheless functions in the same way that an internal representation does in conventional computers. Self-organizing dynamic systems, because of dense local feedback connections, do not require or use teachers. No matching or comparison takes place such as by correlation or completion, and no archetypal set patterns are placed by an external operator into the system as its goals.

Our data indicate that in the olfactory bulb, learning consists in a self-organizing process and not in the manipulation of symbols according to rules: it is the selective strengthening of excitatory connections among neurons (mitral cells) in the bulb leading to the constitution of a nerve cell assembly (NCA) and ultimately to a change of state from local activity in the bulb to a self-organized form of activity globally distributed over the entire set of bulbar neurons that can be related with a particular odor and response. Memory for an odor consists in the set of strengthened excitatory connections of the NCA that, when activated with input, possesses the tendency to produce a spatial activity pattern characteristic of a given odor. These are not mechanisms used by conventional digital computers. No program-specified rule is imposed on olfactory input, the activity is self-organized, there is no central processor, and learning and memory are distributed throughout the system.

On the basis of our data we have suggested that brains do not work in the way in which everyone expected and that new conceptual apparatus will be required to characterize adequately the self-organized (see section 4 below) neural processing that we have observed. With the introduction of alternative models, the identification of symbol processing with intelligence appears to be an oversimplification at best, and we, along with Searle, have argued that it is misleading for both cognitive and neuroscientists to think in these terms when attempting to understand brain function (Freeman and Skarda, 1985; Skarda, 1986; Skarda and Freeman, 1987).

3 Levels of Description and the Neuron Doctrine

We agree with Searle that "[pains] and other mental phenomena just are features of the brain and perhaps the rest of the central nervous system," and that the important requirement for understanding this relationship is the distinction between micro- and macrolevels of neural functioning. The brain produces intelligent behavior, but the crucial question for neuroscientists has always been which level of functioning is relevant for explanations of this behavior? Our research has led us to break with a foundational concept of contemporary research on the nervous system, the "neuron doctrine," that we once accepted in company with the majority of our colleagues, but which we now see as mistaken and as a source of misunderstanding in attempts to comprehend the brain as the organ of behavior (Freeman, 1984).

The nineteenth-century witnessed two main revolutions in biology. The best known is the introduction of Darwinian doctrine; the other is the cellular doctrine of Rudolf Virchow (1871), by which we came to understand that the functional basis of all life is the cell. The teaching and practice of physiology and medicine today are entirely based on this doctrine, and it is undoubtedly correct to say that the great majority of janitorial functions of neurons (processes of growth, repair, general chemical maintenance, metabolic fueling, disposal of wastes, and the modification of connections in molecular and membranal processes) take place and are best understood at the cellular level. The crucial question, however, is whether information used in the elaboration of goal-directed behavior and in controlling interactions with the environment is expressed in or operated on by neurons acting as individual summing and switching devices?

For nearly a century the common answer has been "Of course it is!" The principle reason for believing this has been the assumption that what counts in the production of behavior is the action potential, the most prominent signal generated by individual neurons (Barlow, 1972). Such a cell is called a "unit" with a "spike train," and it is commonly thought that the "message" or "information" transmitted by the cell consists in the temporal patterns of the spikes, in the manner that a message resides in the pattern of dots and dashes in a telegraph wire.

We note, however, that the great bulk of physiological studies cited to support this view come from anesthetized or paralyzed animals in circumstances in which goal-directed behavior is deliberately suppressed. When studies have been undertaken in normally behaving animals, the variability of the observed unit activity has been so great as to be uninterpretable, so that researchers have resorted to averaging their data in such a way that the time base is locked to a stimulus or response. This procedure culls from the data an extremely small fraction of the variance locked to an external event and discards the overwhelming majority of the data as "noise."

Our studies of the behavior of single neurons in respect to the tens and hundreds of thousands of their neighbors indicates that researchers have been searching for neural "information" at the wrong level. While the activity of single cells appears to be largely unpredictable and noisy, the mass of cells cooperates to produce a coherent pattern that can be reliably related with a particular stimulus. In studies of the olfactory systems of small mammals the results are unequivocal: the information expressed by neurons that is related with the behavior of animals exists in the cooperative activity of many millions of neurons and not in the favored few. In the first stage of the system where odor discrimination takes place, the olfactory bulb, there is no evidence that the signaling by the bulb to the rest of the brain is by any small number of neurons unique for each odor. On the contrary, for every discriminable odor *every* neuron in the bulb participates. We conclude that it is incorrect to say that the behavioral information exists in the activity of single neurons; it cannot be observed there. This information exists in patterns of activity that are distributed concomitantly and continuously over tens and hundred of millions of neurons.

The main reason that the cellular doctrine holds so well for most cells but fails for neurons is that neurons are uniquely different from all other types of cells: neurons are involved constantly in widespread activity with other neurons, some at great distances. Each neuron transmits to thousands of others in its vicinity, and in some cases for astonishingly great distances, often thousands of times greater than the diameter of its own axon. It also receives from many neurons in its surround, on the order of 1,000 to 10,000. The key to its interaction lies in this: by virtue of its membrane each neuron has a relatively high degree of automony, yet all that it does is felt by many other neurons, and those neurons provide the environment to which it responds. These widespread actions and reactions lead to the emergence of the constant, ceaseless, ever-fluctuating activity of masses of nerve cells that start talking and never stop. In fact, if they do stop, because they are cut off from interaction with their neighbors, they soon atrophy and die.

Interconnections among neurons are of two main types: local and long range, corresponding to Golgi II and Golgi I neurons. Local connections within areas of the cortex and subcortical nuclei form the basis for interactive masses that create and maintain fluctuating patterns of activity over the entire spatial extent of each mass. Distant connections serve to transmit patterns from one local mass to another and back again, almost always in reciprocal pairs again subserving interaction and not merely action. These reciprocal connections form the basis for feedback loops that are the hallmark of brain structure and function. The overwhelming majority of past and contemporary studies of the brain have omitted these feedback pathways, expressing brain dynamics in terms of flow diagrams that show inferred connections as all being feedforward. But with the introduction of new mathematics and technology it has become possible to simulate the dynamics of neural masses in the brain with large sets of differential equations and to display the solutions as graphic patterns.

These findings have encouraged us to break with the "reductionist" view that the behavior of a system can be explained in terms of the properties and relationships between individual components that constitute the system. Another feature of brain function is also important in this connection: brains use chaotic dynamics in the production of behavior (Skarda and Freeman, 1987). There is a simple recipe for creating this kind of dynamic activity, and it is one that brains use. (1) Assemble together a large number of distinct elements such as molecules, neurons, or even people and allow each to transmit to and receive from many others in the group information, matter, and energy. (2) Specify that the relationship between input and output for each element be nonlinear. This means that if the input is increased in small steps from a low level to a high level, the output changes but not in direct proportion to the input. For example, in the brain if a neuron is stimulated weakly it may release currents but not action potentials, but once a certain threshold of input is reached it will fire. This sudden "jump" or change of behavioral state reflects nonlinearity, i.e., a disproportionately large increase in output for a given input. (3) Make sure that the system is "open", i.e., there is a ready supply of energy, food, blood, and a good disposal system for heat and other wastes. (4) Finally, turn up the temperature, e.g., apply heat uniformly, or infuse an excitatory chemical. Given these conditions, something interesting is likely to happen, and it is likely to be unpredictable. With some initial conditions and arrangements there will emerge new and sometimes fascinating patterns of behavior. Some may congeal and terminate the experiment; others may move, rotate, and reform periodically; but others may dissolve into ceaseless activity without discernable spatial and temporal structure that resembles "noise." This ceaseless activity is chaos.

"Chaos," in its traditional meaning, refers to complete disorder, the formless void from which all order in the universe arose. The new mathematical meaning for the term refers to activity that appears random, but is not. It is deterministic, in the sense that it can be reliably simulated by solving sets of coupled nonlinear ordinary differential equations or generated by building a system to certain specifications and putting energy into it. Chaos exists in many forms and degrees (see e.g., Crutchfield et al., 1987). It can be reproduced with high precision if the initial conditions are identical on repeated runs, but it is unpredictable if new initial conditions are used. Chaos has precisely definable qualities and has relatively small degrees of freedom, meaning that its dynamics can be described by relatively few variables and therefore dimensions or coordinate axes. Most important, it can be turned on and off virtually instantaneously as with a switch.

The physiological basis for the view that brains employ chaotic dynamics involves a hypothesis on the way in which synaptic strengths change during learning under reinforcement. Essentially, when two neurons fire together, i.e., when the action potential of the presynaptic neuron excites the postsynaptic neuron and generates an action potential, the synapse that connects them is strengthened. This is a general form of the so-called Hebb rule of synaptic learning (Hebb, 1949; Viana

Di Prisco, 1984). When many interconnected neurons within a mass of neurons fire together in pairs over repeated stimuli, the selectively co-active neurons are joined together into a network of strengthened connections. This conjoined set is called a nerve cell assembly (NCA), and we believe it is the basis for perception and learning in the nervous system. When perception takes place it is expressed in a reproducible and identifiable pattern of activity that is mediated by the NCA.

When a novel stimulus is presented under reinforcement, a new NCA forms during the first few presentations. However, the background activity state of neural activity that goes on in the absence of the new reinforced stimulus should not be patterned, because this would drive the system into an already existing pattern of activity associated with another stimulus. The kind of activity that is required in order that a new pattern can emerge must be unpatterned yet controllable. This is chaos. It is generated by the nervous system in the presence of a novel stimulus so that the neurons have activity by which the Hebb rule can operate. Thereby a novel pattern can emerge from the chaotic state, and the system is not forced into pre-existing "grooves" or patterns of activity. Chaos has been identified in many areas of the brain (Babloyantz and Destexhe, 1986; Nicolis and Tsuda, 1985; Freeman and Viana Di Prisco, 1986; Garfinkel, 1983; Skarda and Freeman, 1987) with the implication that it may provide the basis for flexibility, adaptiveness, and the trial-and-error coping that make possible the nervous system's interaction with an unpredictable and ever-changing environment.

The observation that brains employ chaos to produce behavior is important in the present discussion because phenomena that are chaotic preclude long-term predictions. Chaotic behavior emerges from the nonlinear interaction of its parts, and global behavior in the system cannot be reduced to or deduced from knowledge about the characteristics and interactions among individual components (Crutchfield et al., 1987). As we have indicated, it is not individual neurons and their activities that explain or cause behavior; it is rather the activity produced by masses of neurons that self-organize to produce new global forms of behavior. As Searle indicates, "just as we need the micro–macro distinction for any physical system, so for the same reasons we need the micro–macro distinction for the brain" (Searle, 1984).

But our agreement with Searle is predicated on an important caveat, namely, that he means the same thing we do by micro/macro descriptions. It isn't always clear that he does mean what we mean. We agree with Searle when he says that while it makes sense to say that a particular organism with its nervous system is experiencing a given stimulus, it does not make sense to say for any particular neuron in that brain that it is experiencing that stimulus (Searle, 1984). The brain, on our view, gives rise to emergent neural phenomena that are responsible for and explain behavior and that are not reducible to the features and relations of its component parts. But sometimes Searle appears to make a further claim, another kind of level distinction, that is not encompassed by the one we have discussed. This distinction is between a microlevel that includes *all* levels of neuronal processing and a macrolevel of purely mental processes. Searle says, "At the higher level of description, the intention to raise my arm causes the movement of the arm. But at the lower level of description, a series of neuron firings starts a chain of events that results in the contraction of the muscles" (Searle 1984).

There are two things to say about this claim. First, it by-passes the role played by global neural activity and conflates the global neural and mental levels. Second, although Searle argues against dualism, he seems to argue here for a level of activity that plays a causal role but is not physiological, a specifically "mental" level. This is philosophically appealing but lacks biological sense. The reason is that as physiologists we cannot make strict causal inferences from the level of neurons to that of neural mass actions (see above); *a fortiori*, we cannot impute cause and effect between the global neural and mental levels. Quite apart from the classical problems concerning causality raised by Hume, Kant, Whitehead, and others, our modern conceptions of feedback necessarily introduce ambiguity and indeterminacy. These are endlessly compounded in our efforts to comprehend distributed networks with large numbers of feedback loops. Already we can build models of brain parts that function in some of the ways that brains do. We can describe them and largely (not entirely) control them, but we cannot explain how they work (Hopfield and Tank, 1986). It appears to us likely that during the next decade or so machines will be constructed that will display useful traits heretofore restricted to biologic intelligence, and the irony will be that we will be unable to understand their processes in causal terms. The problem this raises for Searle is that where he wants a causal explanation there isn't one to be had.

4 The Reflex Model of Behavior

Our data have forced us to reject yet another foundational concept implicit in much of contemporary physiological research: the reflex doctrine. Physiologists and psychologists who work with animals often have the illusion that they control their behavior by use of reinforcement. This belief is based on the model of physiological functioning developed to explain reflex behaviors (Sherrington, 1906) and on the feedforward models that experimentalists use to explain how it is that a conditioned stimulus (CS) that is paired with an unconditioned stimulus (UCS) will elicit a conditioned response (CR) preceding the unconditioned response (UCR). The presumption is that all behavior can be expressed as a sum of responses to stimuli, a view that includes and is ultimately derived from such fundamental behaviors as the slaking of thirst, the satisfaction of hunger, and the titillation of sex.

What experimentalists have failed to note is the essential fact that in the typical experiment it is the animal that is controlling their behaviors: researchers spend, or should have spent, small fortunes on the care, feeding, and housing of their subjects; they tailor the equipment and tasks to the capabilities of the species; familiarize and train them, and then sit waiting for them to deign to stop eating, licking, grooming, or just looking around long enough for the experimenter to get in a CS for a controlled trial; all this can go on for weeks. What is lost in all this is the fact that these animals are continually producing behaviors from within by anticipating external stimuli to guide or pace their actions. These behaviors express internally generated activity of the nervous system and are not deterministic responses to stimuli.

There is a term to describe such internally generated activity. We say that this type of neural activity is "self-organizing". We see self-organizing activity in many inanimate systems around us: in the emergence of patterns of clouds in a previously clear blue sky, in the bubbles that form at the bottom of a heated pan of water, and in the formation of drops of water from a leaky faucet. In the biological sphere we see self-organized dynamics in the earliest stages of development of structure and function from the fertilized ovum on into the growing embryo. Recent findings indicate that behavior can arise from within the system by self-organized patterns of neural activity in interconnected masses of the brain, and that it is not simply the sum of conditioned or unconditioned responses to stimuli (Freeman and Skarda, 1985; Skarda and Freeman, 1987).

In the olfactory bulb, self-organized patterned activity is essential for odor recognition and discrimination, processes that cannot be explained in terms of the reflex model. Molecules of the odorant fall onto the cilia of olfactory receptor cells and, following capture, excite a small subset of receptors that are selectively sensitive to the odorant. This step is called transduction. In the next step of forward excitation the receptors send action potentials into the olfactory bulb that excite the large projection neurons known as mitral cells. Those that have been previously excited by the odorant under reinforcement, and have had their synaptic inter-connections strengthened by the learning process described earlier, preferentially excite each other. This subset of mitral cells forms a nerve cell assembly of strongly interconnected cells. In the third stage of feedback interaction the initial excitation spreads like wildfire through the assembly. Those other mitral cells that have been excited, although not under reinforcement, but that receive excitation from background odorants, excite the bulb further. Both kinds of excitation serve to increase the sensitivity of bulbar neurons to each other and therefore to increase intrabulbar crosstalk. When a critical threshold is reached the fourth step occurs. This is a state change via a self-organized dynamic process in which the entire bulb goes from chaotic activity to an internally generated burst of oscillatory activity that we can correlate with a particular odorant. This globally distributed, self-organized, stereotypical pattern of activity in the bulb is the one that we hypothesize constitutes odor recognition and memory for the rest of the system; this is the pattern that is made available to the rest of the brain and that is behaviorable relevant for the kind of relations that we usually associate with learning and memory (Skarda and Freeman, 1988).

This feature of nervous system functioning, i.e., that it creates something that did not exist before its interaction with the environment, has not gone unnoticed in the past, but before the introduction of the mathematical theory of nonlinear dynamics and computers there seemed no viable alternative explanatory framework to stimulus–response determinism in experimental brain science. Early on, Sherring-ton, who developed the synaptic basis for the concept of the reflex arc, uncovered an internally generated neural process that acted on stimulus input but was not caused by it (Sherrington, 1931). Sherrington suggested that this "central excitatory (inhibitory) state" was internally generated by a mass of neurons that then serve *actively* to coordinate and integrate reflexes that, in themselves, were produced passively by a stimulus.

But physiologists were not alone in recognizing that neural dynamics are more than reactions to external stimuli. Philosophers, too, have realized that the reflex model of physiological functioning is inadequate for explaining behavior. Dewey (1896) can be credited with probably the earliest attack on the notion. As Dewey put it, the stimulus "must already have one foot over the threshold, if it is ever to gain admittance" (Dewey, 1896), and this is provided by a internally motivated activity.

Later Merleau-Ponty (1942) argued that behavior, and hence a neural state generated from within the organism, is the first cause of all stimulation citing the very same data used to support reflex theory by Pavlov (1927) and Sherrington. Perception, on this view, begins within and is not imposed from without by the stimulus. If the opposite view based on the reflex theory dominates our thinking, this is not because we have been convinced by the data but because we interpret all the data to fit the reflex theory we have about how perception must work. At best, Merleau-Ponty suggested, the activity described by classical reflex theories is pathological:

> The reflex as it is defined in the classical conception does not represent the normal activity of the animal, but the reaction obtained from an organism when it is subjected to working as it were by means of detached parts . . . [it is] characteristic not of the fundamental activity of the living being but of the experimental apparatus which we use for studying it. (Merleau-Ponty, 1942)

Our data support Dewey's and Merleau-Ponty's positions. Only under reinforcement, i.e., only in animals who have been motivated to expect certain odorants, does receptor activity initiated by the stimulus lead to changes in the patterned activity of the bulb, the generation of a NCA, etc. In the neural system, if previous, internally generated activity has not laid the groundwork for interaction with the environment, receptor stimulation cannot and will not lead to perception and/or behavior (see also section 5).

We mention this because very often it is overlooked by contemporary philosophers interested in understanding the physiological basis of behavior (Skarda, 1986). The tendency is to adopt a reflex-based model and to generalize it for all behavior. We believe that this move is not only bad physiology; it is misleading for philosophical attempts to understand the biological basis of behavior and the mind/brain relationship (see section 5 below and Skarda, 1986). We think that Searle falls into this trap by focusing on the neurophysiological basis of behaviors that are reflex in nature, e.g., the slaking of thirst or the contraction of muscles, and then adopting this model for all brain function. If reflexes were all that were needed to produce behavior as we know it, we would not find brains generating self-organized behavior and chaos; and certainly, by focusing attention on reflex behavior Searle misses, along with many others, the most distinctive feature of brain functioning in the production of goal-directed behavior, i.e., its self-organizing, creative dynamics. We encourage philosophers and cognitive theorists to take another look at what neurophysiologists have discovered about the neuronal processes responsible for behavior, and we hope that in the future more attention will be given to the excellent work done by distinguished thinkers like Dewey and Merleau-Ponty who pointed out long ago that there is more to behaving than reacting.

5 What's in Perceptual States?

In a recent book on the philosophy of mind Searle discusses what he terms the "intentional contents" of perceptual states (Searle, 1983). He describes these contents as follows:

vis exp (that x with certain features is before me and that x is causing this
perceptual experience)

Whatever else is packed into this description, it implies that what counts as far as
perception (in this case visual perception) is concerned, i.e., the essential features of
the perceptual process, are an internal representation of the object perceived along
with its features and the causal impact that the object has on the system perceiving
it. What does neurophysiology have to say about Searle's description?

The first thing to note about Searle's description of perceptual states is that it
incorporates the reflex model discussed above in section 4. Studies of physiological
functioning, however, reveal that perceptual processing involves more interesting
processes than those described by traditional reflex-based theory and feedforward
processing have imagined. Evidence indicates that when an organism is trained to
respond to a particular odorant a self-organized process in the bulb produces a
spatially coherent activity state that can be modeled as a limit-cycle attractor. Such
attractors mathematically represent the qualitative form of behavior exhibited by a
system, in this case periodic or aperiodic (chaotic) behavior. Topologists say that the
behavior is governed by a stable attractor if the system returns to the same form of
behavior after it is perturbed and is allowed to settle. With each inhalation, after
learning and in the presence of this odorant, this more ordered state repeatedly
emerges from the chaotic background state, only to collapse back again with
exhalation. A separate spatial pattern of periodic behavior forms for each learned
odor given under reinforcement. Each has a latent coexistence in that only one at a
time can find expression or be realized and then only, as far as we have yet been able
to detect, on presentation of its odorant under reinforcement (we have not sought to
explore hallucinations). When the reinforcement contingency is changed in respect
to any one odorant, or if a new odorant is added to the repertoire under
reinforcement, all the spatial patterns undergo small changes during the process of
learning. These changes do not occur in the olfactory bulb if there is no
reinforcement or if the newly learned CS is not olfactory but visual or auditory.
These spatial patterns are manifested in the bulbar EEG and their information
content is measured by assaying the capacity of our measurements on these patterns
to classify correctly the bursts in respect to what CS was given and what CR
occurred on successive conditioning trials (Freeman, 1987).

Several features of the neural dynamics underlying perception are important to
note. First, only when the odorant is reinforced leading to formation of a CR, i.e.,
only when the animal is motivated and the stimulus input has some meaning for the
organism such that it acts on the stimulus, do odor-specific activity patterns form in
the olfactory bulb. Presentation of odorants to the receptor surface in unmotivated
subjects does not lead to any observable changes in the system. Second, the odor-
specific activity patterns are dependent on the behavioral response: changing the
reinforcement contingency changes the activity patterns previously recorded.
Finally, the internally generated odor-specific activity is context-dependent:
introducing new reinforced odorant to the animal's repertoire leads to changes in
the activity patterns of *all* previously learned odorants; in other words, adding a new
odor under reinforcement introduces not only a quantitative change in the number
of learned activity patterns, it also qualitatively alters each of the patterns previously
learned.

How do these findings bear on Searle's claims regarding perception? As mentioned above, Searle's characterization of perceptual contents implies that what is important for the system are the object with its features and the object's causal impact on the perceiving subject. He states that "[t]he story *begins* with the assault of the photons on the photoreceptor cells of the retina, the familiar rods and cones" (Searle, 1983). Our data indicate that perception begins with an internally generated neural process that, by re-afference, lays the ground for processing of future receptor input. The neural activity patterns that we find related to perception are indicative of internal states that reflect reliable forms of interaction in a context. They are sensitive not simply to the presence of an odorant, or to the response, but to both in interaction and to the context of reinforced odorants in which this behavior is embedded. For Searle, perception is something that happens to the system when it is *acted upon* by an object; for us, perception is a process that occurs only when the organism *initiates interaction with* its environment.

In review we suggest that two things are missing in Searle's description: neural interaction and internal context. With respect to the first, causal impact on the system should not be confused with interaction in our sense. As we have indicated, causal stimulation at the receptor level alone does not lead to the formation of odor-specific activity patterns in the bulb that are the basis of odor recognition and discrimination. Only when the odorant is reinforced, when it acquires behavioral significance in terms of a CR, does the internally generated pattern form. Thus, the story of perception cannot be told simply in terms of feedforward causation in which the object initiates neural changes leading to an internal perceptual state. What is missing here is recognition of the role played in perception by self-organizing neural processes and by the dense feedback among subsystems in the brain that allow the organism to initiate interaction with its environment.

Second, internal context is also part of the meaning of the activity pattern for the system: when a new odorant is added to the animal's repertoire *all* previously learned patterns undergo a change. Searle is aware that context plays a role in perception as in all intentional states. He terms this context the "Network" (Searle, 1983), and he claims that each state is embedded in this Network of other states. The problem is that nowhere *within* his description of the intentional content of perceptual states does he include a reference to this Network. For Searle, each perceptual state is located in a Network of other states, but the presence or absence of states in this Network does not effectively alter the content of any one. We have found, however, that neural dynamics are sensitive to, and hence the characterization of their content must include information on, interrelationships within a perceptual system or subsystem, because adding to this Network of perceptual states in the olfactory system leads to a change in the patterned activity of each and every odor-specific state. Thus, we support Searle's insight that perceptual states are always located in a network of states, but our evidence suggests that this network is *internal* to each state. We believe that Searle is on the right track, as usual, but the predominantly reflex-based conception of brain functioning that he has inherited from classical neuropsychology has stymied him. We suggest that brain theories couched in self-organizing nonlinear dynamics will provide the keys he and others need to solve the problem of explaining how intentionality can function with the physiochemical organism.

6　Conclusions

We are greatly encouraged by the attempts of contemporary philosophers of mind to include neuroscience in debates about the mind/body problem and the explanation of behavior. It is high time for a biologically grounded cooperative effort to understand the mind/brain, and Searle has done much to contribute to this project. We are eager to participate, for we believe that there will never be a coherent theory of the mind/brain and its role in behavior as long as philosophers ignore the brain and as long as neuroscientists shy away from the mind. We hope that our remarks on Searle's work illustrate the fruitfulness of cooperative efforts, both with constructive criticism and support based on our data. Without theories neuroscience has no way to explain its data, but without facts about how brains actually function philosophical theories tend to hang in the air. It is only taken together that theories and facts lead to insights and direct future research. We hope this is the way of the future.

REFERENCES

Amari, S. (1983) "Field theory of self-organizing neural nets," *IEEE Transactions on Systems, Man, and Cybernetics, SMC*-13, 5, pp. 741–8.

Anderson, J., Silverstein, J., Ritz, S. and Jones, R. (1977) "Distinctive features, categorical perception, and probability learning: Some applications of a neural model," *Psychological Review* 84, pp. 413–51.

Babloyantz, A. and Destexhe, A. (1986) "Low-dimensional chaos in an instance of epilepsy," *Proceedings of the National Academy of Sciences of the United States of America* 83, pp. 3513–17.

Barlow, H. (1972) "Single units and sensation: A neuron doctine for perceptual psychology?" *Perception* 1, pp. 371–94.

Churchland, P. (1986) *Neurophilosophy: Toward a Unified Science of the Mind-Brain* (MIT Press/ Bradford: Cambridge, Mass.).

Crutchfield, J., Farmer, J. Packard, N. and Shaw, R. (1987) "Chaos," *Scientific American* 256, pp. 46–57.

Dewey, J. (1896) "The reflex arc concept in psychology," *Psychological Review* 3, pp. 357–70.

Earle, D. (1987) "On the differences between cognitive and noncognitive systems," *Behavioral and Brain Sciences* 10, pp. 177–8.

Freeman, W. (1984) "Premises in neurophysiological studies of learning," in *Neurobiology of Learning and Memory*, ed. G. Lynch, J. McGaugh, and N. Weinberger (Guilford Press: New York, NY).

Freeman, W. (1987) "Analytic techniques used in the search for the physiological basis of the EEG," in *Handbook of Electroencephalography and Clinical Neurophysiology*, ed. A. Gevins and A. Remond (Elsevier: New York, NY), vol. 3A, part 2, chapter 18.

Freeman, W. and Skarda, C. (1985) "Spatial EEG patterns, nonlinear dynamics and perception: The neo-Sherringtonian view," *Brain Research Reviews* 10, pp. 147–75.

Freeman, W. and Viana Di Prisco, G. (1986) "EEG spatial pattern differences with discriminated odors manifest chaotic and limit cycle attractors in olfactory bulb of rabbits," in *Brain Theory*, ed. G. Palm (Springer Verlag Berlin).

Garfinkel, A. (1983) "A mathematics for physiology," *American Journal of Physiology* 245: *Regulatory, Integrative and Comparative Physiology* 14: R455–66.

Grossberg, S. (1981) "Adaptive resonance in development, perception, and cognition," in *Mathematical Psychology and Psychophysiology*, ed. S. Grossberg (American Mathematical Society: Providence, R.I.).

Hebb, D. (1949) *The Organization of Behavior* (Wiley: New York, NY).

Hinton, G. (1985) "Learning in parallel networks," *Byte* 10, p. 265.

Hopfield, J. (1982) "Neural networks and physical systems with emergent collective computational abilities," *Proceedings of the National Academy of Sciences of the United States of America* 79, pp. 2554–8.

Hopfield, J. and Tank, D. (1986) "Computing with neural circuits: A model," *Science* 233, pp. 625–33.

Kohonen, T. (1984) *Self-Organization and Associative Memory* (Springer Verlag: Berlin).

Merleau-Ponty, M. (1942) *La Structure du Comportement* (Presses Universitaries de France: Paris).

Nicolis, J. and Tsuda, I. (1985) "Chaotic dynamics of information processing. The 'magic number seven plus–minus two' revisited," *Bulletin of Mathematical Biology* 47, pp. 343–65.

Pavlov, I. (1927) *Conditioned Reflexes* (Oxford University Press: Oxford).

Rumelhart, D., McClelland, J. and PDP Research Group (1986) *Parallel Distributed Processing: Explorations in the Microstructures of Cognition. Vol. I: Foundations.* (MIT Press/Bradford: Cambridge, Mass.).

Searle, J. (1980) "Minds, brains, and programs," *Behavioral and Brain Sciences* 3, pp. 417–57.

Searle, J. (1983) *Intentionality* (Cambridge University Press: Cambridge).

Searle, J. (1984) *Minds, Brains, and Science* (Harvard University Press: Cambridge, Mass.).

Sherrington, C. (1906) *The Integrative Action of the Nervous System* (Yale University Press: New Haven, Conn.).

Sherrington, C. (1931) "Quantitative management of contraction in lower level coordination," Hughings Jackson Lecture of 1931, in *The Selected Writings of Sir Charles Shemington*, ed. D. Denny-Brown (P. B. Hoeber: New York, NY, 1940).

Skarda, C. (1986) "Explaining behavior: Bringing the brain back in," *Inquiry* 29, pp. 187–202.

Skarda, C. and Freeman, W. (1987) "How brains make chaos in order to make sense of the world," *Behavioral and Brain Sciences* 10, pp. 161–73.

Skarda, C. and Freeman, W. (1988) "Research of neural dynamics: Implications for models of learning and memory," in *Systems with Learning and Memory Abilities*, ed. J. Delacour and J. C. Levy (Elsevier: New York, NY).

Viana Di Prisco, G. (1984) "Hebb synaptic plasticity," *Progress in Neurobiology* 22, pp. 89–102.

Virchow, R. (1871) *Die Cellularpathologie in ihrer Begründung auf Physiologie und pathologische Gewebelehre* (A. Hirschwald: Berlin).

8

Consciousness and the Experience of Freedom

ALASTAIR HANNAY

Searle's 1984 Reith Lectures set out to show that with certain important exceptions the common-sense mentalistic view we have of ourselves (as creatures with minds whose conscious contents cause and explain our actions) is consistent with the scientific conception of nature as a whole as a physical system.[1] One expects this concern of a philosopher whose great merit has been to lay bare the conceptual structure of the mentalistic view and particularly the central role given by it to conscious mental representation. Apart from the fact that Searle's naturalist stance would call in any case for some account of the way in which mental concepts can be incorporated into a science of nature, there is the challenge of those who insist that the standing of conscious mental states in explaining actions is at best *sub judice*. Indirectly, the climate of opinion which sees in the progress of cognitive neurobiology and the computer-modelling of human intelligence the reduction of propositional-attitude theory to a convenient manner of speech inevitably throws doubt on the ultimate significance of projects such as Searle's.

It is also worth remarking that nothing in Searle's justly acclaimed accounts of speech acts and intentionality indicates that the idiom of common-sense mentalism, with its central notion of the human being as a rational, free, and conscious agent, should not be accepted as a provisional expression of some ultimate human truth, its proper version awaiting only a perspicuous conceptual analysis of the kind Searle so lucidly provides. Of course that can be explained by his project's having a mainly descriptive focus. But its having that focus could in turn be explained by the assumption that a conceptual probe of this general conceptual area puts you in closer touch with reality. Since that assumption is no longer generally shared, it should be no surprise that Searle feels called upon to show how common-sense mentalism can in general resist reduction and be seen to be, by and large, compatible with the universal physicalism he himself espouses.

Nor is it surprising that he should feel forced to concede important exceptions, or that the most significant of these, and the one Searle's discussion centers on, should be the common-sense intuition of human freedom. Given the prominence of the notions of (speech) "act" and (intention in) "action" in his main corpus, notions which prior to any revisionary metaphysics must surely be read as incorporating just that intuition, this is a point on which Searle's analysis is especially sensitive to the admonitory glare of physicalist science. If he is right in saying that the experience of one's own bodily movements occurring "as caused by" the intention-in-action that they should do so is "the foundation stone of our belief in the freedom of the will,"[2] then the fact that universal physicalism allows no originative mental efficacy to intentions suggests very strongly that the belief should be given up.

Yet, Searle's conclusion on freedom echoes that of Hume on the existence of body. It is skeptical. Just as Hume regards the belief in the existence of body as a principle we are fortunately disposed by nature to accept and "must take for granted in all our reasonings"[3] in spite of its being a notion which lacks any rational support, Searle concedes that although our well-supported conception of physical reality excludes the kind of freedom associated with common-sense mentalism, for reasons he admits he doesn't fully grasp "evolution has given us a form of experience of voluntary action where the experience of freedom . . . the experience of the feeling of alternative possibilities, is built into the very structure of conscious, voluntary, intentional human behaviour."[4]

I shall suggest in the body of this paper that there is some basis for thinking the fact that we have this form of experience to be more readily graspable than Searle allows. But before doing that it is worth picking up Searle's remark about the experience being integral to conscious intentional behavior. By letting the experience (and "conviction") of freedom be an "essential part of the experience of acting,"[5] Searle is able to claim that his analysis of intentionality in terms of the ordinary notion of freedom – the idea associated with action in the common-sense view that in the same circumstances we could have been doing something else – is in order whatever the conflict with our conception of nature as a physical system. For, if he is right, then so long as we can intuitively distinguish in ourselves a kind of behaviour that is voluntary and intentional, contrasted in our own experience with what we catch ourselves doing involuntarily and unintentionally, that is how the former behavior is bound to appear – whether it actually is or not. But Searle goes further. He also claims that we shall in fact always be able to make the distinction so long as we are able consciously to make distinctions at all. Against those who maintain that our common-sense conception may prove radically false, he says that at least it is one of which we shall never be able to free ourselves. Whatever unexpected discoveries we may make about ourselves, "we cannot discover that we do not have minds, that they do not contain conscious, subjective, intentionalistic mental states; nor could we discover that we do not at least try to engage in voluntary, free, intentional action."[6] It looks then as if in Searle's view we are condemned at least to the *experience* of freedom, and will go on, in the Humean vein, acting "on the assumption of freedom" even though "the past three hundred years of science" convince us that the assumption is wrong.[7]

With its participation in any possible human experience guaranteed, the conviction of freedom might, in other hands (say those of a transcendental bent), have been used to turn the tables on universal physical determinism, rendering it rather than common-sense mentalism-with-freedom *sub judice*. But Searle is not out to establish freedom in the required sense as an ultimate constituent of the nature of things; so neither is there any attempt to accommodate the experience of freedom at its face value in some Kantian way by postulating a legitimately moral way of regarding oneself as possessed of free will, in addition to and independently of the theoretical way of regarding oneself as a piece of the natural order. For Searle, any mind–body account which treats the mental as something apart from the physical plays into the hands of the anti-mentalists;[8] while if the mental is part of the physical and the physical is bound deterministically by causal laws, then freedom in the required sense must remain an illusion. Which is why, as his solution to the mind–body problem, Searle proposes that conscious mental states are aspects of certain physical states, namely those (as it happens) biological states which possess the causal powers necessary to produce consciousness or intentionality. Mental states are thus genuine parts of nature, just like any other biological functions, and also like all those surface qualities ("liquidity," "solidity," "warmth," "redness," etc.) which form the world of human experience.

Now to the main issue. It is in terms of an analogy with these latter that Searle elaborates his solution to the mind–body problem; and it is under the imprint of this elaboration that the form of determinism he finds "worrisome" arises. "Since all the surface features of the world are entirely caused by and realised in systems of micro-elements, the behaviour of micro-elements is sufficient to determine everything that happens. Such a 'bottom up' picture of the world allows for top-down causation (our minds, for example, can affect our bodies). But top–down causation only works because the top level is already caused by and realised in the bottom levels."[9] Thus, "the mind can only affect nature in so far as it is a part of nature . . . [but] if so, then like the rest of nature, its features are determined at the basic microlevels of physics."[10]

In the remainder of this essay I wish to question the adequacy of Searle's account of the relation of microlevels to their corresponding macrolevels. The aim is to suggest ways of relieving some of the strain Searle evidently feels in owing allegiance both to mentalism and to physical determinism. I have nothing to say here against "biological naturalism" (Searle's own label)[11] as a fruitful approach to mind–body problems. But I do think that what might plausibly be said about mind on the evidence of mental phenomena themselves could alter our ideas about the kind of thing nature is, and that if there is a sense of freedom as strongly embedded in our experiences of ourselves as agents as Searle assumes (though, as I shall note again later, that sense might weaken if we looked more closely at those experiences), then this might be a case in point.

I think one may, even without abandoning the principle of universal physical determinism, question the adequacy of the "bottom–up" picture presented by Searle. Let us briefly review his use of the picture. According to Searle, conscious mental states are both "*realised in* the structure of the brain" and "*caused by* the operations of the brain."[12] They are "realised" in the brain structure in the sense that to describe something as a conscious mental state is to describe (some aspect or part of) the structure of the brain itself, not something over and above the structure to which the structure has somehow given birth; it is just that we are describing the structure at a higher level of description than that of neurophysiology. They are "caused" by the operations of the brain in the sense that if one effects some change in the operations, a given conscious mental state, or in some cases the state of being conscious itself, will not occur. By analogy liquidity is a property of a certain molecular structure and so realized in that structure, which differs, e.g., from that in which ice is realized, and yet it is caused by the molecular behavior since, if we altered it in a certain way, we would get ice or steam as the case may be.[13] The causation here is "bottom–up" causation simply because the surface features in question correlate with differences at the microlevel.

Now let us observe that in the case of conscious mental states Searle's "bottom levels" are characterized broadly as neurophysiological, and that he is content to refer collectively to these bottom levels and those for surface features generally as the "basic microlevels" of physics.[14] But there is surely a hierarchy of levels in physics. Microphysics is concerned with sub-atomic and sub-nuclear phenomena and with the constitution and behavior of atomic particles quite generally. Its laws do not include those of the behavior of whatever specific body of matter a given particle happens to be part of. Again, sub-molecular properties are of interest to physics but not, say, to chemistry, which assumes that the molecules of any element or compound are of the same size and mass, these being the "bottom level" below which further divisions do not correlate with distinct chemical identities and so fall beneath the purview of chemical laws. Thus the level of structure which maps (relevant) surface changes may be relatively high. While it is of course true that the structures below that level continue to have a constituent role to play in so far as they sustain the structural level whose changes *are* reflected at the surface, in terms of what causes surface phenomena we may well want to say that these are not caused by the merely constituent levels in the same way, or sense, as that in which they are caused by the relatively higher structural level.

More pertinent, however, is the relation between the laws governing the behavior of a molecule, say, in some wider, mechanical or dynamical context. Take a molecule located on the rim of a wheel in motion or at the periphery of a cyclone.[15] Clearly there is a constitutive role played by the laws of microphysics, since the fact that they apply is essential to there being the context in question. But in what sense can it be said that the microphysical laws in question enter in any way into a causal explanation of the actual behavior of the molecule in its context? Is it not rather the case that, given the microstructural explanation of why the corresponding surface phenomenon is wooden or liquid, as well as the sub-atomic and sub-nuclear presuppositions of there being the relevant micro-structures, what causes *that* molecule to be behaving contextually as it does is the applicability of certain mechanical or meteorological laws? Thus liquidity, to take Searle's example, depends on there being a sub-nuclear and sub-atomic level supporting the molecular structure specific to that surface property. Of course if you remove the bottom level here you remove the structure, and this might seem to justify talking of the latter as an effect of the former, and conversely of the former as a cause of the latter. But it is not *the* cause of the latter in the sense of causing the structure specific to liquidity as opposed to, say, ice or steam. And it is, as Searle says, the fact that you are able to produce some specific modification of the surface when you alter the microstructure that makes the relation between the two "clearly causal."[16] However, once you specify a context in which the surface quality occurs, whether a bucket of water, moisture in a cloud, a drop about to enter the ocean, or an eddy in a stream, another level of causal influence comes into play. Take the behavior of a molecule in an eddy.[17] Here the context is in the first place that of a *body* of fluid, and that already means that the molecule is subject to forces other than those affecting, say, liquid particles. But in addition we have to reckon with the forces specific to movement of bodies of water at certain velocities and in given topographical circumstances. Thus it seems undeniable that the behavior of any actual molecule is largely determined by a complex of systemic influences from above.

If this is indeed a form of "top–down" causation, what are the consequences for Searle's use of the microstructure–surface analogy to throw light on the relation of neural microlevels to conscious mental states? Take the first question. Let us remind ourselves that in an obvious sense top–down causation is readily admitted on Searle's account. Intentions in action genuinely cause their conditions of satisfaction and if my intention is to "release . . . the neurotransmitter acetylcholine at the axon end-plates of my motorneurons," I can do that simply by deciding to raise my arm and doing so.[18] But this is causation "over a passage of time" and the problem of freedom arises because we seem to have to say that the decision itself and the intention in action are predetermined by the microlevels that support them. What the above suggestions amount to is the view that the latter relation is not as comprehensively bottom–up as Searle assumes. Still, whatever is not bottom–up but top–down about it is not so by being the converse of the causal relation Searle refers to as "bottom–up." The contextual influences do not affect the micro-structure by altering some surface property in a way analogous to that in which microstructural change may be said to cause alteration in surface features. These micro–macro correlations remain intact, as do whatever reasons there may (or may not)[19] be for taking the dependence to go in only one direction. What any laws which stated these influences would enable us to do is predict when and where, and with what contextual consequences, a given token of a molecular type with its sur-face correlate will occur. Then, to the second question, the parallel in the neural case would be that whatever the contextual influences at work at the surface here, it is they that govern the placement in time and space of a given neural event together with its conscious correlate.

At first glance this may not look promising. So many conscious states – for example thirst, drowsiness, or pain – seem too irremediably bottom–up for this even to enter consideration. But this misses the point. What the laws of a dynamics of conscious mental states would systematically state are the behavioral dispositions of brain cells contexted in some analogue of, say, a body of water subject in turn to the kind of factors that take account of eddies, rapids, undercurrents, sluicing, pollution, or any other relevant "vicissitudes" of the transport of a given body of water. Indeed the case of water transport could prove a particularly apt analogy. The mental surface forms a "stream" (of consciousness) whose "course" and to a considerable degree "contents" are fixed not just by a sustaining infrastructure but by an unfolding environmental topography. According to this picture, all surface-preserving bottom–up relations are maintained, but the microstructural levels relevant for sustaining the surface properties in question (the succession of con-scious mental states) are subject to forces which apply only because there are indeed these surface features. That is, for instance, the biochemical conditions of thirst acquire a new set of determinants, and acquire dispositions correspondingly, by going into a "body" of conscious states which are subject in turn to factors analogous to those brought to bear on a body of fluid by a given topography. Certainly, thirst, drowsiness, and pain are "due to" their underlying chemical and neural origins, but particular activations of their chemistry and neurophysiology, even in the case of such clearly physically dependent mental states as these, are typically owing to whatever forces and factors apply at the level of a putative mental dynamics (plans, projects, decisions, prevailing prejudices, susceptibilities, to mention just a small selection out of any plausibly adequate list).

What this shows is that it is by no means an implication of universal physical determinism that Searle's higher-level facts are "entirely causally explicable in terms of and entirely realised in systems of elements at the fundamental micro-physical level."[20] Since, when applied to psychological facts, it is this claim that constitutes the king of determinism Searle finds disturbing, a top–down structure of the kind outlined would alleviate at least some of his concern. Not only that, we can see how, even under universal physical determinism, some kind of feeling of freedom might come about, as the following argument shows. First, the experience of freedom is one of the psychological facts in question; indeed, if Searle is right about the kind of hold it has on us, it is a particularly pervasive such fact. But then, second, such higher-level facts are those to which the major determinants of the actual motions at the microlevel belong. Since, third, the forces at work here are not ones which work *upon* the surface phenomena and their underlying micro-structures, but are forces that apply to the micro–macro linkages by virtue of the higher-level phenomena the microstructures underlie, the laws of a mental mechanics are statements of dispositions (of attraction and repulsion) of the phenomena themselves. Consequently, fourth, one might well suppose there to be some general feeling of being "where the action is" simply by virtue of belonging *qua* conscious being to the level where the major determinants of the actual motions of contexted molecules exert their influence. But, fifth, since we can assume an evolutionarily established bias in favor of surface-level behavior corresponding to the "conditions of satisfaction" of felt forces of the particular kinds we experience as desire and self-interest, our experience of conscious intentional behavior might reasonably be expected to bring with it some sense of freedom. In the conditions postulated there would of course still be no freedom of the kind expressed by saying "I might in the same circumstances have been doing something else." And indeed the feeling itself might not be a sense of a freedom of that particular kind. But at least we have the beginnings of an explanation of the origin of the sense of freedom in something which might nevertheless genuinely deserve that name.

As indeed another of Searle's formulations of the requirement of freedom suggests. The freedom science excludes is, in this not unfamiliar version, "that the human mind [should] force . . . statistically determined particles to swerve from their paths."[21] Provided the paths are determined only at the microlevel, and the human mind can be regarded as a higher-level system capable of providing supple-mentary determinants of the larger-scale movements of particles, that is just the possibility envisaged. Remember that at the lowest levels, e.g. that of the structures necessary simply to keep my neurons in place in my brain, the specific movements of the particles are irrelevant as far as surface distinctions are concerned; while the swerves that come and go at the junctions between them when particular experiences occur are part of a higher-level system, and according to our hypothesis it is to the determinants of these that their occurrences are subject.

But if we can explain at least some of the sense of freedom we have in experiencing the conditions of satisfaction of our intentions as being caused by the latter, can't we do even better by simply, and without fear of serious opposition, refusing to accept that there is anything like a mental dynamics; i.e. any strict laws of the behavioral dispositions of human beings stated in terms of their conscious states?

A variety of fairly compelling reasons have been offered for the view that mental events are not predictable on the basis of deterministic laws. If the conclusion is accepted, then the hierarchical account adumbrated above, with the higher-level factors responsible for a significant amount of the causal ancestry of events going on in organisms (though also perhaps machines) advanced enough to have structures contextualized at that level, will have significant consequences. For one thing, events outside such organisms but due intentionally or otherwise to their behavior will be amenable to at least partial explanation in terms of such factors. Thus large parts of the world will escape strict determination.

For whatever reasons the very idea of a mental dynamics is rejected (typically that descriptions of mental events do not, e.g. because of internal relations with other such events, fulfill the formal requirements of statements of strict scientific laws), it has been possible to avoid this particular consequence because it has been assumed that identity or strict correlation with the underlying physiology ensures for conscious mental events a place in the world of strict determination. But on the view of hierarchically structured levels of determination outlined here, that assumption is false. And there are fairly persuasive reasons for supposing that it is. The more the search for the principles of a scientific psychology departs from the surface-level, and the greater the trust in a psychology which is ideally indifferent to the surface, i.e. to consciousness,[22] the more mysterious becomes the fact that conscious mental states exist at all. The fact of consciousness, however we describe it and whatever heterogeneity the concept reveals under analysis,[23] cries out for an account of the functions which have given conscious beings a reproductive advantage. Even those who argue that a computer program can duplicate all the control powers of the human brain must concede that. For that argument merely says that the control has been achieved without consciousness,[24] and we are left wondering why nature bothered with conscious mental states when it could have done as well without. Of course the mistake of those who claim we can remain indifferent to consciousness is not that it is not the levels below the surface that should be the concern of psychology, for the topics of psychology begin just as far down as microstructural distinctions correspond to relevant observational phenomena at the surface, and not all psychology need relate to what is conscious in a conscious mental state. The error is to suppose that no explanatory principles are discoverable at the conscious level, while it would be precisely in accordance with evolutionary principles to assume that the acquisition by a physical system of a higher-order property such as consciousness implies some structural modification which leads you to look there for the principles of the consequent improved adaptational performance.

But what if the behavioral dispositions of human beings cannot be stated in terms of strict laws referring to their conscious states? If it is wrong to explain the efficaciousness of mental states at levels *lower* than those which currently give the organism its best overall lead, and the latter are not subject to strict laws, then we are left with a psychology that is no longer a true science; and because we still want to talk of "determinants" at the higher level, we are also left with the notion of a form of efficaciousness, or let us just say causation, which does not conform to the principle that events related as cause and effect fall under strict deterministic laws.

Many will think these are unpalatable consequences. It is one thing to allow that science can be content with rough generalizations until surface regularities are mapped onto an original matrix of strict determination; but it is quite another to accept that nature itself projects beyond any such matrix, so that some not completely reliable surface regularities turn out to be *intrinsically* unreliable.

On the other hand, if the surface regularities in the case of conscious human behavior do prove intrinsically unreliable, or reliable perhaps only in the guise of banal truisms, it is surely more constructive, as far as an investigation into the nature of *these* phenomena is concerned, to ask ourselves just what sort of unpredictability might genuinely be being manifested here, rather than to appeal unquestioningly to a lower level of operations which gives the appearance of being comfortingly continuous with established physical science. Of course, if the hierarchical model outlined above can be defended, this appearance will in any case be illusory. The behavior in a conscious organism of particular microstructures and their elements, e.g. the position in space of its neurons and the timing of firings at its synapses, will be largely determined by factors that come into play only because the structures and their elements have acquired systemic properties at the suspect higher level. The only way to generate any continuity with established physical science in that case will be to make the theoretical innovations necessary for the possibility of physical systems' acquiring systemic properties of the kind in question. Which means, for instance, that if biochemistry views itself as a potential behavioral science, it will have to add intentionality to its stock-in-trade.

What then should we make of what is almost universally agreed to be the inherent unreliability of psychological generalizations? There are a number of possibilities. One is to postulate libertarian freedom. But that would be precipitate. Among other objections, it would be contrary to evolutionary principles. One can admit the emergence of new kinds of control, consistent with properties of high-order brain activity, but not the idea that at a certain stage in development the system as a whole begins to dispose freely over its own control possibilities in a way which implies that in exercising this capacity there is no control over which it does not dispose. Some might prefer to explain the sense of this kind of freedom as due to the factors determining a person's actions becoming so complex that the conscious agent actually *loses* control. If we consider the effect of gravitational change and vicissitudes of weather on the movements of particles in bodies of water, we can imagine how a similar width and depth in the range of determinants of human behavior might leave the conscious agent quite in the dark not only as to what pressures are at work but even as to whether, when we act in the quite normal way that gives as the sense that given the same pressures we might have done otherwise, our "choice" is nevertheless determined.

That would give a negative interpretation of the claim that our conception of freedom is "essentially tied to consciousness."[25] It would tend to show that the level of conscious states is not the one which gives the human organism its overall lead. Consciousness would be, as it is for Dennett, merely a matter of being informed or *mis*informed about "what is actually happening."[26] In saying that freedom is essentially tied to consciousness I suspect Searle has something more positive in mind. Perhaps like many of us he would like to show that free conscious agency is a particularly central kind of determinant of human behavior. The most he can claim, however, is that our *conviction* of freedom is inescapable because conscious agency can give us no phenomenological evidence for an alternative theory.[27] I think the latter claim is at least debatable, and that closer attention to the phenomenology of our own actions might well provide evidence for an alternative theory. There seems no *a priori* reason why the distinction we make in consciousness in marking off an event as due to the special kind of engagement on our part that makes us regard it as an action of ours cannot be *experienced* in some other way than as libertarian freedom. For example, might not the sense we have of an action's being ours be equally well described in terms of some conscious effort, say, to improve on or compensate for past below-par performance? There need be no implication of a past misuse of a capacity for free choice. The experience might be describable simply in terms of the sense of being presently controlled by higher-level determinants which promise an improved performance, determinants to which special significance may be attached in terms of a feeling of personal identity. But whatever scope there may be for alternative descriptions at the phenomenological level, one advantage of the hierarchical view outlined here is that it at least encourages us to seek ways of combining our intuition of freedom with a conception of consciousness which predisposes us to think of it as having some significant directive function. So that if there is indeed an essential link between our sense of freedom and consciousness, we might then conceive it in a way which ties the former to the genuine determination of behavior from the start.

In conclusion I would like to mention an application of the top–down view in a related area: the capacity to recognize grammatical structure. In evolutionary terms it is natural to think of this as an acquired trait which builds upon earlier capacities, such as the ability to use symbols or signs, by superseding them, while these in turn will have built upon and superseded such lower-grade abilities as the ability to distinguish aspects of the visible environment. According to one current approach to higher-level ability, what the cognitive scientist should look for is an analytically structured system, supported by whatever hardware is required for the sustaining of allegedly elemental or "atomic" subcapacities out of which exercises of the more complex abilities are constituted.[28] But if the psychophysical organism is something whose evolution consists in the acquisition of new superstructural levels which actually take over control from the previous top levels, such a procedure is seriously misguided. The elemental operations will belong to the distant past and the analysis will miss the level of complexity at which the hardware currently supports top-level performance. Of course, hardware accounts at levels below the current top will be relevant in cases of impairment of such performance, but in general it will be a mistake to take the analytical parts of some current complex performance such as the recognition of grammatical structure to correspond to real hardware subcapacities working in concert to produce that performance.

The mistake can be repeated at the surface-level. Ever since I first heard John Searle lecture on intentionality, in Oslo in 1972, I have been uneasy about his willingness to describe his project as that of explaining how intentionality is "imposed" on items that are not ("intrinsically") intentional.[29] That sounds as though some special, second-tier capacity of bestowing meaning were exercised upon things already identified by virtue of a first-tier capacity, e.g. imposing syntax or phonology on sequences of marks or sounds. Now we know of course that Searle's account of intentionality is not a causal one; for all his naturalism he is not trying to explain what *biological* complexities could account for the fact that certain physical things have (or are) representational mental states. The focus of the investigation is linguistic. Beginning with the idea of sentences as, in his own words,[30] "considered in one way" merely things in the world, he proceeds by way of speech acts and their representational ingredient to a concept of mental activity which exploits the readily accessible logic of that ingredient, thus arriving at a concept of mind which introduces nothing with which our general ability to use language has not already made us familiar. There is no reliance here at all on the belief that the exercise of this ability involves anything like the imposition of a semantic operation on a syntactic one, or that sentences-in-use really are to be considered in that two-(or more)-tiered way. Any more than Wittgenstein would expect us to answer his question about raising my arm by saying that what is left over when I subtract the fact that my arm went up is something that I add to the fact that it is going up in any case. It just isn't going up in any case, nor, except in extremely articificial circumstances, does our semantic capacity superimpose itself on the prior deliverances of some alleged subcapacity. There are no such prior deliverances. The terminology of "imposition" is misleading because it suggests that the mind "endows" utterances with meaning. But whatever is recognized as an utterance already manifests at least some meaning, even if it may not be the utterer's. Why not conclude that utterances are intrinsically intentional? And why not say the same of sentences-in-use? And, provided we are still considering things in *this* and not Searle's way, why not conclude from the fact that the conditions which have to be satisfied for direct identification of something's being a sentence at all, even just one that *might* be used to make a statement or ask a question, include its having some content or other, that intrinsic intentionality is a feature of sentences in general? Of course, we do find it convenient at a certain level of discourse to discuss aspects of language independently of the context of use or direct identification. But we mustn't take a homonym such as "sentence" generated at that level to be a name of some *thing* we can theoretically subtract from actual linguistic performance, then to ask what needs to be added to the sentence to make the performance possible.

It is because I think Searle would probably agree that there is this other way of considering sentences that I feel he might welcome my suggestions for narrowing the gap between the feeling and the fact of freedom. For this really only calls for a further application of the same argument. One sees how descriptions of low-level functions which ignore their incorporation in higher-level organizations produce the illusion of some independent microlevel process needing a mysterious mentalistic addition to make the whole into a full-fledged intentional state, and which masquerades as a "bottom level" determinant of whatever intentional state is realized in it. Searle has already admitted that higher functional levels than that of "the specific biochemistry of the neurons involved" might conceivably be relevant for the realization of intentional states in the brain.[31] It only remains for him to allow that the levels in question can be subject to determinants which apply only to the intentional level which they "realize", so that in realizing it they become subject to that new level of description.

NOTES

1 John Searle, *Minds, Brains and Science* (Harvard University Press: Cambridge, Mass., 1984), p. 99.

2 Ibid., p. 95.
3 David Hume, *A Treatise on Human Nature*, intro. A. D. Lindsay (Dent/Everyman's Library: London, 1977), pp. 182–3.
4 Searle, *Minds, Brains and Science*, p. 98.
5 Ibid., pp. 97 and 96.
6 Ibid., p. 99.
7 Ibid., pp. 97 and 98.
8 John R. Searle, *Intentionality: An Essay in the Philosophy of Mind* (Cambridge University Press: 1983), p. 262.
9 Searle, *Minds, Brains and Science*, p. 94.
10 Ibid., p. 93. Searle distinguishes this form of determinism from "psychological determinism," the "probably just false" view that all our actions are necessitated by our mental states (ibid., p. 94).
11 Searle, *Intentionality*, p. 264.
12 Ibid., p. 265, original emphasis.
13 Ibid., pp. 265–6.
14 Searle, *Minds, Brains and Science*, p. 93.
15 The wheel example is used by Sperry (see R. W. Sperry, "An Objective Approach to Subjective Experience," *Psychological Review* 77 (1970), p. 589) to illustrate how "the component parts of . . . an excitatory neural process are carried along and thus controlled by the dynamic properties of the whole system." See Charles Ripley, "Sperry's Concept of Consciousness," *Inquiry* 27 (1984), pp. 407–8.
16 Searle, *Intentionality*, p. 265.
17 My comments here owe much to Ripley's excellent reconstruction of Sperry's position as an "emergentist materialism" (see Ripley, "Sperry's Concept," pp. 415ff).
18 Searle, *Minds, Brains and Science*, p. 93.
19 I'm not at all clear as to why Searle takes the relevant micro-to-macrolevel relation to be unidirectional.
20 Ibid., p. 98.
21 Ibid., p. 87.
22 See K. V. Wilkes, "Is Consciousness Important?" *The British Journal for the Philosophy of Science* 35 (1984), p. 239.
23 See Patricia Smith Churchland, "Consciousness: The Transmutation of a Concept," *The Pacific Philosophical Quarterly* 64 (1983), pp. 82, 86, and 92.
24 As Searle himself pointed out in an exchange with Dennett in The *New York Review of Books* following Searle's May 1982 review of Hofstadter and Dennett's *The Mind's I* (Basic Books: New York, NY, 1981).
25 Searle, *Minds, Brains and Science*, p. 94.
26 See Daniel C. Dennett, "How to Study Human Consciousness Empirically or Nothing Comes to Mind," *Synthese* 53 (1982), p. 179.
27 Searle, *Minds, Brains and Science*, p. 97.
28 Robert Cummins, *The Nature of Psychological Explanation*, (The MIT Press/Bradford Books: Cambridge, Mass./London, 1983), defends such an analytical mode of psychological explanation.
29 Searle, *Intentionality*, p. viii.
30 Ibid., p. vii.
31 Ibid., p. 272.

9

Response:
The Mind–Body Problem

JOHN R. SEARLE

I believe that the key to solving the mind–body problem is to reject the system of Cartesian categories in which it has traditionally been posed. And the first step in that rejection is to see that "mental," naively construed, does not imply "non-physical" and "physical" does not imply "non-mental." Once you get rid of the traditional oppositions, it is not a very big step to see that the so-called "mental" properties are both caused by the behavior of lower level elements in the brain and at the same time just are higher level features of the entire brain system (and perhaps the rest of the central nervous system). So on this view, which seems to me a kind of common-sense view, mental processes are caused by "objective" micro-processes in the brain but are at the same time "subjective" macro-level features of the brain.

Consider, for example, consciousness. My present state of consciousness with all its subjectivity, intentionality, causal powers, phenomenology, "qualia", and the rest of it, is just a feature or set of features of my brain. And it is caused by the behavior of lower level elements of my brain in the same unmysterious sense of "cause" that the solidity of this table with all of its features is caused by the behavior at the lower level of molecules and at the same time the solidity is just a higher level feature or set of features of the entire system that is composed of those molecules. This view is not dualism, because it does not say there are two kinds of substances and properties – rather there are lots of kinds. *A fortiori*, it is not monism because it emphasizes the variety in which the world comes. But I must emphasize that it is not materialism, as that view is traditionally understood, since it does not deny that mental features exist, whereas "materialism" has usually been defined in terms of the denial of naive mentalism. The traditional dualist asked how many basic ontological categories are there and counted up to two, the monist got as far as one, I am suggesting that we should reject the question altogether. The real mistake was to start counting at all. Let us make our ontological categories fit the facts as we discover them and not try to prejudge the issues in advance. As far as we know there are lots of different ontological categories, ranging all the way from quarks to superbowl victories, from gravitational fields to balance-of-payments problems. Just to have a name, and to have a name that is totally different from the traditional jargon, I call my view of mind-brain relations "biological naturalism."

Alan Code

I am not sure how far back in history views such as mine go. I have been told that various nineteenth-century philosophers and psychologists held similar views, and some people have even told me that my view is like Aristotle's. I am not competent to discuss the scholarly questions of how to interpret Aristotle's texts on this issue, but Alan Code certainly is. His short but lucid article makes a clear distinction between Aristotle's position, my own position, which is similar to but not identical with Aristotle's, and functionalism, which is quite distinct from both. To his account, I have only one small objection, though it may in the end turn out to be serious. He says "Aristotle's soul, like Searle's mind, is a physical property." That is certainly correct, but that has the consequence that the physical destruction of the brain will destroy the mind with it. For that reason the prospects of immortality, depressingly, do not appear at all promising. My impression is that Aristotle thought that the immortality of *nous* was at least a possibility, and if so, this marks a major difference between my view and his.

Walter Freeman and Christine Skarda

Once you accept something like my view of the mind–body relation, then the question of how exactly mental processes are caused by the underlying neurophysiological processes and how exactly they are realized in the brain becomes a problem more for empirical research in neuroscience than for philosophical analysis. When I wrote my account of the mind–body problem I used the standard textbook accounts of the neuron as the basic functional unit of the brain in order to show how mental processes *could* be both caused by and realized in the brain, rather than to show how they in fact *are*. I take it that even at the present time we do not know how they are in fact. Now, one of the most exciting features of the account given by Freeman and Skarda is that they depart from the traditional neurobiological account of brain functioning. They are anxious to emphasize that their research on the olfactory bulb in rabbits tends to support the view that the traditional account is incorrect. Specifically, they reject "the neuron doctrine"; like me they reject traditional information processing models, and they reject most, but not all, of the current PDP models. Instead, they emphasize that the functional units in the brain consist of large masses of neurons and that the behavior of these masses "cannot simply be explained in terms of the properties and relationships between the individual components that constitute the system." They emphasize, furthermore, that the brain uses chaotic dynamics (in the technical sense of "chaos") in the production of intelligent behavior and that the brain is a self-organizing system.

I find this work very exciting and suggestive, and I can only hope that this publication will have the result that more philosophers will find out about it. I also welcome the suggestion that we should think of perception more as a series of interactions between the environment and the agent, rather than just as a matter of the impact of the environment on the agent. In a sense they are expanding on the idea, familiar both in philosophy and psychology, that you perceive what you are ready to perceive, and the readiness to perceive is a function of your internal context, and not simply a matter of environmental impacts on a passive nervous system.

Is there any disagreement between us? To a certain extent the apparent disagreement is a matter of misunderstanding. I will discuss their views on four topics: the neuron doctrine, the reflex model, perception, and most importantly, the mind–body problem. My main objection to their views will be that it does not seem to me they take anti-Cartesianism seriously enough.

They are mistaken in supposing that I hold what they call "the reflex model" of the behavior of the mind–brain. My conception of the holistic nature of the operation of Intentional states would preclude a mechanical reflex conception at the level of Intentionality, whether conscious or unconscious. As far as the details of brain operation at the neurophysiological levels is concerned I have no original ideas at all; but it is a consequence of my views on the mind–body problem that it would be miraculous if the holistic structure of the mental were realized in neurophysiological systems in a way which did not at all reflect this holism. So, though I do not advance theories in neurobiology, my account of the Intentional, if correct, would make it exceedingly unlikely that the reflex arc is the correct model for all or most brain functioning.

In connection with this they ask whether my use of the distinction between macro and microlevels is supposed to be the same as the distinction between mental and neurophysiological levels. The answer is no. There are lots of different levels of description within both neurophysiology and Intentionality, and there will, of course, be higher levels of description of the neurophysiology which are not mental levels. Furthermore, it seems most unlikely that mental properties could be realized at such low levels as that of the individual neuron or synapse. The familiar arguments against the possibility of a "grandmother neuron" are sufficient to establish this, and such a view is by no means original with me.

Similar remarks apply to the neuron doctrine. My views about Intentionality and the mind–body problem do not commit me to any particular theory about how the brain works at the neurophysiological levels, but my views, if true, would make it seem most unlikely that the only appropriate level for discussing how the brain produces cognition were that of the individual neuron. In any case nothing I say is inconsistent with their hypothesis that the appropriate explanatory level for cognition is that of "masses of neurons."

About perception they object to my account by claiming that "the Network (of Intentionality) is internal to each (perceptual) state." But on my view each perceptual experience only determines its conditions of satisfaction, and thus is only intelligible to the agent, given its *relations* to the Network and the Background. So, in my view, though it is not the Network as such which is internal to the state, it is indeed the relations to the Network which are internal, and in that sense I do not think there is a genuine disagreement between us, only a difference in terminology. Partly the appearance of disagreement derives from the fact that we are answering two different questions. Their claim that perception is a matter of *interactions* between the organism and the environment is an answer to a neurophysiological question. My claim that perception has a particular sort of *Intentional content* which gives the organism information about the environment is an answer to a philosophical question about the analysis of Intentionality. There is no inconsistency between these two views.

My main objection to their account concerns the following passage: "although Searle argues against dualism, he seems to argue here for a level of activity that

plays a causal role but is not physiological, a specifically mental level. This is philosophically appealing, but lacks biological sense. The reason is that as physiologists
we cannot make strict causal inferences from the level of neurons to that of neural
mass actions . . . *a fortiori*, we cannot impute cause and effect between the global
neural and mental levels."

It is precisely in this passage that it seems to me they do not take their anti-
Cartesianism seriously enough. When they say that to speak of causal powers of
Intentionality, of a specifically mental level, "lacks biological sense," it seems to me
they are making the Cartesian assumption that the mental level is not part of the
neurophysiology. I, on the other hand, am suggesting that it is a part of the neurophysiology and that only our acceptance of the traditional Cartesian categories has
blinded us to this fact. I am suggesting, what I think is perhaps a radical view, that
the real subjective conscious mental level is as much a part of the neurophysiology
of our system as are serotonin and Purkinje cells. Furthermore, from the fact that
we "cannot make strict causal inferences from one level to the next," it does not
follow that "we cannot impute cause and effect relations between the global neural
and mental levels." The absence of strict laws which would enable us to make strict
causal inferences does not show that there are no causal relations. I think that the
role of strict causal laws is vastly overestimated and generally misunderstood in
philosophy and science, but for this discussion it is sufficient to point out the following: The absence of strict laws does not imply the absence of causation. Phenomena
ranging all the way from hurricanes to social revolutions in all likelihood cannot be
explained in terms of strict laws, *under any description* and *at any level.* But that does
not imply that such events are not caused. They clearly are. Now, similarly with the
mental and the neurophysiological: mental states, such as my present state of consciousness, are caused by a series of neurophysiological events in my brain; and this
fact is perfectly consistent with the claim that there are no strict laws under any
descriptions correlating the former with the latter. The absence of even the possibility of strict inference does not show the absence of causation.

At bottom I believe the biggest differences between my views and theirs concern
the role of consciousness and the nature of causation. On my view, strict laws play a
very small role in our use of the notion of causation; and the causal powers of consciousness, by which I mean the causal powers of the *neurophysiological* states of
consciousness, are crucial in accounting for human and animal behavior. My biggest disappointment with their paper is the absence in it of any serious discussion of
consciousness.

The two topics of consciousness and causation lead us directly into a discussion
of Hannay's paper.

Alastair Hannay

On my view of the mind–body relation, consciousness is of central importance.
Indeed, if Descartes had not already corrupted the sentence to mean something
quite false, we might say that consciousness is the essence of the mental. I am convinced that we have only just begun to investigate consciousness in philosophy,
psychology, and neurobiology, but even a superficial investigation, or so I claim,
reveals that the conscious experiences of voluntary action give us the impression of

freedom. In such cases we have the experience of acting in one way as opposed to other ways, in which we sense we could have acted. To me the interesting puzzle about free will is how to reconcile those experiences with such facts as we know about the causation of our behavior. It is a general characteristic of the mode of explanation that we have come to accept in the sciences since the seventeenth century, that features of larger systems can be explained in terms of the features and behavior of the micro-elements of which the systems are composed. Of course, in these different levels of explanation it is crucial to be clear about which levels are to be explained and which are to do the explaining. The economic behavior of a dollar bill, for example, cannot be explained in terms of the cellulose fibres and the ink molecules that constitute the dollar bill, but it can be explained in terms of the attitudes and behavior of those who use it.

Hannay, in his subtle article, challenges my account of the relationship between consciousness and freedom of the will, and between the micro- and macrolevels. He relies on examples of the sort used by Sperry in which he showed that within physical systems there can be top–down causation as well as bottom–up causation. Hannay points out, correctly in my view, that within any physical system such as the brain, there are all sorts of different levels of description which are causally real and all sorts of complicated causal relations between them. Hannay thinks that the following sort of example counts against me. Sperry points out that a molecule in a wheel which is rolling downhill will have its behavior determined by the behavior of the wheel even though the wheel is the higher-level phenomenon and the molecule is a lower-level phenomenon. Hannay feels that if we fully appreciate the relationships exemplified by such examples we will come to have a different conception of the problem of free will than the one that I have.

At this point, I fear, I have lost the thread of his argument. Of course, I quite agree that there are lots of different levels and at any given point we can describe the causal impact of the higher on the lower levels as the example of the wheel rolling down the hill illustrates. However, as he concedes, that form of explanation already presupposes that the wheel is a solid and rigid body, and the solidity and rigidity of the wheel have to be explained by the bottom–up causal powers of its molecular structure. So it seems to me that Hannay's very example preserves the primacy of bottom–up forms of causal explanation. In real life, as he points out, we have no hope of explaining economics, say, in terms of molecules; but that was not really the point at issue. The point at issue is whether or not we can give empirical content to the idea of human freedom in a world in which the primary forms of causation work from the micro- to the macrolevels and go in the opposite direction only, and to the extent that, there is a micro-realization of the macrolevel causal phenomena in question.

Now, I am confident that in our entire philosophical tradition we are making some fundamental mistake, or a set of fundamental mistakes in the whole discussion of the free will problem. And I feel also sure that part of the mistake derives from a confusion about the nature of causation, because many of us still mistakenly think that there is some essential connection between the occurrence of a causal relation and the existence of some strict laws which the causal relation instantiates under some description. But I do not see how Hannay's discussion of the complexity of the causal relations among levels of explanation gets us out of our quandary.

One last comment about Hannay's article is in order, because it reveals a misunderstanding of my position which is probably my fault. When I say that the mind imposes Intentionality on entities that are not intrinsically Intentional to start with, I do not mean that speech acts lack intrinsic Intentionality, nor do I mean that we, so to speak, find a lot of sentences just lying around and impose Intentionality on them. On my account, the intention-in-action with which a speech act is performed is partly constitutive of the speech act and is, of course, intrinsically Intentional. The point that I am making is rather that part of the intention that one has in the performance of the speech act is that the sounds that one utters, or the marks one makes on paper, should have Intentionality. The speaker's meaning is a matter of his or her intentions, and the intention in question is in large part a matter of imposing conditions of satisfaction onto utterances. At one level of description, therefore, the speech act is indeed intrinsically Intentional. When we describe it, for example, as a statement or as an order we are describing it in a way which identifies its Intentionality. But if you then decompose the statement into its elements you will find that within its internal structure there is a distinction between the sounds or marks and the meaning or Intentionality with which those sounds and marks are produced. The act of imposing Intentionality is intrinsically Intentional, but the objects, such as sounds or marks, on which the Intentionality is then imposed are not themselves intrinsically Intentional.[1]

NOTE

1   I had hoped that that point was clear in my earlier writings but I now think it is not, since the same misunderstanding is also to be found in an important article by David Rosenthal in "Intentionality," Midwest Studies in Philosophy, vol. 10 (Univesity of Minnesota Press: Minneapolis, Minn., 1986), pp. 151–83.

Part III

Perception and the Satisfaction of Intentionality

10

Intentionality, Perception, and Causality: Reflections on John Searle's *Intentionality*

D. M. Armstrong

John Searle's book, *Intentionality* (1983), seems to me to be a major contemporary contribution to the philosophy of mind. It goes without saying, so I will say it, that I accept his completely naturalistic approach. But what I particularly admire is the way that, while well aware of other work going on in the field, he is always thinking for himself. Furthermore, that thinking is distinguished by a powerful common sense, the "robust sense of reality" of which Russell spoke. The result of this, among other things, is a number of refreshing and useful challenges to some contemporary orthodoxies and fashions.

In the first section of this paper, I shall be concerned with some of the things that Searle says about Intentionality in the first chapter of his book, bringing in his theory of the "Background" in chapter 5, and his remarks on the relation of Intentionality to the brain in chapter 10. The second part of the paper deals with his theory of perception, as set out in chapter 2, together with some mention of his views on causality as expounded in chapter 4.

1 Intentionality

For Searle, mental states in general, although not all mental states, have Intentionality in the classic sense of being directed upon objects and states of affairs, but where these objects and states of affairs need not exist. Intentionality is a genuine and intrinsic feature of these states, not a mere reflection of an "intentional stance" that we take up (!) to the states. The Intentionality of language, on the other hand, is no more than a non-intrinsic and derived Intentionality, derived from the intrinsic and underived Intentionality of the mental. Most of us will applaud these three doctrines.

Searle has much to say, much of it very illuminating, though I will not be going into it, about the nature of Intentionality. But he says that his explanation of this nature: "Is not a logical analysis in the sense of giving necessary and sufficient con-

ditions in terms of simpler notions" (p. 26). Again, on the same page: "Intentionality is, so to speak, a ground floor property of the mind, not a logically complex
feature built up by combining simpler elements." Yet again: "Any explanation of
Intentionality . . . takes place within the circle of Intentional concepts."

Intentionality, then, is a logically irreducible property according to Searle. But
does Searle think that Intentionality is *ontologically* irreducible? It is no part of the
logical analysis of the notion of heat that it is (reduces to) motion of molecules. But
heat is (is identical with, reduces to) motion of molecules for all that. It is true that if
Intentionality *is* ontologically reducible the situation may be more complex than in
such a case as heat. This is because with heat we have a clear case of a *type–type*
reduction. By contrast, Intentionality may be realizable in irreducibly different sorts
of physical structure. However, as far as I can see, this is a *mere* complication. We
could still have ontological reduction even if, to take the worst and utterly unlikely
case, the reduction was token by token.

It will be seen that logical reducibility of concepts entails the ontological reduction of the corresponding entities, but that ontological reduction of entities does not
entail logical reducibility of the concepts. Reductionists thus get two bites at the
cherry.

In his final chapter Searle offers us a model which suggests that he does accept
that, in all probability, Intentionality is ontologically reducible. (Although he has
informed me in correspondence that he does not think that the question of ontological reduction has a very clear sense.) He proposes that intentional states stand
to certain configurations in the brain as liquidity and solidity stand to certain configurations of the molecules of liquid and solid things.

What is the difference between this case and the case of heat? The answer is that
in the liquidity and solidity cases, we have what may be called the *emergence* of the
properties of liquidity and solidity. Because a thing is liquid or solid, it behaves in a
special way: the aggregate of molecules that is the liquid or solid thing behaves in a
new, unitary, way. In the heat case, however, there is just the motion of the individual molecules.

This "emergence" of liquidity and solidity, however, is not something that would
trouble any physicalist. Presumably it is deducible, "in principle" at least, from more
fundamental physical principles. So, it seems to me, Searle does think that Intentionality is ontologically reducible.

It is to be noted that Searle wants to say that the liquidity of a certain sample of
water is both *realized in* the collection of molecules and that the liquidity is *caused* by
the behavior of these molecules. This then, he thinks, licences him to say both that
Intentionality is realized in the brain and caused by the brain.

I am not sure whether Searle is entitled thus to have it both ways. We would
certainly be prepared to say that a certain arrangement of the molecules of the
liquid thing is *responsible* for its liquidity. We might even speak of causing here. But
whether this is ordinary efficient causality is not clear to me. Cause and effect are
a bit too close together!

But this, I take it, is a side-issue. Even if Searle were wrong about the propriety of
running together realization and causation, his analogy might still stand, and might
capture an essential feature of the relation of Intentionality to states of the brain.

It is a bit frustrating that Searle gives us no hint as to what he thinks that the true
scientific theory of Intentionality might be. It is clear what he thinks that Inten-

tionality is not. It is not what a functionalist, or a causal theorist, or anybody like that thinks it is. Perhaps Searle has no theory. Perhaps he thinks that it is just a matter for the neurophysiologists. It would be helpful if he could let us know.

I now leave the question of ontological reduction aside and go back to Searle's clearly stated contention that the notion of the Intentionality of the mental is *logically* irreducible. Should we accept this view? Here I think that Searle dismisses too readily the possibility of *causal* or *functional* logical analyses of Intentionality.

I do not want to deny that the analysis of the mental in intentional terms which stops at the intentional is extremely illuminating, as Searle shows. Furthermore, it seems that any projected deeper analysis will have to change gear in some fashion that is easier to intuit than to explain. We appear to pass from one level of concepts to a wholly distinct level. (Perhaps the transition from social to psychological concepts is similar.) Nevertheless, important *conceptual* relations appear to stretch down from the intentional concepts to simpler, non-psychological, concepts, thus permitting at least partial conceptual analyses of the intentional ones.

(Perhaps it is worth noting that in the case of liquidity and solidity the situation is interestingly similar. The deeper causal and other relations that hold between the molecules are hidden from our sight. But the concepts of liquidity and solidity can be analyzed in some degree. For instance, taking the simpler case, solid things are made up of things whose macroscopic parts tend to stay with each other, to form what we might call a "dynamic unit.")

The intentional states of a single mind, or a single mind at a certain time or over a certain stretch of time, fall into one or more intentional systems. These systems characteristically involve certain purposes, certain beliefs and certain perceptions. (At the intentional level, the beliefs and perceptions involved are those which are relevant to the attempt to carry out the purposes.) These systems cannot be defined in terms of their actual behavioral effects and environmental causes. But it is quite plausible to define them, or partially define them, in terms of the behavior that they are *apt* for producing, and, in the case of perceptions, the distal environmental stimulus that is *apt* for producing them. Furthermore, purposes, beliefs, and perceptions may be differentiated into these three classes by their different type of causal contribution to the behavioral effect that an intentional system as a whole is apt for producing.

I have recently come to think that it is also a promising idea to characterize intentional systems as *functional* systems, where "function" is understood teleologically, as it is in biology. The notion of a teleological system is something that a Naturalist will wish to analyze, of course, and what the true analysis is, is a difficult and disputed matter. But presumably it can be provided with an analysis, and a logical one at that.

At any rate, it seems quite plausible to say that it is a conceptual truth that an intentional system is a functional system. It is true that not all functional systems are intentional systems; indeed, the large majority are not intentional systems. But it seems reasonable to say that all functional systems *approximate*, in their different degrees, to intentional systems. A functional system is something that will, or at least used to, carry out its function in favorable circumstances, and in general is, or was, apt for carrying out its function. (Something like that is analytic.) In unfavorable circumstances, or by sheer bad luck, the system will not carry out its function. This is surely like Intentionality. It is plausible to suggest that intentional systems can be identified with the most complex and sophisticated instances of all those functional systems that we know of.

So, I think that there are prospects for a causal and/or a functional analysis of Intentionality. A *third* point is that intentional systems are revealed on inspection to be extremely complex affairs, a complexity largely given by the fact that they involve numerous cooperating subsystems themselves involving Intentionality or at least functionality. I believe that Searle brings this out, in a somewhat backhanded way, in his discussion of what he calls "the Background" (chapter 5). To this I now turn.

He himself explains the Background as: "A set of nonrepresentational mental capacities that enable all representing [by intentional states] to take place" (p. 143). These nonrepresentational mental capacities are the huge multitude of know-hows (both knowing how things are and knowing how to do things) that one has to have to form the intention, for instance, to do something as simple as going to the refrigerator and getting a bottle of cold beer to drink.

Searle raises the question whether the Background itself consists of intentional states, but says that in fact the states involved lack intentionality. I am inclined to think that his case is weak here, for the following reasons.

Searle mentions on a number of occasions the traditional possibility of a brain in a vat which leads a completely hallucinatory life. He uses the case, in my opinion very plausibly, to criticize certain theories, including the fashionable doctrine that "meanings are not in the head." But now consider the Background of a brain in a vat. It might well be a totally illusory Background, involving "knowings-how" riddled with every sort of error. Now, what of this knowledge of environment and ways of operating in it, that this unfortunate mind–brain takes itself, at a quite un-selfconscious level, to have? Would we not have to describe the non-existent objects, etc., involved as the *intentional* objects of the brain's Background?

Searle's only argument against the Background having Intentionality is this: "If representation [intentional representation] presupposes a Background, then the Background cannot itself consist in representations without generating an infinite regress" (p. 148). This is an argument from within Searle's own system. Why should we not answer it by saying that the central class of cases of Intentionality presuppose a Background which also has Intentionality, but that this Background, or some Background of this Background, *lacks a further Background*? This may involve introducing a doctrine of degrees of intentionality, but that, as I have already suggested, does not seem an implausible idea. (We may note in addition that a change in mere degree of complexity may, in many fields, be *experienced* as a change in quality: an epistemic version of that famous change of quantity which involves change of quality.)

I have said, then, that, *pace* Searle, there are prospects for a logical, or conceptual, analysis of Intentionality along three lines: (1) causal, (2) teleological functional, and (3) by introducing the notion of degrees of complexity in intentional systems.

I proceed to develop the third line of thought somewhat further. As I have said, a natural way to understand degrees of Intentionality is to think of complex intentional systems as complexes of simpler intentional systems. Early in his book, Searle makes light of, rubbishes even, an idea of Daniel Dennett's (p. 21). In *The Concept of Mind* (1949) Ryle developed certain justly famous infinite regress arguments. He argued, for instance, that if you hold that a bodily action, as opposed to a mere bodily happening, requires an *act* of will as a cause, then you must in equity postulate a further act of will to be the cause of the original act of will, and so *ad infinitum*. Dennett pointed out the following way of meeting Ryle's argument (see his 1978, pp. 80–1, 122–5). Suppose we think of the act of will as an act of a mere part of the mind, the act of an homunculus that is less sophisticated than the whole mind. The so-called act of mind is then an act in a diminished sense, springing as it does from an intentional system that is simpler than the mind as a whole. That "act" might in turn be brought about by the "action" of still simpler systems, and so on down to systems that are so simple that their operation can be identified with straightforward causality. At that final point, the intentionality is, as Dennett puts it, "discharged."

Pace Searle, and without accepting the Eliminativism that may be suggested by Dennett's word "discharged," I think that this may be a way to understand the relation of Intentional states to Background. We are inclined to think of the fully developed Intentional states as analyzable, both synchronically and diachronically, into organized complexes of simpler systems. The Background capacities will be typical examples of such simpler systems. These simpler systems will still have Intentionality, but it will be a lower grade of Intentionality. Then so on down the systems to such things as mere negative feedback mechanisms, and below that again to mere dispositions and their manifestations. (Dispositions, which are things which have manifestations *that may not actually be manifested*, have the lowest grade of intentionality of all. But they have a very first approximation to intentionality for all that.)

Here is a great chain of mental being, preferable from the standpoint of evolutionary theory to any saltatory emergence of Intentionality. I do not accuse Searle of saltatory theory, but we naturalists do need a theory of how saltation is avoided, or how we are to be reconciled to it, neither of which Searle provides. An homuncular theory of this sort, which I have suggested may be involved in the very notion of Intentionality, does seem to provide the outline, or part of the outline, for an explanation of Intentionality.

2 Perception and Causation

I will begin by spelling out my agreements with Searle on the topic of perception, agreements that are very extensive, and advance gradually to disagreements.

I completely accept Searle's view that: "The visual experience is as much *directed at* or *of* objects or states of affairs in the world as any of the paradigm Intentional states ... such as belief, fear or desire" (p. 39). Searle extends this to perceptual experience generally. I would extend it even further, to embrace bodily sensations such as pains and tickles, but that is because I think that they are *proprioceptions*, that is, bodily perceptions.

Searle goes on to argue that the (intentional) content of a visual experience, like that of a belief "is always the equivalent of a whole proposition" (p. 40). Speaking of propositions here should not make one think of language. Rather, as Searle says, all that is meant is that "the content requires the existence of a whole state of affairs if it is to be satisfied" (p. 40). Later Searle suggests, correctly I think, that sense-datum theorists wrongly congeal, as it were, this proposition into something perceived (p. 60).

Searle goes on to argue, as is now conventional, that, say, a yellow sensation (better "a sensation of something yellow") is not itself something yellow. The sensation does not interpose itself between the perceiver and the external object perceived. Nor is it the basis or evidence for perceptual judgment (p. 73). I would put it by saying that the sensation is a perceiv*ing* of something (perhaps non-veridical, perhaps even hallucinatory – the something is intentional) rather than something perceiv*ed*.

I first begin to have a moment's hesitation when Searle says that "visual and other perceptual experiences are *conscious* mental *events*" (p. 45). No problem with "events." But do they have to be *conscious*? Perhaps consciousness is built into the word "experiences." It certainly can be so built in if one so chooses. But then I would argue that there is no difficulty in the notion of perceptions that are just like perceptual experiences except that they are unconscious, that is, the perceiver is unaware of having them. Indeed, I think that there is good evidence for the empirical reality of unconscious perception, or subliminal perception as it is called. (See the work of N. F. Dixon, 1971.) Nor do I see any reason for Searle to reject this. He says elsewhere "Some, but not all, mental states are conscious, and the intentional–nonintentional distinction cuts across the conscious–unconscious distinction" (1980, p. 455).

I come now to a very interesting feature of Searle's theory of perception. He holds that it is part of the conditions of satisfaction of, say, a visual experience (the conditions required to satisfy the intentionality of the experience) that the experience must be caused by the putative state of affairs in the world which constitutues the rest of the satisfaction conditions. Thus, my visual experience as of a yellow expanse has as its intentional object not merely *a certain sort of yellow expanse in front of me now*. It does have that state of affairs as intentional object. But it also has as intentional object *that this state of affairs is cause of the visual experience*. The visual experience involves a self-referential element *as part of its intentional content*.

Searle emphasizes that this is not the now familiar point that a perception of a yellow expanse is only a perception of an actual, physical, yellow expanse if that expanse causes the perception (in a non-deviant manner). Searle holds that the experience is an experience *of* this experience being caused by a yellow expanse, even where there is no actual yellow expanse and so, as a result, the content is *purely* intentional.

When I first mastered this, I wondered how Searle reconciled it with the fact that dogs perceive. Searle is properly appreciative of the need for any account of perception to apply to animals as much as to ourselves. But could it be the case, I wondered, that the intentional object of a dog's perceptions should include, besides an external scene including the dog's *bodily* relation to that scene, the self-referential component that the perception itself, something in the dog's mind, should be caused by the external scene? It seems a bit much. What concern has your average dog with its own perceptions? Is it even aware of having them?

But then I thought that Searle could, and should, reply in the following way. He could say that we must distinguish between perception and perceptual experience. Perceptual experience, I hope he would then say, is perception *plus* the perception giving rise to (causing) consciousness of the perception. The intentional object of the bare perception is nothing more than an external state of affairs (including a relation to the perceiver's own body). But when in addition we are conscious of the perception (as human beings normally are), the intentional content of this consciousness includes the perception as caused by the external state of affairs.

If *this* is Searle's view (though I am not sure that it is), then I think that it is true doctrine. But what we have here is pretty much equivalent to a characteristic doctrine of the Causal analysis of the mental concepts. According to the Casual analysis, perceptions are given to us in consciousness (not indubitably given to us, of course, as both Searle and I would insist) as things apt for being produced by a certain particular external state of affairs. It is this state of affairs which constitutes the intentional content of the consciousness of the perception.

However, for the Causal analysis, this characterization of the perception, together with other potential causal relations that the perception has to behavior and to other mental states, *exhausts* the nature of perceivings as they are given to consciousness. Not so for Searle. When he comes to spell out the truth-conditions for "X sees that there is a yellow station-wagon in front of X" he says that these include:

> X has a visual experience which has
> (a) certain conditions of satisfaction
> (b) *certain phenomenal properties* [my italics].

Here is my large disagreement with Searle concerning perception. I do not think that there are any phenomenal properties linked with perceiving, or, indeed, any other mental state or item. As Brian Farrell put it long ago in his article "Experience" (1950), experience (as opposed to what is experienc*ed*) is featureless, transparent, qualityless. Agreeing with Farrell, I think that the only qualities involved in perception are those involved in the intentional content of the perception. These qualities are qualities of *external objects*. The special quality that sighted persons associate with redness *is* redness, a property of external things such as surfaces. (Phenomenologically, by the way, that is what redness appears to be a property of.) This property of external things is epistemically unanalyzable. But as a good physicalist I believe that it is ontologically analyzable, in terms of scientifically respectable properties of red things. I have tried to make that reduction plausible elsewhere (see, especially, my 1987).

Searle, then, accepts the existence of *internal* phenomenal qualities. (Notice that I am not objecting to phenomenal qualities, but only to locating them within.) He must then face the same questions about these qualities that he faces about Intentionality. He denies that any logical analysis can be given of Intentionality. It is obvious that no logical analysis can be given of phenomenal qualities, such as color and warmth. It appears that Searle accepts that there is some scientific, *a posteriori*, reduction of intentional states. It seems that, to be consistent, Searle ought to favor some ontological reduction of the phenomenal qualities. What is a bit puzzling is that he does not say a word on the matter.

His doctrine of the phenomenal qualities also leads Searle into what I think is an unfortunate falling away from his declared Direct Realism. It is to be noted first that Searle does not take the internal phenomenal qualities to be mere accompaniments of perceptions, with no clear role in the mental economy. That is admirable, I think, and contrasts favorably with some other defenders of internal phenomenal properties. But it leads naturally on in Searle to a doctrine that I find dubious.

Searle suggests that his phenomenal qualities are actually the way that intentional content is realized in perception. Redness is a quality of external things, but redness is *given* to us only as that external property which, in appropriate circumstances, causes the phenomenal property. Searle says that this not only holds for a secondary quality such as redness, but also "similarly with the so-called primary qualities" (p. 75). (Note the "so-called." What is going on?) He then says that "this implies that our empirical concepts for describing the world are applied relative to our capacity to receive causal inputs from these very features . . . " (p. 75). But does this not lead to skepticism about our power to know how the world is in itself? Is it not a sophisticated version of the Representative theory of perception? Searle denies that he is involved in skepticism, but he admits that his theory has the consequence that "our very notion of how it [the world] is is relative to our constitution and our causal transactions with it" (p. 76). I think that this is a skeptical doctrine. Searle has moved away from the Direct Realism that he claims to uphold. The world is known to us through its effects on our minds. The effects are known *as* the effects of external causes. But our only clue to the nature of these causes is the nature of the phenomenal properties.

At the end of the chapter on perception Searle says that "it is not possible for something to look red to normal perceivers in normal conditions and not be red" (p. 77). (*En passant*, I would deny this to be a necessary truth. Quite likely, it is not even *true*. See my 1987.) Presumably he would say the same about the "so-called" primary qualities. So it seems that the world is only known as that which causes the phenomenal properties of our perceivings.

Searle would counter-attack, I think, arguing that my denial that perceivings have phenomenal properties would reduce the latter to the mere acquiring of propositional contents, a position which is phenomenologically quite implausible (see his p. 47). There would be no distinguishing seeing from so-called "blind sight," where people can give correct reports about visual events and objects, but claim to have no visual awareness. One possibility here, it seems, is that in blind sight visual perceptions are still occurring, and that these perceptions feed into cognitive systems, but that ordinary reflex awareness (consciousness) of these perceptions, i.e. visual *experience*, is for some reason lacking. But I would concede that those of us who deny the existence of inner phenomenal properties owe the world an account of the very special phenomenology of perception.

One thing that seems useful is to think about the difference between the intentional content of perceptions and the intentional content of other mental states. The propositional content of perception is enormously richer and more specific than the content of other states. (There is good biological reason for this. Consider purposes, for instance. Since the environment is constantly changing, and changing in hard to predict ways, purposes cannot be very specific. For instance, the purpose just to get something to eat can be specific enough. But to achieve this goal, information about the environment and the perceiver's relation to it must be extraordinarily specific.) It is not too surprising, then, that perceptions are often wrongly thought of as involving internal qualities, while other mental states are thought to lack such qualities. Precise and detailed intentional contents of perceivings are mistaken for inner properties.

At any rate, whatever our disagreements, I am in agreement with Searle that "every experience of perceiving and acting is precisely an experience of causation" (p. 123–4). That would appear to have consequences for one's doctrine of causality, or so Searle thinks. I agree with him, and I will finish off what I have to say by making some remarks on his view of causation.

Given this view of the experience of perceiving and acting, it is at least very natural to reject the Humean account of causation. As Searle says, the fundamental notion of cause is making something happen (p. 123), it is a relation holding between tokens, (holding between token states of affairs according to me), and one which cannot be shown *a priori* to involve regularities or laws.

Pace Hume, then, and agreeing with Searle, our impressions of our own mental functioning – impressions of reflection, Hume would have said – constitute impressions from which the idea of cause is derived. But, *contra* Searle, I do not think that this is our only source of impressions of causality.

Searle writes:

> On my account the Humeans were looking in the wrong place. They sought causation (force, power, efficacy, etc.) as the object of perceptual experience and failed to find it. I am suggesting that it was there all along as part of the content of both perceptual experience and experiences of acting. (p. 124)

I do not disagree, indeed applaud, the positive part of Searle's contention. But I think that causation is also the *object* of perception. This was the view of the Louvain psychologist, Michotte (1963). Strangely enough, Searle makes favorable reference to his work (p. 115), but in practice appears unwilling to accept Michotte's conclusions.

Michotte thought, and tried to prove by experiment, that one can observe casual sequences visually. One can argue that in the cases Michotte cites our visual perceptions are infected and theoretically laden by knowledge of the way that the world works, knowledge dervied from other modes of perception, in particular, touch and proprioception. (Though that would be an awkward line for *Searle* to take because of his rather resolutely "ordinary language" line on what it is that we can be said to perceive. We certainly often *speak* of *seeing* that one event causes another.)

But Michotte also refers to tactual perception, and here it is very plausible to say that our perception of causality, although not incorrigible, is as direct a perception as any other perception of a relation. The central cases seem to be those where we are aware of objects exerting pressure on our body. Pressure is causal action, of course; we are perceptually aware of it, and the awareness apparently is as direct, as little theoretically laden, as, say, our visual perception of color.

The overwhelming biological importance of an organism becoming aware of pressures on its body is obvious. A dog is surely aware of such pressures. (But as I have already said, it would seem to be a sophisticated dog that took its visual or tactual *experience* to be caused by something external.)

In general, it seems to me that Searle is too cautious in what he takes perception to make us aware of. I think that we are directly aware of various properties and relations of external things, including some of their causal relations. These properties and relations are not all "relative to our constitution and our causal transactions with it." I think that in Searle's thinking about perception there is an unfortunate residue of phenomenalism (present in many others besides himself). This residue is the doctrine that it is not logically possible for something to appear perceptually to normal perceivers in normal conditions to have a certain sensible quality, yet not in fact to have that quality. I submit that the sensible qualities and relations are as independent of perceivers as any other properties of things.

REFERENCES

Armstrong, D. M. (1987) "Smart on the Secondary Qualities," in *Mind, Morality and Metaphysics: Essays in Honour of J. J. C. Smart*, ed. P. Pettit, R. Sylvan and J. Norman (Basil Blackwell: Oxford).

Dennett, D. (1978) *Brainstorms* (Bradford Books: Cambridge, Mass.).

Dixon, N. F. (1971) *Subliminal Perception: The Nature of a Controversy* (McGraw-Hill: New York, NY).

Farrell, B. (1950) "Experience," *Mind* 59.

Michotte, A. (1963) *The Perception of Causality*, trans. T. R. Miles and E. Miles (Methuen: London).

Ryle, G. (1949) *The Concept of Mind* (Hutchinson: London).

Searle, J. R. (1980) "Minds, Brains, and Programs," *The Behavioral and Brain Sciences*, 3.

Searle, J. R. (1983) *Intentionality* (Cambridge University Press: Cambridge).

11

"I believe that p"

NORMAN MALCOLM

(1)   It is a common philosophical opinion that when a person believes that so and so is the case, his belief is a "mental state" or a "state of mind." John Searle, for example, thinks that if you believe that so and so, your belief is a mental state which has a property that he calls "Intentionality."[1] David Armstrong says that "Belief is a dispositional state of mind which endures for a greater or lesser length of time"; and he says that "there must be some difference in A's state of mind if he believes p from his state of mind if he does not believe p."[2] Both Searle and Armstrong are speaking of belief in the sense of believing *that* so and so; as when the expressions "I believe" or "He believes" are followed by a full sentence that says what the person believes. They are not dealing with the sense of belief in which one may speak of believing *a person*; nor of the sense in which one speaks of believing *in* a person, or in a cause, or in capitalism, or in magic. I also wish to restrict my discussion to belief *that* so and so. (In speaking and writing we, of course, often drop the "that": e.g., "I believe the room is growing colder").

This view that belief, in the above sense, is a mental state or a state of mind, would seem to imply that whenever a person says something of the form "I believe p," he is reporting or referring to a mental state of his, or to his state of mind. I do not wish to deny that this is sometimes so. But I do contend that in a *vast* number of cases this is *not* so.

Suppose that you and I are indoors and about to go out. You are near a window, and I ask you to look out to see whether it is raining. You peer through the window (it is dark outside and you can't see through the glass very well). You turn to me and say "I believe it's raining." Suppose I retorted, "I don't want to know about *your mental state*, but about the weather!" That would be a joke.

Why would it be a joke? Because you were not reporting, or referring to, your mental state or state of mind. You were talkng about the weather! You were saying, *in a tentative or hesitant way*, that it's raining. If, instead, you had said to me, "Yes. It is raining," you would have been making a nontentative, unhesitant, statement about the weather.

The foregoing example illustrates a very common use of "I believe." In this use the function of this prefix to a sentence, is to modify or qualify the sentence that follows it. It is a way of making a *cautious* assertion.

"I believe" is used in other ways. For example, suppose that you are a gentleman

seated next to a lady passenger on an airliner. On arrival at an airport she rises from
her seat to depart, and unknowingly drops her purse. You hand it to her, saying
"Madam, I believe this is your purse." Here the function of "I believe" is not to
make your statement tentative. Instead, it is a formula of politeness. On many social
occasions, the prefix "I believe" serves as a conventional politeness, a bit of good
manners. Certainly the speaker is not saying anything about his mental state.

The philosophical view that a belief that p is always a mental state is quite wrong,
as can be seen from its apparent implication that whenever a speaker says "I believe
that p," he is reporting, or describing, or referring to, some mental state of his, or to
his state of mind. If it seems obvious to a philosopher that the *very meaning* of the
words "I believe . . ." is to say something about the speaker, this is because that
philosopher has not paid attention to how those words are actually *used* in various
contexts. The speaker who, in my example, said "I believe it's raining," was not
saying anything about himself; nor was the speaker who said, "Madam, I believe
this is your purse."

There are contexts in which "I believe that p" is neither a hesitant stating that p,
nor is the "I believe" a prefix of politeness. Suppose that your friend Johnson,
whom you admire and trust, has been accused of dishonesty. If asked for your
opinion of Johnson, you might reply "I believe that Johnson is a *thoroughly honest*
man." This would come to the same as the confident, unqualified, assertion
"Johnson is a thoroughly honest man." Here instead of "I believe that . . .", you
could say "I believe *in* . . ." ("I believe in Johnson's complete honesty.") In contrast,
for the tentative statement "I believe that it's raining," there is no equivalent "I
believe in . . ." Also, in the Johnson example, you would be revealing something
about yourself, namely, your *trust* in Johnson.

(2)   I turn now to a different but related topic. John Searle says that "If I make the
statement that p, I express a belief that p."[3] Searle is holding that whenever anyone
makes a statement, p, that person is expressing the belief that p. Since Searle holds
that any belief is a mental state, his view implies that whenever any person makes
any statement, he is expressing (or giving expression to) a mental state.

The generality of this latter view is far from the truth. If a plumber has been
called in to repair a stoppage of the sink he might, after some investigation, say:
"The trap is clean; the stoppage is further along the line." Here the plumber is not
expressing a mental state of his – as he would be if he broke out in weeping, or
jumped up and down in a rage.

A simple assertion *can* be an expression of a mental state. *It depends on the circumstances!* Suppose a young lad has been joyfully anticipating a family picnic; but
he knows it will be cancelled in case of rain. On the appointed day he looks out of
the window and exclaims, "It's *raining!*" His utterance would be an expression of
his bitter disappointment. His disappointment can hardly be called a "mental state";
but certainly it is a feeling, even an emotion; and it was expressed by his utterance
in those circumstances. If a man in a queue says to his neighbour, "You are standing
on my foot!" his words would probably express indignation. But when the plumber
said what he said about the stoppage, his statement need not have been an expression of any feeling, mood, emotion, or mental state. The utterance "It's raining,"
could be an expression of a mental state. A patient in a mental hospital might utter
those words, obsessionally, every day, no matter what the weather was like. A visitor

to the hospital on a sunny day, astonished by hearing the patient say this, might be told "Those words are an expression of his pathological mental state."

A month after the unexpected death of his son, the father is asked how he is feeling. His reply, "I am terribly depressed," would be an explicit description of his mental state. And his depression might be *expressed* in the listless way he spoke of other things, in the way he walked and sat, in his wanting to stay in bed all day, in his loss of interest in his normal pursuits, in his frequent weeping, and so on.

To think of a *genuine* case where a mental state is expressed, helps to show how extravagant is the view that whenever any person makes any statement, he is expressing a mental state. If a person says, "My neighbors are constantly spying on me," that would, in certain circumstances, be an expression of paranoia; in other circumstances it would be an objective, well-verified, observation.

(3)   I wish to focus now on the puzzle that Wittgenstein called "Moore's paradox."[4] This present essay of mine grew out of a study of section x, part II, of the *Philosophical Investigations*. My explanation of the "paradox" will be different from the explanations offered by Moore and Searle, and is derived from Wittgenstein's remarks in section x, which I hope I have understood correctly.

What is the paradox that Moore brought to light? Moore noticed that it would be "absurd" to make a statement of the form "*p*, and I don't believe that *p*" – *although* it is "logically possible" that the statement is true. Taking as an example the sentence, "I went to the pictures last Tuesday, but I don't believe that I did," Moore says that this

> is a perfectly absurd thing to say, although *what* is asserted is something which is perfectly possible logically: it is perfectly possible that you did go to the pictures and yet you do not believe that you did . . .[5]

In an essay on Russell, published two years later, Moore refers again to the paradox. Taking as an example the sentence "I believe he was gone out, but he has not," Moore says that

> This, though absurd, is not self-contradictory; for it may quite well be true. But it is absurd, because, by saying "he has not gone out" we *imply* that we do *not* believe that he has gone out, though we neither assert this, nor does it follow from anything we do assert. That we *imply* it means only, I think, something which results from the fact that people, in general, do not make a positive assertion, unless they do not believe that the opposite is true: people, in general, would not assert positively "he has not gone out," if they believed that he had gone out. And it results from this general truth, that a hearer who hears me say "he has not gone out," will, in general, assume that I don't believe that he has gone out, although I have neither asserted that I don't, nor does it follow, from what I have asserted that I don't. Since people will, in general, assume this, I may be said to *imply* it by saying "he has not gone out," since the effect of my saying so will, in general, be to make people believe it, and since I know quite well that my saying it will have this effect.[6]

Let us turn now to Searle. He refers briefly to "Moore's paradox."[7] Searle's explanation of why it "sounds odd," or is "logically odd" (as he puts it), to say something of the form "*p* but I don't believe that *p*," resembles Moore's explanation, but also differs from it. Moore's view is that in making a statement, p, a person "implies" that he *believes* that p, although the sense in which he "implies" this does not *entail* that he believes that p. Searle says something different. He says, as previously noted, that "if I make the statement that p, I express a belief that p." Now in saying, "I express *a* belief that p," Searle surely means: "I express *my* belief that p." Searle is talking about what anyone is doing in making any statement. Searle is holding that any speaker in making a statment, p, expresses *that speaker's belief* that p. According to Searle, the belief that p is an "Intentional" mental state that corresponds to the "speech act" of asserting p. Searle says:

> The performance of the speech act is necessarily an expression of the corresponding Intentional state ... The performance of the speech act is *eo ipso* an expression of the corresponding Intentional state; and, consequently, it is logically odd, though not self-contradictory, to perform the speech act and deny the presence of the corresponding Intentional state.[9]

There is an important difference between the accounts of Moore and Searle of why it is "absurd" (Moore) or "logically odd" (Searle) to say something of the form "p, and I don't believe that p." On Moore's account, if your assert p you "imply" that you *believe p*: but the sense in which you "imply" this, says Moore, "simply arises from the fact, which we all learn by experience, that in the immense majority of cases a man who makes such an assertion ... does believe or know what he asserts ..."[10] Moore takes pains to explain that your asserting p does not *entail* that you believe p. It is just a matter of empirical fact that your hearers will assume that you do believe it. Therefore, in saying "p, and I don't believe that p," you are not saying anything self-contradictory.

But on Searle's account of the matter, it seems that it *would* be self-contradictory to say such a thing – although Searle declares that it is *not* self-contradictory. According to Searle, your making the statement that p is *necessarily* an "expression" of your belief that p. Let us consider Searle's words, "express" and "expression." To say, for example, that Paul's slamming the door was an *expression of rage*, would mean that Paul was in a rage when he slammed the door. If Paul was not in a rage, then his slamming the door was not an expression of rage. If Paul was pretending to be in a rage, or was play-acting rage, then his slamming the door was not an expression of rage, even if it looked like it. If this simple point about the normal meaning of the word "expression" is applied to Searle's claim that your statement that p, is *necessarily an expression* of your *belief* that p, we get the following two results: first, that a person cannot make an assertion without believing what he asserts; second, a statement of the form "p, and I don't believe that p," *is* self-contradictory.

Of course Searle does not want to have these consequences. But the step he takes to avoid them is unsatisfactory. He merely says that it is *not* the case "that one always has to have the Intentional state that one expresses. It is always possible to lie or otherwise perform an insincere speech act."[11] Let us apply this to Searle's thesis that your making a statement is necessarily an expression of your belief that the statement is true. From the remarks just quoted, we see that Searle is claiming that your assertion that p is *necessarily* an *expression* of your *belief* that p, even if you do *not* believe that p! It seems to me that Searle's position is very confused. To say that some utterance or action of Paul's "is an expression of Paul's belief that p," is true only if Paul *does* believe that *p*. If Paul doesn't believe that *p*, then his stating that *p* is *not an expression of his belief* that *p*. Searle has run afoul of the ordinary use of "express" and "expression." I will not speculate on how he might try to repair his formulation, since I think that in any case he is on the wrong track in his attempt to deal with Moore's paradox.

(4)   What is the nature of the "absurdity" in saying something of the form "*p*, but I don't believe that *p*," or of the form "I believe *p*, but not-*p*?" Of his example, "I went to the pictures last Tuesday, but I don't believe I did," Moore says that "*what is asserted is something which is perfectly possible logically.*" And of the example, "I believe he has gone out, but he has not," Moore remarks: "This, though absurd, is not self-contradictory." In this respect, Searle has the same idea as Moore. Of such a remark as "It's snowing but I don't believe it's snowing," Searle says that "it is logically odd, though not self-contradictory."[12] Both Moore and Searle think that though it is "absurd" or "odd" to *say* such a thing, *what* is said is *intelligible*. I think their idea is definitely wrong.

If I asked someone what the weather is today, and he, after looking out the window, replied "It's raining but I don't believe it is," I would *not understand* those words. I would think that I had misheard the person, or that he had misspoken, or that he was joking. Of course, in certain special circumstances, people do say things of that sort. Suppose there had been a prolonged drought and everyone was hoping and praying for rain. One day someone rushes into the house shouting, "It's raining! I don't believe it, but it's raining!" There we would understand the words, "I don't believe it!" to be an expression of astonishment and joy.

Leaving aside such special circumstances, an utterance of the form "*p*, but I don't believe that *p*," is not intelligible. It is a mistake to think that although it is an odd or absurd thing to say, nevertheless it is a *meaningful* statement and we would *understand* it. Moore says of such an utterance that "*what* is asserted is something which is perfectly possible logically." But *what* would the speaker be *asserting*? Why does Moore assume that *anything* is being asserted?

It is not difficult to see, part at least, of what led Moore to make that assumption. Take the example of the nonsensical utterance, "It's raining, but I don't believe it is." Now consider, first, the following *supposition*: "Let us suppose that it's raining and I don't believe it is." This supposition makes sense; it postulates a possible state of affairs. Second, consider the *past tense* version of the nonsensical utterance: "It was raining but I didn't believe it was." This makes sense: it describes a possible state of affairs. Third, consider the *third person*, or the *second person*, of the present tense. It might be said *of* someone, "It is raining, but he doesn't believe it"; or *to* someone, "It's raining, even though you don't believe it." This is a possible state of affairs. As Moore says, "it is perfectly possible that you did go to the pictures and yet you do not believe that you did."[13]

Let us designate a sentence of the form "*p*, and I don't believe that *p*," by the letter R. The logical situation is as follows: (1) the *supposition* that R makes sense; (2) the *past tense* of R makes sense; (3) the *third person* and *second person* of R make sense. But despite all this, R itself, a first-person present indicative sentence, does *not* make sense!

I think it is especially significant that the *supposition* that R is the supposition of a possible state of affairs, yet to utter R itself, a present indicative, is to utter nonsense. The particular significance of this, which I have in mind, is the following: When there is a philosophical dispute as to whether some sentence, S, is a meaningful sentence, philosophers frequently resort to what can be *supposed*, or *conceived*, or *imagined*. They say such things as, "It is *conceivable* that S should be the case, therefore S is a meaningful sentence"; or, "The supposition that S is a possible supposition, therefore it makes sense to assert S." An important thing we can learn from a study of Moore's paradox, is that this reasoning is not correct. For it is conceivable that it is raining and I don't believe it is. But if I were to declare, "It's raining and I don't believe it is," I would be making a nonsensical utterance. My sentence would not be just "strange" or "absurd" but really unintelligible.

(5)   *Why* would this be unintelligible? Obviously it has to do with the way in which the first-person present indicative of the verb "to believe" is actually *used*. As I said earlier, a common use (perhaps the most common use) of the form of words "I believe that *p*," is to assert *p* hesitantly or cautiously. (But, as I mentioned previously, there are cases in which that form of words is used to assert *p*, not hesitantly, but emphatically—as in the example, "I believe that Johnson is a *thoroughly honest* man!") A common use of "I don't believe that *p*" is to assert not-*p* hesitantly.

In striking contrast, the form of words "I believe that *p*" (or "I don't believe that *p*") are not used that way in the *supposition*. "Suppose I believe that *p*" is not a hesitant assertion of *p*. Nor is the past tense, "I believed that *p*," a hesitant assertion that *p*. Nor is the third person, "He believes that *p*," a hesitant assertion of *p*. These forms of the verb "to believe" are not used to assert *p* at all.

The fact that "I believe that *p*" is commonly used as an assertion of *p* (either hesitant or emphatic) provides a clear explanation of why it is nonsense to say something of the form, "I believe that *p*, but not-p," or of the form "*p*, but I don't believe that *p*." For what we get is a self-contradictory utterance. In the conjunction, "*p* and I don't believe that *p*," the first conjunct is an assertion of *p*, and the second conjunct is an assertion, hesitant or emphatic, of not-*p*. In "I believe that *p*, and not-*p*," the first conjunct is an assertion of *p*, hesitant or emphatic, and the second conjunct is a denial of *p*. Contrary to Moore's view, and also Searle's, the absurdity of saying such a thing is simply the senselessness of a self-contradictory utterance.

Moore's paradox provides an outstanding illustration of how easily we philosophers can be misled about the meaning of a common sentence of our daily language. If we merely look at the words, not reflecting on how they are actually used, it can seem to us that when a person says "I don't believe it's raining," he is saying something about *himself*. Since "It's raining" is about the weather, and since "I don't believe it's raining" seems to be about the speaker, one could think that in uttering the conjunction "It's raining and I don't believe it's raining" the speaker is referring to two entirely different subject matters. One might even *fail to see* that the conjunctive sentence presents a problem! One might think that, after all, it is common enough for a person to cover more than one subject in a single sentence. It was greatly to Moore's credit that he *perceived* the craziness of saying such a thing, even though he didn't perceive *how* crazy it is, or *how* it is crazy.

(6)   I wish to take up the question of whether a person, in making any statement, *p*, "implies" that he believes that *p*, or "expresses" his belief that *p*. Suppose that I have just come in from a long walk outdoors, I am asked "What is the weather like?" I reply "It's very foggy." "So you believe it's foggy?" A strange question. I might

take it as a joke. If I responded, "Yes, I believe it's foggy," that would be a continuation of the joke.

There is a temptation to think that although I would not *say* "I believe" in such a case; yet just by my saying "It's foggy" I imply or express my belief that it is. One source of this temptation is Moore's paradox. Anyone will feel that there is a *conflict* between the two conjuncts of the conjunction "It's foggy, and I don't believe it is." One may think: How can there be a conflict *unless* by the first part of the conjunction I express or imply, or perhaps "show" my belief that it's foggy?

There may be some philosophers, however, who would disagree with this. They would say that if I have just been walking outdoors, and if it's very foggy out there, then I don't "believe" that it's foggy – I *know* it is. This is why it would be funny for me to say "I believe."

This account is wrong too. I have just come in from a walk outdoors and announced that there is a heavy fog. Suppose someone says, "So you know that it's foggy?" This would be a queer remark. Is it another philosophical joke? Or perhaps this person doesn't realize that I have just come in from a walk. If I thought the latter, my reply would be, not "Yes, I know it" but rather "I have just come from outdoors."

In those circumstances I am not going to say *either* "I believe" *or* "I know." And when I came in from outdoors and reported that it's foggy, I did not *imply* by this either that I "know" or "believe" that it's foggy – nor, of course, did I imply that I *don't* know it or *don't* believe it. I think, therefore, that Moore was mistaken in his assertion that "if I say I went to the pictures last Tuesday, I *imply by saying* so that I believe or know that I did . . . "[14] Moore's assertion is too general. It depends on the circumstances of the particular situation whether by saying "I went to the pictures" I would be implying either that I *believe* I did, or *know* I did, or *neither*. The actual use of "know" and "believe" is too delicate to be captured by generalizations.

(7)   Let us consider the second part of the weird conjunction, "*p*, and I believe that not-*p*." I have just awakened in the morning. My wife, still in bed, asks "Is it foggy again today?" I am trying to peer through the curtains and don't have a good view. But I don't see any fog, and I say "I believe it isn't foggy." In speaking those words, in those circumstances, I was not *saying*, or *implying*, or *expressing*, anything about my state of mind, or anything else about myself. I was speaking only of the weather. I was saying, tentatively or hesitantly, that it isn't foggy.

It might be objected: "*Of course* you were *saying* something about yourself! By your *very words* you said that *you have the belief* that it isn't foggy." But what I was saying by "those very words" depends on the situation in which I said them. In the situation described, they amounted to no more than a cautious assertion that it isn't foggy.

I will add that the words "I have the belief that . . . " are too "heavy" for that situation. "I have the belief that . . . " is a phrase that would more naturally be used to introduce some portentous opinion. For example: "I have the belief that the poverty of the Third World will produce a collapse of the international banking system." "I have the belief" is often used like "In my opinion" or "It is my view." The speaker is about to deliver his viewpoint on some large issue. Now such a speaker *might* say "I believe" instead of "I have the belief" – which means that *sometimes* these phrases are used on the same occasions. But often they are not. My wife would wonder what was the matter with me if, peering through the curtains, I said "I have the belief that it isn't foggy."

To summarize: In the problematic conjunction of the form "*p*, and I believe that not-*p*," there is indeed a *conflict* between the two conjuncts. But both Moore and Searle are wrong in their diagnoses of the conflict. The conflict is not between a belief that is supposedly implied or expressed by the first conjunct, and a contradictory belief that is supposedly asserted in the second conjunct. The conflict is between two assertions – the unqualified assertion of *p* in the first conjunct, and the assertion, either hesitant or emphatic, of not-*p* in the second conjunct. Thus, the whole conjunction is self-contradictory. That is why it is not only "a perfectly absurd thing to *say*" but is actually unintelligible.

(8)   I wish to take a final shot at the assumption that beliefs are mental states or states of mind. I have already argued that although sometimes a belief that *p* is a mental state, or a symptom of one, most commonly this is not so. Here it will be valuable to take note of some remarks by Wittgenstein:

> This is how I think of it: Belief is a state of mind. It has duration; and independently of the issuing (*Ablauf*) of its expression in a sentence, for example. So it is a kind of disposition of the believing person. This disposition is revealed to me, in another person, by his behavior, and by his words. And just as much by his utterance "I believe . . . ", as by his simple assertion.[15]

Surprisingly, some philosophers have taken this passage as an *endorsement* by Wittgenstein of the idea that a belief *is* a state of mind, "a kind of disposition." This is an erroneous reading, as is evident from the remainder of that paragraph, as well as from other remarks in section x. The continuation of the paragraph is:

> Now how is it with myself: how do I recognize my own disposition? That would require me to pay attention to myself as others do; to listen to my words, to be able to draw conclusions from them![16]

Wittgenstein adds: "If I listened to the words of my mouth, I could say that someone else was speaking out of my mouth."[17] And, *before* the paragraph beginning with "This is how I think of it," he says:

> I say of someone else "He seems to believe . . . ", and others say it of me. Now, why do I never say it of myself, not even when others *correctly* say it of me? – Don't I see and hear myself, then? – That can be said.[18]

When section x is read carefully, one sees clearly enough that Wittgenstein was, in the sentences immediately following "This is how I think of it," only describing an *inclination*. He was putting into words a philosophical *picture* of the nature of belief, a picture that tempted him and tempts many others. Both before and after his description of the inclination, he makes observations which show that this picture of belief must be rejected.

The notion that a belief is a dispositional state of a person, implies that certain actions, utterances, facial expressions, would be manifestations of the belief – just as a person's frequent irritated remarks would be manifestations of his irritable state of mind. One can be in an irritable state or mood even though one does not, at every moment, come out with expressions of irritation. In this sense an irritable disposition or mood has a duration independently of its manifestations in behavior or speech. This is a limited independence, however, since a justified claim that a person is in an irritable mood would need to be based on *some* manifestations of irritation. It is even possible for a person to realize that he himself is, or seems to be, in an irritable state of mind – by virtue of his becoming aware of his own expressions of irritation. So he could say, or think: "I seem to be in an irritable mood today."

The concept of belief has *some* similarity to the concept of irritability, in the respect that there can be manifestations of a belief. My belief that a storm is coming might be manifested by my closing the window shutters, putting the car in the garage, calling in the children, and so on. The neighbors, observing this activity, might say of me, "He seems to believe a storm is coming." But it would be senseless for *me* to say "I seem to believe a storm is coming." If a neighbor came over to ask me what the fuss was all about, I could say "I believe a storm is coming": but it would be crazy for me to say this *on the basis of* my observation of my own actions. Thus, the use of the first-person present indicative of the verb "believe" is *incompatible* with the popular philosophical assumption that a belief, such as that a storm is coming, is a mental state or state of mind, i.e. "a kind of disposition."

Can it be that in my own case I observe my disposition "directly," i.e., not by way of its manifestations? No. In the first place, I don't know what could be meant by observing a disposition "directly." Second, my statement, "I believe a storm is coming," would not be based on *self*-observation of any sort but instead on observation of the wind and sky, or on a weather report. Since the logical grammar of the verb "believe" is incompatible with such a belief being a dispositional state, then it isn't one and couldn't be one.

NOTES

1 John Searle, *Intentionality* (Cambridge University Press: Cambridge, 1983), chapter 1, section 1.
2 D. M. Armstrong, *A Materialist Theory of the Mind* (Routledge and Kegan Paul: London, 1968), p. 214.
3 Searle, *Intentionality*, p. 9.
4 Ludwig Wittgenstein, *Philosophical Investigations* (Macmillan: New York, 1971), part II, section x, p. 190.
5 G. E. Moore, "A Reply to My Critics," *The Philosophy of G. E. Moore*, ed. P. A. Schilpp (Northwestern University: Evanston and Chicago, 1942), p. 543.
6 G. E. Moore, "Russell's 'Theory of Descriptions,'" *The Philosophy of Bertrand Russell*, ed. P. A. Schilpp (Northwestern University: Evanston and Chicago, 1944), p. 204.
7 Searle, *Intentionality*, p. 9.
8 Ibid.
9 Ibid.
10 Moore, "A Reply," pp. 542–3.
11 Searle, *Intentionality*, pp. 9–10.
12 Ibid., p. 9.
13 Moore, "A Reply," p. 543.

14   Ibid., p. 541.
15   Wittgenstein, *Philosophical Investigations*, pp. 191–2.
16   Ibid., p. 192.
17   Ibid.
18   Ibid., p. 191.

12

Perceptual Realism, Naive and Otherwise

EDDY M. ZEMACH

The chapter, "The Intentionality of Perception," is the core of Searle's book, *Intentionality*; in it, Searle's analysis of intentionality is applied to its prime instance, where its case is strongest and most plausible. Only after having shown that his analysis works for the mental state of perceiving, can Searle go ahead to apply it in the rest of the book to other mental states as well. An examination of the intentionality of perception as described in "The Intentionality of Peception" is therefore crucially important for grasping, and evaluating, Searle's project as a whole.

In "The Intentionality of Perception," Searle is committed to Metaphysical Realism (the view that there is a real world out there), to Perceptual Realism (the view that we gain information about that world by perceiving it), and to Naive Realism (the view that we perceive that world as it really is). Does Searle argue for these views? Readers of *Intentionality* tend to say that of course he does, since in the said chapter he argues both against Phenomenalism (which rejects Metaphysical Realism) and against Representationalism (which rejects Naive Realism). I am not sure, however, that this answer is quite right; the chapter does seem to contain an argument for Metaphysical and Perceptual Realism, yet it is also possible that the whole chapter is only intended as a clarification of what is logically entailed by endorsing Naive Realism. Being in two minds about that issue (I hope Searle will illuminate it in his response) I shall present here, instead, an argument for Metaphysical and Perceptual Realism which is Searlean in spirit, but is not Searle's own. My argument is one that Searle himself cannot accept, for it is based on a denial of Naive Realism; but Searle, I think, should have never adopted Naive Realism in the first place. In what follows I shall therefore do the following three things. First, argue against Naive Realism, trying to show that it is not only philosophically indefensible, but also that it is incompatible with the most important theses in *Intentionality* itself. Second, argue that *if* "The Intentionality of Perception" constitutes an argument for Metaphysical and Perceptual Realism, then that argument is a total failure. Third, claim that, given Searle's view of causality (with a slight modification) Metaphysical and Perceptual Realism, so essential to Searle's entire enterprise, can be effectively argued for on representationalistic grounds.

I

Representationalists, says Searle, distinguish three kinds of entity involved in the act of perception: the external object, the psychological state of experiencing caused by that object, and the content of the experience, i.e., the phenomenal object that one is directly aware of. Searle, on the other hand, distinguishes only two: the external object and the experience caused by it; the content of the experience is not another kind of object: there are no phenomenal objects. Thus, according to Searle, experiences exist; they are conscious mental events (p. 45)[1] and have phenomenal (p. 61) as well as other properties that determine their satisfaction conditions (pp. 37ff): "the intentionality of a perceptual experience is realized in quite specific phenomenal properties of conscious mental events" (p. 45). But a perceptual experience is not a "representation of the material object" (p. 59) that causes it; according to Searle, the external object is not represented by a phenomenal object, but rather directly presented *via* the experience. Searle says that his reason for taking that view is Berkeley's argument, that "the representative theory is unable to make sense of the notion of resemblance" (p. 60) between a mental object and the real world object that is its cause. Thus, no inference from a mental to an extra-mental object is possible: "once we treat the experience as evidence on the basis of which we infer the existence of the [external] object, then skepticism becomes unavoidable" (p. 74); one cannot "ascertain the presence of the [external] object, as cause, by some further process of inference" (p. 74) from the content of sense experience. Searle concludes that, in order to block the skeptic, one has to hold that the objects of sense perception are external, and reject the representationalist view that the direct objects of perception are phenomenal objects that portray, correctly or incorrectly, their external causes (pp. 58–9). How, then, can one know that there are external objects, and that one's perceptual experiences are not illusory, if not by inference from one's sense data? Searle says (p. 74) that the correct answer is the one given by the Naive Realist; in support of that view, Searle makes the following statement (p. 73):

> When I see the car I can see that it is yellow and when I see the car I have an experience, part of whose content is that it is caused by the car. The knowledge that the car caused my visual experience derives from the knowledge that I see the car, and not conversely. Since I do not infer that there is a car there but rather simply see it . . . it is not correct to say that the visual experience is the "basis" in the sense of *evidence* or *ground* for knowing that there is a car there. The "basis" is rather that I see the car, and my seeing the car has no prior basis in that sense.

How are we to understand that statement? Read in one way, it is platitudinous: indeed, *if* I do see the car, I can see that it is yellow, and *if* I know that I see the car, then I know that the car caused my visual experience. But how do I know that I see (rather than imagine, etc.) the car? Searle says that I do not infer that there is a car there; but do I infer that I see the car? If my knowledge that I *see* the car is inferential, then the claim that I do not infer that there is a car there is disingenuous, since I know that statement (i.e., that there is a car there) only because it follows from one that I do have to infer (i.e., that I see the car). On the other hand, if the statement that I *see* the car is one that I do not infer from any other statement, how do I know whether it is true or not? Perhaps Searle ventures no answer to that question; Naive Realism is assumed, and not argued for. But then how can Searle claim to have answered the skeptic better than the representationalist, who, after all, does attempt to answer it? If Searle does not take it upon himself to answer that question, then his argument in this chapter is seriously incomplete, and his exchange with the representationalist incomprehensible. So perhaps Searle does have an answer to the above question, and the answer is that if I do see the car, then I know that I see the car. Knowledge that I see the car is elementary; on such a construal of the above section, and others like it in *Intentioality*, Searle says that the only basis of my knowledge that I see the car, is that I see the car: "p" entails "Kp."

I find that answer incredible. What theory of knowledge is being assumed here? If it is the standard theory of knowledge as a kind of justified true belief, we have here a claim, that in some cases the mere fact that p (i.e., that I see the car) is sufficient to justify my believing that p. Perhaps the claim can be defended: although extraordinary, such a justification is not impossible; according to some epistemologists there are situations p such that if p, then one is justified in believing that p.[2] Think, e.g., of phenomenalistic propositions like the one expressed by "I am in dire plain"; if it is true, then the person it is true of is *eo ipso* justified in believing it. Believing that proposition is always justified, since as soon as one contemplates it one *knows* whether it is true or not. The trouble, however, is that for Searle the proposition that I see the car is *not* such a proposition, i.e., a proposition that is known if believed, for he holds that (a) "I could be having an experience 'qualitatively indistinguishable' from this one and yet there might not be a car there" (p. 75), and that (b) "in the hallucination cases we don't see anything, though we do indeed *have* visual experiences" (p. 58). From these two premises it logically follows that I can have an experience qualitatively indistinguishable from an experience of seeing and yet not see anything. In an hallucination I see nothing, yet I erroneously believe that I see the car. Thus, that I see the car cannot be an evident truth for which I need no justification; for if an experience of seeing the car is to me utterly indistinguishable from an experience which is not seeing anything at all, then the belief that a given experience is one of seeing the car cannot be self-justificatory. Being fallible in distinguishing between my seeing the car and my not seeing it, I need an additional argument, or evidence, for my belief, that in the present case I do see the car, to be justified.

We must conclude that in *Intentionality* knowledge is not any kind of justified true belief. The other option is to interpret Searle as holding some externalistic, causal theory of knowledge, e.g., Goldman's reliabilism, according to which knowing is being (in a reliable way) caused to have a true belief, by the object of one's belief. That is, S knows that p iff the fact p causes S to believe that p, when the causal route between p and S's belief that p is one that S can regularly use. Justification, on that view, is not necessary for knowledge: I know that the car is yellow iff my belief that the car is yellow is caused in the right way by the fact that the car is yellow. Similarly, then, if my belief that I see the car is caused, in the appropriate way, by the fact that I see the car, then I know that I see the car. That account avoids the contradiction involved in taking Searle's knowledge claim as a claim for justified true belief; yet it is very problematic for other reasons. First of all, externalistic theories (e.g., of meaning) are rejected by Searle (and, I think, quite rightly so) throughout the book. He argues against Putnam that meanings *are* in the head (pp. 197ff.) and insists, against the causal theory of reference (pp. 234ff.), that the satisfaction conditions of what one refers to must be mentally represented by one. Similar attacks on various versions of externalistic and purely causal reliabilism permeate Searle's work. Had Searle adopted a reliabilistic theory of singular reference, e.g., he would have required only that a certain causal connection exists between the car being yellow and one's belief that the car is yellow; his entire discussion of how singular reference is to be internally represented and intentionally specified *by the believer himself* would have been redundant. Resorting to an externalist view of knowledge, having rejected externalism in every other area, is a very odd stance for the author of one of the ablest and most ambitious defenses of internalism in the philosophy of mind.

Moreover, the causal theory of knowledge is worthless as a defense against the skeptic; it is a placebo, not a genuine cure. Believing that I see a yellow car, I am told by the reliabilist that *if* that belief was caused (in the right way) by my seeing a yellow car, then I know that I see a yellow car; but he cannot tell me whether that belief, or in fact any other belief that I have ever had, was so caused by its intentional object. Hence, in the most obvious sense of "know" as implying "being able to tell," I do not know after all whether I do (or ever did) see anything. Second, in order to find our whether the causal route leading to my believing that p is reliable or not, I have to find out whether that route usually produces true beliefs. But how can I find that out, if I have no idea whether any of my perceptual beliefs is or is not true? What I want to know is whether I do see the car, or else my belief that I see it is false. The reliabilist advice is that I should find out whether in other cases, when I was caused in the same manner to believe that I see that car, I was right. That sounds like a bad joke; it is like telling a poor man that he can get a dollar by making a million first, and then pick up the first dollar in the pile. The skeptic doubts whether we ever see anything; an answer which assumes that we know on what occasions we did see something, is question begging. Third, I have no idea in what way perceptual beliefs are being caused in me, now or on any other occasion. No one has yet tracked down the chain of events and kept a record of all the goings on in my brain, and in the world at large, on *any* occasion in which I have perceived something. Fourth, no one has any idea what would count as "the same way" in that context. What processes, in my brain and outside it, are assumed by the reliabilist to be "substantially equivalent" for that purpose? Since no constraints are specified by the reliabilist, no answer to the question, whether my way of perceiving is reliable or not, is possible; the question itself has no clear meaning. Thus Skepticism is enhanced and made immune to all argument, rather than combatted, by the reliabilist; reliabilism makes a very poor defence of Realism.

II

Searle's Naive Realism is also inconsistent with his view that the content of an experience spells out its own satisfaction conditions. Consider again the case of hallucination or other visual illusions: according to Searle, such an experience is not a seeing, but it does specify its satisfaction conditions: "Even if I am having a hallucination, I know what must be the case in order that the experience not be a hallucination, and to say that is simply to say that the Intentional content of the experience determines its conditions of satisfaction" (p. 39). Thus, although while hallucinating one sees nothing, one gets to know what reality must be like in order for the hallucinatory experience to be veridical. But now I wonder how does one get to know that, if one is not seeing anything at all. Surely, to hallucinate is not to become all of a sudden aware of a *sentence* that *describes* (say, in English) satisfaction conditions for that hallucination? What does happen is that one acquires the said information by becoming visually aware of some perceptible item, something that has a pictorial nature; one seems to oneself to be seeing the situation in question. But is it not fairly obvious that to become visually aware of such an image or picture is precisely to *see* it? I understand that Searle may still refuse to *call* such a visual experience "seeing"; he may wish to keep the term "seeing" for veridical visual experiences only, and use a different term (say, "visualizing") for visual, or pictorial, presentations that are not generated in the usual way, or do not present real world objects. In that case, however, visualizing turns out to be the basic phenomenal category, and seeing is just a special kind of visualizing, i.e., a veridical one. To take that position is, for all intents and purposes, to abandon Naive Realism, for "I see a car" must then be analyzed just as the representationalist says, i.e., as a conjunction of "I visualize a car" and (say) "a car is really there and causes my visualizing it." That I see the car could not then be said to be known as an elementary, noninferential truth. Rather, it would be derived from the (noninferentially known) proposition that I visualize the car, and the proposition that the said visualizing is veridical (e.g., because it is caused by the car), when the latter proposition is *inferred* from the first one plus some arguments for Realism.

The above argument can be generalized. Searle holds that perceptual experiences have phenomenal properties that determine their satisfaction conditions. These properties, he says (p. 38), are not the well known properties of being red, or square, etc., for those are properties of materials objects that experiences are *of*, and not properties of the experiences themselves. But Searle never says what the phenomenal properties of experiences *are*. Note that the said properties are such that we are made aware of them by sensory means, i.e., by looking or listening. Moreover, by having an experience characterized by these properties we know that objects that satisfy them are red, or square, etc. What can those properties be, if not the good old properties *red*, *square*, etc.? One may agree that the mental state of experienc*ing* cannot be literally red, or square; but if the content of the experience cannot be red or square either, how can it determine that objects satisfying that experience must be red, or square?

Searle's view of satisfaction is akin to Wittgenstein's picture theory of meaning; Searle uses not only the spirit but also the actual words of the *Tractatus* when he says that "the visual experience does not *say* this [i.e., what are its satisfaction conditions] but *shows* it" (p. 49). But in order for a picture to *show* what reality is like if it is true, it must be *seen*, and manifest the properties it alleges the real object has. Thus, the entire argument leads to the conclusion that visual experiences present us with a phenomenal object, a picture of reality that may or may not be correct; that is how experiences non-verbally determine their satisfaction conditions. That is why representationalists regard experiences (as distinct from experiencings) as phenomenal entities that have visualizable properties. Experiences are not Fodorian Mentalese sentences that run in the experiencer's head. A sense-datum which is phenomenally red and square *shows* that what satisfies it must be red and

square. Searle rightly insists (p. 38), however, that in experience we are not presented with *two* red and square objects, the external object and the phenomenal
object. The conclusion to be drawn, however, is that external objects are not directly
present to us in sense perception. Since what we see may be an incorrect presentation of reality (the external object may be non-red), the properties *red* and *square*
that we are presented with in experience must be properties of phenomena. Had
predicates like "red" and "square" not been literally true of experiences, no experience could determine its satisfaction conditions; for why should a red square
satisfy the experience if that experience is neither red nor square? Why should it
not be satisfied by a blue circle, instead? What other phenomenal properties, except
the properties *square* and *red*, can the said experience have, in order to make it
satisfiable by red squares, and not by blue circles? Searle's account of satisfaction
conditions is so attractive precisely because perceptual experiences do indeed
determine what objects satisfy them; that is clearly shown by the properties of the
mental entity. There is no *a priori* reason why things-in-themselves cannot resemble
phenomena in their visual perceptible properties, although, of course, that need not
be the case.

If experiences are direct presentations of the properties of external material
objects, if the properties present to us in sense perception are the real properties of
external material things, how can we err about external reality? Searle seems to
negotiate that difficulty by adopting Whitehead's view that we can be immediately
aware of how things-in-themselves really are, for the only properties of things-in-
themselves are causal, e.g., how they impact on other things (p. 76). What that view
implies, however, is that perception is always right; no misperception is conceivable.
Yet Searle insists that perceptual experiences may be unsatisfied; such error can
occur only if things may appear to us in a way which is not how they are in themselves (I shall return to that issue later in this paper).

Searle's argument against representationalism is, that if "the predicates which
specify the conditions of satisfaction of the visual experience are literally true of the
experience itself," then "one might as well say that my visual experience is six
cylindered or that it gets twenty-two miles to the gallon as say that it is yellow or in
the shape of station wagon" (p. 43). But that argument is answered by Searle himself, when he makes us "distinguish between those properties where we ascertain
the presence of the property solely or primarily through vision and those where
some further tests are required" (p. 77). "The sentence form 'x looks φ' reports the
presence of a purely visual feature to the extent that 'x really is φ' can be established
by visual inspection" (pp. 77–8). In that manner Searle distinguishes the property,
being intelligent, from the property, looking intelligent; the second property, unlike
the first, is a purely visual feature. Obviously, properties of visual phenomena are
purely visual properties; thus, although a sense datum can be literally yellow or look
like a station wagon, it is neither literally six cylindered nor does it get twenty-two
miles to the gallon. The same holds for properties such as being five inches long,
standing near the fire hydrant, etc.: a phenomenal object may look five inches long
or near the fire hydrant, even though only a physical object can be extended and
have a location in space. Thus, Berkeley's objection can be quickly dismissed.
"How can a mental entity be similar to an external object?" Well, why should a
mental entity *not* be similar to an external object? "How can an idea be red and
square?" Because some ideas are mental pictures, and pictures may be red and look

square. If that is impossible, one might as well claim that red light is a logical impossibility, for light is totally unlike mail boxes: it has no well-defined location in space, it has no surface that is painted red, etc.; yet light can be literally red. An experience whose content is a mental image that is red and looks square can therefore manifest the satisfaction conditions for red squares, i.e., what objects that satisfy that experience must be like.

In a recent article[3] Searle makes the bold, and I think absolutely correct, claim that "Knowledge of those [intentional] contents is not equivalent to knowledge of the matching of public behavior with stimuli nor to the matching of utterances with conditions in the world" ("Indeterminacy, Empiricism and the Third Person," p. 146); the content of a statement can be known to its utterer even if going on external evidence alone no one else can figure out what it is. Searle insists that it is possible for crucially important information about oneself to be accessible to the first person alone, undiscoverable by any of the so-called "objective tests." I would like to see him extend that attitude to perceptual experiences, too. An item that is accessible to its experiencer alone need not be an *unding*, a chimera that ought to be exorcised out of philosophy; sense data are conceptually unobjectionable even though, as Searle says in the above article (about pain), they "are not equally accessible to any observer" (Ibid., p. 146).

III

Let me therefore disregard Searle's stance against representationalism, and assume that perceptual experiences have purely perceptual properties, i.e., properties whose presence "can be established by visual inspection" (*Intentionality*, p. 78). Now, according to Searle, the property of being caused is such a property; in fact, Searle holds that even though other sense properties are not literally possessed by experiences, the property of being caused is (p. 74). Searle does not make a similar claim for the property of causing, but it seems to me that the first thesis (i.e., that if some experience is caused, you can just see that has been caused) is not any more phenomenologically obvious than the second one. If causation is not a matter of statistical data, a Humean constant conjunction of events, but, rather, a palpable exercise of energy by the cause that brings about the effect, then the property of causing is no less phenomenally discernable than the property of being caused. In other words, if there is a perceptible property of being affected, there is a perceptible property of affecting. Let us suppose that you intentionally recite a poem; to you, the recitation then looks caused (it does not look spontaneous), and the intention looks as if it has caused it to exist. Furthermore, under the above anti-Humean assumptions, if a pair of events are given, and one of them causes the other, then that causing may be perceived by a suitably located observer. When the said events are experiences, the experiencer may introspectively know that one of them causes the other. With this modest addition to Searle's view (that being caused is an observable property), it yields an ontological argument for Metaphysical Realism, proving the existence of the external world even without the unfortunate Naive Realism that Searle himself has adopted. It proceeds in the following way:

1   Experiences have phenomenal properties.
2   If P is a phenomenal property of a conscious experience x, its experiencer knows that Px.
3   Being a cause (Cx), being caused ($\overline{C}$x), and causing (Cxy) are phenomenal properties.
4   I know that some experience z of mine is such that $\overline{C}$z, and for every experience y of mine such that Cy, not Cyz.
5   Therefore, I know that z is caused by an external object.
6   Therefore, I know that external objects exist.

The most vulnerable step in this proof is assumption 3; one may claim that it is much too strong. Both Freud and common-sense psychology say that it is possible for me to have two experiences (Freud and the Empiricists call them "ideas"), x and y, such that Cxy, and yet I neither know, nor even believe, that Cxy. I am not sure that the said objection, its current popularity notwithstanding, is valid; but let me not dispute the claim that one may be unaware of such causal relations between one's own experiences. What is needed for the argument above is the much more modest claim, that one need not always be so ignorant. It is enough if I can successfully discern the causal links of many of my experiences, i.e., that it is likely that if an experience, x, of mine is caused by another experience, y, of mine, I observe that Cxy. Thus, if on the overwhelming majority of cases I fail to find any experience y of mine that causes x, although x is palpably caused, then I have a very good reason to believe that x has external causes. That is to say, if I do not observe how my perceptual experiences are being caused, and yet I observe that they are caused, I have a good reason to believe, on the basis of that evidence, that they are not caused by any other mental state of mine. That is to say, I have some evidence that, on the whole, my perceptual experiences are neither hallucinations, nor dreams, nor memories, nor phantasies, nor any other experience that is caused by one's own previous psychological states. In that case I can infer that those experiences are indeed what they seem to be, i.e., perceptual experiences of an external reality, and hence are caused by an extra-mental reality that I confront.

Another objection to the above line of reasoning may be that although Searle is right in holding that causal relations are phenomenologically perceptible, the only causal connections that we perceive are those that hold between the physical objects that we observe, but we do not observe that the said observations themselves are being caused. That objection may start with Searle's contention that phenomenological properties such as being yellow characterize external objects and not phenomenal entities; in that case, why should the property, being caused, be different? Even anti-Humeans, like Anscombe or Armstrong, may hold that we observe only causal connections between items *in* experience (e.g., that the motion of one billiard ball causes another to move), but not that the said experience itself, e.g., of those billiard balls causing each other to move, is being caused by some external objects. Thus, it may be thought that Searle is wrong to maintain that "the visual experience does not represent the causal relation as something existing independently of the experience, but rather part of the experience is the experience of being caused" (p. 74).

It seems to me that this objection does have some power against Searle's original contention, but is powerless against the kind of Searlean representationalism that I have been trying to defend in this paper. If the notion of experience we use is the narrow notion of experienc*ing* favored by Searle, then it is indeed doubtful whether it is caused by anything that is not mental in nature. It is perfectly reasonable to say that what causes one's experiencing is one's desire to observe what goes around and one's general attentiveness, etc. That is to say, if the question "what caused your perception of the cat?" is not understood as, "what caused that cat-like content to be what it is?" but rather as, "what caused that perceiving to occur?" then the answer may very well be that it was caused by some psychological and neurological factors. The cat has nothing to do with the occurrence of that perceiving, for you may have been perceiving even if there was no cat there. One may even say that in that case it would still have been the same act of perceiving, for having a particular content is not an essential feature of a perceiving. Thus, the same act of perceiving that is actually of a cat, may have been of other objects without jeopardizing its self-identity. If experience is as Searle conceives it to be, i.e., a sort of transducer directed at external objects, then the event of activating it is not essentially tied to any particular phenomenal content it may have. It would then be more natural to describe some psychological state or disposition, and not the external object, as "the cause of the experience." But if an experience essentially has phenomenal properties such as being yellow, or square-looking, etc., we tend to say that what is so characterized could not have been caused by a mere psychological factor, and its existence is probably due to the causal efficacy of something in external reality.

It is, after all, quite remarkable that, so far as we know, every man, woman, and child that has ever lived (including even most of the insane) has, in everyday life, been a Realist, who accepts perceptual input as representing an external reality. To my mind, that indicates that Searle's basic contention is right: it is not a mere conjecture that what we see and hear is a world that exists independently of our minds. Rather, that our experiences are externally caused is something that we experience in the same way that we experience sense-qualia. In perception, we *feel* affected by forces that do not depend on our will and that defy our understanding; our experiences are palpably fashioned and determined by what we cannot but term "an exterenal reality." That basic sensation gives some initial corroboration to Metaphysical Realism. Yet we all (with the possible exception of some demented people) tend to hold that we can make perceptual mistakes; that goes to show that we do not assume that reality is as it is revealed to us. That gut-feeling of ours counts against Naive Realism: if what I am visually aware of may, on occasion, be a figment of my imagination, or simply erroneous, then it is impossible that what I am visually aware of is a part of external reality, for external reality cannot be erroneous, nor can it be a figment of my imagination.

Searle has an answer to that (old) argument from illusion and from error. He wishes to reconcile "the most naive of naive realisms" (p. 76) about perception with metaphysical realism by using what he calls "causal relativism." The latter is the daring metaphysical tenet that all properties are essentially diadic. On that view, to say that something is really F is to say that it would F-ly affect some (assumed) observers, under certain conditions: "the very notion of how things are themselves is relative to our capacity to receive causal inputs" (p. 76). Thus Searle can hold that what we perceive is indeed reality as it is in itself; he need not worry about the above argument from error and illusion, for he may say that, strictly speaking, there are no errors. One may be affected by an external object in a way that most other members of one's reference group are not affected by it, but even then one is perceiving reality as it is, for reality does have the property of being such that that person (given his or hers perceptual mechanism) would be affected by it in just that particular way.

Quine (in *Word and Object* (MIT Press: Cambridge, Mass., 1960), pp. 222–5) has argued that such a conception of reality is inconsistent, for disposition-talk makes sense only under the assumption "that there was a hidden trait of some sort, structural or otherwise, that inhered in the substance and accounted for" the said dispositional property. In the same section Quine claims that "redness of things is like solubitily," and must therefore be due to some monadic, inherent properties of things. I am not sure that Quine is right on that point: we have no proof that some ultimate properties cannot be irreducibly dispositional. But what is not possible, I think, is that *all* properties are diadic, in the sense required by Searle. That would undermine the notion of truth as correspondence, which is essential to any form of realism, and imply a relativism of the most pernicious sort. I shall argue that the causal relativism advocated by Searle is open to three objections. First, it is logically unformulable; second, it involves a vicious infinite regress; and third, it is self-refuting.

The first point is this: according to causal relativism, the general form of all ultimate properties of things-in-themselves would be "causes observers of kind S to perceive (or think, or believe, etc.) that p." But that form uses the monadic, non-causal-relative predicate "is of kind S." It will not do, of course, to redefine "being of kind S" as "being such that an observer of kind Q is caused by it to believe that it is of kind S," for in the definition we use again the absolute, non-causal-relative predicate "of kind Q." Hence, causal relativism is logically unformulable.

Second, causal relativism generates an infinite regress. On that view, the monadic predication sentence "F*a*" would be incomplete, for it fails to mention who or what it is that is causally made to take *a* as F. Hence it should be restated, more accurately, as the diadic "*a* appears F-ly to S-observers." Let "G" abbreviate the predicate, "appears F-ly to S-observers." Is "G*a*" adequate? It is not. Indeed, to us it looks as if *a* is G, but causal relativism mandates that we analyze that statement more accurately as a statement about our own causal interaction with *a*. Thus, "G*a*" should be rephrased as "*a* appears G-ly to Q-observers." The same move is now repeated, for how can one attribute the predicate "H" (i.e., "appears G-ly to Q-observers") to *a* without the perspectival *caveat* that that is only the way it causally affects observers of some kind, having a certain kind of interaction with it? So now we have to rephrase our statement once more and put it like this: "*a* appears H-ly to P-observers." Obviously, the process goes on for ever; and since every step on the way is shown to be inaccurate, inadequate, and incomplete, the ensuing regress is truly vicious.

Third, the causal-relative theory is pragmatically self-refuting. Suppose that I believe that the causal-relative theory is true: I believe that the world is such that it causes certain observers, given their perceptual mechanisms, to hold certain views, and there is no further specification of how the world is in itself irrespective of the way it may influence observers. Applying the said theory to my own believing it, I believe that I was caused by the world to hold the causal-relative theory. How, in that case, can I believe that the theory is true? If I think that, given my physical constitution, I was caused to believe that p, while an observer of a different constitution would have been caused under the circumstances to believe that not-p, I can not think that believing that p has any epistemic merit over and above believing that not-p. If I find myself believing that p, but I also believe that I was caused to have the said belief, e.g., by chemical means, then I have an excellent reason to hold my belief that p in abeyance, until I find whether there is any truth in it. Thus, if one finds oneself believing Causal Relativism, one has an excellent reason not to believe it. A realist cannot replace the notion of truth by the notion of an ineluctably forced belief. Thus, if the theory that ultimate properties of the real world are causal-relative is true, then that view of one's, i.e., believing the causal-relative theory, is also a causal-relative property of one's, and hence it says of itself that it has no claim whatsoever to being true. Hence, it is self-refuting.

I conclude that Searle's Causal Relativism, and the Naive Realism is was intended to buttress, are, if I understand them correctly, quite indefensible; I have argued, however, that Searle's major theses need not be seriously affected if the said theories are discarded and replaced by some version of the representationalist theory of experience. On the contrary, I have tried to show that, given that modification, one can argue even more effectively for Searle's Realistic ontology.

NOTES

1   Unless otherwise indicated, all page references are to J. R. Searle, *Intentionality* (Cambridge University Press: Cambridge, 1983).
2   I use italicizing as a nominative device, such that "*p*" is a variable ranging over situations, while "p" is a schematic letter substitutable by sentences.
3   "Indeterminacy, Empiricism, and the Third Person," *Journal of Philosophy* pp. 84 (1987), pp. 123–46.

13

Response:
Perception and the Satisfactions
of Intentionality

JOHN R. SEARLE

I believe that my account of Intentionality has at least the following advantage over other accounts I am familiar with: An enormous variety of different forms of Intentionality ranging from belief and desire to lust, disgust, shame, pride, perception, intentional action, memory and linguistic meaning can all be accounted for within a rather small set of primitive intentional notions, notions such as psychological mode and representative content, conditions of satisfaction, direction of fit, intentional causation, self referentiality, Network, Background and a few others. Each of these is independently motivated. I am always puzzled when some of my critics (not contained in this volume) complain that I lack a *theory*, that I do not explain where Intentionality "comes form." It turns out, under analysis, that I do not answer their question because I think it is misconceived. In general they are hankering after some form of reductionism that will show that Intentionality can be eliminated in favor of . . . well what? Functions, behavior, causation, computer programs, and social relations are all candidates. I do indeed believe that all Intentional states – indeed all mental phenomena – are caused by neurophysiological processes and are realized in the brain; but this view is a consequence of my naturalistic, biological approach to the mind and my rejection of any form of dualism. It does not commit me to "materialism" or "reductionism" as those notions are usually understood.

The real gap in my account is not that I do not get rid of Intentionality in favor of something else but rather that I do not explain the details of the relation between Intentionality and consciousness. This is a problem I am working on now.[1]

The first two articles in this section attack my position from quite different points of view: Armstrong from his well known views on materialism, Malcolm from a Wittgensteinian perspective.

David Armstrong

Armstrong's elegant paper discusses many of the most important issues in *Intentionality*. We agree on many things, but in this discussion I will confine myself to a few main issues where we disagree. The issues are, in order: reduction, causation and perception, and the Background.

Reductionism

I am very suspicious of contemporary philosophical discussions of reductionism because it seems to me the notion is just too unclear; there are too many types of reductionism under discussion. I have similar doubts about the notions of emergence and supervenience. Whenever we say that A-type things are reducible to B type things, it seems to me there are a half a dozen different things we might mean. Of these, *at least* the following three are crucial to this discussion: *Ontological reductionism* says that A-type things do not really have a separate mode of existence, but are just B-type things; there is nothing else there except B-type things. For example, heat (of a gas) just is the mean kinetic energy of molecular motion. *Logical reductionism* says A-type things can be *defined* in terms of B-type things; statements about A-type things are entirely definable in B-type statements. For example, numbers can be defined as classes of classes. Logical reductionism entails ontological reductionism. *Causal reductionism* says that A-type things are entirely caused by B-type things. For example, the solidity of the table is entirely caused by the behavior of the molecules of which the table is composed.

Now, when we ask "Is Intentionality reducible?" what are we asking? Well, it is certainly not logically reducible, at least not on my account. It certainly is causally reducible in the sense that all of the Intentional phenomena are caused by the behavior of the elements of the brain. Is it ontologically reducible? Well, nothing that is a genuine and separate feature of the world can be reduced to anything else. Everything can be reduced to itself and nothing else, because everything is what it is and not another thing. So, if Intentionality is a genuine and separate phenomenon, as I think it is, it is not ontologically reducible to something else.

Armstrong thinks that if a property is causally supervenient on the behavior of the elements of its microstructure then it ought to be ontologically reducible as well. On his view, higher level supervenient properties like solidity and consciousness, because they are subject to the sort of causal reduction involved in causal supervenience, are for that reason ontologically reducible as well. For Armstrong solidity, consciousness, and Intentionality are all in the same boat as heat: there is nothing there in addition to the behavior of the micro elements. Now that is emphatically not my view and I believe it is mistaken. Supervenience, however strict, does not entail reductionism. From the fact that a property is supervenient on the behavior of lower level elements it simply does not follow that there is nothing there except the behavior of the lower level elements. In the case of, for example, consciousness, we have a supervenient, but nonetheless nonreducible property. That, indeed, is the difference between, for example, heat and consciousness. Consciousness is a separate and nonreducible property; and in that sense it is, I guess, "emergent."

Indeed, by agreeing with me that certain features such as liquidity and solildity are "emergent," in this sense, it seems to me Armstrong is committed to denying their ontological reducibility, because by saying the property is emergent we are saying there is a separate phenomenon there, even though the phenomenon may be entirely causally supervenient on other phenomena. Causal reduction yes; ontological reduction no.

Armstrong hopes for a logical reduction along functional lines, but the functionalism in question is not to be merely causal, but also to be teleological, in a sense of "teleology" that is made respectable by biological analogies. Thus, for example, we might agree to call anything a heart if it functioned teleologically, if it served the purpose of pumping blood in an organism in an appropriate fashion. So on this definition artificial hearts are still hearts, and we have logically reduced the notion of a heart to teleological functional notions. Can we do the same thing with the notions of consciousness or belief, desire, etc.? My answer is: No, not without an arbitrary redefinition that eliminates the mental component. Just as an actual human heart has an *intrinsic* structure *and* performs a teleological *function*, so actual intentional states have an *intrinsic* mental structure and perform teleological *functions*. Now, in the case of the heart we can carve off the structure and concentrate on the function, while ignoring the structure; but in the case of the mind, if we ignore the structure we lose what was interesting to us about the mental in the first place. "Well, why can't we capture what was important about the structure just by giving a good teleogical account of the function?" There are two reasons for this, one obvious and one not so obvious.

The obvious reason: you cannot define intrinsic mental structures in terms of functions because a system might perform all the functions, both internally and externally, and not have the structure. For example, a system might behave exactly as if it were conscious and still not be conscious. A system might behave as if it had beliefs and desires, and still not have beliefs and desires. This is the decisive objection to any behavioristically inspired attempt to reduce the "mental" to the "physical." Similarly, a system might have the structure and still for some reason or another not produce the appropriate functions internally or externally. For example, a man might be completely conscious and still not behave as if he were conscious.

The not so obvious reason: a causal phenomenon can only be identified as a *purposive teleological function* relative to some intrinsic intentionality. Whenever we say that such and such serves a certain *purpose*, as opposed to saying it just causes certain *effects*, we are committed to there being an answer to the question "how is the purpose to be identified?" In relation to what is the phenomenon identified as a purpose rather than merely a cause? Hearts do, in fact, pump blood. But hearts know nothing of functions, purposes or teleology. When we say the heart *functions* to pump blood, we are describing a *causal* sequence as a *function*, but such descriptions are always relative to our Intentionality, relative to our interests. So, we cannot eliminate Intentionality in general and replace it with teleological function, because teleological function only exists relative to intrinsic Intentionality.

Causation and Perception

Armstrong, like Burge, objects to my including the causal component within the perceptual content. He thinks that I am ascribing too much intellectual complexity to the content of perceptions, and that, for example, animals and small children could not possibly have the sorts of perceptual contents that I ascribe. Now part, but only part, of the disagreement here rests on a misunderstanding of my views and thus is not a genuine disagreement but a failure on my part to communicate. I am not arguing that the dog thinks to himself "I am having a causally self-referential visual experience," but rather I am claiming that any visual experience, like any tactile experience, is experienced by us *as caused by* its Intentional object. Armstrong actually misstates my position when he says that I want the causation to be the part of the intentional object of the experience. That is not quite right. It is part of the *conditions of satisfaction*, but it does not thereby become an *object*. The idea that I have – and I will say more about it in my reply to Burge and McDowell – is that our perceptual experiences (unlike, e.g., our conscious experiences of acting or day-dreaming) are experienced by us, in such a way that we experience the intentional object as causing the very experience of it. When, for example, I feel a sharp object pressing into my back, the feeling I have is one of a sharp object causing that very feeling.

This much stated, is there still a genuine disagreement between me and Armstrong? Yes, and it is a radical disagreement. The basic disagreement between us derives from the fact that Armstrong holds what I take to be the amazing view that our perceptual experiences have no internal phenomenological properties at all. On this account, there is nothing that it feels like to see something, or touch something, or taste something. When Armstrong uses the word "consciousness," it seems clear that he does not mean what I mean, nor what I take the rest of us to mean, by consciousness. He is simply talking about a kind of inner registering of our bodily states. Conscious states as such for Armstrong have no internal phenomenological feel, no "what it is like" internal phenomenal properties. I am convinced on a close reading of his paper that our really radical differences stem from this view and it is too large to try to settle within the present discussion. I intend to discuss these issues at considerable length in my forthcoming book.

It is Armstrong's refusal to accept the common-sense conception of conscious perceptual experiences and consciousness, in general, that leads him to make a distinction between perceptions and perceptual experiences. A perceptual experience we are to think of as a second order consciousness of a perception. At one point he extends an olive branch to me by suggesting that I "could and should" accept this distinction. But I have to push the olive branch away. Every conscious perception is precisely a conscious perceptual experience.

The Background

Armstrong is suspicious of my argument for the Background; and he wonders why we could not simply postulate that the Background also has Intentionality, but *lacks a further background*. I believe, this answer along with his argument, derived from Dennett, to the effect that we might "discharge" Intentionality by way of reducing it to progressively more stupid homunculi, misses the point made in the original argument. The point of my original argument was that any Intentional content is subject to different interpretations and applications. This would apply to any Background Intentionality. The progressively more stupid homunculi would still have alternative interpretations of their Intentional content. As long as all we have is Intentional content there is nothing to fix one interpretation rather than another.

It really is of no help to characterize the "Background Intentionality" as having "different degrees" of Intentionality or a "lower grade" of Intentionality. What is this supposed to mean? That in the Background I have only a piece of a belief? Or an extremely stupid belief? It ought to be a rule in these discussions that whenever we postulate a form of Intentionality, we are required to state exactly what sort of content that intentionality is supposed to have, and it ought to be a further rule that we be required to clarify any such claims with precisely described examples. Thus, if we are postulating Intentionality possessed by stupid homunculi, what is it exactly, that the homunculi are supposed to believe, suppose, etc.?

Well let's try it with an example. I now believe that George Bush is president. Now that belief I argue, requires both a Network of other beliefs, desires, etc. and a Background of preintentional capacities. To anyone who is patient enough to listen I will tell him what sorts of things are in the Network – that we are in the United States, that the United States is a republic, that is has presidential elections every four years, etc. – but I cannot tell him the beliefs in the Background because I claim that there aren't any. Now Armstrong (following Dennett) tells us that there are beliefs in the Background, but they are possessed by by an army of progressively stupider homunculi until finally they are "discharged." Now what I want to know is, what *exactly* do these homunculi believe at each and every level? The thesis on its face is fantastic and of course we are not supposed to take it literally. We are not supposed to ask who are these homunculi, how old are they, what are their names, etc. But the bit about progressively more stupid beliefs, though part of the fantasy, is meant literally. Otherwise no explanation has been given. Until these obvious questions are answered we have no idea what the thesis is, but from Armstrong (and Dennett) we get no answer.

In any case the infinite regress argument for the Background cannot be evaded by postulating degenerate forms of Intentionality because any intelligible human form of intentionality would still presuppose a Background. As it stands, I believe, Armstrong's only suggestion for evading the infinite regress argument has not been made fully coherent.

Finally, Armstrong asks me the important question, What do I think a "scientific" theory of Intentionality might, in fact, look like? Actually, I do not believe there will be any one simple theory. I think a perfect science of psychology and a perfect neurobiology of the brain would contain a lot different explanations of different aspects of Intentionality and different sorts of Intentional phenomena. So, for example, we expect some day to have both psychological and neurophysiological accounts of memory, and we will, of course, need philosophical or conceptual accounts of the relevant concepts and of their interrelations. I do not look forward to a single all-inclusive theory of Intentionality, but rather a lot of different theories attacking different problems from different points of view.

Norman Malcolm

Malcolm uses a form of philosophical analysis which was very influential in the 1950s, but which I believe was discredited by the mid-sixties.[2] It is the form of analysis that tries to solve philosophical problems by examining the "use" of words. I will now try to say, as succinctly as I can, why I believe his particular application of this method to problems concerning belief does not work and why I think the whole approach is severely limited.

Let us start with a point on which we both agree: Sentences of the form "I believe that p" are characteristically, but not always "used" to make qualified assertions. For example if you ask me "Where is George Bush today?", I might say, "I believe he is in Washington." Now this utterance clearly seems to be, among other things, a qualified assertion about Bush; and as Malcolm points out, it will not do for you to say, "Please don't talk about your mental states, I was asking about George Bush and not about your mental states." To have a name, let's call this point the "agreed fact." Now, what are we to make of it? Malcolm thinks it is an important *result*, providing us with a solution to certain philosophical problems. I think it is not a *solution* at all but part of a problem. It is obviously not a solution to the philosophical problem about the *nature* of belief, because it does not tell us what a belief is, it does not tell us, e.g., what fact about me makes it *true* for me or anyone else to say of me that I believe that p. It is, in addition, puzzling because it is not obvious how we are to square it with a whole lot of other facts we already know about the word "belief" and about beliefs. Now what exactly are these other facts? Well, here are some of them

1   I have a whole lot of beliefs that are totally unconnected to any first person utterances of mine. I have never reported and never will report them in a sentence of the form "I believe that p" or in any other sentence. And I will never make any qualified assertions with the same content that they have. Now these beliefs are not qualified assertions nor anything of the sort. So what are they? The agreed fact does not answer this question, indeed it does not even address it.

2   The agreed fact does not explain the meaning of "believe," because it only concerns one small class of occurences of "believe," those in the first-person present indicative. But it is a condition of adequacy on any acount of the meaning of the word that the word must have the same meaning in "I believe" as it does in "You believe;" it must mean that same in "If I believe p, then I believe that q" as it does in "I believe that p." (Otherwise, *modus ponens* would be invalid); furthermore, it must keep the same meaning in "I used to believe" or "I will believe" as it does in "I do now believe." So, what is the relation between the agreed fact and the meaning of "believe," a meaning it has even in cases in which the agreed fact does not apply? From the agreed fact and from Malcolm we get no answer.

3   Contrary to Malcom's claim,the agreed fact does not solve Moore's paradox. Here is why. Some occurrences of "I believe p" are indeed used to make hesitant assertions, but some are not. Among those that are not are some that are used to state plain facts about the speaker, such as the plain fact that he or she believes that p. Suppose someone says to me, e.g., "We are doing a public opinion survey and we would like to ask you some questions about your political beliefs. First, do you believe that Bush will be reelected?" After some thought I say "Yes, I believe that he will be." Here I am reporting a belief, not making a hesitant assertion. The questioner is asking about my *beliefs*, not trying to elicit hesitant assertions. Malcolm and I agree that sentences of the form "I believe that p" have different uses; and I now want to insist that one of the uses of sentences of the form "I believe that p" is to state the plain fact that the speaker believes that p. (Does anyone deny this?)

Now, let us concentrate on these cases for a moment. Moore's paradox is: why cannot I conjoin one of these reports about my belief with a plain statement about a matter which is logically independent of that report? Why cannot I say, reporting my belief, "I believe Bush will be reelected"; and then add, "Bush will not be reelected." In general, Moore's paradox concerns the oddity of conjoining the report of the belief that p with the assertion that not p. It simply does not answer this puzzle, indeed it is quite irrelevant, to point out that sometimes the primary purpose of uttering the first-person sentence is to make a hesitant assertion.

So, even if we accept the agreed fact, we still do not have an analysis of the nature of *belief*, and we are still left with at least two puzzles. First, why is it that sometimes the statement that I believe that p is a hesitant assertion that p. And second, Moore's paradox: why is it that I cannot conjoin the report that I believe that p with the assertion that not p? Actually, I think these two puzzles have rather simple solutions (indeed, they are really part of a single larger question of the relation of belief and assertion), and as I have stated these solutions and discussed their implications at some considerable length elsewhere,[3] I shall be very brief now.

The verb "believe" and the noun "belief" name certain Intentional phenomena, in particular, beliefs are intentional states of a certain type having a certain sort of direction of fit, conditions of satisfaction, etc. Now, the reason that the sentences of the form "I believe that p" can often be *used* to make hesitant assertions, even though the sentence does not *mean* "I hesitantly assert that p," is that belief is a sincerity condition on the speech act of asserting, and one in general can, by familiar mechanisms of indirect speech acts, perform a speech act by simply asserting that one has the sincerity condition in question.[4] Thus, "I believe that p" can be used indirectly to make an assertion that p in the same way that "I want you to leave the room" can be used to order you to leave the room; "I am sorry I stepped on your foot" can be used to apologize for stepping on your foot; "I intend to come to see you" can be used to promise to come to see you; and so on for many, many such cases. In short, there is a very general phenomenon which is explained in speech act theory, whereby a certain sort of speech act can be performed by asserting that the sincerity condition on that speech act is satisfied.

This, in brief outline, is the answer to the first question. Let us turn to the second. It is a general feature of any speech act that has a sincerity condition that the performance of that speech act is an expression of the psychological state specified in that sincerity condition. Thus, every promise is an expression of an intention, every order is an expression of a wish or a desire, every apology is an expression of sorrow, every assertion is an expression of belief. Moore's paradox is simply one instance of a very large class of cases. The oddity Moore cites about assertion is exactly parallel to "I promise to do A but I do not intend to do A," "I apologize for doing A but I am not sorry that I did A," "I order you to do A, but I do not want you to do A," etc. The explanation in every case is that one cannot, in consistency, express a psychological state, and simultaneously deny the existence of the psychological state expressed.

Now, Malcolm's objection to this analysis is that he is puzzled as to how one can express a psychological state that one does not, in fact, have. He thinks that it is incoherent to say "John expressed the belief that p, but he did not, infact, believe that p; he was lying." I do not find anything at all incoherent or even odd about this, it seems to me perfectly consistent logically and acceptable linguistically. In his article Malcolm systematically and persistently confuses "John expressed *the* belief that p" with "John expressed *his* belief that p." If I say the latter I am indeed committed to the claim that John believed that p, but the former does not commit me to any such claim. Indeed, it is, in general, possible to express a belief without having that belief, and there is a very simple proof of this fact: the verb phrase "express the belief" has a performative occurence. A speaker who says, "I hereby express the belief that p" is expressing the belief that p. But this fact is logically independent of the question of whether or not the speaker actually has the belief that he expresses. The performative utterance can be truly reported by saying "He expressed the belief that p," even though he never had any such belief. Since Malcolm is impressed by the "use" of expressions, he might ponder the difference in use between "the belief that p" and "his belief that p." Occurrences of the second imply that someone believes that p, but occurrences of the first do not imply that anyone believes that p. Thus, for example, the sentence "The belief that triangles have seventeen sides has never been held by anyone" is perfectly OK both linguistically and logically, and for all I know it may even be true. But "John's belief has never been held by John" is inconsistent, at best. In sum, one can easily express beliefs one does not have. People who do this on purpose are called liars or dishonest, etc.

Well, somebody might say that this is just the matter of different intuitions about the word "express." I quite agree with this, and I think the point about the word "express" is of very little importance. The point that I am making could be made without using that word. One could say that anybody who asserts that p commits himself to believing that p, makes manifest a commitment to believing that p, or some such. It does not matter for these purposes. I think my use of the word "express" is perfectly standard and I am absolutely confident that *x expressed the belief that p* does not entail *x believes that p*. But nothing in this particular point about Moore's paradox hinges on these lexical facts about the verb "express."

The general difficulty with the approach exemplified by Malcolm's paper is that you cannot get very far examining the "use" of words without some general theory of meaning and speech acts. A few remarks about the use of words are pretty much useless without a theory of the relations between "use" and meaning. Once you have such a theory, the use will fall into place. But without the theory, you do not know what to make of the "use," and I believe that Malcolm's discussion exemplifies precisely this difficulty.

Eddy M. Zemach

Zemach mistakes the nature of the enterprise of chapter 2 of *Intentionality*, "The Intentionality of Perception." It is not as he supposes, the "core" of the book, and its aim is not, except in passing, to discuss the *epistemological issues* which most concern Zemach. As I said on its first page, "my aim in this chapter is not, except incidentally, to discuss the traditional problem of perception, but rather to place an account of perceptual experiences within the context of the theory of Intentionality that was outlined in the previous chapter." In short, its aim is to situate the Intentionality of perception within a general theory of Intentionality.

If any chapter is the "core" of the book, I would suppose it to be chapter 3 on the Intentionality of intention and action, where I integrate the results of the investigation of both cognition and volition into what I hope is at least a step towards a unified theory of Intentionality. In chapter 2 I make some passing references to the traditional epistemological issues, but my aim was to try to clarify my own views by contrast with certain traditional views, and also to try to show that my account was not subject to certain skeptical objections. But it was, most emphatically, not my aim to develop a general account of the epistemological aspects of perception, nor to answer skepticism, in general. The aim of the chapter, to repeat, is to account for the *Intentionality* of perception. It deals only incidentally and in passing with epistemology.

My objection to the representative theory is the standard objection, going at least as far as Berkeley, that the representative theory has no way of making the notion of representation or resemblance intelligible. My objection to phenomenalism is perhaps new, though I am not sure, because it may be implicit in Wittgenstein. It is that a consistent phenomenalism inevitably leads to solipsism, since the logical reduction of material objects to sense data reduces the publicly accessible real world to sets of private phenomenal worlds. And since for each person the only phenomenal world accessible to him is his internal phenomenal world, it would be impossible on a phenomenalistic account for there to be a public language. However, to repeat, my aim was analytical, rather than epistemological. I was trying to analyze Intentionality, rather than discuss the nature of perceptual knowledge or perceptual evidence. So I have to say that most of the concerns expressed in Zemach's article are really irrelevant to my concerns.

Zemach asks me point blank whether I intend that chapter as offering arguments for Metaphysical Realism ("the view that there is a real world out there"), Perceptual Realism ("the view that we gain information about the world by perceiving it") and Naive Realism ("the view that we perceive the world as it really is"). Actually, I do not use the expression "Perceptual Realism" and my definition of Naive Realism would be a little more cautious than Zemach's. I would simply say that the Naive Realist believes that we sometimes perceive objects directly, and sometimes we perceive them the way they really are. I do not intend chapter 2 as primarily an *argument* for any of these theses, though I will offer a sketch of a transcendental argument for metaphysical realism in this reply. So the answer to his questin is no, except that I do in *Intentionality* argue *indirectly* for Naive Realism by trying to show that phenomenalism and the representative theory of perception (the two chief rivals to Naive Realism) are incoherent and that Naive Realism of the causal variety I present is not subject to skeptical objections.

Zemach finds my discussion of perceptual evidence to be inadequate. He presents me with a dilemma. If I know that there is a car there because I see the car, then how do I know that I see the car? Either this knowledge is inferential or it is not. If, on the one hand, it is inferential, then I can no longer claim that I do not have to infer that there is a car there on the basis of seeing it. If, on the other hand, it is not inferential, then how do I know that it is true? "If Searle does not take it upon himself to answer that question, then his argument in this chapter is seriously incomplete and his exchange with the representationalist incomprehensible" (p. 171). But the point that I was making is as follows: If I say to somebody, "The car is on the street," and he says to me, "How do you know?" it is an answer to his question to say, "I saw it." The statement "I saw it" provides evidence, grounds, or reason for the truth of "I know that the car is on the street." But if somebody says to me, as I am standing there looking at it, "How do you know that you are now seeing it?" there isn't anything that I could provide by way of *evidence* or *grounds* in that sense. That isn't to say that the statement "I see it" or "I am now looking at it" are self-verifying, or that they can't be mistaken, it is just to say that we don't have perceptual evidence for their truth in the way that they provide perceptual evidence for the truth of other claims. But these remarks are not intended as part of a debate with the representational or picture theory of perception. I know that Zemach holds such a theory; but, as I argued in chapter 2, it seems to me incoherent. So it was not the aim of this passage to debate the picture theory.

Near the end of his article Zemach raises some important philosophical issues that I would like to address directly. He points out that I hold two propositions which to him appear to be inconsistent. I do, indeed, accept both propositions, and if they are both true they must be consistent; so I should at least try to explain how they can be consistent and, if possible, remove any appearance of inconsistency.

The two propositions are:

1 Metaphysical realism. There exists a reality whose existence and whose features are independent of our representations of it.
2 Conceptual relativity.[5] Our conception of reality, our conception of how it is, is always made relative to our constitution.

I have not, in print, presented an argument for either of these and it may be that they do not need argument. But at least a sketch of a transcendental argument can be given for the first by saying that metaphysical realism is the condition of possibility of there being public discourse at all. In order that I should address you and say, e.g., "the cat is on the mat" I must presuppose an independently existing world of publicly accessible objects to which expressions like "the cat" and the "the mat" are used to refer. A public language presupposes a public world. And when I address you in what I presuppose is a public language, a language which you can understand in the same way that I understand it, I also presuppose that there exist public objects of reference. In normal discourse none of these "presuppositions" takes the form of beliefs or even, strictly speaking, "presuppositions." They are part of what I call the Background; in the normal functioning of the Background such elements form the conditions of intelligible representation but are not themselves representations.

To state the features of the Background as explicit propositions inevitably distorts the functioning of the Background and is one source of skepticism. If I say "There exists a reality independent of our representations," that naturally invites the question "How do you know?"; and there does not seem to be any non-question begging answer to that. If it is just one belief among others, how would I go about justifying it? But the presupposition of realism is not just one claim among others, it is rather a condition of possibility of my being able to make publicly accessible *claims* at all.

Conceptual relativism, as I have formulated it, is meant to be a trivial truth to the effect that we only form concepts that we are able to form. We have a biological constitution which is quite limited and specific. We have a sensory apparatus of a certain kind and not of other possible kinds. We have a certain level of intelligence and not some other level. Our cultural and social apparatus is simply the form or forms that our biological constitution has taken over the history of the development of our species. In general, it is trivially true that we can only do what we are able to do, and where our conceptual apparatus is concerned we can only form the concepts we are able to form.

Now, Zemach supposes that my version of conceptual relativism commits me to "the daring metaphysical tenet, that all properties are essentially diadic" (p. 177). On Zemach's interpretation, every predicate would have as part of its truth conditions some reference to human constitution. But that is not my view and it is does not follow from my version of conceptual relativism. From the fact that a feature F forms part of the conditions of possibility of the applicability of a concept C, it does not follow that a reference to F is part of the meaning, part of the truth conditions, of C. This point is obvious if you think of examples. Suppose, for the sake of argument, that only beings of a certain level of intelligence can use the concept of "oxidation." That fact would not render the concept diadic. On this supposition it is a condition of possibility of a person's making the statement, "Iron oxidizes," that he or she have a certain level of intelligence; but it does not follow that the meaning of the statement contains a reference to intelligence or that intelligence is now part of the definition of "oxidizes" or "oxidization."

Once this mistake is removed I believe much of the appearance of inconsistency between (1) and (2) is removed: (1) says that there is a real world, (2) says that we can only describe it (represent it, form a conception of it) within our limitations and relative to our concept forming apparatus. Where is the inconsistency? Without some further argument there is no reason to doubt that these are perfectly consistent.

Actually, at least one philosopher, Hilary Putnam, thinks that a version of (2) is inconsistent with (1) and, indeed, he uses conceptual relativism to argue against metaphysical realism and to substitute for metaphysical realism a view he calls "internal realism."[6] I am not suggesting that Zemach has been influenced by Putnam, but since Putnam's argument is the only recent argument I know for supporting Zemach's suggestion that (1) and (2) may be inconsistent with each other, and since I think it is bad argument I will conclude this discussion by briefly considering it. Putnam thinks that because we can only *state* the fact that iron oxidizes relative to a vocabulary and conceptual system, that therefore the fact only *exists* relative to a vocabulary and conceptual system. So, on his view if conceptual relativism is true, then metaphysical realism is false. But the premise of his argument does not entail the conclusion. It is, indeed, trivially true that all statements are made within a conceptual apparatus for making statements. Without a language we cannot talk. It does, indeed, follow from this that given alternative conceptual apparatuses there will be alternative descriptions of reality. For example, not every language will even have a vocabulary for stating that iron oxidizes. But it simply does not follow that *the fact* that iron oxidizes is in any way language-dependent or relative to a system of concepts or anything of the sort. Long after we are all dead and there are no statements of any kind, iron will still oxidize; and this is just another way of saying that the fact that iron oxidizes does not depend in any way on the fact that we can state that iron oxidizes. (Does anyone really, seriously, doubt this?) To repeat a point made earlier, the conditions of possibility of *stating* the facts are not necessarily conditions of possibility of the *existence* of the facts. I am not suggesting that Zemach is making this mistake but I believe that Putnam does. And without making some version of this mistake it is hard to see how anyone could suppose, as Zemach does, that metaphysical realism and conceptual relativism are inconsistent.

NOTES

1 J. R. Searle, *Consciousness* (MIT Press: Cambridge, Mass. forthcoming).
2 J. R. Searle, "Meaning and Speech Acts," (1962); J. R. Searle, "Assertions and Abberations," (1966).
3 J. R. Searle *Speech Acts* (1969), chapters 3, 6, 7, and 8; Intentionality (1983); "Assertions and Aberrations" (1966); "Meaning and Speech Acts" (1962); "Indirect Speech Acts" (1975).
4 J. R. Searle, "Indirect Speech Acts" (1975).
5 He calls this "causal relativity," I do not use that terminology and, in fact, I find it misleading.
6 Hilary Putnam, *The Many Faces of Realism* (Open Court: La Salle, Ill., 1987).

Part IV

Reference and Intentionality

14

Vision and Intentional Content

TYLER BURGE

John Searle's treatment of visual perception and *de re* thought in his book *Intentionality* consistutes a challenging point of view presented in a clear, forthright way. It deserves attention not only for its own merits, but also because it represents an approach to vision and belief that is perenially tempting. In many fundamental respects, it is a revival of Russell's view.[1] In this paper, I shall critically discuss Searle's approach, with special attention to his conception of Intentional content. I shall use this discussion as a basis for replying to his remarks about some of my work on the same subjects.

I

Let me begin by setting a background of agreement. I think that Searle is right to develop issues in the philosophy of language in close conjunction with issues in the philosophy of mind. We differ in our evaluation of the work on reference that grew out of the ideas of Donnellan and Kripke: I think that it is fundamentally right as far as it goes; he thinks that is is fundamentally wrong. But we share the view that much of this work is weakened by largely ignoring the relevance of thought to language.

I am also in substantial agreement with Searle's non-reductionistic, realist approach to Intentional phenomena. I accept the broad but loose analogy between the content of speech and the content of thought that Searle appeals to, and I agree with many of the points he makes in filling out the analogy (pp. 4–13). These analogies do not, of course, answer all questions about the determination of content. But reviewing them reminds one that we share a useable core conception.

A key element in Searle's account of Intentional phenomena is his explication of Intentional content in terms of the conditions for satisfaction of mental states and events. In identifying such phenomena we typically make use of propositional items that may be evaluated as true or false. Searle puts this point by saying that conditions for satisfaction are "internal" to Intentional states:

> just as the conditions of satisfaction are internal to the speech act, so the conditions of satisfaction of the Intentional state are internal to the Intentional state. Part of what

makes my statement that snow is white the statement that it is, is that it has those truth conditions and not others. Similarly part of what makes my wish that it were raining the wish it is, is that certain things will satisfy it and certain other things will not. (p. 11; cf. p. 22)

So stated, I accept this view without serious reservation.

Searle says that a belief "represents" its truth conditions or conditions of satisfaction, and explains this notion by appealing to the notion of a statement's representing its truth conditions (p. 12). Neither notion is transparent to me. But I take it that the idea is that the Intentional content of the belief is, or involves, a certain requirement on what it takes to satisfy the belief. The belief represents its truth conditions in the sense that the requirement "determines" (pp. 12, 19) what states of affairs are required for satisfaction of the belief (cf. p. 13). As long as "determines" is read in a relatively inspecific way, I think that these points can be taken to be correct and relatively uncontroversial.

What is controversial is the application Searle makes of these remarks, or the inferences he draws from them. It appears that he interprets them in a more restricted way than I think that they should be interpreted.

II

The phrase "truth conditions" (similarly – "satisfaction conditions") is one of the most widely and carelessly used phrases in analytic philosophy. The expression has numerous non-equivalent applications. But it is rarely explicated. Consequently, it occasions all manner of mischief – unfocused doctrine, misunderstanding, fruitless disagreement.

Searle uses the expression with more circumspection than most. But I think that it is a source of difficulty in evaluating his account. One reason why the phrase is not clarified in contemporary writing, unfortunately a secondary reason, is that difficult philosophical problems attend any attempt at serious clarification. I shall skirt such problems by approaching the difficulty in evaluating Searle's account through some relatively elementary considerations.

Searle notes the distinction between (1) construing a "truth condition" as a requirement that has to be met for an Intentional state to be veridical (here the truth condition itself has Intentional or referential properties), and (2) construing a "truth condition" as what the requirement makes reference to – what would fulfill the requirement if the Intentional state is veridical (here the truth condition is something like a state of affairs) (p. 13). This is a good distinction, often ignored. I shall always take "truth condition" in the first sense, as a requirement with Intentional properties.

There are many ways of stating what might count as a sentence or statement's "truth conditions." A statement or used sentence occurrence of the form "That F is G" (applied, let us imagine, to a physical object) is true if and only if:

a   that F is G [where one indicates the relevant F]
b   the F that is the referent of the relevant token of "that" is G

c   the object that falls in the extension of (or has the property indicated by) "F"
    and that is the referent of the relevant token of "that," falls in the extension
    of (or has the property indicated by) "G"
d   there is an F, and it is the referent of the relevant token of "that," and it is G
e   there is an F, and it is at the end of such and such a causal chain leading to
    the relevant occurance of "that," and it is G
f   there is an object that fits the concept associated with "F" (or bears such and
    such a causal relation to the relevant occurence of "F") and it is at the end of
    such and such a causal chain leading to the relevant occurrence of "that" (or fits the
    concept associated with the relevant occurrence of "that") and it fits the
    concept associated with "G" (or bears such and such a causal relation to the
    occurrence of "G").

Any of (a)–(f) might be taken to give the "truth conditions" of the statement or
used sentence. Different ones might be given, depending on the point of talking
about "truth conditions." (a) is a homophonic "translation" of the sentence, or
reiteration of the statement. It must be used in a context in which one preserves the
reference of the demonstrative that occurs in the statement whose truth conditions
are being given. (b) involves semantical ascent with respect to the demonstrative.
(c) adds semantical ascent with respect to the predicates. (d) involves the semantical
ascent of (b), but adds a change in the logical form, adding a quantification that
takes a step in the direction of Russell's analysis of the definite article. (e) is like (d)
except that it includes an account of the relation of demonstrative reference, which
is left primitive in (b)–(d). (The form and content of the account are irrelevant to
present purposes.) (f) is like (e) except that it adds an account of the semantical
relation associated with predication left primitive in (c). Clearly permutations
among these ways of giving truth conditions could lengthen the list.

Apart from a homophonic "translation" of the statement, there are various forms
and degrees of semantic ascent, various means of representing logical form, and
various analyses or accounts of those relations between the statement (or sentence-
at-a-use) and the world that constitute the requirements for being true associated
with the statement.

Searle's account of Intentional content is in terms of truth conditions or satisfaction conditions. But he does not say enough about the point of his appeal to truth
conditions to motivate choosing one among various possible types of "truth conditions." The problem is made more complex by the fact that we are concentrating on
the Intentional content of visual experience. There are significant differences
between visual experiences and statements. Nevertheless, there is supposed to be
a fundamental analogy. And we can try to evaluate the account by reference to the
analogy as Searle presents it.

Searle's account gives the following satisfaction conditions to a propositional
visual experience "VE." VE is true if and only if:

(S)   there is an F there and there being an F there is a causing this very
      visual experience (p. 48).

I have some reservations about taking visual experiences to have propositional form.
(Searle argues for his view on this matter (p. 40); but I do not find the arguments
persuasive.) But I shall accept the point for the sake of argument.

It seems to me that (S) bears fairly close comparison to (e). I will take it that "F" remains the same between (e) and (S). And I will assume that "there" (in the sense of "which is there") in (S) approximately plays the role of "G" in (e) – though this latter comparison will not be crucial. In both (e) and (S), the predicates appear in an entirely straightforward manner.[2]

Searle introduces the quantifier "there is" in (S) as an explicit representation of the existential commitments of visual experience, in something like the way that the quantifier has been introduced in (e) as an explicit representation of the existential commitments of demonstrative reference in the statement. This point will not figure prominently in the discussion.

Searle's (S) has a self-referential element, whereas (e) does not, at least not explicitly. This difference derives from special views about visual experience, and from Searle's desire to provide what he calls a "first-person" account of the content. One can provide a parallel to (S) on this count, however:

> (e')   there is an F, and it is at the end of such and such a causal chain leading to this very statement (or sentence occurrence), and it is G.

Like (e) and (e'), (S) involves a certain *ascent*: Reference is made in the truth condition to one of the vehicles of reference in the Intentional item whose truth conditions are being given. In (e) the truth conditions make reference to an occurrence of the word "that," which is a vehicle of reference, within the statement whose truth conditions are being given. In (e') reference is made to the statement itself. In (S) the truth conditions make reference to the visual experience, which is a vehicle for referring to the physical object that is seen.

Also like (e) and (e'), (S) involves an "analysis" or *account* of the referential relation between the vehicle of reference and the physical object referred to. A broadly causal account is gestured toward in both cases.

Intuitively, Searle's proposal is not immediately attractive. Almost anyone will have the initial feeling that the Intentional content that Searle attributes to visual experiences is too complicated or too sophisticated. One instinctively thinks that not every visual experience, including those of babies, higher animals, and unreflective adults, has that complicated and reflective a content. I think that, understood aright, this instinct is correct. My purpose will be to articulate it.

The use of *ascent* (including self-reference) and the introduction of an explicit *account* of reference in Searle's statement of the content of visual experiences are the primary sources of complication in (S). I will ask how these features of the truth condition are motivated and whether the motivation suffices to render Searle's account of Intentional content visual experience superior to alternatives.

III

A project that reflects on truth conditions in order to give an account of Intentional mental states or events is subject to a certain constraint. It must say something plausible about how the objects that the Intentional state refers to are presented to the thinker. Or if the mental states fails to pick out an object, the account must say something about the mode of presentation that fails of reference. The language I am using here is, of course, derived from Frege. But the point does not depend on anything particular in his doctrine. Another way of putting the idea is this: The "requirement" that truth conditions place on the way the world is to be if the mental state is to be veridical, must be in a form that indicates the Intentional (broadly, referential) elements that constitute or identify the thinker's point of view. The point should be uncontroversial. It helps define the project of characterizing Intentional states.

A near corollary of this point constrains any account of the satisfaction conditions of demonstratives that could serve as an account of Intentional content. One cannot simply cite the referent of a demonstrative as its content unless the referent *is* one's way of thinking about the referent. So in giving an account of the satisfaction conditions of the use of a demonstrative that picks out a physical object, one cannot simply cite the physical object as the Intentional content. One cannot do this because it is obvious that in using the demonstrative one thinks of the object from a certain perspective or in a certain way that is not simply identical with the object itself. Some aspect of one's mental state or perspective is relevant to picking out the object. And this aspect must be cited if one is successfully to characterize Intentional content. Precisely analogous observations hold for giving an account of the Intentional content of visual experiences.[3]

I belabor these points because I want to make some preliminary remarks about the "truth condition" (a) listed above. (a) comes closest to representing what I think is the Intentional content most naturally associated with the statement. And in discussing Searle's account of the content of visual experience, I want an analogue of (a) to serve as a foil and rival for his account.

If (a) is to give truth conditions for a statement involving a demonstrative applied to a physical project, and if those truth conditions are supposed to characterize an Intentional content associated by the speaker with the statement, it does not suffice to use (a) and note that one is picking out the same physical object that is picked out in the original statement. Something has to be said about some Intentional element associated with the demonstrative in the original statement, about how the object is picked out in the original statement.

It is not part of my view that the full Intentional content associated by the speaker with the sentence or statement is necessarily what one must assign to it in order to give its "semantics." "Semantics," like "truth conditions," is a term with a bewildering variety of actual (and even legitimate) applications. Certainly, *what is conventionally understood and conveyed* by a used sentence, or a statement, may be less than the Intentional content that the speaker thinks in using it. Perhaps in some theoretical contexts, (a) may suffice for a "semantical" project that aims at accounting for some aspect of what is conventionally understood or conveyed. From a certain point of view, the referent of the demonstrative and its being F and G are all that matters.

But the gloss represented by (a) would fall short of explicating Intentional content. It would say nothing about how the referent of the original statement "That F is G" is indicated. It would not even say that it was indicated demonstratively. And an account of Intentional content must say something about mode of indication or mode of presentation. Moreover, a "semantics" that limited itself in this way would not accomplish all that traditional approaches to semantics (e.g. Frege's) attempted.

How are we to meet the requirement that something be said about some Intentional element associated with the demonstrative in the original statement? The Intentional element might *be* the occurrence of the demonstrative in the statement. It might be a mental demonstrative occurrence. It might be some concept – descriptive visual, or otherwise – or some conceptual complex, perhaps involving or governed by a demonstrative. The point is that (a) must be glossed in some way that indicates an intentional element associated with the statement whose truth conditions are being given.

The constraint that I have been discussing has already been met in (b)–(f). Let us provisionally satisfy the constraint for (a) by revising it to

> (a′)   that F is G [where one indicates the relevant F, and where "that F" is not only used, but stands for the mode of indication used in the statement (or visual experience) whose truth conditions are being given].

Here it is understood that we are not merely using the demonstrative in the unbracketed part of (a′); we are also attributing the demonstrative and its application. The unbracketed part of (a′) – which gives the content of the original statement – displays the content of the statement (or visual experience) by mimicking its demonstrative mode of presentation. The Intentional content involves a demonstrative occurrence (or a type individuated in terms of a demonstrative occurrence) that governs the F-predication and that in fact is applied to the relevant physical object.[4] I will speak of (a′) as the form of a statement of the truth conditions both of statements and of visual experiences.

(a′) provides truth conditions that are relevant to Intentional content. It replicates the Intentional content of the original and gives its "truth conditions" at the same time. I do not intend this as a full explanation of anything. Rather I am merely illustrating a form of account that will guide us as we discuss the Intentional content of visual experiences.

IV

What motivation does Searle offer for fixing on a form of "satisfaction condition" for visual experiences that parallels (e′) rather than (a′)? Nothing in his most direct arguments for his view will serve. Let set out his arguments in his own words:

> it is part of the conditions of satisfaction (in the sense of requirement) of the visual experience that the visual experience must itself be caused by the rest of the conditions of satisfaction (in the sense of things required) of that visual experience. Thus, for example, if I see the yellow station wagon, I have a certain visual experience. But the Intentional content of the visual experience, which requires that there be a yellow station wagon in front of me in order that it be satisfied, also requires that the fact that there is a yellow station wagon in front of me must be the cause of that very visual experience. Thus, the Intentional content of the visual experience requires as part of the conditions of satisfaction that the visual experience be caused by the rest of its conditions of satisfaction, that is, by the state of affairs perceived. The content of the visual experience is therefore self-referential in a sense that I hope to be able to make fairly precise. The Intentional content of the visual experience is entirely specified by

stating the conditions of satisfaction of the visual experience, but that statement makes essential reference to the visual experience itself in the conditions of satisfaction. For what the Intentional content requires is not simply that there be a state of affairs in the world, but rather that the state of affairs in the world must cause the very visual experience which is the embodiment or realization of the Intentional content. (pp. 47–8)

Searle says that the Intentional content of the relevant visual experience has the form: "I have a visual experience (that there is a yellow station wagon there and that there is a yellow station wagon there is causing this visual experience)." He continues:

> The Intentional content of the visual experience determines under what conditions it is satisfied or not satisfied, what must be the case in order that it be, as they say, "veridical." Well, what must be the case in the station wagon scene in order that the experience be a veridical one? At least this much: the world must be as it visually seems to me that it is, and furthermore its being that way must be what causes me to have the visual experience which constitutes its seeming that way. And it is this combination that I am trying to capture in the representation of the Intentional content. (pp. 48–9)

The notion of self-reference that Searle promises to make precise in the first of the quoted passages is given two further glosses:

> the sense in which the visual experience is self-referential is simply that it figures in its own conditions of satisfaction. (p. 49)

> We can say either that it is part of the content of the visual experience that if it is to be satisfied it must be caused by its Intentional object; or, more cumbersomely but more accurately, it is part of the content of the visual experience, that if it is to be satisfied it must be caused by the state of affairs that its Intentional object exists and has those features that are presented in the visual experience. And it is in this sense that the Intentional content of the perceptual experience is causally self-referential. (p. 49)

Searle seems to me entirely right and extremely insightful in his claim that the Intentional content of a visual experience should reflect the fact that the content of a visual experience is satisfied only if the experience is caused by entities of the sort represented as present by the experience. This condition on success or satisfaction must indeed be somehow reflected in the content of the experience, given our assumption that Intentional states' content is identified in terms of the satisfaction conditions of the states.

It is not enough for the satisfaction of the Intentional content that there be some entity in the vicinity that has the visible properties presented by the visual experience. Less obviously, it is not enough for an account of the nature of the experience (and of how the experience refers to entities in the physical world) that one state that the visual experience must be caused by the entities represented by the experience in order for the entities to be seen. In specifying *what experience it is*, one must take account of this condition and somehow reflect it in one's specification of the content of the experience itself. The Intentional content must itself somehow reflect the causal condition of its satisfaction. Searle emphasizes this point and is right to do so. Many have failed to see the point at all; and many others have not seen it as clearly.

What is missing, however, is reason for taking satisfaction conditions in the form of (e') – rather than some other form, such as (a') – to account for Intentional content. For, by including a demonstrative element in the content of the visual experience, in the way that (a') does, one may reflect in the Intentional content the condition that to be veridical the experience must be caused by an entity that is (say) F. An *account* of the semantical or Intentional nature of the visual demonstrative in the visual version of (a') should require that the demonstrative fails to apply to anything unless the experience is appropriately caused. On this view, the Intentional content given in a visual version of (a') *does* require "that the fact that there is an [F] in front of me must be the cause of that very visual experience" (pp. 47–8).

Searle's argument that visual experiences are self-referential is similarly inspecific. He writes that "the sense in which the visual experience is self-referential is simply that it figures in its own conditions of satisfaction" (p. 49). He continues: "it is part of the content of the visual experience, that if it is to be satisfied it must be caused by the state of affairs that its Intentional object exists and has those features that are presented in the visual experience. And it is in this sense that the Intentional content of the perceptual experience is causally self-referential" (p. 49).[5]

But in an ordinary sense, the visual experience does "figure" in its own conditions of satisfaction according to a theory that gives the Intentional content and "conditions of satisfaction" as (a'). Such a theory might add a meta-specification of what it is to be "the relevant F" by requiring that the experience whose content is being given, and which contains the demonstrative element, be appropriately caused by the object being demonstrated. Similarly, in a non-technical sense it is surely true that it is "part of" the conditions layed down by (a') that to be veridical, the visual experience must be appropriately caused. Any theory that treats satisfaction conditions of an Intentional state as token-reflexive will be "self-referential" in this broad sense.

The difference between (a') and (e') is, of course, that in (a') self-referentiality is made explicit only in the background condition (entailed or presupposed by (a')) that *provides a descriptive account of* the semantical workings of the demonstrative in (a'). Someone whose Intentional state was constituted by satisfaction conditions and Intentional content given by the unbracketed part of (a') could reflect on that state and give a descriptive account of what is presupposed by (a'). Such a person would be expanding on the bracketed part of (a'). One could note that implicit in the use of the demonstrative is a background condition that the very experience involving the demonstrative occurrence be appropriately caused. (e') is such a descriptive account; there the self-reference is fully explicit.

In making the critical point, one may say that Searle's argument is inspecific as between the two types of satisfaction condition. Or one may say that the argument tacitly assumes strict notions of "figures in" and "part of" that would rule out (a') – whereas such assumptions are in need of support. Nothing in the argument provides a reason for rejecting (a') as giving "the satisfaction conditions" of the visual experience. For (a') takes full account of the point that motivates Searle's proposals – the point about the need to reflect *in* the conditions of satisfaction, and so in the Intentional content, the requirement that veridical visual experience be caused. The question is why it should be reflected one way rather than another.

V

Now one might be baffled about why the fine distinctions between (a') and (e') matter. After all, I claim that (a') presupposes something like (e'). So it may appear that there is no basis for taking them as rivals. As long as one is talking about satisfaction conditions alone, they are not rivals. In some loose sense, they are just different ways of laying down requirements for veridicality that ultimately determine the same conditions in the world.

But a theory of Intentional content is not just a theory of satisfaction conditions. It is simultaneously a theory of mental states – mental abilities and cognitive point of view. Let us accept the view that "truth conditions" are "internal" to the mental states in the sense that they are the fundamental or "instrinsic" aspects of mental kinds. Let us accept the view that "truth conditions" exhaust the "content" of those states, in the sense that nothing beyond a relevant "truth condition" is thus fundamental. Still, truth conditions that are equivalent in requiring for their veridicality that the same state(s) of affairs obtain may nonetheless differ in the types of mental abilities they individuate. They may, to use Frege's language, constitute different modes of presentation.

A thought of the form (a') – the unbracketed part (see note 4 below) – requires less sophistication, less reflection, fewer conceptual resources than a thought of the form (e'). Yet Searle gives no explicit argument for fixing on (e'), other than the inconclusive one that we have already canvassed.

It seems to me that Searle is guilty of just the thing that he (correctly) accuses his "direct reference" opponents of: concentrating so exclusively on semantical issues that issues in epistemology and the philosophy of mind are distorted or neglected.[6]

Searle does provide some discussion of the mental abilities required by (S), the visual analogue of (e'). He holds a realist position about perception. He claims that although the Intentional content of (S) makes reference to a visual experience, one *sees* only physical objects and properties, not the visual experiences (p. 38). And he holds that although we see such objects by way of our visual experiences, we do not infer the physical object from awareness of the visual experience (p. 73). On the other hand, Searle holds that we do *experience* our visual experiences (p. 74), that we experience them as caused (p. 74), and that we are "directly aware" of the causal nexus between our experiences and the objects that cause them (pp. 123, 125).

It is unclear what distinctions are being drawn here between experiencing and seeing. Both terms, particularly the former, have been construed in many different ways by different philosophers. I think that progress can be made, however, by isolating and discussing two significant issues: One is whether in every instance of vision, the subject experiences causal relations between physical objects and his perceptions in such a way that reference to those relations is a visual ability invariably exercised by his visual apparatus, and made available by that apparatus for the formation of thoughts. The other issue is whether in every instance of vision, the subject experiences, or is directly aware of, his own visual experiences in such a way that visual beliefs automatically are about or make reference to those experiences.

Searle appears to take an affirmative stand on both issues.[7] He must do so if his favored conditions of satisfaction are to provide a general account of Intentional content. I shall concentrate more on the second issue than the first. I shall, however, make a few remarks about Searle's position on causation.

It seems to me implausible in the extreme to claim that we invariably visually experience causal relations between physical objects and our own perceptions. What is Searle's argument for that view? There are some generalized references to the work of Piaget that indicates that our experience of one event following another is different from our experience of one event causing another (pp. 115, 127). This work does not, however, concern experience of causal relations between physical objects and experiences – but rather between "external" physical events and other "external" physical events. So it is relevant at most in suggesting that we sometimes experience causal relations other than those Searle appeals to.[8]

Searle's primary argument for the view is a repeat of the argument that the Intentional content of visual experiences is captured by their "truth conditions," and "truth conditions" make reference to the relevant causal relations: "I get a direct experience of causation from the fact that part of the Intentional content of my experience of perceiving is caused by the object perceived, i.e., it is satisfied only if it is caused by the presence and features of the object" (p. 130; cf. p. 125). This direct move from an "analysis" of truth conditions, one that involves "ascent," to a conclusion about direct experience is illegitimate for the reasons we have developed earlier.

In a footnote Searle produces a supplementary argument that we experience causal relations between objects and our perceptual experiences (p. 124n.). He appeals to the experienced difference between voluntarily producing an image of a house and actually seeing the house (where, presumably the qualitative elements of the two experiences are identical). This argument is inconclusive. The difference can be accounted for by assuming that we experience (as such) our voluntary efforts in the former case and not in the latter. On reflection, we come to realize that passive experience is caused. But unreflective passive experience involves no more than a lack of the experience of our own activity.

I turn now to the second of the issues mentioned above: the issue of whether in every instance of vision, the subject "experiences," or is directly aware of, his own visual experiences in such a way that visual beliefs automatically are about or make reference to those experiences. Again the issue is not settled by the argument from "truth conditions." It depends on further discussion of mental ability.

There are surely various loose senses in which we "directly experience" or are "aware of" our visual experiences. They are part of our conscious, visual life; we react to them in a discriminating way. But Searle's view requires more. *Reference* to those experiences must be part of every visual experience of physical objects. To be part of experience in the relevant sense, it is not necessary, I think, to be conscious. But I take it that experience is something that is available for use by a subject's central cognitive system. Visual experience is what is automatically supplied by the visual system to the rest of the cognitive system for purposes of judgment and intention. The relevant referential events must automatically be part of the references of judgments and intentions that incorporate visual models of presentation. I find this view very implausible.

To make reference to one's visual experiences, over and above the physical objects that one sees by means of them, one must have some means of distinguishing experiences from the objects they are experiences of. There is a sense in which the visual system itself must make some such discriminations in order to have objective reference to physical entities. The system must be capable of screening subjective visual phenomena from the deliverances of the system that have objective significance. But there is no ground for thinking that the system makes systematic reference to causal relations between physical entities and unconscious visual representations of them. And although visual experiences are manipulated within the visual system, they are not thereby referred to by the subject in visual experience. Such manipulations and discriminations are unconscious, automatic, and most important inaccessible to use by other parts of the cognitive system. Empirical evidence and common sense both suggest that they are not supplied to visually based thoughts useable by the central cognitive system. Only the results of the visual system's filtering its information through such discriminations are supplied.[9]

For the subject's judgments to make reference to visual experiences, the subject himself, not merely a sub-system of the subject, must be capable of making discriminations between experiences and physical objects, and of using these discriminations in a wide range of judgments, judgments which presumably would involve reasoning about the discriminations. I think that these are what are ordinarily called "conceptual discriminations." The subject must be capable of making and utilizing these discriminations in a variety of practical and cognitive endeavors.

I see no reason to alter the view of common sense, developmental psychology, and cognitive ethology that these distinctions cannot be drawn by many higher animals, children, and adults of low intelligence that nonetheless have visual experience of physical objects. They lack the conceptual resources to make the distinctions on which reference to their experiences would have to be based. A content like (S) guarantees inferences, available to the whole cognitive system, that distinguish experiences from physical objects that cause them. But such inferences are not guaranteed by the visual experiences themselves. People and animals make reference to physical objects alone in many (most) of their visual experiences and their judgments that incorporate visual modes of presentation. Although (S) approximates a reflective *account* of the semantical principles governing these experiences, it does not represent or provide an equivalent of the mental abilities that are exercised in the experiences themselves.

Searle's account of Intentional content in (S) is nearly the same as Russell's (cf. note 1). But there is a significant difference. Russell combined his account with – and even motivated it by – a distinctive epistemology and theory of mental ability. He thought that all knowledge rested on acquaintance with one's present experiences and with universals. And he thought that acquaintance is a non-propositional, perspective-free, infallible sort of cognition. One makes reference in thought to all entities other than present experiences and universals only by description – only by forming Intentional complexes out of the entities known by acquaintance, complexes that descriptively denote the other entities.

Searle does not appear to be committed to this preposterous theory. He says that we see physical objects "directly." He does not clarify in detail what he means by "directly." But he does not mean that we are "acquainted" with them in Russell's sense. We see them by way of Intentional contents and visual experiences, neither of which we see. And our seeing them is fallible. But seeing physical objects seems to be epistemologically basic. Searle holds that our knowledge that a physical object causes my visual experience is *less basic* than the knowledge that I see the physical object: "The knowledge that the car caused my visual experience derives from the knowledge that I see the car, and not conversely" (p. 73).[10]

On the other hand, reference in thought to particular physical objects, on Searle's view as on Russell's, occurs only through descriptions (descriptions containing demonstratives). And the descriptions are anchored in demonstrative relations to our present experiences. Searle says nothing about our cognitive relations to our present visual experiences, except that reference to such experiences in the Intentional content is by way of an ineliminable demonstrative element ("this").

The lack of discussion of the demonstrative relation between the thinker and present experiences is a serious deficiency. In view of the fact that this is the only sort of demonstrative relation, according to Searle's theory of Intentional content, one would expect there to be a serious account of the cognitive and mental abilities that correspond to this unique sort of reference (or Intentionality) in thought.

There is an apparent mismatch here between Searle's epistemology and his theory of Intentional content. If seeing physical objects is epistemologically fundamental, then the most basic form of cognitive reference should correspond to that relation. The most basic form is demonstrative (or indexical) reference. So a realist view of perception should, I think, be combined with an account of Intentional content that countenances demonstrative relations between the thinker and physical objects. Assuming agreement on the basic outlines of Searle's theory of perception, this point favors a theory of satisfaction conditions and Intentional content for ordinary visual experience along the lines of (a'), rather than (e') or (S).[11]

The same basic critical point can be put another way. We noted above that knowledge of the causal relation between visual experiences and physical objects seems posterior to the experience (and knowledge of the experience) of seeing physical objects (cf. p. 73, and note 10) We gain knowledge of the causal relation, and indeed of our own visual experiences, by reflecting on unreflective visual experience. If this is to be possible, there must be a cognitive *step* of some sort between the unreflective experience and the knowledge gained by reflection. Searle's theory collapses the step by attributing to the unreflective visual experience satisfaction conditions that are the result of reflection. The theory of satisfaction conditions does not match the facts of mental ability.

Russell's theory does not involve these mismatches. But it is committed to a highly implausible theory of perception, knowledge, and mental ability. If one gives up these theories, one should give up his strategy for representing Intentional content. One should recognize demonstrative reference in thought to physical objects.

VI

The distinction between the mental abilities backing satisfaction conditions of the forms (a') and (S) can be further elucidated by standing back from special issues regarding reference to causation or visual experiences. It is possible to have a perceptual belief that that yellow station wagon is self-identical and yet be in a position to reason about whether to accept the view that the yellow station wagon causing this very experience is that yellow station wagon. One might, for example wonder whether two yellow station wagons are causing this very experience – whereas only one of them is *that one*. On Searle's account such doubt, described in the way I have described it, is not really possible. For the perceptual model of presentation that I have expressed by "that yellow station wagon" has the *same* content as "the yellow station wagon that is causing this very experience." (I am happy to enrich these contents by assuming that "yellow station wagon" is a stand-in for a concrete visual model of presentation that images the object. The point still stands.)

The argument, a variant of Frege's argument for distinguishing senses, indicates that the Intentional content of the visual mode of presentation must be different from that of the account of that content stated in (S).

The case suggests a mare's nest of problems about causal theories of perception. Searle suppresses these problems when he presents his analogue of (S), and only takes them up briefly later (pp. 135–40). There he makes some suggestions about how to deal with problems. He holds, with some diffidence, that cases of deviant causation can be ruled out by such conditions as the following: the object that is seen must cause the visual perception by a plannable, regular pattern of causation. It is not important for our purposes whether such conditions deal with all the cases. What is important is that the conditions must be incorporated into the account of the Intentional content of visual perception if one is to provide a correct account of "satisfaction conditions". (Searle does not note this. Perhaps he regarded it as obvious.)

Incorporating the fruits of reflecting on deviant causal chains into the account of Intentional content provides a more nearly accurate account of the satisfaction conditions of visual experience. But it provides an even less plausible account of the perspective, and mental abilities, involved in having visual experience. It is obvious that one arrives at an account of non-deviant causation only after reflecting on numerous cases that most people have never thought of. And it is obvious that one is reasonable in being uncertain (as Searle is) that one's account is correct. This very uncertainty, expressed in the material mode (i.e. without semantic ascent), counts against theories of Intentional content gotten by supplementing (S) or (e') with more conditions. Even if a thought like "that [visually presented] yellow station wagon is the yellow station wagon causing this experience in a plannable, regular way" is firmly believed, it is informative in a way that the associated self-identity is not.

One is tempted to note here that supplementations of (S) or (e') are arrived at by reflection, not by induction from ordinary empirical observations. Many would hold that they are knowable *a priori*. Some would infer from this that everyone already knows them. Does this line of reasoning help such accounts?

I do not think so. In the first place, it does not follow from the assumption that the accounts are discoverable by *a priori* means that everyone already knows them. Much *a priori* knowledge is new knowledge (witness the growth of mathematical knowledge). If someone managed to provide a correct and known "account" of non-deviant causation, it would constitute new knowledge in philosophy.

In the second place, even if everyone with a visual system always knew, in some unconscious way, things of the form

(Frege)   that [visually presented] F is [necessarily] the [visually presented]
           F causing this experience in a plannable, regular way,

that knowledge would still have different and greater cognitive value than a mere
thought of self-identity (that that [visually presented] F is [necessarily] self-identical).
The former thought connects the seen object to the very most general conditions
for seeing it. The latter, self-identity thought provides no philosophically interesting insight at all. This indicates, I think, that the cognitive content of the latter
phrase in the identity (Frege) is not identical with the former.

VII

(a') (from section III) is essentially analogous to the explication of demonstrative or
indexical beliefs, including perceptual beliefs, that I gave in "Belief De Re."[12] On
my view, demonstrative elements – which I contrasted with conceptual elements –
should be taken as primitive in mental states, or their Intentional contents. In order
to have a reference, demonstrative elements must be part of a particular thinker's
thought or experience in a particular context. The individuation of a demonstrative
element, its intentional properties, and its referent normally depend on some one
particular mental event. In this regard, demonstrative elements contrast with conceptual elements, which have a constant reference or extension regardless of who
thinks them or when they are thought. To be *de re*, a thought should both contain
a primitive demonstrative element in its content and involve successful reference
(application) through a demonstrative element to an object or *re*. Relevant *res* may
be physical or mental.

The two requirements for being a *de re* thought are separable. It is possible for an
applied demonstrative element to fail to have a referent. Since thoughts are individuated in terms of their contents (including the token applications of demonstrative
elements in thought), some demonstrative thoughts are not *de re*. Moreover, since
some demonstrative token applications that in fact have a referent might have failed
to have had one (if the contextual circumstances had been different), some thought
tokens that are in fact *de re* are not essentially *de re*. The very same demonstrative
thought might have lacked a referent if the world beyond the thought had been
different.[13]

In my terms, Searle's account treats perceptual belief as *de re*. He treats the contents of such beliefs as irreducibly demonstrative and as having successful demonstrative applications. It is just that he holds that the only possible demonstrative
applications in perceptual thoughts are to perceptual states. I hold that demonstrative applications may be directly to the objects of vision – physical objects.

Searle sees himself as attacking all views that take any beliefs to be irreducibly
"*de re*." Obviously he uses the terminology differently. In his discussion of my
views, this difference in terminology leads to his overestimating how much we
disagree, and prevents his precisely identifying the points of disagreement.

Searle thinks that it is characteristic of a philosopher's believing in *de re* belief
that the philosopher hold that such beliefs are not individuated solely in terms
of their mental contents (pp. 198, 208, 210–11). He thinks I hold this view:

According to Burge such beliefs cannot be completely or exhaustively characterized in terms of their Intentional contents, because, as he puts it, there are contextual, non-conceptual elements which are crucial to the identity of the belief. (p. 211; cf. also p. 214, no. 3)

This remark contains a misunderstanding. I think that characterizing a *de re* belief as *de re*, requires reference to the *re*, which may indeed be outside the Intentional content. But as I have noted, the property of being a *de re* belief is not in general essential to the identity of the belief. I do not think that a physical *re* in the empirical world beyond the thinker is itself "part of" the belief. (I am familiar with this way to talking, but find it artificial and unilluminating; cf. section III and note 3.) In my view, the Intentional side of a belief is its only side. In many cases, in my view, a belief that is in fact *de re* might not have been successfully referential (could have failed to be *de re*) and still would have remained the same belief. Moreover, the belief itself can always be individuated, or completely characterized, in terms of the Intentional content. Thus the Intentional content *is* crucial to the identity of the belief.

It is true that I think that there are contextual, nonconceptual elements that are crucial to the identity of the *de re* belief. But these are not the physical individuals, the *res*. Nor are they the causal relations between physical object and perceiver. (They are critical for reference, but not in every case for belief identity.) They are the demonstrative element and the token act of application in the demonstrative belief. These are part of the Intentional content.

Searle's own position involves acknowledging that there are contextual, non-conceptual elements, in this sense, that are crucial to the identity of the belief. He also appeals to ineliminable demonstrative elements in thought. On these important points we are in fundamental agreement. Thus my examples and arguments were not directed against a view such as his that already recognizes such elements. They were directed against pure descriptivist views and against views, such as Frege's, that hold that all elements of Intentional content have their intentional properties timelessly and independently of any particular person's doing any thinking.

Searle is right to think that his sort of view can accommodate my examples (granted an adequate account of deviant causal chains). He is wrong to think that I thought otherwise. My objection to the sort of view that he proposes is not that it cannot accommodate the examples, and not that it tries to individuate all belief in terms of Intentional content. It is that it does not match the theory of Intentional content with the theory of knowledge, and gives a misleading picture of mental ability.

A characterization of a disagreement that is closer to being accurate concerns reference, not belief identity. Searle characterizes "*de re* theorists" as holding that

internal Intentional content is insufficient to determine what [the thinker] is referring to. They share the view that in order to account for the relations between words [thoughts] and the world we need to introduce external contextual, non-conceptual, causal relations between the [thinking of thoughts] and the features of the world that the [thought] is about. (p. 199) they mistakenly suppose that [contextual features on which perceptual and indexical beliefs depend] cannot themselves be entirely represented as part of the Intentional content. (p. 214)[14]

These quotations point toward a genuine disagreement. But they do not identify it precisely. The notion of "introduction" in the first quotation is really not very clear. Searle's own account of the relation between thoughts and the world makes reference in the satisfaction conditions for visual experience to plannable causal regularities between external objects and visual experiences. Such regularities are contextual and non-conceptual. And if there were no such regularities, there would be no relations between perceptual experiences and the world. In a straight-forward sense he too "introduces" causal relations in order to account for refer-ential relations.

Of course, Searle specifies these in what he calls the Intentional content of the visual experience, whereas I would specify them in rules governing (and presup-posed by) the thinking of demonstrative thoughts. But Searle's notion of Intentional content as the "satisfaction condition" for thoughts is not sharp enough to locate the disagreement. For I too count my presupposed rules of reference as "satisfac-tion conditions" for demonstrative thoughts.

The real issue once again is whether these relatively complex satisfaction condi-tions, which analyze the mechanism of reference to physical objects, articulate the mental abilities exercised in visual experience. I take a clear negative position on this issue. Searle does not squarely identify the issue. But in so far as his view is intended as a distinctive alternative, it would appear that he is committed to a positive position.

As I have argued, a positive position blurs an important distinction between what visual experience itself transmits to us – or more generally what cognitive abilities are exercised in a particular *de re* thought – and what we obtain by reflection on that experience. Such reflection makes use of philosophical analysis and reasoning that clearly go beyond any particular visual experiences or particular *de re* thoughts. It makes use of knowledge summed up from visual experience. The problem with Searle's apparent view is not that "the contextual features on which perceptual and indexical beliefs depend *cannot* themselves be entirely represented as part of the Intentional content" (p. 214, my emphasis), for any possible notion of Intentional content. The problem is that the notion of Intentional content that one obtains by including such features does not correspond to our cognitive states or mental abilities.

NOTES

1   The historical Russell, not the approach of neo-Russellians, often called "direct reference" theorists. Cf. Bertrand Russell, "On the Nature of Acquaintance" and "The Philosophy of Logical Atomism," in *Logic and Knowledge*, ed. Robert Charles Marsh (Allen and Unwin: London, 1956); "Knowledge by Acquaintance and Knowledge by Description," in *Mysticism and Logic* (W. W. Norton and Co.: New York, 1929). The general type of approach bears comparison with one defended by Stephen Schiffer, "The Basis of Reference," *Erkenntnis* 13 (1978), pp. 171–206. Numerals surrounded by parentheses in the text will refer to page

numbers in John Searle's *Intentionality* (Cambridge University Press: Cambridge, England, 1983).

2   Actually, I think that use of the word "there" may constitute a slip on Searle's part. The spirit of his account of the Intentional content of visual states is to hold that only the states themselves may be the referents of primitive demonstratives. "There" obviously is meant to refer to a place. A fuller Searlean analysis would presumably analyze "there" in terms of some specified relation of the place to "this" visual experience.

3   Searle is fully aware of these points. Cf. e.g. *Intentionality*, pp. 63, 214. He is right to complain that some of his opponents pay too little heed to them. As I shall indicate more fully below, one of the ways in which he misconstrues my view is that he fails to see that I am also fully aware of these points.

4   In discussing (a′) in the rest of the paper, I shall often refer to (a′) as giving the Intentional content of a statement or thought or visual experience. This will be shorthand. I will always mean that the *unbracketed part* of (a′) gives or displays or mimics the Intentional content; the bracketed part provides instructions to the reader for understanding how the unbracketed part is to be understood. In saying that (the unbracketed part of) (a′) gives the Intentional content of a thought, I will not be assuming that a demonstrative is explicitly tokened in some inner language of thought. I assume only that the thought or visual experience involves the exercise of a demonstrative ability and that this exercise has the formal and semantical properties of an applied demonstrative. Obviously, this ability need not to consciously exercised. As will later become clear, there is much more to be said about the Intentional content in (a′). For example, "relevant" can be glossed in terms of conditions on the original demonstrative's picking out the right object. Moreover, the Intentional content does not include any physical object that is actually picked out: the content is a demonstrative applications of something of the form "That F is G." Sometimes a demonstrative content fails to pick out any object. And sometimes, even when it does, it can be individuated independently of that object. The satisfaction conditions require that there be a relevant demonstrated object if the Intentional content is to be true. I shall discuss these matters further in sections IV and VII.

5   Both passages are quoted above. See also the passage quoted from pp. 47–8 that relies on the phrase "makes essential reference." This phrase may be treated in a way parallel to the way I treat "figures in," "part of," and "is self-referential" in what follows.

6   Searle is perhaps indirectly acknowledging the worry that the satisfaction conditions in (S) are unexpectedly complicated in his insistence that (S) "is not in any sense a translation."

> It is rather a verbal specification of what the Intentional content requires if it is to be satisfied. The sense then in which the visual Intentional content is self-referential is not that it contains a verbal or other representation of itself . . . . Rather, the sense in which the visual experience is self-referential is simply that it figures in its own conditions of satisfaction. (pp. 48–9; cf. p. 213)

What Searle asserts here is inspecific in the same way the argument for his form of truth conditions is. Any view that takes indexicality (or "token reflexivity") as ineliminable will at some level require that the relevant token (here, the visual experience) figure in its own conditions of satisfaction. Part of Searle's denial in this passage is uncontroversial. The reference in (S) is obviously not to the content, but to the visual experience itself. It is less clear what Searle means by denying that (S) is a translation. "Translation" does perhaps carry inappropriate connotations: visual experience is non-verbal; one may think that comparison of visual experience to an "inner language" is misleading; and certainly not all the concrete visual modes of presentation can be captured in ordinary English expressions. But it seems to me that what is wanted is a representation of the content of a mental state that *is* the closest possible cognitive equivalent.

I am inclined to think that Searle's denial of the translation analogy is not meant to excuse the account from the considerations regarding mental ability. Some readers have taken Searle in this way. On such a reading, Searle is only giving an account of abstract truth conditions that does not purport to correspond in any fine-grained way to mental abilities. I think that such a reading would render Searle's account irrelevant to some of the theories of *de re* belief (such as mine) that he criticizes as alternatives. Cf. section VII.

7   Searle's commitment to the view that reference to causation and to the experiences them-selves is made available to the formation of thoughts – that is, accessible to the central cogni-tive systems of a person or animal – is clear throughout the discussion. Cf. e.g. *Intentionality*. pp. 69–70.

8   The relevance of Piaget's work to the present issue is further attenuated by the fact that the discriminations that Piaget discovers are acquired. Searle is arguing that such "experience" of causation is part of the content of *every* visual experience. So if there are visual experiences in a child before it acquires the ability to make the discriminations, Searle must *argue* that the experience of causation is present before the ability to discriminate it is acquired.

9   For detailed discussion of empirical findings on this and related matters, see David Marr, *Vision* (W. H. Freeman and Co.: San Francisco, 1982).

10 I think that Searle would do well to explain how this claim is to be represented within his theory. Since the Intentional content of seeing the car is couched in terms of the car's causing my visual experience, it is not evident how knowledge of the latter can be *derived* from know-ledge of the former. It appears that knowledge of the former just is, on Searle's account, knowledge of the latter. They appear to be equally basic. This apparent mismatch between Searle's epistemological remarks (with which I am sympathetic) and his account of Intentional content seems to me symptomatic of the larger problem with the view that I will go on to develop.

11 I am, of course, glossing over many complex issues in the theory of perception. Although I very much agree with Searle's basic approach, I think a more thorough account of the senses in which perception of physical objects is "basic" needs to be given. The primary point of agreement is that perception of physical properties is not a product of inference on the part of the perceiving subject from experience of visual experiences. (It is, however, the product of inference-like transformations carried out by the subject's visual system.) I add two other points here. I think that we obtain knowledge of – and make reference to – the visual experi-ences only long after we have perceptual knowledge of physical objects. I think that physical properties are the primary "objects" of vision in the sense that obtaining information about them is the primary objective of the visual system; and I think that an account of vision should be centered on this fact.

12 "Belief De Re," *Journal of Philosophy* 74 (1977), pp. 338–62.

13 This point is made in "Belief De Re". But it is more prominent in my "Russell's Problem and Intentional Identity," in *Agent, Language, and the Structure of the World*, ed. Tomberlin (Hackett Publishing Co.: Indianapolis, 1983).

Although I think that some demonstrative occurrences might have lacked a referent (cf. note 14 below), the nature and intentional content of a demonstrative may in some cases be fixed by the identity of the referent. This is always true of indexicals like "I": the same index-ical occurrence could not have occurred with a different referent, or without a referent. My views on the individuation of demonstrative occurrences bear a complex relation to my anti-individualistic views on concept determination. (On the latter, cf. e.g. my "Other Bodies," in *Thought and Object*, ed. Woodfield (Oxford University Press: Oxford, 1982); "Individualism and Psychology," *The Philosophical Review* 95 (1986), pp. 3–45; and "Intellectual Norms and Foundations of Mind," *Journal of Philosophy* 83 (1986), pp. 697–720.) Empirical concepts for physical objects are, I think, always determined to be what they are by causal and inten-tional relations that the individual bears to satisfiers of empirical concepts (though sometimes these relations are indirect – through other empirical concepts, or even through other members of the species). Someone sympathetic with this anti-individualistic view of concept individua-tion might think that an anti-individualistic view of demonstrative elements is straightforward and simple. There are views that individuate *all* demonstrative occurrences in such a way that it is impossible for such occurrences to be the same if a different referent is present or if there is no referent. For a variety of reasons, I think that this simple view is incorrect. My anti-individualistic views on the individuation of concepts do not transfer in this simplified and unqualified way to demonstrative elements in thought. But I will reserve discussion of these issues to another occasion.

14   Searle sometimes seems to take the opposition position on reference to dictate an opposing position on belief-identity. He seems to treat the two questions in the following passage as equivalent and answers both negatively: "Do some beliefs relate the believer directly to an object without the mediation of an Intentional content which is sufficient to individuate the object? Are they such that a change in the world would necessarily mean a change in the belief even if what is in the head remained constant?" (p. 214).

   I think that no beliefs relate the believer to an object without mediation of an Intentional content. But my answer to the former question is nevertheless "yes." The Intentional content is not always sufficient to individuate the object, at least in this sense: the Intentional content considered on its own, independently of the contextual circumstances (including events out-side the thinker's mind or body) in which it occurs, is sometimes insufficient to individuate the object. That is, in some cases the demonstrative element in the content that is in fact success-fully applied to a physical object might have failed to apply to that object (and either would have applied to nothing or applied to some other object); yet the demonstrative element and its token application would have been the same. Thus the demonstrative element does not by its nature and individuation always suffice to individuate the object: the surrounding cir-cumstances in which the element is applied play a supplementary role. What the demonstra-tive applies to depends not only on the nature of the Intentional content but on the context in which it is thought. On this point, Searle and I are indeed in disagreement. But Searle seems to think that disagreeing with him on the first question in the quoted passage entails disagreement on the second. In fact, my view is that in those very cases in which the demon-strative element fails to individuate its object, in the sense just specified, a change in the world (in the referent) would not necessarily mean a change in the belief.

15

Intentionality *De Re*

JOHN MCDOWELL

(1)   In his characteristically trenchant and forthright book *Intentionality*,[1] John Searle urges an account of how minds are directed at particular objects which he describes as "Fregean in spirit" (p. 197): given the way in which Searle reads Frege, the description is appropriate. In Frege's account, a mind is directed at a particular by virtue of grasping a Thought which has as a constituent a sense of the appropriate kind, determining that object as its associated *Bedeutung*. According to Searle's reading of this, a sense of the appropriate kind determines its associated *Bedeutung* by fixing something like a specification or set of conditions which the right object fits.[2]

It seems clear that Searle means formulations on these lines (for which see, e.g., p. 197) to suggest an idea we can usefully put like this: Frege's conception of the relevant sort of sense exploits, in anticipation, something like the leading idea of Russell's Theory of Descriptions. Russell's aim was to isolate a sort of significance that could be attributed to the terms he considered (a partial determinant of the propositions expressed by sentences containing them, and hence – to move to a quasi-Fregean way of putting things – something suitable to be regarded as an element in the contents of possible mental states) whether or not there was anything answering to the specifications that figured in making such a significance explicit.[3] Russell's thought was that the very possession of content, on the part of the relevant statements or mental states, ought not to be undermined if the speakers or thinkers were wrong in supposing appropriate objects to exist. So it would be out of line with the point of Russell's construction to allow cases in which the conditions an object must fit, in order to be determined by a significance of the relevant sort, are partly themselves determined by the object itself, in such a way that the conditions could not be stated or entertained in thought if the object did not exist; this would make content vulnerable to non-existence in just the way the construction is meant to prevent. At any rate this object-dependence of the conditions must be disallowed if the threat of loss of content which Russell's construction is designed to avert would be, failing Russell's construction, a live one – that is, if the object in question (if there is one) is of such a kind that subjects can be wrong in supposing one of its members to exist (for instance, if it is an item in the perceived environment). Now in Searle's reading of Frege, the conditions expressed in expressing a singular sense are evidently conceived on the lines of the significance of a Russellian definite

description: that is, as something available to be expressed or entertained independently of any object – at any rate, any "external" object – that might fit them.
Thus Searle takes it that Fregean object-directed Thoughts (at any rate those
directed to objects that are not "in the mind" of the subject himself) would still be
thinkable even if the objects to which they are directed did not exist: as he graphic-
ally puts it, all the Fregean beliefs that his position countenances could be had by a
brain in a vat (p. 230; see also pp. 209, 212).[4]

(2)   Such specificatory (or "descriptive")[5] conceptions of how mental states (and
utterances) are directed to particulars have come under attack, especially since the
ideas of Saul Kripke's 1969 Princeton lectures became generally known.[6] The gist
of the attack, so far as our present purposes are concerned, is that the materials
available in the minds of subjects for constructing the envisaged specifications are
insufficient to secure the right particular-directedness for their mental states.
("Right" in the light of what is required to make proper sense of people, which is
what the attribution of mental states is for in the first place.) In some cases, according to the objection, the specificatory conception will require us to take a subject's
mental state to be directed to a particular other than the right one; in others, although
making proper sense of someone will demand crediting him with a particular-
directed mental state, the specificatory conception will leave us with materials
insufficient to determine any one object as that to which his mental state is directed.
   In Searle's view, this kind of objection is based on a failure to take full account of
the resources available to the specificatory conception. I shall illustrate the general
strategy of his response in connection with what is probably the simplest possible
case for it, where a mental state is directed to a particular in a way that exploits the
fact that the particular is currently in the subject's field of vision. If we formulate a
specification by making explicit, in general terms, how the visual experience represents the object as being, we make ourselves vulnerable to an objection of the
relevant kind. The result will often be too unspecific even to seem to stand a chance
of individuating something (think of things seen at a distance in poor conditions
for vision): and even if the content of the experience is highly specific, a specification constructed by making that content explicit in purely general terms will fit
the right object no better than it fits a Twin Earth *Doppelgänger*.[7] (This objection
obviously belongs to the second of the two kinds I distinguished in the last paragraph: it cites a case where, allegedly, specificatory content is insufficient to individuate an object at all. It will be clear that the materials of Searle's response would
equally apply to an objection of the first kind, where specificatory content is, allegedly, such as to individuate the wrong object.)
   Objections of this sort misfire, Searle argues, because they ignore the possibility
of anchoring the particular-directedness of the mental states in question to the
particularity of the relevant experiences themselves. Thus, he suggests, the content
of a belief that someone who dimly glimpses a man in the distance might express
by saying "That man is wearing a red cap" can be expressed (in the right circumstances) in this way: "There is a man there causing this visual experience and
that man is wearing a red cap" (p. 212). There is no risk that the specificatory
material made explicit here might be satisfied by the wrong man.[8] (Searle builds
here on his discussion of the content of visual experience in chapter 2 of *Intentionality*: the very same form of words just cited as giving the content of a belief, in

the case envisaged, might equally be used, according to that discussion, in making partly explicit the content of the visual experience itself – see p. 48.)[9]

(3)   But what about the particular-directedness signalled here by "this visual experience"? How is this to be made out to conform to the general "Fregean" picture?

This kind of demonstrative expression is enormously important at several points in *Intentionality* (see chapters 2, 3, 8, and 9); and that makes it remarkable that the book contains no discussion at all of the questions I have just posed. When he discusses the content of visual experience, Searle insists that a formulation of the sort in question makes explicit what is *shown* by an experience (p. 49; there are similar moves elsewhere, e.g. pp. 213, 223). He seems to be suggesting that these formulations do not actually *give* the content of the mental states in question, but make it available to us by a kind of indirection. But he does not make this man-oeuvre with respect to the content of the perceptually based belief (p. 212, cited above). And in any case, even where he does exploit the notion of showing, that does not obviously make it legitimate (nor indeed does Searle suggest it does) to duck questions about how expressions like "this visual experience" should be conceived as working in these formulations. Whatever the formulations do, they do it by reminding us of a way in which explicit expression can be given to a certain sort of thinkable content when one is in the right perceptual situation, and even if this content is not itself supposed to *be* the content of the mental state originally under discussion (the visual experience, say), its particular-directedness ought to conform to the general picture.

Notice that it matters how the visual experience is referred to. Consider the claim that one of Searle's formulations, uttered by me in suitable circumstances, might capture the content of a visual experience or a perceptually based demon-strative belief of mine, whether directly, by being a specification of that content, or indirectly, by making explicit what is shown. This claim would lose plausibility if "this visual experience" were replaced by something designating the visual experience in question as, say, that enjoyed by John McDowell at such-and-such a time. I could have this sort of experience or belief without knowing that I am John McDowell. (For a parallel point, accepted by Searle from John Perry and David Kaplan, see pp. 218–9.)

(4)   In the absence of help from Searle on this point, then, let me suggest that the best account of the sort of particular-directedness that is, perfectly intelligibly, signalled by phrases like "this visual experience" in those formulations of his exploits the fact that the experience itself – the very object to which those contents are directed – is a possible focus of the mind's attention, simply by virtue of being enjoyed.[10] In the right circumstances, namely that one is having a visual experience, the experience itself can be a determinant of the mode of attention or directedness that one might indicate, at least to oneself, by "this visual experience". It is not a matter of a specification intelligible independently of the object specified: the pres-ence to the mind of the object itself enters into any understanding of these demon-strative modes of presentation.

This notion of the presence of an object to the mind is reminiscent of Russell's notion of acquaintance – a relation which, according to Russell, makes possible a direct targeting on objects of propositions that do not need to be spelled out in terms of the apparatus of the Theory of Descriptions. So one way of expressing the idea that Frege's conception of singular senses is to be understood as a partial anticipation of the Theory of Descriptions (see section 1 above) would be to suggest that if one appeals, as I have done, to what looks like a version of Russell's *contrast* or *foil* to the kind of case where he takes propositions to bear on objects by way of descriptions, one is suggesting that in these demonstrative cases the notion of Fregean sense is simply dispensable. What need is there of a Fregean sense to target the mind on the object of its thought, one might ask, if the object is itself present to the mind as a possible focus of its attention?

But this would be a mistake. There is still the standard Fregean reason for saying that *how* the object is presented in a Thought makes a difference to which Thought it is. As we have seen (section 3 above), it matters for my getting hold of the right contents to make Searle's proposals plausible that I take the visual experience they concern to be presented as *this visual experience*, and not as, say, the visual experience had by John McDowell at such-and-such a time. There is nothing unFregean here – no appeal to the apparatus of "direct reference" and "singular propositions" that Searle is (rightly, to my mind) concerned to avoid (see p. 220). The point is that this recognizably Fregean insistence on discriminating contents more finely than that apparatus does – by modes of presentation, not by objects – is in no way disrupted by our envisaging modes of presentation which exploit the presence to the mind of objects themselves.

Even the idea of fitting or satisfying specifications or conditions can perhaps be made out to apply here. The condition an object must satisfy to be what one of the relevant contents concerns is the condition of being (as only the subject can put it, and only at the time) *this visual experience*, where that form of words is used in a way that essentially exploits the subject's having the very visual experience that is in question. The condition is not one that could be expressed or entertained even if the experience in question did not exist.[11]

(5)   The suggestion is, then, that "this visual experience" can signal a way in which a visual experience can be presented in a thought, made possible by the fact that the experience itself is present to the mind by virtue of being enjoyed. And now I want to raise the question why it cannot be fully Fregean to parallel this idea for the case of perceived objects. The upshot would be to build on a plausible account of Searle's apparatus, in such a way as to yield a different account of the contents which he uses the apparatus to explain. Why should we not suppose that "that man" – when a man is in one's field of vision – expresses a way in which a man can be presented in a Fregean Thought, made possible by the fact that the man himself is present to the mind by virtue of being seen? As before, the idea is that such a demonstrative mode of presentation is not capturable in a specification that someone could understand without exploiting the perceived presence of the man himself. In answering the question how the man is presented in such Thoughts, there is no substitute for saying "He is presented as *that* man", exploiting his perceived presence to make oneself understood. The condition an object must meet to be what such Thoughts bear on – the condition of being *that* man, as one can put it if one is in the right perceptual circumstances – is not one that could be expressed or entertained even if the man in question did not exist. As before, this suggestion does not involve sliding into the apparatus of "direct reference" and

"singular propositions", individuated by the objects they are about rather than by modes of presentation. Standardly Fregean arguments still allow us to discriminate a Thought expressible in suitable circumstances by "That man is wearing a red cap", understood in this object-dependent way, from Thoughts expressible by concatenating the same predication with different designations of the same man.

It is not my aim in this paper to argue positively for this sort of view.[12] For present purposes, the point is simply that it is a possibility. Apart from one notable difference (which I shall come to in section 7 below), it simply parallels a plausible suggestion for filling a gap in Searle's explicit discussion of his own apparatus. So what is there to prevent Searle accepting it?[13]

(6) Part of the answer is that Searle's reading of Frege precludes a view of this sort. As I suggested in section 1, he takes Frege's idea of singular sense, at any rate where the associated *Bedeutung* is "external", to match Russell's idea of the significance of "denoting phrases", at least in that he supposes singular senses to be independent of the existence of an object determined. Searle does not cite chapter and verse in support of this. I believe the basis of this reading of Frege, in which of course Searle is far from alone, is not specific texts so much as a philosophical train of thought which convinces people that Frege's idea *must* have been on these lines. I shall come to Searle's version of this philosophy in section 7 below. Meanwhile, although the exegetical issue is less important than the underlying philosophical one, let me briefly try to sow some preliminary doubts about Frege himself.

It is obvious that Frege's guiding aim, in using the concept of singular sense, was to secure a fineness of grain in object-directed contents that could not be achieved if they were individuated simply by the objects they concern.[14] Russell's main point in the Theory of Descriptions, by contrast, was to postulate a kind of significance that is independent of the existence of associated objects: one notable upshot is that Russell could handle existential statements containing the relevant kind of terms in a way that is consistent with the doctrine that existential statements attribute the second-level property of instantiation. Russell's apparatus does secure a fineness of grain, but it is easy to see that as a bonus. The basic motivations diverge.

Now it is not simply given that these two aims – securing fineness of grain and dealing with the issues about existence – *had* to be met by the same apparatus. However neat one finds Russell's use of, in effect, the notion of specification in order to secure at one stroke significances which are existence-independent and fineness of grain, one should be aware that there is a grave risk of anachronism in assuming that a notion of specification used to gloss *Frege's* way with fineness of grain must similarly involve existence-independence. If it does not, then of course a Fregean needs a different treatment of existential statements involving proper names; but it seems clear in any case that Frege did not suppose that the attribution of sense to names by itself accommodated such statements, in something like the way in which the Theory of Descriptions does.[15] It is time philosophers stopped taking for granted that the notion of singular sense is a half-baked forerunner of the Theory of Descriptions, and started considering the possibility that the fineness of grain which Frege was basically concerned to register can be had with senses which are not independent of the existence of the objects they present.[16]

(7)   The philosophical train of thought that underpins Searle's reading of Frege starts from the thesis that an Intentionalist account of content, such as Frege's notion of Thoughts patently is, must be "internalist" (see especially p. 198). In effect Searle glosses "internalist" in terms of the idea of locating meanings, and more generally contents, "in the head" (see chapter 8 of *Intentionality*, "Are Meanings in the Head?", and the discussion therein); what this amounts to in his argument is that the contents that an "internalist" account can countenance must be capable of being entertained by a brain in a vat (see p. 230, cited in section 1 above). This would clearly not be the case with contents that could not be entertained or expressed if certain perceived environmental items did not exist. Whereas if a brain in a vat can have content-involving mental states at all (something Searle evidently sees no difficulty in supposing), the requirement would not preclude contents partly determined by object-involving modes of presentation of those mental states, such as those I envisaged – offering Searle a plausible account of his unexplained appeal to demonstrative phrases like "this visual experience" – in section 4 above. This is the difference I alluded to at the end of section 5 above, between that suggestion and the similar suggestion I aired, about demonstrative modes of presentation of perceived "external" objects, also in section 5. Searle could exploit this difference to claim that modes of presentation which are object-involving (not existence-indifferent) may pass muster – that is, be acceptable to "internalism" – when the objects are "in the mind", but not when they are not.[17]

I think this line of thought begins with an insight, but distorts it into a mistake. The notion of what is "internal" undergoes a shift between what it must amount to in order to make "internalism" clearly incumbent on an Intentionalist and what it amounts to in Searle's requirement about brains in vats.

The insight is best understood in terms of the style of objection against "descriptive" accounts of object-directedness that I mentioned in section 2 above. Many philosophers, as Searle notes, have taken such objections to show that Intentionalistic views of content do not have the resources to individuate the objects on which mental states should be taken to be targeted. They have concluded that individuation requires an appeal to extra-Intentional considerations: notably facts about the context and causation of the mental states in question, conceived as investigated "from the third-person or external point of view" (see pp. 62–5 – this phrase is from p. 65 – and chapter 8).[18] In Searle's view, this "externalist" approach simply shirks facing the right question (see especially pp. 64–5). Directedness to particulars, he insists, is an aspects of the *contents* of some *mental* states; and if giving an account of something requires this sort of stepping outside the subject's point of view, then whatever it is that is being explained, it cannot be the contents of mental states. We can put the point like this: attributing content-involving mental states, including those whose contents are particular, is delineating the contours of a subjectivity, and it does not make sense to suppose that executing that task could require "external" considerations over and above the whole truth about how the subjectivity in question is arranged.[19]

This line of thought of Searle's strikes me as absolutely right. One could oppose it, on behalf of an "externalist" position, by claiming that there is some strict sense of the notion of mental content according to which mental contents do not have particularity, at any rate if "externally" directed, as a feature. But put baldly like that, this seems like a denial of mental directedness at "external" objects, which is hard to swallow. A less bald denial allows for a kind of object-directed content, which is conceived as having an "internal" and an "external" aspect. But as long as the "external" aspect is taken to come into sight only when we step outside the subject's own point of view (as it usually is, more or less explicitly, in views of this type),[20] this "double aspect" kind of position is vulnerable to a form of Searle's objection: it does not accommodate, but indeed simply flouts, the connection on which Searle implicitly insists between content and subjectivity. It is no good protesting that the connection is respected with regard to the supposed "internal" aspect: it is the complete "double aspect" contraption that positions of this kind put to a sort of use – specifically, giving the contents of propositional attitudes – which is genuinely intelligible only if the connection with subjectivity is respected.[21] Outright "externalism", as Searle suggests, seems merely to abandon the topic of mental content.

Searle's "internalism", then, embodies what seems to be a genuine insight. But the right way to understand the insight, as indeed some of Searle's own formulations make clear, is by glossing "internal" with "first-personal"; what is wrong with "externalism" is that it steps outside the delineation of the relevant subjectivity. Searle's "in the head", and his "brain in a vat" requirement, are quite another matter. On Searle's own account, visual experience provides "direct access" to seen objects (pp. 45–6). What is present to the mind, when one sees an object, is not some mental surrogate for it but the object itself. This "direct realism" (see p. 57) yields a perfectly intelligible sense in which the first-personal truth about a subject – the truth about the layout of his subjectivity – is not independent of the external objects that perceptually confront him. One's subjectivity is partly constituted by one's point of view on the objects in one's environment. There is thus no shift to a point of view other than the subject's if we countenance object-dependent contents on the lines suggested in section 5. There is certainly a violation of the "brain in a vat" requirement, but that looks simply irrelevant to the good point Searle makes against "externalism".[22]

Glossed in terms of "first-personal" and "third-personal", the contrast between "internal" and "external" makes a point about perspective. It takes a slide to get from there to a literally spatial interpretation of the contrast, under which whatever is outside the subject's body is *eo ipso* "external"; and this spatial reading is what Searle's "brain in a vat" requirement involves. Searle contrives to obscure the slide with appeals to a "biological naturalism", which he expresses in remarks like this (p. 230): "The brain is all we have for the purpose of representing the world to ourselves and everything we can use must be inside the brain." But on any normal understanding of the words he uses here, this remark is straightforwardly and obviously false. We have all kinds of things other than the brain for the purpose of representing the world to ourselves: sounds, marks on paper, arrangements of models (as in the law-court goings-on that impressed Wittgenstein), in short all kinds of bits of the world outside our brain. (In fact the brain is one thing that we do not exploit for any representative purposes that we have.) It is as if Searle has here forgotten, or perhaps never quite took the measure of, the "direct realism" that he resolutely espouses, in an earlier chapter, about perception. When we control our actions by what we see (for instance homing in on an object), the right thing to say, in the spirit of that "direct realism", is that we have no need to represent the relevant bit of the world to ourselves, as if in order to have something by which to guide what we do: we can guide what we do by the relevant bit of the world itself, directly presented as it is to our view. And our other uses of bits of the world, whether in constructing representations or for any other purpose, can be just as direct.

Searle goes on from the passage I have just quoted with this amazing remark: "Each of our beliefs must be possible for a being who is a brain in a vat because each of us is precisely a brain in a vat; the vat is a skull and the 'messages' coming in are coming in by way of impacts on the nervous system" (ibid.). Surely no sane naturalism can possibly compel us to accept the idea that being in the world, for *us*, is being inside our own heads. The idea has a comical ring; and the indirectness which it imposes on how we have to picture our dealings with the world (the talk of "messages" coming in) sits ill with Searle's earlier commendable rejection of intermediaries. There is certainly something attractive about his suggestion that mental states need to be understood in the context of a "biological naturalism": the point of attributing mental states is to make sense of the actions – which make up the lives – of creatures such as ourselves. But the natural biological phenomena that we understand in the light of mental states figure in the lives of creatures that engage, as we do, in direct dealings with the objects in their environment; not in something we can call "life" only derivatively, the functioning of organs of behavioural control which relate only mediately to environmental objects.[23]

(8)   The upshot of these considerations is that it may be possible after all, contrary to what Searle claims, to return an affirmative answer to his question (p. 208), "Are there irreducibly *de re* beliefs?" As Searle rightly says, the terminology here has been used in many different ways. In the interpretation I intend, an irreducibly *de re* propositional attitude (belief figures in Searle's question only as an example) is one whose content would not be thinkable if the relevant object did not exist. The twist is that there can be contents that relate in this way to "external" objects but which are fully Intentional, contrary to Searle's claim that Intentional content must be thinkable by a brain in a vat.[24] In making room for this rejection of Searle's "brain in a vat" requirement, I have argued that we can respect Searle's insistence that an Intentionalist account of content must be "internalist". I have tried to drive a wedge between two interpretations that he gives of this, one in terms of subjectivity and one in terms of literal interiority. My claim has been that we should applaud the former, but discard the latter, partly on the basis of Searle's own admirable insistence that our access to environmental objects in perception is direct.

NOTES

1 Cambridge University Press: Cambridge, 1983.
2 Searle makes room also for mental states whose Intentional content is less than an entire proposition (p. 7): in Fregean terms, these would involve senses smaller than Thoughts figuring otherwise than as constituents of whole Thoughts. I do not know whether Frege himself envisaged this extension of his apparatus. But even if not, this is clearly no problem for Searle's claim to be recommending a position that is Fregean in spirit.
3 See "On Denoting", *Mind* 14 (1905), pp. 479–93; reprinted in Bertrand Russell, *Logic and Knowledge*, ed. R. C. Marsh (Allen and Unwin: London, 1956), pp. 41–56.
4 Russell hardly figures in *Intentionality*, and not in this context. But Searle's gloss on Fregean

singular sense, in terms of fit, does not by itself secure the object-independence he insists on; this will emerge below. A tacit Russellian influence (which is plausible in any case) helps to explain why Searle apparently supposes otherwise.

5   This terminology is familiar, and Searle allows himself to use it (e.g. in chapter 9); but it is potentially misleading in suggesting that the specificatory conception is limited to what can be verbally expressed, in purely general terms (see pp. 232–3). I shall not trade on any such assumption.

6   "Naming and Necessity", first printed in Donald Davidson and Gilbert Harman (eds), *Semantics of Natural Language* (Reidel: Dordrecht, 1972), pp. 253–355, 763–9; issued as a monograph by Basil Blackwell, Oxford, 1980. Another early landmark in the revolt against "descriptive" accounts of reference and singular thought was Keith Donnellan, "Proper Names and Identifying Descriptions", in Davidson and Harman, *Semantics*, pp. 356–79.

7   This way of dramatizing objections of this kind is due to Hilary Putnam, "The Meaning of 'Meaning'", in *Mind, Language and Reality* (Cambridge University Press: Cambridge, 1975), pp. 215–71.

8   It might seem that there is a risk of cases where such a formulation would not select between several candidates (because there are several men in view). I think Searle would respond that "there" functions to select the right aspect of the visual experience and so secure that the specification selects the right man. See the discussion of Donnellan's case of the two seen patches at pp. 253–4.

9   In sticking to this case, I shall be avoiding some extra complexities introduced by Searle's discussion of indexicality, which imports a reference to the current *utterance* (as "this utterance") in a specification of "conditions of satisfaction": see pp. 220–8. The simpler case I have rehearsed from Searle contains enough to reveal the shape of his strategy, and to enable me to make the points I want to make. (In passing, I note that it is a curiosity of Searle's discussion that he deals with the first person, for instance, only in the context of his treatment of indexical *expressions*, as if the first-person mode of presentation – to use Fregean terminology – was in play only when one speaks and not also in unexpressed thought. There is no reason to suppose that the general strategy, exemplified in the passage I have focused on, requires this. I note also that the case discussed at p. 212 suggests that the "problem of particularity" – in the content of visual experience – that Searle discusses at pp. 62–71 ought to include more than what he there considers. The explicit discussion of the "problem of particularity" is limited to cases where the particularity relates to a *prior* identification. But one can see something that might be expressed by saying, in suitable circumstances, "That man is wearing a red cap" – that is, the content of one's experience can be particular in a way that the demonstrative indicates – without any prior identification of the man in question being involved.)

10 It is a good question what makes this sort of attention possible, and the best answer may not in the end be congenial to the use to which Searle puts these demonstratives: see n. 12 below.

11 Philosophers who are gripped by the idea that singular sense must be independent of the existence of the relevant object will need to consider, instead of "this visual experience", specifications of the general form "the visual experience which . . .". One candidate that might have some attraction is "the visual experience which I am now having"; with its indexicality, this would not be vulnerable to the objection against "the visual experience which John McDowell is having at . . ." and the like (see section 3 above). But this suggestion would at best postpone the facing of an issue like the one that I am addressing in this section, about the modes of presentation expressed (by me, on an occasion) by "I" and "now". In Searle's treatment (which relates exclusively to uses of those indexical *expressions*: see pp. 220–8), the issue would in the end be shifted to one about "this utterance". In a modification of Searle's treatment, preserving its spirit but taking account of the fact that first-person thinking need not be expressed (see n. 9 above), the issue would be shifted to one about something like "this thought"; it is natural to suggest that we might as well stay with "this visual experience". ("This utterance" raises extra questions, in view of the fact that utterances are not "in the mind" in the way that experiences are: see section 5 below. Searle's taking it for granted

is accordingly perhaps even more remarkable than his taking "this visual experience" for granted.)

12 I do believe it points the way to a general view of object-directed Intentionality that is a great improvement over what Searle suggests. In Searle's picture, "externally" directed particularity in content is secured indirectly, by way of contents targeted on "internal" items, with this latter targeting hardly discussed, as if it can stand unproblematically on its own. In a different view, the targeting of content on "internal" items like experiences is not intelligible independently of the targeting of content on the self. Searle's treatment of indexicality, however acceptable in itself, simply bypasses the deep issues that first-personal content raises (see n. 9 above). The different view of "externally" directed demonstrative content which I have sketched permits us to register a plausible role played in a full explanation of first-personal content by the capacity to locate and orient oneself in a perceived environment. This inverts the priority that Searle's discussion suggests of "this visual experience" and the like over "that man" ("rock", "tree") and the like. (Particularly in the context of this comparison, Searle's priority has a rather Cartesian feel.) For more detail about the sort of different view I have in mind, see Gareth Evans, *The Varieties of Reference* (Clarendon Press: Oxford, 1982), especially chapters 6 and 7.

13 I should note that this sort of view of perceptual demonstratives figures here only as one example (though probably the most immediately attractive) of a way of making sense of the phrase I have used for the title of this paper. A fuller discussion would need to look into other possible examples (to say nothing of much more detailed treatment of this sort of case). Compare n. 8, p. 141, of my "Singular Thought and the Extent of Inner Space", in Philip Pettit and John McDowell (eds), *Subject, Thought, and Context* (Clarendon Press: Oxford, 1986), pp. 137–68; and Evans, *Varieties of Reference*.

14 See, of course, "On Sense and Reference", in P. T. Geach and Max Black, *Translations from the Philosophical Writings of Gottlob Frege* (Basil Blackwell: Oxford, 1960), pp. 56–78.

15 Frege did not even allow that "NN exists (does not exist)" can be well-formed with the name functioning in its normal way. In *Speech Acts* (Cambridge University Press: Cambridge, 1969), p. 165, n. 3, Searle acknowledges this, but makes it an occasion to chide Frege for not seeing that his conceptual equipment permitted a broadly Russellian approach to existentials: Searle's suggestion is that the attribution of sense to names removes all reason for not allowing such existential statements to be well-formed. It would have made for better exegesis if Searle had tried to comprehend Frege's notion of singular sense in a way that warranted his assignment of ill-formedness. The idea of singular senses as object-dependent (but fine-grained) accommodates the texts much better. (Positive support for the idea that Frege envisaged object-dependent singular senses comes from his doctrine of truth-value gaps: see my "Truth-Value Gaps", *Logic, Methodology and Philosophy of Science VI* (North-Holland; Amsterdam, 1982), pp. 299–313.) Frege's own treatment of the issues raised by apparent singular terms with no bearer (the existence issues) is sketchy and unsatisfactory, but it does not follow that we do him a favor by equipping him with a conception of singular sense inspired anachronistically by the Theory of Descriptions; for a better (neo-Fregean) treatment on no such basis, see Evans, *Varieties of Reference*, chapter 10.

16 On object-dependent Fregean singular senses, see further chapter 1 of Evans, *Varieties of Reference*, and my *"De Re* Senses", *Philosophical Quarterly* 34 (1984), pp. 283–94.

17 I have no idea whether Searle would accept something like the suggestion of section 4. The point is only that it supplements his silence about an important part of his own apparatus, and in a way that is not ruled out by his "internalism", so long as we grant his own assumption that brains in vats can have content-involving mental states.

18 The idea of reference as an extra-Intentional relation is made vivid by Richard Rorty, in chapter 6 of *Philosophy and the Mirror of Nature* (Basil Blackwell: Oxford, 1980). Rorty himself does not endorse the idea: he contrives to remain aloof, above the controversy between Intentionalists and "externalists" (to put it in Searle's terms), while leaving unchallenged the "externalist" view about the individuative insufficiency of the Intentionalists' resources, by,

in effect, separating the needs of interpretation from the aim of delineating the true contours of mental states. For some discussion, see section 9 of my "Singular Thought and the Extent of Inner Space".

19   I have put it like this in order to allow for a possibility that factors outside a subject's ken might partly determine what I have described (more impressionistically than Searle) as the contours of his subjectivity. What Searle finds intolerable is the idea that *after* noting the whole truth about the contours of a subjectivity (however they are determined), we might *still* need to look outside it in order to establish any particular-directedness of the subject's mental states.

20   For a particularly explicit example, see Colin McGinn, "The Structure of Content", in Andrew Woodfield (ed.), *Thought and Object* (Clarendon Press: Oxford, 1982), pp. 207–58, at pp. 254–5.

21   I cannot recall anywhere in the now vast literature urging this kind of position where the idea of a general connection between content and subjectivity is so much as considered, let alone attacked. Searle is engagingly selective in his targets: from his discussion alone, one would not realize the baroque proliferation of options now on offer in this very poorly understood area of philosophy. There is a little more elaboration than I have allowed myself here in my "Singular Thought and the Extent of Inner Space".

22   Searle's "brain in a vat" requirement dictates that one's visual experience when one sees, say, a station wagon is something that could have been exactly what it is even if there had not been a station wagon in one's vicinity: this very experience might have been a hallucination. It is hard to see how this is consistent with his admirable "direct realism". How can a mental state which would have been exactly what it is even if there had been no relevant environment constitute, when there *is* a relevant environment, one's being directly presented (see p. 46) with objects and states of affairs in it? (It is beside the point that hallucinations can be indistinguishable, from a subject's point of view, from "veridical" experiences.) This question suggests a doubt about the idea – which Searle evidently does not see as even needing defence – that brains in vats could have dealings with content, so long as it was not dependent on the existence of "external" particulars. See, further, my "Singular Thought and the Extent of Inner Space".

23   Avoidance of dualism does not justify Searle's readiness to identify us with our brains and so impose the "brain in a vat" requirement: there is nothing to stop us saying that a mental state can be "realized in" a brain state (compare p. 265) even though not any case of the brain state in question will "realize" a case of the mental state in question (specifically, not cases in which the brain is not normally related to the environment, for instance if it is in a vat).

24   The confused appeal to "exported" forms that Searle rejects (pp. 216–17) can simply fall away. For more on this, see section 7 of my "*De Re* Senses".

16

Response:
Reference and Intentionality

JOHN R. SEARLE

One of the central questions in contemporary philosophy of language in particular, and in the theory of Intentionality in general, is how do Intentional entities, whether mental or linguistic, relate to reality? Since the early 1970s, one of the central points at issue within his larger philosophical question has been whether the inner contents of mind are sufficient to account for the relationship between representations and reality, or whether some external – "causal," "contextual," etc. – element has to be introduced to supplement the inner mental contents. Narrowing that question down even further, we can say that a central question within that central question is whether or not the particularity of reference, i.e., the fact that our intentional contents and linguistic expressions are sometimes directed at quite specific particular objects, can be accounted for with purely internal mental contents.

The standard answer to that question since the 1970s has been "no." And the most commonly given grounds for the negative answer have been that mental contents are not adequate to determine unique reference (e.g. the twin-earth arguments) and would often fix the wrong reference (e.g. arguments against descriptivist theories of proper names). Now, in *Intentionality* I claimed that every argument I knew against internalism in the theory of reference could be answered, and I tried to answer the arguments of Burge, Donnellan, Kripke, Putnam, and others.

Regardless of whether or not I am right about that, the discussion raises another set of difficult but curiously neglected questions about how to specify exactly the relations between Intentional entities such as beliefs, statements, or perceptual experiences; and their Intentional contents (e.g. meanings), the conditions of satisfaction (e.g. truth conditions) and the actual world that in some cases at least correspond to these Intentional entities in virtue of their contents. On the one side, we have the world, blind, uncomprehending, indifferent, and in a sense, undifferentiated; on the other side we have human beings, conscious, linguistically equipped, culturally prejudiced, and biologically predisposed to certain capacities for perception, recognition, description, etc. What is the correct *form* for specifying the Intentional relations between the two? Part, but only part, of our difficulty is that we lack an adequate vocabulary. It is hard to avoid discussing these issues except in terms that are a weird mixture of terminology derived from Descartes, Frege, and Russell, all of whom were in various ways interested in a whole lot of other problems besides this one and did not have a vocabulary designed to pose and answer our questions. I have to say in advance that the vocabulary in the subsequent paragraphs is inadequate, but I hope that readers of this volume will be able to figure out what I am talking about.

When I wrote *Intentionality* I used a notation borrowed from speech act theory to represent the structure of Intentional states, S(p), where the "S" marks the psychological mode and the "p" the representative content that determines the conditions of satisfaction. Using this notation I tried to capture the way the content of the Intentionality in the case of perception and action has a causal component which relates the intentional state itself causally to the rest of its conditions of satisfaction. In the case of a visual experience it comes out like this. If I see that the F is G then the representation is:

> Vis Exp (that the F is G and the fact that the F is G is causing this visual experience)

Probably no claim in the book has been misunderstood as much as this one, and if three philosophers as shrewd as Armstrong, Burge, and McDowell misunderstand it then there is clearly some failure in my expoisition, if not in my theory. A standard objection is that it is "too complicated or too sophisticated" (Burge, p. 198) and that for example dogs, small children, and many adults could not have anything as complicated as this. But this objection is based on a misunderstanding. I am not claiming that the perceiver thinks to himself in words the sentence in the brackets or even that the perceiver has any consciousness of this articulation of these conditions at all. The theoretical representation is a second-order characterization of a set of first order psychological facts. I am trying to specify *in a language* the content of a *nonlinguistic visual phenomenon*; for this reason the complexity is a matter of the theoretical representation and not a matter of the first order psychological facts. The first-order facts are quite simple. They would normally be expressed by the agent in a sentence such as "I see that that man is wearing a red hat." But in the theory of Intentionality we are uncovering complexities in the actual content which may not be immediately available to the agent. He may be, in fact, unconscious of the actual complexities of his own Intentional phenomena.

Furthermore, when I say "this visual experience" I am not, of course, claiming that, for example, a dog who sees something has running through his head the words "this visual experience," or some translation in Caninese; nor am I suggesting that a subject who has a visual experience performs a speech act of indexical reference to his experience. What I am suggesting rather is that the visual experience itself functions self-referentially in fixing its conditions of satisfaction. Now, as a theorist, I can from the third-person point of view represent that in words from, so to speak, the animal's point of view as "this visual experience." But it is emphatically not part of my claim that dogs or people have to have some verbal equivalent of "this visual experience" or references to their visual experiences or thoughts about causation in order to have visual experiences. I tried to state the original thesis naively, but perhaps it will be clear if I try now to be even more naive. Imagine that our visual experiences could talk. Imagine that they could tell us what they were doing. What would they say? I think they would say something like the following:

This is how things are and the fact that this is now things are is causing me to tell you that this is how things are.

Perhaps my original notation can be made to work, but as a tool of exposition it certainly failed with Burge and McDowell. They both think I am committed to the view that there is some second-order indexical or demonstrative reference by a subject to an experience whenever there is an experience and Burge even thinks my view is – Heaven forbid! – like Russell's theory of acquaintance.

The issues are so important and the claims are so easily misunderstood that before I answer the specific objections of McDowell and Burge it is worth going over the nature of the enterprise, in general. Burge and I (and to some extent McDowell) are trying to find a notation for representing the facts about intentional content. When we are trying to specify the relations between Intentional contents, conditions of satisfaction and the world, it is essential to make certain distinctions at the very beginning. Burge and I both agree that when discussing conditions of satisfaction, it is essential to distinguish the requirement from the thing required. But even confining the notion of conditions of satisfactions to the notion of the requirement, and thus enabling ourselves to say that the conditions of satisfaction are internal to the Intentional content, it is still a tricky question to specify exactly the relationships between the Intentional content, conditions of satisfaction and the world. It will not do to say simply that, for example, a belief, when true, represents the state of affairs in the world that makes it true, because there are many features of any state of affairs that are not specified in the content of the belief. It is not enought to say, for example, that the belief that snow is white, when true, represents the state of affairs that makes it true, because any state of affairs which makes it true is also a state of affairs in which atmospherically formed water crystals in flake forms reflect light of all wave lengths, but the belief in question does not represent the state of affairs under that description. Furthermore, it will not even do to say that the Intentional content represents what *must* be the case in the world if the Intentional content is satisfied because, trivially, any necessary truth must be the case, and thus any necessary truth would be represented by any Intentional content whatever. The belief that two plus two equals four is different from the belief that snow is white, even though it must be the case that two plus two equals four, if it is true that snow is white, because it must be the case that two plus two equals four under any circumstances. We can make a preliminary groping effort to specify the sorts of relation between Intentional contents and the world if we say that the Intentional content sets certain *requirements* which must be met if the Intentional entity is to be satisfied.

This formulation enables us to introduce something like Frege's notion of the "mode of presentation." So we can distinguish an Intentional content which represents the Evening Star from an Intentional content which represents the Morning Star, even though the Evening Star and the Morning Star are identical. In the specification of Intentional content we thus specify not only *what* is represented, but *how* it is represented. And the notion of how things are represented introduces the notion of the *aspects* under which they are represented. The Evening Star aspect of an object will be different from the Morning Star aspect of the very same object. However, even these distinctions are not going to be enough, because within the notion of aspects, we will need a further "what–how" distinction. We will need to distinguish not only *what* aspects are represented but *how* those aspects are represented. So, for example, the belief that an object in front of me is red, represents redness in a different way from the visual perception that a red object is in front of me. To one approximation the conditions of satisfaction are the same, since both require that there be a red object in front of me; but the contents are nonetheless different, because perceptual contents are different from belief contents. Furthermore, we can continue to make our specification of the Intentional content even more fine-grained. There is, for example, clearly *some* difference between the thought that John loves Mary and the thought that Mary is loved by John, yet in some sense their conditions of satisfaction are the same, because the same requirement is placed on the world by each thought.

The situation is further complicated by the fact that not all of the internal mental conditions which fix the conditions of satisfaction of an Intentional state are internal to that state. On my view, relations to the holistic Network of Intentionality and to a nonintentional Background are crucial in determining conditions of satisfaction, but neither Network or Background is part of each state.

So, we appear to be in all kinds of deep water, and there is no easy way out. Now, as far as linguistically realized Intentional entities are concerned, we have a simple way of fudging the issue. We simply specify the conditions of satisfaction homophonically, or by disquotation. So, we can say the conditions of satisfaction of the belief that snow is white are *that snow is white*. And the identity of the right-hand side with the left-hand side guarantees that we have the specifications of the conditions of satisfaction right. However, this does not really solve our problems, because by *exhibiting* the conditions of satisfaction rather than describing how they work we do not explain anything; we simply exploit the reader's prior understanding including his Network and Background capacities. There is nothing wrong with specifying the conditions of satisfaction homophonically, but it is not explanatory. For certain theoretical purposes we need to be able to describe the *functioning* of the intentional content in fixing certain conditions of satisfaction and not others. Suppose, for example, we are explaining in one language how the thought is expressed in another. Suppose that a man believes in German what he would express by saying "Schnee ist weiss." Now, if we are specifying the conditions of satisfaction of the belief, more is involved than simply saying that the man has the belief that snow is white, because, in addition, there is a certain way that that state of affairs is represented. It is part of the *content* of the man's intentional state that (using our vocabulary to describe it) the German word "Schnee" is used to refer to snow. And that is part of the man's Intentional content: he is using "Schnee" to refer to snow even though he may not have the second-order concept of reference, and may not even understand the English word "snow." The fact that we use expressions in a theoretical vocabulary to describe what is consciously going on in his head does not imply that what is going on in head is going on using this terminology or some equivalent.

The discussion so far has been designed not only to show the complexity of specification of conscious Intentional content but to begin to justify my claim that an adequate specification of conscious Intentional contents can use concepts that are not available to the agent, and that a complexity in the specification does not imply complexity in the phenomenon specified. With these thoughts in mind, let us now turn our attention more directly to Burge's account.

Tyler Burge

Burge thinks that his (e') is like my (S) and that both involve "semantic ascent." He also thinks that his (a') is perferable to my (S). I believe he is mistaken on all these points, but since the notational issues and the substantive theories are intertwined I have to say something about his conception of representing Intentional contents. Burge, if I understand him correctly, accepts two conditions on the specification of Intentional content which I would reject. First he believes that any *specification* of an Intentional content, where the Intentional content is a conscious state of the agent, should contain only features which are available to the possessor of the intentional state; he thinks that the description of a conscious intentional content should be given in terms which are part of the immediate consciousness of the agent. In the case of conscious visual experiences, he thinks that if you have to reflect in order to see that a certain condition is part of the conditions of satisfaction of ordinary unreflective visual experiences, then that condition cannot be part of the visual experiences. Second, because of this feature, he has a preference for homophonic or disquotational forms for representing Intentional contents. His preferred method of representing an Intentional content simply is to give the words that are available to the agent, and then, outside the content, he gives stage directions as to what further conditions are imposed on the use of those words, or what background requirements we are also taking into consideration. His example (a') exemplifies these principles.

I do not accept these requirements. They seem to be mistaken in the example we considered earlier of explaining to somebody who did not speak German how German expressions determine their conditions of satisfaction. And I think the point is perfectly general. And agent may have a conscious Intentional content and that Intentional content may determine the conditions of satisfaction under certain aspects, that is with a certain "mode of presentation," where the agent may not himself have a *second-order* awareness of how the conscious Intentional content functions to determine the conditions of satisfaction under those aspects. I believe examples of this are easy to find. To make the point clear in general, I will give three sorts of examples. First, an agent may use a word referringly without having the second order concept of "reference." Indeed, this was illustrated in the above example of describing the intentional content of the German speaker while using English. Second, an animal or a human will perceive objects from a *point of view* without necessarily having the concept of a "point of view." The point of view is a feature of the Intentional content in determining the mode of presentation, but it does not follow that the agent has to have the second-order concept of a point of view.

The third example I wish to give is the most important because it also illustrates causal self-referentiality. An agent who gives an order or makes a promise issues a speech act which has causally self-referential conditions of satisfaction. So, for example, if I order that you leave the room, then the Intentional content of my order, stated homophonically, will be

I order (that you leave the room).

But if you spell out the conditions of satisfaction you find that they contain a causally self referential component, which might be made fully explicit as follows:

I order (that you leave the room because of this very order).

Now, notice that in this case these are the conditions of satisfaction of the order and they are intended by the agent as such, but the agent need not be conscious or aware, or even able to specify, that these are the contents of the order. The *specification* may indeed be the result of a difficult philosophical analysis.

So far it might seem that Burge and I have simply opted for two alternative notations for describing exactly the same set of facts, and that consequently there is no substantive difference between us. Burge points out that since both options will determine the *same* state of affairs in the world, "one might be baffled about why the fine distinctions between (a′) and (e′) matter. After all, I claim that (a′) presupposes something like (e′). So, it may appear that there is no basis for taking them as rivals" (p. 203). He answers this by saying "But a theory of Intentional content is not just a theory of satisfaction conditions. It is simultaneously a theory of mental states – mental abilities and cognitive point of view" (p. 203). I agree with this latter claim of Burge. I think it matters which features in the overall account of Intentionality are specified as part of Intentional content strictly speaking and which are specified as further conditions on the applicability of the Intentional content.

With this point we reach what I think is the crux of the disagreement between me and Burge. At this point we are no longer just arguing about alternative notations for representing the same facts, but what the facts are. And some notations are better than others at getting at the facts.

First, I claim that it is essential to distinguish those features of content which function to determine conditions of satisfactions from features outside the content which also serve to fix conditions of satisfaction. Specifically, on my view elements of the Network and the Background are crucial in determining how Intentional content determines conditions of satisfaction, but they are not themselves part of the intentional content of each intentional state.

Now I cannot see how Burge can make this distinction. He says, "Searle seems to me entirely right and extremely insightful in his claim that the Intentional content of the visual experience should reflect the fact that the content of a visual experience is satisfied only if the experience is caused by entities of the sort represented as present by the experience" (p. 201). But how exactly is the "content" supposed to "reflect" the fact? On his notation for expressing Intentional content there is no obvious way that he can express this fact. His notation puts it outside the content as a stage direction for interpreting the content; but there is a substantive difference between maintaining, as I do, that causal self-referentiality is internal to content and that it is external. If he thinks, as the passage implies, that it is internal, then the notation should reflect that fact. His objection to my notation is that he finds it misleading to describe the contents of consciousness in terms that are not available to the agent, but I have already given reasons for rejecting that condition.

Second, once you see the difference between mental conditions which are internal to content and those which, though internal to the mind, are external of specific Intentional contents, then you can see that his (e′) is really not like my (S). Formulations like (e′) were introduced as part of the "causal theory of reference" precisely to have a form of external causation which was not represented in the internal mental contents at all. They are part of an externalist theory that claims that the determination of reference cannot be done by the contents of the mind. And the form of causation which they employ is quite different from Intentional causation. On my view, on the other hand, it is absolutely essential that the causal conditions in reference are internal to the contents of the mind and do involve Intentional causation. Intentional causation is a form of causation which is quite different from Humean or billiard ball causation.

Third, because of his failure to grasp the distinction between the mental preconditions for determining the applicability of intentional content and intentional content itself, he misunderstands the role of the Background in my theory. He mentions my discussion of how the Background is supposed to solve the problem of "deviant causal chains" and then remarks, "What is important is that the conditions must be incorporated into the account of the Intentional content of visual perception if one is to provide a correct account of 'satisfaction conditions' (Searle does not note this. Perhaps he regarded it as obvious.)" (p. 207). But on the contrary, I did not mention it because I thought it was obvious from everything I said that the Background is *not* part of the intentional content. One of the recurring themes of the book is that relations of Intentional states to the Network and the Background, though crucial for the functioning of Intentionality, are not part of intentional content. To repeat, *not everything which is an internal mental precondition for determining the conditions of satisfaction of an Intentional state is itself part of a content of that very Intentional state,* as my entire discussion of the Network and the Background was designed to show. I will return to this point at the end of my reply to Burge.

Part of the difficulty is probably my fault. When arguing in favor of "internalism" and against "externalism" in the philosophy of mind and language, I sometimes use the expression "Intentional content" as a shorthand for Intentional content including Background and Network conditions on its application, all of which are internal to the mind. I rely on the context to make the point clear. The point is to contrast an internalistic account of reference which says that the innter contents of the mind including Background and Network are sufficient to determine conditions of satisfaction and hence sufficient to determine reference with an externalist account that says that the contents of the mind are insufficient to fix reference. In any case this misunderstanding turns out to be crucial in several respects, because Burge takes my solution to the problem of "deviant causal chains" to be the specification of some external condition in the world. But that is not right; for me there is no such thing as a deviant causal chain *per se.* The deviance is only relative to the conditions set by the mind including background conditions.

Fourth, another reason for rejecting Burge's method is that I think that, in fact, it is impossible to carry it out. When we are discussing one form of Intentionality such as visual experience using another device such as language, it is, strictly speaking, impossible to use homophonic translation. How, for example, is his analysis of visual experience supposed to work for dogs, who do not have a language? It is worth pointing out that, in spite of his extensive discussion, he never actually states what he thinks the conditions of satisfaction of the visual experience are. Nowhere does he actually try to answer the question that I am answering. And it would not be easy to do, given his assumptions.

Now with this much in hand I hope to clear up some misunderstandings fairly quickly:

Burge attributes two views to me, only one of which I hold; the first is that in perception the subject experiences causal relations. I do hold this view and will say more about it in a moment. The second is that the "subject experiences, or is directly aware of, his own visual experiences in such a way that visual *beliefs* [my italics] automatically are about or make reference to those experiences" (p. 203). I do not hold this view and I do not know why he thinks I do, unless it is supposed to be a consequence of my remarks about self referentiality, which as I said, I believe he has misinterpreted.

Several arguments in his article depend on this misunderstanding and I will run through them briefly:

1   Burge says (p. 205): "Although visual experiences are manipulated within the visual system, they are not thereby referred to by the subject in visual experience. Such manipulations and discriminations are unconscious, automatic, and most important inaccessible to use by other parts of the cognitive system."

I believe this objection is just irrelevant to me. It is not part of my claim that *the subject refers* to his visual experiences. I think Burge's claim here depends on the same misunderstanding I mentioned earlier.

2   "For the subject's judgments to make reference to visual experiences, the subject himself, not merely a sub-system of the subject, must be capable of making discriminations between experiences and physical objects, and of using these discriminations in a wide range of judgments, judgments which presumably would involve reasoning about the discriminations" (p. 205).

But again, it is not a consequence of my view that the subject must have any "judgments" at all about his visual experiences. For all I know, dogs, small children, and most adults never reflect on their visual experiences. So, once again, this objection is simply irrelevant.

3   According to Burge, Intentional contents of the sort that I propose would "guarantee inferences, available to the whole cognitive system, that distinguish experiences from physical objects that cause them. But such inferences are not guaranteed by the visual experiences themselves" (p. 205).

But there is nothing in my account that guarantees any inferences at all. Of course, a *theorist* may be able to make inferences about what the conditions of satisfaction would commit the subject to. But the subject himself need have no knowledge of this theory at all, nor even be able to make the inferences.

4   Burge objects that in order to know of the causal relation between the visual experience and the external world, there has to be some reflection: "We gain knowledge of the causal relation, and indeed of our own visual experiences, by reflecting on unreflective visual experience. If this is to be possible, there must be a cognitive *step* of some sort between the unreflective experience and the knowledge gained by reflection. Searle's theory collapses the step by attributing to the unreflective visual experience satisfaction conditions that are the result of reflection" (p. 206).

I believe this simply expresses the same misunderstanding. The agent himself need have no "knowledge of the causal relation." The causal feature is simply a feature of the content of the unreflective visual experience. By analogy, all visual experiences are from a certain point of view, even though the agent in having the visual experience may not be aware of this point of view, i.e., he may not have a *second-order* awareness of the point of view. Nonetheless, the point of view is a feature of the visual experience in the sense that it is part of the visual mode of presentation of the objects perceived. Similarly with causation: the agent need have no second-order *knowledge* of the causal relation. It is simply part of the content of his own unreflective experience.

5   Burge (ingeniously!) imagines a Frege-style argument of the following form: "It is possible to have a perceptual belief that that yellow station wagon is self-identical, and yet be in a position to reason about whether to accept the view that the yellow station wagon causing this very experience is that yellow station wagon. One might, for example wonder whether two yellow station wagons are causing this very experience – whereas only one of them is *that one*. On Searle's account such doubt, described in a way I have described it, is not really possible" (p. 207). As I understand this argument, it is simply the "paradox of analysis" repeated. That is, what it says is that an analysis such as mine might be denied by the agent who has the experience I am analyzing. I believe that it is true, but notice that it is characteristic of any analysis of perception (or any other philosophical analysis of a concept) that an agent might have the perception and yet make claims which are inconsistent with the specific features of the analysis. So this does not seem to me a forceful objection.

6   According to Burge "Searle says nothing about our cognitive relations to our present visual experiences, except that reference to such experiences in the Intentional content is by way of ineliminable demonstrative element ('this')" (p. 206). But this passage betrays the same misunderstanding. As I said in *Intentionality*, and have repeated here, I do not think that we perform the speech act of referring to our visual experiences when we have them, it is simply that their conditions of satisfaction are token-reflexive or self-referential in the sense that I have tried to explain. But Burge goes on to say that "this is the only sort of demonstrative relation, according to Searle's theory of Intentional content" (p. 206). But that is simply not true. I think there are all sorts of demonstrative relations and I have attempted to analyze them in the section on indexicality in *Intentionality*. I think that this misunderstanding on Burge's part is connected to the way that he tries to relate my views to Russell's. As I understand Russell's views about knowledge by acquaintance and knowledge by description, his views are not like mine.

So far I have claimed that most of Burge's difficulties derive from the difficulties I encountered in trying to explain one mode of Intentionality, namely visual experience, using the resources of another mode of Intentionality, namely linguistic expressions. Of course, linguistic expressions are not going to be the same as the perceptual experiences. What I was trying to represent are the essential features of the experience construed both phenomenologically and Intentionalistically, where the phenomenology determines the Intentionality. Now, phenomenologically, the natural way for the agent to describe his experience would be to say, e.g., "I see that man in the red hat." But what I am trying to do is to show how the actual experience determines the conditions of satisfaction. The first step was to see that the whole content must be propositional (even though phenomenologically it seems a matter of just perceiving an object). Second, that the proposition contains a causal component, and third, that the whole set of conditions is causally self-referential.

So far, in this reply to Burge, I have tried to establish that one could have a notation in which all of the causally self-referential conditions are part of the *content* of the experience, rather than as a set of background stage directions about how to interpret the content of the experience. But, it seems to me, Burge might object that though I have shown how one *might* be motivated to include them as part of the content; nonetheless, I have not shown why we *must* so include them. It takes a separate argument to show that they are actually part of the content of the experience, and about this Burge is extremely skeptical.

I do not know of a demonstrative argument to show that visual perception includes a causal component in such a way that the analysis of the content must contain the causal self-referentiality that I allude to. But I do in *Intentionality* give various considerations which incline me to this view. In the end, perhaps, it is one of those points in philosophy where you either see it the way I do or you don't. But there are some arguments that I find are quite compelling, and here is a sketch of one.

Let us begin by considering the case of perceptual experiences other than vision. Suppose that I feel a sharp object pressing into my back. Suppose I can't see it, but I can feel it. Now what exactly is the perceptual character of my experience and what exactly is its perceptual content and what exactly is the relation between perceptual character and intentional content? Well, in this case it seems to me we would normally express this in ordinary speech by saying "I feel a sharp object pressing into my back." And that is surely right as far as it goes, but what exactly is the "mode of presentation"? Well, of course, I *feel* the object in question. Yes, but what is the intentional content of that feeling? Here is seems to me pretty clear that the "mode of presentation" is such that there is a sharp object pressing into my back and the fact that there is a sharp object pressing into my back is causing me to have this very feeling, this very sensation. I feel the object *as causing me* to have this sensation. But now what this example shows us is that it is at least possible that there can be a causally self-referential mode of presentation contained in the actual content of the perceptual experience. Notice that in this case we did not feel that we were ascribing any special sophistication to the agent. We simply describe now things seem to him perceptually, and there seems to be no difficulty in claiming that how they seem involves more than just that there is an object there, but also the fact that there is an object there is making him have that feeling. Notice, furthermore, that we do not have any hesitation here about supposing that one can have these sorts of feelings without being able to theorize about them. A small child or an animal could have sensations with exactly these features, or so at least I would claim. The child would not be able to theorize about it to the extent of describing it as causally self-referential; nonetheless, the way it feels to the child is the same as the way it feels to the adult: i.e. in a way that is causally self-referential.

So as far as perception in general is concerned there does not seem to me any special difficulty in construing the causal self-referentiality as part of the content of the experience. The remaining question is whether or not vision is relevantly like tactile experiences. Well, of course, vision is in many respects different. But what I wish to argue is that the content of the visual experience is just as much a matter of things happening to me; i.e. in vision, as in touch, *the world is making things happen to me.* But the relevant notions of making things happen and things happening to me, are, I suggest, causal notions. It is the fact that the world is the way that it is that causes me to experience it that way.

Such considerations do not constitute a demonstration that our visual experiences have the causally self-referential feature that I have been referring to. Indeed, as I said, I doubt that it is possible to demonstrate this thesis in the sense of giving a demonstrative argument. All one can do, as I have been trying to do, is assemble a set of reminders.

Turning finally to Burge's discussion of the *de re–de dicto* distinction I must confess that I am puzzled. If I understand his present account, we are not really in disagreement. I have been all along insisting that "meanings are in the head," i.e. in this case the intentional content, entirely internal to the mind of the agent, is sufficient to fix reference, and this goes for all of the so-called "*de re* propositional attitudes." Now, does Burge agree with this? That is, does he think that all of the *de re* intentional states could be had by a brain in a vat?

There are at least three different possible positions:

1 *Externalism.* What is inside the head is insufficient to determine the identity of our various beliefs, meanings, etc. The reason for this is that there are contextual causal conditions in the world which are totally unrepresented inside the head, and which nonetheless fix the identity of our beliefs, etc. This view is held by Putnam, among others.
2 *Holistic Internalism.* What is inside the head is entirely sufficient to determine the identity of each of our intentional states. The various "causal" and "contextual" conditions referred to by the externalists are entirely represented by the mind. However, the conditions of satisfaction of each intentional state are only fixed relative to the Network and the Background which is not part of each intentional state though, of course, the Network and the Background are nonetheless parts of the mind.
3 *Atomistic Internalism.* Each intentional state fixes its conditions of satisfaction in a way that is independent of the functioning of any other intentional state.

Now, I took Burge to be arguing in favor of (1) against (2) and (3). I gather from some of his remarks that he takes me to be defending (3) against (2) and (1). But my own view is (2), and perhaps that is his view as well. And if that is so, we are both holistic internalists.

John McDowell

It is a consequence of my account of Intentionality that one could have all of the mental contents one has, and still the objects that in fact correspond to those contents in the world, the objects which "fit" the contents and thus are "referred to" by the representations in question, might not even exist. Mental contents, in short, are existence-independent, in the sense that one could have exactly the contents one has, and yet the objects referred to by one's representations might not exist. Thus, for example the thought that Santa Clause comes on Christmas Eve, is existence-independent in the sense that one can have exactly that thought even if Santa Claus does not exist.

The issue between McDowell and me precisely concerns "existence independence." McDowell thinks I am mistaken in supposing that subjectivity implies existence independence, that the first-person point of view in Intentionality entails existence independence of thoughts, and that all my thoughts could be had by a "brain in a vat." He further thinks that a natural way for me to preserve both my realism about perception and my attempt to describe Intentionality in a way that accounts for "the contours of subjectivity" would be one which acknowledges the existence *dependence* of a certain class of *de re* thoughts.

I believe that McDowell misunderstands certain crucial views of mine, but more importantly, I believe that there is a philosophical error involved in his proposal of an alternative way of describing the contours of subjectivity.

McDowell, like Burge, is puzzled about how I hope to get away with using expressions like "this visual experience" in the analysis of the content of visual experience. McDowell asks "But what about the particular-directedness signalled here by "this visual experience"? How is this to be made out to conform to the general "Fregean" picture? This kind of demonstrative expression is enormously important at several points in *Intentionality* . . . and that makes it remarkable that the book contains no discussion at all of the questions I have just posed" (p. 217).

The reason I did not offer much by way of explicit discussion is that I, mistakenly, assumed that it was reasonably clear. To repeat the point made earlier, when I say "this visual experience" I am not claiming that the subject refers to his own visual experience. Rather the claim is that the visual experience itself functions self-referentially in fixing the conditions of satisfaction.

McDowell takes this particular objection quite seriously, and so, perhaps the point is worth going over again in light of his discussion. I have a certain visual experience which sets certain conditions of satisfaction. The conditions of satisfaction are internal to the visual experience in the sense that it could not be that very visual experience if it did not set these conditions of satisfaction. Now, the specification of the content of the visual experience involves a reference to the visual experience itself as caused by the state of affairs in the world which is seen. But to say this is not to say that the visual experience is itself a speech act that refers to itself. Rather, when *we describe* its contents we are forced to refer to it as functioning as part of the determination of its own conditions of satisfaction. So I do not really think there is a problem here about how it is referred to because, of course, in that sense it is not referred to by some separate representation; rather it just functions in a self-referential way in determining its own conditions of satisfaction. I put this, I fear, inadequately by saying that the self-referentiality is *shown* but *not stated* by the visual experience, but perhaps it would have been better to try to state the point without using the notion of reference, but e.g. that of token-reflexivity.

McDowell seems to accept this interpretation a few pages later when he says "The experience itself – the very object to which the contents are directed – is the possible focus of the mind's attention, simply in virtue of being enjoyed." But now he wants to use this point to make a general criticism of me. The idea, if I can put it in my own words, is this: since I acknowledge that expressions like "this visual experience" are not "existence independent," why don't I make a similar generous acknowledgement for demonstrative thoughts referring to cars, chairs, tables, dogs, mountains, etc.? He says "The suggestion is, then, that "this visual experience" can signal a way in which a visual experience can be presented in a thought, made possible by the fact that the experience itself is present to the mind by virtue of being enjoyed. And now I want to raise the question why it cannot be fully Fregean to parallel this idea for the case of perceived objects" (p. 218). In the same paragraph he asks "Why should we not suppose that 'that man' – when a man is in one's field of vision – expresses a way in which a man can be presented in a Fregean Thought, made possible by the fact that the man himself is present to the mind by virtue of being seen . . . ?" And later he says "In answering the question how the man is presented in such Thoughts, there is no substitute for saying 'He is presented as *that* man', exploiting his perceived presence to make oneself understood" (p. 218).

Furthermore, McDowell claims that such an approach would be much more consistent with my general realism about perception, my view that in perception we characteristically directly perceive objects and states of affairs in the world. "This 'direct realism' yields a perfectly intelligible sense in which first-personal truth about a subject – the truth about the layout of his subjectivity – is not independent of the external objects that perceptually confront him" (p. 221). On this account, says McDowell, we can keep my general first-person internal approach but abandon the existence-independence principle and abandon the brain in a vat fantasy as a possible way of describing our intentional contents. In short, McDowell is trying "to drive a wedge" between my commitment to subjectivity and my commitment to existence-independence. One can have subjectivity with internal Intentional contents and still, according to McDowell, abandon the principle of existence-independence; and indeed McDowell concludes that we should abandon this principle.

I believe there is a profound mistake involved in McDowell's suggestion, but it is not easy to identify it exactly. As a first approximation we might say the following: it is indeed true that even from a first-person point of view I would characteristically specify the Intentional contents of my demonstrative thoughts by mentioning the object they are directed at. Thus, I would specify the content of my thought by saying "that man is wearing a red hat." But this fact does not violate the principle of existence independence. Because the existence and content of the thought are in no way dependent on the existence of the thing the thought is about. I can have exactly that thought even if it is a hallucination, even if the man does not exist. The difficulty in appreciating this derives from the usual fact that we tend to confuse features of the phenomenon itself with features of the way the phenomenon is described; and this is particularly tempting to us where the phenomena in question are Intentional contents. For an Intentional content of a demonstrative thought we would naturally *describe* the content of the thought by making reference to actual objects. But it simply does not follow that the content of the thought depends on the existence of those objects. The feature in question derives from the fact that the content is directed at an *object*, and if satisfied, the object will exist. But notice – and this is crucial – the content can be exactly the same even if no such object exists. In short, existence-independence is essential to the account of intentionality because it is necessary to preserve the insight that one can have exactly these Intentional contents even if their purported Intentional objects do not exist.

But what about such contents as "this visual experience?" Surely, they are not existence independent. This distinction that I have been making throughout is between the representation and the thing represented, between the Intentional state and the Intentional object. Now, of course, as a "thing" Intentional states have to exist, if there are to be Intentional contents at all. That is trivial. But it does not follow that the Intentional object has to exist. In the self-referentiality of visual perception, the visual experience is not the object. When I say "I see that car" the object of my visual experience is the car. The visual experience figures self-referentially in determining its conditions of satisfaction, but it is not thereby seen. When I have a visual experience I do not see the visual experience. So, it is in no way inconsistent with the principle of the existence-independence of the Intentional objects of Intentional states to say that, of course, the Intentional states themselves are existence-*dependent*. Indeed, it is trivially true that in order for an Intentional content to exist the Intentional state of which it is the content has to exist.

For these reasons I reject McDowell's effort to drive a wedge between internalism and existence-independence. I believe that he thinks an argument for doing that is that the self-referentiality of certain Intentional contents already abandons the thesis of existence-independence. But that is not quite right. The thesis of existence-independence is that we could have exactly the *representations* we do and yet the *objects* represented in the world might not exist. But, of course, it is not an answer to that thesis to say, "well, all the same the representations have to exist." Of course the representations have to exist, and where representations are self-referential then there will be an internal reference to some feature of the representation. But the thesis of existence-independence is the thesis that we could have the *representations* we do have even if the *objects* that allegedly exist in the world independent of our representations did not, in fact, exist. So, the thesis of the self-referentiality of a certain class of representations is not itself inconsistent with the thesis of existence-independence.

McDowell also objects strongly to my discussion of the "brain in a vat" fantasy. I maintain that in a sense we are, in fact, brains in vats because "the brain is all we have for the purpose of representing the world to ourselves, and everything we use must be inside the brain" and, of course, the brain is inside the skull, which for these purpose is a "vat." Now, according to McDowell, on a normal understanding this is obviously false. He points out, correctly, that we also have all kinds of other things such as words, sentences, marks on paper, pictures, etc. for the purpose of representing the world. To this I want to answer as follows: Of course, we have all these other things, but it is important to notice that they only function by way of impacting on our nervous systems. If you take away our nervous systems, then all the sounds, marks on paper, pictures, etc., will no longer function to represent anything. McDowell claims "no sane naturalism can possibly compel us to accept the idea that being in a world for us is being inside of our own heads. That has a comical ring." But in reply to this it is important to notice that I do not say that being in a world consists in being inside our own heads. Rather, what I want to say is, we are *identical* with our own bodies, and the part of our body most important for our Intentional relations with the world is inside our skulls. It is not that, so to speak, we crawl inside our own heads, rather in a sense we *are* our own heads. So, I continue to maintain my position that the contents of our brain are all we have for representing the world.

The last point is about Frege: It is not my aim to offer an interpretation, account, or gloss on the works of Gottlob Frege. My interest is philosophical not historical. Nonetheless, at several points I disagree with McDowell's interpretation of Frege and of the relation between Frege and Russell. One point is important enough to be mentioned explicitly. Since Frege grants that proper names have senses, he has the resources of allowing that sentences of the form "NN exist" and "NN does not exist," where "NN" is a proper name, can be well-formed. So, why does Frege not allow it? McDowell believes that it is because for Frege sentences using proper names are object-dependent. He thinks that this view derives in turn from Frege's thesis about truth-value gaps in sentences containing proper names which suffer from reference failure.

My own interpretation of Frege is quite different and I believe that it fits the Fregean texts better. Frege's doctrine about truth-value gaps did not derive from Strawsonian arguments concerning reference failure, though at one point, I concede, he does mention such considerations. But Frege's main motivation derives from the fact that he believed the relation between subject and predicate expressions in sentences is a species of the relation of function expressions and argument expressions as used in mathematics. For Frege, predicates refer to concepts, and a concept just is a function whose value always is a truth-value. But on this model of the subject-predicate sentence, a sentence containing a proper name which fails to refer would contain a predicate which refers to a function to which no argument has been assigned. And since a function without an argument does not determine a value, the concept referred to by the predicate expression in the sentence will not determine a truth-value. In short, the doctrine of truth-value gaps is a direct consequence of Frege's claim that predicate expressions are a species of function expressions. Now, since existence is a second-level concept (*Begriff der zweiten Stufe*), it takes only first-level concepts as arguments. But proper names, though they have a Sinn, cannot be used to refer to concepts. They cannot be used as concept expressions, and therefore they cannot occur in sentences of the form "NN exists" or "NN does not exist". What I am arguing, in short, is that Frege's overall application of mathematical concepts to natural languages precludes what I think he would have been able to argue for otherwise, namely that sentences of the form "NN exists" and "NN does not exist" are well-formed sentences.

I believe both papers in this section directed against my views are powerful and indeed brilliant. I am sorry I was not able to discuss all of the issues they raised but I hope to have answered at least the central thrust of their arguments.

Part   V

The Background of Intentionality and Action

17

The Background of Thought

BARRY STROUD

There is a simple and, to me, conclusive demonstration that thinking, or intentional phenomena generally, cannot be accounted for or even fully described by speaking exclusively of "representations" or "intentional contents" or "objects" present to the mind. The metaphor of presence before the mind is not the real source of the difficulty. Even if "representations" were little plastic flash-cards and "the mind" was a special little pocket they fit into, and an "object's" being "present to the mind" was defined as a card's being in that pocket, we still could not explain someone's thinking that p as just a matter of there being a card with 'p' on it in that person's special pocket.

I think everyone after a moment's thought would agree with this. It seems obvious that "representations" alone are not enough because, at the very least, the person also has to understand what is on his card, he has to "grasp" the "content" that is represented there. That suggests that thinking involves both "representations" or "contents" and a grasp or an understanding of them. But then those graspings or understandings are themselves presumably psychological phenomena, so it would seem that a complete theory of the mind ought to account for them as well. To say that they too consist of nothing more than the presence before the mind of "objects" or "representations" would lead eventually to a regress. Either nothing but "representations" or "contents" would be mentioned, and so still no account of what a person's thinking something amounts to would be forthcoming, or psychological phenomena would have to be appealed to which were not themselves explained as merely the presence before the mind of certain "representations" or "intentional contents." Or if they were, there would be still others which were not. The point is not that there are some particular kinds of psychological phenomena that simply cannot be described that way; it is rather that not all psychological phenomena can be described that way. The theory of "representations" or "intentional contents" alone is by itself inadequate, however far it is taken.

The strategy of deflating the theory of mental objects in this way is prominent throughout Part I of Wittgenstein's *Philosophical Investigations*. I believe that its true force and significance have not really been absorbed into philosophy. To what extent this or that current theory of the mind is vulnerable to difficulties like those he raises is always a nice question that ought to be pressed more often and more persistently than it usually is.

It is a question some of us were raising about John Searle's *Speech Acts* in seminars in Berkeley in the late 1960s and early 1970s. That book was meant to develop and so to test the hypothesis that "speaking a language is engaging in a (highly complex) rule-governed form of behavior" (*Speech Acts*, p. 12), and the question was just how far the scope of those rules was supposed to extend and what exactly it meant to say that the behavior was "governed" by them. Some of the rules are what Searle called "constitutive," serving to define the different kinds of speech act we perform. Other rules are straightforwardly grammatical, distinguishing between a correctly and an incorrectly formed sentence. Still others are strategic or instrumental. We all comply with such rules in our talk, and we do so intentionally. At least in that sense we apply the rules, so we must somehow know what they are. The question was whether exercising that essential further knowledge or expertise or ability is in turn a matter of our engaging in rule-governed behavior. If it is, we must in some sense know or grasp the rules we are following in doing that in turn, so the question arises again. It arises at each stage at which rule-following alone is invoked. Rules for following rules are no better than "representations" allegedly showing how other "representations" are to be understood. So what did the hypothesis that speaking a language is engaging in a rule-governed form of behavior really amount to? Did it mean that our linguistic behavior could be fully captured and so made intelligible by an appeal to nothing but rules alone? But how could that be? And if it could not, what import remained to the hypothesis that our speaking as we do is rule-governed? Our behavior could not be *everywhere* governed or guided by rules.

These are large, intricate, and difficult problems. It was no shortcoming of *Speech Acts*, of or our discussions, that they remained unresolved. But in *Intentionality* Searle leaves no doubt where he now stands on these large questions, at least negatively. He endorses the regress argument and so explicitly rejects the hypothesis that "all Intentionalistic mental life and all cognitive capacities could be entirely reduced to representations" (*Intentionality*, p. 152). That rejected view he identifies as "the converse" of something he calls "the hypothesis of the Background" which he therefore thinks there are good reasons to accept.

Strictly speaking, it would seem that what is established by the regress argument ought to be nothing more than the negative idea that "representations" alone are never enough. Searle does seem to agree that the regress argument is sound. But he also finds other considerations even more convincing in supporting a "hypothesis" to the effect that intentional states are "underlain" by a "Background" of "skills, abilities, preintentional assumptions and presuppositions, stances, and nonrepresentational attitudes" (ibid., p. 151). That too he calls "the hypothesis of the Background." It appears to be a positive, substantive thesis that goes well beyond the negative point supported by the threat of a regress. It tells of a previously neglected domain that must be seen to figure in any fully adequate theory of the mind. Searle even sketches a "minimal geography" of the newly exposed area, recommending a distinction between the "deep" and the "local Background," and between those aspects of it which have to do with "the way things are" and those which have to do with "how to do things" (ibid., pp. 143–4). He speculates about how best to study this "Background" and how to understand how it works.

It is very difficult to describe, and therefore to understand, what sort of thing this "Background" is supposed to be. I think Searle would be the first to insist that he has not really been able to explain it satisfactorily so far. But he is certain that it must be there and that it must be acknowledged and incorporated into any full account of human intentionality. And however little is known about it at the moment, he is certain that it must be regarded as "mental." Failure to understand its nature and operation he finds to be the source of many philosophical problems which, when properly understood, will presumably simply go away.

I want to take up some of these points in the hope of encouraging Searle to say more. My ruminations accordingly focus at least as much on the general question of what can reasonably be expected of any positive treatment along these lines as on the detail of what Searle has already said. I simply take for granted the negative thesis that any theory invoking nothing but "representations" or "intentional contents" would be regressive and therefore inadequate. The question is what to do in the face of that inadequacy. It is a question about what a full account or theory of human intentionality is supposed to be, whether there is reason to think such a thing is possible, and whether it could be the key to important philosophical misconceptions if it were.

It is not easy to tell where the negative thesis leaves off and Searle's positive "hypothesis" begins, or exactly how much the considerations he finds more convincing really support. One thing he appeals to is the way we acquire physical skills. It is certainly true that human beings must have some capacities or abilities in order to do anything, or even to learn to do anything. We could not walk if we did not have the ability to walk, and we could not even learn to walk, or acquire the ability to walk, if we did not have the further capacity to acquire that skill. In that sense there are conditions that must be fulfilled if we walk or if we acquire the ability to walk. Those capacities and abilities could therefore perhaps be said to lie in the background of what we do and to make our actions possible. The same is true of speaking a language, expressing our desires, communicating with others, and so on; there too there are many conditions that must be fulfilled if we do those things. Of course we can look for the sources or bases of our many capacities – muscle control, reflexes, balance, and so on in the case of walking, and other no doubt more complicated features of the organism in the other cases. But that does not seem to be what Searle has in mind when he speaks of studying the "Background."

What he says about physical skills that is meant to support or explain the positive idea of the "Background" seems to be at most that learning how to do something cannot be understood as solely a matter of "internalizing" a set of rules or instructions which become increasingly unconscious while functioning as "representations" from which we read off what we are supposed to do. That view does seem clearly unacceptable, but what makes it unacceptable appears to be the threat of a regress. "Representations" or rules alone could never be enough without some further rules for applying them. "Practice makes perfect," Searle says, "not because practice results in a perfect memorization of the rules, but because repeated practice enables the body to take over and the rules to recede into the Background" (ibid., p. 150). This last phrase is puzzling. It suggests that for Searle there *are* rules in the "Background," and if the "Background" is essential to a proper account of physical skills, as he claims, it would seem that those rules would have to come into the story after all. And then the regress threatens. No "Background" of rules alone would be enough.

If, as seems better, we drop that last phrase and say only that "the body takes over," we would be saying simply that, with practice, we do acquire various physical skills. That is true, but it says nothing about doing it by being guided by rules, and nothing about a "Background" that rules recede into either. Searle expresses the point perhaps best of all two sentences earlier when he says that as the learner gets better and better any rules he might have been given "become progressively irrelevant" (ibid., p. 150). It is not that they recede into a "Background" and function unconsciously, or even that they function as part of the "Background" at all; they simply play no explanatory role in an account of what the person is doing or how he learns. But that, as it stands, is no more than a negative thesis. It could perhaps be said, positively, that certain capacities and abilities must be present, or else the body couldn't "take over," but it is hard to find in this consideration alone a reason to believe that such capacities and abilities constitute a "Background" as Searle understands it.

Another consideration that helps convince him of the need for his "Background" is our understanding of the literal meanings of sentences. There are several different points here. One is that it is possible to grasp the meanings of each of a number of words without understanding an apparently grammatical sentence made up of those words alone. Another is that in understanding the literal meanings of those sentences that we do understand we tacitly take for granted a certain context or range of contexts; that "the literal meaning of a sentence is not a context-free notion" (ibid., p. 145). Behind both points is the idea that not everything it takes for us to understand the literal meaning of a sentence can itself be made part of that literal meaning, so something more than literal meaning must be appealed to in accounting for our understanding of sentences.

The conclusion again seems to me undeniable, but what makes it so, as Searle himself argues, is the threat of a regress. If we try to state all the facts we think would suffice to fix the meaning of a given sentence, he says:

> those facts will be stated in a set of sentences, each with its own semantic content. But now those sentences themselves have to be understood and that understanding will require yet more Background. If we try to spell out the Background as part of the semantic content, we would never know when to stop, and each semantic content we produce will require yet more Background for its comprehension. (Ibid., p. 148)

That is the regress argument, and it could be stated with no mention of what Searle here calls "Background" (simply replace the word "Background" throughout with the word "sentences"). Such reasoning supports only the negative thesis that "representations" or "semantic contents" or sentences alone are never enough.

A third consideration he finds convincing is our immediate understanding of certain kinds of metaphor. We recognize what is meant by the phrase "a lukewarm reception," for example, even though our understanding "does not rely on any perception of literal similarity between lukewarm things and the character of the reception so described" (ibid., p. 149). Searle thinks that must be so because he thinks there simply are no such "literal similarities" in this case. He might seem then to be allowing that if there were "literal similarities" between the items in question our understanding of the expression might well be explained by appeal to rules we follow for interpreting metaphors on the basis of such similarities. He argues only that since not all metaphors are like that, we could not be relying on such rules in every case. But the regress argument shows that even in cases in which there are "literal similarities" our understanding of metaphors cannot be explained by appeal only to rules we follow in interpreting them. Further rules would be needed to explain how we interpret those rules in turn. So we can't be relying on nothing but rules in any case.

With that negative conclusion in hand, we could even grant that there are some "literal similarities" in the particular case in question. And in fact that seems to be true. Similarities, after all, are fairly easily come by, if you are allowed sufficiently abstract terms in which to express them. A lukewarm reception and a lukewarm thing could be said to be similar in at least this respect: the ardor with which the reception is carried off and the heat of the thing are both roughly half-way between the highest and the lowest degrees of it that we are normally familiar with. I do not suggest that this similarity provides us with a rule that we rely on in understanding the phrase "a lukewarm reception." But that is no reason to deny that the similarity is there. Nor do I suggest in general that rules alone can explain our understanding of something. That is the point that really matters for Searle's case for his "Background." But the regress argument is enough to establish the point, and in itself it is purely negative. It is not easy to see, then, what positive ideas of a "Background" are added by what he says about metaphor, or indeed about the other two considerations he mentions.

It is perhaps better to turn to the general theoretical project Searle is engaged on and to the role he thinks an appeal to the "Background" should play in an account of intentional phenomena.

One thing he does not want to say is that the "Background" explains intentional phenomena in the way rules or "representations" were said to do by the theories he rejects. It is not that, rather than relying on rules or "representations" alone in our understanding of something, we rely instead or as well on the "Background." That would put the "Background" into the foreground and would be the very opposite of what he has in mind. The threat of a regress undermines the idea that our intentional activities are guided by the "Background" just as it does the idea that they are guided by rules or "representations" alone. It implies that, in general, our mental activities are not in the relevant sense guided by anything at all. But still Searle thinks a "Background," positively conceived, must somehow be invoked.

The idea from which his whole theory of intentionality begins is that "every Intentional state consists of an *Intentional content* in a *psychological mode*" (ibid., p. 12). But even to understand how intentional states, so understood, are possible, the "Background" must be brought in. Those elements that constitute the "Background" are what "enable all representing to take place" (ibid., p. 143); without them there would be no intentional states at all. Intentional states "only are the states they are, against a Background of abilities that are not themselves Intentional states" (ibid., p. 143). So it appears that our understanding of intentional psychological phenomena generally depends on a grasp or acknowledgement of a "Background" which makes them all possible.

This is perhaps one reason why for Searle the "Background", whatever it is, cannot be made up of intentional contents possessed in some psychological mode. No set of intentional states could explain how *any* intentional states at all are possible. Whatever can be understood as an intentional state already requires the presence of a "Background" for what Searle calls its "functioning," for its determining "the conditions of satisfaction" which make it the particular intentional state it is (ibid., p. 143). He therefore repudiates his own natural description of the "Background" as made up of "assumptions," "presuppositions," or "attitudes," since to have any of those, it seems, is to be in an intentional state. We can always select a particular part of the "Background" and make its presence explicit by identifying it as an assumption or presupposition, but as soon as we have done that we can no longer think of it as part of the "Background" as Searle understands it. It looks as if that is because invoking such intentional states could not do what he thinks an appeal to the "Background" is meant to do. It could not help explain how there could be any intentional states at all. The explanatory function of the "Background" would be lost.

He would prefer then to describe the elements of the "Background" as "abilities," "capacities," or "practices." That is presumably to render them non-propositional, and so to avoid the danger of their slipping into the foreground as states involving a propositional content held in some psychological mode. But he finds even those descriptions inadequate in another way; "they fail to convey an appropriate implication that the phenomena are explicitly mental" (ibid., p. 156). For Searle it is crucial that "the Background consists of mental phenomena" (ibid., p. 154).

Even if the "Background" must be "mental", why is it not right to say that abilities, capacities, and practices are what make up the "Background"? Aren't many of our abilities and capacities mental abilities and capacities? My ability to do long division in my head, for example, seems to be something purely mental. My ability to remember the English words for those things we typically sit on or those things we eat off also seems to be something mental. I don't just mean my competence in using the correct words on the appropriate occasions – although I don't see why that cannot be called mental as well – but my ability to remember what the correct English words are. Without abilities or capacities like that we probably could not think or get into any intentional states at all.

It could perhaps be argued that what disqualifies abilities from being part of the "Background" that Searle insists must consist of "mental phenomena" is that an ability is not a "phenomenon," and it is not itself something mental, even if it is an ability to do something mental. When I do long division in my head, it might be said, the actual thoughts I have are all mental phenomena, but the ability I am exercising in thinking those thoughts in that activity is not itself something mental. This is a possible line of argument, but I don't think it can be what Searle has in mind. Or if it is, it is not enough.

For one thing, although it is true that an ability is not a "phenomenon" in the sense of an occurrence, a state of affairs, or something that happens, he does not want to say that "mental phenomena" in that sense are what the "Background" does consist of. Particular mental occurrences or happenings do not make up the "Background"; they are the sorts of things Searle thinks the "Background" makes possible. So abilities and capacities are not to be disqualified as "mental pheno-mena" because they are not occurrences or happenings.

Furthermore, to deny that an ability, even an ability to do something mental, is itself something mental would presumably mean that an ability to do something physical is not itself something physical either. The ability to walk or to ski would not be something physical any more than the ability to do long division in one's head would be something mental. Even if this were Searle's reason for denying that abilities and capacities are appropriately "mental" – which I doubt – he would still have to explain why abilities and capacities so understood cannot be what makes up the "Background." Why must the "Background" consist of something "mental" rather than something that is neither mental nor physical? Again, I suggest that it is because of the explanatory role it is meant to play. Brute abilities or capacities alone could not do that job.

It is undeniable that we must have certain abilities or capacities if we are able to do anything at all, and so in particular if we think, speak, believe, wish, hope, and so on. In that sense there are human abilities and capacities that are necessary for our being in any intentional states. We might even identify some of the capacities lying behind particular kinds of intentional state by producing or imagining the absence of the capacity and then seeing which particular intentional states a person can no longer achieve. This sounds like a way to "study the Background" as Searle thinks of it (ibid., p. 155), but he is reluctant to call such capacities or abilities part of the "Background."

It seems to me that the source of his reluctance could be the thought that the presence of such abilities and capacities, although necessary, would not really explain *how* the intentional states of which they are preconditions are possible. "The Background provides a set of enabling conditions that make it possible for particular forms of Intentionality to function," Searle says (ibid., p. 157), but an appeal to the "Background" seems meant to do more than simply bring that fact to our attention. The "Background" has detail, articulation; it is somehow supposed to make intelligible to us precisely how we can get into the particular kinds of intentional state we can be in. It would not be enough to see only that there are, or even must be, such conditions; we must in addition be able to understand *how* those "enabling conditions" enable us to have the forms of intentionality we have. Our being in intentional states must make sense to us, and it must do so in "mental" or intentional terms. The presence of the "Background" seems somehow meant to explain it in that special way. I think that is what Searle must have in mind when he insists that the phenomena in the "Background" must be seen as "explicitly mental" (ibid., p. 156).

I ascribe this general explanatory role to Searle's "Background" on admittedly shaky grounds. It is the only thing I can find that would explain the conflict he feels among the various things he wants to say about it. He admits that "there is a real difficulty in finding ordinary language terms to describe the Background" (ibid., p. 156), but there seem to be no technical terms that can be coherently introduced to describe it either. "Practices," "capacities," and "habits" are not right, because they must somehow be understood as "explicitly mental" phenomena. "Assumptions" or "presuppositions" are not right, because they imply that there are propositional contents which we entertain in some psychological mode. What is in the "Background" must be thought of only as "preintentional" or "nonrepresentational" – in other words, as "assumptions" or "presuppositions" that are not really assumptions or presuppositions at all.

Searle is fully explicit about his difficulty, but he seems to me to underestimate it. He says the price of trying to describe the "Background" is "metaphor, oxymoron, and outright neologism" (ibid., p. 157). But to me it does not look like a question of linguistic nicety or insufficient vocabulary; it looks more like contradiction. What are found to be the best terms to describe the "Background" must immediately be qualified in ways that contradict their literal application. Terms like "assumption" and "presupposition," for example, "must be literally wrong" (ibid., p. 156), although they otherwise seem to do exactly what reference to the elements of the "Background" is supposed to do.

Searle asks a good question about his conception of the "Background," but I do not find his answer satisfactory:

> The fact that we have no natural vocabulary for discussing the phenomena in question and the fact that we tend to lapse into an Intentionalistic vocabulary ought to arouse our interest. Why is it so? (Ibid., p. 156).

His answer is that just as "language is not well designed to talk about itself, so the mind is not well designed to reflect on itself" (ibid., p. 156); this means that "the only vocabulary we have available is the vocabulary of first-order mental states" (ibid., p. 157). We are therefore tempted to think of the elements of the "Background" as "representations" or intentional states.

He does not say what is wrong with the linguistic resources we possess for talking about language or our mental resources for thinking about the mind. They seem pretty rich to me. But even leaving aside those dubious claims I don't think his answer goes far enough. What needs to be explained is why intentionalistic vocabulary is declared unavailable to us. Why would its use be a "lapse?" It seems to be the most natural vocabulary for describing the phenomena in question. Searle agrees that when he lifts his mug of beer in a restaurant and is surprised by its near weightlessness, "we would naturally say I *believed* that the mug was made of glass, and I *expected* it to be heavy" (ibid., p. 157). But he thinks that what we say in that case is wrong. He does not say why. He declares rather that he "simply acted," but that does not seem to preclude an intentional description's being true of him. It is not wrong to say he was surprised; why doesn't the surprise betoken an expectation or other similar attitude? That seems to be the only way to make sense of it.

He acknowledges that "we can and do, treat elements of the Background as if they were representations" (ibid., p. 157). As noted earlier, we might select a part of what Searle thinks of as the "Background" and make its presence explicit as an assumption or belief or presupposition. That seems to be what happens in this case. But he insists that "it does not follow from that, nor is it the case that, when these elements are functioning they function as representations" (ibid., p. 157). What we identify as an expectation was not necessarily "functioning" as an expectation, or as any intentional state, when it was part of the "Background."

But even if that is so, it equally does not follow that when we do speak explicitly of someone who is surprised by the mug as having expected it to be heavy, what we are saying is not true. The most that follows is that we are not speaking of an element of what Searle calls the "Background." Or rather, we are not speaking of the expectation *as* an element of the "Background." That is because it is a condition of something's being an element of Searle's "Background" that it not be described in intentional terms; if we report the presence of an intentional state we are not describing the "Background." But in describing the mug-lifter as being in the intentional state of expecting the mug to be heavy we could still be saying something that is true.

I have suggested that Searle excludes intentionalistic vocabulary from the description of the "Background" because he sees that no set of intentional states could fulfill the explanatory function his "Background" is meant to perform. The "Background" must make intelligible to us how we come to be in any of the intentional states we are in, and it must do so in "mental" terms. But once we put the demand in this way the conflict he points to seems inevitable. We want to understand how any of our intentional states come to be what they are; we want a theory of intentionality. Our abilities and capacities in themselves explain nothing; they are necessary, but their presence does not explain any particular exercises of them. But to use intentionalistic vocabulary and so to appeal to intentional states would mean that not all intentional states could be so explained. They would not be explained by anything lying "behind" them; one such state would only be explained by some others. So no intentional states can be thought of as part of the "Background"; and no brute non-mental or non-intentional phenomenon could be part of the "Background" either, since they could never explain our being in the intentional states we are in.

My answer to Searle's question would therefore be that on the one hand we "lapse" into intentionalistic vocabulary because we are looking for an explanation that will make the phenomena intelligible to us in that intentional way; but since the "Background" is also something that is supposed to explain how any intentional states are possible, we see that it cannot be made up of intentional states in turn. There is therefore no vocabulary left for describing it at all.

The suggestion that he is imposing such explanatory demands on anything that could count as a "Background" would help explain why Searle is so sure that a "Background" as he understands it must be there, even if nothing fully satisfactory can be said about what it is. He would be giving expression to the almost irresistible thought that our having the kinds of intentional states that we do must after all be an intelligible phenomenon. If it is a fact that we are and can be in such states, there simply must be some explanation of that fact. The "Background" will then turn out to be whatever could provide the right kind of explanation. But what could do that? No explanation in non-intentional terms could make intentional phenomena intelligible in the right way; no explanation in intentional terms could explain intentional states in general. The quest for a general theory of intentionality along these lines would seem to involve demands that cannot possibly be met.

The dilemma appears in its starkest form in Searle's brief application of his doctrine of the "Background" to the solution or dissolution of traditional philosophical problems. He mentions the problem of "realism" and argues that a proper understanding of the "Background" shows that the question whether there exists a world independent of our representations of it is not even fully meaningful. If we think of "realism" as a doctrine we hold or a hypothesis we can look for evidence for, we seem immediately faced with the problem of how we can ever show that it is true, or even reasonable. But for Searle:

> Realism, I want to say, is not a hypothesis, belief, or philosophical thesis; Realism is part of the Background in the following sense. My commitment to "realism" is exhibited by the fact that I live the way that I do, I drive my car, drink my beer, write my articles, give my lectures, and ski my mountains. (Ibid., p. 158)

There is not, he says, in addition to these manifestations of his intentionality, an additional hypothesis or belief that he holds to the effect that there is a world independent of his representations. "My commitment to the existence of the real world is manifested whenever I do pretty much anything" (ibid., p. 159).

But if his *commitment* to "realism" or to an independent world is what is manifested in his behavior, then he must certainly have such a commitment, since he certainly does drink his beer, give his lectures, and ski his mountains. And what could it be a commitment to, if not to the existence of an independent world, or to the truth of the proposition that such a world exists? But if there is a problem of "realism" at all – if thinking of "realism" as something we believe or hypothesize leaves its truth or its reasonableness problematic – then thinking of it as something we are committed to would leave it equally problematic for us. The question would not have gone away.

The trouble comes, Searle thinks, from misconstruing the nature of the "Background." If we treat what is part of the "Background," and is therefore "preintentional," as if it were an intentional state or the "intentional content" of such a state, the traditional difficulty immediately arises. But what Searle says is exhibited in the way he lives his life is described as just such an intentional state – commitment. So his *commitment* to an independent world could not be strictly speaking part of the "Background"; no intentional states are in the "Background." At most what is in the "Background" must be a "pre-" or "non-intentional" commitment. But then that could not be a commitment *to* anything; nor could it be a *commitment* to anything. Words simply fail us.

Even if the "Background" did contain a commitment to something – to the existence of an independent world, say – the problem of "realism" as Searle understands it would not be dissolved by appealing to that commitment. He thinks the problem of showing or demonstrating that there is an independent world is rendered meaningless by the fact that "any *showing* or *demonstrating* presupposes the Background, and the Background is the embodiment of my commitment to realism" (ibid., p. 159). But even if our commitment to "realism" is necessarily involved in trying to show or demonstrate anything, it does not follow that what we are thereby committed to is true, or that our commitment to it is reasonable. We could still wonder about the credentials of that presupposed commitment, just as we might wonder about the credentials of a belief in "realism" or a hypothesis of an independent world. Talk of commitment rather than belief or hypothesis changes nothing, if there is a problem of "realism" in the first place. The problem does not vanish even if our commitment to "realism" is indeed presupposed in any attempt to show or demonstrate anything.

Searle seems to acknowledge this when he switches to speaking of "realism," and not our commitment to it, as what is presupposed. The very posing of any question at all, he says, "presupposes the preintentional realism of the Background" (ibid., p. 159).

> There can't be a fully meaningful question "Is there a real world independent of my representations of it?" because the very having of representations can only exist against a Background which gives representations the character of "representing something." This is not to say that realism is a true hypothesis, rather it is to say that it is not a hypothesis at all, but the precondition of having hypotheses. (Ibid., p. 159)

What is here said to be a precondition of anyone's having any hypotheses, because it is a precondition of anyone's having any "representations" or thoughts at all, is "realism," or the existence of a world independent of our representations of it. Now we know that people do have many thoughts and hypotheses, so we know that the preconditions of their doing so must be fulfilled. So if we could know, as Searle here claims, that "realism" *is* a precondition of there being any representations, we would be able to conclude that "realism" is true, that there is a world independent of our representations of it. Far from the question's not being fully meaningful, an affirmative answer to it would be directly derivable from anyone's thinking anything.

This kind of response to the problem of "realism" would require that it be proved, or at least made plausible, that the existence of an independent world is indeed a necessary condition of anyone's having any hypotheses, thoughts, or representations. Not only does Searle not attempt such a proof; he denies that one can be given. In insisting that the "Background" must be "mental" he explicitly rejects the idea that an independent world is itself part of the "Background" and so is presupposed by our being in any intentional states.

> Even if I am a brain in a vat – that is, even if all of my perceptions and actions in the world are hallucinations, and the conditions of satisfaction of all my externally referring Intentional states are, in fact, unsatisfied – nonetheless, I do have the Intentional content that I have, and thus I necessarily have exactly the same Background that I would have if I were not a brain in a vat and had that particular Intentional content. *That* I have a certain set of Intentional states and *that* I have a Background do not logically require that I be in fact in certain relations to the world around me ... (ibid., p. 154)

This is meant to be true of all of us. That we are in intentional states, and that those states have the "intentional contents" they have, does not on Searle's view imply that the world independent of us is any particular way rather than some other, or even that there is such a world at all. But if that is so, "realism" itself is not part of the "Background" that makes our intentional states possible; "realism" says that there is a world independent of us. This is consistent in another way with what I am suggesting must be Searle's view of the "Background." The existence of an independent world would never be enough to explain how anyone could get into any intentional states with respect to it. A "Background" that contained "realism" in that sense would not be something "mental" and so could not be the "Background" as Searle understands it.

Appeal to a "Background" containing "realism" therefore would not work. But appeal to a "Background" containing only a commitment to "realism" would not eliminate the problem. Nor could it be literally correct to speak of the "Background" that way, since the "Background" does not consist of intentional states. So it seems that only something somehow in between the truth of "realism" and a commitment to "realism" could do the job. But what could that be?

In a recent discussion of Wittgenstein Searle identifies as the single most disappointing feature of the later work its opposition to philosophical theory, to "the idea that we should be seeking a general theory or general explanation of the phenomena which puzzle us, specifically the phenomena of language and mind" (Bryan Magee, *The Great Philosophers* (Oxford University Press: Oxford, 1988), pp. 342–3). He says his natural response to someone who says he cannot have a general theory of speech acts or of intentionality is to go out and prove that person wrong, as he has tried to do: "to write general accounts of speech acts and of intentionality" (ibid., p. 343). But he also thinks the most powerful part of Wittgenstein's later work is its attack on the traditional idea that all our meaningful activities are the product of some inner theory – a theory of action and value by means of which we act, for example, or a theory of language by means of which we speak and understand the things we say. Wittgenstein by contrast reminds us that a great deal of what we do is "biologically and culturally primitive" – we just do it (ibid., p. 346). Those "animal reactions" he finds Wittgenstein appealing to Searle identifies as elements of his own "Background" – "non-representational, non-theoretical mental capacities and dispositions" (ibid., p. 346). His doctrine of the "Background" develops what he thinks is Wittgenstein's most important point.

Searle denies any inconsistency in his attitude to Wittgenstein, since he holds that the recognition of a non-theoretical set of background capacities is not inconsistent with developing a theory of language or of mind. "The claim that we often in real life proceed without a theory is itself a theoretical claim" (ibid., p. 346), he says. But that does not completely dispose of the threat of inconsistency. The claim that we often or even always proceed without a theory is not a "theoretical" claim in the sense in which Wittgenstein is said to be opposed to philosophical theory. It is purely negative. It says nothing about how we do proceed, or what explains our proceeding as we do. It does not attempt to explain our behavior at all. In that sense, it does not offer or promise a theory that would explain how language or thought or anything else is possible.

But Searle apparently does offer or at least aspire to such an explanatory theory. He does not content himself with pointing out that when we speak or think we do so (or even must do so) without applying a theory or following rules; he seeks a positive account of how we do proceed. His theory is that although we do speak and think and get into intentional states without a theory, we do not do so without a "Background." That is what makes it possible for us to proceed as we do, and only when we understand the workings of that "Background" will we understand intentional phenomena.

Because of the threat of regress, that ingredient of Searle's theory of language or mind which is supposed to explain in general how our speech acts or our intentional states are possible cannot be something that *guides* us or *directs* us to act in certain ways. We cannot be said to rely on the "Background" in the way the rejected traditional theory says we rely on a theory or on rules. So the question is *how* an appeal to the "Background" is supposed to make our being in intentional states at all intelligible to us. That is how the negative conclusion that we do not rely on a theory or on rules or on anything else that could guide us or direct us begins to raise the question whether there can be any general theory of speech acts or of intentionality that can do what Searle thinks such a theory should do. If it is supposed to explain intentional phenomena in "mental" or intentional terms, then that negative conclusion does seem to be inconsistent with developing a general theory or a general explanation of the phenomena of language and mind.

The threat of a regress is not of course inconsistent with explaining any particular intentional phenomenon or set of such phenomena in intentional terms. The mug-lifter was surprised, and what partly explains his being in that state is that he was expecting the mug to be heavier. That helps make sense of his present condition in a way that no purely non-intentional cause could do. Even large classes of someone's, or everyone's, intentional states might be similarly explained by appeal to further intentional states not mentioned in the original class. We expand the beam of our intentional gaze to take in more and more such phenomena if they are connected in intelligible ways with those we want to understand.

In this way, perhaps no intentional phenomenon is necessarily beyond the reach of an explanation that would make it intelligible to us in the right way. But in fact and in practice we find a great deal about human behavior that we do not or cannot explain further. But even the "biologically and culturally primitive" reactions and ways of thinking at which our understanding typically stops and which are appealed to to explain other things we do are usually themselves intentional phenomena, described in intentional terms. We naturally raise our hands to avoid a blow. We naturally react to the gesture of pointing by looking in the direction of the line from wrist to fingertip. It comes natural to us to understand the order "Continue the series '+2'" by putting "1,002" after "1,000." We have not left the domain of the intentional in describing ourselves and others in these ways.

This picture of understanding intentional states and other intentional phenomena does not require any "Background" in Searle's sense. What is appealed to to explain intentional phenomena are other intentional phenomena, not "pre-intentional" or "non-representational" assumptions, presuppositions, stances, or attitudes. From what he says about "realism" it looks as if one reason Searle resists this picture and seeks a non-intentional "Background" is that he thinks certain philosophical problems would otherwise be inevitable and unsolvable. To say that when he is drinking his beer and skiing his mountains he is presupposing that there is a real world independent of his representations of it suggests to him that he knows that his beer and his mountains are there only if he knows that there is a real world. And Searle thinks that to know such a thing he would have to solve the problem of "realism."

But that would seem to me to be so only if there were not a perfectly innocuous way in which he does or can know that there is an independent world if he knows that his beer or his mountains are right there before him. Beer and mountains, after all, are objects that are independent of Searle's and everyone else's representations of them, so anyone who knows that fact will know that there are independent objects if he knows that beer or mountains are present. In this innocuous sense of presupposing, he can know the more general proposition (There are independent objects) is true by knowing that the more particular propositions (Here is some beer. Here is a mountain.) are true. It would just be a matter of inferring the "presupposition" from what presupposes it, or of moving from the more specific to the more general. I think Searle would insist, as he does in the mug-lifting case, that it is simply not true that he is presupposing or assuming the existence of an independent world. But I do not find that he has given a good reason for saying that. It does not follow from his theory of intentionality; all that follows is that no such presupposition could be part of the "Background." And simply granting that we do have such general beliefs or assumptions is not in itself enough to generate the problem of "realism."

I do not mean to suggest that this would be a way of trying to answer the philosophical problem of the existence of a world independent of our representations of it. That problem is meant to bring into doubt one's putative knowledge of particular facts about beer and mountains just as much as one's general presuppositions or assumptions about the world. If those particular bits of knowledge have been revealed as problematic, as the philosophical problem seeks to do, then even if Searle is right that our believing them does not presuppose more general beliefs about the world, the problem would remain. Nor would saying that they do presuppose general assumptions about the world be any help in explaining how they are known. The philosophical critique comes to encompass everything thought to be known about the world, particular and general alike. So if there is a question of "realism" at all, the presence or absence of general assumptions or presuppositions about the world will not really matter. But that in itself does not show that it is always wrong to say that we have such general beliefs or make such general assumptions or presuppositions. If the philosophical problem of "realism" could be defused or dissolved in some other way, it could be perfectly correct, and philosophically innocuous, to describe ourselves that way.

Even if its apparent potential for dissolving philosophical problems evaporated I think the real source of the appeal of Searle's "Background" would seem to remain. It looks to be the only sort of thing that could possibly explain, in general, how any intentional states at all are possible. Since it is a fact of the world that there are beings who are in intentional states, we feel that there must be some explanation of that general fact. In that thought or aspiration we are making a stronger demand than the natural intellectual expectation that every intentional state should be, at least ideally, explainable. It looks more like the requirement that all intentional states should be explainable at once, and in the same way. No intentional states could be used to explain them, so the "Background" must be "pre-" or non- intentional. But it seems that no non-intentional phenomena could explain them in the right way. This has all the hallmarks of a philosophical demand.

Is this really what a philosophical theory of intentionality is supposed to do? How could it? Must it explain the whole domain of the intentional in non-intentional terms? Could anything satisfy that demand? Whether Searle can give satisfactory answers to these large, intricate, and difficult problems depends on something we still do not understand well enough – what the "Background" is supposed to be, or what kind of explanation he has in mind.

18

Intentionality and the Phenomenology of Action

JEROME WAKEFIELD AND HUBERT DREYFUS

What is an action, and what is it like to perform an action? We will argue that John Searle's brilliant account of the logic and phenomenology of action in *Intentionality*[1] substantially advances our understanding, but that it prematurely forecloses some important philosophical options.

We will begin by arguing that Davidson's account of action (as bodily motion caused by reasons) has trouble accounting for two features of the phenomenology of action, the fact that actions feel different than nonvoluntary bodily motions, and the fact that we sometimes know directly and without observation what we are doing. We will then summarize Searle's solution to these puzzles via his concept of an "intention in action," a representation of the goal of one's action that both causes the action and is directly experienced as causing the action. Next, we will challenge the generality of Searle's account by suggesting that the experience of an intention in action causing one's action does not appear to occur in many spontaneous, habitual, skillful, and otherwise nondeliberate actions. (While no term seems quite right, we will use "nondeliberate" to refer to all the sorts of actions we describe below in which there is no representation of the goal.) We will outline an alternative account of such actions, inspired by certain strands of the Continental tradition of phenomenological description. Finally, we will consider potential Searlian replies to our counterexamples.

Two Puzzles about the Phenomenology of Action

Three things that happen in a typical action are: (1) one's body moves; (2) the movement is due to one's own muscular activity, and not to some external force acting upon one's body; and (3) the movement serves some purpose of the person acting. However, these conditions by themselves fail to capture either what an action is or what it is like to act. For example, a reflex can satisfy all these conditions without being an action. Suppose the doctor strikes one's knee with a mallet. The leg moves; it moves not because the doctor lifts it, but due to the organized contractions of one's own muscles; and that movement may be precisely what one wants the leg to do in order to provide evidence of health. Yet the reflexive raising of the leg is not an action. Moreover, the leg's motion is not experienced as an action. The leg feels like it moves of its own accord, it does not feel like one is moving it.

Analogous to the reflex case are instances of "Penfield motion," with which Searle is much concerned, in which the subject's bodily motion – including organized muscular activity such as hand motion or vocalization – is caused by the firing of an electrode implanted in the subject's brain. Penfield motions are not actions. Moreover, their phenomenology is not the phenomenology of action. The subjects in Penfield's experiments immediately reported to Penfield, "You did that," and their reports seem to have been based upon their experiences and not on observations of the inappropriateness of the motion to the situation, or knowledge of Penfield's experimental manipulation. We may assume that even if the subjects had been thirsty and their hands had been made to move toward a nearby glass of water just as they wanted it to do, the motion would still not have been experienced by the subjects as their own action.[2]

The Penfield and reflex cases establish that an action is not like one's body simply moving, even in a desired and useful manner. Some logical element in the concept of action, and some corresponding phenomenological characteristic of action, are lacking in these motions. The missing logical and phenomenological features have to be specified in order to have a viable account of action as opposed to other bodily motion.

Donald Davidson's account of the logic of "action" explains why the reflex and Penfield motions do not meet the logical criteria for being actions, but Davidson's account fails to address the phenomenological issue. Davidson's view is that an action is a bodily motion that is caused (in the right way) by the psychological state which constitutes the reason for that action.[3] Davidson's account explains why reflexes and Penfield cases are not actions, namely, because the relevant bodily motions are not caused by reasons. But what of the phenomenological puzzle? Why is it that reflexes and Penfield motions do no feel like actions? There is nothing within the Davidsonian framework to answer this question. So far as the Davidsonian account goes, the phenomenology of bodily motion could be exactly the same in motions that happen to be caused by reflexes or electrode firings as it is in cases of motions that happen to be caused by reasons.

If we were to try to construct within the Davidsonian perspective an explanation of how Penfield's subjects or the person experiencing a reflex manage to judge correctly on the basis of their own experience that the respective bodily motions are not actions, the best account might be the following. In the case of an action, the agent would be aware of his or her reasons for the action before the bodily motion occurs, and from the relation between the content of the reasons and the nature of the action, the person could infer that the reasons likely caused the bodily motion. In the reflex and Penfield cases, however, at the time of the motion the subject would not be aware of having an appropriate reason for the motion, and thus would infer that the motion is not caused by a reason and is therefore not an action. This inferential account does not depend on the person's direct awareness of any phenomenological feature of the action itself. Rather, it suggests that the conclusion that one is performing an action results from a special kind of "third-person" interpretive inquiry into the causes of one's own action, using as evidence the memory of one's antecedent representations, the observation of one's motion, and a variety of background information.

The inferential account seems to ignore the fact, emphasized by Searle, that we know what we are doing directly from the experience we have of acting, and not via some causal inference. Moreover, as stated earlier, in either the reflex case or the Penfield case, the subject might indeed be entertaining representations of the sort which would constitute appropriate reasons for the movement (e.g., wanting the leg to move to verify health, wanting the hand to move toward the glass of water). If we accept as a phenomenological fact that even under such conditions the movement need not feel like an action, then it is hard to see how the inferential account can be made satisfactory.

In sum, Davidson's approach to action fails to explain two salient facts about the phenomenology of action. First, how do we know that we are acting rather than moving involuntarily? Second, how do we know what we are doing when we are acting?

Searle on the Phenomenology of Action

We now want to focus on the solutions to the phenomenological problems with Davidson's account that Searle provides via his concept of the intention in action. After elaborating Searle's approach, we will suggest a modification of Searle's account which does not give up the strengths of his approach but which we believe is truer to the phenomenology of action.

Searle suggests that two further conditions, beyond the basic Davidsonian criterion, must be met before a bodily motion qualifies as an action. First, the bodily motion must not merely be caused by a prior representational state as in Davidson's account; instead, a representation of the goal of the action must continue to exist throughout the motion and must play a continuing causal role in shaping the action.[4] Searle calls this continuing representation of the goal the "intention in action," thus differentiating it from the "prior intention" which corresponds to the initial representation of the goal of the action prior to the initiation of motion.

Second, Searle maintains that, in cases where the experience of acting is entirely conscious (we will consider cases of unconscious intentions in action later), the subject continuously experiences the causal connection between the intention in action and the bodily motion. Indeed, according to Searle, the experience of acting itself contains within it the experience that the bodily motion is being caused by the intention in action. On Searle's view, it is this experience of the causal relationship between the intention in action and the bodily motion that is lacking in the Penfield cases. Penfield's subjects experience a bodily motion, but they do not experience their own mental representation of the goal as causing the bodily motion, and thus do not experience themselves as acting.

Note that in his account of action, as elsewhere in his account of Intentionality, Searle attempts a unique integration of linguistic analysis and phenomenological description. The standard pre-*Intentionality* analysis of action is "bodily motion caused by a reason." Searle incorporates a phenomenological analog of this analysis into his account of action by maintaining that the experience of an action must include a direct experience of the causal relation between the intention in action and the bodily motion. If, when acting, the agent is directly aware of the causal connection between his intention and his motion, this links the phenomenology to plausible criteria for ascription of actions and thus provides for a unique explanation of first-person access to one's own actions. This sort of linkage of linguistic analysis and phenomenology is distinctively Searlian.

According to Searle, an action is generally caused by a prior intention to perform the action, although there exist cases of spontaneous action that do not involve a prior intention. But the action itself, whether caused by a prior intention or not, consists of a bodily motion and an intention in action, where the intention in action continues to cause the bodily motion during the entire duration of the motion. The fact that consciously acting agents continuously experience themselves as acting is explained on Searle's account by the fact that the intention in action continues throughout an action.

Searle elaborates the Intentional content, or conditions of satisfaction, of the prior intention to raise one's arm as follows: "This prior intention causes an intention in action which is a presentation of my arm going up, and which causes my arm to go up" (*Intentionality*, p. 93). That is, the prior intention is a representation that has as its conditions of satisfaction that it cause an intention in action which in turn has as its conditions of satisfaction that it cause the relevant bodily motion. Note that in this passage the intention in action is equated with the presentation of one's arm going up. This means that Searle's phrase, "presentation of one's arm going up," is not meant to refer simply to a kinesthetic perceptual presentation of the arm rising and the associated muscular effort, for that presentation occurs in the Penfield and reflex cases. The phrase "presentation of my arm going up" is meant by Searle to capture the presentation that constitutes the experience of the arm intentionally being raised, that is, the experience of acting. Now, elsewhere, Searle states that "the experience of acting just is the intention in action" (ibid., p. 91; see also the chart on p. 97). Since the intention in action causes the bodily movement, it is also true that "the experience [of acting] causes the [bodily] movement" (ibid., chart, p. 91). In sum, the intention in action to raise one's arm, the experience of acting in raising one's arm, and the presentation of one's arm going up (in Searle's sense of this phrase), are all identical, are all the cause of one's arm going up, and are all experienced as the cause of one's arm going up. Note that the experience of acting, which is an experience of one's intention causing one's bodily movement, comes pretty close to capturing what would be traditionally called an experience of volition or an experience of willing.

The intention in action resolves the two fundamental phenomenological puzzles about action mentioned earlier. First, why are some bodily motions experienced as actions while others are not? Searle's answer is that only those bodily motions experienced as caused by an intention in action are experienced as actions. Second, how is it that we always know without observation what it is that we are doing? This is just another way of asking for an explanation of what has traditionally been called "first-person access" to our actions. Searle's answer is that the very experience of acting contains within itself a representation of the goal of the action, which means the experience of acting is in part an experience of what it is that we are trying to do. This explains "the fact that at any point in a man's conscious life he knows without observation the answer to the question, 'What are you now doing?'" This knowledge of what one is doing "characteristically derives from the fact that a conscious experience of acting involves a consciousness of the conditions of satisfaction of that experience" (p. 90).

Action without Intention in Action

In this section, we will attempt to construct a plausible case, largely through the use of examples and analogies, that actions can occur without being continuously caused by a simultaneous intention in action.[5]

Searle's account of the intention in action explains how it is that we know what we are doing, and it identifies the special experience of action that is missing in the Penfield cases, thus explaining what differentiates experiences of actions from experiences of motions that are not actions. Despite these advantages, the claim that the intention in action is a universal feature of action goes against phenomenological intuitions. Some actions, especially those actions that are unfamiliar and therefore deliberate, surely do have the structure described by Searle. However, Searle ignores the Continental tradition of phenomenological description, which suggests that many actions do not have this structure. From the perspective of this tradition, by requiring that an intention in action exist throughout an action Searle has created too strong a criterion which "overrepresentationalizes" action. Many actions appear to take place without this kind of representational "monitoring," or so we will argue.

Phenomenological examination strongly suggests that in a wide variety of situations human beings relate to the world in an organized purposeful manner without the constant accompaniment of representational states which specify what the action is aimed at accomplishing. Possible examples are skillful activity, like walking or playing the piano or skiing; habitual activity, like driving to the office or brushing one's teeth; casual unthinking activity, like rolling over in bed or making gestures while one is speaking; and spontaneous and emotionally laden activity, such as jumping up and pacing during a heated discussion or fidgeting and drumming one's fingers anxiously during a dull lecture. In all these cases of action it is possible to be without any representation of the near- or long-term goal of the action as one performs the action. Indeed, at times one is actually surprised when the action is accomplished, as when one's thoughts are interrupted by one's arrival at the office. These unthinking actions seem to be at least as typical of the activities in a normal day as their opposite. In fact, they provide the non-salient background of activity that makes it possible deliberately to focus on what is unusual or important or difficult.

Often, perception of one's body's situation is critical to action, and one responds to such perceptions with exquisite refinement, resolving the set of tensions which they produce. For example, when spontaneously rolling over in bed, one responds to the moment-to-moment tensions distributed over the surface of the body, moving until an acceptable equilibrium is reached. In this and similar cases, one does not actually represent to oneself where one is heading or what one is doing. One just does it, responding to the moment-to-moment local forces acting upon one. The moment-to-moment response may be "aimed" in a functional sense at achieving some larger purpose, just as the activity of rolling over in bed is aimed at achieving a more comfortable position, but no ongoing representation of that purpose need be involved in the regulating of the activity.

If it seems impossible that complex actions could be accomplished without representational monitoring, consider the fact that such representations need not be involved in complex physiological adjustments to the environment. For example, the complex dilations of the pupil function to provide optimal use of ambient light, but this complex function does not require that the eye be guided by a representation of the visual outcome that is desired. The pupil is built so as to function to optimize use of light, but it is built to do so without accessing semantic representations concerning light and its uses. Of course, the pupil dilation system functions more or less according to built-in programming that is set for life, whereas the response tendencies of the voluntary musculature change dramatically with context and are largely learned. Nonetheless, once action within a specific context is set going by a prior intention, it might well be the case that during the resulting episode of activity the body simply functions to accomplish a preset goal without semantic regulation of the activity.

Another useful analogy might be the *gestaltists'* favorite example of a perfectly spherical bubble forming from an initial hodgepodge of soapy film. The bits of soap are not guided into place by a representaton of the end-result; they are not like guests at a formal dinner party, running around with a seating chart telling them where they should go. The bits of soap just respond to local forces according to laws which happen to work so as to dispose the entire system to end up as a sphere. The sphericity of the result is not semantically accessed and does not play a causal role in producing the bubble. Now, let our perceptions be the forces acting on us, and our musculature be a response system, and suppose that our bodies have a capacity to respond to moment-to-moment stimulation in a way which tends to promote an optimal fit between perception and action. Of course, unlike pupil dilation and bubble formation, where the outcome is rather rigidly determined, the body's tendencies to respond are learned and infinitely varied according to context. Whereas bubbles always form into spheres, the response tendencies of the body are attuned to the context and can function to approach a myriad of possible end-points. The action-perception *gestalt* which the body pursues in a given context may be set spontaneously and without prior thought, as in emotional reactions like getting up and pacing when anxious, or they may be set through a prior intention which represents the goal of the action. But once the response function is set, it may operate for some time without the need for any further representational resetting. One may be dimly aware of a sense of "wrongness" or tension when one deviates from the preset goal, and of rightness when one moves toward the goal, but that is not the same as having a continuing representaton of the goal. Our actions might beautifully fit the situation so as to produce a certain end result just as the movements of the soap film beautifully fit the pattern of movements required to form a sphere, but our actions might be no more continuously caused by representations of the end state than is the formation of a bubble.

We are emphasizing the nonrepresentational aspects of action, so it is important to make clear that representations certainly do have a prominent place in the overall explanation of how it is that we manage to act so effectively in such a range of situations. Indeed, when the situation is new or especially complex or a deviation from the expected, manipulation of representations seems to be the primary way we have of carefully reconsidering our options and reorienting ourselves. There are unquestionably certain forms of problem-solving which require representing future circumstances and thus cannot be accomplished merely through reactions to immediate perceptions, no matter how contextually sensitive. Representationally nonmediated behavior is often limited in intelligence, and then mainly consists of overlearned responses. Nonetheless, it is remarkable how "intelligent" our actions can be even when they are not mediated by representations of intentions. For example, consider gestures of emphasis made while speaking. One generally does not think ahead and figure out how one is going to gesture in order to emphasize one's point, nor does one normally representationally regulate one's gesture while performing it, yet the gesture adjusts itself finely to the nuances of the situation and the meanings of the words being spoken. Or consider Boston Celtic basketball player Larry Bird's description of the experience of the complex act of passing the ball in the midst of a game: "[A lot of the] things I do on the court are just reactions to situations . . . I don't think about some of the things I'm trying to do . . . A lot of times, I've passed the basketball and not realized I've passed it until a moment or so later."[6] Such phenomena are not limited to strictly muscular responses, but exist in all areas of skillful functioning, including intellectual functioning. For example, some instances of apparently complex problem-solving which seem to be implementing a long-range strategy, as in making a move in chess, may be best understood as direct responses to familiar perceptual *gestalts*.[7] Here, the "tension" model must be taken not in the literal sense of muscular tension, but as a metaphor for other kinds of deformations from *gestalt* equilibrium and for the tendency to return to equilibrium.[8] Mustn't such adaptive behavior require an explicit and continuous representation of what is wanted, in order to regulate the performance? Apparently not; indeed, the overregulation of such performances by explicit representations may well interfere with the smoothness of the performance (the "centipede syndrome"). The feeling of deviating from some optimal *gestalt* and responding so as to conform with the *gestalt* may occur without a representation of the *gestalt* endpoint of the action.

If our description of nondeliberate action is correct, it implies that we can sometimes consciously experience ourselves as acting (as opposed to not acting) but at the very same time not be explicitly aware of what we are trying to do. That is, one can have the feeling of one's musculature purposefully adjusting to one's perceptions and the resulting "tensions" without being aware at the same moment of the *gestalt* that determines the sense of tension (or the sense of rightness) of the body–world relationship. Spontaneously gesturing for emphasis while talking might be a good example of this. In this regard it seems that our description is in conflict with Searle's intuitions, for he asserts that the experience of acting contains within it a representation of what we are trying to do, the intention in action, so that to experience oneself consciously as acting must, on his account, involve a conscious awareness of what one is trying to do.

What we are saying about action is not such a radical departure from what Searle himself says about background skills. Searle holds that an intention in action can "reach down" and organize the body's skillful activity in a way that helps to achieve the intended action, but as long as the context does not change and there is no breakdown, there need be no additional intention in action at the level of the skill. For example, one might intentionally ski downhill, during which time one might react skillfully to potential obstacles, but these skillful movements in themselves might be all background skill and not representationally mediated, in the sense that there is no intention in action concerning the details of the obstacle-evading movements. One simply performs such movements without any particular intention in action to, say, bank right. However, these skillful movements are done by way of accomplishing the overarching action of skiing downhill, for which one does continuously experience an intention in action. In sum, Searle allows that representational states often "set" the workings of nonrepresentational skills which themselves need not be representational, but that in any action at some level there must be an intention in action which "organizes" the nonrepresentational skill components. Now, it appears that a large part of the motivation for Searle's account of skills in terms of the nonIntentional background is precisely the sort of phenomenological observation that we are making here about certain actions. It is simply the case that one does not experience intentions in action regarding the details of the skillful performance when one skis, plays the piano, and so on. However, once Searle's account of background skills is accepted, it seems arbitrary to resist the phenomenological evidence that at certain moments in certain actions there is what is tantamount to Searlian background skills all the way up, so that at no level is an intention in action experienced.

Nondeliberate Action and First-Person Access

Several questions arise about the type of nondeliberate activity we have described above, once it is accepted that no intention in action is experienced during such activity. First, can Searle simply argue that our examples are all cases of unconscious intentions in action, so that there is an intention in action, albeit unexperienced, involved in all of them after all? Second, if no intention in action is involved, and perhaps no prior intention is involved either, what is the justification for calling such activity "intentional"? Third, what of Searle's central point that an intention in action is required to explain how we can always say what we are doing? Fourth, how does our account manage to avoid the phenomenological problem with Davidson's account that Searle's intention in action resolved, that is, how do we explain the fact that even those actions lacking an intention in action are experienced as actions, rather than in the way that reflexes and Penfield motions are experienced?

First, then, how would Searle account for some of the phenomenological facts cited above, where it appears that there is no experience of an intention in action? It seems likely that if he accepted the phenomenological claims, he would argue that the intentions in action do exist in the cited cases, but that they are simply unconscious. The intentions in action would not necessarily be unconscious in the Freudian dynamic sense, but they might just be unattended to or otherwise unnoticed. If this move is possible for Searle, then Searle's view is trivially compatible with any phenomenological facts that could be cited.

Without independent motivation, the "unconscious intentionality" reply would obviously be a questionable way for Searle to deal with apparent counterexamples to his phenomenological account. Moreover, the very logic of Searle's position seems to preclude any such motivation and makes this reply extremely problematic. On Searle's account, the experience that one is acting directly depends upon an *experience* of the causal connection between the intention in action and the bodily motion. If the intention in action is unconscious, then the causal connection between it and the motion cannot be conscious, and it would seem that there can be no experience of acting. It would thus seem to follow from Searle's account that, whenever an intention in action is unconscious, the actor would not feel that he or she is acting, and would experience his or her bodily motions much as did Penfield's subjects. This is exactly the position of some of Freud's hysterical patients whose "symptoms," which do not feel like actions, are really unconsciously motivated actions. As Freud remarks concerning one of his patients: "If she is executing the jerks and movements constituting her 'fit,' she does not even consciously represent to herself the intended actions, and she may perceive those actions with the detached feelings of an onlooker."[9] But the cases we have discussed are cases where we fully experience ourselves as acting, and not as moving involuntarily as in a fit, or as having a reflex response, or as being manipulated by an experimenter, and so on. Consequently, these cases cannot be dismissed by Searle as cases of unconscious intentions in action.

Second: If, at a given moment, no Intentional states are actively involved as intentions which guide the action, why should the activity be considered intentional action? (We follow Searle's convention here of using "Intentional" with a capital I to refer to directedness of mental states in general, and "intentional" to refer to a specific property of voluntary actions.) Now, Intentionality is initially defined by Searle and others as a form of intrinsic directedness. Searle, along with the vast majority of writers on the topic, then identifies that directedness with representationality, on the traditional and seemingly plausible assumption that the only way a brain state could be intrinsically directed at some state of affairs outside of itself is if it realized a representation of that state of affairs. However, it should not be forgotten that representationality is just a theory of how the initially identified phenomenon, Intentional directedness, can work. It is by far the dominant theory, so that representationality and Intentionality may seem to be virtually synonymous, but in fact the Continental tradition of philosophy has explored other possible options for the nature of Intentional directedness. In particular, as suggested earlier, a plausible account of another kind of Intentional element in intentional action might be framed in terms of a sense of deformation from and return to an optimal form or *gestalt* of the body–world relationship. We cannot present here a full analysis of such nonrepresentational Intentionality. Instead, we are simply suggesting that such an approach is possible and seems to fit the phenomenology of some instances of intentional action better than Searle's representational account, so that such an alternative should be taken seriously.

If we are right, then Searle's identification of Intentionality with representationality is problematic because it prematurely excludes potential nonrepresentational approaches from discussion. Thus, rather than excluding nondeliberate action of the sort we have described from the realm of intentional behavior, we would suggest rethinking the limits of both Intentionality and intentionality in view of the actual nature of the phenomena described earlier. For convenience, we will call the representational form of Intentionality described by Searle "R-Intentionality," and the Intentional directedness which consists in the tendency of the muscular–perceptual system to promote certain *gestalts* (or the analogous processes in intellectual functioning) "G-Intentionality."

Third: Searle's point that we always know what we are doing is central to his case that R-Intentionality, and not simply G-Intentionality, is involved in an ongoing way in every action. However, there is no reason to think that, in the relevant sense, we always do know what we are doing. In the cases we have cited, it certainly does not appear that at the moment of the action the person is consciously aware of the point of the action. In order to defend the idea that an intention in action nonetheless exists in all actions, Searle might cite the fact that when people are asked, they are always able to say what they are doing. Thus, he might argue, there must always be an awareness of the point of the action. We agree that when asked, people do give an account of what they are doing. However, Searle's explanation of people's ability to say what they are doing in terms of an intention in action is not at all mandatory, and Searle himself gives the reason why in his own discussion of the background. To put the point in our vocabulary, G-Intentionality and R-Intentionality clearly have complex interactions and are geared to each other. R-Intentional states can set G-Intentional processes going, and interrupting a G-Intentional process often yields immediate R-Intentional translations of the goals of the action. When someone is asked what they are doing, or just stops and thinks about what they are doing, they experience a form of such interruption of ongoing behavior. A representation of the goal can occur at the point of interruption without any implication that the representation existed all along. Searle accepts this point with respect to background skills. For example, the interruption of routine or skillful activity, as when the doorknob to your office door falls into your hand as you are trying to turn it, leads to an immediate awareness of what one is doing; however, Searle does not think that that implies that one has an explicit representation of the goal of opening the door, for that qualifies as a background skill. We are arguing that certain episodes of action have the same structure as background skills, and the fact that we can always explain what we are doing when we are stopped does not, on Searle's own logic, provide a cogent objection to our claim that an intention in action need not exist throughout the action.

Fourth: What, then, of the fact that raising one's arm is experienced differently than its merely going up? By suggesting that there are cases of action in which there is no ongoing intention in action, it may seem that we have landed ourselves back in the problem from which we started, the problem of distinguishing the experience of acting from the experience of reflex or Penfield motion. After all, the nondeliberate activity we have described above is nonetheless experienced as one's own action. Even as one drives unthinkingly to the office, the working of the car's controls is dimly experienced as one's own action, as are the spontaneous hand gestures one makes while speaking. We agree with Searle that there is a phenomenological difference between one's arm rising and raising one's arm, even during non-deliberate activity. Although at certain times during an action we may not know what we are doing, we do always seem to know during an action that we are acting, at least in the sense that we experience ourselves as acting rather than as being passively moved about. But in nondeliberate action the experience of acting does not consist of the experience of an intention in action causing one's movement. Instead, the experience of acting during nondeliberate action appears to consist simply of the experience of a steady and immediate flow of skillful activity in response to one's sense of the environment and one's internal state. Searle is correct that one feels differently than Penfield's subjects because one experiences the connection between one's bodily motions and a cause of the motion. But no intention in action is necessary to explain such as experience. One can simply be experiencing the causal connection between one's motion and one's perception of one's body's situation in the world. Part of that experience is a sense that one's situation deviates from some optimal body–environment relationship, and that one's motion takes one closer to that optimal form and thereby relieves the "tension" of the deviation.

Think of walking along a familiar path, absorbed in thought. There is the dim feeling of doing something, of walking, but that experience is not the experience of a representation of the goal of walking causing the walking. The experience of causality in such activities might be partitioned into two components. First, there is an experienced causal connection between our perception of the environment's eliciting conditions and the exquisitely organized response of our body. The texture of the ground, the slope of the path, and all the other contextual factors are in constant interaction with our muscular dispositions so as to produce a complex response. Second, there is a feeling that our motion "fits" or is "appropriate" to the environmental context. We do not simply feel that our motion was caused by the perceived conditions, but that it was caused in such a way that it is constrained to reduce a sense of deviation from some satisfactory relationship, even though the nature of that satisfactory relationship is by no means represented. Like our ability to see that something is wrong with a picture without being able to identify what is wrong, we can have a sense of the rightness or wrongness of our body's relationship to the world without at the same time being aware of the criterion which determines our sense of the quality of that relationship. What we experience while walking is just the smooth body-in-environment functioning constrained by that preset disposition. The feeling of causal efficacy in action – and thus the basis for first-person authority about whether we are acting – is simply the presentation of the causal link between the perception of the inner and outer environment and the musculature's organized motion, as mediated by a set of muscular response dispositions which function to produce a goal which need not be represented.

We began with the observation that contemporary analytic accounts of the nature of action, such as Davidson's, do not account for certain phenomenological features of action, especially the experience of acting. We then outlined how Searle's account of action solves such problems in the case of deliberate action. In particular, Searle maintains that the experience of acting is the experience of a causal connection between an intention in action and a bodily motion. However, we argued that Searle's approach does not work in cases of nondeliberate action, where no intention in action is evident. Our own account attempts to solve the phenomenological problem for nondeliberate actions. We argue that the experience of acting in cases where no intention in action exists is the experience of the causal connection between our perceptions of our internal and external situation and our bodily motion, along with an experience of the appropriateness of our motion to the circumstances. If we are right, then, contrary to Searle's account, the experience of acting does not necessarily contain an experience of what we are trying to bring about. Thus, Searle's account supplemented by our account can explain the intuitive distinction in experience between action and nonaction over the entire spectrum of actions, from the most to the least deliberate.

NOTES

1 John Searle, *Intentionality: An Essay in the Philosophy of Mind* (Cambridge, University Press: Cambridge, 1983). All page references to Searle's writings will be to this work.
2 Of course, if the right brain state – namely, the one which corresponds to the experience of acting – were induced to fire by Penfield's electrodes, then the patient would presumably experience the motion like an action. We assume that the electrode is producing the motion through stimulation of the neurons directly controlling muscular action, and that the electrodes do not stimulate the more central processes involved in the experience of action.
3 See D. Davidson, "Actions, Reasons, and Causes," reprinted in *Essays on Actions and Events* (Clarendon Press: Oxford, 1980).
4 Exactly how this representation manages to regulate ongoing behavior is not addressed by Searle, and we will not consider that thorny question here.
5 We are relying heavily in these suggestions upon an analysis of Merleau-Ponty's *gestalt* phenomenology developed primarily by Wakefield, reinforced by Heideggerian insights developed primarily by Dreyfus.
6 Quoted in L. D. Levine, *Bird. The Making of an American Sports Legend* (McGraw Hill: New York, 1988).
7 For a full discussion of the chess example, see H. Dreyfus and S. Dreyfus, *Mind Over Machine* (The Free Press: New York, 1988).
8 There may be a basis for this approach in recent neurological work on what are called "basins of attraction" in the activity of the brain, which may directly map situation perception onto response without intermediate representations. See, for example, C. A. Skarda and W. J. Freeman, "How brains make chaos in order to make sense of the world," *Behavioral and Brain Sciences* 10 (1987), pp. 161–95.
9 S. Freud, "A Note on the Unconscious in Psychoanalysis," in S. Freud, *General Psychological Theory*, ed. P. Rieff (Collier Books: New York, NY 1963) (orig. pub. 1912), p. 51.

19

Searle's Theory of Action

BRIAN O'SHAUGHNESSY

There is much in John Searle's theory of action that I welcome and endorse. Above all, his insistence that there is a characteristic "experience of acting:" a phenomenon noteworthy for its absence in the theories of Chisholm and Davidson. In this respect Searle's theory constitutes a significant advance upon its two predecessors. However, all three writers eschew "acts of the will." To my mind, this is a grave weakness in their respective theories: tantamount to a Hamlet without The Prince himself. Thus, Searle explicitly disavows any identification of the experience of acting with "volitions or acts of the will or anything of that sort;"[1] adding that "they are not acts at all, for we no more *perform* our experiences of acting than we *see* our visual experiences."[2] Later in this paper I will address myself to this issue. But before I do so I must first consider Searle's theory of intentions, since this bears directly on his theory of the structural constitution of physical actions.

1 "Intentions in Acting"

Two Possible Construals of Searle's "Intentions in Acting"

Let us call the event of arm rise ϕ, and the familiar act of arm raising Φ; and let I stand for intention. Now according to Searle we "need first to distinguish those intentions that are formed prior to actions and those that are not."[3] The first variety of intention he calls "prior intentions" (I_p), the second variety "intentions in acting" (I_Φ). The theory is that, while each type of intention can occur in the absence of the other, when I_p's occur and find expression the following is what happens. The prior intention causes the intention in acting, while the latter is at once part of the act *and* cause of the bodily event which the act is the active producing of. Thus, the prior intention of raising my arm at one swoop causes the intention in acting of raising my arm – which is part of that act Φ *and* cause of the desired arm movement ϕ – and the act Φ.

In general I experience perplexity over the role that is allotted to the intention in acting. But first I am unsure as to what it actually *is*. I say so because at one point Searle writes that "the intention in action just is the Intentional content of the action."[4] This construes it as nothing more than an Intentional content. I find such a suggestion perplexing in the extreme. How can any sort of intention be merely that? And in any case other things that Searle writes seem, at least by implication, inconsistent with this reading. Thus, he claims that "sometimes one performs intentional actions without any conscious experience of doing so; in such a case the intention in acting exists without any experience of acting."[5] It follows that on such occasions that intention in acting cannot be the Intentional content of an experience of acting. Then to me this strongly suggests that the intention in acting can be no kind of Intentional content. For what if, on such an occasion, everything necessary for bodily act Φ occurred – except bodily movement ϕ, which was actually prevented? What would be the bearer of the Intentional content then? If the answer is that nothing is, this is tantamount to saying that in the absence of the experience of acting, nothing is the bearer of the Intentional content of Φ until ϕ! But what sort of Intentional contents can these be, that wait upon their goal and effect to exist? If the answer is that something is, seeing that the Intentional content must have preceded ϕ and cannot float around unattached like a Cheshire cat smile, what can that something be? Not Φ (*ex hypothesi*). And not the experience of acting (again, *ex hypothesi*). Meanwhile, the intention in acting must obtain prior to the occurrence of the intended event ϕ, seeing that "the intention in action . . . causes the movement."[6] Then surely that intention must be the bearer of the Intentional content on those special occasions when the experience of acting is absent and ϕ is actually prevented. What else is there left that could play the role of bearer? Then surely the intention in acting must be the bearer, whether or not ϕ occurs. Accordingly, intentions in acting must be bearers of content rather than mere contents. And this is a feature they will share with prior intentions. And it is consistent with their causal properties.

In sum: the fact that Searle allows intentions in acting in the absence of any experience of acting; and the fact that he asserts that "the intention in action causes bodily movement;"[7] together with the fact that prior intentions are autonomous mental existents that are bearers of Intentional content rather than being mere contents of some other bearer-entity – all this suggests that we should opt for a similar construal of intentions in acting. That is, construe them also as autonomous bearers of Intentional content. Yet having said this, it must now be admitted that just as many passages in the text support the alternative construal: namely, that they *are* the Intentional content of the action, and, where it exists, of the (embedded) experience of acting. Thus, "the experience of raising your arm has intentionality,"[8] "the act of raising my arm involves two components, an intentional component (the experience of acting),"[9] and above all: "the action . . . contains two components, the experience of acting and the movement, where the Intentional content of the experience of acting and the intention in action are identical,"[10] and (already quoted) "the intention in acting just is the Intentional content of the action."[11]

Let us call the latter construal of "intention in acting" construal α, and the former construal, construal β. Then it is instructive at this point briefly to spell out both the content and immediate implications of these two theories concerning the contemporaneous intentions of the intentionally acting agent. Thus, if I_Φ is that intention:

Theory α
1   I_Φ is a mere Intentional content, always of act Φ where that act occurs, and

always of the experience of action where (as is characteristic) it also occurs.

2 I_Φ causes the bodily movement ϕ, but not the bodily moving act Φ.

3 I_Φ differs in type from I_p, the former being a mere Intentional content of an event (Φ, and characteristically also of the experience of acting), the latter being an autonomous mental state? process? bearer of such a content.

Theory β

1 I_Φ is an autonomous mental state? process? constituent of act Φ.

2 I_Φ causes the desired bodily movement ϕ, but not the bodily moving act Φ.

3 I_Φ shares with prior intentions I_p the property of being the bearer of an Intentional content, and thus of being an autonomous mental state? process?

The Distinction Between Two Kinds of Intention

(1) Donald Davidson has described intentions we never deliberate or act upon as "pure intendings."[12] I have never seen the point of this locution (just as I have never understood the arcane sense of "judgment" involved in his characterization of intentions as "all-out judgments").[13] "Pure intendings" turn out to be nothing more nor less than – intentions, with the accidental property of being at once spontaneous and barren. Why this combination should be dubbed "pure" escapes me. Somewhat similarly I cannot bring myself to suppose that the distinction between "intentions that are formed prior to action and those that are not"[14] is anything more than a distinction between intentions with different temporal properties. Yet the text seems to suggest otherwise. It is clear that it does if construal α is correct; but on either construal the type of their appointed causal properties is so widely dissimilar as to suggest that I_p's and I_Φ's are in themselves grossly dissimilar items.

Now my difficulty is not just that I cannot accept that there is any significant difference between "intentions which are formed prior to action and those that are not." It is that I cannot in any case discover anything that meets the specifications for being an intention in acting. To bring this out it will help at this point to consider a concrete example. We shall suppose that on Monday I reach a decision to swim the English Channel on Tuesday (starting at 6 a.m.). This decision is the onset of a prior intention that endures at least until the onset of the act. What, according to Searle, happens to prior intentions as their act-object begins? Do they expire at that point? Or do they endure until the act ends? I cannot say for certain, but the text suggests the former, and so does Searle's claim that "the characteristic linguistic form of expression of a prior intention is 'I will do A' . . . and of an intention in acting is 'I am doing A' ".[15] In any event, Tuesday arrives and I start swimming. Then whatever is true of prior intentions or intentions in acting, the following is true of my intentions as I swim. Half-way across I *still have* the intention of swimming from Dover to Calais; for this intention ("plan," "project," etc.) which came into being on Monday, endures until the act is completed or abandoned or forgotten. And it continues to cause the act all the way through that act. After all, an intention does not cause an act in the way a kick sets a football in motion: that is, its causal contribution is not exhausted in the initial instant of its effect. Rather, it takes up its task from instant to instant; for one's freedom to change, and therefore to *abide by* one's practical mind, is in no way compromised as the act unfolds. Delete the intention at *any* point in the crossing and the act fizzles out, e.g. I join my friends in the boat. In a word, the intention that came into being on Monday, endured until Tuesday morning when it caused the beginning of the act, and persisted all through Tuesday when it kept causing the continuation of the act until, as we shall suppose, completion occurred. Plainly, this particular intention fails to match the specifications for being an intention in action. The reason being, that although it is ensconced in the mind as the act unwinds, it was formed prior to the act, it causes the act, and it is therefore of course no part of the act.

The difficulty is to discover anything that matches Searle's specifications for being an intention in action. Yet his theory requires that such an intention be present even in this highly self-conscious situation, since his structural theory states that the intention in action is the first and causally efficacious part of every act. We need at the very least an intention that is contemporaneous with action. Then what others are there? Consider the particular intentions that are directed towards particular acts of extending my swimming arms. It is a moot point precisely when such intentions begin. Maybe as the act begins, but more likely an instant or so before (for do I not know, a moment before the act begins, that it is indeed about to begin?). If so, this seems already to disqualify them from the class of intentions in action. But let us set this difficulty to one side. How do these intentions relate to the acts of extending one's arms? Surely as cause – and once again for the same kinds of reasons. For would not the act spasmodically seize up if I caught sight of an evil-looking jellyfish just where I was about to insert my forearm? And did not a change of act-intent, wrought by the acquisition of a novel cognitive attitude, mediate the perceptual experience and the resulting abortion of the deed? Was there not method in my madness? This likewise excludes them from the class of intentions in acting. And so does one other trait. Thus, Searle says of the intention in acting that "the movement is the 'Intentional object'."[16] But what is the "Intentional object" of those short-lived intentions that express themselves in swimming movements? What "must be the case in order that the Intentional content be satisfied?"[17] Not just that the arms move, but that I move them; and so on this count too these intentions cannot be intentions in acting. Finally, they are disqualified on the grounds that they cause the experience of acting. In sum: even though these intentions are contemporaneous with the act, and may even have originated only as the act began, they cannot be the elusive intention in acting – first because they cause the act, second because they cause the experience of agency.

One other contemporaneous intention must be considered in our search for the intention in acting. Namely: the intention of getting from where one is sited in any action to the point that constitutes the completion of the act which is the object of the overarching or governing intention. Take the present example: at each instant I have the intention of swimming from "here" to Calais. How could I *not* have such an intention if I "now" believe I am at a determinate point somewhere in the midst of such a still-intended deed? Yet whereas the overarching intention has as object a particular deed which I believe extends in part into the forever buried past, this present intention takes as object a part-act which exclusively extends from the "now"-present to some appointed place in the future. So whereas the first intention is an enumerable existent directed to one act entire, these sliding-by intentions are a continuity of non-enumerables directed to thought-sliced non-enumerable part-acts with different temporal properties. And yet they are realities which are essential to the expression of the single enumerable governing intention. In short, they are realities, not to be confused with the overarching intention of swimming the Channel, caused by the latter, and cause of – what? Surely, of "taking up one's bundle" in the ever changing "now." That is, of a continuous acting or striving and in any case of *the continuation* of the deed, and with it the continuation of *the experience of agency*. For once again is it not true that, should I cease to harbour such intentions, say through being convinced that my feet were here and now scraping the sands of Calais beach shallows, my labours and my strainings and my immediate awareness of either would on the instant stop? Here, too, we seem to be dealing with a contemporaneous intention that falls outside the confines of the act, that is responsible both for its occurrence and the occurrence of a characteristically co-present experience of agency. That is, with a mental state of intending that fails to measure up to the requirements for being an intention in acting.

(2)   The above are more or less all the intentions I can discover. Then where in this story do we find a point of application for the concept, "intention in acting?" Consider the two construals of Searle's theory of intentions. If construal α is correct we are to look for an intention, contemporaneous with the act and formed contemporaneously; that *is* the Intentional content of the act; that is part of the act, and hence no type of cause of the act; and that is directed to and putative Intentional cause of the bodily movement (rather than the act). If construal β is correct we are to look for an intention, contemporaneous with the act and formed contemporaneously; that is an autonomous mental state? process? bearer of an Intentional content; that is part of the act, and thus no type of cause of the act; and that is directed to and putative Intentional cause of the bodily movement (rather than the act).

Construal a   Let us begin by discussing the first construal. The question immediately arises: what justifies our describing the Intentional content of the act/experience of acting as *an intention*? We have just now noted that there are intentions present and operative contemporaneously with the act· to wit, the long-term and organizing intention of swimming from Dover to Calais, together with the subsidiary intentions it fathers upon a welter of perceptually acquired beliefs, such as the intention to now extend my right arm, and the intention to swim from here to Calais, and the intention to avoid a wave, etc. These are indeed intentions, active projects, practical plans, commitments to doing, or what have you; and they all tend to engender self-consciously executed deeds which would not have seen the light of day were it not for the inherence in the mind of that practical mode of internal assent that *is* intending. But what justifies us in describing the Intentional content of the characteristically present experience of acting as a further example of *the same*? Certainly not the mere fact that Intentionality is exhibited in this phenomenon, otherwise visual and many other experiences would rate as intentions; and not even the fact that it tends to cause the desired bodily movement, otherwise we would classify act-desires as intentions. It is clear that these conditions are insufficient. And I can think of no other property that might strengthen the case for describing the Intentional content as an intention.

In fact if construal α is the correct reading of "intention in acting," there is I suggest every reason for classifying that "intention" as an altogether different type of phenomenon from any of the *bona fide* intentions we have thus far considered.

While this particular item is an Intentional content characteristically of the experience of acting and necessarily of the act-event, these *bona fide* intentions look to be something altogether different. Thus, these intentions not merely have Intentional content, they *are* intentions, which is to say something roughly of the ilk of a practical mode of internal assent; and they are *bearers* of Intentional content, rather than being Intentional contents themselves; and these intentions neither are nor indeed could be either experiences or the content of experiences; and they are "apt for" causing both actions and experiences of action; and can exist in the complete absence of actions or experiences of action; etc. To me this looks like sufficient justification for saying that if we describe intentions in acting on construal α as *intentions*, then the word "intention" has become ambiguous.

Construal β   Turn now to the second construal of "intention in acting." The problem here is, to discover anything in the situation in which I am engaged in swimming from Dover to Calais that measures up to the several requirements for being an intention in acting on construal β. The first two of those several requirements were, that the item be an intention, and contemporaneous with the act. Well, we encountered three distinct phenomena which satisfied this dual requirement: namely, intentions to swim from Dover to Calais, to move my right arm, to swim from "here" to Calais. Meanwhile the third and fourth requirements for being an intention in acting on construal β were, that the intention was part of the act, and that it was not cause of the act. Then it is clear that the above three intentions founder on both counts. And so we have yet to discover anything that is an intention in acting, on construal β.

It is worth spelling out what exactly we are seeking at this point. Let us assume that the act is that of extending my right swimming arm. Then we are looking for an intention, that came into being only as the act did, that takes as Intentional object the arm movement, that does not take the act of arm moving as Intentional object, that is Intentional cause of the arm movement, that is part of the act, and therefore no cause of the act. Now we know that there exists a contemporaneous intention that takes as Intentional object the act of arm moving (which is an event that necessitates and includes arm movement), that causes and thus lies outside the confines of the act-event of arm moving. Therefore if theory β of intentions is correct, we are compelled by the above to suppose that as the act begins there exist *two* intentions directed either in part or *in toto* to arm movement: an arm moving *and* an arm movement intention; and that the first intention engenders the second. Is this not a little strange? I say so because, if the first intention is ensconced, what need of the second? Assume for a moment that intentions are roughly of the ilk of a practical commitment, of a practical internal assent, or some such. Then to assent in such a practical internal mode to arm moving is, surely, not to harbor a state that *causes* a comparable internal assent to arm movement. It *is* to assent to an arm movement – plus ... But if it is thus to assent to arm movement, how can there be work or scope or function for a second resultant internal assent to arm movement? Must it not of necessity be otiose? And is not otiosity here tantamount to inexistence?

To be sure, this vague analysis of intending as a sort of practical internal assent may be disallowed, whether on the count of imprecision or other grounds. But the point remains: *what need* of an intention toward arm movement if an intention *already inheres* whose object explicitly encompasses precisely that same arm movement? What is there left to cause? To this it may be replied that these two intentions have nonetheless highly diverse causal functions: one being to cause action, the other to cause a mere bodily movement. Now I do not for a moment believe that this reply meets the above difficulty. But in any case my response to this claim would be to point out that, to the extent that there exists such a radical diversity of function, to such an extent there exist indications of a parallel diversity in nature. If it is indeed the case that there exists a psychological phenomenon that is effect of the act-intention and Intentional cause of the arm movement, this marked divergence in the causal propensities of the two "intentions" evidences an inherent unlikeness in type. Thus, the very factors which may be adduced as evidence that the act-intention toward arm moving does not render otiose the intention toward arm movement, tend by the same token to undermine the force of precisely that claim. And we must in any case recognize the need to *substantiate* the thesis that the supposed "intention in acting" is indeed of the type, intention. It is, I submit, not enough to show that there exists an Intentionally directed phenomenon that is "apt for" the causation of an actively engendered arm movement. Give or take a few adjustments, I personally believe in the existence of such a phenomenon; but I, for my part, cannot see how it can be *an intention*. A striving or willing, that is what I should say. And its causal propensity to lead to the desired and intended arm movement, coheres with that view.

I do not wish to urge the latter theory at this point in the discussion. But it seems that the hypothesis of a second intention, directed like the act-intention towards an actively originated arm movement, is seriously in need of substantiation. What we need to know is, why the presumed causal powers of this phenomenon suffice to ensure that it is of the type, intention. It is not that I doubt that there is a psychological phenomenon ushered into being when the act-intention finds expression. And neither do I doubt that this psychological phenomenon is uniquely conative in type, i.e. pertaining uniquely to the phenomenon of action. Nor that it causes or (anyway) is "causally crowned" in the pre-appointed goal-event of arm movement. All of these claims of Searle's are congenial to my way of thinking, and I have advanced reasons elsewhere[18] in favor of each of these propositions. What I seriously question is that there exist reasons for categorizing the psychological phenomenon in question as of the type "intention." And I have just now advanced reasons why we should *not* so classify it: namely, on any agreed connotation of "intention," the inherence in a mind of an act-intention toward φ-making renders otiose any intention toward φ. To which I now add: that the very idea of building an intention into an act, into a *doing*, is surely unacceptable. If Davidson makes the mistake of de-practicalizing intentions, to the point where intentions might be adjudged "right" or even perhaps as "true," Searle seems to me to make the opposite error in injecting the intention into the very heart of the deed itself, to the point where the intention must be adjudged "active" and even as "a doing." If intentions in action constitute the very first part of the deed, they must be both "chosen" and "done", *pace* Searle;[19] and this runs counter to any usage I am acquainted with. But so too does the suggestion that there exist intentions which are not act-directed. Or that necessarily cannot precede the act.

A Summary Statement

In sum: If construal α is the correct interpretation, and intentions in acting *are* the Intentional content of the act, then there is every reason to believe that prior intentions and intentions in acting are not two sub-varieties of the one type, intention. Too many properties divide them; indeed, the very categories of their being are unlike: one being the bearer of Intentional content, the other no more than such a content. That is, "intention" is not univocal in "prior intention" and "intention in acting." Intentions in acting simply are not – intentions.

If construal β is the correct interpretation, and "intention" is indeed univocal across these usages, then there is every reason to suppose that intentions in acting are a myth. A first indication of their mythical character is to be found in the undeniable fact that *all* intentional acts are the immediate effect of distinct and wholly contemporaneous intentions. The highly self-conscious act of swimming from Dover to Calais merely highlights this property, found alike in heavily premeditated highly self-conscious *and* infinitely spontaneous high-speed "automatic" – intentional actions. Indeed, it was with this in mind that we elaborated that situation in some detail. Then the indications are that Searle's distinction rests upon the assumption that intentions in acting are *not* accompanied by contemporaneous intentions which are their cause. Rather, the prior intention is supposed to expire as action begins, whereupon intention-function is at that point passed like a torch to the intention in acting. I say so, partly because Searle introduces the distinction as between "those intentions that are formed prior to action and those that are not,"[20] and asserts that "the characteristic linguistic form of expression of a prior intention is 'I will do A' . . . [and] . . . of an intention in action is 'I am doing A' ".[21] But also because a contemporaneous act-intention cause would render the intention in acting otiose: it would rob it of *rationale*, of rationale of being. It is for this reason that I say that the actual co-presence of wholly contemporaneous act-intentions is strongly suggestive of the mythical nature of the intention in acting. But so too are the properties of the latter: namely, necessarily never preceding the act, having no act-object, etc.

My reading of Searle's thinking on this matter is as follows. He has with perspicacity perceived the phenomenon of willing, and noted that it has Intentional content; he has grasped that it is the causal explanation of the willed bodily movement, and not of the act itself; and he has divined in addition that there is *something* the matter with traditional volition theory. Out of these well-formed parts he has fashioned a questionable theoretical edifice. And the reason is, the insights are something short of total. They lead him to deny the phenomenon of willing; and, as it seems to me, to confuse that reality with a wholly mythical variety of intention. Thus, this supposed intention is credited with almost all of the properties of the outlawed phenomenon of willing. Notably: necessarily never preceding the act, characteristically being experienced, being part of the act, and hence not cause of the act, being the immediate effect of an intention, being of its very nature a putative causal explanation of the willed bodily movement, and being endowed with Intentional content. Complacently at this point I add: the difficulties in Searle's theory more or less vanish if he substitutes willings for intentions in acting. I shall cap this with the even more complacent observation that they would vanish in their entirety were he to embrace the dual-aspect theory of the will for which I have argued elsewhere.[22] It remains at this point to substantiate the nub of these diagnostic suggestions. Namely: to back up my claim that it is willings that in reality play the part he allots in his theory to intentions in acting.

2 The Experience of Acting

Searle writes that "raising your arm characteristically consists of two components: the experience of raising your arm, and the physical movement of the arm."[23] And: "where I actually succeed in raising my arm the experience of acting causes the arm to go up."[24] Further: "there is no term for that which gives us the Intentional content of an intentional action, but [we] have to invent a term of art, 'the experience of acting'."[25] And: "the term would mislead if it gave the impression that such things were . . . like what some philosophers have termed volitions or acts of willing or anything of that sort. They are not acts at all, for we no more *perform* our experiences of acting than we *see* our visual experiences."[26]

The Concept of an Experience

Before I discuss these claims, it is necessary to say a few words about our use of the term "experience." Now it is I think natural to say that "all experiences are experiences *of* something," even "experiences are *the* constituents of the stream of consciousness." And it is I think equally natural to say that "while beliefs and memories are not experiences, sensations and images are experiences," even "if x is a sensation then x is an experience." Then it is evident that "experience" is being put to two different uses here, and I will reserve the expressions "experience$_1$" and "experience$_2$" for these two senses. Roughly experiences$_1$ are actual constituents of the stream of consciousness: thoughts, images, emotings, dream emotings, noticings; and these are items that we naturally and even necessarily know of at the time, and event-remember for at least some short span of time afterwards. The concept of the experience$_2$ is broader and at the same time a little more elusive. Roughly, experiences$_2$ are those psychological events which are epistemologically immediately available to their owner at the time, which in effect is to say they are *either* experiences$_1$ *or* possible immediate psychological material objects of awareness-type experiences$_1$. Thus, images are both experiences$_1$ and experiences$_2$, whereas sensations are merely experiences$_2$ (being no part of the stream of consciousness). The distinctness of the two concepts of experience shows in the fact that we could have the experience$_2$, sensation of contact, in the absence of the experience$_1$, awareness of that sensation. Because pain is essentially obtrusive to the attention, the distinction is more liable to elude us with pain; and for the most part when people remark that "pain is an experience," they fail to draw the distinction and so fail to make a determinate claim. Is an unnoticed pain an experience? An unnoticed pain is an experience$_2$, as is a noticed pain; and neither are experiences$_1$. An unnoticed pain is an experience$_2$, occurring in the absence of the characteristically and closely associated experience$_1$, awareness of pain. Meanwhile we should note that cognitive attitudes like believing, affective attitudes like loving, practical attitudes like intending, cognitive phenomena like forgetting, together with character traits like generosity, are none of them either experiences$_1$ or experiences$_2$. Hence the utility of the concept of the experience.

Which Act-Experience is Characteristically Present when We Act?

(1)   In what sense of "experience" is there *characteristically* an experience of acting? Absolutely *all* mental activities, activities like thinking or listening or phantasizing, *are* of necessity both experiences$_1$ and experiences$_2$: and are not just *characteristically* experiences – in either sense of the term. But what of physical actions like raising an arm? In what sense of "experience" is there merely characteristically an experience of acting when we physically act? I have argued elsewhere[27] that trivial "sub-intentional" activities can occur of which the executor is *wholly* unaware, e.g. idly moving one's tongue about in one's mouth. I think such trifling phenomena destroy the Davidsonian theory that "a man is the agent of an act if what he does can be described under an aspect that makes it intentional"[28] (which is, of course, circular if intended as a definition, leaving the concept of action forever swathed in darkness). However, some will dispute that such goings-on are activities, or done wholly unawares, or intentional under no description, etc. Well, I cannot enter into the matter now. But no one will dispute that there are *degrees of awareness* of physical activities. Think of a statement like "as I lost my footing and fell, I was vaguely aware of uttering a cry." Or activities like tapping one's feet to music. These are phenomena of which we can be less than fully aware – at the very least. That is, they can occur in the absence of fully fledged awareness-experiences$_1$ of them. Thus, the awareness-experience$_1$ looks as if it is only characteristically present when we physically act. Meanwhile, we are in agreement with Searle that when we physically act there at least usually occurs an experience of acting – call it X. Therefore when we engage in action there typically occur *two* experiences: the experience X which we have all along been calling "the experience of acting;" and the awareness of X. These experiences could in different senses each be termed "experiences of acting." Then the question is, which of these two "experiences of acting" is only characteristically present when we physically act? My answer is, the awareness of X; and I adduce as justification the fact that we can be more or less unaware of X when we act. Searle's answer seems to be, X (at least).

Let me now amplify the above a little. Both Searle and I seem to be in agreement that when a physical action occurs, there occurs a psychological phenomenon X that is peculiar to action. Then since the bodily movement φ happened because X, X is the causal explanation of φ. Now it is clear that X cannot be of the type, awareness, for it is not mere awarenesses that lead to active bodily movements. On the other hand, it is possible to be aware of X, and this awareness must be rated a psychologistically immediate awareness of a contemporary psychological event. On these grounds X must be classed as an experience$_2$. But is X an experience$_1$? If the act were a mental act like listening it would be; but because the act is physical, X cannot be part of the stream of consciousness, and so cannot be an experience$_1$. In a word, X is an experience$_2$ but not an experience$_1$. Now experiences$_1$ cannot recede epistemologically out of view, since in a broad sense they are already consciousnesses; but the same is not true of experiences$_2$. Therefore we should in principle be prepared for the situation in which X occurs in the absence of an awareness-type experience$_1$ of acting. Why not? It may be uncharacteristic, but when the act is simple and the attention engrossed elsewhere it seems to be a real possibility. Thus, the act can occur in the absence of a proper awareness of it. Then is the same true of X? Can the act occur without X? I shall have to wait until the next section, The

Nature of "the Experience of Acting," to advance reasons supporting the following claim; but it is to me evident that the physical act cannot occur in the absence of X. And so the position as I see it is this. I suggest that whenever we physically act there *necessarily* occurs an "experience of acting" that is an experience$_2$ but not an experience$_1$, i.e. not even broadly a "consciousness." And whenever we physically act there merely *characteristically* occurs an "experience of acting" that is an experience$_1$/experience$_2$: namely an awareness of acting.

(2)   I shall have little more to say on this specific issue, except to express once again my perplexity over Searle's claim that the experience of acting is only characteristically present when we physically act. I am perplexed because I am unclear as to what *motivates* this claim.

If by "experience of acting" Searle meant "awareness-experience of acting," the claim would of course be readily comprehensible; but how could such a reading be squared with his additional claim that "the experience of acting causes the arm to go up?"[29] As noted above, awarenesses do not produce active bodily movements. In any case, everything suggests that Searle does *not* understand the experience of acting to be an awareness of acting. But if that is the correct reading, why suppose the experience to be only characteristically present? One feels that it must in *some* way be motivated by the fact that some acts occur in the absence of a full or proper awareness of acting. Yet how could that be a motivation if he does not take the experience of acting to be an awareness? One possible interpretation is, that Searle endorses something like the following claim: where there exists no awareness of acting, there exists of necessity no act-experience object of that awareness. If he does, presumably it would be because he endorses the following wider claim: Where there exists an experience, there exists of necessity an awareness of that experience. However, we earlier saw that there was a familiar sense of "experience" in which this latter principle was false. The sensation of contact decisively demonstrates this.

The above is mere surmise. And the following diagnostic suggestion is also no more than surmise. I suspect that Searle has not drawn the distinction between experience$_1$ and experience$_2$; indeed, he may for all I know completely reject it. Meanwhile, he has noted three important truths: that often when we act we are the experiencers of an experience E that is distinctive to active situations; that occasionally and uncharacteristically we act in the absence of that experience; and that willed bodily movements occur because something X psychological and experiencable and distinctive to active situations took place. I have no doubt that these three propositions are true. Then what more natural than to identify E with X? That is, identify the experience that is the subject of the first two propositions, with the experience that is the subject of the third. After all, they are each as wholly distinctive to active situations as the other. But to do so would be to confuse one phenomenon – a consciousness of a willing – with another phenomenon – the willing itself. So it seems to me that what is really going on is this. Searle mentions but one "experience of acting." Thus, he appears to distinguish neither the two types, nor the two tokens of act-experience. Accordingly, he conjoins some of the features of one act-experience with features of the other, supposing them to belong to a single entity. In this way he arrives at a qualitatively hybrid phenomenon that is said to be at once part of the act and cause of the bodily movement *and* as such "a conscious experience with Intentional content"[30] that is only characteristically present when we act. This is the "experience in acting," and I suggest that nothing answers to the specification. Rather, two distinct "experiences in acting" share out the above parcel of properties.

Of course this diagnostic criticism rests in part on the assumption that the act-experience constituent of the act is in fact a necessary constituent of the act. This remains to be shown. But before we attempt to do so, it is worth asking the question: what is to be the bearer of the Intentional content of the act, on those occasions on which the experience in acting uncharacteristically is absent? The answer Searle gives is: the intention in acting. But we have earlier seen that this concept has serious problems of its own, and we in addition come up against the sheer incomprehensibility of the claim that an intention bearer of Intentional content could actually enter the precincts of the act itself! Then if the intention in acting cannot play such a role, it looks as if the experience in acting will have to be reinstated to play the part instead. In short, there are reasons in advance, besides my diagnostic claims, for supposing the act-experience cannot just be character-istically present when we act.

The Nature of "the Experience of Acting"

(1)   I come now to the nature of "the experience of acting." There is much common ground here between Searle and myself. Thus, we both agree that charac-teristically at least an experience that is distinctive to active situations occurs when we physically act. And we agree that such an experience is part at least of the act. And we agree also that the occurrence of that distinctive experience is the causal explanation at least of the active bodily movement.

The differences between us are less marked. I think the active experience that is part of the act is an experience$_2$; whereas Searle, since he describes it as "a conscious experience of acting,"[31] presumably meaning that it is *as such* a conscious experience, in all probability sees it as part of the stream of consciousness and therefore as an experience$_1$. So we probably differ on the question of its relation to consciousness. But we certainly differ on the following issues. I think the experience occurs of necessity whenever we physically act. Indeed, I think the experience is actually identical with the act. And I think the occurrence of the experience is the causal explanation, though not the separate cause, of the active bodily movement. Finally, and most importantly, he believes that we do not *do* or *perform* or *carry out* the event that we are calling "the experience of acting," that it is nothing of the ilk of volition or act of the will or *doing* of any kind; while I am of the opinion that, in a reasonably patched-up sense, it is a volition, and certainly a doing or act of the will or willing.

I would have my and the reader's time cut out trying to debate all these issues – and must set some to one side. In particular, I will not argue the merits of "double aspectism." Thus, I shall not try to demonstrate that the act and experience are one, nor that the act is causal explanation rather than separate cause of the active bodily movement. I shall instead restrict my efforts, first in support of the thesis that the experience is a doing, second in arguing that the act-experience is a necessary constituent of any physical action. Before I do so however, a word or two on Searle's suggestion that there is no "native" term for the experience of acting.

(2)   I shall begin by assembling a series of quotations which seem to be saying the same thing. Thus, Searle writes: "If I have the experience but the event doesn't occur we say such things as that I *failed* to raise my arm, and that I *tried* to raise my arm but did not succeed."[32] And: "his experience is one of *trying* but *failing* to raise his arm."[33] And: "he knows what he is trying to do and he is surprised to discover that he has not succeeded."[34] And: "the experience of moving one's hand has certain conditions of satisfaction. Such concepts as 'trying', 'succeeding', and 'failing' apply to it in ways that they do not apply to the experiences the patient has when he simply observes his hand moving."[35] And: "Even in a case where a man is mistaken about what the result of his efforts are he still knows what he is *trying* to do."[36]

Somewhat mysteriously Searle also writes: "there is no term for that which gives us the Intentional content, and . . . [we] have to invent a term of art, 'the experience of acting'."[37] I find this mysterious, because after inspecting these quotations one surely wants to ask: Why the need of a term of art? Why not describe the experience of acting as a "trying," as an "attempt," even as a "having a shot at?" The above quotations suggest very strongly to me that that precisely is the truth of the matter. Why should not a trying be an experience? After all, "his experience is one of trying,"[38] and "Even in a case where a man is mistaken about what the result of his efforts are he still knows what he is *trying* to do."[39] Is not this exactly what we should look for in the case of an experience? Then what is it that holds Searle back from taking such a step? I cannot answer this question, but the following suggests itself. Searle puts to use *a battery of terms* on those occasions on which we try and fail: "try," "fail," "not succeed." In the light of his belief that there is no "native" term for the experience of acting, this suggests that he thinks that "fail" applies to the situation in just the same way as does "try," and that the same may be said of the negative concept of not-succeeding. Then since the latter concept looks at first blush not to be the concept of an event type, the same must be true of the concept of trying. That is, "try" has a more complex or at any rate *outré* function than that of merely classifying an event by type.

I do not know if this is Searle's view. Very likely it is not. I merely fumble for it in an attempt to understand why, given the above sequence of quotations and as I would say insights, he declines to avail himself of the world "try" and turns instead to a "term of art." In any case the view is surely wrong. A few simple phenomena demonstrate beyond all doubt that the above cannot be the general function of "try." Witness the situation in which a person is trying to remember a name, or trying to move a hitherto paralyzed limb. Are we not in these cases in the presence of determinate events, and is not the designation of those events as "tryings" a designation of event-type? What would one put in its place? It is not merely a *property* – to use that protean and much mangled term – of the event of trying to remember a name that it is a trying: it *is* what it *is*. And the same is true of the patient trying at a signal to move his hitherto immobilized limb.

But now let us suppose this patient fails in his attempt. And he fails *as* he tries. So his trying is a failing. Then was the event *as much* a failing as a trying? How could it be? How could an event be in the first place a failing, and only secondarily a trying? Plainly, the event was first of all a trying and secondly a failing. Plainly, it was first and in all probability essentially a trying, and secondly and certainly inessentially a failing. For the truth is, that failing entails trying, but trying does not entail failing.[40]

Now it may just be that "fail" is like "try" in being an event-type designation; but if it is, of necessity it always inessentially characterizes, whereas "try" always of necessity applies essentially or at least as a "first of all" characterization. But more likely "fail" is not an event-type designation at all: more likely being a failing is being a trying with the inessential negative property of not managing to be what is the act-object of the trying that is itself. Either way, "fail" applies to the event differently from "try." It follows that we cannot conclude from the fact that a battery of concepts, "try," "fail," "not succeed," apply in a situation at one stroke, that they all work in the same way. Therefore we cannot deduce that "try" is not an event-type designation on the grounds that "not succeed" looks as if it might not be.

But if "try" is indeed an event-type designation, and if we systematically reach for this concept on all those occasions on which the act-experience *lies openly exposed to view* – such as situations of epistemological error or active failure, surely it should be descriptively applied to the act-experience? Tryings are phenomena, in time, being events, of which one is immediately aware, irrespective of attendant non-psychological events, etc. Significantly, these are the marks of experiences. I conclude: the experience of acting is a trying, striving, attempting. It follows from this that the experience of acting has, *pace* Searle, already been singled out by the common public language. In a word, we have no binding need of the term of art, "experience of acting."

(3)   Now it must at this point be admitted that tryings can *wholly* fail. To try is not as such to succeed at anything, least of all at trying; for trying is no mode of succeeding, despite the fact that trying can be difficult to do. Even when I stand over myself and succeed in getting myself to try, that trying is not a succeeding at trying, precisely because the trying was not a trying to try. Rather, the act of trying to get myself to try is the act that succeeds – not the resultant trying. Thus, trying is consistent with succeeding in performing *no* act whatsoever. Now here we have an acceptable sense for Searle's "they are not acts at all."[41]

If that was all that Searle had to say on the matter, we could agree with him. But he caps the above with several additional claims which imply that he is saying something other than what we affirm when we assert that trying is not as such a succeeding at doing anything. Thus, he also says of experiences of acting that they are not "acts of willing or anything of that sort,"[42] adding that "we no more *perform* our experience of acting than we *see* our visual experiences."[43] Now it is one thing to say that tryings are not as such succeedings at doing anything, it is quite another thing to say that we do not perform them, or that they are not active doings. For surely they are. It is surely certain that tryings are things that we do or perform. Do we not choose, decide, intend, and desire, to try; and are we not occupied or engaged or busy trying? Is not a phenomenon like trying to remember a name, an activity, a doing, a performance, quite irrespective of whether it is successful or not? That is, irrespective of whether we perform *an act* of jogging our memory? Thus, being an active doing is not as such being an action. It is therefore open to tryings to be active doings *as such*. And I think it clear that they are.

My suggestion thus far is, that the experience of acting that is at least part of the action and causal explanation of the active bodily movement is an experience$_2$ but not an experience$_1$, that it has a common public linguistic designation, that it is a striving or trying, and that it is as such an active doing and therefore something that we *perform*. I say therefore because the event of performing an active doing is not an event *linking* the performer with the performed: it *is* the performed, precisely because it *is* the active doing itself. How do these assertions sort with Searle's additional claim that experiences of acting are not "like what some philosophers have called volitions or acts of the will or anything of that sort."[44] I think they are inconsistent with it. It is true that the concept of the volition has a somewhat uncertain history, and we ought perhaps to disengage ourselves from it. Whether or not this is so, the same cannot be said of the concept of an act of the will. All that we require to legitimise this concept is, show that something which measures up pretty much to its received content is instantiated in reality. That is, demonstrate that something in reality matches up to the following specification: namely, an event, a psychological experience, of a type peculiar and essential to active situations, that is irreducible to non-active categories, that is causal explanation of the active bodily movement. No more, it seems to me. Thus, I do not think that we need in addition to prove that the event in question is an *interior* psychological phenomenon. While this has been the usual unspoken presumption in the past, none of the other properties of the supposed psychological event *obviously* entail interiority. Then I suggest that the event of bodily striving or trying fits the bill. I suggest that it is an act of the will. Why should not bodily tryings be acts of the will? Certainly not because they are not as such successful actions of any kind – as we noted above. And not because they may well not be accounted "interior" (in some acceptable sense of that (here) unexplained term). After all, double-aspect theories of the bodily will are not *obviously* false. But why call them *acts* of the will, if they are not as such actions? Because they are as such doings that are active, done, performed, etc. Then why call such phenomena *willings*? Well, there may be an element of stipulation here, but the term has the advantage of reminding us of the fact that the event in question is irreducibly *psychological*, and irreducibly of its own *sui generis* kind. Are not bodily strivings just that?

(4)   The last issue on which I wish to make a very brief comment is, my earlier suggestion that the experience of acting is a necessary and not merely characteristic element of the act. At first blush the claim appears dubious, bearing in mind that some actions are almost certainly performed unawares. Is not the concept of an "unawares experience" a contradiction? We shall consider the latter question first. Then I think it clear that the problem vanishes once we distinguish experiences$_1$ from experiences$_2$; for the intelligibility of "unnoticed sensation of contact" shows that "unawares experience$_2$" is unexceptionable as "unawares experience$_1$" is not.

Then why suppose that this experience$_2$ is actually necessary for action? Well, we have in the interim as it seems to me unearthed the nature of the experience: namely, as a trying, striving, or willing. Accordingly, the question now transforms to: Why suppose bodily trying a necessary condition of bodily action? I shall not at this late stage of the paper launch into a serious discussion of this question. Suffice it to say that a simple old traditional home-spun argument from illusion and failure discloses the common constant presence of a bodily striving whenever we physically act. I will not rehearse the details of the argument, but would like to make the following particular observation. Suppose a man unawares is tapping a foot to music as he reads, and suppose improbably that scientists duplicate the kinaesthetic sensations of foot movement even as they bring (merely) that foot movement to a halt. Would it not be true to say of this man that, in despite of his near or even total unawareness, he was nonetheless striving to move his foot as he read? After all, motor impulses are still travelling foot-wards through his nervous system in response to the insistent thud of the music. Examples like this demonstrate that physical striving is essential to, and not merely characteristic of physical action. Such a striving is an experience$_2$, occurring in the presence of a malformed or even no-formed awareness-experience$_1$ of itself.

NOTES

1 Intentionality (Cambridge University Press: Cambridge, 1983), p. 88.
2 Ibid., pp. 88–9.
3 Ibid., p. 84.
4 Ibid., p. 84.
5 Ibid., p. 92.
6 Ibid., p. 94.
7 Ibid., p. 94.
8 Ibid., p. 87.
9 Ibid., p. 88.
10 Ibid., p. 93.
11 Ibid., p. 84.
12 *Essays on actions and events* (Oxford University Press: Oxford, 1980), p. 83.
13 Ibid., p. 99.
14 Searle, *Intentionality*, p. 84.
15 Ibid., p. 84.
16 Ibid., p. 93.
17 Ibid., p. 93.
18 *The Will* (Cambridge University Press: Cambridge, 1980), vol. 2, pp. 39–146, 303–57. Also "Trying (as the Mental 'Pineal Gland')", *Journal of Philosophy* (1973).
19 *Intentionality*, pp. 88–9.
20 Ibid., p. 84.
21 Ibid., p. 84.
22 *The Will*, vols 1 and 2.
23 Ibid., p. 87.
24 Ibid., p. 88.
25 Ibid., p. 88.
26 Ibid., pp. 88–9.
27 *The Will*, vol. 2, pp. 58–74.
28 *Essays on actions and events*, p. 46.
29 *Intentionality*, p. 88.
30 Ibid., p. 91.
31 Ibid., p. 90.
32 Ibid., p. 88.
33 Ibid., p. 89.
34 Ibid.
35 Ibid., p. 90.
36 Ibid.
37 Ibid., p. 88.
38 Ibid., p. 89.
39 Ibid., p. 90.

40 We must distinguish "fail" meaning little more than "not," from "fail" meaning "unsuccess-
    fully attempt." In the first sense I failed to go to Mars last year, in the second sense I did not;
    and in both senses I failed to understand a certain passage in Hegel. No one would count the
    former brand of failure amongst his "recent string of failures." Then the entailment of which I
    speak applies of course only to the other brand.
41 Ibid., p. 88.
42 Ibid.
43 Ibid., p. 89.
44 Ibid., p. 88.

20

Response: The Background of Intentionality and Action

JOHN R. SEARLE

One of the least well understood chapters in *Intentionality* is the one called "The Background." I must be partly responsible for this because I did not express myself clearly enough. However, I also think that part of the lack of clarity is due to the sheer difficulty and obscurity of the subject matter. The main thesis of that chapter is that intentional states only function, they only determine their conditions of satisfaction, given a pre-intentional or non-intentional Background of abilities and capacities that do not themselves consist in intentional phenomena and therefore are strictly speaking not part of the holistic Network of intentional states. I give a variety of reasons for this claim and I try to explore some of its consequences. However, I think the whole discussion is still very unsatisfactory.

Barry Stroud

Stroud's provocative and ingenious article is the most extensive discussion that I have seen of my views on this topic and I am not sure that I can answer all of the questions he raises. However, I can at least correct some misunderstandings and misapprehensions. I think much of Stroud's argument is based on a series of subtle, but nonetheless profound misunderstandings. My guess is that he is interpreting my questions in terms of his own deep concerns with problems in epistemology, but in any case, I believe he mistakes both the questions I am asking and the answers I am giving in such a way that it appears to him that I am making contradictory claims. The best way for me to try to answer him is to state his misreadings against the statement of what I am, in fact, trying to do in that chapter:

1   Searle presents a theory of Intentionality designed to enable us "to understand how any of our intentional states come to be what they are" (p. 253). He wants a theory that will "explain, in general, how any intentional states at all are possible" (p. 258).
2   Searle postulates the Background, because "it is somehow supposed to make intelligible to us precisely how we can get into the particular kinds of intentional states we can be in" (p. 251).

3   A theory of Intentionality must explain intentional phenomena in "mental" (p. 253) or intentional terms. Stroud says, "No explanation in non-intentional terms could make intentional phenomena intelligible in the right way" (p. 253).

4   But the Background cannot be intentional because of the threat of regress. "No explanation in intentional terms could explain intentional states in general" (p. 253).

5   Therefore, Searle is making contradictory demands on his theory. "On the one hand, we 'lapse" into intentionalistic vocabulary because we are looking for an explanation that will make the phenomena intelligible to us in that intentional way; but since the 'Background' is also something that is supposed to explain how any intentional states are possible we see that it cannot be made up of intentional states in turn" (p. 253).

All of these five statements express misunderstandings both of the overall nature of the enterprise and the specific claims being made. In answer to these points:

1   I am definitely not looking for the sort of theory that Stroud has in mind. On the contrary, my whole approach is naturalistic: I start with the assumption that we all have real intentional states such as beliefs, desires, etc., and I want to know how they work. I am asking such questions as "What sort of structures do they have and how do their structures relate them to the world?" I am trying to get an *account* of mental states, but I am not trying to answer such questions as "How do they come to be what they are?" or "What makes them intelligible?" I am not even sure I know what such questions mean, but in any case they are not my questions. I think most of Stroud's misunderstandings come from a basic misconception of the nature of my enterprise.

2   I do not *postulate* the existence of the Background out of some theoretical need, I just claim to discover its existence as a matter of fact. That is, I claim that if you follow out the threads in the Network of intentional states you will discover that the whole system of Intentionality only works against the set of capacities, abilities, etc., that are not themselves Intentional. I do give various "arguments" for this, but I confess that it is not the arguments that are really important to me. I am certainly not trying to "make it intelligible how we can get into the Intentional states that we are in."

3   I am not using "mental" and "intentional" as equivalent. And I do not seek some explanation of Intentionality in Intentional terms. I do say that the Background is "mental" and Stroud takes this to be the main source of the contradiction he claims to discover, because he thinks "mental" must imply "intentional."

Since this, I believe, is the central issue in the disagreement between Stroud and me, I will explain my position in more detail: In what sense can the Background be mental if it does not consist of Intentional phenomena?

The reason I am so insistent that the Background capacities must be mental is not that I am making some self-contradictory demand to the effect that they both be intentional and that they not be intentional; the reason, rather, is that I take it to be a condition of adequacy on any account of the functioning of intentionality that the account must be given independently of any presupposition as to whether or not the agent is, in fact, getting things right with his or her Intentional states. An account of belief in general, for example, has to be independent of the question of which, if any, of my beliefs are true. At this point I am in agreement with various philosophers who are trying to get at Intentionality with such notions as "methodological solipsism," "the transcendental reduction," or simply the fantasy of "the brain in the vat." Now, it is only in this sense that I am claiming that the Background is mental. It does not consist of actual objects or states of affairs in the world and it is not located in Kansas City or at the North Pole. I could have all of my Background abilities even if I am radically mistaken about how the world is; and in that sense my Background abilities are independent of how things are in fact in the world that I represent to myself with my Intentionality.

Many people find it uncomfortable to describe such things as my ability to swim or ski as "mental" capacities. I share this reluctance and, in fact, I am unsatisfied altogether with the traditional vocabulary of "mental" and "physical." Nonetheless, it is important to emphasize that Background abilities are not dependent on how things in fact work in the world. All of my Background capacities are "in my head," and in that sense I use the word "mental" to describe them. In short, when I say the Background is mental without being Intentional there is no inconsistency implied or presupposed. I am simply saying that the Background is not iself a feature of the world independent of the mind.

4   There is a regress argument for the Background, but Stroud's argument is not really the same as mine, though there are some similarities. His argument is that if we imagine the contents of the mind as consisting of mental representations we would still have to assume acts of *grasping* these representations, but these graspings cannot themselves consist of further representations without an infinite regress. I think that argument is acceptable as far as it goes but I am trying to go a bit farther. I think that the standard accounts in the literature think of mental representations not just as a set of mental objects, not just as a set of, e.g. mental "pictures," but rather they think that the mental representation somehow combines both the picture and its grasping. Such authors would be unmoved by Stroud's objection. They would say that there cannot be any question about the representation as grasped, because the representation just includes its own grasping. In the case of Jerry Fodor, for example, as I interpret him, the question whether or not the internal representations have to be *grasped* cannot even arise.[1] I was trying to answer even this stronger version of representationalism.

I give a number of arguments in favor of the hypothesis of the Background, one of which is this: Intentional contents are not self-interpreting or self-applying. Even, for example, if someone understood (grasped) all the meanings of words and thus to that extent understood (grasped) the meaning of a sentence containing those words, the sentence is still subject to an indefinite range of different interpretations. The sentence is not self-applying, and sometimes a meaningful sentence with meaningful words admits of no literal interpretation at all. Even "grasping" the meaning does not fix the interpretation or the application. In both my account and Stroud's a regress argument comes in, but on my account it comes in at a later stage. If someone tries to *answer* my argument by saying that we can have, in addition to the literal meaning of sentences, rules for the interpretation of sentences, pragmatic rules, for example, then, it seems to me that we get a rather simple regress argument, because the rules themselves are subject to further interpretation.

5   So, there are no contradictions or contradictory impulses in my account. There are real difficulties in it, and I am acutely aware of its inadequacies; but I do not think that the apparent inconsistency that Stroud professes to find is one of them.

When it comes to the discussion of realism we once again find that I have not succeeded in making myself understood. Specifically, when I talk of a "commitment to realism" Stroud misunderstands what I am driving at. Stroud thinks that when I talk about a "commitment to realism" I am thinking of a commitment to the "truth of the proposition that the real world exists." But that is precisely the point I am concerned to deny. The point that I am making is not that realism is "true" theory, but rather that as long as the Background is functioning normally, there is no question about having a commitment to any hypothesis, belief, or theory at all. Stroud says that the commitment must involve the commitment to *truth*, but that again is precisely the point that I am denying. It is not one of my claims that this solves the epistemological problem of skepticism about realism; but rather I am trying to cast doubt on the motivation and intelligibility of one of its traditional formulations. A certain form of the problem in this case arises when we take features of the non-representational background to be representations.

My idea is not that by skiing or drinking beer I somehow imply that I hold a commitment to the truth of a certain proposition: namely, that the real world exists. Rather, I am suggesting any "commitment" is simply *constituted* by the way I behave. There need not be anything else. And the picture that I was militating against is this: it looks as if in order for me to intend to drink beer or go skiing I must first believe that there is a real world, a world existing independently of my intentionality. After all, if I disbelieved that there was such a thing as the real world, if I disbelieved in its existence, then I could not intend to drink beer or go skiing. But now, if I have to presuppose the existence of the real world, or if I am committed to the belief in the existence of the real world, surely I must ask the question "what justifies that belief?" But then it seems I cannot justify that belief.

The picture that I was trying to put in its place is this: in the end, as Wittgenstein says, we just act. We just speak, ski, drink beer, etc. We do not *in addition* have a belief in a metaphysical thesis to the effect that the real world exists. Part of the puzzle arises because we suppose that if we believe in the negation of the realism, then we could not intelligibly have the Intentional states that we do. So we suppose that because the belief in the negation of the realism would undermine the intelligibility of our behavior, that therefore the behavior involves a commitment to the *truth* of realism. Having a "commitment" to realism in the sense I am discussing does not imply a commitment to the truth of any proposition. I would like eventually to be able to make clear the connection between this point and the point that the denial of realism is not fully intelligible. I think that denials of realism deny the conditions of intelligibility of publicly assertable propositions.

The final point concerns Wittgenstein. In his discussion of Wittgenstein, Stroud makes a distinction between "negative" and "theoretical" claims. I do not make this distinction, since for me a theoretical claim can be negative; and indeed many of my theoretical claims are negative. For me, a theory is just a set of systematically related claims about any given subject matter. Here, for example, is a theoretical claim: The functioning of Intentionality cannot be Intentionalistic right down to the ground, but rather this functioning must presuppose a set of capacities that are not themselves representational. Indeed, this is the essential theoretical claim in my thesis of the Background. I call these capacities collectively the Background. My own view (and in this I think I do depart from Wittgenstein) is that ultimately our explanations of these capacities will be biological. That is to say, the existence of Intentional states is explained by the fact that we are creatures with the certain sort of neurophysiological structure, and certain sorts of biological capacities.

Jerome Wakefield and Hubert Dreyfus

Wakefield and Dreyfus present some very interesting objections to my account of the Intentionality of voluntary action. They claim that my views are more suited to deliberate cases but do not provide us with a general account; since, so they claim, non-deliberate action does not exhibit the sort of representational Intentionality that I claim for deliberate action.

Actually, I think the problems here are so complex and subtle that I will not be able to discuss all of them within the confines of the present format. However, I want to begin by introducing three themes that are not present in *Intentionality* but which I have come to believe since the book was published.

First, it seems to me a general point that *Intentionality rises to the level of the Background abilities.* This is true both for perception and action, but the phenomenon is easiest to observe in a case of actions. If, for example, I am a skillful skier, I do not need to form a separate intention to move each leg, or even to make each turn. I simply decide to ski down the mountain and I do so. If, however, something goes wrong, if I lose my skill because of a pulled leg muscle or a broken ski, then my intentionality will lower to the level of my diminished ability. Then I have to think about moving the left leg and moving the right leg. Again, in the case of language, the skillful speaker of a language does not have to form a separate intention for each letter or even each word. He simply puts his thoughts in naturally flowing words and sentences.

Second, this leads to the idea that Intentional behavior exhibits what I call *"the flow."* When we talk about Intentionality, we naturally tend to describe it in a serious of verbal snapshots, but the actual phenomena are more like a continuous cinema. As I walk to my office, eat lunch, or give a lecture there is a continuous flow of intentional behavior governed by the experience of acting.

And third, *The Intentionality reaches down to the bottom level of the voluntary actions.* Thus, for example, the skillful skier has his Intentionality at the level of getting down the mountain. But each subsidiary movement is nonetheless an intentional movement. Each movement is governed by the Intentionality of the flow, even though there is not, and need not be, any explicit representation of the intentional movement. Furthermore, even if we accept all these three points we need also to add that in skillful behavior there will be a lot of things that are not at the focus of one's attention but are still Intentional phenomena and are part of the flow. Thus, for example, if I am driving a car, I may be carrying on a conversation at the same time. The bulk of my attention is focused on the conversation, and I drive the car more or less "automatically." Nonetheless, it seems to me wrong to say that my driving the car is not intentional, that I do not have continuous intentions in action and the experience of the phenomenology of voluntary movement. Thus, when I shift gears I do not have a *separate* intention to go from second to third, but all the same I shift *intentionally*. This phenomenology, as Wakefield, Dreyfus, and I all agree, is essential to intentional action and is present in this sort of case.

But they suggest that I should think of these cases as cases where the Background is so to speak present all the way up to the top, and there is no Intentionality. But I think that is mistaken. Indeed, as I use the notion of "the Background" such a thesis would be incoherent. There is nothing, of course, that guarantees that my terminology is the right terminology; perhaps we can think of something better. But as I use these notions, the Background only functions when it is activated by genuine Intentional contents.

It is not at all obvious what exactly the difference between their view and my view is. They say "but, in non-deliberate action, the experience of acting does not consist of the experience of an intention-in-action causing one's movement. Instead, the experience of acting during nondeliberate actions appears to consist simply of the experience of a steady and immediate flow of skillful activity in response to one's sense of the environment and one's internal state . . . But no intention-in-action is necessary to explain such an experience. One can simply be experiencing the causal connection between one's motion and one's perception of one's body's situation in the world" (p. 268). My problem with this passage is that the description they give to exemplify the absence of an intention-in-action is precisely sort of description that I would give as an example of an intention-in-action. In my terminology they have already characterized the experience as containing an intention-in-action, when they describe it as an "immediate flow of skillful activity," and when they further concede that "Searle is correct that one feels differently than Penfield's subjects, because one experiences the connection between one's bodily motions and *a cause of the motion*" (my italics, p. 269). The only cause in question could be the fact that I am actually *doing it* intentionally as opposed to passively experiencing it. And that difference derives from the fact that in the case of doing it intentionally there is an intention-in-action. They say that "no intention in action is necessary to *explain* such an experience." But of course one does not explain that experience with some further intention in action: that very experience *is* an intention-in-action; that is precisely what I mean by an intention-in-action. It seems to me, in short, that the difference that they cite is not between cases where there is an intention-in-action and cases where there is not, but rather cases where there are, for example, varying degrees of attention and focus, and varying degrees of skill involved in the behavior in question.

They claim that their views are inspired by certain Continental traditions of phenomenology. I think that is surely right, but I would like to suggest that perhaps their objection to me is based on understanding my views within that same Continental tradition. When they contrast what they call "G-intentionality" and "R-intentionality" I believe they are thinking in terms of certain Continental paradigms. On my account, both G-intentionality and R-intentionality are forms of Intentionality in the sense that they can succeed or fail. They have conditions of satisfaction. In fact, I think it may have been unwise of me to have used the word "representation" at all, since it tends to evoke uses of this word by other authors who use it in ways quite unlike my own. The word does not occur essentially in my account, since it can be completely dispensed with in favor of all of the notions that are used to explain it. It is simply a device for coordinating those notions (I mean here notions such as "propositional content," "direction of fit," "conditions of satisfaction," "causal self-referentiality," "Network," etc.). But my use of the word "representation" has naturally led people to suppose that I must be using it in a sense that goes back several centuries in Continental philosophy.

Brian O'Shaughnessy

O'Shaughnessy presents the most extensive and powerful set of objections to my account of action that I have seen. From my point of view his objections can be divided into three types: (1) Those that are based on misunderstandings or different uses of terminology; (2) those that express genuine disagreements; (3) those that I do not understand. I will confine this discussion to (1) and (2).

First, a misunderstanding arises from his notion of the "bearer of Intentional content." When I say that the intention-in-action is the Intentional content of the action, he asks, what is the bearer of the Intentional content? Well, I do not, in fact, ever use this expression. But if I did, the only bearer of Intentional content would be the brain. It might be possible to imagine beings who lack brains who also had Intentional contents, but in the world we live in, the only Intentional contents are possessed by human and animal brains, so that only "bearer of Intentional content" is the brain. Why then is there a problem for O'Shaughnessy about the bearer of Intentional content?

On my account, intentional states in general have the structure $S(p)$, where S marks the psychological mode or type, such as belief, desire, intention, etc.; and p marks the representative content. Thus, the belief that it is raining will have the form

BEL (it is raining).

Sometimes I talk as if there were two *components* to the belief, but it is more accurate to think of the whole package as simply consisting of a *content* in a certain *mode*. The intentional state just is an Intentional content, though, of course, the Intentional content can only exist in a certain intentional mode.

When I say, in the passage that puzzles O'Shaughnessy, that the intention-in-action is the Intentional content of the action, I mean the whole package in the form $S(p)$ is the Intentional content of the action. I do not mean p by itself. On my account it makes no sense to suppose that the content could exist without occurring in some psychological mode or other.

However, it is clear that the talk of content has misled, so let us simply abandon it for this discussion, and let us say that the intention-in-action is the Intentional *component* of the action. This eliminates any problem about "bearers". I believe we then do not need to worry about his alternative interpretations *alpha* and *beta* of my discussion of intention-in-action.

Before turning to the genuine disagreements between me and O'Shaughnessy I need to repeat some elements of my account of human action: An intention-in-action just is an Intentional event that consists in a representational content in a certain psychological mode. If the action is a simple bodily action, such as raising one's arm, then the structure of the intention-in-action looks like this (using "ia" as an abbreviation for intention-in-action, "bm" as an abbreviation for bodily movement):

ia (this ia causes bm)

And if the action is successfully performed, then the action will consists of two components. The intention-in-action and the bodily movement, where the bodily movement is both caused by and Intentionally presented by the intention in action. So the picture of the whole action would look like this, using small letters for the "mental" component and capitals for the "physical" component and square brackets to mark the boundaries of the whole action:

[ia (this ia causes bm) CAUSES BM]

With this much apparatus in mind I want to turn to what I take to be genuine disagreements between O'Shaughnessy and me. I believe that the disagreements are almost entirely due to the fact that O'Shaughnessy never takes seriously my notions of conditions of satisfaction and Background. I think that if you take these notions very seriously and ask yourself what are the conditions of satisfaction of the Intentional phenomena involved in the perfomance of an action, you will see that there are two distinct types, which I call respectively: prior intention and intention-in-action. If I form a plan to raise my arm, I have formed a prior intention to perform a whole action. The conditions of satisfaction of prior intentions are quite different from the conditions of satisfaction of intentions-in-action. The prior intention represents the whole action and not just the bodily movement, but since the whole action consists of an intention-in-action and the bodily movement, the prior intention represents the whole package consisting of both the intention-in-action and the bodily movement. So its form is (using "pi" as an abbreviation for prior-intention):

pi (this pi causes action)

And if it actually succeeds then the whole pattern of plan plus action looks like this:

pi (this pi causes action) CAUSES ACTION

And since the action represented by the prior intention has two components, ia and bm, the internal structure of the pi is like this:

pi (this pi causes [ia (this ia causes bm)])

(I am here summarizing a very extensive account; see chapter 3 of *Intentionality* for the details.)

O'Shaughnessy clearly objects to this analysis, but my difficulty is that I do not see what alternative he is proposing. He grants me, I guess, that there is an intentional content to the action itself but he never tells me *exactly* what its conditions of satisfaction are. What *exactly* is its intentional structure? To make the disagreement more precise let me express his points as two related objections. First, he cannot see any adequate reason for the distinction between the prior intention and the intention-in-action; and second, he cannot see any grounds for calling the intentional component of an action an intention.

Let me take up both of these in order. The key of Intentionality is conditions of satisfaction. It ought to be a rule in all of these discussions that nobody is allowed to talk about an Intentional phenomenon without telling us what its conditions of satisfaction are. So if I am to vindicate my account I need to show first that intuitively there are two different types of phenomena, and that corresponding to the intuitive difference there is a difference in conditions of satisfaction. The intuitive difference is this: there is a difference between the plans that one forms prior to an action (what I call the prior intention) and the actual mental component of the action itself (what I call the intention-in-action). Forget for the moment whether we should call either of these an intention or not. I do not want to beg any questions. The intuitive point is simply that in *many* cases, not all, of intentional action there is an Intentional content functioning *outside* the action itself; and in *all* cases of intentional action there is an Intentional component functioning *inside*. There is, to my mind, a conclusive argument for the distinction between the two types, and that is, that one can exist without the other. A man can form an external prior intention and not act on that intention, and a man can act intentionally without any prior intention or any outside intention at all. For example, a man might just spontaneously raise his arm for the hell of it. In such a case there is no prior intention at all. He simply performs an intentional action, without any external intention. Now once you grant me an intuitive difference between the plan and the mental component in its execution, between the external and the internal Intentional element, then, I believe, it is easy to see the difference in intentional content is as I have described it above. If a prior intention could talk, it would say "I am going to cause an action" and if the intention in action could talk it would say, "I am part of an action and I am going to cause the bodily movement which is the rest of the action."

In sum, there is a conclusive argument for this distinction which O'Shaughnessy has not met: You can have the one without the other, you can have the outside intentions without ever acting on them, and you can have an intentional action with an inside Intentional component and no outside Intentional content whatever. That is exactly what happens when a man just spontaneously raises his arm without thinking about it at all, he just hauls off and does it.

But now, the question arises why should we call this interior Intentional content an "intention?" At one level, it does not matter. The notion "intention-in-action" is just a technical term. As long as you recognize the nature of the component, and in particular its causally self-referential conditions of satisfaction, it is not of very great interest what we choose to call it. However, there is an argument to show that it is an intention which seems to me quite compelling. Here it is: there are classes of intentional actions which are performed without any outside intention whatever. These are cases of spontaneous action, cases in which the agent just acts spontaneously. But what fact about these actions make them intentional? Since there is no outside intention involved at all, they are not caused by any exterior intention. I think the answer is obvious: A spontaneous intentional act is none-theless an act done with a certain intention. The man who raises his arm sponta-neously, raises his arm with the intention of raising his arm. Now, that intention I call an intention-in-action. There is nothing mysterious about it. However, since all intentional actions have this feature, namely an interior intentional content which causes the bodily movement (or other conditions of satisfaction), we can say that every intentional action contains an intention-in-action.

These are the main disagreements between me and O'Shaughnessy, at least as I understand them. There are, however, a number of other issues that are important enough to require a special mention:

1   I reject O'Shaughnessy's distinction between experience$_1$ and experience$_2$. For me, the notion of experience implies the notion of consciousness. The distinctions he is making seems to involve different degrees of attention, focusing, or awareness; but these are not two different senses of experience or two different types of experience. A man who is tapping his foot in time to music is only marginally or peripherally conscious of what he is doing. But he is still marginally or peripherally conscious of it. His tapping is not at all like the secretion of enzymes in his stomach, of which he is totally unconscious. Where the foot tapping is concerned, he is not a zombie; he just is not paying any attention to what he is doing.

2   I need both the notion of intention-in-action and experience of acting, because, since for me experience implies consciousness, I need a more general notion to mark the intentional component of an action, than that of a conscious intention-in-action. There are many actions that are performed intentionally, where the agent is quite unconscious of the intention. These are the cases in which the agent does something quite unconsciously even though he does it intentionally. All cases of the experience of acting are cases of an intention-in-action but the notion of an intention-in-action is a more general notion since not all intentions-in-action involve an experience of acting.

3   O'Shaughnessy has convinced me of a point I was not aware of before: At least in the cases of complex extended actions, the prior intention can exist and continue to function after the onset of the action. So to take the case of a man who is swimming from Dover to Calais, his prior intention will consist in the plan: On Tuesday beginning at 9 a.m. I will swim from Dover to Calais. When he is half-way through swimming from Dover to Calais, he no longer has that whole prior intention, since the action is half-way completed. Nonetheless, he still has the remains of the prior intention which continues to regulate his behavior as he continues to swim from Dover to Calais. The onset of the sequence of subsidiary intentions-in-actions when he began swimming does not necessarily eliminate the prior intention.[2]

4   "Well, why not call these intentions-in-action all cases of 'trying'?" I think, in fact, that the most general term in English for the intention-in-action is simply "trying". When I was writing *Intentionality* I was aware of this point, but I was reluctant to use the notion of "trying" because of all the Wittgensteinian debates that had gone on around that notion. Furthermore, the notion of "trying" is rather tricky, and it has some features that are not appropriate for intentions-in-action. For example, a man may try to remember something, or even try to believe something, even though "remembering" and "believing" are not names of actions. In such cases the notion "try to believe" does not really name the content of an intention-in-action. The intention-in-action would represent the steps or procedures that the man takes in order to produce the effect of his believing. But

"believing" here is not the name of the content of an intention-in-action. The phrase "try to x" does not always name an intention-in-action, even though, as I said, the most general term in English for intentions-in-action is indeed "trying."

Why could one not call all these cases of "willing" or "volition"? Perhaps one could. I was reluctant to use these expressions because of the history of combat surrounding these notions. I was brought up philosophically in the Oxford of the fifties, and by that time the traditional talk of "volitions" and "willings" had already been discredited. For example, I assumed that volitions were subject to Rylean infinite-regress arguments. As O'Shaughnessy says: "It is true that the concept of the volition has a somewhat uncertain history, and we ought perhaps to disengage ourselves from it" (p. 285). However, if we can purge these notions of their "uncertain history" and get rid of the idea that every action has to be preceded by a separate act of willing or volition, then I really have no objection to calling intentions-in-action cases of volition or willings, because they are, after all, in general, cases of trying.

NOTES

1 J. Fodor, *Representations* (MIT Press/Bradford Books: Cambridge Mass., 1981).
2 Actually, this claim is already implicit in my comparison of the relation of prior intention to intention-in-action with the relation of memory and perceptual experience. As far as complex experiences are concerned, one can have memories of part of the experience before the entire sequence is completed. On my view, the relation of prior intention to intention-in-action is the mirror image of the relation of perceptual experience and memory (see *Intentionality*, p. 97). In any case, I am grateful to O'Shaughnessy for calling my attention to this point.

Part   VI
Social Explanation

21

On Searle's Argument against the Possibility of Social Laws

RAIMO TUOMELA

(1)   In his recent book, *Minds, Brains and Science* (1984), Searle discusses the philosophical nature of the social sciences and he claims that there can be no social laws. I shall critically examine his argument for substantiating this claim. By a scientific law Searle means a universal generalization "about how things happen" (ibid., p. 71). He also says that a law is explained by deducing it from a higher order law. Thus I take it that Searle accepts the so-called standard conception of theories and laws. Accordingly, the nomicity which in this contrual is supposed to distinguish between accidental generalizations and genuine laws is due to the systemicity of laws, namely, the fact that they belong to nomological networks where laws and theories of different generality occur and stand in the mentioned kind of explanatory relationships. This is roughly the conception one finds in Braithwaite's *Scientific Explanation* (1953), and, although Searle is not explicit about this matter (and does not speak about the distinction between laws and accidental generalizations at all), it seems that this is more or less what he accepts and takes to be involved in what he calls the standard theory of scientific explanation.

As Searle puts it, "there will be no laws of wars and revolutions in a way that there are laws of gases and of nutrition." By this he means roughly that the relationship between the social level and the individual level is not relevantly analogous to the relation between the macroproperties of gases, for example, (cf. Boyle–Mariotte's law) and their microproperties as specified by the kinetic gas theory. "The phenomena in the world that we pick out with concepts like war and revolution, marriage, money and property are not grounded systematically in the behaviour of elements at the more basic level in a way that the phenomena that we pick out with concepts like fat-deposit and pressure are grounded systematically in the behaviour of elements at the more basic level" (p. 77). But why is this so? Let us consider Searle's answer (cf. Searle, 1984, chapter 6, esp. pp. 75–85).

Searle argues that in order to see why there cannot be social laws in the mentioned sense we must look at the fundamental principles on which we categorize psychological and social phenomena. And he claims that one crucial feature is this:

> For a large number of social and psychological phenomena the concept that names the phenomenon is itself a constituent of the phenomenon. In order for something to count as a marriage ceremony or a trade union, or property or money or even a war or revolution people involved in these activities have to have certain appropriate thoughts. In general they have to think that's what it is.

Social terms, unlike any terms used in the physical and biological sciences, have the peculiar kind of self-referentiality. Thus "money" refers to whatever people use and think as and think of as money. Thus people must have certain thoughts and attitudes about something in order for it to counts as money and these thoughts and attitudes are art of the very definition of money. Another important consequence of Searle's view is that this defining principle of such social phenomena sets no physical limits whatever on what can count as the physical realization of them. Therefore there cannot be any systematic connections between the physical properties and the social or mental properties of the phenomenon. The social features are determined in part by the attitudes people have toward them, and these attitudes are not constrained by the physical features of the phenomena in question. Therefore, Searle concludes, there cannot be any matching of the mental level and the level of the physics of the sort that would be necessary to make strict laws of the social sciences possible.

Actually, here is a further twist to this argument. Suppose a critic of Searle now says that his account does not really need a strict match between social and psychological properties and, on the other hand, things in the world. All that is needed is such a match between the former and feature of the brain: The real grounding of economics and sociology in the physical world is not in the properties of the objects we find around us, it is in the physical properties of the brain. So even if thinking that something is money is essential to its being money, still thinking that it is money may well be, and indeed on Searle's account is, a process in the brain.

Searle's response to this is the following. From the established fact that, e.g., money can have an indefinite range of physical forms it follows that it can have an indefinite range of stimulus effects on our nervous systems. But then it would be a miracle if they, in all cultures and societies, all produced exactly the same neurophysiological effect on the brain. Paradoxically, Searle says, the way the mental infects the physical prevents there ever being a strict science of the mental.

Before going to a more detailed discussion of this interesting argument let me follow Searle in clarifying its basic structure and set it out as follows:

1   For there to be laws of the social sciences in the sense in which there are laws of physics there have to be some bridge principles between the higher and lower levels, namely there must be some systematic correlation between phenomena identified in social and psychological terms and phenomena identified in physical terms.

2   Social phenomena are in large part defined in terms of the psychological attitudes that people take.

3   This has the consequence that these categories are physically open-ended.

4   That implies that there cannot be any bridge principles between the social and physical features of the world.

5   Furthermore, it is impossible to get the right kind of bridge principles

between phenomena described in mental terms and phenomena described in neurophysical terms, that is, between the brain and the mind. And this is because there is an indefinite range of stimulus conditions for any given social concept, and this enormous range prevents concepts which are not built into us from being realized in a way that systematically correlates mental and physical features.

6 It follows from (4) and (5) there cannot be bridge laws of the kind required by (1).

7 Hence there cannot be laws in the social sciences in the sense there are laws in physics.

I will below claim that (1), (4), and (5) (and hence (6)) are problematic if not clearly false, while premises (2) and (3) will be regarded as more or less acceptable. There are two broad issues to be considered. One is the impossibility of bridge laws, and I will start with a discussion of this alleged fact, supposed to follow from the key premise (2). (Possibly many philosophers would like to quarrel with premise (2), but I accept it, although I do not accept psychologism and take this to be consistent; cf. Tuomela, 1987.) The remainder of the paper will concern premise (1) and the conception of science on which it relies. But I will start with bridge laws and thus for the sake of argument accept that they are needed in the sense premise (1) specifies.

(2) Searle's arguments against bridge laws (of the standard kind) are based on the possibility of multiple realization of social and psychological predicates (premises (3) and (5)). Let us first consider the possibility of macro–micro laws where the microbasis is taken to consist of suitable psychological, social psychological, and physical properties (or predicates). What effect does the open-endedness argument have here? My first suggestion is that we take the relation between the social and the individual level to be a suitable kind of supervenience relation (cf. e.g. Kim, 1984; Tuomela, 1989c for the notion).[1] To put the matter crudely, the supervenience thesis says that if a putatively social object or system and it replica share all their microproperties, then they will (and under so-called strong supervenience, necessarily so) share all their macroproperties. Now strong supervenience even gives necessary coextension, namely each macroproperty is necessrily coextensive with a possibly infinite disjunction of microproperties. The existence of this kind of necessary bridge connection is compatible with the open-endedness argument. Of course we may not know (nor generally have epistemic or conceptual access to) this infinite basis and in this sense we may fail to have macro–micro laws. But we would still have a required kind of connection, for we are here only discussing the world in metaphysical terms not in terms of its accessibility to us. (See Tuomela, 1989b,c, for a detailed argument of this in the case of actions predicated to collectives.) If again we do not get strong supervenience, we might still have weak supervenience, in which case the microbasis does not determine (in the sense of supervenience) the macrobasis, but there is still a kind of macro–micro connection which might satisfy an individualist. So I conclude that supervenience may give a suitable macro–micro connection which is immune to Searle's argument. Whether it is reasonable to think that we indeed have supervenience (or even can have it) still requires more investigation, but I have in any case tried to make a case for it in Tuomela (1989c).

Thus we have here grounds for doubting (4) and (5) and thus (6) and (7) of Searle's above argument.

At this point it is appropriate to note that Searle is claiming more than that there cannot be any holistic social laws. He is also claiming that there cannot be any psychological and social psychological laws in many interesting cases. Put in terms of the individualism–holism debate as it is typically conducted nowadays within the philosophy of social science, Searle's first claim concerns the impossibility of holistic social laws while his second claim concerns the impossibility of individualistic laws. (This sense of individualism is of course quite different from the kind of individualism currently discussed within the context of methodological solipsism in the philosophy of cognitive science.) Those interesting cases where we do not get even individualistic laws involve so-called wide (or noninternal) psychological and social states or properties, roughly speaking states or properties which logically presuppose the existence of other entities than the person (or entity) having them. States of belief about money are a good example of such states. They are not supervenient on internal psychological states nor are they supervenient on internal brain states (see e.g. Kim, 1982, for a good discussion). So it seems that while my above point about explicating macro–micro connections in terms of supervenience seems to work in the holistic social case (cf. Searle's premise (1)), it does not work in the case of connecting the microbasis of that analysis, namely internal and noninternal psychological and social psychological states and properties, with brain states (see, e.g., the discussion in Tuomela, 1989a). Do we then have to undertake this larger project of supervenience as well? We do (in some sense of supervenience closely connected to at least token materialism) if we accept Searle's premise (2) (as I do) and his general idea of – should I say – unity of science in the sense of successive microgroundings down to the level of microphysical entities or at least molecular physical entities (cf. his premise (2)).

Let us here go with Searle at least for the sake of argument. What should we – and can we – say concerning the problem of open-endedness? To give this matter a little airing consider again Searle's argument about seeing or believing that something is money. Searle claimed, we recall, that because of its indefinite range of physical forms money will have an indefinite range of stimulus effects on people's nervous systems. And it would be a miracle if they all produced exactly the same neurophysiological effects on the brain. But now a critic of Searle could argue as follows in response to this. Searle's point about the "miracle" is weak, he would say. For the fact that diverse physical forms of money are possible just involves, to put the matter in rough terms, that the brain makes them relevantly similar, and thus we have what is needed. After all, isn't it the product of the brain that we have this indefinite physical set of realizations of money, in accordance with premise (2)? For, the critic continues, we conventionally take money to be represented by such and such physical forms. The similarity here lies in the internalized convention or taking, understood as a mental fact or, better, as an internal brain fact. And, furthermore, consider, for example, seeing a stone, a stree, or whatever nonsocial. We seem to have an indefinite set of stimulus conditions here as well, and we need about the same amount and kind of learning in all these cases to establish the relevantly similar brain connections. So in all Searle's argument proves too much. So says our critic, at least.

While the critic's position is at least conceptually possible. I regard it as false in general. For it amounts to accepting the so-called Explanatory Thesis of methodological solipsism (cf. Kim, 1982; Stich, 1983), and I have elsewhere argued that this thesis is incorrect (see Tuomela, 1989a). It claims that psychological laws and explanations can be stated in terms of internal psychological states only. Furthermore, these states are argued by methodological solipsists to be supervenient on internal brain states, and this, if true, would satisfy Searle, too. I shall not here discuss this possibility in detail. Instead I would like to point out another line of thought. It is that while believing that something is money and analogous noninternal psychological states are not supervenient on internal brain states, nor in any other way connectable by means of bridge principles to such brain states as Searle's premise (5) requires, perhaps they are still supervenient on the basis consisting of brain states and relevant environmental physical states (involving for example the different physical forms of money and what have you). Searle has not presented any arguments against this possibility, which I regard – *prima facie* – as a viable candidate (which still is individualistic in my mentioned sense of the word). Yet I shall not here investigate it more deeply. So my conclusion concerning Searle's premise (5) is that it seems acceptable when understood to concern only brain states on the physical side. But if other relevant physical states are allowed in the basis it may well prove to be false.

(3)   I will now proceed to Searle's premise (1). It can be criticized from various points of view. First, a social holist may refuse to accept the requirement of individualistic reduction in the sense of this premise. He can even accept the standard account of theories but deal only with holistic terminology (cf. Searle's examples of social laws involving holistic social concepts such as revolution, war, etc.). A social holist does not need the kind of individualistic backing required by Searle. However, if one accepts Searle's premise (2) or is otherwise an individualist one needs some kind of microgrounding – at least ultimately and in principle. And as this is my position (and as I don't know how to defend holism), I will not consider further this potential criticism of (1).

The next possibility concerning (1) that interests us is that one indeed needs macro–micro bridge laws or principles but that they need not be of the kind Searle envisages. Above we in fact discussed this possibility in terms of supervenience. We noted that supervenience may give bridge connections which however need not be epistemically accessible or manageable. This would give a way of falsifying (1) which falls within the standard construal of theories. A third possibility is simply to give up the standard account of theories while at the same time accepting some kind of requirement of individualist grounding of holistic social talk. This is the position I advocate (see Tuomela, 1985, chapters 5 and 9, and cf. Sellars, 1963). One can give both philosophical and scientific grounds to give up the standard account (and Searle's account, to the extent it does not quite coincide with the standard account). My philosophical reasons are to a great extent Sellarsian. The standard account is wrong as it relies on an unacceptable levels-view of science ultimately relying on an unacceptable version of the Myth of the Given (cf. Tuomela, 1985, chapters 4 and 5). Instead, explanatory theories explain laws and generalizations (e.g. holistic social ones) not by subsumption, as in the standard account, but by explaining directly the individual instances of the generalizations by redescribing them in the terminology of the reducing theory and by showing them to be instances of the explaining theories in question to the extent that the generalization in question is a correct one (and thereby both falsifies and corrects that generalization). I shall not here make an attempt to justify this eliminativist approach – see the mentioned works.

Accordingly I claim that one could possibly have individualistically acceptable social laws given the eliminativist view of scientific explanation. This can be, and is, backed not only by philosophical considerations but also by scientific ones (see below). We can and should be eliminativists – and let folk sociology be as wrong or right as it may and will turn out to be. To present a couple of scientific examples favoring our eliminativist and correctivist view, consider first Searle's physical example, the micro-reduction of phenomenological gas laws in terms of the kinetic theory of the gases. This is not as smooth a case as Searle argues. For we really have two different macro gas concepts here. For instance, we have phenomenological gas temperature and then the macro temperature construed as mean kinetic energy. There is no strict and smooth reduction of phenomenological gas laws into kinetic theory in the old-fashioned positivistic sense. Instead we have counterpart laws for phenomenological laws construed in terms of micro-notions (i.e. laws of kinetic theory that preserve some image of the format structure of the laws in the reduced theory) and strictly speaking gases and their phenomenological properties as originally construed are eliminated from the reducing theory, or so at least a realist may interpret the situation (cf. Churchland, 1979). Analogously macrophysical things (conceived in terms of classical or even in terms of relativistic physics) do not reduce as smoothly to microthings as Searle seems to think and as his premise (1) requires. (In those situations Planck's constant must counterfactually be required to approach zero in order to have reduction.) In general, in physical cases of macro–micro reduction there will be some slack and the picture painted by Searle of the physical situation is not correct. In fact, we seem not to have any factual reductions in science which would be smooth and strict and accord with the standard conception of explanation.

As to the social sciences, there is accordingly no good reason to expect smooth microreductions either. And it would not matter so much even if there is – as there probably will be – more slack in the social case than in the physical cases. So whether or not Searle is right in that there cannot be strict bridge laws, we may still possibly have social laws in a weaker, individualistically acceptable sense (namely, individualistically redescribed sense). Or if not, that is, if folk sociology turns out to be irreparably wrong, we may still possibly get counterpart social laws as it were, e.g. laws construed on the basis of a brand new cognitive (social) science.

Let me still note a couple of consequences ensuing from the acceptance of an eliminativist position. First, related to the above open-endedness problem we now get new possibilities for blocking it, for new categorizations of the individualistic basis may help make it finitely or (somehow) recursively treatable. Second, no bridge laws are needed as the social realm is described directly in individualistically acceptable terminology. Accordingly the new possibilities that future cognitive science may or will give us may change the situation as the explanadum, holistic social talk, will (or at least may) be redescribed and recategorized. Then the examples on the basis of which Searle's argumentation has proceeded may also change in some sense affecting his argument, for example "belief" (or whatever linguistic item plays its counterpart role) would then refer to a somewhat different notion, and so on.

Let me just add here that if my argumentation is correct (that is, if his premise (1) is not acceptable and if either no bridge laws are needed or if they are, openendedness does not block that) it follows not only that – despite the difficulties posed by contextual dependencies and historicality, and what have you – there can be social laws but also that nomological social science and intentionality can coexist. There is, by the way, no necessity to insist on a strict dichotomy of law-like versus accidental generalizations, and we can be happy with, say, probabilistic social laws or tendency laws with varying degrees on nomologicality (cf. contextual dependency and historicality). I accept what Searle says about the role of intentionality in the social sciences, and have in fact analyzed that role much as Searle, but I shall not here go into those intricate issues.

NOTES

1   The notions of weak and strong supervenience can be characterized as follows, where A and B are respectively the supervening property-set and the base set:

Weak supervenience: The set A supervenes on the set B if and only if necessrily for any state F in A, if an entity x has F, then there exists a state G in B such that x has G, and if any y has G it has F.

Strong supervenience: The set A supervenes on the set B if and only if necessarily for any state F in A, if an entity x has F, then there exists a state G in B such that x has G, and necessarily if any y has G it has F.

REFERENCES

Braithwaite, R. B. (1953), *Scientific Explanation* (Cambridge University Press: Cambridge).
Churchland, P. (1979), *Scientific Realism and the Plasticity of Mind* (Cambridge University Press: Cambridge).
Kim, J. (1982), "Psychophysical Supervenience", *Philosophical Studies 41*, pp. 51–70.
Searle, J. (1984), *Minds, Brains and Science* (British Broadcasting Corporation: London).
Stich, S. (1983), *From Folk Psychology to Cognitive Science* (MIT Press: Cambridge, Mass.).
Tuomela, R. (1985), *Science, Action, and Reality* (Reidel: Dordrecht).
Tuomela, R. (1989a), "Is Methodological Solipsism a Tenable Doctrine?", *Philosophy of Science* 56, pp. 23–47.
Tuomela, R. (1989b), "Actions by Collectives", in *Philosophical Perspectives 3*, ed. J. Tomberlin (Ridgeview Publishing Co.: Atascadevo, Cal.), pp. 471–96.
Tuomela, R. (1989c), "Collective Action, Supervenience, and Constitution", *Synthese* 80, pp. 243–66.

22

On Explanation in Psychology

IRVIN ROCK

In one of the chapters in John Searle's book *Minds, Brains and Science* (1985), he argues that there is no need for explanatory concepts about thought and behavior other than those given in terms of neurophysiology, of events in the brain or those of common-sense intentional psychology. His target is cognitivism, which, by his definition, is the belief that the best way to study cognition is to study computational-symbol-manipulating programs. Presumably, though, he would apply the argument to any other kind of theorizing about cognition and behavior that falls between common-sense explanations in the language of intentionality and neurophysiological explanations. "All the gap-filling efforts fail because there isn't any gap to fill" (Ibid., p. 72). In taking this position, Searle challenges the entire enterprise of psychology as it has been practiced since its inception as an experimental science 100 years ago.

This essay should be read as the thoughts of an investigator of cognition reacting to the thoughts of John Searle the philosopher as to what kinds of explanation are necessary in psychology. It may be worth noting that not every investigator in the field of cognition subscribes to the tenets of information processing, cognivitism (as defined by Searle), or the computational approach. There is a tradition in psychology that antedates these approaches and it seems to me to be important to examine how Searle's imperative about the inexistence of an explanatory gap between folk psychology and brain theory would apply to this traditional approach.

To begin with, we should not confuse two meanings of "level." It is true, with respect to mind, that there is no ontological level of events other than intentional on the one hand and neurophysiological on the other. That is, there are mental events and there are brain events (some would collapse these into one). However, that does not imply that there is no useful level of *explanation* other than those that can be given in mental terms or in terms of neurophysiology. I shall argue that not only is such a level of explanation possible, but that it is absolutely indispensable.

Psychologists will agree with Searle that all cognition, feeling states, motivation, and behavior, in short anything and everything that is psychological, is caused by neural events in the nervous system. Therefore, we can maintain that *ultimately* we will arrive at explanations at the level of brain events. Nonetheless, there are reasons why this argument is misleading. First, such explanation is a long way off, and there is much in the way of gap-filling theorizing that can be done in the meanwhile that

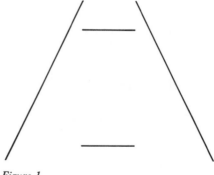

Figure 1

has the character of explanation. Second, and more importantly, it is deceptive to think that an explanation couched purely in terms of neurophysiology would be an intelligible explanation unless it is accompanied by an explanatory statement in non-physiological language. In fact, I will argue that without the achievement of such a non-physiological explanation, investigators of brain processes would not even know what to look for. In the remainder of this paper I shall try to illustrate these points with examples drawn from the study of perception and cognition.

In figure 1, illustrating the Ponzo illusion, the upper horizontal line looks somewhat longer than the lower one. No doubt we will some day be able to say that the neurophysiological correlate underlying our perception of the upper line is such-and-such and that the lower line is a different such-and-such, presumably smaller along some dimension that corresponds to length. But such an explanation in and of itself would be incomplete. We would want to know why these neural correlates differ with respect to magnitude. In any event we are a long way from achieving any kind of brain explanation of even such a circumscribed phenomenon as this illusion.

In the meanwhile, psychologists have been studying illusions. One hypothesis is that the Ponzo illusion is the result of inappropriate depth processing (Gregory, 1968; Gillam, 1980). We now know that size perception is based not only on the visual angle subtended by an object at the eye (or the size of the retinal image representing it) but by the distance at which the object is perceived to be. Thus, the constancy of perceived size in daily life despite variation in the distance of an object – and thus variation in its visual angle – is based on a process that integrates visual angle and distance information. Something like a multiplication of visual angle times encoded distance information occurs. The corollary of this same process of integration is that when the visual angle remains *constant* with variation of distance, the object must appear larger the greater its perceived distance. This corollary is roughly equivalent to what has been referred to as Emmert's Law. In passing, I might mention that the corollary can explain the moon illusion, the fact that the moon over the horizon looks much larger than the moon in elevation. The presence of the terrain below the horizon moon provides information that it is quite far away, whereas the elevated moon is an isolated object surrounded by sky, thus excluding information about its distance (Kaufman and Rock, 1962; Rock and Kaufman, 1962).

The explanation as applied to the Ponzo Illusion is this: The converging lines suggest depth based on the perspective cue. Therefore, the upper line is taken to be farther away than the lower one. If farther, given its visual angle *equal* to the lower line, it must appear longer. But since we are looking at a two-dimensional drawing not intended as a picture of a three-dimensional scene, the depth effect is inappropriate and so we call it an illusion. What we have here is a functional explanation, one that describes the kind of process that is assumed to occur.

Let us assume that this explanation is correct at least qualitatively and that all investigators agree about it. (In point of fact, it is probably at least part of the story, but not all of it.) Is this *not* an explanation according to the position Searle takes? Note that it is certainly not a common-sense or intentionalistic explanation either. I would say that it not only is an explanation, but that without it we would neither understand nor know what to look for at the level of brain process. Moreover, it will have to accompany the explanation at the level of brain events once we achieve it, if the latter is to be at all intelligible.

The argument here about explanation is analogous to one that can be made about explanation of the origin of species. Darwin's theory was a functional explanation stated in terms of concepts such as common ancestry, adaptation to the environment, survival of the fittest, variation and natural selection. When he advanced his explanation he had no knowledge about the genetic mutations that accounted for the emergence of species variation. The genetic change explains the variation that Darwin knew was necessary to explain evolution. Now that we do know about the mechanism, it does not mean that we no longer require Darwin's principles to explain evolution. The genetic mechanism cannot stand alone as explanation because in and of itself it only explains the emergence of altered characteristics in the species.

To the argument about the necessity of functional explanation in psychology, Searle may respond by maintaining that they are couched in the language of intentionality. Thus, they only masquerade as a different level of explanation but in fact are intentional statements using somewhat more precise or sophisticated language. The statement "the integration of visual angle and distance information" in size perception can be restated as "inferring perceived size by taking account of distance."

Well there is some truth in this argument but it suggests that we need to make certain distinctions within the domain of intentional statements. On the one hand we have common sense, folk psychology explanations such as those that make sense of behavior by inputing motives, emotions and beliefs to people. These seem to me to be very different from explanatory statements that (a) have not been known by grandmothers no matter how wise they may be, (b) are based on careful controlled observation and represent generalizations or hypotheses about the nature of a psychological process, (c) are subject to experimental test and are stated so as to be disconfirmable, (d) often entail quantitive relationships (e.g. perceived size = visual angle × perceived distance), (e) lead to predictions of new phenomena (e.g. we could predict the moon illusion from the law of size constancy even if it had never been observed), and (f) are considered to be statements that refer to processes that ultimately can be stated in terms of brain events, indeed that tell us what kind of brain events to look for. Therefore, it would seem to be evident that the enterprise associated with the achievement of functional explanations follow the dictates of scientific method. The psychology of perception and cognition is advancing, ever so slowly, beyond folk psychology. In fact folk psychology has had relatively little to say about cognitive aspects of mind. I, therefore, submit that we should distinguish folk psychology intentional explanations from functional explanatory statements that may sometimes make use of intentional language.

If the understanding of brain mechanisms depends upon the prior explication of the relevant process in non-physiological terms, the opposite is also true: the discovery of a brain mechanism prior to an understanding of the process more often than not leads to the peculiar situations of our not understanding precisely what the discovery means. A good example of this state of affairs is the landmark discovery of cortical cells that seem to be detectors of certain stimulus patterns on the retina, such as an edge or contour in a particular orientation (Hubel and Wiesel, 1962). The question is how such detectors explain the perception of form and the organization of the visual field into discrete objects or figures on background. For example, should we now believe that the perception of a triangle is based on the firing of those cells in the cortex that detect the three-edges in their particular orientation? There would be many difficulties with such an elementaristic approach. There are now different speculations about what these orientation detector cells are "doing" at the functional level (DeValois and DeValois, 1980; Koenderink & Van Doorn, 1987).

A discovery of this kind often leads to what the *Gestalt* psychologists Karl Duncker (1945) and Max Wertheimer (1945) referred to as problem-solving from below. In the example under discussion, the nature of the thought process is this: What role in perception should we assign to these cells? How can the firing of these cells explain perception? By way of contrast, in problem-solving from above, one asks how the organized perception of objects in the visual field might come about (without being fettered by the knowledge of edge detectors) and only after formulating a plausible account does one look for a specific mechanism by which the process could be achieved. For all we now know, the "edge detector" cells may not enter into the process of parsing of the field into distinct objects or the achievement of phenomenal shape but may play some entirely different role. In that event thinking "from below" in terms of edges would be a tactical scientific error.

In contrast to this example about the discovery of edge-detector cells is the recent discovery of cells that apparently detect retinal disparity (Barlow et al., 1967). In this case we have known a good deal about depth from Wheatstone's (1838) brilliant (but non-physiological) analysis and demonstrations with the stereoscope. Thus we already understood what kind of stimulation of the two eyes gave rise to the perception of depth. With such knowledge in hand we knew to look for a certain kind of mechanism and, once found, knew how to interpret it.

Another example underscores the fact that brain theorizing is usually premature. Consider the fact that the appearance of objects and figures is a function of their orientation, as noted by Ernst Mach in the case of the square that looks like a diamond when tilted by 45 degrees, shown in figure 2. We now know that this is a very general phenomenon often resulting in failure to recognize an object when it is oriented differently than its customary one (see figure 3). Suppose investigators

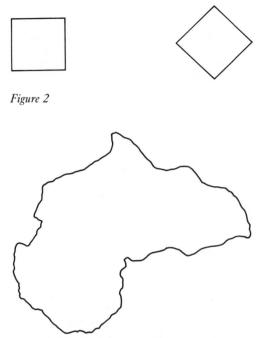

Figure 2

Figure 3 This figure is not as such readily identifiable. However, if rotated through 90 degrees clockwise it will immediately be recognized as the shape of: ʇo ʇuǝuᴉʇuoɔ ǝɥʇ ˙ɐɔᴉɹɟⱯ

following the Searle imperative begin searching for an explanation in terms of neurophysiology. A very obvious fact immediately comes to mind. The disoriented figure stimulates the retina in an orientation very different from that yielded by the figure when it is upright. Therefore, one might say that the stimulus of the disoriented figure impinging on the retina is totally different and that consequently the figure ought to look different. Thus, one might think that this phenomenon is no more of a problem than the fact that geometrically different shapes give rise to differently perceived shapes.

However, Wolfgang Köhler (1940), one of the founding fathers of *Gestalt* psychology, was puzzled by the orientation effect because he and his fellow *Gestaltists* had emphasized the transposability of forms both visual and auditory as illustrating the importance of stimulus relationships. If a figure does not look different when it is enlarged or diminished, why should it look different when it is tilted or inverted? The internal geometry of the figure is unchanged. As a possible answer, he suggested that the visual cortex is not isotropic. There is a biochemical gradient within it whose direction is fixed. In changing a figure's orientation we change the orientation of the projection of its retinal image to the visual cortex. The projection thus "sits" quite differently with respect to the gradient for a figure that

Figure 4

is, let us say, inverted than when it is upright. Using + and − to characterize the gradient, figure 4 shows that an upright A points toward one direction of the gradient and an inverted A to a different direction. Therefore, the neural processes are quite different in the two cases.

The trouble with this theory is almost embarrassingly simple. If one tilts one's head by 45 degrees in viewing a figure such as a square, the orientation of the retinal image is also transformed to that of a "diamond." Does the square look like a diamond? I have shown by simple experiment that it does not. In further research I have shown that what matters for orientation effects in perception is not the orientation of the object's image on the retina but the manner in which the mind assigns directions to the object. If sensory and other kinds of information suggest that a corner of the square is its top and not one of the sides, then it will look like a diamond, regardless of the orientation of the figure's image on the retina. Further work advanced our understanding of orientation effects and the kind of mechanism that leads to them but there is no need to go into this research here (see Rock, 1973.) Suffice it to say that the explanations advanced are functional, i.e. they are couched in language that describes the *kind* of event that occurs and not directly in terms of neural processes. These explanations are independent of any facts about neurons and the workings of the brain and they presuppose nothing about the details of the underlying neural causes. The lesson here would seem to be that there is much progress that can be achieved, indeed that *must* be achieved, before we try to translate explanation to the level of neurophysiological events.

Still another consideration is this. Physiological explanations of psychological phenomena are bound to be constrained by our limited knowledge of the brain. Thus, they will generally be simplistic and not do justice to the psychological facts. Certainly the history of perception is replete with examples of this kind. For example, it was once thought that the explanation of the perception of lightness of surfaces on the white–gray–black continuum was the rate of firing of the neurons emanating from the region of the retina stimulated by the surface in question. But this account can hardly do justice to the fact that a white surface in shadow will continue to look white and a black one in sunlight will continue to look black. The luminance of the latter (a physical measure of the intensity of reflected light) can easily be thousands of times greater than that of the former. We refer to this fact as lightness (or, formerly, brightness) constancy.

Therefore, some time later a more sophisticated theory was proposed based on the known fact that the neural firing in one region can suppress or inhibit the firing in another neighboring region (Hering, 1905; Hurvich and Jameson, 1964;

Cornsweet, 1970). This physiological fact, referred to as lateral inhibition, was then used to explain lightness constancy. Suppose the black surface is on a white background. When the black-on-white surface is in sunlight, while the black surface does reflect much more light to the eyes than when it is indoors or in shadow, the white background reflects even more. The latter thus inhibits the former so that the effective rate of firing of the black region remains low even in sunlight.

There are many difficulties with this theory that are discussed elsewhere (Rock, 1975, 1983; Gilchrist, 1979) and I believe it is incorrect. Thus it illustrates the prematurity of physiological explanation by virtue of our very limited knowledge of the brain. In contrast to this kind of theory much progress has been made in understanding what kind of process goes on in the perception of lightness without recourse to neurophysiology. The task for a physiological explanation of the perception of lightness is then seen to be much more difficult than has been thought to be the case.

An interesting example of a construct employed by psychologists over the past century is that of the memory trace. All that is meant by trace is some enduring state in the brain that represents a prior experience. Logically it has seemed to psychologists that it is absolutely necessary to assume that some state of the brain must endure over time that represents prior experiences. Otherwise how can we explain the causal effect of the past on the present. Thus, the trace construct is compatible with the widely accepted notion that the cause of an effect is cotemporaneous with the effect. Therefore, there is virtually no alternative to the assumption of the memory trace. Although the definition above acknowledges the trace's ontological status as a neural or biochemical state of the brain – which in principle is eventually knowable – the concept has been put to good use without attempting to say exactly what the state of the brain is that is the correlate of the memory. Indeed, since we have no idea about the physiological underpinning of traces, we could not theorize at all if that were a requirement. Moreover, to begin with some theory about the trace *qua* physiological state is to place ourselves unnecessarily in a straitjacket insofar as dealing with the many known facts about memory is concerned.

An argument that Professor Searle is likely to make, indeed has made in discussion if not in print, is that what I am here calling a level of explanation other than a brain-event level is nothing more than speculative neurophysiologizing. One might say, for example, that a "trace" is indeed a state of the brain. Well, to the extent that psychological events are always caused by brain events, of course all attempted explanations in psychology can be regarded as temporary substitutes for brain-process explanations. But this would miss the point. We need to understand what kind of process occurs when we have a certain kind of experience or when we behave in a certain way and we need to know about it in functional terms. To repeat what I have already said, without it we will neither know what to look for in the brain nor understand how the brain event, once uncovered, explains the experience or the behavior.

How have psychologists made use of the trace concept? One example derives from *Gestalt* psychology. It was argued by the *Gestalt*ists that perception is governed by a tendency for it to become as simple and regular as the prevailing conditions allow. This was their notion of prägnanz. By "prevailing conditions" they meant chiefly the nature of the impinging stimulus. Thus, an irregular quadrilateral image on the retina of a figure in the frontal plane could not be expected to lead to the perception of a regular square despite the tendency for perception to be directed at that end-state. But an *ambiguous* figure that has the potential to be perceived in either of two ways can be expected to be perceived in whichever of these ways is simpler. Moreover, to return to the irregular square example, once the stimulus is removed, the constraint no longer applies. Now the memory trace can be expected to transform itself in the prägnant direction. How can we test this prediction? By requiring subjects who have been shown the irregular quadrilateral to draw it from memory and to do so at varying intervals. The prediction is that sisnce the trace is undergoing transformation over time in the direction of increasing regularity, the mental representation during the moment of remembering must reflect that state of the trace. Research on this theory has been carried out over the past half-century with various improvements in methodology that need not concern us here. One improvement worth mentioning, however, is the use of recognition to test the prediction. If a trace whose initial state was condition A and later is changed to condition B, then a figure in a recognition test that resembles A should not be recognized whereas one that resembles B should be recognized.

Let us suppose that the *Gestalt*ists were correct about prägnant memory change. Then we have added to our construct of trace the notion of forces at work that transform traces toward simpler configurations in the manner that soap bubbles, crystals and other physical structures illustrate the tendency toward a regular or symmetrical end-state.

It is quite valuable to be able to theorize in cognition in terms of the trace concept. It tends to bring certain problems into sharp focus that otherwise might escape us. For example, suppose one believes, as many do, that perception is affected by prior experience. There are some – but not many – experiments that show this. We might translate this belief and say that traces of prior perceptions affect ongoing perceptions. But just this simple re-statement of the past-experience view is to immediately make clear a very difficult problem. If a trace is to affect perception we must assume that it is accessed or aroused or contacted because, after all, there are countless other traces which presumably have no effect on the perception in question. We must assume that only the appropriate trace is at work. Well then how is that trace activated *before* the current perception under study is achieved? After all, in the ordinary course of events, we would say that a perception occurs first. Then, if there are traces that are similar to it, we recognize the object. Note in passing that we are explaining recognition on the basis of the accessing of an appropriate trace. It is widely believed by investigators of perception and cognition that recognition is based on the similarity of a percept of a memory trace (or entire family of traces if the object has been seen repeatedly in the past).[1]

If, therefore, traces are normally accessed *after* the perception has taken place – or how else would the necessary similarity come about – then how can it be that the reverse would happen, that the appropriate trace would be accessed *before* the perception was realized? Unless that occurs beforehand how could it be that the trace can affect the perception? I do not propose to try to answer that question here, although it would be nice to believe that I have aroused the curiosity of the reader about this problem. The important point is to show that the concretization of memory into the trace construct is heuristic.

Another example of the utility of the trace concept concerns forgetting. Suppose you cannot remember a woman's name on meeting her again. One might think that the physical repository of the memory has been lost. However, the fact is that you feel that you do have the memory but cannot now access it. You may feel that the name is on the tip of your tongue and you may (correctly) believe that, for example, it is a one syllable name beginning with a particular letter. Moreover, if now given several alternative names, you can immediately tell which is correct. To deal with these facts it is plausible to believe that (1) the trace is indeed still intact, as it were, unchanged in fact from the time it was formed, (2) traces are readily accessed by a high-similarity percept and that is why you can do so when told the name, and (3) traces are sometimes difficult to access by the associative connection that exists between them and other items. Thus, we can conclude that the associative connection between face and name has been formed. It endures in the form of trace connection. Nonetheless, accessing the face portion of the overall face–name trace (which results in recognition of the face) does not guarantee easy passage to the name portion of the trace although (4) some general aspects of that name trace do rise to consciousness, as witness the content of the tip-of-tongue experience.

Continuing with the topic of memory for the moment, it seems to me that we did learn one very important fact about it from the tradition launched by Ebbinghaus (1885/1913) of studying memory with the use of nonsense syllables. We learned that the major cause of forgetting was not the mere passage of time following the stage at which material is learned, a kind of erosion of the trace by metabolic processes or the like, but rather was the result of the interference brought about by the learning of other similar content either after the original learning (retroactive inhibition) or before that learning (proactive inhibition). I might add that the nature of this forgetting is primarily that the interference with the *accessing* of the material in question rather than that of obliterating the traces of this material, because, if recognition or matching tests are used rather than recall tests, there is much less forgetting evidenced in spite of the interference generated by the learning before or after of other material.

Moreover, we can make some general statements about the temporal relationships between the interfering and interfered with material, about similarity relationships, and about various other relevant parameters. So one might fairly say that we have uncovered various lawful relationships about forgetting. And, surely this goes well beyond folk psychology which, if anything, seems to emphasize the wrong idea, namely that the passage of time is the cause of forgetting.

To be sure, we are talking here about lawful generalizations about forgetting derived from controlled experimentation rather than theoretical explanation that would make these generalizations understandable. Nonetheless, these generalizations constitute scientific knowledge about mental phenomena although they say little about specific brain mechanism. Besides, one can go on to theorize about traces and how the interaction or amalgamation of them can lead to difficulty in accessing the required one. Indeed the *Gestalt* psychologists did just this in their reference to what they called the "crowding" of traces when they were similar to one another as compared to the "isolation" of those that were distinctly different.

Investigators of brain correlates of remembering and forgetting would be well advised to address the question of how the presence of other, similar material has the deleterious effect that it does on remembering. When and if such correlates are uncovered, a complete explanation, I should think, would be one that refers to interference and to how it is manifested in neurophysiological terms such as to make assessing of memories difficult.[2]

It seems to me that the concept of trace is more immune to the criticism that one might make of some of the other examples of psychological explanations I have given in this eassy. As I noted, some of these explanatory statements can be said to be formulated in the language of intentionality. However, "trace" is an example of a hypothetical construct analogous to such constructs as atom and gene. If a trace (atom, gene) is assumed to exist with such and such properties then it would explain such and such facts about memory and recall (matter, inheritance). The trace is the bearer of intentional content, but has properties independent of specific content and is independent of any particular neurophysiological realization. Speaking for myself, I have the feeling that we are truly explaining various memory phenomena when we are grounding them in the behavior and properties of the memory trace.

These examples suffice to illustrate the argument that explanation in psychology must be such as to refer in nonphysiological terms to the kind of process that is taking place. When and if we have said all there is to say on this level, the ultimate explanation underlying these uncovered processes will be in terms of brain events. I would argue that the history of psychology both before and during the 100 years since its birth as an experimental science in Wundt's laboratory at Leipzig is a history of a succession of theories cast in language that is not physiological, such as: association; unconscious inference; the law of effect; perceptual organization; prägnanz; relational determination; repression; super ego; priming and spreading activation; suggestion; cognitive dissonance; imprinting; conservation; and so forth.

The issue is not whether any of these concepts endured or were fruitful, but whether they have the status of explanation and go beyond intentional psychology. I have deliberately chosen these examples because they are not simply matters of common sense. As to whether they have the status of explanation, I submit that they do, even if incorrect. To be sure, these concepts have the potential of being translated into events in the brain but, in the meanwhile, they can stand on their own and, to repeat what I've been saying throughout, such ultimate brain-process statements would be wholly unintelligible without accompanying statements of the kind of process they are generating.

Summary

It is time to sum up. Searle has argued that there is no gap to be filled between common-sense explanation of mind in the language of intentionality and explanations of mind in terms of neurophysiological processes in the brain. While agreeing that from the standpoint of *ontology* there is no level other than mind and brain, I have maintained that there is an indispensable level of *explanation* between the two. Before we search for brain-process accounts of mind we must first achieve an understanding of what kind of process occurs that gives rise to a particular phenomenal experience or behavior, a functional explanation.

Among the arguments I have made in support of this position are these:

We will not be able to understand the meaning of the neurophysiological event that underlies a mental event unless the former is accompanied by a functional explanation.

We will not know what kind of brain process to look for unless we first clarify what it is that the brain event is supposed to achieve. Intentional or folk psychology accounts of what kind of process causes a psychological phenomenon are generally inadequate.

Explanations offered in terms of brain mechanism at this time are bound to be simplistic and premature and, if the mandate is to seek only this kind of explanation, we are restricting ourselves unnecessarily by requiring that we think in terms of the little that is now known about the brain.

Discoveries of brain mechanisms in advance of understanding functionally how perceptions and cognitions work often leaves us in the odd situation of not knowing what to make of the discovery.

While functional descriptions of psychological processes may sometimes be couched in the language of intentionality, that does not mean that they are no more explanatory than folk psychology as practiced by our grandmothers.

Moreover, some functional explanations are not couched in intentionality language but make use of hypothetical constructs analogous to explanation in physics or biology.

Such explanations ought not to be dismissed as nothing more than speculative neurophysiology simply because it is true that anything we say now about mind in non-physiological language will some day be translatable into such language.

Ultimately, when there is nothing more to explicate on a psychological level, brain mechanisms will provide an explanation of mind, but even then such deeper explanations cannot stand alone.

NOTES

1   Professor Searle (1985) brings up the example of face recognition and concludes that it may be "as simple and as automatic as making footprints in the sand" (p. 52). The brain just does it, he says. Analogously, in discussing vision in general, he says. "We are neurophysiologically so constructed that the assault of photons on our photoreceptor cells enables us to see – " (p. 53). He may well be right that, however the brain achieves facial recognition, it does not entail a complex computational process or the utilization of rules. But the process must surely be such that a certain memory is accessed on the basis of similarity.
2   I should think that Professor Searle would like the concept of trace for the following reason. The trace must be the repository of meaning. The first time a child sees a hammer it is simply a certain three-dimensional shape. So the memory of that perception will represent little more than the shape. But after many experiences in which the child sees how the hammer is used, memories are acquired that refer to such things as the swinging of the hammer by an arm, the driving of nails into wood, the noise it makes, and so forth. These memories are also represented by traces and they are all associated with the shape of the hammer. Eventually then we can say that the hammer has meaning for the child because the mere sight of it leads to the accessing of these associated trace components. Still later, the *word* hammer has the potential of eliciting these traces. Thus, traces would be the embodiments of the associated intentional states that Searle (1983) refers to as the network. Therefore, trace theory can deal with semantic content whereas computer programs are by definition purely syntactical; the symbols that are manipulated have no meaning. To be sure, states of the machine can be said to represent memories, but they too are purely syntactical and, in any event, that does not do

322   *Irvin Rock*

justice to the conscious experience that accompanies associated trace evocation that occurs when an observer sees a hammer.

REFERENCES

Barlow, H. B., Blakemore, C. and Pettigrew, J. D. (1967) "The neural mechanism of binocular depth discrimination," *Journal of Physiology* 193, pp. 327–42.
Cornsweet, T. N. (1970) *Visual Perception* (Academic Press: New York).
DeValois, R. and DeValois, K. (1980) "Spatial vision," *Annual Review of Psychology* 31, pp. 304–41.
Duncker, K. (1945) "On problem solving," *Psychological Monographs* 58, pp. 1–112.
Ebbinghaus, H. (1885/1913) *Memory*, trans. H. A. Ruger and C. E. Bussenius (Teachers College: New York).
Gilchrist, A. (1979) "The perception of surface blacks and whites," *Scientific American* 240, pp. 112–26.
Gillam, B. (1980) "Geometrical illusions," *Scientific American* 242, pp. 102–11.
Gregory, R. (1968) "Visual illusions," *Sciencitific American* 219, pp. 66–76.
Hering, E. (1905/1964) *Outlines of the Theory of the Light Sense*, translated by L. Hurvich and D. Jameson (Harvard University Press: Cambridge, Mass.).
Hubel, D. H. and Wiesel, T. N. (1962) "Receptive fields, binocular interaction, and functional architecture in the cat's visual cortex," *Journal of Physiology* 160, pp. 106–54.
Hurvich, L. and Jameson, D. (1964) "Theory of brightness and color contrast in human vision," *Vision Research* 4, pp. 135–54.
Kaufman, L. and Rock, I. (1962) "The moon illusion, I," *Science* 136, pp. 953–61.
Koenderink, J. J., and Van Doorn, A. J. (1987) "Representation of local geometry in the visual system," *Biological Cybernetics* 55, pp. 367–75.
Köhler, W. (1940) *Dynamics of Psychology* (Liveright: New York).
Rock, I. (1973) *Orientation and Form* (Academic Press: New York).
Rock, I. (1975) *An Introduction to Perception* (MacMillan and Co.: New York).
Rock, I. (1983) *The Logic of Perception* (Bradford Books/MIT Press: Cambridge).
Rock, I. and Kaufman, L. (1962) "The moon illusion, II," *Science* 136, pp. 1023–31.
Searle, J. (1983) *Intentionality* (Cambridge University Press: Cambridge).
Searle, J. (1985) *Minds, Brains and Science* (Harvard University Press: Cambridge, Mass.).
Wertheimer, M. (1945) *Productive Thinking* (Harper and Bros: New York).
Wheatstone, C. (1838) "Contributions to the physiology of vision; On some remarkable, and hitherto unobserved, phenomena of binocular vision: Part I," *Philosophical Transactions* pp. 371–94.

23

Intentionality, Narrativity, and Interpretation: The (New) Image of Man

CAROL FLEISHER FELDMAN

For twenty years now, Searle has occupied a crucial role in Anglo-American philosophy: his has been the central voice attempting to explain human mental life in terms of human agency expressed in patterned action. His early well-known work on the patterned expressed of human agency in linguistic acts is taken in his more recent work on intentionality as a special case. In *Intentionality* (1983) he generalizes from his discoveries about speech acts in order to develop a working model of human agency expressed in human action. These are my words, not his. His goals are more focused, for his approach to the general problem of agency is through the specific, but central, notion of intentionality.

Intentionality, for Searle, is "that property of many mental states and events by which they are directed at or about or of objects and states of affairs in the world" (ibid., p. 1). States that can be intentional states include belief, fear, hope, desire, love, and so on. They may be conscious or not, and the object that they are directed at need not exist. Although intentional states do not reduce to belief and desire, all intentional states nonetheless contain a belief or a desire or both, and "in many cases the intentionality of the state is explained by" the constituent belief or desire (ibid., p. 35). But "beliefs and desires are not primary forms, rather they are etiolated forms of more primordial experiences in perceiving [perception] and doing [action]" (ibid., p. 36).

An "intention is satisfied iff the *action* represented by the content of the intention is actually performed" (p. 79). In "cases where an agent is acting on his prior intention there must be a close connection between the prior intention and the intention in action . . ." (p. 85).

Suppose I intend to raise my arm. The content of my intention can't be . . .

(that I perform the action of raising my arm)

because I might perform the action of raising my arm in ways that had nothing to do with this prior intention. I might forget all about this intention and later raise my arm for some other independent reason. The intentional content of my intention must be at least

(that I perform the action of raising my arm by way of carrying out *this intention*). (Ibid., p. 85)

From where I stand, there seems to be an important new beginning in the air shared among a minoritarian group of psychologists, anthropologists, and philosophers. It can take the form of preferring natural to artificial thinking, of wanting to import notions from literature, literary theory, and history into the human sciences, of treating culture as text, or of an interest in the non-logical, non-computational aspects of thinking. Obviously, all of these new interests are not exactly alike, but they cluster together as a set of related concerns – we can allude to them as the (new) image of man. And they do share one deep and specific concern: that the discovery of human capacities in the empirical sciences is being hindered and entrapped by a thoroughly inappropriate (positivist) philosophy of science. The hope is widely shared that significant progress in any one of these areas, say narrative thinking, should not only help to explain it itself, but might also point the way toward a more appropriate set of conceptions of the empirical enterprise in the human sciences. Here is Searle's statement of the problem:

> One nagging problem remains that is not addressed directly in the book, but was one of my main reasons for wanting to write it. Ordinary human behaviour has proven peculiarly recalcitrant to explanation by the methods of the natural sciences. Why? . . . There are many attempts to answer this question in contemporary philosophy, none of them in my view completely satisfactory. I believe that the direction of the correct answer lies in seeing the role of Intentionality in the structure of action; not just in the description of action, but in the very structure of human behaviour. (Ibid. p. x)

Let me be more specific about this minoritarian interest in the field where I see it most closely. Cognitive psychology today is rapidly moving along two divergent paths. The majority path is toward computability or Turing machine reductions of epistemic states. But there is lately a growing minority interested in the non-computational capacities of mind – in creative, divergent, and "narrative" thought. For them, thinking is not reducible to something else,[1] but is rather, as intentionality is for Searle, a ground-level property of the mind. Searle puts it well: "In my view it is not possible to give a logical analysis of the Intentionality of the mental in terms of simpler notions, since Intentionality is, so to speak, a ground floor property of the mind, not a logically complex feature built up by combining simpler elements" (ibid., p. 26).

Being non-reductivist about mental states or about intentions can seem to require a specification of metaphysical commitments concerning the exact nature of the reality of mental states or intentions as it does to Searle: "I believe people really do have mental states, some of them conscious and some unconscious, and that, at least as far as the conscious ones are concerned, they pretty much have the mental properties they seem to have" (ibid., p. viii). Strangely, Searle nonetheless rejects the two standard mentalist metaphysical positions – Cartesian dualism and simple mental realism of the Peircean kind. Instead, he offers us a new metaphysical formulation: a mind caused by and realized in the brain – a single substance with two expressions. "On my view mental phenomena are biologically based: they are both caused by the operations of the brain and realized in the structure of the brain" (ibid., p. ix). This formulation gives rise to baffling complexities.[2] Is it really necessary?

For Goodman (1984), in contrast, no metaphysical stance has seemed to be necessary, or to put it another way, Goodman adopts the "irrealist" view that all we have are versions, and that there is no independent reality that lies outside of them. Mind is a range of constructive procedures that makes the versions, but whatever we can say about it will just be another version. And, if Goodman's view is too quirky for many tastes, Rorty (1979) has argued for the possibility of studying such matters as psychology without making any commitments one way or the other about the nature of reality. I agree with them.[3] Moreover, I think the particular "caused by and realized in" metaphysics is unhelpful to Searle's important undertakings in *Intentionality*. So, for present purposes, let me simply extract the non-reductivist commitment from its metaphysical frame and preserve it as a *stipulation* of intentional states that may explain human action. So altered, Searle's analysis of intentionality lies squarely in the center of the current discussion across disciplines and offers an analysis that could be taken as central to the various enterprises.

The notion of intentionality is a central one in that an interest in intentional states could be said to characterize thick interpretation in anthropology as well as studies of narrative thinking in psychology. It works this way because it isolates an important aspect of human agency – its directedness. Tolman (1949) created an important anti-behaviorist alternative in an earlier era by showing that behavior of rats in mazes could not be explained without invoking a closely related notion – the purposes of the rats.

And much more recently, Morton (1980) gives this picture of psychology: there

"is little that is psychologically unique in the attribution of states of mind. One has cognition, just cognition as it is everywhere, and beliefs, just beliefs, though they have a particular subject matter. The object of interest now becomes these beliefs and how they are structured. The standard view is that they are structured as . . . a body of beliefs, most of which everyone has, concerning the relations between different attributes. . . . When these hypotheses in the theory of attribution are combined with claims elsewhere in social psychology, for example in the writings of Heider, that people possess a conception of human action as caused by intentions to produce changes in the world operating with the against causal tendencies of the world itself, one gets the outline of a fairly extensive commonplace psychological theory, concerned both with dispositional traits such as those of character and mood and with the intentions that produce action. (*Frames of Mind*, p. 13)

Intentionality is one of a cluster of related notions – among them, action, cognition, belief, consciousness, purposiveness, and text. It would be nice to be able to decide which of these is the most basic concept and to announce accordingly a general agenda for research on the (new) image of man, but a universal ground-level concept is likely to elude us here. The best approach will vary for different problems, and for problems approached from different points of view. It is bound to be sensitive to context. But if basic concepts elude us, and if intentionality is not the first and last step in the derivational chain, that is due to the clustered nature of the problems to which it speaks. Nothing ever could be that final step.

So let us begin with Searle's proposal that intentionality can explain human action and see how it bears on the the common and particular enterprises that constitute the study of the (new) image of man. I propose now to consider each of these in turn. First, as to the common enterprise, I want to spell out some of the interesting consequences of an intentionalist stance for a new philosophy of science. For to begin with intentionality is immediately to shift the ground of empirical methods in psychology from an old physical or biological paradigm and is immediately to suggest some alternative criteria. Second, I will turn to one of the particular areas most familiar to me – the study of narrative thinking – and explore the consequences of an intentionalist stance for its study.

The simple formulation of the problem in the philosophy of science is this. In physics and biology causal relations may be discovered between antecedent physical conditions and consequent physical conditions. These causal relations take the form of law-like or general regularities. Once discovered, the identification of a particular instance of physical conditions known to be antecedent in some such law permits us to predict the consequent physical condition and serves as an explanation for it. Leaving aside a host of issues, the thing to be noted is that the antecedent and consequent conditions are presumed to be physical and (therefore) observable, observable independently of one another, and observed as the same from all points of view. In contrast, intentionality and human action are not physical phenomena and (therefore) are not observable, are not observable independently of one another, and are not seen as the same from all points of view. In consequence, we cannot formulate general laws under which, in a particular instance, some antecedent condition, say an intentional state, predicts some consequent condition, say an action, in the same sense in which we can do this with physical states. This gives rise to a host of problems and solutions, but the general problem for the student of mind is this: How (in what form) is it possible to explain what humans do?

The paradigm case of explaining human doings that I have in mind is when some intentional state, say an intention, is offered as an explanation for some action (not a behavior, its strictly physical counterpart). Even today the great majority of the solutions to this problem offered both by working empiricists and by philosophers have been attempts to recast mental events as physical events. Experimentalists often recast human action as human behavior though it may be seen as explained by states of mind, as among cognitivists.[4] Modern philosophers more often recast mental causes as physical – say, intentions as brain states. The various forms of these recastings need not trouble us here. Let me just say that they range from frank reductionism (acts treated as behaviors, minds treated as brains) to subtler efforts to preserve the scientific enterprise as we know it in the physical sciences by finding a physical constituent that lies within or behind human intentionality and is capable of entering lawlike statements. Peacocke's (1979) version will do as an example of this: mental states are realized in (but not reduced to) physical states. Causal relationships exist between the physical states in which they are realized. These causal relations make it possible to give explanations of action with intention in the same (or very similar) way that we give explanations of physical events. "My own . . . suggestion would be that for a kind of explanation to be explanation in the same sense in which physical explanation is explanation, it is a necessary condition that" [(successive) mental states are realized in (successive) brain states that are explanatory of one another] (*Holistic Explanation*, p. 168).

The chief problem physicalism solves is the problem of how we can explain mental events in the same sense as we can explain physical events – by prediction within the context of general causal laws. Very roughly speaking, all of the alternative solutions involve giving up physicalism of all forms in favor of non-physicalism. The chief motive for preferring this alternative is the sense that by focusing on the non-physical aspects of intention and action, it will be possible to develop a richer and more principled understanding of them. There is a steep price to be paid for this. Once we give up physicalism, we give up the possibility of being able to explain, in the same sense that we can explain the physical, the nature of human action. If physicalism leads to the familiar form of scientific explanation, roughly, by objectification, non-physicalism blocks that form of explanation: there may be no observable antecedent and consequent, they may not be independent of one another, and they may not be the same from all points of view. If so, we may then have to give up the hope for general causal laws of the kind familiar in physicalism and therefore of the possibility of prediction. As others have noted, the new physics has similar characteristics, and is similarly ill-served by the old model of doing science. The problem here may not be specific for the human sciences or mental states, but rather a general one about the form of explanation of non-mechanical causality between non-objective (in the sense of non-billiard ball-like) phenomena. But this is another matter.

What would explanations of human action consist of then? Could we tell good ones from bad ones? How? Would they all be inferior to all explanations of physical phenomena? Could we ever really *know* anything about them in the same sense or in any real sense or acceptable sense? Could there be anything properly called a human science? And, is there any coherent metaphysical position compatible with this approach? The considerable successes of the old model lead to a deep pessimism about the possibility of a happy resolution to these questions once we are cut adrift, but the pessimism seems to me to be premature. There are possibilities here that we haven't begun to explore yet. These questions could be the agenda for a new philosophy of science that framed the (new) study of man. I suggest that we philosophers, psychologists, and anthropologists start to take them on, and see where we can get.

Searle's *Intentionality*, minus its metaphysics, is an outline of how we can explain intentional states. In connection with these particular proposals, he avoids making any ontological claims: We have a mistaken model of intentionality if "we are . . . searching for a thing to correspond to the word 'intention' . . . [T]he only thing that could correspond is an intention, and to know what an intention is . . . we do not need to know its ultimate ontological category but rather we need to know: first, what are its conditions of satisfaction . . ." (ibid., p. 16). Here then is the general program: What "we want to know is, what is an intention? What is an action? And what is the character of the relation between them that is described by saying that one is a condition of satisfaction of the other?" (ibid., p. 81).

"An intentional state only determines its conditions of satisfaction – and thus only is the state it is – given its position in a *Network* of other Intentional states . . ." (ibid., p. 19). If this partakes of "holism" as we encounter it elsewhere, Searle's position goes beyond it.:[5] "There is no neutral standpoint from which we can survey the relations between Intentional states and the world and then describe them in non-Intentionalistic terms. Any explanation of Intentionality, therefore, takes place within the circle of Intentional concepts" (ibid., p. 26). Moreover, "in the case of prior intention and intention in action the cause contains a representa-tion or presentation of the effect in its conditions of satisfaction . . ." (ibid., p. 126). Thus, Searle's solution gives up the orthodox requirement of independence of antecedent and consequent. But if intentionality is taken as a ground-level concept, one that cannot be constituted of other non-intentional concepts, he has no choice. For the consequence to be explained, the action, is intentional, and it can only be explained by intentional concepts – namely an antecedent intentional state. This sacrifice then is one crucial commitment and it is likely to be of some general interest for many non-physicalistic approaches.

Searle also gives up the requirement that a particular instance of causation can only be interpreted with respect to a general law: "When I said that my being thirsty caused me to drink the water, was it part of what I meant that there is a universal law? . . . It seems to me quite unlikely that there are any relevant purely psycho-logical laws . . ." (ibid., p. 118). In the end, he gives up this requirement for causa-tion of all kinds – physical as well as intentional. Causation of all kinds is simply a matter of "some things making other things happen" (ibid., p. 135) and does not entail that there are general causal laws. Nevertheless, the concept of causation is only applicable in a universe where a high degree of causal regularity is presup-posed. What is *special* about *intentional* causation is this: "we can be directly aware of the causal nexus in some of these cases,[6] there is a 'logical' connection between cause and effect, and these cases are the primitive forms of causation as far as our experiences are concerned" (ibid., p. 135). Whether general or particular, this model departs from orthodoxy in giving up causal laws. So, Searle's proposal for the shape of a new human philosophy of science is that we permit the explanation of actions with intentional concepts, and that we accept as causal explanations particular claims that something (intentional) made something else (intentional) happen.

Leaving other matters aside, the great virtue of causation for the empiricist is that it permits prediction. But if intentional causation does not entail any general statements and therefore does not permit prediction in new cases, we can just as well do without it. If we did without causation altogether, what would we have left? What remains then is explanation within an intentional network. Explanation of this kind, if not causation, may characterize the way one intentional state accounts for another within a network of intentional states. This is a radical proposal for a new beginning, and I want briefly to explore what its consequences might be for a new philosophy of science.

Again oversimplifying, we might get a kind of explanation without prediction, an accounting for, an interpretation. A pattern of particular causation, where the cause contains the consequent, is more like a text than like an experiment involving bil-liard balls. It is a complexly patterned kind of thing, hard to produce *in vitro*, and in which it is hard to find a beginning and an end. It seems less suitable for the application of deductive procedures than for procedures of unravelling: start any-where you can find a thread, pull on it slowly, and see how it held things together. In some areas of intellectual life, especially in literary theory, procedures of this kind exist. They are procedures of interpretation. This is not, of course a novel suggestion. But where it is solidly established, for example in literature and the law, the practitioners are not trying to be scientists. They do not try to generate the data experimentally. At most, they hope to be able to explain the data as they find them. Moreover, they don't (or shouldn't) expect to be able to predict anything.

Perhaps actions, or at least patterned actions, should be viewed as texts, in some expanded sense of text. Scientific study would consist of interpretation. The patterns revealed through interpretation would discover the intentional states that lay behind the interpreted text. It would make no sense here to say that they *caused* the text. And since in a certain sense they lay within it as well, it might be better to think of them as *constituting* it. In that case the task of the scientist who studies human action is to *interpret* patterned human action construed as a text in order to discover its patterns and particularly how those patterns are constituted of intentional states.

Let us turn now to one set of psychological implications of the Searlian programme. Searle tells us that in everyday life we make use of explanations in terms of intentional states to make sense of human actions. As a matter of fact subjects in psychological studies don't *always* do this. In particular if the actions in question are isolated and seem not to be situated in a narrative framework then subjects may revert to accounts in terms of categories. For example, if we ask of a picture of an isolated action "Why did the woman hand the toy to the child?", subjects may reply, "She is nice", or "She likes children", or "She feels guilty."

There is intentionality here to be sure, but not much, and there are two interconnected reasons why not. First, there is the nature of the task. We seem to be asking the subject for a category or a name rather than to be asking for a narrative. It we set up tasks like this in such a way as to suggest that what we want from the subjects is a narrative, then they produce stories that situate the action in a network of interconnected intentions. Second, there is a problem with the materials. We present the subjects here with an isolated, single action and no context. This seems to violate an essential condition on intentionalist explanation, namely, that it be applied to patterned action. Patterned action is not a matter of mystical interconnections, but is rather a framework that disambiguates the many possible actions that a single behavior might express. At the same time it clarifies that it is an action interpretation of the behavior that is wanted and not a mere physical description of the behavior itself. Patterning does this by situating the behavior in a set of actions.

From these data to the contrary then I want to draw two conclusions about the psychological implications of the Searlian model: People explain actions in terms of intentions when (a) they see the nature of an appropriate account as narrative-like rather than categorical or nominal. This in turn presupposes that people in general have available to them two kinds of accounts. Without taking much time on this matter here, let me just say that data showing that the same subject can be shifted from one kind of explanation to the other, by introducing conditions that suggest that what is wanted are either logic or stories, are what I have in mind. And (b) people give intentional explanations when the behaviors/actions to be explained are seen as actions; one way to encourage this is to situate them in a network of interconnected actions. The evidence I have in mind here lies in tasks where a subject is given a series of simple line drawings that tell a simple story about an agent with one overriding intention – for example to grow flowers. An example (from Scopinski, 1985) is reproduced in figure 1.

Figure 1

While any one of the pictures could adequately be given a purely behavioral description, no one of them should be when it is presented as part of a seriated pattern because this pattern itself implies that there is some purpose, or *telos* or intention – we can call it directedness – that the individual steps serve. Normal children conform to this pattern. Autistic chidlren, in contrast, give non-intentional accounts. Here is one autistic subject's reponses when asked what was happening in each of the six pictures:

1 A sun, the cloud, the house, a boy.
2 He watering – the plants.
3 The clouds, the sky, the sun.
4 A flower.
5 The clouds, the sun a house, the plants.
6 The house, the plants – they grow.

Apart from any implications they have for the nature of autism, there is something instructive about these data for an understanding of the conditions on intentional explanation: that intentional explanation requires or is evoked by recognition of directed or intentional patterning of human action. Autistic subjects do not see the story line or patterned connectedness of the actions, nor therefore do they explain them with (underlying) intentions.

Now this brings me to a general point about human mental processes. Intentional explanation is one of two natural kinds of explanation.[7] It is normally evoked by patterned action – that is, by narrative. The other, categorical or logical explanation, is ordinarily given for acting things rather than for acting agents, and is used to explain physical states rather than patterned actions. So my central claim is that narrative evokes intentional explanation, and that more intentionally patterned narratives evoke more intentional explanations. However, the narrative in question cannot do any evoking if it is in a book rather than in our explainer's head, so what is at issue here is human action *understood* as narrative. My final version then is this: human action patterned in such a way that it is undertood as narrative evokes intentional explanations. It has an interesting implication that I won't develop here: that narrative organization is a form of mental organization, that it is a kind of cognition.

In Feldman et al. 1990, I have recently collected a set of data that can perhaps exemplify this formulation. Rather than comparing narrative and non-narrative versions to see what kinds of accounts they would evoke, we compared more and less richly patterned narratives. We created these by creating two versions of a single published story. The "conscious" version is just the story as it was written. The other version, the "non-conscious" version, was created by deleting mental verbs and other simple lexical expressions of mental state. We read each subject one version of the story and asked various interpretive questions as we went along – "What's the most important thing I've told you so far?" and "What are the way this could be going?" We probed answers to both questions with "Why?" Then we asked them to retell the story. We analyzed these retellings for propositions that were not in the original story – that went beyond the information given. We also analyzed them for accuracy – the number of core propositions in the story-as-told that they included in their retellings. There was no difference in accuracy between subjects getting the conscious and non-conscious versions. It is against this background that we turn now to the group differences that went beyond the information given in the presented story.

The total number of codable units in the retellings that were coded as beyond the information given was somewhat larger for the conscious version (210) than for the non-conscious version (143). These were then coded in subtypes: intentional characterizations of characters, physical actions, and traits. Conscious stories elicit more intentional than physical inferences (43.8 percent to 36.7 percent), while non-conscious stories elicit more physical inferences than inferences of intention (44.7 percent to 30.7 percent). Trait inferences differences between the two groups were not remarkable.

In summary, the more richly narrativized, conscious version evokes somewhat more generative thinking but whether the total number of inferences is greater or not, inferences from the conscious version are characteristically about intentional states, while those from the less richly narrativized non-conscious version are more likely to be about physical states.

Finally, are we justified in assuming that the conscious version is generally seen by subjects as more richly patterned than the non-conscious version, or is it just more conscious? We looked therefore at an independent measure of narrative patterning – temporality. We coded responses to the question "What is the most important thing I've told you so far" as static or temporal. Our reasoning was that the rich narrative of the conscious version would lead subjects to see more sequential connectivity between events, even though the conscious version was not itself more sequentially connected – it differed only in the number of mental verbs. Subjects given the conscious version gave 15 temporal and 9 static replies. The relationship was reversed for the non-conscious version – 8 temporal and 16 static. This suggests that the conscious version is seen by subjects as more richly patterned in general.

We may be justified then in supposing that what we have here is an empirical illustration that bears on Searle's claim that explanations of human action are given in terms of intentional states. If I am justified in thinking, as I argued above, that explanation of action hinges on behaviors being seen as actions by virtue of their being situated within a narrative framework, then these data can be seen as asking how action is explained by asking how narratives are explained. The answer we find here is that they are explained with statements about intentions and with statements about physical states. But the more richly textured is the (understood) narrative to be explained (here, the more conscious and the more temporal), the more likely are subjects to explain it with appeals to intentional states.

Finally, a *caveat*. This study speaks to or illustrates the claim that there is a basic level of explanation of human action, and that it includes intentional states. It doesn't prove it, and the study isn't a real experiment.[8] Intentions aren't physical or subject to control, and as we know more about our own than anyone else's, they are not the same from all points of view. We can't and we probably shouldn't want to manipulate them like a well-behaved independent physical variable. Most import-ant, intentional causes cause intentional effects – in this case, greater intentionality in the form of conscious versions led to greater intentionality in the explanations. It looks circular, rather than like science. Given these realities, intentional explana-tions are going to look a little strange when compared with an ideal type of scientific explanation that we all share. But we all live in a world and in a culture that we see as constituted of agentive actions that can be construed as narratively patterned. We try to explain or account for narratively patterned actions in terms of inten-tions in literature and in art as in life. So we will have to try to make some kind of sense out of what we are doing when we do this, to explain this sense of "explain." Searle's work takes us all a giant stride forward in giving shape to this foray into the future.

ACKNOWLEDGEMENTS

First I want to thank John Searle for the exciting beginning he gave my academic life, now 25 years ago. I also thank the following people with whom I have had conversations on related matters: Jane Atkinson, William Kessen, David Olson, Renato Rosaldo, Brian Stock, and Annette Weiner. None of them heard about this paper, and it may not in any sense reflect their views. Finally, I want to thank Carol Tittle for her helpful reading of this paper, Robert Van Gulick for his editorial advice, and Jerome Bruner with whom I have had extensive discussions about narrative, and who kindly read and commented on the draft.

NOTES

1   And particularly not to a machine state, but usually not to a brain state either.
2   And the ugly whiff of physicalism. For Peacocke's analysis of causation eventually assigns causal

connectedness to mental states by assigning it to the sequence of physical states in which mind is realized. Though there are big differences here in the analysis of causation itself, the analogy with Peacocke is too close for comfort.

3   I have defended this point of view elsewhere, most recently in Feldman and Bruner (1987).

4   All too often they then convert the mental cause into a machine state, by reduction. An awful lot of psychology today that calls itself cognitive fails to consider the mental antecedents as supplying a basic level of explanation not decomposable into non-mental constituents. In this rather crucial sense cognitive science, for example, is at best only indirectly a study of cognition.

5   Searle tells us that this is Peacocke's holism, but it differs in that the network of intentional states here is composed not just of putatively causal states or potential explanations but also of the intentions in action that are to be explained. Searle observes that his holism goes beyond Peacocke's but he attributes this to his additional claims about the "background," a set of non-intentional knowings how that is presupposed in the workings of the system of intentional states.

6   This claim that we understand intentional causation directly in our own case and and the related more general implication that we have a special form of direct access to our own intentional states is a very important one for a new science, perhaps even as important as the non-independence of explanation and thing explained that I make so much of. For it suggests that explanation will have to be grounded in particular points of view rather than in some putative objective posture. But it raises another whole set of questions that didn't seem to bear directly on the main argument I wanted to make here.

7   For further discussion of these two natural kinds, see Bruner (1986), especially chapter 2.

8   This is because we cannot manipulate the variable of *perceived* narrativity directly, and because we cannot ask the same subject to hear the story in two forms, and because we cannot get fully objective measures of the subject's inferences about intentionality, among other reasons. Moreover, the perceived narrativity of the stories is not independent of attributed intentionality since they are part of a network of connected states.

REFERENCES

Bruner, Jerome (1986) *Actual Minds, Possible Worlds* (Harvard University Press: Cambridge, Mass.).

Feldman, Carol, Bruner Jerome, Renderer Bobbi, and Spitzer Sally (1990), "Narrative comprehension", in B. K. Britton and A. D. Pellegrini (eds) *Narrative Thoughts and Narrative Language* (Lawrence Erlbaum Associates, Hillsdown, N.J.).

Feldman, Carol and Bruner, Jerome (1987) "Overview," in James Russell (ed.), *Philosophical Perspectives on Developmental Psychology* (Basil Blackwell: Oxford).

Goodman, Nelson (1984) *Of Mind and Other Matters* (Harvard University Press: Cambridge, Mass.).

Morton, Adam (1980) *Frames of Mind* (Clarendon Press: Oxford).

Peacocke, Christopher (1979) *Holistic Explanation* (Clarendon Press: Oxford).

Rorty, Richard (1979) *Philosophy and the Mirror of Nature* (Princeton University Press: Princeton).

Scopinski, Heidi (1985) "A study of narrative patterns of autistic subjects," unpublished Masters Thesis, Department of Psychology, New York University.

Searle, John (1983) *Intentionality* (Cambridge University Press: Cambridge).

Tolman, Edward (1949) *Purposive Behavior in Animals and Men* (University of California Press: Berkeley).

24

Response:
Explanation in the Social Sciences

John R. Searle

I have argued that in explaining human behavior we need both a mentalistic and a neurophysiological level of explanation. Within each of these levels there will, in all likelihood, be many sublevels. Thus, for example, in the Intentionalistic explanation of human behavior we need to account for both the levels of individual Intentionality and collective Intentionality. We need the individual level if, for example, we are trying to explain why a particular human being engaged in a certain course of action. But if, for example, we are examining wars, revolutions, or collective economic behavior, we will also have to investigate collective forms of Intentionality. Furthermore, there are all sorts of complicated interrelations between the levels of Intentionality and of neurophysiology. For example, if we are examining the psychology of perception, we will find, I believe, an intermingling of Intentionalistic and physiological phenomena.

I making these claims I am not trying at all to be dogmatic, nor to prescribe to social scientists how they ought to conduct their investigations. However, if I am right, my claims have two important consequences which have proved controversial. First, it is unlikely that there is an intermediate level of explanation between the levels of neurophysiology and the level of Intentionality of the sort that is postulated, for example, by various computational and informational processing models. Second, if my particular account of Intentionality is correct it has the consequence that we do not have laws in the social sciences comparable to the sorts of laws that we have in physics and chemistry.

The argument for the second of these claims is somewhat different from standard arguments against bridge laws between the "mental" and the "physical" that are given in philosophy, and it may be worth repeating its basic premiss at least in bare outline. The basic idea is simply that most of the important social concepts, concepts such as money, property, marriage, war, revolution, exchange, game, rule, election, cocktail party, etc., are self-referential in a special way. These phenomena are only the phenomena they are if people think they are those phenomena. That is, unless the people involved have a certain set of attitudes towards an event, it does not constitute an election, a war, a marriage, a judicial decision, or a purchase. And unless they have a certain attitude toward a certain object, it does not constitute money or property. And in such cases, the representations of the phenomena by the participants are partly constitutive of the phenomena represented. Now, this has the consequence that there is nothing physically in common to all of those objects that we call, e.g., money, and indeed, there is no interesting set of physical disjuncts that all money has in common, since roughly speaking anything that can be regarded as money can be used as money and hence can be money. Physical instantiations of money are potentially unlimited in their variety. Now, this has the consequence that there cannot be any physical feature, or even a disjunction of physical features, which all money has in common which would constitute the principle that enable us to connect the laws of money with the laws of physics, and it further has the consequence that there is no shared physical stimulus that all money produces on our nervous system.

This argument applies only to social phenomena. I think that it is not true of, for example, pain or visual perception that it has to be regarded in a certain way in order to be a pain or a visual perception.

Raimo Tuomela

Most of Tuomela's paper concerns possible objections that someone might make to the argument I sketched above, namely the argument against the possibility of laws in the social sciences of the sort that we have in physics and chemistry. Most of his arguments consist of considerations about how a *possible* critic *might* make an objection that *may* ultimately have some force. In the end it seems to me he comes down on my side in just about all of these hypothetical debates, so I am not quite sure how seriously he wants me to take these fantasized "refutations." My puzzlement is increased when I note that the possible objections are very vaguely sketched without much by way of illustrative examples. His discussion of supervenience, in particular, is extremely puzzling because the sort of supervenience that he suggests is quite unlike standard cases of the supervenience of, e.g., the "mental" on the "physical." For example, I take it that he agrees with me that, e.g., being a dollar bill, is not supervenient on any set of purely physical properties, since two objects could have all their physical properties in common and yet one be a genuine dollar bill, and the other be a counterfeit; and an object might cease to be a dollar bill without any change in its physical properties, if, for example, the United States Treasury declared it to be void. But then Tuomela makes the following extremely puzzling claim: "perhaps," he says, believing that something is money is "still supervenient on the basis consisting of brain states and relevant environmental physical states (involving e.g. the different physical forms of money and what have you)" (p. 307). In this connection he also suggests that for the supervenience basis we should consider not just physics but "suitable psychological, social psychological, and physical properties" (p. 305). He concludes that I have not "presented any arguments against this possibility." I certainly have not, but a simple reason for that is that I cannot figure out what "this possibility" is supposed to amount to. What social psychological and environmental facts could possibly be a non-question-begging basis for thinking that something is money? Is the fact the people think of this thing in my pocket as a dollar bill and they treat is as a dollar bill the sort of facts he had in mind? If so, it is quite hopeless as a "microbasis" for solving the questions about the relation of "higher level" social phenomena to "lower level" facts of physics and chemistry, since the "microbasis" is already too macro. And it is no help at all to be told that we can include "the relevant environmental physical states (involving, e.g., the different physical forms of money and *what have you*" (my italics). If the question is, "What have you?" then as far as argumentation in this case is concerned, I fear, the answer is, "Not much!"

Only at the end of his article does Tuomela come out with an argument against me that he fully endorses. I believe this argument is based on a misunderstanding of my position, and is in any case invalid. The central issue is this; he takes me to be claiming that in order for there to be laws of social science there has to be a reduction of higher order social laws to lower order laws of physics by way of bridge laws. He also think I hold the traditional hypothetico-deductive model of scientific laws and explanations. But, in fact, I never endorse the traditional view and I explicitly deny that the issue is about what he calls "smooth" reductions by way of strict bridge laws. My arguments are intended to hold against both smooth and rough reductions. In fact, I explicitly criticise certain views, such as those of Jerry Fodor, which reject the idea of smooth reductions in favor of loose disjunctions of bridge laws; and indeed I presented an example of a loose set of bridge laws that connect princples of nutrition with principles of physics and chemistry. I argue that this is precisely the sort of example which cannot be matched in the relationship between the social and the physical. The issue under discussion, to repeat, is not about the strictness of the bridge laws, or smoothness of the reductions.

Well then what is the issue about? When you cut through all the jargon about "supervenience," "smooth reductions," etc., there is still a real issue: suppose we had what we thought were iron laws of wars and revolutions, of the sort that some Marxists thought they could get. Now, the puzzle is, how is this sort of law supposed to fit with the laws of physics such as those concerning molecules? After all, at one level of description a revolution is just the movement of a whole lot of molecules. You cannot have a revolution if nobody brings the molecules. So any law couched in the vocabulary of revolution must be systematically related to laws couched in the vocabulary of microparticles, because both laws must systematically predict the same events, even though the predictions are made in different vocabularies. There would have to be some systematic explanation of the fact that on the day of the revolution the molecules will all be blowing in exactly the right directions in order for the revolution to take place, otherwise it would be a miracle, a matter, for example, of divine preestablished harmony, that the laws of physics and the laws of revolution both predicted exactly the same result, in their different vocabularies.

Now, I argue that there cannot be such systematic principles connecting social phenomena with micro-physics. There are indeed such principles at various places within the hard sciences. So, for example, we can explain why the story about a gas told in terms of pressure and volume matches the story told in terms of the movements of molecules. This is the famous "reduction" of the gas laws to the laws of statistical thermodynamics. Tuomela thinks it is important that the reduction is not smooth, but I do not think it matters at all for this discussion. You can forget about the issue of "smooth reduction," because it is irrelevant to this issue. The case of gas laws is just an example to illustrate how the same phenomena can be accounted for in terms of scientific laws at different levels.

Now here is Tuomela's answer my to argument, and this I believe is the crux of his paper: "explanatory theories explain laws and generalizations (e.g., holistic social ones) but not by subsumption, as in the standard account. Rather they explain directly the individual instances of the generalizations by redescribing them in the terminology of the reducing theory and by showing them to be instances of the explaining theories in question to the extent that the generalizations in question are correct."

But this objection fails to meet my point. Every instance of a revolution is indeed an instance of molecular movement and so is redescribable in the terminology of molecular theory and is, presumably, also an instance of the explaining theory of revolutions. But so what? The point at issue is whether the theory of revolutions can have "iron laws" when there can be no systematic set of matching correlations between the supposed iron laws of revolutions and the iron laws of physics. As far as I can tell Tuomela's argument simply does not address this issue.

What has gone wrong here? My diagnosis of the misunderstanding is that he thought my argument depended on some particular theory about scientific laws and about bridge laws connecting them and so could be answered by stating a rival theory of these matters. But my argument does not depend on endorsing any particular theory of scientific laws and bridge principles. If the argument is valid it should be consistent with any sane theory of the nature of scientific laws. It simply rests on the common-sense point that if two different sets of laws are supposed to predict the same sets of events, and to predict them universally, systematically, and uniformly under two independent sets of descriptions, there has to be some systematic set of relations between the two sets of laws.

The upshot of this discussion is not that there cannot be useful generalizations in the social sciences. There can. And it is up to us whether we wish to call them "laws," such as "Gresham's Law" in economics. The motivating force behind such laws is not, e.g., molecular or gravitational relations, but Intentional causation. The principle that binds the diverse phenomena of social laws into a single conceptual realm is not some jointly shared physical property or disjunction of physical properties stated in physical terms, but rather Intentionality.

Irvin Rock

I agree with almost everything in Irvin Rock's impressive article. My only disagreement concerns those areas in which he is summarizing my views. On his summary it would appear that we are in disagreement. I think we are not, and therefore I will spend at least a little space explaining how I think he may have misunderstood me.

Rock begins his summary of his objections to me as follows: "Searle has argued that there is no gap to be filled between commonsense explanation of mind in the language of Intentionality and scientific explanations of mind in terms of neurophysiological processes in the brain" (p. 320). Now, this is not quite a statement of my actual views, because it makes two equations which I reject. I do, indeed, believe that there is no "gap to be filled between" the levels of intentionality and the levels of neurophysiology. But I do not accept the view implied in his summary that Intentionalistic explanations are co-extensive with "common-sense" explanations, which what he sometimes calls explanations in "folk psychology;" and I do not suppose that the only "science" of human beings will necessarily be neurophysiological. One way to put the difference between my views and the views he attributes to me is to say that I reject the idea that the distinction between Intentionality and neurophysiology is the same as the distinction between common sense and science. Since I believe Rock's misunderstanding of my views can be corrected very simply, perhaps the best way is to just set out what I do think and what I do not think as a series of propositions.

First, I do not claim that there is a perfectly adequate "folk psychology" which is quite sufficient for a science of human beings and needs only to be supplemented by scientific neurophysiology. Actually, I doubt that there is any such well-defined phenomenon as "folk psychology." If you were to make a list of popular sayings such as "A stitch in time saves nine" or "Easy come, easy go" it seems to me extremely unlikely that you would find anything of much serious intellectual merit.

Second, I do not claim "that there is no need for explanatory concepts about thoughts and behavior other than those given in terms of neurophysiology of events in the brain of those of common sense Intentional psychology." On the contrary, I have in my own work found it frequently both useful and necessary to introduce technical terms to described psychological and linguistic phenomena. I use terms like "illocutionary act," "propositional content," "direction of fit," "conditions of satisfaction," etc. all of which go beyond our common sense vocabulary. And this necessity for technical terms seems to me pervasive in psychology and in other social sciences. Thus, consider, for example, terms such as "marginal propensity to consume," or "dissonance." I think there is no doubt much to criticize in economic theory or in dissonance theory, but it would certainly be anti-intellectual to suggest that the theorists should not even introduce terms to describe the phenomena that they believe they have discovered.

Third, I do not think that the only systematic or "scientific" accounts of human beings can be given in neurophysiological terms. On the contrary, I see no objection to quite systematic sciences of economics, linguistics, psychology, etc. In the work that Rock cites I was very anxious to argue against certain prevailing computational conception of the mind and of psychological explanation. But Rock interprets my objection to computational and to earlier "gap-filling" attempts at a science of human beings in way that seems to me to make my view look excessively simple minded, even anti-intellectual, and I certainly did not intend any such result. I have struggled to get systematic accounts of, for instance, speech acts and Intentionality, and though I do not much care whether or not these are called "science," it is important to me that we do not rest content in a lot of common sense intuitive explanations. An intellectual grip on a subject matter requires a systematic account of that subject matter, and any such account is almost bound to go beyond common sense.

Actually, I think the use of the word "science" here is probably a source of confusion. What we are trying to get in general is knowledge and understanding, and about human beings we are trying to get knowledge and understanding of human beings. I do not think we should worry too much if the result is called "science" in the sense in which physics is a science. But I do think that Intentionalistic concepts are appropriate for giving systematic accounts of human beings, and I think, in fact, his examples illustrate this.

But what about functional explanations? Rock claims to discover a level of functional explanation in psychology which he thinks, is neither at a level of neuro-physiology, nor at a level of Intentionality. I believe that this is Rock's central argument against me, so I will devote the rest of my reply to this issue.

I believe with Rock that there are functional explanations of human behavior and cognitive capacities which are crucial to psychology and other disciplines. But I reject the idea that the functions in question are neither specifiable in neuro-physiological nor Intentionalistic terms. Let us consider his example of the Ponzo illusion to illustrate my point. Standard textbook explanations of the illusion ascribe to the perceiver a level of unconscious Intentionality and inference. We are sup-posed to think that in order to explain the Ponzo illusion the subject first makes an unconscious inference to the effect that the top line is further away from him than the bottom line, and he does this following a rule of perspective. And second, that the subject infers that the top line is larger because it appears to be further away. And he does this following the rule specified in Emmert's Law. This "func-tional explanation," as given in Rock's excellent book on perception,[1] is certainly consistent with my view that there are many Intentionalistic explanations of many psychological phenomena.

However, there is another possible functional explanation of the illusion which makes no reference to unconscious Intentionality. The Ponzo illusion might be explainable in terms of functions of the neurophysiology that have no Intentionality. Perhaps the correct explanation is that our visual system just functions in such a way that perspectival cues give us the impression of distance and certain distance per-ceptions are correlated with size appearances. On this neurophysiological account of the functioning of the visual system, we do not need to postulate any unconscious inferences or unconscious rule following. We just describe *what* the mechanism does without knowing the details of its physical realization or how it does it. In short, on my account there are at least two different possible functional explana-tions of the Ponzo illusion. One is in terms of the functioning of the Intentionality, and the other is in terms of the functioning of the neurophysiology. It doesn't matter for the purposes of this discussion which is right; perhaps they are both wrong. The important point for this discussion is that the two sorts of functional explanations are precisely at the two levels of neurophysiology and Intentionality, respectively. Neither supports the idea of a middle level between the neurophysiology and the intentionality, because the idea of such a middle level is the idea of a causal ontology which, though implemented or realized neurophysiologically was supposed to have causal properties not specified in Intentionalistic or neurophysiological terms. In various ways computer programs, information processing, and stimulus response patterns were supposed to meet these conditions. But neither of our functional explanations gives us a gap-filling functional level which is neither neurophysio-logical nor Intentionalistic.

Now, what is the source of the misunderstanding here? Why does Rock think that the functional level must be between these other two levels? I don't know, but I think it may be because he supposes that a neurophysiological account would have to consist in describing the details of the actual micro-anatomy of the brain. But, as he has repeatedly and effectively pointed out, in most cases we simply do not know enough to give an anatomical account of neurophysiological functioning. Most such efforts are quite premature.

Rock's point, I believe, is that often we need to know *what* the brain does, before we know the details of *how* it does it. Furthermore, we sometimes need to postulate functional mechanisms in the brain long before we have any idea about how those mechanisms might be physically realized in the actual anatomical structures. A good example of this is the idea of "memory traces." I am very puzzled that Rock supposes that I might have an objection to the idea of memory traces. On the contrary, it seems to me absolutely essential to suppose that experiences cause some change in the brain if there is to be a subsequent memory or behavior, such as face recognition, which requires a prior memory. Given everything we know about how the world works we have to suppose that the memory of prior experiences is only possible because of some change or other in the brain. Furthermore, I have no objection to what I sometimes call "speculative neurophysiology." He seems to think that I am sneering when I use this expression. I think, in fact, that in our current state of knowledge we have no choice but to speculate about the brain. For example, Chomsky's idea that there are specific structures in the brain that account for the child's ability to acquire language seems to me a prime example of "speculative neurophysiology" and one I would wholeheartedly support.

Carol Fleischer Feldman

I agree with so much Carol Fleischer Feldman's article that it will seem churlish of me to concentrate on our few areas of disagreement, but they may be important.

Agreements first: We both believe that Intentionalistic explanations are the correct form of explanation for (most) human behavior, that Intentionalistic explanations are holistic in form, not only in the sense that the intelligibility of the explanation depends on situating the explanans within a holistic Network of Intentional contents and against a holistic Background, but also in the sense that the phenomena to be explained, the explananda, only exist within the Network and against a Background. To these agreed points Feldman adds what I think is the exciting idea that where human behavior is concerned much of the holistic structure of intelligibility is provided by *narrative structures*. We characteristically understand other people's behavior, and even our own, by situating particular acts within a structured narrative.

So far so good; but now she says things that I find extremely disquieting. First, she rejects metaphysical realism, in the sense that I have defined, and she even cites Rorty and Goodman as holding views similar to her own. Second, she accepts the Cartesian categories of the mental and the physical, and throughout her paper she persistently contrasts the mental with the physical, even to the point of calling Intentionalistic explanations "non-physical." At one point she says, "intentions are not physical," and later, in the same paragraph, "Intentional causes cause Intentional effects." And third, perhaps most disquieting of all, she seems to deny that the ordinary notion of causation, in which phenomena in the real world cause other events, has any application to human behavior. In place of this she believes we should think more in terms of "literary theory" according to which human actions are "texts."

Now, against these disturbing tendencies I want to say the following: First, metaphysical realism is not, so to speak, a theory that is up for grabs like any other theory. It is, among other things, the presupposition of the intelligibility of public discourse. Denials of realism are not so much false as they are unintelligible; and affirmations of realism are, at best, misleading; because they make a feature of the non-representational Background look as if it were just a theory like any other. It is easy, though misleading, to present arguments in favor of realism – I sketched one in my reply to Zemach – but the difficulty in presenting answers to irrealism is that it is difficult to find a coherent formulation of a thesis to answer. Putnam[2] at least tried to present an argument, even if it is a bad one, but in the absence of specific arguments it is hard to take irrealism seriously.

Second, I do not know how Feldman makes her acceptance of the Cartesian categories of mental and physical consistent with her denial of realism. How can there be real mental and physical things if there are no real things at all? But that issue apart, I have argued at length that it is wrong and confused to think of reality as coming in two flavors, the mental and the physical. There is just one world, and it contains, among other things, people with conscious states such as thoughts, pains, perceptions, etc. Some of these states are Intentional, and these frequently cause certain effects in virtue of their Intentional contents. Often Intentional causation produces perfectly ordinary "physical" events such as my body movements.

Third, once you overcome the Cartesian categories then it is easy to see that Intentional causation is just a species of what Aristotle called *efficient* causation. It is one of the ways in which some things in the real world make other things happen.

If there are some solid results in "literary theory" that help us to understand better such facts, say, by getting us to have better interpretations of Intentional phenomena, such results are unknown to me. Literary theory as currently practiced is something of an intellectual basket case, an intellectual disaster waiting for help to come. It is, at best, unlikely that cognitive science will find help by looking to literary theory. Specifically, the metaphor of treating actions as texts may be useful up to a point – both texts and actions, like all Intentional phenomena, are subject to interpretations. But if you try to take the metaphor literally, to think that there is nothing there except texts, you get confusion and incoherence.

The point I most wish to emphasize is this: Feldman's real insights into the narrative structure of much holistic Intentional explanation is in no way dependent on these various confused philosophical views, for which she is not responsible anyway. She can keep the insights of her theory and the results of her experiments and simply jettison the bad philosophy. She – and the rest of us – are much better off without it.

NOTES

1   Irvin Rock, *The Logic of Perception* (MIT Press: Cambridge, Mass., 1983).
2   H. Putnam, *The Many Faces of Realism* (Open Court press: La Salle, Ill., 1987).

Part VII

Applications: Ontology and Obligation

25

Searle on Ontological Commitment

PETER VAN INWAGEN

This paper is not about any very important aspect of John Searle's philosophy. That is, if I am right in my criticisms of Searle, this will not force him to undertake any large-scale revision of his philosophy. Nevertheless, the points on which I shall attempt to show that Searle is mistaken are philosophically important ones.

In *Speech Acts*, Searle has argued for the following theses about "ontological commitment:"[1]

1   The only acceptable criterion of ontological commitment is trivial: A *person* is committed to the existence of what he says there is (or, at most, to those things whose existence is entailed by what he says); a *theory* is committed to the existence of what it says there is (or to those things whose existence is entailed by what it says).

2   This trivial criterion fails to be "objective," for what a person (or theory) "says" can be a matter of philosophical dispute; moreover, there are many vexed philosophical questions about what entails what.

3   Quine attempts to construct an objective (and, for that reason, non-trivial) criterion of ontological commitment. He proposes certain features of sentences in a certain notation as determinative of the ontological commitments of the person who accepts, or of the theory that contains, those sentences. He further proposes that the commitments carried by a sentence that is not in this "certain notation" (call it "the canonical notation") can be revealed only by translating that sentence into, or "paraphrasing it in," the canonical notation. One important consequence of this thesis (according to Quine) is that paraphrasing certain sentences of ordinary English in the canonical notation will show, objectively, that these sentences do not in fact "say" that there are entities that (on the face of it) it looked as if these sentences said that there were.

4   Quine's attempt is a failure, and any such attempt – any attempt at a notational, and hence objective, criterion of ontological commitment – must be a failure, because it will be provably inconsistent with the trivial criterion stated in (1) above.

These theses, in my view, embody several misapprehensions concerning Quine's views on "ontological commitment." Because I think that these views are both true and important, I am eventually going to try to correct Searle's misapprehensions.

Let us begin, however, by laying aside the question whether Searle has got Quine right. Let us examine the arguments he brings against the position that – rightly or wrongly – he attributes to Quine.

I

The core of Searle's argument for the thesis that "Quine's attempt is a failure" is a point that was made very early in the history of the discussion of "Quine's criterion of ontological commitment" by William P. Alston.[2] In Searle's words,

> [T]here is something very puzzling about [the suggestion that it is possible to construct a notational, and hence objective, criterion of ontological commitment] because of the following consideration: sometimes a statement couched in one notational form can involve a commitment which, in some intuitively plausible sense, is exactly the same as the commitment involved in a statement couched in some quite different notational form. By way of commitment, there may be nothing to choose between them. Furthermore, there may be no paraphrasing out procedure that determines that one is more primitive, or is preferable to the other. Yet on the criterion the two statements, though they involve the same commitments in fact, would involve different commitments. (*Speech Acts*, p. 107)

Searle proceeds to an example, a pair of statements that are supposed to display this puzzling feature of Quine's thesis. The example is embedded in a dialogue, which, to avoid disputes about the interpretation of Quine and Alston, he attributes to two imaginary philosophers, Q and A:

> Q: We can eliminate apparent commitments to unwelcome entities by paraphrase into a notation which makes explicit our real ontological commitments. For example, the apparent commitment to the existence of miles which occurs in the statement, "There are four miles between Nauplion and Tolon," can be eliminated with the formulation: "Distance in miles between Nauplion and Tolon = four."

> A: There is no commitment in the first which is not in the second. How could there be? The second is just a paraphrase of the first, so if the first commits you to the existence of miles, so does the second. A man's existential commitments depend on the statements he makes, not on the sentences he uses to make them.

The debate between Q and A does not end here. The rest of it may be summarized as follows. Q replies that he is not contending that two synonymous sentences – whatever *that* means – carry different ontological commitments. Rather, he is contending that the original *seems* to carry a certain commitment, and that the paraphrase reveals this seeming as mere seeming. A dithers and fails to meet this point (which is rather remarkable, since he is Searle's creature and surrogate). The reader is invited to test this judgment of mine by examining the whole of the dialogue between Q and A that is laid out on pages 108 and 109 of *Speech Acts*. A may be given some interesting philosophical assertions to make, but none of them effectively meets the seeming/mere-seeming point. And that point is a simple and powerful one. Suppose our topic were not existence but motion. Isn't there a sense in which "The sun rose at 6:25 this morning" appears to imply that the sun moves? Isn't there a sense in which "The sun became visible at the horizon at 6:25 this morning" counts as a "paraphrase" of the first – whether or not the two sentences are "synonymous?" Isn't it obvious that the paraphrase does not even appear to imply that the sun moves? Doesn't that show that one who utters the former sentence is not committed to the thesis that the sun moves?

We should note that the concept of a "canonical notation" does not figure in the debate between Q and A. Despite the fact that Q talks of "paraphrase into a notation that makes explicit our real ontological commitments," no special notation (other than the identity sign) appears in the paraphrase he offers, and if A's point were valid, it would entail that no paraphrase (whether or not it were in a special notation) could ever show that the apparent commitment to something carried by a certain sentence was only apparent. And, surely, the astronomical example shows that that's false.

Before we leave the debate between Q and A, let us raise the question of what would actually be involved in an attempt to represent "There are four miles between Nauplion and Tolon" in what Quine calls "the canonical notation of quantification." I think that there is something to be learned from such an attempt. The sentence looks like an existential quantification. It appears to say that there are objects of a certain description – miles – and that exactly four of them bear the spatial "betweenness" relation to two Greek towns.[3] That is to say, it looks a lot like "There are four churches between Nauplion and Tolon," which certainly does say that there are objects of a certain description – churches – and that four of them bear "betweenness" to those two towns. Suppose that, on that assumption, we tried to translate "There are four miles between Nauplion and Tolon" into the quantifier-variable idiom. The translation would be rather long (any logic text shows how to produce it); it would start

$$\exists x \exists y \exists z \exists w \ (x \text{ is a mile and } y \text{ is a mile} \ldots)$$

and it would contain, among other things, six non-identity statements and a universal quantification whose consequent was a disjunction of four identity-statements. And it would be either nonsense or false. We should begin to suspect that it might be nonsense when we asked ourselves what open sentences like "x is a mile" meant. What sort of object would satisfy such sentences? By a desperate application of the principle of charity, we might decide that we should understand someone who uses "x is a mile" this way: he means this sentence to be satisfied by mile-long line-segments. (There could no other way to understand him.) But on that far-fetched interpretation of "x is a mile," our long sentence starting with four existential quantifiers is just false: An indenumerable infinity of such "miles" lie between Nauplion and Tolon.

"There are four miles between Nauplion and Tolon," therefore, is unlike "There are four churches between Nauplion and Tolon." And this difference is not a mere difference of subject matter. It is not that one of these sentences says that four physical objects (churches) satisfy a certain condition, while the other says that four "abstract" or "ideal geometrical" objects (miles) satisfy that condition. Rather, the former is not about the spatial arrangement of *four* objects of any sort whatever; it is about the spatial separation of two towns; it tells how the English system of linear measure and the number four combine to assign a measure, a thing subject to arithmetical manipulation, to the spatial separation of two Greek towns. This is what a paraphrase of the original as an identity-sentence is supposed to show,[4] for another way of putting what I have just said is that "four" and "the unique x such that x measures the distance between Nauplion and Tolon in miles" are alternative names for a certain number. It is instructive to notice that this number is a real, as opposed to a natural, number: it specifies (relative to a system of measure) the size of a physical magnitude and not the cardinality of a set. There can as easily be 4.012 miles as four miles between two towns; but the assertion that there were 4.012 churches between Nauplion and Tolon could only be some sort of joke.

Now one might object that one does not have to try to render the two sentences into the quantifier-variable idiom to discover this difference between them. (One could easily imagine an essay by Ryle on the difference between "There are four miles between Nauplion and Tolon" and "There are four churches between Nauplion and Tolon" that concealed the same discovery somewhere within a thicket of ornamental Oxonian shrubbery.) But if the discovery is a rather obvious one, might that not be because the example was a rather simple one? What about, say, "There are six moves by which John can get out of check, one of which will allow him to checkmate his opponent within three moves." Does this assert the existence of six objects (albeit "abstract" objects) as it appears to, or is this appearance an illusion, as it is an illusion that "There are four miles between Nauplion and Tolon" asserts the existence of four objects? Is it like or unlike "There are six doors by which John can leave the room, one of which will allow him to reach the street by going through at most three more doors?" Can you do this one in your head? Can you answer this question by informal reflection on the two sentences, without guidance from a formal technique like an attempt to translate both of them into the quantifier-variable idiom? If you can, your capacity for arriving at the truth by informal reflection greatly exceeds mine.

This digression has, I hope, shown something of the utility of attempting to translate sentences of doubtful ontological import into "the canonical notation of quantification," a topic to which we shall return. As to Searle's fictional skirmish between Q and A – which, as I have noted, does not involve the notion of a canonical notation of quantification, but is about the very idea of the relevance of paraphrase to ontology – I award the victory to Q (who, like Searle, I am unwilling to identity with Quine). The opposition (Searle and his fictional lieutenant A) have not met his argument that, since the only point of ontological paraphrase is to settle the question whether the ontological commitments a sentence apparently carries are ones it really carries, it is therefore no criticism of his thesis to point out that a (correct) paraphrase must carry exactly the same commitments as its original. The "kinetic commitments" carried by "The sun rose at 6:25 this morning" and "The sun became visible at the horizon at 6:25 this morning" are, let us suppose, exactly the same. Well and good; that shows that someone who utters the former is not, as one might have thought, committed to the thesis that the sun moves. And the same point applies to what can be revealed about ontological commitment by paraphrase.

II

But the skirmish is only a skirmish. The main action is elsewhere. Searle thinks he has a general *proof* of the thesis that, if we accept the notion of a purely objective or notational criterion of ontological commitment, "we can show that any ontological commitment you like is merely apparent by paraphrasing it in the spirit of Q's paraphrase of the mile example" (ibid., p. 109). The proof goes like this:

> I shall prove . . . that as far as the criterion goes, we can assert all existing scientific knowledge and still remain committed only to the existence of this pen.
> Let "K" be an abbreviation for (the conjunction of statements which state) all existing scientific knowledge.
> Define a predicate "P" as follows:
>
> Px = df x = this pen & K
>
> Proof: 1   This pen = this pen (axiom)
>   2   K (axiom)
>   3   ∴ This pen = this pen & K
>   4   ∴ P this pen
>   5   ∴ ∃xPx
>
> Thus, in the spirit of Q's ontological reduction [Searle is alluding to the Nauplion–Tolon example] we demonstrate that, in terms of Q's criterion of ontological commitment, the only commitment needed to assert the whole of established scientific truth is a commitment to the existence of this pen. (Ibid., pp. 109–10)[5]

Taken literally, this passage does not seem to make much sense. What Searle has done is to derive an existential quantification from a certain sentence, and then to tell us that, if Q is right, it follows that in asserting the original we are committed to the existence only of what is asserted to exist by the derived existential quantification. But you might just as well argue that because "∃x x is a cat" follows from "∃x x is a cat. & ∃x x is a dog," someone who utters the latter sentence is (according to Q) committed thereby only to the existence of cats. Q is Searle's creature and he can make him believe what he likes, but I doubt whether he intended to represent him as believing *that*. What Searle should have said, I think, is that just as "∃xPx" follows from "this pen = this pen" and K, so K follows from "this pen = this pen" and "∃xPx." Thus, the biconditional "∃xPx. ↔ K" follows from the trivial identity-sentence "this pen = this pen;" and "∃xPx" and K are therefore in a very strong sense equivalent. This argument can be put much more succinctly if one notes that in "Fregean" systems of logic, systems in which it is stipulated that every term denotes something,

∃x (x = a & *p*) ↔ *p*

is a theorem; and, of course,

∃x (x = this pen & K) ↔ K

is an instance of this theorem. (The fact that we had to use a Fregean system of logic to get this result[6] introduces some complications that I shall not discuss.) But what can we deduce from the result that "∃x (x = this pen & K) ↔ K" is true, and, in fact, logically true? (I'm not sure what role the abbreviation of "x = this pen & K" as "Px" is supposed to play in Searle's argument. I can't think of a role for it to play, so I shall ignore it.)

What Searle plainly *wants* us to deduce is that someone who accepts Q's ideas about ontological commitment should reason as follows.

> Let's see. I accept K. I see that K is equivalent to "∃x (x = this pen & K)". The latter sentence is in canonical notation, since it consists of an open sentence bound by an existential quantifier. And in accepting "∃x (x = this pen & K)", I commit myself only to the existence of this pen. I therefore conclude that the apparent commitment to entities other than this pen that is carried by K is only apparent.

An obvious weak step in this reasoning is the assertion that one who accepts "∃x (x = this pen & K)" is thereby committed to the existence only of this pen. There must be some suppressed premise here, one that is supposed to be endorsed by Q. I think it has to be this:

> An existential quantification ∃xFx commits those who accept it to *and only to* the existence of things that satisfy the open sentence Fx.[7]

Whatever Q may believe, I can find no evidence that *Quine* accepts this thesis, and, in any case, it is certainly false. The italicized words reflect a failure to consider the fact that in accepting certain sentences we are constrained to accept others. Consider, for example, the sentence "∃x (x is a cat & ∃y y is a dog)." If we accept this sentence, we are constrained to accept its logical consequences, including "∃y y is a dog," and therefore – Quine would certainly agree – to accept the existence of dogs. But, by the above principle, accepting this sentence would commit us to *and only to* the existence of cats, owing to the fact that the open sentence "x is a cat & ∃y y is a dog" is satisfied by, and only by, cats. To decide what an existential quantification – or, for that matter, a sentence of any sort – commits those who accept it to, one must examine all of the existential quantifications that follow formally from it, and not simply that existential quantification itself.

"Well, all right. But let's get back to '∃x (x = this pen & K).' Suppose that K is not in canonical notation. Then for every existential quantification ∃xFx that follows formally from this sentence, Fx will be satisified by this pen and only this pen, or else by everything – as is the case with, e.g., '∃x (x = x & K).' So doesn't it remain true that we could (if Quine is to be believed) accept all of science and still be committed only to this pen?"

K, which we cannot actually write out, is something of an impediment here. Let us replace it with the sentence "There are dogs," which contains no quantifiers or variables – in the formal sense, anyway – and whose intuitive ontological implications are reasonably clear.[8] And let us ask the question again.

"What about the sentence '∃x (x = this pen & there are dogs)?' This sentence is in canonical notation and the only object that satisfies 'x = this pen & there are dogs' is this pen, and, for every existential quantification ∃xFx that follows formally from '∃x (x = this pen & there are dogs),' Fx will be satisfied by this pen and only this pen, or else by everything – as is the case with, e.g., '∃x (x = x & there are dogs).' Doesn't Quine's criterion of ontological commitment therefore entail that someone who accepts '∃x (x = this pen & there are dogs)' is (thereby) committed to the existence of *and only of* this pen?"

III

This question seems to me to be founded on two false presuppositions. The first is that when Quine talks of "canonical notation" he is talking about something that a given sentence is either "in" or "not in" – as a given sentence might be in (or not in) Hebrew characters or the French language or italics. The second is that Quine has a certain *thesis* called (appropriately enough) "Quine's criterion of ontological commitment," a thesis about when people in general, or perhaps only philosophers who are familiar with canonical notation, are, and when they are not, committed to the existence of things of various descriptions.

Let us first examine the idea that a sentence is either in or not in canonical notation. Which sentences are "in canonical notation?" Searle's answer to this question is, apparently, contained in the following footnote:

Notice that 5 [the sentence so numbered in Searle's "proof," i.e., "∃xPx"] . . . satisfies Q's condition of being in canonical notation, that is, it employs only quantificational logic and predicates. (Ibid., p. 110)

I think we may fairly take the final clause to be intended as a definition of "in canonical notation." The trouble with this definition is that Searle has not said what he means by "predicate." The footnote suggests that a "predicate" is a capital letter of the roman alphabet, or perhaps a capital letter followed by one or more variables, or perhaps a capital letter followed by one or more (differentiated) blank spaces (cf. the notation used by Quine for "predicate-schemata" in *Elementary Logic*, of which "P 1 2" is an example). But that suggestion can't be right. "∃xPx" is simply an abbreviation for "∃x (x = this pen & K)." The real "predicate" in Searle's argument must be "= this pen & K" or "x = this pen & K" or "1 = this pen & K" or something like that. And the "predicate" in "∃x (x = this pen & there are dogs)" must be "= this pen & there are dogs" or "x = this pen & there are dogs" or "1 = this pen & there are dogs." That is to say, "predicates" contain words drawn from the vocabulary of English (or other natural languages). Presumably, therefore, sentences in canonical notation will contain such words.

If we must have a notion of canonical notation such that a sentence can be said, without qualification, to be in that notation or not to be in it, the only natural way to define "canonical notation" seems to me to be this: A sentence is in canonical notation just in the case that it is the result of replacing the predicate-letters in a symbolic formula with the items with which they are paired in some scheme of abbreviation. The technical terminology in the preceding sentence is that of Kalish and Montague's *Logic: Techniques of Formal Reasoning*, to which the reader is referred for a fuller account of it.[9] But an example should make it clear enough for our purposes. The sentence "∃x∀y (x is a person & .y is a person → x loves y)" is, by the terms of our definition, "in canonical notation" because it is the result of replacing the predicate-letters in the symbolic formula "∃x∀y (Fx & .Fy → Gxy)" with the items with which they are paired in the scheme of abbreviation.

> F: **1** is a person
> G: **1** loves **2**.[10]

But this reasonable and natural definition has the consequence that all declarative sentences of English are "in canonical notation." For example, "There are dogs" is in canonical notation because it is the result of replacing the predicate-letter in the symbolic formula "*p*" (the formula "*p*" contains – in fact it consists of – a single zero-place predicate-letter) with the item with which it is paired in the scheme of abbreviation

> *p*: There are dogs.

We might, of course, impose some sort of restriction on the notion of canonical notation to rule out cases of this sort, but this would, to my mind, be a wholly arbitrary procedure. There is a great deal of utility and power in the idea that, just as "**2** loves **1**" and "**1** is a peron" are, respectively, two- and one-place English predicates, so "There are dogs" is a zero-place English predicate – that a declarative sentence is just a zero-place predicate. And why insist that sentences "in canonical notation" must be formed entirely from one-or-more-place predicates? But if all declarative sentences of English are "already" in canonical notation, then a distinction between sentences that are and are not in canonical notation is not likely to be of much use to someone interested in ontological commitment (or in anything else, I suppose).

Let me suggest another way of understanding "canonical notation," one that I believe *is* of some use, and is, moreover, Quine's. Consider the following sequence of sentences, a sequence of a type familiar to anyone who has taught logic:

> Every planet is at any time at some distance from every star
> ∀x if x is a planet, x is at any time at some distance from every star
> ∀x (x is a planet → ∀y if y is a star, x is at any time at some distance from y)
> ∀x (x is a planet → ∀y (y is a star → ∀t if t is a time, then x is at t at some distance from y))
> ∀x (x is a planet → ∀y (y is a star → ∀t (t is a time → ∃z (z is a distance & x is at t separated from y by z)))

Let's not think of "canonical notation" as something that a sentence is "in" or "not in." Let's think of "canonical notation" as something that there's *more and more of* in each of the successive sentences in this sequence. In ordinary English, there are various devices and constructions that do the work that "∀" and "∃" and "x" and "y" and "t" and "z" do in the above sentences. We can transform an English sentence into a sentence that is not (strictly speaking) English by replacing some of these devices and constructions with these symbols – with "canonical notation." (But it might be more instructive to say that we are introducing not canonical *notation*, but rather devices and constructions belonging to a canonical *grammar*. Cf. Quine, *Word and Object*, p. 231.) And if the English sentence is of any very great degree of complexity, there may be several "sites" within the sentence that afford opportunities to do so. In a given case, one or some or all of these opportunities may be taken; how *much* the original sentence is transformed – how many of the available opportunities for the introduction of canonical notation are taken – will depend on the purposes of the person who is introducing the notation.

The introduction of canonical notation may be, but is not always, a mechanical procedure. For one thing, a choice will sometimes have to be made between alternative ways of introducing the unambiguous canonical notation of quantification into a sentence that is ambiguous as to quantificational import. But there is a more interesting way in which the task of introducing canonical notation can be more than mechanical. Sometimes the task requires a certain amount of creativity. For a rather minimal instance of this, consider the four-place open sentence in the final sentence in the above sequence. Where did the word "separated" come from? A computer program – any program a human being could actually write, anyway – for the introduction of canonical notation would probably have "ended up" with a sentence containing the following open sentence: x is at t at z from y. Why didn't I? Well, just because that sounds funny. For one reason or another, while you can say in English, "A is at some distance from B," you can't say of some distance, "A is at it from B." Or you can hardly say it. Recognizing that a slavish adherence to the "at" idiom of the original was going to bring me up against this fact of English usage, I cast about for an idiomatic alternative and came up with the "separated from . . . by . . ." locution. This is creativity, if you like; not a very impressive example of creativity if it is measured against many of the daily achievements of human beings, but (I think) greatly in excess of anything a computer could be expected to achieve.

The introduction of canonical notation, however, can be accomplished in ways that involve greater creativity than this. Consider the final sentence in the above sequence. In my opinion, the open sentence "z is a distance" does not make much sense, owing to the fact that I can't give a coherent account of the properties that an object that satisfied it would have.[11] And since I think that the obvious intelligibility of the first sentence, the English sentence, in the above sequence, does not presuppose that, e.g., "ten miles" is a noun-phrase that denotes a particular "distance," I am inclined to think that the final sentence in the sequence misrepresents the first sentence – although the second, third, and fourth sentences *don't* misrepresent it.

I *could* say that the fourth sentence is "as far as we can go" in the introduction of canonical notation into the first sentence, that the predicate "1 is at 2 at some distance from 3" simply affords no opportunity for the introduction of a quantifier. But if that is so, what about a sentence like "if x is at some distance from y, and x is at some distance from z, then the distance between x and y is greater than the distance between y and z or the distance between x and y is equal to the distance between y and z or the distance between x and y is less than the distance between y and z?" Are we to say that this sentence – which obviously expresses a truth – is formed from *four unrelated* predicates, the one we have already mentioned, and three others ("the distance between 1 and 2 is greater than the distance between 3 and 4," etc.)? Surely this is incorrect. The logical structure of the antecendent and the consequent are more closely related that *that*. We could exhibit an intimate logical relation between the antecedent and the consequent if we were willing to assume that there are things called "distances" that "separate" physical objects from one another, and that one and the same "distance" may simultaneously separate A and B (on the one hand) and A and a third object C (on the other). But we need not be willing to make that assumption to exhibit such a relation. There are a lot of alternatives. One of them would be to introduce the predicate "**1** is **2** times farther from **3** than **4** is from **5**." Then our sentence can be expressed using only *one* predicate involving the notion of spatial separation:

> If x is 1 times farther from y than x is from y, and x is 1 times farther from z than x is from z, then ∃n x is n times farther from y than y is from z and n > 1 or n = 1 or n < 1.

And this predicate allows us to replace the last clause in the final sentence in our sequence with "at t, x is 1 times farther from y than x is from y," thus enabling us to escape the awkward question, "Just what does 'z is a distance' mean, anyway?"

So: the transition between "being in" and "not being in" canonical notation is not sharp but gradual – or, better, the "introduction of canonical notation" consists in one's seizing some or all of the opportunities afforded by a given English sentence for replacing certain constructions within that sentence by constructions involving canonical notation. And this is a procedure that may require a certain amount of creativity; one may find certain ways of introducing canonical notation objectionable, owing to the fact that the result of choosing one of these ways may formally entail ∃xPx for some P such that, on reflection, one can't bring oneself to admit that there are things that satisfy Px. Creativity comes in in finding some way of introducing canonical notation that has no such unwelcome consequence.

Let us now turn to the question whether Quine has propounded a *thesis* that goes by the name "Quine's criterion of ontological commitment." I want to suggest that Quine has no such thesis, but only a *strategy* for getting people to make their ontological commitments clear. The strategy is this; take sentences that the other party to the conversation accepts, and, by whatever dialectical devices you can muster, get him to introduce more and more canonical notation into those sentences. If, at a certain point in this procedure, it emerges that ∃xPx can then be formally deduced from the sentences he accepts, one has shown that the sentences he accepts, and the way of introducing canonical notation into these sentences that he has endorsed, formally commit him to there being things that satisfy Px.

"But if someone doesn't believe in P's, and if he sees that a certain introduction of quantifiers and variables into his sentences would have the result that ∃xPx could be formally deduced from the result, why shouldn't he simply refuse to introduce canonical notation in that way and say, 'Thus far and no farther?' Why can't he stop playing Quine's game at will? In fact, why should he play in the first place?"

Well, any philosopher is perfectly free to resist the application of any dialectical ploy. But the following four points are in order.

Sometimes, in simple cases involving little or no creativity, a refusal to accept the obvious proposal for the introduction of canonical notation can border on the unintelligible. The symbol "∃," after all, is essentially an abbreviation for the English "there are," just as "+" is essentially an abbreviation for the English "plus." Suppose, for example, that a certain philosopher maintains (contrary to Searle)[12] that "there are irreducibly existential sentences." And suppose he is also a fanatical nominalist who has been known to say that there are (strictly speaking) no sentences. There is a perfectly obvious proposal for the introduction of canonical notation into the English sentence "There are irreducibly existential sentences":

$\exists x$ (x is a sentence & x is irreducibly existential).

But the philosopher who accepts "There are irreducibly existential sentences" and denies that (strictly speaking) there are any sentences had better resist this proposal. And yet, given that "$\exists$" just *means* "there are" (as "+" just *means* "plus") it is very hard to justify such intransigence. (How would we understand someone who claimed to accept "Two plus two equals four" and refused – and *not* because he was unfamiliar with the canonical notation of elementary arithmetic – to accept "$2 + 2 = 4$?") As a matter of historical fact, Quine seems to have begun to talk of "the canonical notation of quantification" in ontological contexts because he was confronted with philosophers who accepted English sentences whose obvious "symbolization" was of the form "$\exists x$ (Gx & Hx)" and who, nevertheless, rejected the corresponding English sentences of the form "$\exists xGx$."[13]

In more complicated cases, a refusal to go beyond a certain point in introducing canonical notation may leave English predicates that seem intuitively to be intimately logically related without any logical relation. We have seen an example of this above.

A refusal to go beyond a certain point in introducing canonical notation may leave one without any way to account for the validity of inferences that seem, intuitively, to be logically valid. (This is really a consequence of the previous point, the point about leaving intuitively logically related English predicates unrelated.) An example may make this clear. Here I venture to touch on my own work.[14] Suppose a certain philosopher denies that there are any fictional characters – like Mr Pickwick or Tom Sawyer. Suppose I ask him whether he accepts [insert here a long list of English sentences, of which "Some fictional characters are closely modeled on real people, while others are wholly products of the literary imagination" is representative]; suppose he says he accepts them all. I then point out that, given the obvious way of introducing canonical notation into these sentences, the result in each case permits the formal deduction of "$\exists x$ x is a fictional character."

Now suppose our philosopher refuses to endorse the "obvious" way of introducing canonical notation into the English sentences he has accepted. And suppose that he does not simply refuse to say another word on the matter. Suppose he instead offers various *paraphrases* of the original sentences. Suppose, for example, that he offers the following paraphrase of the sentence given as "representative" above: "Some literary works are such that if they were historical records there would exist people who do not actually exist but who had properties very like those of certain actual people, *and* some literary works are such that if they were historical records there would exist people who do not actually exist and who have properties wholly unlike the properties of any actual people." "*There*," he says, "I'll accept any (reasonable) introduction of canonical notation into *that* sentence, and, of course, any formal consequence of any such introduction." (Note that a "paraphrase," one designed to avoid the appearance of unwelcome ontological commitments, need not be "into canonical notation," or, better, need not contain "$\exists$" or "x." The language of paraphrase may well be ordinary English. The point of such a paraphrase is that – or so the paraphraser hopes – no reasonable way of introducing canonical notation into it will have formal consequences starting with "∃" that he is unwilling to accept.)

Anyone who proceeds this way is playing Quine's game. But this game is like chess: The move that takes one out of check may have consequences that one has not anticipated and which one may not like. Consider the following two sentences.

> There is a fictional character who, for every novel, either appears in that novel or is a model for a character who does.

> If no character appears in every novel, then some character is modeled on another character.

The second sentence seems, intuitively, to be a logical consequence of the first. If it is, how can we account for that fact? *One* way to account for it would be (a) to accept the following two sentences as resulting from legitimate introductions of canonical notation into the two sentences above, and (b) to point out that the second is a *formal* consequence of the first:

> ∃x (x is a fictional character & ∀y (y is a novel → (x appears in y ∨ ∃z (z is a fictional character & z appears in y & x is a model for z))))

> ~∃x (x is a fictional character & ∀y (y is a novel → x appears in y)) → ∃x∃y y is a model for x.

This sort of account of the validity of inferring the second sentence from the first is not open to the philosopher who accepts the "counterfactual-history" paraphrase mentioned above: There is no way in which canonical notation can be introduced into "counterfactual history" paraphrases of our two sentences in such a way as to exhibit the second as a formal consequence of the first. And, *a fortiori*, the same is true of any philosopher who refuses to accept a formal paraphrase of the first sentence in which an existential quantifier binds the free variable in occurrences of "x is a fictional character" and who refuses to suggest an alternative formal paraphrase.

This, then, is how Quine's strategy works. There is a philosopher who insists that the sentences he accepts don't commit him to the existence of P's – or who insists that certain sentences *do* commit those who accept them to the existence of P's. You are doubtful about this. You find out what ways of introducing canonical notation into those sentences your partner in ontological inquiry will accept. In the former case, you point out (if it indeed transpires that this is true) that ∃xPx is a formal consequence of what he has conceded to be a correct introduction of canonical notation into sentences that he accepts. Then it's his move – and he is in check. In the latter case, you point out (if it indeed transpires that this is true) that ∃xPx is *not* a formal consequence of what he has conceded to be a correct introduction of canonical notation into those sentences that, he has alleged, commit those who accept them to the existence of P's. Then it's his move.

Admittedly, however, he is not in check. There is an asymmetry between the two cases, an asymmetry that arises from the obvious fact that if *q* follows formally from *p*, then *q* follows from *p*, but not conversely. Nevertheless, it is a plausible thesis that if *q* follows from *p* and does not follow formally from *p*, then there must be certain other sentences, sentences that are in some sense analytic or necessary truths, such that *q* follows formally from those sentences *and p*. If, therefore, some-one tells you that, in virtue of accepting *p* you are committed to the existence of P's, even though (he concedes) ∃xPx is not a formal consequence of any reasonable way of introducing canonical notation into *p*, then – if you resist this contention – your obvious move is to ask him to specify a set of sentences (sentences that it is reasonable to regard as being in some sense necessary truths) such that one can deduce ∃xPx from some acceptable "formal version" of *p* together with those sentences. (It is at this point that hidden philosophical disagreements usually come to light.)

And, remember, at any point in this procedure, either party may appeal to the following consideration: There *should* be a way of introducing canonical notation into a sentence that accounts for its logical consequences.

The examples Searle considers are all of the second type. Let us return to the case of "∃x (x = this pen & there are dogs)," which was our more perspicuous surrogate for "∃x (x = this pen & K)." Suppose one insists that one is, in accept-ing this sentence, committed thereby only to the existence of this pen. If one's opponent is an adherent of Quine's strategy, the debate will proceed as follows.

> You admit that "There are dogs" is formally deducible from the sentence you accept? And that you are, as a consequence, committed to the truth of "There are dogs"?
> Yes.
> Well, is "There are dogs" equivalent to "∃x x is a dog"?

If the respondent says "Yes," he is committed to the existence of dogs. If he says "No," there is little we can do, beyond trying to find out what on earth he means by "There are dogs." And the same goes for K – in a sense. But the introduction of canonical notation into K will be no trivial matter. There will be an enormous number of alternative ways of doing this, and the problem of determining the scien-tific and philosophical acceptability of at least some of them will raise questions of great subtlety.[15] But it seems clear that all ways of introducing canonical notation into K that have any hope of exhibiting as valid the inferences that scientists regard as valid will allow the formal deduction of sentences of the form ∃xPx, where Px is not satisfied by this pen.[16]

NOTES

1 *Speech Acts: An Essay in the Philosophy of Language* (Cambridge: Cambridge University Press, 1969), pp. 103–13.
2 In "Ontological Commitment," *Philosophical Studies* 9 (1958), pp. 8–17.
3 I am indebted to W. V. Quine for saving me from having said "two French villages."
4 Or this is what I should expect was the intention of a real philosopher who produced this paraphrase; but no real philosopher has produced it, for it is the work of the fictional Q. Searle appends the following note to the speech of Q's that I have quoted in the text: "Cf. W. Quine, *Word and Object*, p. 245." But the example on p. 245 of *Word and Object* (M.I.T. Press: Cam-bridge, Mass. 1960) is a paraphrase of "length of Manhattan = 11 miles" as "length-in-miles-of Manhattan = 11." Note that in this case the "original" is an identity-sentence and does not contain "there are." Quine's intentions on p. 245 of *Word and Object* are clear enough – to

illustrate his preferred way of dealing with sentences that contain "defective nouns" like "mile" – but the two examples of paraphrase are sufficiently dissimilar that Quine's intentions are no guide to Q's intentions.

5 I have changed the logical notation employed in Searle's "proof" to the logical notation of the present paper.

6 As, in effect, did Searle. That is what allowed him to call, "this pen = this pen" an "axiom." In some non-Fregean systems, that sentence is not an instance of a theorem; in others it is, but the inference from "this pen = this pen" to "∃x x = this pen" is valid only if "∃" represents a kind of quantification that does not imply existence.

7 Here and in the sequel, "Quine corners" or "quasi-quotation marks" are invisibly present wherever they are appropriate.

8 Searle has allowed such a replacement. See n. 2 on p. 109 of *Speech Acts*.

9 Donald Kalish and Richard Montague, *Logic: Techniques of Formal Reasoning*, 1st edn (Harcourt, Brace and World: New York 1964), chapter 4.

10 Kalish and Montague do not use bold-face numerals. Since the items on the right-hand side of what they call a "scheme of abbreviation" are just exactly what Quine calls "predicates" in *Elementary Logic*, I retain the notation already introduced. I have made other minor modications of their notation.

11 This statement requires a subtle qualification. Suppose we give a functional account of what a "distance" is; suppose, that is, that we define "distances" in terms of what they are supposed to do for us. What we want them to do is (roughly) this: we want them to serve as abstract "counters" that uniquely measure the spatial separation of spatial objects. It is easy enough to "construct" (as philosophers say, although the objects have been there all along) objects that can be used for this purpose. For example, if we know what it is for the pair of (spatial) objects (x, y) and the pair of objects (z, w) to be "equally separated" – an equivalence relation – then we can say that a "distance" is any equivalence class of pairs defined by that relation. And we can say that x is "at" the distance d from y just in the case that |x, y| is a member of d. But, of course, "the set of distances" is a merely conventional designation for the set of all such equivalence classes. A vast number of other sets have as good a claim to be called "the set of distances," for a vast number of other sets could be used as counters that uniquely measure spatial separation, given an appropriate specification of the "at" relation. When I say that I can't give a coherent account of the properties that a "distance" would have, I mean that I can't give a coherent account of the properties that an object that was intrinsically, or non-conventionally, a distance (as the spatial objects that are "at" distances from one another are intrinsically, or non-conventionally, spatial objects) would have.

12 *Speech Acts*, p. 112.

13 See, for example, Quine's discussion of Carnap's distinction between "internal" and "external" questions, a distinction that allowed Carnap to dismiss as illegitimate the question "Are there numbers?" but to regard the question "Is there a largest pair of twin primes?" as legitimate. The discussion occurs in "On Carnap's Views on Ontology," *Philosophical Studies* 2 (1951) pp. 65–72.

14 "Creatures of Fiction," *American Philosophical Quarterly* 14 (1977) pp. 299–308; "Fiction and Metaphysics," *Philosophy and Literature* 7 (1983) pp. 67–77; "Pretense and Paraphrase," in Peter J. McCormick (ed.) *The Reasons of Art/L'Art a ses raisons* (University of Ottawa Press: Ottawa 1985) pp. 414–22.

15 Consider, for example, the various controversies engendered by Hartry Field's book *Science Without Numbers* (Princeton University press: Princeton 1980).

16 I am grateful to W. V. Quine and Ernest Lepore for comments on a draft of this paper.

Note added in proof: the circled numerals used by Quine in *Elementary Logic* have been replaced in the present paper by bold-face numerals.

26

Prima Facie Obligation:
Its Deconstruction and Reconstruction

BARRY LOEWER AND MARVIN BELZER

Moral philosophers commonly appeal to the concept of *"prima facie* obligation" or *"prima facie* duty" when attempting to describe reasoning concerning moral conflicts and their resolution. W. D. Ross, who usually is credited with explicitly introducing the term *"prima facie"* into moral theory characterizes it this way:

> I suggest *"prima facie"* duty . . . as a brief way of referring to the characteristic . . . which an act has . . . in virtue of being of a certain kind, of being an act which would be a duty proper if it were not at the same time of another kind which is morally significant.[1]

The idea that some obligations are *prima facie* can be found prior to Ross. Kant, for example, writes:

> a conflict of duties and obligations is inconceivable . . . But there can, it is true, be two grounds of obligation . . . both present in one agent and in the rule he lays down for himself. In this case one or the other grounds is not sufficient to oblige him . . . and is therefore not a duty.[2]

Onora Nell commenting on this passage remarks

> The problem may be stated in more modern terms, without much distortion as that of determining which of two *prima facie* duties is an actual duty.[3]

Harman points to a similar distinction saying

> Just as we can distinguish mentioning a consideration that is a reason, not necessarily the only relevant one, from saying what someone has reason to do all things considered (Davidson's all-out judgment, or Williams' all-in judgment), we can distinguish saying what someone ought *"prima facie"* to do from what he or she ought to do "all things considered."[4]

And Joseph Raz emphasizes the importance of this distinction in a theory of practical reasoning:

Much of the work in deontic logic, useful as it is, is of marginal interest to those concerned with practical reasoning because it is altogether oblivious to the problems presented by conflicts of reasons . . . the main task of a theory of practical reason is to establish what one has (*prima facie*) reason for doing and how to resolve conflicts of reasons and establish what one ought to do all things considered.[5]

As Ross says, an act is *prima facie* obligatory in virtue of its possessing a certain characteristic which would make it obligatory proper if it were not for the existence of other moral considerations. A *prima facie* obligation may be overridden by considerations which favor some incompatible alternative act. In contrast to *prima facie* obligations some obligations are said to be actual, or proper, or absolute, or all things considered. As we will see these terms suggest different contrasts but the common idea is that these are obligations which are not overridden. The task of practical reason, as Raz says, is to show how one can validly infer conclusions about such obligations from premises about what one has *prima facie* reason to do. That is to show how to go from the various grounds for acts to a conclusion about what one is obligated to do "all things considered."

In spite of its popularity, John Searle thinks that "we would do well in philosophy to abandon the terminology of *prima facie* obligations and duties."[6] He has argued that the distinction between *prima facie* obligation and whatever it is contrasted with (actual, absolute, all things considered) is hopelessly confused. Searle does, however, grant that there is a genuine point that Ross and others are attempting to make concerning moral conflicts and attempts to make this point himself without resorting to the distinction. In the course of his interesting discussion he produces an account of moral conflicts and in particular how they should be formalized. We generally agree with Searle's criticisms of some ways of drawing the distinction and we think his positive proposal is on the right track. However, we will argue that his attempt at formalizing what he takes to be that correct distinction in deontic logic is inadequate. We will sketch a deontic logic in which moral reasoning from what one has *prima facie* reason to do to what one ought to do all things considered (the reasoning that interests Raz) can be represented and evaluated. Within that framework we will be able to clarify the notion of "*prima facie*" and its role in moral reasoning.

Searle reasonably says that in explaining a new technical concept (which he takes *prima facie* to be) it is important to specify both the point of introducing the term and also what other terms it is supposed to contrast with. Ross et al. are fairly explicit about the first point. They introduce the term in order to describe conflict situations in which one is under two obligations which cannot both be satisfied. One of these obligations may possess greater moral weight and in that case one has only a *prima facie* obligation to act on the weaker obligation. For example, suppose that Jones has promised to play tennis with a friend. His primise provides grounds for his being obligated to meet his friend and so he has a *prima facie* obligation to do so. But suppose also that later his child falls and needs to be taken to the doctor. This grounds an obligation to take his child to the doctor which, we may suppose, overrides the first obligation. Finally, it may be that all things considered Jones ought take his child to the doctor. It is important to note that in examples like this there is what we will call "moral residue" remaining from the first, *prima facie*, obligation. Once Jones has decided not to meet his friend he incurs a new obligation to call him to tell him so.

Searle observes that *prima facie* obligations have been contrasted with both actual and absolute obligations. The two contrasts suggest accounts of *prima facie* obligation which, Searle argues, are confusing and misleading.

The *prima facie*/actual contrast suggests that a *prima facie* obligation is not an actual or real obligation at all. The use is analogous to the the contrast between the *prima facie* and the actual guilt of the accused. When one says that the accused is *prima facie* guilty one means that there is evidence in favor of his guilt. Furthermore, there is a suggestion, perhaps a conversational implication, that he is not actually guilty. Similarly, on this account of the distinction, Jones having made a promise provides some, although not conclusive, evidence for his being obligated to meet his friend. As in the case of *prima facie* guilt, it is suggested that in fact he really has no such obligation. Let's call this way of understanding "*prima facie*" the "evidentiary construal."

The evidentiary construal fits in nicely with act utilitarianism. For an act utilitarian the fact that an act is the keeping of a promise provides no moral grounds for doing it. At best there may be an evidentiary connection between promise keeping and maximizing utility. Fred Feldman, who has recently developed a sophisticated form of act utilitarianism, thinks that moral principles like "If someone makes a promise then he ought to keep it" express rules that we teach to children.

As we get a bit older, we begin to realize that, however useful it may be to believe these [rules], none of them is actually true . . . Childhood training has made us unwilling to reject [them] outright . . . We need a way to maintain a commitment to the sentences, while acknowledging that they are subject to exceptions. In this sad situation, we hear some phrase such as "other things being equal" or "inasmuch as", or "*ceteris paribus*." Although we don't know what these things mean they seem to resolve the perplexity.[7]

It is clear that this is completely at odds with the way Ross understands "*prima facie* obligation." Ross thinks of the fact that an act is a promise keeping as providing distinctively moral grounds for doing it, grounds that would require doing it if there were no overriding moral considerations. Furthermore, as Searle observes, if the obligation to meet his friend is not a real one then it is senseless to say that the obligation to bring his child to the doctor *overrides* the obligation to go to meet his friend – for the latter obligation is nonexistent. Further

This view is unacceptable because it makes it mysterious and inexplicable that I should have any "compunction" about breaking the promise and that I should have "a duty to make up to the promisee for breaking the promise".[8]

That is, this way of characterizing *prima facie* obligation completely fails to account for the fact that there frequently is "moral residue" in situations in which *prima facie* obligations are violated. Of course, one of the traditional objections to utilitarianism is precisely that it fails to account for moral residue and more generally for the existence of genuine moral conflicts. Thus, it is not surprising that from Feldman's utilitarian perspective "*prima facie* obligation begins to look like a moral mirage" (*Doing the Best We Can*, p. 144). But whether or not utilitarianism is a plausible moral theory, it is clear that the evidentiary construal of *prima facie*/actual distinction does not clarify the distinction that Ross was after.

The second way of characterizing *prima facie* obligations examined by Searle contrasts them with absolute obligations.

> (5) *Prima facie* obligations are a species or kind of obligations. They are inherently subject to being overruled or overriden by other obligations (and other reasons for acting in conflict situations). And obligation that overrides them is called an absolute obligation. Relative to a given situation a *prima facie* obligation can become an absolute obligation if it overrides all other obligations.[9]

Searle's characterization is a bit confusing since, on the one hand, he seems to claim that absolute obligations are ones that always override other obligations while *prima facie* obligations are inherently overridable, and on the other hand he says that an obligation is absolute in a particular situation if in that situation it overrides other conflicting obligations. The difference is between a situation independent and a situation dependent characterization of absolute. In any case, Searle argues that the situation independent account of the *prima facie*/absolute distinction is not satisfactory.

> The question we are now asking is can we make any sense of the distinction between *prima facie* and absolute obligations construed as species of obligations . . . ?"[10]

His answer is negative since an obligation "may be absolute relative to one conflict situation and *prima facie* relative to another" (p. 87). His point can be made by noting that if we embed Jones' obligation to take his child to the doctor in various situations (i.e. alter the "facts" that surround it) we will find that it overrides other obligations in one situation but is overridden in other situations. If we assume that any two obligations can conflict then, as Searle argues, there can at most be one obligation that overrides all other obligations in all situations. Since absolute obligations are ones that override others in all situations he concludes that "we [do not] get a useful classification of obligations into two kinds, *prima facie* and absolute" (p. 87).

If an absolute obligation is one that overrides other obligations in every possible situation while *prima facie* obligations are the rest we do not obtain a useful classification. But there are two other classifications that are useful. One is between those obligations that are never overridden and those that can be. A second is the distinction between obligations which in a particular situation are in fact overridden and those which in that situation are not overriden. Neither of these have been shown by Searle to be without interest. In fact, he goes on to sketch an account of the second distinction although he recommends jettisoning the "*prima facie*/absolute" terminology. Instead, he suggests that we attend to the following statements:

(a) Jones has an obligation to do A
(d) Jones ought, other things being equal, to do A
(f) All things considered Jones ought to do A

Searle claims that (a) implies (d) but does not imply (f). The first point, that (a) implies (d) is certainly correct. If Jones is under an obligation to do A then he has a reason which, other things being equal, commits him to doing A. Incidentally, the converse implication does not hold. For example, it may be that Jones ought, other things being equal, give $100 to a particular charity but he may be under no obligation to do so. The second point, that neither (a) nor (d) entails (f) is also correct. As Searle says they are compatible with

   (g)   All things considered, Jones ought not to do A.

He continues:

> In characteristic conflict situations statements of the form (a) and (g) are both true. That is what is meant by saying that the obligation to do A is overridden by some more important considerations. The truth, then, that underlies the *prima facie* jargon is that in conflict situations one can both have an actual (real, valid, honest-to-John) obligation and yet one ought not, all things considered, to do what one is under an obligation to do. (p. 88)

Searle concludes that there is a third distinction underlying the traditional terminology – between what one has an obligation to do and what one ought to do all things considered. Statements like (a) and (d) express that one has some moral reason (in the case of (a) a particular kind of moral reason, being under an obligation) for acting in a particular way, while (f) expresses what one ought to do all things considered. Searle claims that those who introduced the *prima facie*/absolute distinction were really groping for this distinction – in any case, it is a valid distinction according to Searle and is best expressed without resorting to the term "*prima facie*."

Searle now asks how the distinction between (a) and (f) should be formalized. His answer is to introduce a series of deontic operators O_1p, O_2p, etc. and O^*p where the subscripts represent various obligations that Jones has to do A and O^*p says that all things considered Jones ought to do A. Searle observes that O_1-p, O_2-p, and O^*-p might all be true.[11] In this case Jones has an obligation to do A (say because he promised to A), an obligation not to do A (say because he promised something which conflicts with A), and all things considered he ought not do A. This might be because the second obligation is weightier than the first. In Searle's view then what is right about the *prima facie* jargon is captured by indicating that O_1p expresses a real obligation even though O^*-p is true. It is not that one has a special kind of obligation, an absolute one, not to do A, it is just that in the conflict situation weighing all one's obligations and other considerations one ought not do A.

Searle's criticisms of the two ways of drawing the *prima facie*/actual or absolute distinction seem to us to be basically correct. Neither illuminates the kind of moral conflicts that Ross was concerned with. And we also agree that for discussing moral reasoning the pertinent distinction is between statements (a) and (d) on the one hand and statements (f) and (g) on the other. However, we think that Searle's way of formalizing these statements fails to illuminate logical connections among them which are central to moral and practical reasoning. To make this clear, consider again the scenario involving Jones. We want to say that since he promised to meet his friend he ought, other things being equal, to meet him. We also want to say that since his child needs to be taken to the doctor, he ought other things being equal take his child to the doctor. Things aren't, in this example, equal, since there is a conflict. Jones cannot both meet his friend and take his child to the doctor. We want to be able to express that conflict and say that the second obligation outweighs the first and that in this situation all things considered (since the promise and the child's need are all that are required to be considered) he ought to take the child to the doctor. Now the statement that all things considered Jones ought to take his child to the doctor seems to follow logically from the statements of his obligations, that the second outweighs the first, and that there are no other relevant considerations. But Searle's suggested symbolization provides no way even of representing that the second obligation outweighs the first or that there are no other relevant considerations let alone that there is a logical connection between O* and the O_is. That is, it fails at what, according to Raz (in the passage quoted on p. 360), is the main task of a theory of practical reason.

It would be nice if we could find within standard deontic logic (SDL) the resources to represent *prima facie* obligation statements (or more generally, statements like (d)) and all-things-considered-ought statements and the logical relations between them. There is an attempt to do precisely this suggested by Jaakko Hintikka and effectively criticized by Searle. It will be useful to sketch this attempt before presenting our own proposal. Hintikka thinks of *prima facie* obligations as basically conditionals of a certain sort.[12] He focuses on the difference between two principles that he numbers (11) and (12):

$$(11) \quad O(p \to q)$$

and

$$(12) \quad Op \to Oq.$$

His suggestion is that when p is true (11) represents *prima facie* it ought to be that q, while since (12) and p entail Oq, (12) represents all things considered it ought to be that q. Presumably what suggests this to him is that (11) and p may be true even though $O-q$ is true so that (11) can be "overriden." In contrast Oq cannot be overriden. Searle roundly criticizes Hintikka's suggestion for reasons with which we basically agree. The idea behind the *prima facie*/all things considered distinction is that *prima facie* it ought to be that q when there is some, perhaps overridden, reason that q. But, as Searle's discussion makes clear, (11) and p may be true even though there is no moral reason at all in support of q. If p is Jones murders Smith and q is Jones murders everyone in the room and $O-p$ and unfortunately p then $O(p \to q)$ is true. But of course we do not want to say that Jones' murdering Smith results in his having a *prima facie* obligation to murder everyone in the room. He has no moral reason at all to do that – it is not that he has a reason which is overridden. Hintikka's representation also fails to capture the ways in which *prima facie* ought statements are defeasible (are overridable). Jones ought *prima facie* to meet his friend given that he promised. He ought not meet his friend given that although he promised to do so he is required to take his child to the doctor. On Hintikka's account the first is formalized by $O(p \to m)$ and the second by $O(p \& d \to -m)$. The trouble is that $O(p \to m)$ entails $O(p \& d \to m)$. So on Hintikka's formulation Jones also ought to meet his friend given that he promised to do so and he is required to bring his child to the doctor. But this completely misses the feature of the story that d overrides the obligation m. Furthermore, the only way to conclude what one ought do all things considered from statements like O(p & d → m) is to have the additional premise O(p & d). But this completely fails to capture the reasoning involved in our example (and similar cases) since it might very well be that −O(p & d). So Hintikka's theory no more than Searle's can capture reasoning from *prima facie* obligations to what one ought to do all things considered.

Although we agree with Searle in the view that Hintikka's formal representation of the *prima facie*/all things considered distinction is inadequate, we do think that there is one thing right about Hintikka's suggestion. It is that statements which express that we *prima facie* ought to do something because we have an obligation to do it involve conditionality. The conditionality is made explicit in statements like "Given that Jones promised to meet his friend he ought, other things being equal, do so." The main problem with Hintikka's account is that the system of deontic logic that he is working with, SDL, is inadequate for representing the kind of conditionality involved. We will remedy this by constructing a system we call "General Deontic Logic," GDL, which contains a genuinely conditional deontic operator. We will use $O(q/p)$ to stand for p is a moral reason requiring q. This is supposed to capture the force of Searle's statements of the form (d). It expresses that if p is true and there is no other consideration that overrides the requirement for q (i.e. if all other things are equal) then all things considered it ought to be that q. $O(q/p)$ is a "defeasible" conditional since it is compatible with $−O(q/p \& r)$. We will also employ $O^*_t q$ to mean that all things considered at t it ought to be that q. The reason for the subscript t is that what considerations are to be among those eligible for consideration varies with respect to time. This is an important point which is neglected by Searle's formalism. So, for example, at one time t before his child has fallen it might be that $O^*_t m$ but at a later time t', after his child has fallen, it might be $O^*_{t'} −m$. Exactly what considerations are considered eligible in determining what one ought to do all things considered will be discussed shortly. In order to symbolize our example scenario we will also need a way of saying that at a given time certain considerations, say p and d, are all that are relevant to determining whether or not all things considered Jones ought meet his friend. We will use $R_t(m, p \& d)$ mean that at t, p & d are sufficient to settle whether $O^*_t m$ or $O^*_t −m$ or neither. Finally we will use $S_t p$ to mean that at t p is a consideration which is eligible for consideration in determining what one ought to do all things considered.

The central semantical ideas for interpreting these expressions are a function F which assigns to propositions p a set of propositions F(p) and a function $\$(t)$ which assigns to a time t the set of propositions that are eligible for consideration at t. We will suppose that $\$(t)$ is closed under the usual Boolean operations. F(p) is the set of propositions morally required by p. We will, for the moment, suppose that F need not be defined for all propositions and place no restrictions on F with the exception that it be defined for the tautological proposition. The key truth clauses read as follows:

(1) $O(q/p)$ is True iff $q \in F(p)$
(2) $S_t p$ is True iff $p \in \$(t)$

(3) $R_t(q, p)$ is True iff there is no $r \in \$(t)$ such that not $O(q/p \ \& \ r)$.

(4) $O^*_t p$ is True iff there is a $p \in \$(t)$ such that $O(q/p)$ and $Rt(q, p)$

GDL is a comprehensive formal system for representing practical and moral reasoning. It will be instructive to mark some of the differences between it and SDL. We saw that two difficulties with Hintkka's account of *prima facie* ought statements is that the following are theorems of SDL

$$-p \rightarrow (p \rightarrow Oq)$$
$$(p \rightarrow Oq) \rightarrow (p \ \& \ r \rightarrow Oq)$$

But neither of the following analogous formulas are theorems of GDL

$$-p \rightarrow O(q/p)$$
$$O(q/p) \rightarrow O(q/p \ \& \ r)$$

$O(q/p)$ is a genuinely defeasible conditional. As we will see this enables it, unlike SDL, to express that one moral requirement overrides another.

In GDL moral principles are formulated by conditionals $O(q/p)$ which say that p provides moral grounds, other things being equal, for bringing about q. The fundamental idea is that in deciding what one ought to do all (moral) things considered at t one needs to look at the considerations eligible for consideration at t. On our account $O^*_t q$ iff there is a consideration p eligible at t for which $O(q/p)$ which is not overridden.[13] We have shown elsewhere how GDL can be used to represent various kinds of practical reasoning, how it avoids the familiar paradoxes of deontic logic, and how it compares with other systems.[14] Here we want to sketch how it can represent moral conflicts and reasoning with moral conflicts. In our story we have $m \in F(p)$ and $-m \in F(d)$ and $-m \in F(p \ \& \ d)$ and $\$(t) = \{p, d \ldots\}$. So we also have $O^*_t -m$. Given suitable definitions of validity the following inference scheme is valid:

(Key) $O(q/p)$
                $S_t p$
                $R_t(q, p)$
        So $O^*_t q$

Key connects statements that say that one has some moral reason to bring about a certain state of affairs with conclusions about what one morally ought to do all things considered. Thus it fills the lacuna that Raz pointed to in his remarks (quoted on p. 360) on the inadequacy of deontic logics for representing practical reasoning.

There is a natural way of represent "other things being equal" statements (Searle's (d)) in GDL. These express a *prima facie* ought since they can be overriden. As a first approximation we suggest the following:

Jones ought, other things being equal, do A, $PF_t q$ is true iff there is a condition $p \in \$(t)$ such that $O(q/p)$ (q stands for Jones does A)

This captures the idea that one has *prima facie* reason for q just in case there is some moral reason that is eligible for consideration at t and morally requires q. On this characterization $PF_t q$ is compatible with there being no other eligible conditions which override p so that $O^*_t q$ is also true. But sometimes, as we have seen, an obligation (or reason) is called *prima facie* to indicate that it is *merely prima* *facie* and is in fact overridden in particular circumstances. If we want we can add this to the definition by requiring that there is an available condition r which entails p such that $-O(q/p \ \& \ r)$. We say that this is only a "first approximation" because in some situation there may be a moral reason requiring q without there being a *prima facie* obligation that q not because the moral reason is overriden by other considerations but because it is "cancelled."[15] For example, Jones has promised to meet his friend but his friend has called up to cancel the meeting (c). In this case we presumably have $O(m/p)$ but $-O(m/p \ \& \ c)$ while $p \in \$(t)$ and $c \in \$(t)$. If so our definition of *prima facie* says that Jones prima facie ought to meet his friend. This seems inappropriate. The difference between an obligation's being cancelled and its overriden by other considerations typically will show up in terms of other obligations, moral residue, that arise when the original obligation is overridden. In our example, if Jones fails to meet his friend because his obligation is overriden by his obligation to take his child to the doctor then this gives rise to an obligation to call his friend and apologize (a). This is expressed by $O(a/-m \ \& \ p)$. On the other hand if the friend calls and cancels the date then no new obligation arises; $-O(a/p \ \& \ c)$. In any case, we can improve our definition of *prima facie* ought statements by adding to it the clause that there is no $c \in \$(t)$ such that c cancels $O(q/p)$.

Recall that Searle distinguishes statements that express obligations (his (a)) from statements that say what someone ought, other things being equal, to do (his (d)). As he says (a) Jones has an obligation to do A implies (but is not implied by) (d) Jones ought, other things being equal, to do A. Our account of *prima facie* ought statements applies to statements of the latter sort. PF_tq says that at t there is *prima facie* for q (for Jones' doing A); but doesn't necessarily say that Jones is under an obligation to do A. However, we can capture Searle's point within our framework by introducing statements o(q) which say that Jones has an obligation to q. Then $O(q/o(q))$ is true since having an obligation to do q is a reason which, other things being equal, requires doing q.

Our account of *prima facie* ought statements comes very close to the situation-dependent account that Searle briefly discusses. Relative to one situation t, $O(q/p)$ may ground a merely *prima facie* requirement since there may be another rule $O(-q/p \ \& \ r)$, where r is eligible at t, that overrides it. Relative to another situation t' this conditional ought statement may yield an all things considered ought statement since there may be no eligible considerations that override it at t'. Further, as in Searle's formulation, $O(q/p) \ \& \ S_tp$ (the conjunction says that Jones ought at t, other things being equal, do q) does not imply O^*_tq.

In GDL conflicts between *prima facie* obligations are represented by $O(q/p) \ \& \ S_tp$ and $O(-q/r) \ \& \ S_tr$. The second overrides the first if $O(q/p \ \& \ r)$.[16] Not only can there be conflicts between *prima facie* oughts but we can also represent in GDL conflicts between all things considered ought statements – that is, situations in which O^*_tq and O^*_t-q both hold. Searle himself apparently thinks that this is impossible since he adopts

(NC) $\quad O^*q \rightarrow -O^*-q$

as an axiom. (NC) is not valid in GDL. Searle argues in support of (NC) that in a conflict situation where one has moral grounds for conflicting actions "one obligation has to override another if one is to satisfy either" ("*Prima Facie* Obligations," p. 85). While it is true that one cannot satisfy both obligations in such a situation it doesn't seem correct that one obligation must always override the other. For example, Jones may have promised his friend to meet him (f) and he also may have promised his mother to meet her (m) not realizing that it turns out that it is impossible to satisfy both obligations. Now one can say as Searle would that in this situation one obligation must override the other but we see little motivation for requiring this. It may be that the two obligations are of equal weight and so relative to all eligible considerations we may have both O*f and O*m.[17] This holds in GDL (for time t) if the following are the (only) rules and the eligible statements:

$$O(m/p), \qquad O(f/q), \qquad S_t(p \ \& \ q).$$

In this case neither obligation overrides the other. The result is a genuine conflict, one in which no matter what the actor does he violates a non-overriden obligation.[18]

In GDL we can also characterize a notation that comes close to the notion of an "absolute" obligation which Searle, at one point, contrasts with *prima facie* obligation. Recall that he characterizes an absolute obligation as one that overrides all other obligations and proves that there can be at most one such obligation. In GDL this characterization amounts to this:

@q iff for all conditions r for which $F(r)$ is defined $O(q/r)$, and if s is incompatible with q then $-O(s/r)$.

As Searle argues there can be on this account at most one independent absolute obligation. But there is another, slightly weaker account as follows:

@q iff for all r for which $F(r)$ is defined, $O(q/r)$.

This says that no condition overrides the obligation that q while the stronger account also says that q overrides conflicting obligations. Since (NC) fails in GDL it is possible for there to be a number of independent absolute obligations.

Notice the difference between @q (it ought absolutely to be that q) and $O^*_t q$ (it ought all things considered at t to be that q). The former is situation-independent and says that the obligation that q is not overridden in any possible situation while the latter is situation-dependent and says that in situation t the obligation that q is not overridden.

We think that we have shown that GDL is an appropriate deontic system for representing deontological ethical views such as Ross's that hold that an act's possessing a certain feature grounds its obligatoriness.[19] Searle himself is committed to such a view in his famous argument that "is" implies "ought." He claims that in virtue of an act's being a certain kind, the keeping of a promise, it is obligatory. Now the obligation involved here, as Searle is well aware, cannot be described by an all things considered ought statement. So his view must make room for a distinction between what one has moral reason to do and what one ought to do all things considered. Searle marks this distinction by introducing various ought operators, the O_is and the all things considered O^*. What we have done here is to show how to develop his considerations into a full blown deontic system in which one can represent logical connections among the various O_is and O^*. Within this framework the concept of *prima facie* obligation can be used without confusion.

NOTES

1 W. D. Ross, *The Right and the Good* (Oxford University Press: Oxford, 1930), p. 19.
2 Quoted in Onora Nell, *Acting on Principle: An Essay on Kantian Ethics* (Columbia University Press: New York 1975), p. 133.
3 Ibid., p. 133.
4 Gilbert Harman, *Change in View* (MIT Press: Cambridge, Mass., 1986), p. 132.
5 J. Raz, "Introduction," in J. Raz (ed.), *Practical Reasoning* (London University Press: Oxford, 1978), p. 11.
6 J. Searle, *"Prima facie* Obligations," in Raz (ed.), *Practical Reasoning*, p. 84. An expanded version of the article appears with the same title in Z. van Straaten (ed.), *Philosophical Subjects*, (Oxford University Press: Oxford, 1980) pp. 238–59.
7 Fred Feldman *Doing the Best We Can* (Philosophical Studies Series in Philosophy: Reidel: 1986), p. 143. Feldman argues against an account of defeasible obligation due to Chisholm which is similar in a number of respects to the account that we develop later in this paper. While Feldman's criticisms of Chisholm are sound they do not hold against our account. Cf. Chisholm, "Practical Reason and the Logic of Requirement," in Raz (ed.), *Practical Reasoning*, pp. 118–27. For a fuller discussion see M. Belzer's review of Feldman in *International Studies in Philosophy*, forthcoming.
8 *"Prima Facie* Obligations," in Raz (ed.), *Practical Reasoning*, p. 83.
9 Ibid.
10 Ibid., p. 87.
11 Searle stipulates that the deontic operators take propositional variables as arguments while granting that this may be an oversimplification, at least for the description of obligations; cf. van Straaten (ed.), *Philosophical Subjects*, p. 243.
12 J. Hintikka, "Some Main Problems of Deontic Logic," in Risto Hilpinen (ed.), *Deontic Logic: Introductory and Systematic Readings* (Reidel: Dordrecht, 1971), pp. 59–104.
13 Of course, it is important to say what makes a consideration eligible for consideration at t. One idea (an idea that we employed in the system of deontic logic 3-D, a precursor to GDL which we described in Belzer and Loewer, "Dyadic Deontic Detachment," *Synthese* 54 (1983), pp. 295–318) is that the eligible considerations at t are those propositions that are settled as true at t. Fred Feldman would count eligible also those propositions not settled at t but nonetheless "unalterable" by an agent x (in this way Feldman characterizes a notion of the "ought to do" for agent x at t), cf. Feldman, *Doing the Best We Can*, p. 22ff. Intuitively the unalterable propositions for x at t is supposed to be that class of truths that would hold independently of what actions x chooses at t or later. Both 3-D and Feldman determine "objective" obligations where the eligible propositions are settled truths or truths unalterable for an agent. There also are "subjective" obligations determined by belief states, where the propositions eligible to be considered are those believed by the relevant agent.
14 GDL is presented in "General Deontic Logic," and compared with Castañeda's system in "HECTOR Meets GDL: a Diaphilosophical Epic" (unpublished).
15 So there are a number of ways in which a circumstance r may override the obligation that p given q: (a) r may be a reason weightier than p which favors a state of affairs incompatible with q; (b) r may be a condition which cancels the obligation, e.g. if the match is called off; (c) r may be a reason which favors q's being permissible even though r is not a reason for −q being obligatory, as e.g. if O(q/p) but −O(q/p & r). Walter Sinnott-Armstrong discusses the distinction between (a) and (b) in *Moral Dilemmas* (Basil Blackwell: Oxford, 1990).
16 Overriding is related to the relative weight of the competing norms. In general: O(q/p) has greater relative weight than O(s/r) iff O(q/p & r & −(q ↔ s)) and −O(s/p & r & −(q ↔ s)).
17 Whether or not there can be conflicts of this sort is a matter that has received much discussion in recent moral theory. For a survey of the arguments both pro and con see Walter Sinnott-

Armstrong, *Moral Dilemmas*. Sinnott-Armstrong himself argues that there are situations in which moral reasons for conflicting actions are perfectly balanced and that such situations should be described as ones in which b̲ ̲h O*p and O*−p are true. We are not taking a stand on this issue here but are content to point out that in GDL (unlike SDL) O*p and O*−p are consistent.

18   Granting the possibility of "all things considered" conflicts means having to give up at least one of two commonly accepted principles concerning all things considered permissibility, P*. It is easily proven that either

(a) $P^*_t q \leftrightarrow -O^*_t -q$

or

(b) $O^*_t q \rightarrow P^*_t q$

must fail given the consistency of $O^*_t q$ amd $O^*_t -q$. The defender of the possibility of genuine all things considered conflicts probably should reject (b).

19   Although GDL is appropriate for representing deontological ethical theories it is also capable of representing consequentialist theories that rank worlds in accordance with their intrinsic value. F can be defined in terms of the ranking in this way: $q \in F(p)$ iff the most highly ranked p worlds are q worlds. On this consequentialist construal F will satisfy certain conditions i) $q \in F(p)$ and $r \in F(p)$ iff $q \& r \in F(p)$, and ii) $q \in F(p)$ and not $-r \in F(p)$ implies $q \in F(p \& r)$. The result is a deontic system for $O(-/-)$ similar to David Lewis's, cf. *Counterfactuals* (Harvard University Press: Cambridge, Mass., 1973). In the consequentialist system "rules" $O(q/p)$ may tend to be uninteresting.

27

Non-literal Speech Acts and Conversational Maxims

DANIEL VANDERVEKEN

As John R. Searle pointed out, the primary units of meaning in the use and comprehension of language are speech acts of the type called by Austin illocutionary acts. Whenever a speaker makes a meaningful utterance, he always means to perform a certain illocutionary act. In literal utterances, the speaker's meaning is identical with the sentence meaning; the speaker only means to perform primarily the literal illocutionary act expressed by the sentence that he uses in the context of his utterance.

However, in ordinary conversations speaker meaning is often different from sentence meaning, because the primary speech act is different from the literal illocutionary act (as in the cases of metaphor, irony, and indirect speech acts), or because the speaker means to perform in addition to the literal speech act a secondary non-literal illocutionary act (as in the cases of conversational implicatures). For example, whenever by saying "Do you know the way to the Metropole hotel?" the speaker indirectly requests the hearer to tell him the way to the hotel, the primary speech act is the indirect request and not the literal question.

Unfortunately, there has not been much progress until now in the development of a theoretical Pragmatics capable of constructing the speaker's meaning in the case of non-literal utterances. Grice and Searle made some important remarks in the analysis of non-literal meaning by exploring the idea that language use is governed by certain maxims on which the speaker relies in order to get the hearer to understand his non-literal utterances. But their informal analyses of speaker meaning remain largely heuristic and partial, and lack a precise theoretical content. The purpose of this essay is to contribute to the *foundations of Pragmatics* by formulating the principles of a general logical theory of speaker meaning capable of constructing the ability that speakers have to make and understand non-literal utterances. As I will show, the general theory of speech acts that Searle and I have developed in *Foundations of Illocutionary Logic* can be used and further developed in Pragmatics in order to formalize the basic laws that govern the non-literal per-

The editors wish to point out that John R. Searle has been unable to respond to Daniel Vanderveken's paper in this volume.

formance of speech acts. In doing this, I will generalize and explicate results obtained by Grice and Searle in their analyses of non-literal utterances and I will also discuss the general role and place of speech act theory in semiotics.

Pragmatics conceived as the theory of speaker meaning must answer the following two fundamental questions:

1   How does the speaker succeed in getting the hearer to understand that what he means is not identical with what the sentence that he uses means in the context of the utterance?

2   Once the hearer has understood that, how does he succeed in identifying the non-literal speech acts?

From a logical point of view, one can say that a speaker who means to perform non-literal speech acts in a context of utterance intends to get the hearer to understand him by relying on various mental states and abilities of the hearer. Roughly, the speaker relies (1) on the hearer's knowledge of the meaning of the sentence that he uses and on his ability to understand the nature of the literal speech act, (2) on their mutual knowledge of certain facts of the conversational background, and (3) on the hearer's capacity to make inferences on the basis of the hypothesis that the speaker respects conversational maxims in the context of the utterance. On this account, it is not possible to understand the primary non-literal speech act without having first identified the literal speech act and without having understood that this literal act cannot be the primary speech act in the context of the utterance, given that the speaker respects the conversational maxims in that context. Thus, *Pragmatics* conceived as the *theory of speaker meaning* incorporates *Semantics* conceived as the *theory of sentence meaning* as well as a *theory of conversational maxims* and an *analysis of the conversational background* of utterances.

In this essay, I will use speech act theory in order to answer the first fundamental question of Pragmatics. After a few preliminary remarks on literal meaning, I will analyze precisely the conditions which are necessary and sufficient for non-literal speaker meaning. I will first characterize how a speaker can get a hearer to make inferences on the basis of the hypothesis of respect of the conversational maxims in the context of an utterance. Next, I will propose a generalization of the conversational maxims of quantity and of quality which makes their theoretical content precise by explicating them in terms of notions already defined in illocutionary logic. Finally, I will apply the theory to irony and I will make a few methodological remarks on the conversational background of utterances.

1   Illocutionary Acts and Sentence Meaning

Meaning and use are logically related in language. It is part of the meaning of each sentence that it can be used literally to perform illocutionary acts of certain forms in certain contexts of utterance. For example, it is part of the meaning of interrogative sentences like "Is it raining?" and of imperative sentences like "Please, come!" that they serve respectively to ask questions and to make requests. One cannot understand the meaning of these sentences without understanding that their literal utterances serve to perform such speech acts. On this view, any sentence of a natural language (whenever its logical form is fully analyzed) expresses with respect to each possible context of utterance one or (if it is ambiguous) several illocutionary acts which are uniquely determined by the linguistic meaning of that sentence and by the relevant contextual features.

From a logical point of view, illocutionary acts, like assertions, questions, promises, declarations, and orders, have conditions of success and of non-defective performance as well as conditions of satisfaction. First, attempts to perform illocutionary acts, like attempts to perform other human actions, can *succeed* or *fail*. For example, an attempt to fire the hearer by an utterance of the performative sentence "You are hereby fired" is not successful in a context in which the speaker does not have the authority to make such a declaration. In illocutionary logic, the *conditions of success* of an illocutionary act are the conditions that must obtain in a possible context of utterance in order that the speaker succeed in performing that act in that context. As Searle and I pointed out, the conditions of success of elementary illocutionary acts are entirely determined by the components of their force and by their propositional content. Thus, an illocutionary act of the form F(P) is *successfully performed* in a context of utterance if and only if the speaker in that context achieves the *illocutionary point* of the force F on the proposition P with the proper *mode of achievement* of F, and P satisfies the *propositional content conditions* of F, and if the speaker moreover presupposes the propositions determined by the *preparatory conditions* of F and manifests with the required degree of strength the psychological states determined by the *sincerity conditions* of F. For example, a speaker makes a request by uttering a sentence if and only if (1) the point of his utterance is to make an attempt to get the hearer to carry out a future course of action (illocutionary point); (2) in his attempt to the speaker gives the option of refusal to the hearer (mode of achievement); (3) the propositional content is that the hearer will carry out a future course of action (propositional content conditions); (4) the speaker presupposes that the hearer is capable of carrying out that action (preparatory conditions); and finally (5) he manifests with a medium degree of strength a desire that the hearer carry out that action (sincerity conditions). Now a speaker can presuppose a proposition which is false or manifest a mental state which he does not have, and this is why one distinguishes in illocutionary logic between a *successful* and a *non-defective* performance of an illocutionary act. An illocutionary act is *non-defectively performed* in a context of utterance if and only if it is successfully performed in that context, and moreover, the preparatory and sincerity conditions obtain in that context.

In addition to conditions of success and of non-defective performance, illocutionary acts also have *conditions of satisfaction*. In the successful performance of an illocutionary act, the speaker generally expresses the propositional content with the aim of achieving a success of fit between language and the world. For example, a speaker who gives an order attempts to get the hearer to carry out a future course of action so that the world matches the propositional content of his utterance. Similarly, a speaker who makes an assertion expresses a proposition with the aim of representing how things are in the world. In illocutionary logic, the notion of satisfaction is a generalization of the notion of truth which is needed to cover all forces. Just as an assertion is satisfied if and only if it is *true*, an order is satisfied if and only if it is *obeyed*, a promise is satisfied if and only if it is *kept*, a request is satisfied if and only if it is *granted*, etc . . . The notion of satisfaction is based on the notion of correspondence. When an illocutionary act of the form F(P) is *satisfied* in a context of utterance, there is a *success of fit between language and the world*, and the propositional content P is *true* in that context because it corresponds to an existing state of affairs.

Now, given the logical form of illocutionary acts, the two single most important goals of semantics are the formulation of *general recursive theories of success and of satisfaction* under an arbitrary semantic interpretation. As I have shown in my new book *Meaning and Speech Acts*, the semantic theory of truth advocated by Montague, Davidson, and others for ordinary language is just the particular sub-theory for assertive utterances of the more general theory of satisfaction for utterances with an arbitrary illocutionary force.

2   Inference of Speaker Meaning

As Grice pointed out, the non-literal speech acts that a speaker means to perform in the context of an utterance are in general *contextually cancellable*, in the sense that there are other possible contexts where the same speaker could use the same sentences without having the intention of performing these non-literal speech acts. For example, in a context where the speaker has a room at the Metropole Hotel and has invited the hearer to come and visit him, an utterance of the sentence "Do you know the way to the Metropole Hotel?" is just a literal question about the hearer's state of knowledge. Furthermore, non-literal speech acts are also in general *not detachable*, in the sense that it is not possible to imagine that the utterance of another sentence expressing the same literal illocutionary act in the same context would not also have generated them.

From a pragmatic point of view, these facts are important for the following reasons: First, if non-literal speech acts are in general cancellable, certain conditions must be *necessary* in order that a speaker who uses a sentence in a context with a certain conversational background can mean something other than what the sentence that he uses means in that context. When such conditions are not fulfilled in the conversational background, the speaker's meaning can only be literal in the context of an utterance. Second, if non-literal speech acts are not detachable, certain conditions relative to the form of the literal speech act and to the conversational background must be *sufficient* in order that a speaker mean something other than the literal speech act in the context of an utterance. When these conditions are fulfilled in the conversational background, the speaker's meaning cannot be entirely literal. The aim of this section is to analyze precisely the conditions that are both necessary and sufficient for non-literal speaker meaning.

Grice was the first to make definite progress in the analysis of non-literal meaning. I will first briefly explain his ideas. Next, I will try to reformulate and integrate his analysis of conversation in terms of illocutionary logic. On Grice's account, any conversation is governed by certain general *conversational maxims* that the speaker and hearer must necessarily respect if they want to pursue successfully a conversation without being liable of misleading. According to Grice, the speaker and hearer not only respect these conversational maxims in conversations where they co-operate, but moreover it is also reasonable for them to respect such maxims if they want their conversations to be successful and efficient language games.

Grice lists the various maxims by making reference to Kant's categories of quantity, quality, manner, and relation.

Maxims of quantity: "Be as informative as is required (for the current purposes of the exchange)!", "Do not be more informative than required!"
Maxims of quality: "Speak the truth!", "Do not say anything you believe to be false!", "Have evidence for what you say!"
A maxim of manner: "Be perspicuous!"
A maxim of relation: "Be relevant!"

Although Grice gives many examples of derivations in which the non-literal speaker's meaning is inferred from the hypothesis of the respect of such conversational maxims, he does not analyze in detail the nature of such derivations. Using speech act theory, his general approach can be summarized as follows: In the context of a non-literal utterance, the speaker intends to get the hearer to understand him by relying (1) on the hearer's ability to *understand the meaning in context* of the uttered sentence, (2) on their *mutual knowledge of certain facts of the conversational background*, and (3) on the hearer's *ability to make inferences* on the basis of the hypothesis that the speaker respects the conversational maxims. The conclusion of such inferences is always that the speaker means to perform non-literally certain illocutionary acts because their performance is required for the respect of the maxims, given the nature of the literal speech act and the existence of the facts of the conversational background.

Now, from a logical point of view, there are two main ways in which a speaker can get the hearer to make inferences in order to get him to understand non literal speech acts. These are what I will call hereafter the exploitation and the use of a conversational maxim.

The Exploitation of a Maxim

My notion of exploitation of a maxim is more general than that of Grice. On my analysis, a speaker *exploits a conversational maxim* in a context of utterance if and only if three types of conditions obtain in that context. First, certain facts of the conversational background that the speaker presumes to be mutually known by him and by the hearer are such that he intends that the hearer recognize that he cannot respect that conversational maxim in the context of utterance if the primary speech act is the literal speech act and these facts exist. Second, the speaker is capable of respecting that maxim without violating another maxim (because of a clash) and he wants to pursue the conversation. Third, the speaker also intends that the hearer believe that they both have a mutual knowledge of all this.

In the case of exploitation of a maxim, whenever the hearer recognizes the facts of the conversational background that the speaker has in mind, he makes an inference on the basis of the existence of these facts and gets to the conclusion that the speaker means to perform a primary illocutionary act which is different from the literal one. From example, a speaker who says "Julius is a pig" exploits the maxim of quality which requires him to speak the truth in a context of utterance in which he refers to a human being. He relies on the fact that his literal assertion is obviously false in the conversational background in order to get the hearer to understand that he means to assert non-literally something else. As we will see later, in the case of exploitation of a maxim, there is often only an apparent violation of that maxim. At the level of the literal speech act, the speaker obviously violates the maxim, but at the level of the primary speech act, on the contrary, he respects the maxim, or at least it is not obvious given the conversational background that he fails to respect it.

The Use of a Maxim

A speaker *uses a conversational maxim* in the context of an utterance if an only if certain facts of the conversational background that he presumes to be mutually known by him and the hearer are such that he intends that the hearer recognize that, given the existence of these facts, he respects that maxim in performing the primary speech act in the context of his utterance only if a certain non-literal illocutionary act is performed, non-defective and satisfied in that context, and if he intends that the hearer believe that this is the content of mutual knowledge. When a speaker uses a maxim and the hearer recognizes the facts of the conversational background that the speaker has in mind, the hearer makes an inference and comes to the conclusion that the speaker intends to get him to understand that he makes a secondary non-literal speech act in addition to the primary illocutionary act. Thus, for example, a speaker who answers the question "Where is Michael?" by saying "He is in Paris or in London" in general uses the maxim of quantity "Be as informative as required!" by relying on the fact of the conversational background that he did not answer "Michael is in Paris" or "Michael is in London" in order to implicate conversationally that he lacks evidence for saying in which of these two cities Michael is. From the point of view of speech act theory, such a conversational implicature is a secondary non-literal assertion.

As in the case of literal speech acts, non-literal attempts of performance of illocutionary acts can be misunderstood. The speaker can wrongly believe that the hearer is aware of the facts of the conversational background on which he relies in order to exploit or use a conversational maxim. In such cases, the hearer does not fully understand the speaker's meaning and can even fail to recognize the speaker's intention to perform a non-literal speech act. Moreover, even when they are understood, non-literal speech acts can also fail to succeed or to be satisfied.

3   A Generalization and Explication of the Maxims of Quality and of Quantity

In spite of its incontestable merits, Grice's theory is defective in various aspects. Grice's maxims are too vague, without precise theoretical content and apply only to utterances with an assertive illocutionary force. Grice also tends to identify the exchange of information as the sole aim of conversation. Moreover, he does not provide any justification of the completeness of his system of conversational maxims and does not explain the relationships between the various maxims and sub-maxims. These seem to be arbitrarily chosen. Finally, Grice purely and simply confuses the primary non-literal speech acts and the conversational implicatures.

I will now try to improve his analysis by formulating generalizations of the maxims of quality and quantity.

The Maxim of Quality

Let us measure the qualitative value of an utterance by the quality of the speech act that the speaker attempts to perform in the context of his utterance. From a logical point of view, an illocutionary act is of *perfect quality* if and only if it is both non-defectively performed and satisfied. This leads to the following simple generalization of the maxim of quality in illocutionary logic: "*Let the illocutionary act that you mean to perform in the context of an utterance be successful, non-defective and satisfied!*" As there is an inductive definition of the conditions of success, of non-defective performance and of satisfaction of speech acts in illocutionary logic, the maxim of quality, as I have just formulated it, is both precise and general. It can be applied to utterances with any possible illocutionary force and not only to assertive utterances. Thus, there is a particular sub-maxim of quality for each possible illocutionary force. For example, there is the sub-maxim of quality for promises: "Let your primary promise be a promise that is successful, sincere and that you can and will keep!" There is the sub-maxim of quality for assertions: "Let your primary assertion be successful, supported by evidence, sincere and true!" and so on. On this account, Grice's formulation of the maxim of quality is just the particular case of quality for assertions.

In the case of an *exploitation of the maxim of quality*, the speaker intends the hearer to recognize that there are in the conversational background of his utterance certain facts which are relatively inconsistent with conditions of non-defective performance or of satisfaction of the literal speech act. These facts prevent the speaker from meaning to perform the literal speech act in the context of his utterance. Whenever the hearer understands that the speaker's intention is to get him to recognize all this and that the speaker moreover wants to continue the conversation, the hearer also understands that the speaker means to perform a primary non-literal speech act with other conditions of non-defective performance and of satisfaction than the literal conditions which are violated in the conversational background. The hearer then identifies these non-literal conditions by drawing them out of his knowledge of the same or of other facts of the conversational background that the speaker intends him to recognize. For example, in a context where the teacher says imperatively to his pupil "Please, leave the classroom immediately!" without giving him any option of refusal, he exploits the maxim of quality by the fact that he obviously does not achieve the directive illocutionary point with the polite mode of achievement of a request. In such a context, the hearer understands that the speaker means to perform primarily a directive illocutionary act with an opposite mode of achievement (where no option of refusal is given to him) and he identifies that non-literal mode of achievement from the background as that of a command. Thus, in cases of an exploitation of the maxim of quality, the primary speech act often differs as little as possible from the literal speech act. It has instead of the literal conditions of success, of non-defective performance and of satisfaction which are obviously violated in the conversational background other non-literal conditions which are not only compatible with the background but also obviously fulfilled in it.

Of course, a speaker can quietly violate a maxim like the maxim of quality without meaning *eo ipso* to perform a non-literal primary speech act. He can, for example, lie unostentiously or give an order that he does not want to be obeyed. Such utterances are not cases of exploitation of the maxim. Indeed, even if the hearer is aware of such facts, it is not part of the speaker's intentions to draw the hearer's attention to them in these contexts. In such contexts, the speaker may want to mislead the hearer.

In the case of *use of the maxim of quality*, the speaker intends that the hearer recognize certain facts of the conversational background (which he presumes to be mutually known) and that the hearer make an inference on the basis of the assumption of the existence of these facts and of the hypothesis that the primary illocutionary act of the utterance is successful, non-defective and satisfied. Whenever the hearer recognizes the speaker's intention, he comes to the conclusion that a secondary non-literal illocutionary act which is relevant at that moment in the conversation is successful, non-defective and satisfied in the context of the utterance. For example, a speaker who answers the question "Did Jones vote Conservative?" by saying "He is communist" uses the maxim of quality in a conversational background where he relies on the hearer's knowledge that communists do not vote for the Conservative Party. By giving that answer, the speaker means to implicate conversationally that Jones did not vote Conservative. Indeed, if his primary literal assertion is successful, true, and sincere and the fact of the conversational background exists, then the non-literal secondary assertion that Jones did not vote conservative, which is a relevant answer to the question, is also true and non-defective.

The Maxim of Quantity

Each illocutionary act is a natural kind of use of language which can serve to achieve linguistic purposes in the course of conversations. From a logical point of view, an illocutionary act is of *perfect quantity* in the context of an utterance if it is as strong as required to achieve the current linguistic purposes of the speaker in that context. Given their logical forms, certain speech acts are *stronger than* others, in the sense that they have more conditions of success, of non-defective performance or of satisfaction. For example, a supplication to a hearer that he give a bottle of champagne is stronger than a simple request that he give a bottle. Similarly, an assertion that it is necessary that $2 + 2 = 4$ is stronger than an assertion that $2 + 2 = 4$. Stronger speech acts serve to achieve stronger linguistic purposes. Thus, a speaker who would like to supplicate the hearer to give a bottle of champagne but who simply requested that he give a bottle, would perform a speech act which is too weak to achieve his linguistic purpose.

On the basis of these considerations, I propose the following generalization of the maxim of quantity: *"Let your speech act be as strong as required (i.e. neither too strong nor too weak) to achieve your current linguistic purposes in the context of each utterance!"* As the relation of greater strength between illocutionary acts is explicitly defined in terms of their conditions of success, of non-defective performance and of satisfaction, this definition of the maxim of quantity is precise, general and covers all possible illocutionary forces of utterances. For example, there is the sub-maxim of quantity for directives: "Let your primary directive be as strong as needed!" Moreover, that definition of the maxim is sound from a logical point of view because the relation of being a stronger illocutionary act is a relation of strict order.

It might of course be the case that the linguistic purposes of a speaker in the context of an utterance are not appropriate for the current purposes of the conversation in which that utterance takes place. Thus, for example, the speaker might be overinformative or perform a speech act which is not a useful contribution to the progress of the conversation. Following Grice, I believe such utterances can be better viewed as violations of the maxim of relevance.

On my account, a speaker respects the maxim of quantity in a context if and only if his utterance constitutes the literal and/or non-literal performance of illocutionary acts which serve to achieve all his linguistic purposes in that context (even if these linguistic purposes are not entirely appropriate or relevant at that moment in the conversation). Thus, in certain contexts, there might be a clash between the two maxims of quantity and relevance.

In the case of *exploitation of the maxim of quantity*, the speaker intends in general to get the hearer to recognize that the literal speech act is not strong enough to achieve all his linguistic purposes in the context of his utterance. In such contexts, the speaker wants to draw the hearer's attention to facts of the conversational background whose existence implies that certain non-literal conditions of success and of non-defective performance are fulfilled in the context of his utterance. Thus, he intends that the hearer recognize that he means to perform another non-literal speech act. For example, a speaker who says "That painting is not bad!" exploits the maxim of quantity in order to make an understatement in a context where he intends that the hearer recognize that he is obviously very impressed by the painting and that he believes that it is very good. In such a context, the hearer concludes that the speaker means non-literally to make indirectly a primary assertion stronger than the literal one.

In the case of *use of the maxim of quantity*, on the other hand, the speaker intends the hearer to make an inference on the basis of the hypothesis that the primary speech act that he performs in the context of the utterance is actually the strongest illocutionary act that he intends to perform in that context. Usually, the conversational background is such that the speaker has performed that primary speech act instead of other stronger illocutionary acts that were also relevant or expected at that convesational moment in the context of the utterance. Thus, the hearer comes to the conclusion that the speaker intends to implicate conversationally that these non-literal stronger speech acts are not performed because they would be defective or not satisfied in that context. For example, a speaker who answers the question "Do you promise to do it?" by saying only "I will try" usually exploits the maxim of quantity by relying on the fact that he did not answer that he promised, in order to implicate conversationally that he does not promise or does not want to obliged to keep such a promise.

Like A. Kasher, I believe that the conversational maxims are *pragmatic universals of language use* and are not relative to a particular human culture, mainly because language and reason are inseparable in the very performance of illocutionary acts. Indeed, the respect of conversational maxims can be derived from the hypothesis that the *speaker is a rational agent*. This is particularly obvious for the maxims of quantity and quality because they concern the logical form of speech acts. As I said earlier, an illocutionary act is a means of achieving linguistic ends in the course of conversations. Now just as certain means must be used under certain conditions in order to be fully effective, an attempt of performance of an illocutionary act is defective unless certain conditions are fulfilled in the context of an utterance. Moreover, the performance of illocutionary acts also serves in general to express a propositional content with the aim of achieving a success of fit between language and the world from a certain direction. Speakers perform illocutionary acts with the aim of bringing about or representing states of affairs. It would not be reasonable for a speaker to attempt to perform an illocutionary act whose conditions of satisfaction are mutually known to him and the hearer to be violated in the conversational background of the utterance, because the two protagonists of the utterance would then know that no success of fit can possibly be achieved by the performance of that illocutionary act. Finally, the respect of the maxim of quantity is also reasonable in the use of language if one accepts the idea that any rational agent must respect a principle of the effective means. Indeed to each possible linguistic purpose corresponds a unique illocutionary act which serves fully and most effectively that purpose, and a speaker who would attempt to perform a weaker or stronger illocutionary act in a context where he has that purpose would not act most effectively to attain his ends.

4 Irony and Conversational Background

On the basis of the previous considerations, one can say first that a speaker *means to perform a primary non-literal speech act* if and only if he *exploits one or several conversational maxims* and second that he *means to implicate conversationally* something if and only if he *uses one or several maxims* in the context of his utterance. As I show in a forthcoming paper on "Irony, indirect speech acts, and conversational implicatures," this account of non-literal speech acts together with my generalizations of the maxims of quantity and quality enable pragmatics to define the nature of important figures of non literal meaning. I will now briefly apply the theory to irony.

Irony is a limit case of exploitation of the maxim of quality. In the context of an ironic utterance, the speaker exploits the maxim of quality by relying on facts of the conversational background whose existence implies that non-literal conditions of non-defective performance and of satisfaction that are incompatible with conditions of the literal speech act are fulfilled in the context of the utterance. In general, the speaker's irony concerns one or several conditions of non-defective performance or of satisfaction of the literal illocutionary act. It is not only part of background mutual knowledge that these literal conditions are violated in the context of the utterance, but also that the speaker is in a position to perform a non-literal illocutionary act with relatively inconsistent conditions of non-defective performance and of satisfaction. Thus, for example, the speaker is ironic whenever he says "Thank you very much for your help" in a context where it is part of background mutual knowledge that he intends that the hearer recognizes that he is very dissatisfied with the fact that the hearer did not give him any help. In such a context, the speaker's irony concerns both the illocutionary force (the literal sincerity condition that the speaker is grateful to the hearer is violated) and the propositional content (the hearer did not give the speaker any help). The speaker exploits the maxim of quality by relying on the hearer's knowledge of these facts in order to complain ironically about the fact that the hearer did not help him.

The characteristic logical feature of irony is then the following: In an ironic utterance the speaker intends to perform a primary non-literal illocutionary act which differs from the literal speech act by the fact that it has instead of literal conditions which are obviously violated in the context of the utterance the opposites of these conditions, whenever such a non-literal ironic speech act exists and is performable. Otherwise, the speaker means simply to perform the denegation of the literal speech act. Such a definition of irony explains why in the case of irony the speaker's meaning is always in opposition to the meaning of the sentence that is used. Moreover, this definition of irony also accounts for the two main kinds of irony that can occur in language use, namely: the irony as to the illocutionary force, and the irony as to the propositional content of the literal speech act.

As I will show in a future work, there is an effective method of decision for constructing the primary non-literal speech act from the literal speech act and the relevant facts of the conversational background in the cases of ironic utterances. In the simple cases, the algorithm which enables us to understand the ironical speech act is the following:

1 Identify in the background knowledge the literal conditions of success, of non-defective performance or of satisfaction to which the speaker's irony is directed.
2 Identify the components of the literal illocutionary force or of the literal propositional content which determine these conditions (to which the speaker's irony is directed).
3 The ironic speech act is obtained from the literal speech act by replacing such literal components by their opposites when such opposite complements exist and the obtained non-literal illocutionary act is performable.
4 Otherwise, the ironic speech act is the illocutionary denegation of the literal speech act.

Grice and Searle have given examples of derivations of non-literal speech acts which reconstruct the process of understanding of speaker meaning. Here is a derivation which analyzes in detail the interpretation of an ironic utterance of the sentence "Please, get out of the classroom immediately!" made in a context where a teacher invokes his position of authority in his attempt to get a pupil to leave the classroom.

Step 1 The speaker has uttered a sentence which expresses literally in the context of his utterance a request that the hearer get out of the classroom. (Facts about the conversation and about the meaning of the sentence uttered.)
Step 2 The speaker is cooperating in the conversation. (Hypothesis of respect of the conversational maxims.)
Step 3 Consequently, the speaker intends to perform a primary illocutionary act which is relevant, successful, non-defective, satisfied, and as strong as needed. (Consequence of step 2 and of the definitions of the conversational maxims.)
Step 4 A condition of success of a request is that the speaker gives option of refusal to the hearer. (Definition of a request.)
Step 5 The speaker did invoke his position of authority over the hearer and

did not give him any option of refusal. (Facts about the conversational background.)

Step 6   Consequently, the speaker does not respect the maxim of quality if the primary speech act is the literal speech act. He must intend to perform another illocutionary act. (Consequence of steps 2, 3, 4, and 5.)

Step 7   In particular, the speaker must intend to perform a primary non-literal speech act which does not have the condition of success relative to the literal mode of achievement of the force of request, since that condition is obviously violated in the context of the utterance. (Consequence of 2, 5 and 6).

Step 8   The other conditions of success, of non-defective performance and of satisfaction of the literal speech act are not violated in the conversational background and there is no other fact than the one mentioned in step 5 on which the speaker relies in the context of the utterance. (Fact of the conversational background.)

Step 9   Invoking a position of authority over the hearer in making an attempt to get him to do something is a special mode of achievement of the directive point which is in opposition to the mode of achievement of a request. (Fact about the directive forces.)

Step 10 This non-literal mode of achievement of the directive point is achieved on the literal propositional content in the context of the utterance. (Consequence of steps 5 and 9)

Step 11 A command is a directive speech act which differs from a request only by the fact that it has the special mode of achievement which consists in invoking a position of authority over the hearer instead of the mode of achievement which consists in giving option of refusal to the hearer. (Definition of a command.)

Step 12 The speaker respects the conversational maxims in the context of the utterance if instead of requesting he commands the hearer to get out of the room and if this non-literal command is the primary speech act of the utterance. (Consequence of steps 8, 10, and 11.)

Step 13 The hearer knows that the speaker knows that he will come to that conclusion and he does not give him any reason to think that he intends to perform another primary speech act. (Consequence of 8, 12 and of a cognitive principle about speaker meaning.)

Step 14 Consequently, the speaker must ironically intend to *command* the hearer to get out the room. (Consequence of step 9 and 13.)

It goes without saying that in a conversation the speaker and the hearer do not consciously go through all the steps of such a derivation of the primary non-literal speech act any more than they consciously go through all the steps of the construction of the literal speech act. However, the necessary existence of such derivations and their systematic generation by recursive rules enables pragmatics to explain the creative abilities that speakers have in making and understanding ironic utterances.

I will end this paper by making a few *methodological remarks on the conversational background* which are important for the purposes of a logical pragmatics. As Wittgenstein pointed out, to speak a language is to engage in various *forms of life*. Thus, one cannot separate the speaker's meaning from the conversational background of utterances. However, when one tries to analyze conversational backgrounds, one is struck by the great variety of the forms of the facts which can be relevant for the understanding of the speaker's meaning. Most facts of the conversational background which are relevant for understanding the non-literal speech acts performed in an utterance do not have a form which is semantically determined by the sentence uttered and which is invariant from one context of utterance to another. Moreover, it seems to be impossible to formulate an exhaustive theoretic description of any conversational background. There seems to be an open infinite series of facts in each conversational background.

On the basis of such considerations, philosophers like Wittgenstein and Searle have tended to argue that pragmatic (or even semantic) theories of language are impossible. In opposition to such anti-theoretic views, my pragmatic approach leaves space for a constructive theory of speaker meaning, once an arbitrary finite description of the conversational background is associated to each utterance in pragmatic interpretations. Indeed, on my account of non-literal meaning, only a *finite number of facts of the conversational background* can be relevant for interpreting a non-literal utterance, since these facts must enter as empiric premises in a derivation and derivations are of finite length. Moreover, these relevant facts are the *contents of propositional attitudes*, since the speaker intends that the hearer recognize them when he uses or exploits conversational maxims. Consequently, they belong to the conceptual part of the conversational background (which Searle calls the *network* of intentionality) and they can be formally represented in Pragmatics by propositions. Finally, since the relevant facts of the conversational background are *empiric premises* which are *absolutely necessary for the derivation of non-literal speaker meaning*, they must have something to do with the conditions of non-defective performance and of satisfaction of the literal speech act (when they are relevant for understanding the primary speech act), and with the conditions of the primary speech act (when they are relevant for understanding conversational implicatures).

Now, there may not be a theoretical mental level underlying the abilities that hearers have to recognize all the facts of the background that the speakers intend them to recognize. However, the number of these facts is finite and they are represented in the speaker's head. Moreover, once hearers have recognized these facts, their mastery of the conversational maxims enables them to infer the non-literal speech acts of the utterance. Consequently, some theorization can be achieved in pragmatics. One can decide to represent the conversational backgrounds of utterances in pragmatic interpretations by arbitrary finite sets of propositions, assume that hearers recognize the corresponding facts and then try to construct the formal rules that are constitutive of the ability that hearers have to infer the non-literal speech acts from the assumption of the existence of these facts, the conversational maxims and the literal speech acts.

REFERENCES

Grice, H. P. (1975) "Logic and Conversation," in P. Cole and J. L Morgan (eds), *Syntax and Semantics*, vol. 3, *Speech Acts* (Academic Press: New York, NY).

384 *Daniel Vanderveken*

Kasher, A. (1982) "Gricean Inference Revisited," *Philosophica* 29, III.
Searle, J. R. (1979) *Expression and Meaning* (Cambridge University Press: Cambridge).
Searle, J. R. and Vanderveken, D. (1985) *Foundations of Illocutionary Logic* (Cambridge University Press: Cambridge).
Vanderveken, D. (1990) *Meaning and Speech Acts*; vol. 1: *Principles of Language Use*; vol. 2: *Formal Semantics of Success and Satisfaction* (Cambridge University Press: Cambridge).
Wittgenstein, L. (1953) *Philosophical Investigations* (Oxford, Basil Blackwell: Oxford).

This research was supported by grants from the FCAR Foundation and from the Social Science and Humanities Research Council of Canada.

28

Response: Applications of the Theory

JOHN R. SEARLE

Two papers in part VII deal with applications of my views to traditional philosophical problems. Specifically, the article by Peter van Inwagen addresses criticisms I made of Quine's conception of ontological commitment, and Barry Loewer and Martin Belzer in their article try to resurrect the notion of *prima facie* obligation and to answer the criticisms I have made of his notion.

The Ontology Game

The dispute about "ontological commitment," to which van Inwagen addresses his paper, began as part of a particular phase in the history of analytic philosophy. I do not believe you will understand the issues fully unless you are aware of some of the prevailing winds in the intellectual climate of that period. There were at the time three commonly accepted theses all of which seem to me then, and still seem to me, mistaken.

First, it was widely supposed that there was some interesting and meaningful dispute between nominalists and platonists.[1] It was also supposed, though more tacitly, that somehow or other it was better, all things being equal, to be a nominalist rather than a platonist. Roughly, the nominalists were the good guys; the platonists were the bad guys. But as usual it was hard to be good. And many people who would have preferred to be nominalists, found that they had to accept the existence of classes, for example. Still, it was regarded as preferable to accept classes rather than properties or universals: it was somehow closer to nominalism.

Second, it was also a feature of that era that many philosophers thought that we should seek "objective," or even "behavioral," criteria for ascertaining the presence of philosophically puzzling phenomena. So there were efforts to get objective criteria for meaningfulness, synonymy, analyticity, etc.

Third, it was also supposed to be the case that there was a special class of commitments called "ontological commitments." In a way that people would not have thought it philosophically interesting to talk about "subject-predicate commitments," or "past participle commitments," or "left-handed commitments," or "bald-headed commitments", they thought that it was philosophically interesting to talk about their "ontological commitments." These were the commitments one had to the existence of certain sorts of entities.

Quine's criterion of ontological commitment, as I interpret it, combined aspects of all three theses. It was supposed to be an objective criterion for the existence of the ontological commitments which would distinguish our real commitments from our merely apparent ones by translating them into the canonical notation of quantification. This would help in turn to clarify the debates about nominalism by exhibiting genuine from merely apparent commitments.

I thought then, and I think now, that all three of these theses are mistaken:

First, it seems to me that the dispute between platonists and nominalists, as it is traditionally conceived, is utterly empty. It is a case, as Wittgenstein would say, of the bewitchment of our intelligence by means of language. The nominalist says "Socrates is bald," the platonist says "Socrates has the property of baldness." This is because the nominalist believes that only concrete particulars exist; the platonist believes that universals also exist. But the facts in the world which correspond to these two claims are exactly the same. There is no commitment involved in one that is not involved in the other. How could there be, since exactly the same state of affairs in the world corresponds to both claims? The only difference is in the notation with which we represent this state of affairs.

Perhaps one can construct a meaningful dispute between platonists and nominalists but, as traditionally construed, the dispute is empty. We are misled, as usual, by language into thinking that the question "Do universals exist?" is like the question, e.g., "Do dinosaurs exist?"

Second, the search for objective criteria for puzzling philosophical phenomena such as analyticity, meaningfulness, ontological commitment and synonymy was doomed from the start, because the most that the criterion could ever produce would be a test for the criterion. The most we would be ever able to grind out of any such enterprise was an answer to the question whether or not the criterion matched our pretheoretical intuitions, but then there was no way to apply the criterion without depending on the intuitions that the criterion was supposed to replace. I think this enterprise is largely forgotten now, but it is important not to forget that it was once taken quite seriously.

The third issue is actually quite deep and I will try to say a little bit more about it. The mistake in thinking that there is a special class of commitments called "ontological commitments" is a matter of confusion about the unit of commitment. The unit of commitment in question is that of a total speech act, but the notion of ontology in question is tied to the notion of a thing or an entity. And confusion arises because thing-hood or entity-hood is not the unit in which one is committed by one's claims. Our notion of a thing or an entity is just the shadow cast by certain sorts of noun phrases. Thing-hood is the metaphysical correlative of naming and referring. But the unit of commitment is not that of simply naming or referring; rather, to repeat, it is minimally an entire speech act (more holistically, it is probably a set of speech acts; but at the very minimum, you can only be committed by performing at least one whole speech act). So there could not be any separate category of commitments that is especially tied to noun phrases, because the noun phrase only functions as part of the total speech act.[2]

These three problems come together if we try to get an objective criterion for a special class of commitments called ontological commitments. Any such criterion is bound to fail, because what one can express in one syntactical form can also be expressed in a completely different syntactic form. Thus, one could, for example, refuse to quantify over either properties or concrete particulars, and simply treat, e.g., "Socrates-is-bald" as a single predicate construed as true of Reality. Let that predicate be "*F*," and instead of saying "Socrates is bald" just say "Reality is such that *F*."

I am not, of course, suggesting that this is a useful way to talk. I do not think it is. But I do suggest that there is nothing in the nature of the facts in the world that precludes it as a possibility. If we prefer one notation over another, as we surely do, it is for practical reasons, not because the facts that correspond to the notation are any different.

In the passage van Inwagen is criticizing I suggested that you could take the whole of the known truths about the world and treat them as a single predicate true of my pen. In response to this van Inwagen says, correctly, that that would not be playing the game. And I quite agree that it is not. That is, someone is simply not being cooperative if he refuses to split up his sentences in ways that enable us to operate on them with our usual linguistic and logical apparatus. But there is nothing in any criterion of ontological commitment that by itself tells us whether someone is playing the game. The only way that we can decide whether or not they are playing the game is whether or not they intuitively agree to accept the sorts of paraphrases and renditions of their utterances that we find natural.

So, the dilemma that I want to present to van Inwagen in this: Either you try to have an objective criterion of ontological commitment or you do not. If you try for objectivity it will not work, because it is always open to anybody to be uncooperative and simply produce formulations that intuitively carry commitments that the criterion fails to detect. Such a person can, for example, assert all of science and still, on the criterion, be committed only to the existence of this pen. If, on the other hand, you insist, as van Inwagen does, that it is essential that the person play the game, then we have given up any idea of an objective criterion of ontological commitment. What we now accept is the trivial criterion of ontological commitment of the form that I suggested in *Speech Acts*.

The really deep point that I tried to address is not discussed by van Inwagen at all. There are no such things as "ontological commitments," there are just commitments, and these are normally expressed in assertions. Some of these assertions will naturally take an existential form, others will not. But a commitment is always to what must be the case in the world. Sometimes in making assertions you can select from two different notational forms that will suggest different commitments, but if for those two forms, what must be the case in the world is the same for the two, then the two differing notations can be just differing ways of expressing the same commitment. Van Inwagen clearly believes that the apparent commitment in "There are four miles between Nauplion and Tolon" is just a manner of speaking and in that respect it differs from "There are four churches between Nauplion and Tolon." I quite agree that the first is just a manner of speaking, but what I am trying to emphasize is, *every manner of speaking is just a manner of speaking.*

Van Inwagen presents an argument from analogy against my view: apparent commitments are like apparent sunsets. We get rid of the idea that the sun actually raises and lowers itself; and we can similarly rid ourselves of ontological optical illusions. But I believe the analogy does not work. It is literally *false* to say that the sun moves up and down relative to a fixed horizon, but none of the analogous ontological claims are literally false. On the contrary, it is literally true that there are four miles between Nauplion and Tolon;[3] and that there exists a property, namely baldness, such that Socrates had it; etc. The really deep mistake we are making is to think that our craving for an alternative notation is based on the apprehension of some fact which is concealed by the ordinary notation. But the facts are the same for either notation, and that is why the philosophical worries about ontology are quite unlike genuine worries. "Do universals exist?" is very different from "Do dinosaurs still exist?" in spite of the surface similarity.

I think, in fact, that his discussion of the ontological commitment to fictional characters reveals precisely the point that I am getting at. If one person says "Fictional characters do not exist" and the other one says "Fictional characters do exist," what fact in the world is supposed to make the one right, and the other one wrong? What fact about the world is supposed to settle the dispute? One philosopher is struck by the fact that you cannot see Sherlock Holmes or shake hands with him, the way you can with real people. The other philsopher is struck by the fact that you can still say lots of true things about Holmes. But they are agreeing on all of the actual facts in the world: about authors and books and literature, etc. And, as is usual in these philosophical disputes, they are really fighting for one notation as opposed to another. The suggestion I am making is: the facts are not in the notation, rather one notation may be preferable to another, not because one commits us in the way that another does not, but one gives us a better way of coping with the facts that another.

Prima Facie Obligations Revisited

Barry Loewer and Marvin Belzer agree with my criticisms of the existing literature on *prima facie* obligations but they think they can still rescue the notion from confusion and incoherence. To do this they describe a fragment of a system of deontic logic, GDL, which they have developed more fully in other writings. In this system they introduce an operator they think will express the notion of *prima facie* obligations by capturing the special *conditional* nature of "*prime facie*" deontic statements.

In my article I had introduced two operators and claimed that *at least* these two are required to account for certain distinctions. Using their notation, my operators are: O(p) for the deontic notion that occurs, for example, in

Jones has an obligation to do A;

and O* p for the notion in

All things considered Jones ought to do A.

I gather that they agree with the need for these two, but they want to add a third operator as follows:

"We will use O(q/p) to stand for p is a moral reason requiring q."

And they add, "This is supposed to capture the force of Searle's statements of the form (d)":

Jones ought, other things being equal, to do A.

I have not studied their system enough to have an intelligent opinion about it as a whole, but it has two features that I like immediately: first they introduce a time index to mark the fact that relevant moral considerations can vary with time; and second they try to formalize the type of inference by which we go from sets of statements of the form:

(a)   Jones is under an obligation to do A.

to

(f)   All things considered Jones ought to do A.

That is, from $O_1(p)$, $O_2(p)$ . . . to O^* p.

But do they rescue Ross's notion of a *prima facie* obligation or *prima facie* duty? I do not see how they do, and I will try to say why:

At first face, "*prima facie*" is an adverbial sentence modifier meaning roughly, at first face. It is not an adjective modifying nouns. Ross borrowed it from the law, where its use is epistemic. For example, "The plaintiff has a *prima facie* case" means "*Prima facie* the plaintiff has a case," which means "The evidence is such that it appears that the plaintiff has a case."

Now if you try to take this usage over and apply the expression as an adjective of "obligation" the result is only confusion. Suppose we try interpreting "Jones has a *prima facie* obligation" to mean *prima facie* (Jones has an obligation).

But on an epistemic reading this will not do, because it means something like:

On the evidence it appears that Jones has an obligation.

We might want to talk this way to describe cases where we weren't sure about the facts. (Did Jones really make a promise? He wasn't talking loudly enough for us to hear.) But, as Loewer and Belzer are aware, these are not the cases that worried Ross or us because they have nothing to do with moral *conflict*.

Interestingly Loewer and Belzer use this expression both as an adjective modifying "obligation," or "duty," and sometimes they speak of "*prima facie* ought statements" and once of a "*prima facie* requirement." I doubt very much that these are all equivalent, but in any case what are they supposed to mean?

If we are going to have a use for the expression "*prima facie* ought statements," there would have to be a distinction between what one ought to do *other things being equal*, and what one ought to do *prima facie*. Otherwise, the expression is just redundant and confusing. We should not confuse one Latin expression, *prima facie*, with another, namely *ceteris paribus*.

It is clear that they think that their notation $O(q/p)$ is the key to justifying the introduction of the *prima facie* talk because they think that it enables them to express what they think of as the special *conditional* nature of *prima facie* obligations. They tell us "it is a genuinely conditional deontic operator." But the difficulty is that they offer different readings of this operator and it is not at all obvious to me that these different readings are really equivalent. Their preferred reading, the one that fits their semantics, is

$O(q/p) =_{df} p$ is a moral reason requiring q.

But that is not much help without an explanation of the notion of a *requirement*; and intuitively, there is nothing conditional about the notion of a requirement. But they then offer a further explanation of their operator in terms of its conditionality. They say: "it expresses that if p is true and there is no other consideration that overrides that requirement for q (i.e. if all other things are equal) then all things considered it ought to be that q (p. 365)."

Now here is my puzzle: It does not seem to me that these two explanations are equivalent nor does it seem to me that either motivates the introduction of the notion of a *prima facie* ought statement. Intuitively, to repeat, there is nothing conditional at all about the notion of a requirement (or an obligation or a duty or what one ought to do). You can always embed any of these notions in conditionals, as you can any notion, and some statements using these notions will imply conditionals. E.g., "If you make a promise you are under an obligation" uses the word "obligation" in a conditional; and "Making a promise requires keeping it" implies "If you make a promise, you are required to keep it." But this does not show that any of these deontic notions *by themselves* are conditional.

So where is there room for any special conditional deontic operator? Well, the other explanation they give for $O(q/p)$ is that it is equivalent to:

> IF p and IF other things are equal, then all things considered it ought to be that q.

And that certainly is conditional. But notice that on that explanation we can now eliminate $O(p/q)$ by defining it in terms of O^*. Here is the definition:

$O(q/p) =_{df}$ if p and if other things are equal then O^* q.

But this equivalence would also seem to eliminate any claim that we have a "genuinely conditional deontic operator." To make this clear, imagine that somebody had said:

> In addition to regular dogs there are conditional or *prima facie* dogs. The property of conditional doghood, CD, is a genuinely conditional property different from categorical doghood, D, because it is defined as follows:
> $CD(x/p) =_{df}$ if p then Dx.
> Where this is to be read as:
> X is a conditional dog relative to p $=_{df}$ If p then x is a dog.

My tentative conclusion is that they have not given us any justification for reintroducing the notion of a *prima facie* obligation.

Now, what is going on here? Well, it seems to me we need to make the following distinctions at the beginning: First, obligations (as well as duties, requirements, etc.) are *reasons for action*. Reasons for action can in general conflict with other reasons for action. Now, the word "ought," as dictionaries say, is used to "express reasons for action." That is why my (a) Jones is under obligation to do A entails (d) Jones ought, other things being equal, to do A. But because of the possibility of conflicting obligations, and other sorts of conflicting reasons for action, (a) does not entail (f) all things considered Jones ought to do A. But neither the notion of an obligation, nor the notion of what one ought to do is a conditional notion. Now, (d) is genuinely a conditional statement, because "All things being equal Jones ought to do A" means "If all things are equal Jones ought to do A." But the "If" here, is not part of the deontic notions of ought or obligation, rather the "if" occurs because the deontic notions are embedded in an ordinary conditional statement.

Despite these criticisms, I nonetheless believe that they are on to something important. What it seems to me they are really driving at is that the notion of a practical "ought" statement is, we might say, *reason dependent* or *reason relative*. "X ought to do A" entails "There is some reason for X to do A"; and any system of deontic logic ought to capture that feature. It seems to me this is the correct insight implicit in their account; and I see no reason why they should confuse this valid point with the unnecessary and futile effort of revive the notion of *prima facie* obligation.

Finally, there are two misunderstandings of my position which may be of some importance. First, they think that I hold the view that in situations of conflicting obligations "one obligation must always override the other." But I do not actually hold that view. It seems to me quite possible that there may be a complete stand-off. My claim was only that "one obligation has to override another if one is to satisfy either." That is, by the definition of conflicting obligations, one can only act on one, and not on both. In that sense one has to override the other, if one is to satisfy either. Second, this is not my ground for saying that

O*q → ~O* ~q.

Rather, I believe, this formula simply expresses part of the meaning of the notion of what one ought to do all things considered. What it says in plain English is: "If one ought, all things considered, to do A, then it is not the case that one ought, all things considered, not to do A." And that, I hope, is obvious.

NOTES

1   The word "platonists," in small letters, was introduced as a substitute for the traditional medieval term "realist," because of the multiple ambiguities in that term.
2   Perhaps, this is what Frege meant when he said: "Nur im Zusammenhang eines Satzes bedeuten die Wörter etwas": It is only in the context of a sentence that a word has meaning.
3   I wrote the passage he is criticizing on Tolon Beach in the summer of 1964. The geographical claims are approximate but the philosophical point is intended to be exact.

Selected Bibliography
of the Works of J. R. Searle

1956

(1) "Does It Make Sense to Suppose that All Events, Including Personal Experiences, Could Occur in Reverse?" Analysis Competition – Ninth "Problem". *Analysis*, 16(6), new series no. 54, June.

1958

(2) "Proper Names," *Mind* 67. Reprinted in the following collections: *Philosophy and Ordinary Language*, ed. Charles E. Caton (University of Illinois Press: Urbana, 1963); *Philosophical Logic*, ed. P. F. Strawson (Oxford University Press: Oxford, 1967); *Readings in the Philosophy of Language*, ed. Jay F. Rosenberg and Charles Travis (Prentice-Hall, Englewood Cliffs, NJ, 1971); *Präsuppositionen in Philosophie und Linguistik*, ed. J. Petöfi and D. Franck (Athenäum: Frankfurt am Main, 1973); *Causal Theories of Mind*, ed. Steven Davis (Walter de Gruyter: Berlin, 1983); *The Philosophy of Language*, ed. A. P. Martinich (Oxford University Press: Oxford, 1985).
　　Translation　French: "Les Noms Propres" in *Theories du Signe et du Sens*, ed. Alain Rey (Ed. Klinksieck: Paris, 1973–6). German: "Eigennamen" in *Philosophie und Normale Sprache*, ed. Eike von Savigny (Verlag Karl Alber: Freiburg, 1969). Reprinted in: *Philosophie und Sprache* (Philipp Reclam, Jun.: Stuttgart, 1981). Italian: "Nomi Propri" in *La Struttura Logica Del Linguaggio*, ed. Andrea Bonomi (Valentino Bompiani: Milano, 1973).
(3) "Russell's Objections to Frege's Theory of Sense and Reference," *Analysis*, 18, 1957–8. Reprinted in: *Essays on Frege*, ed. E. D. Klemke (University of Illinois Press: Urbana, 1968).
　　Translation　Spanish: Ediciones Universitarias de Valparaiso: Valparaiso.

1959

(4) "Determinables and the Notion of Resemblance," *Proceedings of the Aristotelian Society*, Supplement.

1961

(5) "The Lessons of Black Friday," *The Bridge: Youth in Revolt*, Institute of International Relations, (Stanford University: Stanford, 1961).
(6) Review of "Logical Positivism," ed. A. J. Ayer *Philosophical Review* 70, July.

1962

(7) "Meaning and Speech Acts," *Philosophical Review*, 71, October. Expanded version appeared with comments in: *Knowledge and Experience*, ed. C. D. Rollins (University Pittsburgh Press: Pittsburgh, 1962). Original version reprinted in: *Theory of Meaning*, ed. Adrienne and Keith Lehrer (Prentice-Hall: Englewood Cliffs, NJ 1970). Reprinted in Bobbs-Merrill reprint series in Philosophy, Phil-193, Indianapolis, Indiana.

1964

(8) "How to Derive 'Ought' from 'Is'," *Philosophical Review*, 73, Janurary. Reprinted in numerous anthologies, among them: *Theories of Ethics*, ed. Philippa Foot (Oxford University Press: Oxford, 1967); *Readings in Contemporary Ethical Theory*, ed. Kenneth Pahel and Marvin Schiller (Prentice-Hall: Englewood Cliffs, NJ 1970); *Philosophy Today*, no. 1, ed. Jerry H. Gill (Macmillan: New York: Collier: London, 1968); *The Is-Ought Question*, ed. W. D. Hudson (Macmillan: London, 1969); *Approaches to Ethics*, ed. Jones, Sontag, Bekner, Fogelin (McGraw-Hil: New York, 1969); *Readings in Ethical Theory*, ed. Wilfred Sellars, John Hospers (Appleton-Century-Croft: New York, 1970); *Ethics Now, A Contemporary Anthology*, ed. Struhl and Struhl (Random House: New York, 1975); *Concepts in Social and Political Philosophy*, ed. Richard E. Flathman (Macmillan: New York, Collier: London, 1973); *Introduction to Moral Philosophy*, ed. Philip E. Davis (Charles E. Merrill Publishing Co.: Columbus, Ohio, 1973); *Philosophy: A Contemporary Perspective*, ed. R. Hoffman, S. Gendin (Wadsworth Publishing Co.: Belmont, California, 1975); *An Introduction of Ethics*, ed. R. E. Dewey and R. H. Hurlbutt III (Macmillan: New York, 1977); *Moral Philosophy*, ed. A. G. Oldenquist (Houghton Mifflin Co.: Boston, 1978); Bobbs-Merrill reprint series in Philosophy, Phil-192, Indianapolis, Indiana; *Contemporary Ethics*, ed. James E. Sterba (Prentice Hall: Englewood Cliffs, NJ, 1988).
  Translation Spanish: *Problema de Etica*, by Instituteo de Investigaciones Filosoficas (Mexico, D. F. Mexico, 1975); *Teorias Sobre la Etica*, ed. Philippa Foot (Fondo de Cultura Economica: Mexico, D. F. Mexico, 1973). Polish: *Etyka*, 16 (Warsaw, 1978). Swedish: *Filosofin genom Tiderna, efter 1950*, ed. Konrad Marc-Wogau (Bonniers: Stockholm, 1980). Hungarian: *Tenyek es Erterek* (Gondolat Kiado: Budapest, 1981).

1965

(9) "What is a Speech Act?" *Philosophy in America*, ed. Max Black (Cornell University Press: Ithaca, NY; George Allen and Unwin: London. Reprinted in: *An Introduction to Philosophical Inquiry*, ed. J. Margolis (Alfred A. Knopf, 1968: New York, 2nd ed. 1978); *The Philosophy of Language*, ed. J. R. Searle (Oxford University Press: Oxford, 1971); *Readings in the Philosophy of Language*, ed. Jay F. Rosenberg and Charles Travis (Prentice Hall: Englewood Cliffs, NJ, 1971); *Language and Social Context*, ed. Pier Paolo Giglioli (Penguin Books: Harmondsworth, Middlesex, 1972); *Contemporary Analytic and Linguistic Philosophies*, ed. E. D. Klemke (Prometheus Books: Buffalo, NY, 1983); *The Philosophy of Language*, ed. A. P. Martinich (Oxford University Press: New York, 1985); *Critical Theory Since 1965*, ed. H. Adams and L. Searle (Florida State University Press: Tallahassee, Fla. 1986).
  Translation German: "Was ist ein Sprechakt?" in *Sprachhandlung-Existenz-Wahrheit*, ed. Matthias Schirn (Problemata, Fromann Verlag: Stuttgart, 1974). Greek: *Deucalion*, 17, 1977. Spanish: "Que es un acto de habla?" in *Revista Teorema* (Valencia, 1977). Dutch: "Wat is een taalhandeling?" in *Studies over Taalhandelingen*, ed. F. H. van Emeren and W. K. B. Koning (Boom: Amsterdam, 1981). Japanese: *Bunseki Tetsugaku no Kompon Mondai* (Koyo-Shobo, Kyoto, 1985).

(10) "The Faculty Resolution," *The Revolution at Berkeley*, ed. Michael V. Miller and Susan Gilmore (The Dial Press: New York; Dell Paperback: New York).
(11) Review of the *Coherence Theory of Truth*, Haig Hatchadourian, *Philosophical Review*.

1966

(12) "Assertions and Abberations," *British Analytical Philosophy*, ed. Bernard Williams and Alan Montefiore (Routledge and Kegan Paul: London, 1966). Reprinted in: *Symposium on J. L. Austin*, ed. K. T. Fann (Routledge and Kegan Paul: London, 1969).
(13) Review of Mats Furberg's *Locutionary and Illocutionary Acts*, in *Philosophical Review* 75, July.

1967

(14) "Determinables and Determinates," *The Encyclopedia of Philosophy*, ed. P. Edwards (Macmillan: New York, 1967; Collier: London, 1967).
(15) "Proper Names and Definite Descriptions," ditto
(16) "Strawson, P. F.," ditto
(17) "Human Communication Theory and the Philosophy of Language," *Human Communication Theory*, ed. Frank E. X. Dance (Holt, Rinehart and Winston: New York, 1967). Reprinted as: "Words, The World, and Communication," *Philosophy in the Age of Crisis*, ed. Eleanor Kuykendall (Harper & Row: New York, 1970).
(18) "Freedom and Order in the University," *Freedom and Order in the University*, ed. Samuel Gorovitz (The Press of Western Reserve University: Cleveland, Ohio, 1967).

1968

(19) "A Foolproof Scenario for Student Revolts," *The New York Times Magazine*, December 29. Reprinted in numerous newspapers and magazines including: The *Spectator*, London, 1969; *Ha Aaetz*, Tel Aviv, 1969; *San Francisco Chronicle*, 1969; *Boston Globe*, 1969; *Protestas y Estilos*, Mexico, 1969; *Worcester Sunday Telegram*, 1969. *Daily Californian*, Berkeley, 1969; *Minerva's Kuartalsskrift*, Oslo, 1971. Also reprinted in numerous anthologies, including: *Starting Over, a College Reader*, ed. Frederick Crews, Orville Schell (Random House: New York, 1970); *The University Crisis Reader*, vol: 2, ed. I. Wallerstein and Paul Starr (Random House: New York, 1971, Vintage Books: New York, 1971); *The Radical Left: The Abuse of Discontent*, ed. Gerberding Smith (Houghton Mifflin Co.: Boston, 1970); *In Defense of Academic Freedom*, ed. Sidney Hook (Pegasus: New York, 1971).
(20) "Austin on Locutionary and Illocutionary Acts," *Philosophical Review*, 77, 4. Reprinted in: *Readings in the Philosophy of Language*, ed. J. F. Rosenberg and Charles Travis (Prentice-Hall: Englewood Cliffs, NJ, 1971); *Essays on J. L. Austin*, ed. G. J. Warnock (Clarendon Press: Oxford, 1973).

1969

(22) *Speech Acts, An Essay in the Philosophy of Language* (Cambridge University Press: Cambridge, 1969, reprinted: 1969, 1970, 1972, 1974, 1976, 1977, 1978, 1980, 1982, 1983, 1984, 1985, 1987, 1988, 1989). Pirated editions published in Taiwan and in South Korea. Part of chapter 2 reprinted as: "The Verification of Linguistic Characterizations," *Philosophy and Linguistics*, ed. Colin Lyas (Macmillan: London, 1971); "Expressions, ed. meaning and speech acts," *Communication Studies*, ed. J. Corner and J. Hawthorn (Edward Arnold: London, 1980), (reprinted

1982, 1983; 2nd edition 1985); part of chapter 6 reprinted as: "The Assertion Fallacy," *Readings in Semantics*, ed. F. Zabeech, E. D. Klemke, A. Jacobson (University of Illinois Press: Urbana, Illinois, 1974). Part of chapter 7 reprinted as: "The Problem of Proper Names," *Semantics, an Interdisciplinary Reader*, ed. Danny D. Steinberg and Leon A. Jakobovits (Cambridge University Press: Cambridge, 1971). Part of chapter 8 reprinted as: "Objections and Replies" in *The Is-Ought Question*, ed. W. P. Hudson (Macmillan: London, 1969).
  Translation   German: *Sprechakte, ein Sprachphilosophischer Essay*, (Suhrkamp Verlag (Theorie): Frankfurt am Main, 1971, reprinted 1973, reprinted in Taschenbuch Wissenschaft, 1983). Part of chapter 7: *Präsuppositionen in Philosophie und Linguistik*, ed. J. S. Petöfi, D. Franck (Athenäum Verlag: Frankfurt am Main, 1973). Part of chapter 1 reprinted in: *Sprechanalyse und Soziologie* (Suhrkamp: Frankfurt, 1975). French: *Les Actes de Language, Essai de Philosophie du language* (Hermann (Collection Savoir): Paris, 1972). Italian: *Atti Linguistici, Saggio di Filosofia del Linguaggio* (Boringhieri: Torino, 1976). Dutch: *Taal-handelingen, Een taalfilosofisch essay* (Het Spectrum: Utrecht, 1977). Spanish: *Actos de Habla, Ensayo de filosofia del lenguaje* (Ediciones Catedra, S. A.: Madrid, 1980). Portuguese: *Os Aotos de Fala, Um Ensaio de Filosofia da Linguagem* (Livraria Almedina: Coimbra, 1984). Japanese: 1986. Korean: 1987. Polish: *Czynnosci mowy, Rozwazania z filozofi jezyka* (Pax: Warsaw, 1987). Russian: chapter 4 translated as: "Referenciya kak rechevoy akt" in: *Novoye v zarubeschnoy lingvistike* (Raduga: Moscow, 1982). Chinese: portions translated, 1987.

1970

(22) "Reply to 'The Promising Game'", *Readings in Contemporary Ethical Theory*, ed. Kenneth Pahel and Marvin Schiller (Prentice-Hall: Englewood Cliffs, NJ)

1971

(23) Editor of *The Philosophy of Language* (Oxford University Press: London) with an introduction by the editor. Pirated edition published in South Korea.
(24) *The Campus War* (The World Publishing Co.: New York). Published in England in Pelican Books (Penguin Books, Ltd.: Harmondsworth, Middlesex, 1972). An expanded section of chapter 5 submitted at their request to the President's Commission on Campus Unrest (The Scranton Commission) (US Government Printing Office: Washington, DC, 1970). Chapter 6 reprinted in *The Concept of Academic Freedom*, ed. E. L. Pincoffs (Texas University Press: Austin, Texas, 1975).

1972

(25) "Chomsky's Revolution in Linguistics," *The New York Review of Books*, 17, June 29. Reprinted in: *Editorial Anagrama*, Barcelona; *Hamburger Phonetische Beiträge* 13 (1974); *On Noam Chomsky*, ed. Gilbert Harman (Anchor Doubleday: Garden City, NJ, 1974).
  Translation   French: "Chomsky et la revolution linguistique," *La Recherche*, March 1973. Greek: in *Deukalion* 27/28, December, 1979. Swedish: "Chomskys Revolution i Linguistiken" (Göteborgs Universitet Kompendier: Göteborg, 1980).

1973

(26) "Linguistics and the Philosophy of Language" *Linguistics and Neighboring Disciplines*, ed. Renate Bartsch and Theo Vennemann (North Holland Publishing Co.: Amsterdam, 1975).

Translation German: "Linguistik und Sprachphilosophie," in *Linguistik und Nachbarwissen-schaften*, ed. Renate Bartsch and Theo Vennemann (Scriptor Verlag: Kronberg, 1973).

1974

(27) "The Role of the Faculty," in *The Idea of a Modern University*, ed. Sidney Hook, Paul Kurtz, Miro Todorovich (Prometheus Books: Buffalo, NY, 1974).

(28) "Agenda for the Future," *ibid.*

1975

(29) "The Logical Status of Fictional Discourse," *New Literary History*, 6, February. Reprinted in: *Contemporary Perspectives in the Philosophy of Language*, ed. French, Uehling, Wettstein (University of Minnesota Press: Mineapolis, 1979).

Translation Spanish: "El estatuto logico del discurso de ficcion," in *Linguistica y Literatura*, ed. R. Prada Oropeza (Universidad Veracruzana: Xalapa, Ver., Mexico, 1978). Italian: "Statuto logico della finzione narrativa," *Versus* 19/20, 1978.

(30) "Indirect Speech Acts," in *Syntax and Semantics 3: Speech Acts*, ed. Peter Cole and J. L. Morgan (Academic Press, New York, 1975). Reprinted in: *The Philosophy of Language*, ed. A. P. Martinich (Oxford University Press: Oxford, 1985).

Translation Spanish: "Actos de Habla Indirectos," *Teorema* 7/1, 1977. Italian: "Atti linguistici indiretti", in *Gli atti linguistici*, ed. Marina Sbisa (Feltrinelli: Milano, 1978). Dutch: "Indirecte Taalhandelingen" in *Studies over Taalhandelingen*, ed. F. H. van Emeren and W. K. Koning (Boom: Amsterdam, 1981).

(31) "A Taxonomy of Illocutionary Acts," in *Language, Mind and Knowledge*, Minnesota Studies in the Philosophy of Science 11, ed. Keith Gunderson (University of Minnesota Press: Minneapolis, 1975). Reprinted as: "A Classification of Illocutionary Acts," in *Language in Society* 5, 1975. Reprinted in: *Proceedings of the Texas Conference on Performatives, Presuppositions, and Implicatures*, ed. Andy Rogers, John P. Murphy, Bob Wall (Center for Applied Linguistics: Austin, 1977).

Translation Spanish: "Una Taxonomia de los actos Illocucionarios," *Teorema*, 6/1, 1976. Italian: "Per una tassonomia degli atti illocutori," in *Gli Atti Linguistici*, ed. M. Sbisa (Feltrinelli: Milano, 1978). German: "Eine Klassifikation der Illokutionsakte" in *Sprechakt Theorie*, ed. P. Kussmaul (Athenaion: Wiesbaden, 1980). Dutch: "Den Taxonomie van ed. illocutionaire handelingen." in *Studies over Taalhandelingen*, ed. F. H. van Emeren and W. K. B. Koning (Boom: Amsterdam, 1981).

(32) "Speech Acts and Recent Linguistics," in *Developmental Psycholinguistics and Communication Disorders*, Annals of the New York Academy of Sciences.

(33) "The Grammar of Dissent," review of Ian Robinson, *The New Grammarian's Funeral*, in *Times Literary Supplement*, November 21: letters answering criticism thereof *TLS*, December 12; January 30, 1976.

1976

(34) "The Rules of the Language Game," review of Noam Chomsky, *Reflections on Language*, in *Times Literary Supplement*, September 10; letters answering criticisms thereof *TLS*, October 22; December 17.

(35) Review of J. Sadock, *A Linguistic Theory of Speech Acts* in *Language*, December.

1977

(36) "Re-iterating the Differences: A Reply to Derrida," *Glyph*, 1, 1.

1978

(37) "Entrevista sobre libertad humana y libertad academica," (with Stuart Hampshire), *Teorema*, 7/3–4 (Universidad de Valencia).
(38) "Sociobiology and the Explanation of Behavior," in *Sociobiology and Human Nature*, ed. Gregory, Silvers, and Sutch (Josey-Bass: San Francisco).
(39) "Prima Facie Obligations," in *Practical Reasoning*, ed. Joseph Raz (Oxford University Press: Oxford) An expanded version printed in: *Philosophical Subjects* ed. Zak van Straaten (Oxford University Press: Oxford, 1980).
(40) "The Philosophy of Language," in *Men of Ideas*, ed. Bryan Magee (British Broadcasting Corporation: London) Also taped as a program in TV series on BBC rebroadcast several times in England. Also broadcast in Canada and elsewhere in the British Commonwealth.
Translation Korean: 1985. Chinese: 1988.
(41) "Mind and Language," in *Prospects for Man: Communication*, ed. W. J. Megaw (York University: Toronto)
(42) "Literal Meaning," *Erkenntniss* 13. Reprinted in: The Philosopher's Annual 2 ed. Boyer, Grimm, Sanders (Rowman & Littlefield: Totowa, NJ, 1979).
Translation French: "Le Sens Litteral," *La Langue Française* 42, May, 1979.
(43) "Psychology Group Report," (co-author) in: *Morality as a Biological Phenomenon*, ed. Gunther S. Stent (University of California Press: Berkeley: revised, 1980).
(44) "A More Balanced View," in: *The University and the State*, ed. S. Hook, P. Kurtz, M. Todorovich (Prometheus Books: Buffalo, NY)

1979

(45) "Intentionality and the Use of Language," in *Meaning and Use*, ed. A. Margalit (Riedel: Dordrecht, Holland) Also printed in: *Linguistics in the Seventies*, ed. Braj B. Kachru, Special Issue of *Studies in the Linguistic Sciences* (University of Illinois: Urbana, 1979).
Translation German: "Intentionalität und der Gebrauch der Sprache," in *Sprechakttheorie und Semantik*, ed. G. Grewendorf (Suhrkamp: Frankfurt am Main, 1979).
(46) "What is an Intentional State?" *Mind* 88, 349, January. Reprinted in: *The Philosopher's Annual* 3, ed. Boyer, Grim and Sanders (Ridgeview: Atascadero, California, 1980); *Husserl, Intentionality and Cognitive Science*, ed. Hubert L. Dreyfus (MIT Press: Cambridge, Mass., 1982).
(47) "Metaphor," in *Metaphor and Thought*, ed. A. Ortony (Cambridge University Press: Cambridge). Reprinted in: *Philosophical Perspectives on Metaphor*, ed. Mark Johnson (University of Minnesota Press: Minneapolis, 1979); *The Philosophy of Language*, ed. A. P. Martinich (Oxford University Press: Oxford, 1985).
(48) *Expression and Meaning: Studies in the Theory of Speech Acts* (Cambridge University Press: Cambridge; reprinted 1979, 1986). Pirated edition published in South Korea.
Translation French: *Sens et espression; études de theorie des actes du language* (Les Editions de Minuit: Paris, 1982). German: *Ausdruck und Bedutung; Untersuchungen zur Sprechakttheorie* (Suhrkamp: Frankfurt am Main, 1982). Chinese: in selected articles forthcoming.
(49) "The Intentionality of Intention and Action," *Inquiry* 22, Autumn. Reprinted in: *Language, Logic and Philosophy* (Holder-Pitcher-Tempsky: Vienna, 1980): *Manuscrito* (Campinas: Brasil, 1981); *Perspectives on Cognitive Science*, ed. D. A. Norman (Ablex Publishing Corp.: Norwood, New Jersey, 1981).

Translation   French: "L'intentionalite' de l'intention et de l'action," *Critique*, Paris, October, 1980.
(50) "Re⁵erential and Attributive," *Monist* 62, 2, April.
(51) "Reply to Fodor on Methodological Solipsism," *The Behavioral and Brain Sciences*.
(52) "Reply to Chomsky on Rules and Representation," *The Behavioral and Brain Sciences*.
(53) Chairman's opening address and concluding remarks in: Proceedings of the CIBA Conference on *Brain and Mind* (Excerpta Medica: Amsterdam)

1980

(54) "*Las Meninas* and the Paradoxes of Pictorial Representation," *Critical Inquiry* 6, 3. Reprinted in: *The Language of Images*, ed. W. J. Mitchell (The University of Chicago, 1980).
(55) *Speech Act Theory and Pragmatics*, ed. with F. Kiefer and M. Bierwisch (Reidel: Dordrecht, Holland) Pirated edition published in South Korea.
(56) "The Background of Meaning," *Speech Act Theory and Pragmatics*, ed. J. R. Searle, F. Kiefer and M. Bierwisch (Reidel: Dordrecht, Holland, 1980).
(57) "Minds, Brains, and Programs," *The Behavioral and Brain Sciences*, 3, pp. 417–57. Reprinted in: *Mind Design*, ed. John Haugeland (Bradford Books: Cambridge, Mass., 1981); *The Mind's I*, ed. D. R. Hofstadter and D. C. Dennett (Basic Books: New York, 1981); *Introduction to Philosophy*, ed. J. Perry and M. Bratman (Oxford University Press: Oxford, 1986); *Artificial Intelligence, the Case Against*, ed. Rainer Born (Croom Helm: London, 1987); *Readings in Cognitive Science*, ed. Allan Collins and Edward E. Smith (Morgan-Kauffmann: San Francisco, 1988); *Argument and Persuasion*, ed. Howard Kahane (Wadsworth Publishing Co.: Belmont, California, 1988); *The Philosophy of Artificial Intelligence*, ed. Margaret A. Boden (Oxford University Press: Oxford, 1989).
Translation   Japanese: 1983. Dutch: "Geest, hersenen en programmas" and published in *Wijsgerig perspektief op maatschappij en wetenschap* 4, 1983/4. Italian: "Menti, Cervelli e Programmi," in *Menti, Cervelli e Programmi*, ed. G. Tonfoni (CLUP: Milano, 1984). French: "Esprits, cerveaux et programmes", *Quadreni*, 1, 1987.
(58) "Intrinsic Intentionality," reply to criticisms of "Minds, Brains and Programs," *The Behavioral and Brains Sciences* 3.
(59) "The Chinese Room Revisited", response to further commentaries on "Minds, Brains and Programs," *The Behavioral and Brain Sciences* 5, 2.
(60) Interview with John Searle in *Versus*, Quaderni di studi semiotici, 26/27.

1981

(61) "Analytic Philosophy and Mental Phenomena," *Midwest Studies in Philosophy* 6. ed. French, Uehling, and Wettstein (Minnesota University Press: Minneapolis). Reprinted in *Historical Foundations of Cognitive Science*, ed. J. C. Smith (Kluwer Academic Publishers: Dordrecht, Holland, 1990).
(62) "Intentionality and Method," *Journal of Philosophy* 78, November.

1982

(63) "The Myth of the Computer," *New York Review of Books* 29, April 29.
(64) "The Myth of the Computer: An Exchange," *New York Review of Books* 29 June 24.
(65) "Proper Names and Intentionality," *Pacific Philosophical Quarterly*, 63, 3, July.
(66) "Meaning", *Colloquy 44*, Center of Hermeneutical Studies (G.T.U.: Berkeley, 1982).

Selected Bibliography

1983

(67) *Intentionality: An Essay in the Philosophy of Mind* (Cambridge University Press: Cambridge) Translation Italian: *Della Intenzionalità* (Bompiani: Milano, 1985). French: *L'Intentionalité: Essai de Philosophie des Etats Mentaux* (Les Editions de Minuit: Paris, 1985). German: *Intentionalität: Eine Abhandlung zur Philosophie des Geistes* (Suhrkamp Verlag: Frankfurt am Main, 1987).
(68) "The Word Turned Upside Down," *New York Review of Books*, 30, October 27.
  Translation Swedish: *Clarté* (Stockholm, 1984). Roumanian: *Caiete critice* (Bucharest, 1988).

1984

(69) "An Exchange on Deconstruction," *New York Review of Books* 30, February 2.
(70) Interview "Von der Sprechakttheorie zur Intentionalität," *Information Philosophie*, January, March.
(71) *Minds, Brains and Science*, "The 1984 Reith Lectures" (British Broadcasting Corporation: London; Harvard University Press: Cambridge, Mass., 1985; Pelican, Penguin Books: London, 1989) Portion of Chapter 2 reprinted in: *Philosophy and Contemporary Issues*, ed. J. R. Burr and M. Goldinger (Macmillan: New York; Collier: London, 1988).
  Translation French: *Du Cerveau au Savoir* (Hermann, Collection Savior: Paris, 1985). Spanish: *Mentes, Cerebros y Ciencia* (Catedra, Colección Teorema: Madrid, 1985). German: *Geist, Hirn und Wissenschaft* (Suhrkamp, Taschenbuch Wissenschaft: Frankfurt am Main, 1986). Portuguese: *Mente, Cérebo e Ciência* (Edições 70, Biblioteca de Filosofia: Lisbon, 1987). Italian: *Mente, Cervello, Intelligenza* (Bompiani: Milan, 1988). Hebrew: Am Oved Publishers: Tel Aviv, Israel 1988. Chinese: chapters 1 and 2 in: *Philosophical Translation Series*, 4 & 6, 1987. Complete Chinese translation forthcoming.
(72) "Intentionality and Its Place in Nature," *Synthese*, October. Reprinted in: *Dialectica* 38, Fasc. 2–3, 1984; *Philosophy, Mind, and Cognitive Inquiry*, ed. David Cole, James H. Fetzer and Terry L. Rankin, (Kluwer Academic Publishers: Dodrecht, the Netherlands, 1990).
(73) "Has Artificial Intelligence Research Illuminated Human Thinking?", *Annals of the New York Academy of Sciences* 426, "Computer Culture: The Scientific, Intellectual, and Social Impact of the Computer," ed. by Heinz R. Pagels, panel discussion with Hubert L. Dreyfus, John McCarthy, Marvin L. Minsky, Seymour Papert, pp. 138–160.

1985

(74) With Daniel Vanderveken: *Foundations of Illocutionary Logic*, (Cambridge University Press: Cambridge).
  Translation Russian: chapter 2 *Novoe v Zarubezhnoy Linguistike* 18, ed. V. V. Petrov (Progress: Moscow, 1986).

1986

(75) "Discusija John Searle, Karl-Otto Apel," *Theoria*, Beograd.
(76) "Meaning, Communication and Representation," *Philosophical Grounds of Rationality, Intentionality, Categories and Ends*, ed. R. Grandy and R. Warner (Clarendon Press: Oxford)
(77) "Notes on Conversation," in *Contemporary Issues in Language and Discourse Processes*, ed. D. G. Ellis and W. A. Donohue (Lawrence Erlbaum Associates: Hillsdale, NJ)

1987

(78) "Indeterminacy, Empiricism and the First Person," *Journal of Philosophy*, February. Reprinted in *The Philosopher's Annual*, ed. Patrick Grim, Gary Mar, and Michael A. Simon (Ridgeview Publishing Company: Atascadero, California, 1987).
  Translation   French: L'indetermination, l'empirisme, et la première personne," in *Revve de Théologie et de Philosophie*, Geneva, 1987.
(79) "Wittgenstein," in *The Great Philosophers*, ed. Bryan Magee (BBC Books: London). Also broadcast as a program in a television series by BBC.
  Translation   Portuguese: *Os Grandes Filósofos* (Editorial Presença: Lisabon, 1989).
(80) "Minds and Brains without Programs," in: *Mindwaves*, ed. C. Blakemore and S. Greenfield (Basil Blackwell: Oxford, 1987).

1988

(81) Interview in *World Literature*, 9, p. 188ff., in Korean.
(82) "Turing the Chinese Room,"'in *Synthesis of Science and Religion, Critical Essays and Dialogues*, ed. T. Singh (Bhaktivedenta Institute: San Francisco, 1988).

1989

(83) "Artificial Intelligence and the Chinese Room: An Exchange", *New York Review of Books*, 36, February 16.
(84) Interview with Bill Moyers in *A World of Ideas* (Doubleday: New York) Also broadcast as a program in a television series by P.B.S.
(85) "Consciousness, Unconsciousness and Intentionality" *Philosophical Topics* 17, 1, Spring.
(86) "Reply to Jacquette", *Philosophy and Phenomenological Research*, June.
(87) "How Performatives Work", *Linguistics and Philosophy* 12, pp. 535–56.
(88) "Individual Intentionality and Social Phenomena in the Theory of Speech Acts", *Semiotics and Pragmatics*, ed. Gérard Deledalle (John Benjamins: Amsterdam/Philadelphia).

1990

(89) "Is the Brain's Mind a Computer Program?", *Scientific American*, January.

FORTHCOMING

(90) "Conversation," an expanded version of (76), *Journal of Pragmatics*.
(91) "Collective Intentionality and Action," *Intentions in Communications*, ed. P. Cohen, J. Morgan and M. E. Pollack, (Bradford Books, MIT Press, Cambridge, Mass).
(92) "Cognitive Science and the Computer Metaphor", in a volume to be edited by Bo Göranzon. Swedish translation of an early draft appeared in 1988, in *Dialoger* 7–8/88, pp. 57–88; Italian translation of an early draft apeared in 1988 in *Nuova Civiltà delle Macchine*, Anno VI, 1/2 (21/22) pp. 53–61.
(93) "Yin and Yang Strike Out", *The Nature of Mind*, ed. David M. Rosenthal (New York: OUP)
(94) "Epilogue to the Taxonomy of Illocutionary Acts", in: ed. *Cultural Communication and Intercultural Contact*, Donald Carbaugh (Erlbaum).
(95) "The Causal Powers of the Brain", *Behavioral and Brain Sciences*.
(96) "Consciousness, Explanatory Inversion, and Cognitive Sciences," *Behavioral and Brain Sciences* 13, 4.

Selected Bibliography

MAJOR WORKS ABOUT THE WORK OF JOHN R. SEARLE

Reinhard B. Nolte: *Einführung in die Sprechakttheorie John R. Searles* (Verlag Karl Alber: Freiburg/ München, 1978).

"Speech Act Theory: Ten Years Later," *Special Issue of periodical devoted to the work of John R. Searle: Versus* 26/27, 1980.

William Garnett: *The Springs of Consciousness. The 1984 Reith Lectures of Professor Searle critically examined* (Tabb House, Cornwall, 1987).

Index